LEARNING AND INSTRUCTION

Theory Into Practice

FOURTH EDITION

Margaret E. Gredler
University of South Carolina

Merrill
Prentice Hall

Upper Saddle River, New Jersey
Columbus, Ohio

Library of Congress Cataloging in Publication Data
Gredler, Margaret E.
    Learning and instruction: theory into practice / Margaret E. Gredler.—4th ed.
        p.   cm.
    Includes bibliographical references and indexes.
    ISBN 0-13-012227-0
    1. Learning. 2. Cognition in children. 3. Teaching.   I. Title.
    LB1060.G73   2001
    370.15'23—dc21   00-036175

Vice President and Publisher: Jeffery W. Johnston
Executive Editor: Kevin M. Davis
Editorial Assistant: Christina M. Kalisch
Production Editor: Julie Peters
Copy Editor: Key Metts
Design Coordinator: Diane C. Lorenzo
Text Designer: Ed Horcharik/Pagination
Cover Designer: Rod Harris
Cover art: © Image Bank
Production Manager: Laura Messerly
Electronic Text Management: Marilyn Wilson Phelps, Karen L. Bretz, Melanie N. Ortega
Illustrations: Christine Haggerty
Director of Marketing: Kevin Flanagan
Marketing Manager: Amy June
Marketing Services Manager: Krista Groshong

This book was set in ITC Garamond by Prentice Hall and was printed and bound by R.R. Donnelley & Sons Company. The cover was printed by Phoenix Color Corp.

Merrill
Prentice Hall

10 9 8 7 6 5 4 3 2
ISBN: 0-13-012227-0

In memory of my beloved daughter,
Margaret Lynn,
and for her sister,
Elizabeth Lee

Preface

Against the tapestry of changing educational and social events, theories of learning continue to address the complexities of human learning and cognitive development. Rapid popularity of a theory, typically followed by misinterpretations, is sometimes followed by corrected perceptions and, as the theory matures, a legacy of one or more major concepts that enter the mainstream of educational thought. New in this edition are current applications of classical conditioning and Gestalt psychology, new developments in contemporary theories, and similarities and differences between each theory and other perspectives. In addition, the concepts in Vygotsky's theory are clarified, particularly the role of the teacher and subject-matter learning in cognitive development.

I would like to thank the following individuals for their review of this edition: Kay W. Allen, University of Central Florida; Michael Bloch, University of San Francisco; Michael T. Dealy, New York University; and Fernando Hernandez, California State University, Los Angeles. In addition, I would like to thank the reviewers of the previous edition, Joyce Alexander, Indiana University; Scott W. Brown, University of Connecticut; and Michael J. Wavering, University of Arkansas—Fayetteville, for their helpful comments.

Margaret E. Gredler

Contents

Chapter 10
Lev S. Vygotsky's Cultural-Historical Theory of Psychological Development   275

PART IV
Social-Context Theories

Chapter 11
Albert Bandura's Social–Cognitive Learning Theory   315

PART I

Introduction

The human capacity for learning is an important characteristic with far-reaching implications for both the individual and society. Discussed in chapter 1 are the role of learning in human life and the various sources of knowledge about learning. Described are the limitations of traditional wisdom, maxims, and fragmented data in expanding knowledge about learning. Also discussed is the role of theory in developing information about the process of learning, the design of instruction, and the analysis of classroom situations.

By the 1920s, learning had become a major focus of study for American psychology. Until the 1950s, two broad perspectives sought to develop the one theory that would explain all learning. Behaviorism, the dominant perspective during this period, is described in chapter 2. This perspective views learning as behavioral change, and researchers attempt to identify the environmental events and conditions responsible for such change.

A different perspective, discussed in chapter 3, is Gestalt psychology. Initiated in Germany, Gestalt psychology maintains that learning is a sudden perceptual reorganization of a problem situation. Gestalt theorists named this process insight.

By the mid-1950s, efforts to develop the one comprehensive learning theory began to decline. New developments redirected psychologists to other problems. Chapter 4 describes these developments and current trends in theory development, and it also introduces the seven contemporary theories presented in this text.

CHAPTER 1
The Role of Theory in Learning and Instruction

Man's power to change himself, that is, to learn, is perhaps the most impressive thing about him (Thorndike, 1931, p. 3).

The human capacity for learning sets the species apart from all others. Lev S. Vygotsky, a well-known scholar, described three unique characteristics of human intelligence. First, humans can learn about the discoveries, inventions, and ideas of great thinkers and scientists of the past (referred to as inherited experience) (Vygotsky, 1924/1979). This capacity enriches one's knowledge and also makes possible the development of new discoveries and inventions that build on prior accomplishments.

Second, humans can develop knowledge about places and events they have not experienced personally through the experiences of others (social experience). That is, an individual can know Berlin or Mars although he or she has neither traveled nor looked through a telescope (Vygotsky, 1924/1979, p. 13).

Finally, humans adapt the environment to themselves, rather than merely adapting to it, and they do so by first building mental models in their heads. Examples include a variety of activities from quilt making to architecture. This creation of products from mental patterns was named repeated experience (Vygotsky, 1924/1979, p. 14).

WHY IS THE STUDY OF LEARNING IMPORTANT?

First, learning is important to the individual. It begins in infancy with the baby's acquisition of a few simple skills, such as holding its own bottle and recognizing its mother. During childhood and adolescence, competencies in various subject areas as well as a number of attitudes, values, and social interaction skills are acquired.

Classroom scenes, for example, may include two 8-year-olds comparing their separate approaches for determining the age of a book written in 1980 or middle school students checking various web sites on the Internet for information relevant to their term papers on human body systems. In adulthood, the individual is expected to have mastered a knowledge base relevant to his or her chosen profession or career.

Learning also can contribute to a rich and diverse lifestyle for the individual. Sewing, basic home repair, water skiing, playing Scrabble, and mountain climbing are only a few of the leisure-time activities acquired through learning. In our society, we are not surprised to find engineers who are gourmet cooks and college professors who grow prize-winning roses.

The capacity for continued learning is particularly important for the individual in today's information age. New developments in technology are increasing both the store of knowledge and the ways that information and knowledge are transmitted. Continued learning is important both for changing job markets and taking advantage of new opportunities to access information.

Second, learning is essential for societies to preserve the values, language, and contributions of the particular culture. Adults, by continuing the customs and practices of their culture, make them available for the next generation.

In addition, learning makes possible new discoveries and inventions by subsequent generations that build on past developments (the inherited experience described by Vygotsky). Robots journeying to Mars, satellites that record wind and sea patterns, and laser surgery are only a few.

The third reason that the study of learning is important is that both the individual and society have a vested interest in the successful management of learning. Individuals who become skilled at self-directed learning are able to acquire expert knowledge in their chosen fields, to change careers, and to endow their lives with creativity and variety.

Society, on the other hand, cannot risk leaving the acquisition of learning to chance. Some system is needed to teach the cultural heritage to the young and to train them to take on productive adult roles. In early societies, the collective wisdom and folklore often were acquired by each member, usually by word of mouth. In technological societies, the available knowledge and information is so vast that no one can begin to learn all of it. Instead, formal educational systems address both broad areas of knowledge and areas of particular expertise that individuals select for further study. This process requires several years and often includes the learning of particular prerequisite knowledge, such as chemistry for pharmacists and music theory for symphony conductors.

The importance of learning to society is conceptualized in two ways. First, suppose that each new generation would only be able to learn those things that are half as difficult as the things currently learned (Thorndike, 1931). For example, instead of members of the present generation learning calculus, they would learn only algebra. Then the next generation would learn only arithmetic, and so on. The result is obvious. Most of human civilization's accomplishments would be unusable in one generation, and civilization itself would soon disappear from the face of the earth (Thorndike, 1931).

Another analysis of the importance of learning to society is derived from the perspective that learners construct their own meanings for themselves from the contexts in which they live. That is, individuals select information from interpersonal and other interactive events occurring in the family, school, peer, community, and work environments. Individuals then relate the selected information to their prior knowledge, analyze it, and construct a representation in memory. In this view of learning, the knowledge in the mind is coextensive with the relationships that compose one's interpersonal and societal environments. From this perspective, each new generation constructs a new society for itself (Meacham, 1993, p. 259). The key question then becomes, Can adults in democratic societies, for example, be confident that the next generation will construct society so as to reproduce the society's traditions, values, commitments, and hopes? (p. 264). For example, how will farm children in the Midwest, growing up in an environment of worry, hopelessness, fear, and alienation as large numbers of independent family farms collapse, construct society? Or others of the one in four children under the age of 6 whose families are below the poverty line? According to Meacham (1993), these and similar questions have serious implications for any discussion of learning.

Discussed in the remainder of this chapter are the sources of knowledge about learning, the role of research and theory in knowledge development, and the functions of learning theory. The chapter concludes with an overview of the organization of the text.

WHAT ARE THE SOURCES OF KNOWLEDGE ABOUT LEARNING?

Each generation seeks an explanation of the contemporary reality to which it belongs. Early societies sought to explain the mysteries of the four seasons, thunder, lightning, and other natural forces in their lives. Contemporary cultures, in contrast, are seeking to understand the causes and effects of global viruses, the effects of and countermeasures to widespread pollution, and the ramifications of cloning.

The search for understanding by any generation is restricted by the methods available at the time. Early societies lacked the methods to systematically analyze events. Instead, they developed different beliefs to explain the world. First were folklore and myths, which gradually gave way to logically reasoned explanations referred to as philosophies. In the 20th century, empirical research and formal theories have replaced these early types of beliefs as sources of knowledge.

Folklore, Traditional Wisdom, and Myths

Folklore consists of customs, tales, or sayings that typically are preserved orally among people. Traditional wisdom, a subset of folklore, consists of proverbs and maxims that often are derived from experience. An example is, "Spare the rod and spoil the child." However, one problem with this information is that it may be interpreted in a variety of ways. Therefore, such sayings are inadequate as guidelines for educational practice.

Some individuals, however, contend that good teaching practice constitutes a "traditional wisdom" that can inform others about learning and instruction. According to this view, more can be learned from good teachers than from either research or psychology. Of course, much can be learned from skilled teachers (Hilgard, 1964). However, ignoring the possibility of improving instruction through well-designed research is like "returning medical practice to the prescientific physician because we still value the bedside manner" (Hilgard, 1964, p. 404).

Several cultures explained events in the natural world by creating myths about powerful gods and goddesses who were responsible also for particular events in both the natural world and human affairs. The early Greeks, for example, believed that ocean storms were caused by Poseidon, the sea god, and lightning bolts were Zeus' arrows unleashed in punishment. In human affairs, the goddess Aphrodite was believed to influence love relationships, and wisdom was the gift of Athena. Such a system led to activities to placate the gods and goddesses, so that events would go well. However, these myths did not advance society's knowledge about the actual workings of the physical or social environment.

The Original Role of Philosophy

The early myths were replaced gradually by logically consistent belief systems known as philosophies. Unlike folklore and myths, which tend to be loosely organized, philosophies are structured belief systems based on reasoned judgment and logic. The purpose of a philosophy is to provide a coherent set of values that describes the relationship between the human race and the universe.

A philosophy first describes the nature of reality and then defines the nature of truth and beauty consistent with the stated assumptions about reality. Some philosophers also developed views about the human role in society, the function of the mind, and the nature of knowledge. The questions addressed are, What is knowledge? What is the origin of knowledge? and What does it mean "to know"? The answers, of course, are required to be logically consistent with the philosopher's view of reality.

One of early views on learning was developed by the Greek philosopher Plato (417–327 B.C.). His philosophy (idealism) describes mind or spirit as basic to everything that exists. Reality, therefore, consists of the pure ideas of the mind. Thus, human knowledge is derived from the ideas and concepts that are present in the mind at birth in the form of shadowy images. Learning, then, is the process of developing these innate or inborn ideas into a knowledge system. In Plato's view, the mind was developed through the study of the pure forms of mathematics, such as the circle and the square, and the classics.

Aristotle, Plato's pupil, developed a contrasting view of learning. According to Aristotle, reality exists in the physical world, not in the mind's conception of it. Universal laws are not innate ideas. Instead, they are the relationships observed in nature. The source of knowledge, therefore, is the physical environment, and learning occurs through contact with the environment. In Aristotle's system, the individual initially acquires knowledge by forming images of sensory experiences and by making associations among the images.

From 400 B.C. to the 19th century, philosophy served as the primary source of information about the human mind. Although experimentation on the physical world began in the 16th century, research methods were not applied to the study of mental activity for another 300 years. First, the mind, like the soul, was viewed as the gift of God. To conduct research on the mind would call into question the gift of God. Second, the primary function of the mind was to become attuned to the universe, the ultimate reality. Therefore, descriptions of reality developed by philosophers were sufficient for this task.

Two problems arise, however, when philosophy is used to develop knowledge about real-world events. First, the information is likely to be limited because only general questions are addressed, such as the nature of learning. For example, learning, according to Plato, is the development of the innate or inborn ideas in the mind. Methods for identifying these innate ideas, however, are not described.

Second, a philosophy develops information about major concepts (e.g., virtue, truth, knowledge, learning) using logic and reasoning. The resulting definitions, however, are only required to be logically consistent. They are not explicit hypotheses about the processes that are components of learning.

Current Influences of Philosophical Beliefs

Early philosophical beliefs about knowledge and learning have influenced theoretical developments and educational practice in various ways. First, some general concepts developed by early philosophers in their efforts to describe the nature of knowledge have appeared in contemporary theories. For example, Aristotle's recommended practice, in which public orators were taught to form vivid, active images of ideas to be remembered, is a device currently used to recall foreign language words and their meanings. Similarly, the association of ideas described by early philosophers reappears later in behaviorism. However, instead of the association of ideas, the behaviorists describe learning as the association of responses to particular objects or events known as stimuli.

Second, philosophical beliefs about the origins of knowledge have influenced educational practice. The belief in the innate nature of knowledge led to the development of and reliance on only intelligence tests for major educational decisions about students in the early 20th century.

In addition, different views on the origins of knowledge contributed to the nature/nurture controversy. For several years, the debate revolved around whether intelligence is an inborn trait (Plato) or is developed through experience with the environment (Aristotle). John Dewey, a well-known American philosopher, psychologist, and educator, noted that this focus on origins of knowledge had led to 30-year cycles of different emphases in educational practice. That is, American education has swung in a wide arc from the view that education is development from within to education as formation from without (Dewey, 1939, p. 5). One problem with a reliance on philosophical beliefs about the origins of knowledge, according to Dewey (1929), is that the focus is like looking in a rearview mirror. Instead, the factors that convey value on one's thoughts or ideas are the results of outcomes they produce (Dewey, 1929; Prawat, 1998).

Philosophical concepts also have influenced aspects of the cognitive–development theories developed by Jean Piaget and Lev S. Vygotsky. For Piaget, answering the philosophical questions, What is the nature of knowledge? and What is the relationship between the knower and reality? are essential to establish a framework for theory development and research. Knowledge, according to Piaget, is not a static objective reality. Instead, knowledge is synonymous with human intelligence as it constructs the structures it needs to adapt to the environment (Piaget, in Bringuier, 1980, p. 3). Also, the learner and the world cannot be separated in the individual's construction of cognitive structures because the relationship cannot be specified in advance and it is always changing. The infant, for example, learns about the world by putting objects into its mouth and other similar actions whereas researchers develop information about the world through detailed experiments.

Vygotsky, in contrast, drew on the beliefs about dialectical change described by the German philosopher, G. W. F. Hegel. That is, a movement or event (thesis) is countered by an opposing force (antithesis). The resolution, which is a qualitatively new phenomenon, combines elements of both and is referred to as a synthesis. According to Vygotsky (1930/1966), cognitive development is "a complex dialectical process characterized by disproportion in the development of some (cognitive) functions, metamorphoses or qualitative transformations of some forms into others, . . . and a complex process of surmounting difficulties and of adaptation" (p. 36). Specifically, primitive or natural cognitive functions were transformed into higher cognitive functions referred to as categorical perception, logical memory, conceptual thinking (verbal and mathematical), and voluntary (self-regulated) attention.

In summary, a philosophy provides a coherent set of values about the nature of reality, truth, beauty, and knowledge. Philosophies do not develop testable hypotheses about causes and effects in real-world settings. However, some of the concepts and ideas developed by philosophers have influenced the thinking of contemporary learning theorists.

Empirical Research

In the mid-16th century, experimentation with objects emerged as a new method of developing knowledge about the physical world. Introduced by Galileo in the 1500s, it is referred to as the scientific approach. One of Galileo's experiments, for example, involved dropping several objects from the top of a tower and calculating the rate of descent. This experiment contradicted the philosophical belief that a pound of lead and a pound of feathers fall to earth at different speeds.

Conducting experiments greatly expanded knowledge about the physical environment. Mystical beliefs and untested maxims gradually were replaced by reliable laws and principles. The science of chemistry supplanted the practice of alchemy, and the methods of astrology were replaced by the science of astronomy.

Rationale for Psychological Research

For almost 300 years, research methods were confined to the natural sciences. One reason was that to conduct research on the mind would call into question the gift of God. Second, philosophy was an adequate knowledge base for the mind's task of becoming attuned to an ultimate reality.

Two events in the 19th century set the stage for scientific investigations of mental functions. One was the publication of Charles Darwin's *Origin of Species* in 1859, in which his theory of evolution was set before the public. The theory states that the biological species found on Earth are not a preestablished set or group. Instead, species survive, perish, or develop variations as a result of their ability to adapt biologically to changing conditions. Thus, the theory defined a new reality, one in which change rather than some static order predominates. One result was that the formerly accepted views about the mind were altered; that is, if the human mind is part of the evolutionary process, then defining the static relationship between the human mind and the mind of God is no longer a major issue.

The second key event that set the stage for psychological research of mental functions was Hermann von Helmholtz's introduction of the concept of scientific empiricism. Von Helmholtz, a medical doctor, scientist, and philosopher, maintained that because ideas are products of human experience, they are subject to human observation and analysis. The term *scientific empiricism* refers to the accumulation of facts through carefully designed experiments. He demonstrated the usefulness of experimentation on ideas by his invention of the ophthalmoscope for observing the operations of the eye.

From research on the senses, which are living tissue, to research on the mind was only one short step. That step was taken by Wilhelm Wundt. In addition to publishing a text that summarized the research on sensory functions, Wundt established the first psychological research laboratory in 1879 at the University of Leipzig. The first studies included research on reaction time, sensation, auditory perception, and attention. Individuals from around the world, including the United States, came to study and conduct research in Wundt's laboratory.

However, the shift in ideas from the mind as the gift of the Creator to that of the brain as the key to mental activity was gradual rather than immediate. Books on psychology at the end of the 19th century continued to assert that psychology could not be an exact science because humans could never predict the interventions of the Creator to produce particular mental events in an individual's life (Reed, 1997).

Although Wundt's work on sensations captured the attention of Western scholars, he also advocated a "second psychology" that should address higher psychological functions, such as deliberate remembering, reasoning, and language (Cole, 1996). This second psychology was based on the concept proposed by two other German scholars that collective mentality exerts a powerful influence on individuals (see Jahoda, 1993, for a discussion). Referring to the second psychology as *Völkerpsychologie* (roughly translated, folk psychology), Wundt maintained that this area required historical and anthropological methods rather than experimentation. The purpose was to study reasoning and language which are created by a community of individuals. Although Wundt used the term *Kultur* (*culture*), the term referred to art, science, and sophistication, the products of advanced civilizations (Jahoda, 1993). From this perspective, some societies would be more cultured than others.

Wundt's early writings on Völkerpsychologie were not translated into English. Further, the primary interest of the new discipline of psychology was to develop a scientific knowledge base which required experimentation. Thus, his work (although it later grew to 10 volumes) fell into oblivion (Jahoda, 1993). The identification of culture as the primary agent in the individual's development of higher psychological functions reemerged in the theory of Vygotsky in the early 20th century. However, his ideas did not enter the mainstream of educational psychology in the United States until the 1980s.

Only Wundt's text on physiological psychology and his laboratory dominated Western thought. These developments initiated psychology as an experimental discipline and formally marked its separation from the discipline of philosophy. By 1895, 24 laboratories were in existence in the United States as well as 3 journals and several textbooks, including *Principles of Psychology* (1890) by William James, the father of American psychology.

An educational study conducted in the 1920s illustrates the contributions of empirical research to the development of knowledge and learning. The experiment, conducted by Edward L. Thorndike, tested the "mental discipline" concept derived from Plato's philosophy. The mental discipline perspective maintained that courses such as mathematics, chemistry, and Latin improved thinking (i.e., disciplined the mind). Thorndike compared the achievement of high school students enrolled in classical curricula with those enrolled in vocational curricula. He found that the type of subject taken by the students did not influence their thinking skills.

Pitfalls

By the early 20th century, empirical research had become a primary mechanism for generating information about psychological processes. However, the difficulty with the use of empirical research as the *sole* source of knowledge is that data collection does not necessarily advance knowledge about important phenomena. Vygotsky (1993) decried the pedagogical anarchy that resulted from efforts to use "uncoordinated compendia of empirical data and techniques."

Further, Suppes (1974) refers to the educational research of the 1920s as "the golden age of empiricism." This period was characterized by questionnaires, surveys, and studies on almost every aspect of school life. These efforts, referred to as "the scientific movement in education," obtained data on such topics as the number of Latin verbs learned by students in one year and the amount of time required to learn the multiplication tables. However, the extensive data collection did not contribute to an understanding of the basic processes of learning and instruction.

Theory

A fourth source of knowledge about learning is theory. Of importance are the criteria that a well-constructed theory should meet and the differences between theory and other sources of knowledge.

General Criteria

Clark Hull (1935), a behavioral theorist, identified three criteria that are essential in theory construction. First is a set of explicit assumptions that are the theorist's basic beliefs about the phenomenon to be addressed by the theory. For example, three basic assumptions of Robert Gagné's (1972; 1977) conditions of learning are (1) learning is the acquisition of increasingly complex structures of learned capabilities that build on prior learning, (2) no one set of characteristics can be applied to all learning, and (3) an adequate conception of human learning should apply to all the various contexts in which learning occurs. Included are home, school, business, trade occupations, military training, information situations, and others.

The second criterion is that key terms are explicitly defined. For example, the term "capabilities" is the focus of Gagné's (1972; 1977) conditions of learning. He defined capabilities as the skills, knowledge, attitudes, and values that are acquired by human beings. They are the outcomes of learning.

The basic assumptions and definitions set the framework for a theory, according to Hull (1935). The next step for the theorist is to derive specific propositions (principles) that are testable from the assumptions. These propositions, the third criterion, form the body of the theory and they are tested by collecting data on them through research. For example, based on the assumption that no one set of characteristics can describe all human learning, Gagné (1972, 1985) identified five distinct varieties of human learning. Principles of the theory describe the particular type(s) of capabilities generated by each variety of learning as well as the teaching and testing requirements for each. Research indicates, for example, that the strategies for teaching verbal information are ineffective in producing attitudinal change (Gagné, 1984).

Learning Theory

The prior criteria apply to a theory in any discipline. A fourth requirement is unique to theories of learning. Specifically, a theory should explain the underlying psychological dynamics of events related to learning. For example, prospective teachers are sometimes told that praising students is important. However, Brophy (1981) notes that teachers often use excessive public praise for right answers and global reactions, such as, "What a good group you are." These reactions are at best ineffective and, at worst, counterproductive (Brophy, 1981). B. F. Skinner's (1968) principles of reinforcement address the factors that govern the effectiveness of consequences and the relationships of consequences to other environmental events. Familiarity with these principles can help teachers avoid misuses of praise and other behavioral consequences.

Of importance for the researcher or practitioner in evaluating theories is first to determine that the theory meets the four criteria. The purpose is to avoid "theory"-labeled fashions that simply restate common-sense knowledge (Van der Veer & Valsiner, 1991, p. 2).

Comparisons of Theory with Other Knowledge Sources

Theories share some characteristics with other sources of knowledge about learning, but they also differ from them in important ways.

Learning Theory and Philosophy

First, both theories and philosophies are derived from assumptions and include hypothetical statements. A key difference, however, is that a philosophy is basically a value system, whereas a theory seeks to explain real-world events. Examples of real-world events addressed by theory include (1) the ways that children of different ages approach problems that require logical inference (Piaget's cognitive-development theory), (2) the types of events responsible for increased responding in a learning situation (Skinner's operant conditioning), and (3) learner explanations of the causes of academic success and failure (Weiner's attribution theory).

A second difference between philosophies and theories is that only theories can be certified through scientific investigation (Hull, 1937). For example, Vygotsky developed a theory about the role of signs and symbols used by each culture in the development of children's thinking processes. He also maintained that learning to use signs and symbols to direct and regulate one's thinking was both a long-term and ever-changing process. Vygotsky (1934/1978) designed memory experiments in which colored pictures and other symbols were available to the subjects in assisting them later to recall a set of words. He found that young children were unable to use the memory aids and that school children used them with varying levels of success. In contrast, adults used the aids only to develop complex verbal sequences that themselves became the cues for word recall (Leont'ev, 1959).

Learning Theory and Models of Teaching

Joyce and Weil (1996) define a model of teaching as a description of a learning environment (p. 11). Examples include cooperative learning (methods for organizing students to work together), advance organizers ("umbrella" statements that conceptually link learner knowledge and new learning), and direct instruction (an approach with objectives, related activities, monitoring, and feedback). Some are specific, such as advance organizers, whereas others are more general (direct instruction). Further, some are applicable to only certain subject areas and age levels. An example is the jurisprudential model that was created for secondary social studies. Students study cases involving social problems in areas that may benefit from public policy (Joyce & Weil, 1996, p. 14). Although the model may be used in any area with public policy issues, this model is not appropriate for young children.

Further, models of teaching are approaches to the management of some aspect of instruction in the classroom. Mastery learning, for example, describes an approach for accommodating individual differences that includes mastery-based assessments, whereas advance organizers are a particular type of introductory material to a lesson.

Theories of learning, in contrast, are independent of subject area, grade level, age of the student, and learning setting. More important, theories consist of specific principles about the learning process, not management, organization, or other events tangential to the processes of learning.

Summary

The three essential criteria for theory are (1) an explicit set of assumptions, (2) explicit definitions of key terms in the theory, and (3) specific testable propositions derived from assumptions. In addition, a fourth criterion for theories of learning is that they address the underlying psychological dynamics of learning. The importance of these criteria is to assist the researcher or practitioner to recognize common-sense ideas labeled as theories.

Theories differ from both philosophies and models of teaching. A philosophy is a value system, whereas a theory seeks to explain real-world events and can be certified through scientific investigation. Models of teaching are approaches to the management of some aspect of classroom instruction and they may not be independent of subject area, grade level, age of the student, or the setting for learning.

WHAT ARE THE FUNCTIONS OF LEARNING THEORY?

Several functions for learning theory may be identified. Included are general functions fulfilled by theory in any discipline as well as specific roles for theories of learning.

General Functions of Theories of Learning

Four general functions of theory have been identified by Suppes (1974): (1) to serve as a framework for conducting research, (2) to provide an organizing framework for specific items of information, (3) to reveal the complexity of apparently simple events, and (4) to reorganize prior experience. A fifth function is to serve as working models of complex events.

A Framework for Research

This function is related to the requirement that a theory consists of testable principles. That is, an essential requirement of a good theory is that it can be translated into concrete research designs (Bronfenbrenner, 1993). Serving as a framework for research is important because this practice facilitates data collection that contributes to an understanding of events. Simply collecting data in the absence of an organizing framework is referred to by Suppes (1974) as bare empiricism. It is a mental form of streaking, and nudity of body is much more appealing than nudity of thought (Suppes, 1974, p. 6).

The First Educational Scientist.   Edward L. Thorndike, referred to as the father of educational psychology, is a model of the use of theory to guide experimentation. The range of Thorndike's contributions in more than 400 books and articles includes the first learning theory and the formulation of laws of learning applied to the curriculum (as well as a variety of tests and measurements for the schools). Thorndike's contributions began with his dissertation study, "An Experimental Study of the Associative Process in Animals" (1898). The study was the first experimental analysis of the relationships among stimulus situations, behaviors, and consequences—key concepts in Thorndike's learning theory. The research demonstrated the feasibility of behavioral research in generating principles about mental events. (See chapter 2 for a description of the theory.)

Organization of Knowledge

The second function of theory is to provide an organizing framework for specific items of information. For example, why are some students happy to earn a "C" in a difficult course and others despondent about a "B"? Why do children entertain naive beliefs about the world, such as that the moon walks with them at night? Why does simply learning a rule not guarantee that the child will be able to use it in solving a problem? These questions are addressed respectively within the frameworks of Bernard Weiner's attribution theory, Piaget's cognitive-development theory, and Gagné's conditions of learning.

Identification of Complex Events

The third general function of theory is to reveal the complexity and subtlety of apparently simple events. This function is related to the characteristic that learning theories address the underlying dynamics of events related to learning.

An example is the situation in which young children are busily engaged in trying to topple a plastic dummy using a ball on a string suspended from the ceiling. A few of the children will be able to observe the arc that is made by the ball, modify their pitches, and successfully strike the dummy. Others, however, will tend to verbalize contradictory and often illogical explanations for the ball's actions. They might say, for example, "The string is too short," "The string is too long," or "The ball isn't heavy enough."

The tendency of the typical adult is to attempt to correct the child's illogical statements. Jean Piaget's (1963) extensive analyses of children's thinking, however, have revealed that these "illogical" statements are a natural and essential stage in the development of logical thinking. Repeated interaction and experimentation with concrete objects by the child will contribute to the subsequent development of more logical modes of thinking.

Another event that was regarded as fairly simple on the surface is the fact that young children frequently made errors in responding to questions on the Stanford–Binet intelligence test. However, Jean Piaget, a young Swiss psychologist who was working at the Binet Institute in the 1920s, became intrigued with the children's wrong answers. He began to study their responses, and his research eventually led to a description of the prelogical ways that young children use to explain the world.

Reorganization of Prior Experience

A theory often can bring new insights to a situation such that existing principles or theories are reorganized. For example, learning from models was once viewed as that of simple mimicry. That is, the learner immediately imitates the model and is rewarded for the behavior. However, Albert Bandura's (1971) social–cognitive theory found that imitation often was not immediate. Instead, the observer executed the modeled behavior days or weeks later. Bandura then proceeded to identify the factors that account for this form of observational learning.

Theories as Working Explanations

From the 1920s to the 1950s, psychologists had hoped to develop the one "grand theory" that would explain all learning. The prototype for this goal was classical physics (also known as Newtonian mechanics). This theory was viewed by physicists and others as the explanation of the actions of physical forces throughout the universe.

However, psychologists were not successful in developing eternal principles of learning. In the 1940s, their laboratory-based efforts were challenged, and eventually eclipsed by the practical training needs of military personnel in World War II and the development of high-speed computers. These events raised new questions about human learning and thinking and led to the development of theories that address the ways learners process new information.

In other words, a theory does not stand for all time. As new information is discovered and new questions emerge from the changing social context, early theories give way to redefined relationships and new generalizations. Therefore, at one point in time, a generalization may adequately describe a particular system, but at a later point in time, it may be valid only as history (Cronbach, 1975).

The redirection or replacement of theories is not unique to psychology. For example, classical physics was insufficient to describe *precisely* the actions of physical forces in the entire universe. In classical physics, time is treated as a constant. With Einstein's discovery of the theory of relativity, in which time is a relative variable, classical physics became a special case of that theory. Classical physics is sufficiently accurate for activities on our planet, and it was sufficient for a civilization undertaking an industrial revolution. Interplanetary travel, however, requires a more precise theory of time and motion.

Similarly, in psychology, the experiments on reflexes conducted by Ivan Pavlov initially were believed to hold the key to the learning of complex behaviors. Today, his views, referred to as classical conditioning, are a special case in behaviorism. Classical conditioning explains the learning of many emotional responses, but it does not explain the acquisition of complex behaviors.

Specific Functions of Theories of Learning

A characteristic of learning theories is that they address the underlying psychological dynamics of events. Thus, they provide a mechanism for understanding the implications of events related to learning in both formal and informal settings.

In addition, learning may involve any of a variety of internal mental processes, social interactions, and interactions with information in the environment. No single theory can adequately account for these myriad events. Therefore, each theory describes the key features of learning as the theorist defines them and focuses on identifying the factors that will lead to those outcomes. Skinner's operant conditioning, for example, addresses the role of consequences in bringing about behavioral change. In contrast, Gagné's conditions of learning describe the environment and internal mental events necessary for the learning of different skills and attitudes.

The coexistence of different theories is not unique to the field of learning. Sfard (1998) notes that the existence of several theoretical outlooks of the same entity occurs in science where chemistry and physics provide different, but not incompatible, accounts of matter. Further, perspectives that often may be viewed initially as incompatible may instead be considered as incommensurable. That is, no one set of vocabulary and no one set of rules explains them (p. 11). An example is

Euclidean and non-Euclidean geometries. Examples in learning theory are Gagné's conditions of learning and Vygotsky's cultural–historical theory.

The importance of more than one theory of learning is that each offers insights that are not provided by others. Therefore, understanding and taking account of more than one theory guards against the pitfalls and shortcomings of relying exclusively on any one perspective.

Regardless of orientation, learning theories may fulfill any of four specific functions listed in Table 1.1. In addition to the two examples that serve as a guide to planning instruction, other major theories also provide information on particular aspects of planning.

In summary, learning theories are useful in planning and evaluating instruction, and in diagnosing problems in classroom instruction. They also are useful in determining if research that purports to test a particular theory in the classroom setting is in accordance with the theory.

TABLE 1.1
Specific functions of learning theory

Function	Example
1. Serves as a guide for planning instruction	a. Robert Gagné's conditions of learning provides a set of nine specific steps that parallels the sequence in which information is received from the environment, processed (encoded), and stored in long-term memory.
	b. Jean Piaget's cognitive-development theory provides insights into classroom practices that facilitate the development of logical thinking.
2. Evaluates current products for classroom use and current practice	Theories helpful in the evaluation of computer-based instruction include information-processing principles, Skinner's operant conditioning, Gagné's conditions of learning, and Bandura's social-cognitive theory.
3. Diagnoses problems in classroom instruction	Difficulties experienced by low achievers often include low self-esteem and inadequate learning strategies. Weiner's attribution theory, Bandura's social-cognitive theory, perspective on problem solving, and Vygotsky's sociohistorical theory address various aspects of this problem.
4. Evaluates research conducted on theories	One study implemented models for prosocial behavior and post-tested the children at the end of the experimental session. The children's lack of model imitation was taken as evidence that Bandura's theory does not apply to certain social situations. However, according to the theory, children do not enact everything they learn.

HOW DOES THIS TEXT PRESENT KNOWLEDGE ABOUT LEARNING?

The primary purpose of this text is to reflect the current state of the art in theory development related to classroom learning against the backdrop of early theory development. Toward this end, behaviorism and Gestalt psychology are discussed first, followed by seven contemporary perspectives. They are B. F. Skinner's operant conditioning, Robert Gagné's conditions of learning, cognitive learning principles, Jean Piaget's cognitive-development theory, Lev Vygotsky's cultural-historical theory, Albert Bandura's social–cognitive theory, and Bernard Weiner's theory of motivation (known as attribution theory).

These theories were selected because they each describe particular psychological mechanisms of importance to classroom learning. B. F. Skinner details the role of reinforcement in behavioral change, and Robert Gagné describes the internal processes and environmental conditions essential for different kinds of learning outcomes. The ways that individuals process and remember information received from the environment, learn to solve problems, and become experts in a knowledge domain are addressed by the cognitive learning perspective. In contrast, Albert Bandura describes the ways in which human beings learn from observing the behaviors of others and the role of perceived self-efficacy in learning.

The other three theories in this text technically are not categorized as learning theories. Nevertheless, they have important implications for classroom practice. Jean Piaget describes the development of logical thinking processes from infancy to adulthood. Lev Vygotsky describes the unique role of each culture in determining the nature and level of the thinking processes attained by the child. Bernard Weiner, on the other hand, presents the ways in which individuals identify the causes of success and failure outcomes. Each of these theories has been applied to particular issues in the design and implementation of instruction.

Psychological Models of Reality

Learning is a complex set of processes that may vary according to the developmental level of the learner, the nature of the task, and the context in which the learning is to occur. As already indicated, no one theory can capture all the variables involved in all learning.

Each theory, therefore, begins with an assumption or set of assumptions about the nature of learning and then proceeds to develop a set of principles consistent with the assumptions. The behavioristic perspective, for example, assumes that the environment is the primary agent responsible for learning. These theories describe the various ways that events in the environment influence behavior (see Figure 1.1).

In contrast, the cognitive theories assume that the learner's mental processes are the major factor in learning. These theories therefore emphasize the ways that the learner's processing and application of information change one's thoughts and internal mental structures.

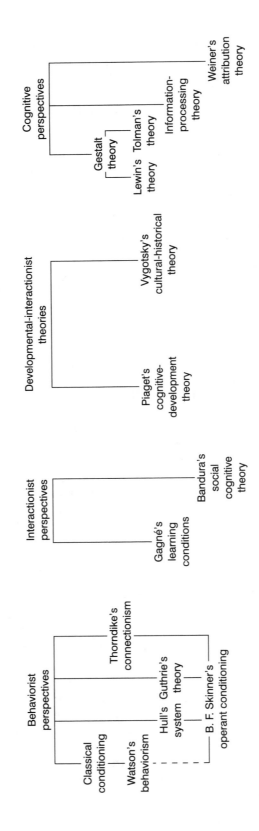

FIGURE 1.1
Psychological models of reality related to learning

The interactionist perspectives, however, assume that behavior, mental processes, and the environment are interrelated. Thus, they describe the interactive role of these elements during learning.

Two of the theorists in this text, Jean Piaget and Lev Vygotsky, focus on the development of thinking. Learning, in their view, is related to, but is not the same as, cognitive development. Piaget describes the stages from birth through adolescence that lead to the development of logical thinking. Vygotsky, in contrast, discusses the development of conceptual thinking, logical memory, and self-regulated attention. In his view, the signs and symbols developed by a particular culture and the child's interaction in learning these symbols are essential in developing these higher mental functions.

Organization of the Text

The 1920s to the 1950s have been described as the period of the "great debate" among learning theories. During that period, two broad perspectives sought to develop the one theory that would explain all learning. These perspectives are behaviorism and Gestalt psychology. Behaviorism, the dominant perspective during this period, is described in chapter 2. This perspective views learning as behavioral change, and researchers attempt to identify the environmental events and conditions responsible for such change. Gestalt psychology, a cognitive perspective, is discussed in chapter 3. Initiated in Germany, Gestalt psychology maintained that learning is a sudden perceptual reorganization of a problem situation. Gestalt theorists named this process *insight*.

By the mid-1950s, efforts to develop the one comprehensive learning theory began to decline. New developments, such as high-speed computers and changing social conditions, redirected psychologists to other problems. Chapter 4 describes the developments since mid-century and introduces the contemporary theories presented in the text.

Chapters 5 through 12 present the selected contemporary theories. These theories are categorized into three broad groups: learning-process theories, cognitive-development theories, and social-context theories (see Table 4.1, p. 70). Skinner's operant conditioning is discussed in chapter 5. Skinner's principles, developed in the 1930s, successfully made the transition from the laboratory to classroom practice, and were dominant in the late 1950s and 1960s. Gagné's theory is discussed in chapter 6. Gagné's conditions of learning addressed the curriculum redesign priorities that emerged in the 1960s following the launch of Sputnik by the U.S.S.R. Also, Gagné's perspective, which incorporates both learning outcomes and the processing of information by the learner, serves as a bridge between operant conditioning and the cognitive theories that follow.

Chapter 7 discusses information-processing theories, which describe the ways that individuals take in information from the environment and then process, store, and later retrieve the information when needed. This chapter is the first part of the cognitive perspective that seeks to identify universal processes of learning. Chapter 8, the second part of this perspective, discusses the processes identified in metacognition, problem solving, and expert knowledge.

Chapters 9 and 10 discuss two theories that focus on cognitive development. Chapter 9 presents Piaget's theory of the development of logical thinking, and chapter 10 presents Vygotsky's sociohistorical theory.

The last two theories, discussed in chapters 11 and 12, are referred to as social-context theories. Both of these perspectives focus on the abstraction of information by the learner from the immediate social setting. Bandura's social-cognitive theory describes the processes of learning from observing the behavior of others and the consequences and the learner's development of a self-regulatory system to manage learning. Bernard Weiner, in contrast, addresses the individual's perceived causes of events or outcomes. His perspective, attribution theory, is a motivational theory. The text concludes with a brief summary of the theories and a discussion of current issues in learning theory (Epilogue).

CHAPTER QUESTIONS

1. Self-directed learning is important to the individual because it contributes to a varied and creative lifestyle. What are some reasons for the importance of self-directed learning to society?

2. One of the activities undertaken in the data collection efforts of the 1920s was determining the cost of teaching certain topics, such as Latin verbs. What is the problem with this particular piece of research, according to Suppes?

3. A maxim sometimes provided to novice teachers is "Don't smile until Christmas." Why is such a directive of little help in the classroom?

4. The view that one should study great books to improve one's mind is consistent with which philosophy?

5. What is the major difference between the methods used by philosophy and the new psychology?

6. A collaborative learning group in seventh grade, using print resources and the Internet, develops a travel brochure on South America. Included are major historical sites. According to Vygotsky, what type of experience is this?

REFERENCES

Bandura, A. (1971). *Social learning theory*. Upper Saddle River, NJ: Prentice Hall.

Bringuier, J. C. (1980). *Conversations with Jean Piaget* (B. M. Gulati, Trans.) Chicago: University of Chicago Press.

Bronfenbrenner, U. (1993). The ecology of cognitive development: Research models and fugitive findings. In R. H. Wozniak and K. W. Fischer (Eds.), *Development in context: Acting and thinking in specific environments* (pp. 3–44). Hillsdale, NJ: Erlbaum.

Brophy, J. (1981). Teacher praise: A functional analysis. *Review of Educational Research, 51*, 5–32.

Cole, M. (1996). *Cultural psychology*, Cambridge, MA: Belknap Press of Harvard University Press.

Cronbach, L. J. (1975). Beyond the two disciplines of scientific inquiry. *American Psychologist, 30*, 116–127.

Dewey, J. (1929/1988). The quest for certainty. In J. A. Boydston (Ed.), *John Dewey: The later works, 1925–1953, Vol. 14*. Carbondale, IL: Southern Illinois University Press.

Dewey, J. (1939/1988). Experience and education. In J. A. Boydston (Ed.), *John Dewey: The later works, 1925–1953, Vol. 14*. Carbondale, IL: Southern Illinois University Press.

Gagné, R. M. (1972). Domains of learning. *Interchange, 3*(1), 1–8.

Gagné, R. M. (1977). *The conditions of learning* (3rd ed.). New York: Holt, Rinehart, & Winston.

Gagné, R. M. (1984). Learning outcomes and their effects: Useful categories of human performance. *American Psychologist, 37*(4), 377–385.

Gagné, R. M. (1985). *The conditions of learning* (4th ed.). New York: Holt, Rinehart, & Winston.

Hilgard, E. R. (1964). A perspective on the relationship between learning theory and educational practices. In E. R. Hilgard (Ed.), *Theories of learning and instruction: The sixty-third yearbook of the National Society for the Study of Education, Part I* (pp. 402–415). Chicago: University of Chicago Press.

Hull, C. L. (1935). Conflicting psychologies of learning: A way out. *Psychological Review, 42,* 491–516.

Hull, C. L. (1937). Mind, mechanism, and adaptive behavior. *Psychological Review, 44,* 1–32.

Jahoda, G. (1993). *Crossroads between culture and mind.* Cambridge, MA: Harvard University Press.

James, W. (1890). *Principles of psychology.* New York: Henry Holt.

Joyce, B., & Weil, M. (1996). *Models of teaching.* Boston, MA: Allyn & Bacon.

Leont'ev, A. N. (1959). *Problems in mental development.* Moscow: Academy of Pedagogical Sciences AFSFR.

Meacham, J. A. (1993). Where is the social environment? A commentary on Reed. In R. H. Wozniak and K. W. Fischer (Eds.), *Development in context: Acting and thinking in specific environments* (pp. 255–267). Hillsdale, NJ: Erlbaum.

Piaget, J. (1963). *The origins of intelligence in children.* New York: Norton.

Prawat, R. S. (1998). Current self-regulation views of learning and motivation viewed through a Deweyan lens: The problems with dualism. *American Educational Research Journal, 35*(2), 199–226.

Reed, E. S. (1997). *From soul to mind: The emergence of psychology from Erasmus Darwin to William James.* New Haven, CT: Yale University Press.

Skinner, B. F. (1968). *The technology of teaching.* New York: Appleton-Century-Crofts.

Sfard, A. (1998). On two metaphors for learning and the dangers of choosing just one. *Educational Researcher, 27*(2), 4–13.

Suppes, P. (1974). The place of theory in educational research. *Educational Researcher, 3*(6), 3–10.

Thorndike, E. L. (1931). *Human learning.* New York: Century.

Van der Veer, R., & Valsiner, J. (1991). *Understanding Vygotsky: A quest for synthesis.* Cambridge, MA: Blackwell.

Vygotsky, L. S. (1978). *Mind in society.* Cambridge, MA: Harvard University Press. (Original work published 1934).

Vygotsky, L. S. (1979). Consciousness as a problem in the psychology of behavior. *Soviet Psychology, 17*(4), 3–35. (Original work published 1924.)

Vygotsky, L. S. (1993). *The collected works of L. S. Vygotsky: Vol. 2. The fundamentals of defectology (abnormal psychology and learning disabilities)* (J. E. Knox and C. B. Stevens, Trans.). New York: Plenum.

CHAPTER 2

Early Behaviorist Theories

At any one time, a science is simply what its researches yield, and the researches are nothing more than those problems for which effective methods have been found and for which the times are ready. Each step in scientific progress depends on the previous one, and the process is not much hurried by wishing (Boring, 1950).

Wilhelm Wundt's laboratory for research on the senses initiated the separation of psychology as a discipline from philosophy. One year later, 1875, Harvard University introduced the first graduate course in psychology. By 1900, 24 laboratories, 3 journals, and the new American Psychological Association indicated the rapid growth of American psychology.

Major questions for the new discipline were What should be the focus of study? and What should be the scope of psychology? Several perspectives proposed answers and competed to be the major voice of the new discipline. Psychologists also aspired to develop a precise science, like physics and chemistry. However, many of the directions suggested for psychology lacked defined research methods. Into that breach came behaviorism, championed by its founder, John R. Watson. From the 1920s to the 1950s, behaviorism was the dominant movement in psychology and with it, the study of learning became a major focus.

CLASSICAL CONDITIONING AND CONNECTIONISM

The research method that initiated behaviorism was reflex or classical conditioning. Discovered by two Russian physiologists in independent experiments and adapted by John Watson, classical conditioning seemed to be the precise methodology sought by psychologists. The other approach implemented in the early 20th century was Edward Thorndike's connectionism.

A Rationale for Behaviorism

The inability of early views of psychology to establish a clearly defined subject matter and specific research methods set the stage for behaviorism and established the climate for change. In that context, John Watson launched the movement to study behavior rather than mental processes or states.

In the 1913 article "Psychology as the Behaviorist Views It," Watson made a case for the study of behavior. He noted that in some 50-odd years, psychology had failed to establish itself as a natural science. The focus on consciousness and mental processes had led psychology into a dead end where the topics were "threadbare from much handling" (Watson, 1913, p. 174). Furthermore, when human consciousness is the reference point for research, the behaviorist is forced to ignore all data that do not relate to human mental processes. Other sciences, such as physics and chemistry, he noted, do not restrict their definitions of the subject matter to the extent that information must be discarded.

The starting point for psychology, therefore, should be the fact that all organisms adjust to the environment through responses (Watson, 1913). Because certain responses follow certain stimuli, psychologists should be able to predict the response from the stimulus, and vice versa. When this goal is achieved, according to Watson, psychology will then become an objective, experimental science. In addition, the discipline also would provide useful knowledge for the educator, physician, business leader, and others.

After the appeal to study behavior, Watson discovered the motor-reflex research of V. M. Bekheterev, a Russian physiologist. Bekheterev's work was important because he had successfully manipulated simple behavioral reactions in the laboratory. On reading the research, Watson was convinced that behavioral control in the real world was within reach. His prediction was wrong, but his views were a major force in the use of precise methods of research and measurement by psychologists (Kratochwill & Bijou, 1987).

Basic Assumptions

The term *behaviorism* refers to several theories that share three basic assumptions about learning. They are:

1. Observable behavior, rather than internal mental events or verbal reconstructions of events, should be the focus of study.

2. Behavior should be studied in terms of its simplest elements, e.g., specific stimuli and specific responses. Examples of behavioral reactions investigated by different researchers include reflexes, observable emotional reactions, and motor and verbal responses.

3. The process of learning is behavioral change. That is, a particular response becomes associated with the occurrence of a particular stimulus. In other words, the response occurs in the presence of a particular stimulus.

Reflex or Classical Conditioning

The motor reflex experiments conducted by Bekheterev "trained" reactions such as finger retraction to respond to a variety of sights and sounds associated with an electric shock stimulus (Murphy, 1949). The best-known experiments, however, were conducted in the research laboratories of Ivan Pavlov.

The story handed down through the years about Pavlov's research features the lonely scientist who, quite by accident, discovered that an involuntary reaction, salivation, could be trained to respond to sounds unrelated to food. However, far from being a lonely scientist, Pavlov directed several physiological laboratories, which produced more than 530 research papers from 1897 to 1936. As director, Pavlov assigned research topics to co-workers and students and monitored their work, but he rarely experimented himself (Todes, 1997; Windholz, 1997).

Pavlov and the Bolsheviks

The years of the Bolshevik revolution (1917–1921) were particularly difficult for Pavlov, his family, and his laboratory. Pavlov's home was searched several times, he scavenged for firewood, and fed his family from a garden he tended at the Institute of Experimental Medicine. The Nobel Prize money he had received in 1904 for the work on digestive processes was confiscated and work in his laboratories almost ceased for lack of electricity, kerosene, and candles (Todes, 1995, p. 384).

In June 1920, at the age of 70, Pavlov wrote to the government for permission to emigrate. Considering the emigration of an internationally known scientist impermissible, the government accorded Pavlov special status. He received improved living quarters, liberal food rations for himself and his co-workers, and extensive laboratory support (Todes, 1995).

Of interest is that throughout the 1920s, Pavlov attacked state policies in public, including the ouster of various scientists from academic positions. Because of his special status, Pavlov was not silenced. Although his public criticisms tempered somewhat in the 1930s, Pavlov did not relinquish his basic criticisms of governmental actions (Todes, 1995, p. 46).

The Research in Pavlov's Laboratory

The accepted belief about the salivary reaction was that (1) food texture did not influence the reaction, and (2) contact between food and the animal's sensory receptors is essential to produce salivation. However, an early laboratory finding by a student indicated greater salivation for dry foods placed in a dog's mouth than for moist foods. Another student testing this finding serendipitously discovered that "teasing" dogs from a distance with dry and moist foods produced the same greater and lesser amounts of salivation (Windholz, 1997, p. 942). Pavlov initially named the reaction to sight of the food as a conditional reflex.

Subsequent research by V. N. Boldyrev found that the salivary reflex also may be conditioned (trained to respond) to stimuli (objects or events) from virtually any sensory modality (sight, sound, touch) (Windholz, 1997). An often-described experiment is that of sounding a tuning fork moments before the placement of meat powder on the animal's tongue. After several such pairings, the tuning fork alone elicited the salivation reaction.

The research in Pavlov's laboratory was important for two reasons. First, it demonstrated that the salivation reaction is a reflex. That is, it is a spontaneous reaction that occurs automatically to a particular stimulus. Second, to alter the "natural" relationship between a stimulus and a reaction was viewed as a major breakthrough in the study of behavior. To manipulate even a simple reaction held out the promise that the causes of complex behaviors also might be discovered. Thus, the research demonstrated the potential of laboratory studies to discover new knowledge.

The Classical Conditioning Paradigm

The process by which new events or stimuli acquire the power to trigger responses became known as reflex or **classical conditioning**. In the classical conditioning methodology, the naturally occurring stimulus and the reflex response are unconditioned. That is, they occur together without training and are referred to as the **unconditioned stimulus (UCS)** and **unconditioned response (UCR)**. The UCS is said to *elicit* the UCR; for example, a foreign object in the eye elicits an eye blink.

After training, the new stimulus that elicits the reflex response is referred to as the **conditioned stimulus (CS)**. The reflex, formerly unconditioned, became known as a **conditioned** (instead of conditional) **response (CR)** after training (see Table 2.1).

The development of classical conditioning introduced a number of variables and new relationships that could be researched and precisely measured in the laboratory setting. Included are the amount or strength of the response (referred to as amplitude), the length of time between the stimulus and the response (latency), and the tendency of similar stimuli to elicit the reflex (stimulus generalization). For example, studies indicated that a reflex conditioned to a sound pitch of 256 also is conditioned to sound pitches of 255 and 257 (Murphy, 1949).

TABLE 2.1
Examples of classical conditioning

Preexperimental ("Natural") Relationship		Experimental Trials		Postexperimental (Conditioned) Relationship	
UNCONDITIONED (ELICITING) STIMULUS (UCS)	ASSOCIATED REFLEX RESPONSE (UCR)	PAIRED STIMULI	REFLEX RESPONSES	CONDITIONED STIMULUS (CS)	CONDITIONED REFLEX (CR)
Meat powder	Salivation	Meat powder Tuning fork	Salivation	Tuning fork	Salivation
Air puff	Eye blink	Air puff Bright light	Eye blink	Bright light	Eye blink
Electric shock	Finger retraction	Electric shock Buzzer	Finger retraction	Buzzer	Finger retraction

Two other relationships introduced in classical conditioning include **resistance to extinction** and **inhibition**. Resistance to extinction is the tendency of a response to persist for a time after the supporting conditions are withdrawn. Inhibition refers to the reduction in a response caused by the introduction of extraneous stimuli.

Current Applications.   In addition to the discovery of new variables that have become part of the foundation of behavioral psychology, Pavlovian research had three other enduring effects. One is the research on animal survival mechanisms in the natural environment in which an animal learns to respond to cues that precede biologically important events (Hollis, 1997). An example is the particular locations or sites that signal the likely presence of a predator.

Second, Pavlovian research in the 1920s identified animal neuroses and methods to counter maladaptive reactions. Animal neurosis develops when powerful conditioned environmental stimuli (such as repeated mild electric shock) overwhelm an animal's typical reactions and elicit anxiety or neurotic reactions (such as howling and rapid pacing). However, pairing an aversive stimulus, such as mild electric shock, with the presentation of food precipitated salivation instead of the animal's defensive behaviors. Termed counterconditioning, this finding, along with the Pavlovian research on animal neuroses, became the foundation for clinical behavior therapy for these problems in humans (Wolpe & Plaud, 1997).

Third is the research into drug reactions which has identified the cues that signal different human responses. Pavlov found that conditioned responses (CRs) associated with drug injections also were elicited by cues that precede the injection. Contemporary research by Siegel (1991) and others indicates that reliable cues associated with the ingestion or injection of several drugs (including opiates, alcohol, and caffeine) elicit a set of CRs that counter the physiological and biological reaction to the particular drug. The result is drug tolerance, the decreasing effect of a drug over several administrations (Hollis, 1997, p. 960).

John Watson's Behaviorism

Watson's contribution to psychology is that he organized the findings of current research into a new perspective and persuaded other psychologists of the importance of his views. Behaviorism, as Watson viewed it, should apply the techniques of animal research (i.e., conditioning) to the study of human beings. He therefore redefined mental concepts (which he considered to be unnecessary) as behavioral responses. Thinking, for example, was identified as subvocal speech, and feeling was defined as a glandular reaction (Watson, 1925).

Watson also believed that the human personality developed through the conditioning of various reflexes. He maintained that the human infant at birth possesses only three emotional responses (Watson, 1928). They are fear, rage, and love. The fear response, for example, begins with the jumping or starting of the body and an interruption in breathing. Then, depending on the infant's age, crying, falling, and crawling or running away follows. The fear response was observed in the natural environment after a loud noise or loss of support for the infant. According to Watson (1928), an adult's complex emotional life is the result of the conditioning of the three basic responses to a variety of situations.

Conditioning Experiments with Infants.   While at Johns Hopkins University, Watson and his graduate assistant, Rosalie Raynor, conducted a controversial experiment with an 11-month-old child named Albert (Watson & Raynor, 1920). This experiment, unethical by today's standards, conditioned Albert's fear reaction to several soft furry objects.

Albert was tested first to confirm that live animals and objects (such as a human mask and cotton) did not elicit his fear response. Then, for several trials, a white rat was presented to Albert, and a laboratory assistant behind Albert struck a steel bar with a hammer. On the first pairing of the two stimuli, the infant jumped violently; on the second trial, he began to cry. On the eighth trial, the white rat alone elicited crying and crawling away (Watson & Raynor, 1920).

Five days later, the fear reaction also appeared in response to a white rabbit. Non-furry objects, such as the child's blocks, did not elicit the fear response, but mild fear reactions occurred in response to a dog and a sealskin fur coat. The child's emotional response had transferred to furry animals and objects, and it persisted for longer than a month.

In recent years, questions have been raised about the experiment because the requirements for classical conditioning were not strictly followed. The loud noise was not paired with the presentation of the rat; instead, the noise occurred as Albert reached out his hand to touch the animal. However, the experiment demonstrated that emotions could be studied by controlled research methods, and it promoted research on conditioning (Kratochwill & Bijou, 1987).

A related topic, the elimination or "unconditioning" of children's fear reactions, was pioneered by Mary Cover Jones. She found that efforts to talk the child out of the fear or relying on extinction to eliminate the fear were ineffective (Jones, 1924). Instead, a planned program was required. The two successful strategies were (1) the child's observation of other children's acceptance of the feared object, and (2) the gradual presentation of the feared object during a favorite activity, such as eating.

Watson's Predictions.   Watson concluded from his experiment that behaviorism was the mechanism that could provide a foundation for living. In his usual persuasive style, Watson (1925) made the following claims for conditioning:

> Give me a dozen healthy infants, well formed, and my own specified world to bring them up in, and I'll guarantee to take any one at random and train him to become any type of specialist I might select—doctor, lawyer, artist, merchant-chief—regardless of his talents, penchants, tendencies, abilities, vocations, and race of his ancestors (p. 65).

Needless to say, behaviorism became immediately popular. The simplicity of the method for conditioning responses and the novelty of the procedure led to a multitude of applications and experiments. In the 1920s, almost every psychologist seemed to be a behaviorist, and none appeared to agree with any other (Boring, 1950). The term behaviorism became attached to several developments, including a particular research method, objective data in general, and a materialistic view of psychology.

Watson also believed that behaviorism would place psychology in the ranks of the "true" sciences, along with zoology, physiology, physical chemistry, and others.

These same views on the potential of behaviorism were to be reiterated in the 1950s by B. F. Skinner.

In fact, conditioned reactions were not shown to add up to complex voluntary behavior. However, it was *believed* that they would, very likely because the resulting conception of psychology responded to the general scientism of the times (Baars, 1986, p. 53).

Conditioned Emotional Reactions

Through paired association, positive and negative reactions may be conditioned to a variety of objects and events. For example, a whiff of the paste used to fasten labels to bottles brought back painful memories of a miserable childhood for the well-known author Charles Dickens (Ackerman, 1990). The bankruptcy of Dickens' father had driven him to abandon the young Charles to a workhouse where such bottles were made.

Emotional reactions may, in certain situations, be conditioned in a single pairing of stimuli. An example is an automobile driver who narrowly misses a fatal accident with a large truck on a particular S-shaped curve. He experiences a rapid pulse, sweating palms, and increased blood pressure. A few days later, on approaching the same S-shaped curve, he experiences the same physiological reaction.

However, "pure" examples of classical conditioning to aversive stimuli are difficult to find in the natural setting. Typically, individuals are not "trapped" by emotion-producing stimuli. They may engage instead in escape behaviors that may, in some situations, produce satisfying outcomes. For example, Albert's fear responses of crying and whining (conditioned response) to the furry object (conditioned stimulus) were followed by crawling away (escape behavior). In the natural setting, the baby's mother would likely pick him up and comfort him, perhaps even rock him a few minutes. Thus, a selected response, the escape behavior of crawling away, is followed by receiving the mother's attention and comfort.

A positive example of classical conditioning is the nostalgic reaction (response) to a song (conditioned stimulus) that was a hit during a former love affair. The song has acquired the power to elicit some of the same feelings originally associated with the person in the former relationship. Such emotional reactions often occur without the awareness of the individual; thus, their origin may be difficult to identify.

Classical Conditioning in the Classroom

An essential step in developing the appreciation of literature, art, science, and other subjects is that of associating students' early experiences with positive reactions (Estes, 1989). However, the problem is that negative emotional reactions may become attached to the same situations and lead to the passive escape behaviors of apathy and "tuning out."

One strategy is to make use of already-established relationships that elicit positive reactions. For example, sustained reading is an important activity in learning to appreciate literature. Carpeting one corner of the room and furnishing it with large sofa cushions to create an area for sustained reading may, over time, elicit positive reactions to the free-time reading included in the daily schedule.

Such strategies are particularly important in situations in which a particular setting or activity is expected to elicit a negative reaction. For example, the anxiety of children on the first day of school may become associated with certain subjects, particularly if a difficult activity is introduced the first day. Positive strategies observed in some elementary school classes included greeting the children warmly as they arrived and starting the day with drawing or coloring activities (Emmer, Evertson, & Anderson, 1980). In addition, no difficult activities were introduced the first week while the children were becoming accustomed to classroom routines. The potential for anxiety is reduced by repeatedly pairing the unfamiliar setting with warm greetings and enjoyable activities (Figure 2.1).

Summary

Reflex conditioning began with the motor-reflex experiments of Bekheterev and the research on salivation in Pavlov's laboratory. Early studies on dogs found that dry foods elicited greater salivation than moist foods and that "teasing" the animals from a distance with food also elicited the salivary reflex. Subsequent research indicated that the salivary reaction could be trained to respond to a variety of sights and

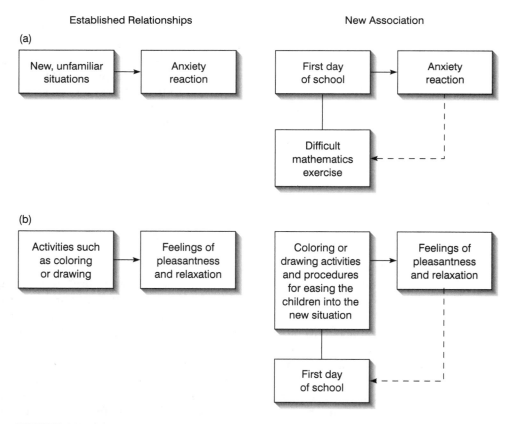

FIGURE 2.1
Applying classical conditioning in the classroom

sounds. The importance of this research is that it demonstrated salivation is a reflex and the "natural" relationship between a stimulus and the associated reflex could be altered. These manipulations held out the promise that reflex conditioning might lead to the causes of complex behaviors.

The paradigm by which a reflex is trained to respond to a new stimulus involves the repeated pairing of the new stimulus with the stimulus that naturally elicits the reflex. In addition, Pavlovian research indicated that particular objects or events can precipitate reactions in several areas of psychological functioning. Among them are animal responses to cues associated with danger, the associations that become the basis for counterconditioning, and the drug reactions referred to as drug tolerance and enigmatic overdose.

John Watson applied the concepts of classical conditioning to emotional reactions. Maintaining that newborns possess only three emotional responses, Watson believed that an adult's complex emotional life resulted from the conditioning of these responses to various situations. His now-famous experiment with baby Albert reportedly conditioned the fear reaction to several soft furry objects. Of interest is that another researcher, Mary Cover Jones, demonstrated the unconditioning of children's fear reactions through the gradual presentation of the feared object during a favorite activity.

Although Watson's prediction about the role of classical conditioning was not realized, positive and negative emotional reactions may be conditioned to a variety of objects and events. In the classroom, for example, the teacher can utilize already-established relationships to elicit positive reactions.

Edward Thorndike's Connectionism

Although typically referred to as a behaviorist theory, Edward Thorndike's connectionism differs from classical conditioning in two major ways. First, Thorndike was interested in mental processes and his first experiments were designed to provide information about the nature of the thought processes of animals. Second, instead of reflex or involuntary reactions, Thorndike researched voluntary or self-directed behaviors.

The publication of Thorndike's doctoral thesis in 1898 was a breakthrough in the study of behavior in North America (Galef, 1998). Prior to his research, the literature in comparative psychology was a morass of questionable anecdotes and engaging tales (p. 1128). Thorndike (1911) noted that "dogs get lost hundreds of times and no one ever notices it or sends an account of it to a scientific magazine. But let one find his way from Brooklyn to Yonkers and the fact immediately becomes a circulating anecdote" (p. 24).

Instead of depending on chance observations of intriguing bits of behavior and attempting to describe the animal's likely mental processes, Thorndike insisted on experimentation under controlled conditions. In the experiments, animals were confined in cages or food was placed in a latched box. The task for the hungry animal was to open the box or cage and get to the food. Thorndike referred to his experiments as **instrumental conditioning** to reflect the differences from classical conditioning. The theory also is known as **connectionism** because connections were established between particular stimuli and voluntary behaviors.

Experimental Procedure

Thorndike experimented with baby chicks, dogs, fish, cats, and monkeys. (While he was a student at Harvard, his landlady forbid him to continue hatching chicks in his room. William James offered the basement of his home for Thorndike's research, to the dismay of Mrs. James and the excitement of the children.) The typical experimental procedure required each animal to escape from a confined space to reach food. A puzzle box was used that required the tripping of a latch or some other mechanism to effect escape (Figure 2.2).

When confined, the animal often engaged in a variety of behaviors, including scratching, biting, clawing, and rubbing against the sides of the box. Sooner or later the animal tripped the latch and escaped to the food. Repeated confinements were characterized by a decrease in the behaviors unrelated to escape and, of course, a shorter escape time. The most dramatic change was observed with monkeys. In one experiment, a box containing a banana was placed inside the cage. The monkey took 36 minutes to pull out the nail that held the wire fastener closed. On the second trial, the monkey successfully released the fastener in only 2 minutes 20 seconds (Thorndike, 1911).

The experimental data from a series of trials were recorded as a learning curve illustrating the faster escape times. Thorndike concluded from this data that the escape response gradually became associated with the stimulus situation in trial-and-error learning. For this reason, his theory is referred to as an *association* theory.

The Laws of Learning

During the series of trials in the experiment, the correct response was gradually "stamped in" or strengthened. Incorrect responses were weakened or "stamped

FIGURE 2.2
Puzzle cage used in some of
Thorndike's experiments

out." In other words, problem solving involves establishing associations or connections between the stimulus (the problem) and appropriate responses.

Thorndike originally identified three major laws of learning to explain this process. They are the law of effect, the law of exercise, and the law of readiness. The *law of effect* states that a satisfying state of affairs following the response strengthens the connection between the stimulus and the behavior, whereas an annoying state weakens the connection. Thorndike later revised the law so that punishment was not equal to reward in its influence on learning.

The *law of exercise* describes the conditions implied in the adage "Practice makes perfect." Repetition of the experience, in other words, increases the probability of a correct response. However, repetition of a task, such as drawing lines blindfolded, does not enhance learning in the absence of a satisfying state of affairs (Thorndike, 1913b, p. 20).

The *law of readiness* describes the conditions that govern the states referred to as "satisfying" or "annoying" (Thorndike, 1913a). Briefly summarized, the execution of an action in response to a strong impulse is satisfying, whereas the blocking of that action or forcing it under other conditions is annoying.

Thorndike's views were not immediately accepted. Galef (1998) notes that one early review maintained he has studied "starved, panic-stricken cats and dogs that had temporarily lost their normal wits, so that their intelligence was grossly underestimated" (Mills, 1899 in Galef, 1998, p. 1130). However, Thorndike's work became better known and laboratories to study comparative psychology were established.

Applications to School Learning

In the laboratory, Thorndike researched the relationship between physical stimuli and physical actions, and his interpretations of learning were based on these behavioral studies. However, his theory also includes references to mental events. It thus occupied a middle ground between the concerns of some early views of psychology and the "pure" behaviorism of other researchers.

Thorndike described human mental life as composed of both mental states and movements with connections between each type (Thorndike, 1905, p. 12). In his view, connections between ideas accounted for the major portion of "knowledge" in its popular sense (Thorndike, 1913b, p. 19). The process of learning, in other words, is simply that of connecting: "The mind is man's connection system" (Thorndike, 1913b, p. 122). This connection system includes both specific examples, such as $9 \times 5 = 45$, and connections to multiple cofigurations. An example is the concept that $1 \times 1 = \frac{1}{2} \times 2 = \frac{1}{3} \times 3$ (Cox, 1997). Other examples include events and dates, such as Columbus and 1492 and persons and characteristics, such as John and blue eyes.

Thorndike's rules for teaching arithmetic, for example, identify the requirements for establishing connections between stimuli and responses. Examples are (1) do not form a bond that will have to be broken, and (2) form bonds in the way they are later required to act (Thorndike, 1922, p. 101). He also described five minor laws that are the first effort to account for the complexity of human learning. These subsidiary laws and their applications to school learning are summarized in Table 2.2.

TABLE 2.2
Application of Thorndike's minor laws to education

	Law	Description	Example
1.	Multiple response or varied reaction	A variety of responses often occurs initially to a stimulus	Pronunciation of foreign language Skill in tennis Coherence in English composition
2.	Attitudes, dispositions, or states	Condition of the learner that influences the learning; includes stable attitudes and temporary factors of the situation	Individual competing to throw a ball the longest distance or throw a player out in a baseball game Instructions for the problem $$\frac{\begin{array}{r}7\\6\end{array}}{}$$ to add or to subtract
3.	Partial or piecemeal activity of a situation	The tendency to respond to particular elements or features of a stimulus situation (also referred to as analytic learning)	Responses to the qualities of shape, color, number, use, intent, and others Responses to relations of space, time, causation, and others
4.	Assimilation of response by analogy	The tendency of situation B to arouse in part the same response as situation A	The foreigner pronouncing English
5.	Associative shifting	Successively altering the stimulus until the response is bound by a new stimulus	*abcde* is altered to *abcdef* to *abcdefg* and so on

Note: From *Educational Psychology: Vol. II. The Psychology of Learning* (pp. 19–31) by E. L. Thorndike, 1913. New York: Teacher's College Press.

These laws were believed to interact with the laws of effect and exercise to account for human learning.

Connectionism, with its emphasis on establishing bonds between stimuli and responses, was particularly relevant for school learning in the early 20th century. At that time, the emphasis was on the learning of information and specific procedures.

The application of connectionism to school subjects is an example of Thorndike's focus throughout his career—that of developing an educational psychology based on empirical data (Beatty, 1998). A series of studies on **transfer of learning** conducted by Thorndike and Woodworth (1901) found that training in particular tasks facilitated the later learning only of similar tasks, not dissimilar ones.

Some behaviorists interpreted the findings to be the result of identical stimulus elements between the training and transfer tasks. However, Thorndike and Woodworth (1901) viewed the commonality to be that of similar mental actions or habits related to stimuli (Cox, 1997, p. 42).

Thorndike also investigated the popular "mental discipline" concept originally described by Plato. According to this view, the study of certain difficult subjects, such as Greek, Latin, or geometry, functioned as kinds of mental exercises that would enable students to think clearly and deeply (Cox, 1997, p. 42). That is, such school subjects were believed to discipline the mind. Thorndike (1924) tested the concept by comparing the postcourse achievement of high school students enrolled in classical and vocational curricula and found no significant differences. This finding refuted the belief that learning a particular subject, such as Greek, would benefit intellectual performance in other areas.

Thorndike (1924) also noted that the main reason that certain school studies superficially seemed to produce good thinkers was that good thinkers tended to enroll in those courses. That is, good thinkers tend to enroll in physics and trigonometry and these courses, therefore, seem to produce good thinkers. However, students became better thinkers because of the "inherent tendency of the good to gain more than the poor from any study" (Thorndike, 1924, p. 98). In succeeding years, Thorndike's research was named as a major influence in turning curriculum designers away from the mental discipline concept and toward the practice of designing curriculum for more useful purposes (Cushman & Fox, 1938; Gates, 1938).

In addition to founding the *Journal of Educational Psychology* and developing tests of mathematics and handwriting, Thorndike produced more than 500 publications in his career, including 50 books (Dewsbury, 1998). His son later noted that his father was a workaholic primarily because he enjoyed analyzing data more than anything else (R. L. Thorndike, 1991).

Summary.   Seeking to determine the nature of mental life in animals, Thorndike confined animals in cages with food nearby. Observing the faster escapes in repeated confinements, he concluded that the correct response is "stamped in" through association with eating the food, a satisfying state (the law of effect). Describing human mental life as the connections between ideas, Thorndike described five minor laws that further address human learning.

Thorndike's school-related research illustrates his goal of developing an educational psychology based on empirical data. His research on the transfer of learning found that training on particular tasks facilitated only the learning of similar tasks. Other studies demonstrated that the learning of difficult subjects, such as Greek, Latin, or geometry, does not function as a type of mental exercise that enhances thinking skills.

THE RETREAT TO THE LABORATORY (1930–1950)

Thorndike cautioned his fellow psychologists that the proper laboratory for research was the classroom and the appropriate experimental subject was the student (Shulman, 1970). For the most part, however, the theorists from 1930 to 1950 ignored Thorndike's advice. Research was conducted instead on animals and human beings in artificially contrived situations: Rats ran mazes, rats escaped from boxes, and humans were given puzzles to solve.

The goal of the research also shifted in this period. In this "era of grand theories," the goal was to integrate all known facts around the principal theme of describing, predicting, and controlling learning (DiVesta, 1987, p. 207). In other words, the purpose of research was to develop the one comprehensive theory that would explain all learning.

The Refinement of Behaviorism

The dominant movement in the 1930s and 1940s continued to be behaviorism. However, it was by no means a unitary theory, nor was it the only approach to behavioral analysis. Some psychologists, influenced by Sigmund Freud's psychoanalytic theory, were searching for deeper meanings in behavior beyond observed relationships between events and responses. Included were Robert Woodworth's "dynamic psychology" and William McDougall's "hormic psychology." McDougall described "drives" as behavioral activators. For example, the "thirst drive" activates the go-to-water mechanism (Boring, 1963, p. 723). In contrast, McDougall developed an extensive list of instincts that he identified as goal directed (flight, fear, reproduction, and so on).

Three theories emerged from the 1930s and 1940s. They are Clark Hull's behavior system, Edwin Guthrie's contiguity theory, and B. F. Skinner's operant conditioning. They are referred to as *S–R theories* because they define learning as an associative link between a particular stimulus and a particular response. They differ, however, in the identification of the specific factors believed to be of primary importance in establishing the S–R association. Hull's theory emphasized processes within the organism, specifically, intervening variables. Guthrie, however, maintained that the temporal relationship between the stimulus and the response was the critical factor in learning. Skinner, on the other hand, began with Edward Thorndike's law of effect. He redefined "reward" as reinforcement and described behavioral change as a function of response consequences. These three theorists also are known as "neobehaviorists," to distinguish their work from that of Thorndike and Watson.

Two S-R Theories

Hull's behavioral system and Guthrie's contiguity theory are in sharp contrast to each other. Hull's theory is rigorous, abstract, and complex; Guthrie's theory is informal and loosely organized. Practical advice for parents and teachers also is included in Guthrie's work.

Clark Hull's Behavior System

Hull's theory is a rigorous example of his recommendations for theory development, the hypothetico–deductive method. That is, testable propositions are derived from explicitly stated assumptions. Then controlled experimentation either verifies or fails to support the propositions.

Influenced by the concept of evolution, Hull (1943) maintained that behavior functions to ensure the organism's survival. Therefore, the central concepts in his theory revolve around biological needs and need satisfaction, which is essential for survival. Needs were conceptualized by Hull (1943, 1952), as "drives", such as hunger, thirst, sleep, relief from pain, and others. Stimuli, referred to as *drive stimuli* are associated with primary drives and therefore "motivate" behavior. For example, stimuli associated with pain, such as the sounds of a dentist's drill, can also arouse fear, and the fear motivates behavior.

Reinforcement was also incorporated into the theory; however, reinforcement is a biological condition. Satisfaction of the biological need, referred to as **drive reduction**, strengthens the link between the drive stimulus and the response. For example, giving an animal a sip of water after turning right in a maze reduces the drive stimulus of a dry mouth. The water, therefore, strengthens the link between the dry mouth and turning right in the maze.

The final version of Hull's theory combined 17 assumptions into 133 propositions on theorems (Hull, 1952). Also included in the system are concepts such as incentive, generalized habit strength, the power of a stimulus to elicit a particular response, and others. However, the testable propositions in the theory often were not verified. Further, Hill (1990) notes that, depending on which assumption is used, the theory yields conflicting predictions. More important for educators, the theory did not generalize beyond the laboratory. Although dominant into the 1940s, Hull's system was eclipsed in the 1950s by Skinner's operant conditioning (discussed in chapter 5).

Edwin Guthrie's Continguity Theory

A refreshing contrast to the other theories of this period, continguity theory relied on one major learning principle. Known as the **law of contiguity**, it states that a combination of stimuli accompanied by a movement will tend to be followed by the same movement on its recurrence (Guthrie, 1952, p. 23). Movements are muscle contractions, and movements also can generate stimuli for subsequent movements in a complex action. For example, the ringing of the telephone leads to standing up followed by walking to the telephone, then lifting the receiver (Guthrie, 1935, p. 34). The movements, in other words, form a series and they bridge the distance between the initial stimulus (ringing of the telephone) and the response (lifting the receiver).

Guthrie also defined acts as combinations of movements. Examples are eating a meal or throwing a ball. He further defined skills as combinations of acts, such as playing golf and typewriting (Guthrie, 1942). Although a single movement may be acquired in one learning trial, time and practice are required to learn all the associations in a skill. The reason is that "many specific movements must be attached to many different stimulus situations. A skill is not a simple habit, but a large collection of habits that achieve a certain result in many and varied circumstances" (Guthrie, 1952, p. 59). Guthrie and Horton (1946) noted that even a simple act such as grasping a rattle requires different movements depending on the distance, direction, and position of the rattle. One successful experience is insufficient because the movements acquired might not be successful on the next occasion (p. 8).

Reinforcement, however, is not an essential factor in learning. Instead, learning occurs because the last movement that is made changes the stimulus situation and no other response can occur. For example, in solving a puzzle, the last action changes the stimulus (i.e., completes the puzzle). Similarly, in the earlier example, lifting the telephone receiver changes the stimulus condition (the ringing) and no other response can occur. Therefore, in the same situation again, the same response will be repeated. Reinforcement simply protects the new learning from unlearning by preventing the acquisition of new responses (Guthrie, 1942, 1952).

Breaking Habits.   A habit is defined in the theory as a response that is associated with several different stimuli (Guthrie, 1952). The greater the number of associations, the stronger the habit because the response is "cued" on many different occasions. Smoking is an example of a strong habit because so many different cues trigger lighting up a cigarette. Included are finishing a meal, taking a coffee break, sitting down to watch television, and so on.

Breaking habits requires breaking the associations between the cues (eliciting stimuli and the response). To break a habit, one must practice another response in the presence of the cues that elicit the undesirable response. The three methods suggested by Guthrie (1938) are the threshold method, the fatigue method, and the incompatible response method. These three methods are summarized in Table 2.3. They are equivalent, according to Guthrie (1938, p. 62), because they all involve presenting the cues that typically elicit a particular undesirable response while preventing the performance of the response.

Guthrie (1938) suggests that the threshold method is appropriate for introducing new foods to a young child. That is, the child may react to certain foods by spitting them out. However, parents should begin with small tastes that are not enough to cause rejection and gradually build toward a teaspoonful. However, it is not clear that this method will be successful if the child has already developed a strong dislike for a food, such as spinach.

TABLE 2.3
Summary of three methods for breaking habits

Method	Characteristic	Example
Threshold method	1. Introduce the eliciting stimulus at weak strength 2. Gradually increase the stimulus strength, always keeping it below the response "threshold" (i.e., strength that will elicit the response)	*Breaking a horse to the saddle*: Begin with a light blanket, then heavier blankets, and finally, a light saddle
Fatigue method	"Exhaust" the response in the presence of the eliciting stimulus	*Breaking a horse*: Throw the saddle on the horse and ride him until he quits kicking, bucking, and trying to throw the rider; the saddle and rider become the stimulus for walking and trotting calmly
Incompatible response method	Pair the eliciting stimulus (S^1) for the inappropriate behavior with a stimulus (S^2) that elicits appropriate responses; the appropriate behavior associated with S^2 becomes linked to S^1	Overcome fear and avoidance by pairing the frightening object, such as a large toy tiger, with a stimulus that elicits warm feelings, such as mother

The fatigue method involves executing the response in the presence of the stimuli until it is no longer fun. However, practical applications of this method for parents and teachers are difficult to identify. For example, the student who is caught writing notes in class should not be punished by having to write sentences on the blackboard for an hour after school. As discussed later in the chapter on operant conditioning, such practices evoke resentment and other undesirable emotional reactions.

The incompatible response method, however, does have practical applications. It is appropriate for overcoming the fear of a particular object. The method used by Mary Cover Jones earlier in this chapter for unconditioning children's fears by introducing the feared object during a favorite activity is an example.

Uses of Punishment.   A contribution of Guthrie's (1952) work is his perspective on punishment. To be effective, punishment (1) must be delivered appropriately in the presence of a stimulus that elicits inappropriate behavior, and (2) cause the subject to do something different. Guthrie (1935) describes the example of the girl who came home repeatedly from school each day and threw her hat and coat on the floor. The girl's mother made her put her hat and coat back on, go back outside, come in again, and hang up her wraps. After a few occasions, the response of hanging up the coat and hat became associated with the stimulus of entering the house.

Suggestions for Educators.   Associating stimuli and responses appropriately is the core of Guthrie's advice to teachers. The student must be led to perform what is to be learned. Students, in other words, learn only what the stimuli in lectures or books cause them to do (Guthrie, 1942, p. 55). Therefore, if students use notes or textbooks simply to memorize quantities of information, books will be the stimuli that cue rote learning.

In managing the classroom, the teacher is cautioned not to give a directive that is permitted to be disobeyed. A request for silence, if followed by a disturbance, will become the cue for disruptive behavior.

SUMMARY

At the beginning of the 20th century, the newly formed discipline of psychology was searching for a direction and major focus. Unlike other proposed courses of action, behaviorism, advocated by John Watson, was represented by the newly discovered reflex or classical conditioning. Watson's directive to discover the mechanisms that explain why certain responses follow certain stimuli soon became the dominant perspective. Demonstrations of the new linkages established between stimuli and reflex reactions by classical conditioning led to application of the paradigm to emotional reactions and application to animal neuroses and counterconditioning. Classical conditioning, however, was unable to explain the mechanisms that account for complex, self-initiated behaviors.

The advent of Thorndike's connectionism initiated the study of voluntary behaviors and set the stage for Skinner's operant conditioning. According to

Thorndike, positive consequences in the form of a satisfying state of affairs establish connections between stimuli and appropriate responses. Thorndike also demonstrated the applicability of research methods to school learning through his studies of transfer of training and the mental discipline concept.

Contrary to Thorndike's advice, the neobehaviorist theories retreated to the laboratory. Hull's behavior system, which incorporated biological needs, drives, and need satisfaction, did not generalize beyond the laboratory. Guthrie's perspective analyzed the movements in acts. However, he provided little direction for establishing appropriate connections, suggesting instead methods for breaking already-established habits.

APPLICATIONS TO EDUCATION

The behaviorist and neobehaviorist theories of the early 20th century differed in their research goals and methods. As a result, their suggestions for education address different aspects of behavior. Classical conditioning, which relies on stimulus pairing to link reactions to new stimuli, identifies the importance of avoiding the association of anxiety and other negative feelings to the school setting. Implementing activities that elicit positive feelings the first few days of kindergarten or elementary school is suggested.

In contrast, Thorndike emphasized the importance of establishing connections between ideas and the avoidance of introducing opportunities to establish inaccurate bonds or connections. Guthrie's contiguity theory also focused on the link between the stimulus and the response. Of importance in the classroom is that (1) students learn what they do, and (2) teachers should ensure that stimuli do not cue wrong responses. For example, the teacher should ensure that directives such as to begin seatwork or to line up for lunch are not followed by disruptive behavior. The problem is that these directives can become the cues for disruptions in the future. If punishment is to be used for inappropriate responses, then it must "undo" the association between a stimulus and the inappropriate behavior. In other words, if students are disruptive following a directive to line up by rows for lunch, they should be sent back to their seats to respond appropriately to the teacher's statement.

CHAPTER QUESTIONS

1. What are the implications for the classroom inherent in the major differences between Thorndike's connectionism and classical conditioning?

2. At summer camp, a spider is thrust in a child's face at the same time that some girls scream and shout, "Boo!" The next night, the girls scare her just as she turns down the sheet and finds a spider. Diagram these events and predict the outcome of these experiences.

3. Identify a school activity that may tend to elicit negative reactions. What prior relationship may be the basis for this reaction?

4. Apply Guthrie's "incompatible response method" to address the problem in question 2.

5. A student who relies on coffee to wake up in the morning finds, over time, that he requires a stronger brew to be alert. How does classical conditioning explain the problem?

6. In the 1980s, some advocates of teaching computer programming skills maintained that such learning would promote the broad skills of rigorous thinking (Cox, 1997). These beliefs reflect what concept that was refuted in the early 20th century?

REFERENCES

Ackerman, D. (1990). *A natural history of the senses.* New York: Random House.

Baars, B. J. (1986). *The cognitive revolution in psychology.* New York: Guilford.

Beatty, B. (1998). From laws of learning to a science of values. *Celebrating E. L. Thorndike: American psychologist, 53*(1), 1145–1152.

Boring, E. G. (1950). *A history of experimental psychology* (2nd ed.). New York: Appleton-Century-Crofts.

Boring, E. G. (1963). *History, psychology, and science: Selected papers.* New York: Wiley.

Cox, B. D. (1997). The rediscovery of the active learner in adaptive contexts: A developmental–historical analysis of transfer to training. *Educational Psychologist, 32*(1), 41–55.

Cushman, C. L., & Fox, G. (1938). Research and the public school curriculum. In G. Whipple (Ed.), *The scientific movement in education. The thirty-seventh yearbook of the National Society for the Study of Education, Part II* (pp. 67–78). Chicago: University of Chicago Press.

Dewsbury, D. A. (1998). Celebrating E. L. Thorndike a century after animal intelligence. *Celebrating E. L. Thorndike: American Psychologist, 53*(1), 1121–1124.

DiVesta, F. J. (1987). The cognitive movement and education. In J. A. Glover & R. R. Ronning (Eds.), *Historical foundations of educational psychology* (pp. 203–233). New York: Plenum.

Emmer, E., Evertson, C., & Anderson, L. (1980). Effective classroom management at the beginning of the school year. *The Elementary School Journal, 80*(5), 219–231.

Estes, W. (1989). Learning theory. In A. Lesgold & R. Glaser (Eds.), *Handbook of research on teaching* (pp. 1–49). Hillsdale, NJ: Erlbaum.

Galef, B. G. (1998). Edward Thorndike: Revolutionary psychologist, ambiguous biologist. *Celebrating E. L. Thorndike: American Psychologist, 53*(1), 1128–1134.

Gates, A. (1938). Contributions of research on the general methods of education. In G. Whipple (Ed.), *The scientific movement in education. The thirty-seventh yearbook of the National Society for the Study of Education, Part II* (pp. 79–80). Chicago: University of Chicago Press.

Guthrie, E. R. (1935). *The psychology of learning.* New York: Harper.

Guthrie, E. R. (1938). *The psychology of human conflict.* New York: Harper.

Guthrie, E. R. (1942). Conditioning: A theory of learning in terms of stimulus, response, and association. In N. B. Henry (Ed.), *The psychology of learning: The forty-first yearbook of the National Society for the Study of Education, Part II* (pp. 17–60). Chicago: University of Chicago Press.

Guthrie, E. R. (1952). *The psychology of learning.* New York: Harper & Row.

Guthrie, E. R., & Horton, G. P. (1946). *Cats in a puzzle box.* New York: Rinehart.

Hill, W. F. (1990). *Learning: A survey of psychological interpretations* (5th ed.). New York: Harper & Row.

Hollis, K. L. (1997). Contemporary research on Pavlovian conditioning. *American Psychologist, 52*(9), 956–965.

Hull, C. L. (1935). Conflicting psychologies of learning: A way out. *Psychology Review, 42,* 491–516.

Hull, C. L. (1937). Mind, mechanism, and adaptive behavior. *Psychological Review, 44,* 1–32.

Hull, C. L. (1943). *The principles of behavior.* New York: Appleton-Century-Crofts.

Hull, C. L. (1952). *A behavior system.* New Haven, CT: Yale University Press.

Jones, M. C. (1924). Elimination of children's fears. *Journal of Experimental Psychology, 7,* 382–390.

Kratochwill, T. R., & Bijou, S. W. (1987). The impact of behaviorism on educational psychology. In J. A. Glover & R. R. Ronning (Eds.), *Historical foundations of educational psychology* (pp. 131–157). New York: Plenum.

Mills, W. (1899). The nature of animal intelligence and the method of investigating it. *Psychological Review*, 6, 262–274.

Murphy, G. (1949). *Historical introduction to modern psychology.* New York: Harcourt, Brace, & World.

Shulman, L. (1970). Reconstruction of educational research. *Review of Educational Research, 40,* 371–396.

Siegel, S. (1991). Feedforward processes in drug tolerance. In R. G. Lister & H. J. Weingartner (Eds.), *Perspectives in cognitive neuroscience* (pp. 405–416). New York: Oxford University Press.

Thorndike, E. L. (1905). *The elements of psychology.* New York: A. G. Seiler.

Thorndike, E. L. (1911). *Animal intelligence.* New York: Macmillan.

Thorndike, E. L. (1913a). *Educational psychology: Vol. I. The original nature of man.* New York: Teachers' College Press.

Thorndike, E. L. (1913b). *Educational psychology: Vol. II. The psychology of learning.* New York: Teacher's College Press.

Thorndike, E. L. (1922). *The psychology of arithmetic.* New York: Croswell-Collier and Macmillan.

Thorndike, E. L. (1924). Mental discipline in high school studies. *Journal of Educational Psychology, 15,* 1–22, 83–98.

Thorndike, E. L., & Woodworth, R. S. (1901). The influence of improvement in one mental function upon the efficiency of other functions I, II, & III. *Psychological Review, 8,* 247–261, 384–395, 553–564.

Thorndike, R. L. (1991). Edward L. Thorndike: A professional and personal appreciation. In G. A. Kimble, M. Wertheimer, & C. White (Eds.), *Portraits of pioneers in psychology* (Vol. 1, pp. 139–151). Washington, DC: American Psychological Association.

Todes, D. P. (1995). Pavlov and the Bolsheviks. *History and Philosophy of the Life Sciences, 17,* 379–418.

Todes, D. P. (1997). From the machine to the ghost within: Pavlov's transition from digestive physiology to conditioned reflexes. *Commemorating Pavlov's work: American Psychologist, 52*(9), 947–955.

Watson, J. B. (1913). Psychology as the behaviorist views it. *Psychological Bulletin, 20,* 158–177.

Watson, J. B. (1925). *Behaviorism.* New York: Norton.

Watson, J. B. (1928). Chapter I. What the nursery has to say about instincts; Chapter II. Experimental studies on the growth of emotions. In C. Murchison (Ed.), *Psychologies of 1925* (pp. 1–37). Worcester, MA: Clark University Press.

Watson, J. B., & Raynor, R. (1920). Conditioned emotional reactions. *Journal of Experimental Psychology, 3,* 1–14.

Windholz, G. (1997). Ivan P. Pavlov: An overview of his life and psychological work. *Commemorating Pavlov's work: American Psychologist, 52*(9), 941–946.

Wolpe, J., & Plaud, J. J. (1997). Pavlov's contributions to behavior therapy. *Commemorating Pavlov's work: American Psychologist, 52*(9), 966–972.

CHAPTER 3

Gestalt Psychology:
The Cognitive Perspective

A general theory in psychology is something like a political platform, in that its policies are stated as of larger scope, and in a form to encourage enthusiastic adherents, and often equally committed opponents. (Hilgard, 1987, p. 416)

The dominant perspective in the first half of the 20th century was behaviorism. In the early years, under Watson's influence, it had acquired some of the characteristics of a political platform. However, the rise of behaviorism was not completely unchallenged. The opposing view was that of Gestalt psychology, which, ironically, had originated as a reaction against the study of sensations in psychology. When transported to this country, Gestalt psychology became the reaction to the behaviorist perspective. The primary reasons for the attention of American psychologists to Gestalt psychology were dissatisfaction with the strictures of behaviorism and the limited intellectual appeal of Thorndike's connectionism (Hilgard, 1996).

MAJOR CONCEPTS

The original focus of Gestalt research was the experience of perception. Max Wertheimer, the founder of Gestalt psychology, initiated the movement with an innovative experiment that illustrated the differences between visual perceptions and physical phenomena. Together with Kurt Koffka and Wolfgang Köhler, Wertheimer proceeded to develop the laws of perception and to apply these concepts to learning and thinking.

The theory was introduced in the United States in 1922, 10 years after its inception. In the 1930s, the three leaders left Germany to continue their writing and teaching in the United States. In general, Gestalt theory was viewed by American psychologists as interesting but by no means the final solution to major issues. However, the theory established the experimental study of perception and social psychology, neglected topics in the heyday of behaviorism (Baars, 1986, p. 71). In addition, the theory raised new questions about problem solving and thinking.

Origins of the Gestalt Perspective

The foundation for Gestalt psychology was established in an 1890 paper by a German named Christian von Ehrenfels. He maintained that qualities appear in perception in addition to the separate sensory elements that are components of the experience. For example, when the same melody is played in different keys, the tone sensations (sensory elements) change but the melody is recognized as the same.

The term applied to this process was *Gestaltqualität* which may be translated roughly as "the quality conferred by a pattern" (Murphy, 1949, p. 226). The familiar melody played in a different key has no single element in common with the original, but the melody is recognized instantly (Murphy, p. 227).

Several questions were left unanswered by this perspective, however (Murphy, 1949). For example, what is meant by "the same"? A melody sung by the voice or played by the violin, for example, may be recognized as "the same" (p. 286). However, a particular note, such as middle C, does not sound the same when it appears in different chords or is played by different instruments. The result is that an almost infinite number of "qualities" given by each structural total may be identified. For psychologists, such a process that yields an infinite number of patterns is no more useful than the analysis of separate elements.

The solution to these problems was found quite by accident some years later by Max Wertheimer (Watson, 1963). He was traveling by train from Vienna to Germany for a vacation. Leaving the train at Frankfurt to follow up a sudden hunch, he bought a toy stroboscope. A stroboscope is an instrument that presents pictures at such a rapid rate that the illusion of motion is created; it was popular before the invention of motion pictures. As a result of this preliminary investigation, Wertheimer canceled his vacation plans and took his research to the laboratory.

What characteristic of this event led Wertheimer to launch a new movement in psychology? Specifically, it was the perception of motion from the rapid successive presentation of stable images. In a subsequent laboratory experiment, Wertheimer presented his subjects with many variations of the same basic situation. First, light was projected through a small vertical slit and then through a slit inclined 20 or 30 degrees to the right. The time intervals were varied between the two projections. Logically, the subject should see two brief illuminations. However, depending on the time interval, the subjects saw differing illuminations, including one projection moving toward the other, two simultaneous projections, and one projection "falling" from right to left (Heider, 1973, p. 68). The perception of motion was named the *phi phenomenon* in a 1912 publication of the research.

The discovery was important because it demonstrated the relationships between stimulus configurations and "experienced wholes." In other words, the relationships between stimulus configurations and perceptions were not haphazard. Instead, they could be studied and categorized.

Basic Assumptions

Four basic assumptions support the Gestalt perspective (see Table 3.1). First, unlike the behaviorists, Gestalt theorists maintained that "molar" behavior should be studied, rather than "molecular" behavior. Chemical processes illustrate these concepts. Suppose, for example, that HNO_3 is produced in one part of a factory out of its elements and that the product is used in another part of the factory to dissolve silver (Köhler, 1929, p. 180). Do we say that the silver reacts to nitrogen, hydrogen, and oxygen? Of course not, because the effect on the silver depends on the chemical organization of the product. The effect on the silver cannot be understood either as a reaction to the individual elements or to their sum.

Examples of the related assumption (organisms respond to organizations of stimuli or "segregated sensory whole") include the names of groupings of stars in

TABLE 3.1
Basic assumptions of Gestalt Theory

Assumption	Example
1. Molar behavior, rather than molecular behavior (muscle contractions or gland secretions), should be studied.	1. A college student's performance that occurs in a classroom in which a lecturer holds forth (Koffka, 1935, p. 27).
2. Organisms respond to "segregated sensory wholes" or *Gestalten* (Kohler, 1929, p. 174) rather than to specific stimuli as isolated and independent events.	2. A geometrical arrangement of 11 dots is perceived as a cross.
3. The geographical environment, which is the way things are, differs from behavioral environment, which is the way things appear to be. The behavioral environment is the individual's subjective reality.	3. Koffka (1935, p. 29) describes the incident of a man on horseback who rode across a windswept plain in a snowstorm to arrive safely at an inn. When asked where he came from, the man pointed in the direction away from the inn. Amazed, the landlord asked the man if he knew he had ridden across a lake. The story goes that the man dropped dead from the shock that he had ridden miles across thin ice.
4. The organization of the sensory environment is a dynamic interaction of forces within a structure that influence an individual's perception.	4. The three patterns below are projections of the same wire-edged cube, but are perceived differently because of the relationships of the lines to each other.

 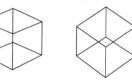

a   b   c

the sky. These names, such as the hunter Orion, reflect the particular images suggested by the star clusters. Similarly, cloud formations often are perceived as faces, mountains, and other familiar objects.

The third assumption, the differences between the geographical and the behavioral environments, provides the foundation for studying individuals' perceptions. As illustrated in the examples in Table 3.1, the individual responds to his or her perception of the environment, not to the geographical environment.

Finally, the organization of stimuli in the environment is itself a process and this process influences an individual's perception. Koffka (1935, p. 159) noted that when pattern a in the example in Table 3.1 is presented without the others, it is seen as a plane figure, either as a hexagon with diagonals or as a type of cross or starlike pattern. In pattern a, the plane figure is both symmetrical and simple; therefore, it is dominant.

In contrast, pattern c appears as a three-dimensional cube. Here, the plane figure is very irregular and difficult to see. Pattern b, on the other hand, is seen as either two- or three-dimensional. It may be seen as a plane figure in which the pattern

is lying on top of a hexagon or it may be seen as a cube. The reason is that the two- and three-dimensional forces are more balanced in pattern b than in the others. Figure 3.1 illustrates another example in which the forces within the perceptual field are balanced. In this figure, the viewer typically sees either a black Maltese (German iron) cross or a white propeller (Hartmann, 1942, p. 176).

The description of the behavioral environment and the dynamic organization of the sensory equipment illustrate Gestalt efforts to apply the concept of field theory in physics to psychology. Briefly, a field is a dynamic interrelated system in which every component influences all the other components. In the psychological theory, the behavioral environment is a field and small groups of stimuli (such as the examples in Table 3.1) are each a small field.

In summary, Gestalt theory emphasized wholeness and organization. For example, individuals respond to complete geometric figures rather than the separate lines. Also, because individuals may perceive a situation in particular ways, the behavioral environment (the perceived field) rather than the geographical environ-

FIGURE 3.1
Geometrical figure with balanced forces in the perceptual field

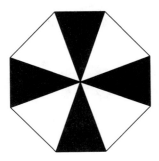

ment should be studied. Therefore, psychological research should identify the dynamic interaction of elements in a field that influence the individual's perception.

The Laws of Perceptual Organization

The primary task for psychology, according to the Gestalt theorists, was to answer the question, How does the individual psychologically perceive the geographical environment? First, Gestalt psychology defined the process of perception as that of organizing the observed stimuli. That is, the observer conveys meaning on the stimulus array.

Second, the arrangement of elements in the total stimulus is a major factor in perception (Koffka, 1935). For example, 11 dots distributed in the shape of a parallelogram would be perceived as a four-sided figure. The next step was to determine the characteristics of the stimulus display that influence perception. These influences are described in a basic law, the law of Prägnanz, and four related primary laws.

The Law of Prägnanz

The term **Prägnanz** refers to essence. The law of Prägnanz, introduced by Wertheimer, states that "a psychological organization will only be as 'good' as prevailing conditions allow." In this definition, the term *good* is undefined. It embraces such properties as "regularity, symmetry, similarity, and others" (Koffka, 1935, p. 110).

In other words, in any particular group of stimuli, the organization that prevails is the one that is the most comprehensive and the most stable and one that is also free of the casual and the arbitrary (Murphy, 1949). An example is a particular type of puzzle picture popular several years ago. The picture, a line drawing, typically portrayed a landscape, and hidden in various parts of the drawing were faces and sometimes objects. However, the structure that prevailed was that of the overall scene and often much searching was required to find the "hidden" objects.

Related Laws.   A principle closely related to the law of Prägnanz is the law of membership character. Specifically, each element manifests particular qualities depending on its place in the total structure of context. For example, a patch of color in a landscape depends for its value on the context in which the artist places it (Murphy, 1949, p. 288). Similarly, "faces" are so difficult to find in a line drawing of a forest because the lines that make up the faces take on the character of roots, leaves, and other aspects of the forest context that surround them. In other words, important aspects of the components of a structure are defined by their relationship to the system as a whole.

Another example of membership character is the presentation of a red cross in a gray field. After viewing the cross for 20 seconds, the subject perceives a green border around the cross. Then the subject is asked to predict the color if a notch is cut in one of the arms of the cross. The logical answer is green, like the border. The Gestaltists, however, predict accurately that the color will be red. The cross is an organized whole that forces the elements within it to take on those attributes that support the total structure (Murphy, 1949, p. 288).

This example also illustrates the dynamic nature of the organization of the sensory environment. That is, the sensory field includes forces that exert particular effects on the individual stimuli. The definite outline of the arms of the cross have a higher degree of Prägnanz than the outline of the notch (Murphy, 1949). Therefore, the organization of the cross prevails and the notch "disappears."

Four primary characteristics of the visual field that influence perception were also identified by Wertheimer (1938). They are *proximity, similarity, open direction,* and *simplicity.* Specifically, the nearness of elements to each other (proximity), shared features such as color (similarity), the tendency of elements to complete a pattern (open direction), and the contributions of stimulus elements to a total simple structure (simplicity) are factors that govern the perception of groups from separate elements (Figure 3.2).

The laws of perceptual organization operate in conjunction with the general law of Prägnanz. That is, psychological events tend to be meaningful and complete, and the four characteristics influence the completeness.

FIGURE 3.2
Examples of four primary laws of perceptual organization

1. **Proximity**: The lines tend to be perceived as three columns or three sets of two lines.

2. **Similarity**: Although the letters are equidistant from each other, they tend to be perceived as columns.

```
x o x o
x o x o
x o x o
x o x o
x o x o
x o x o
x o x o
```

3. **Open direction**: The figure on the right tends to be perceived as a circle although it is not a closed figure.

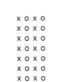

4. **Simplicity**: (total structure): The total structure (a) is perceived, rather than the hexagonal figure (b) that is embedded in it.

(a)   (b)   (c)

The "Insight" Experience

Perhaps the best-known contribution of Gestalt theory to the study of learning is the so-called "insight" experience. Introduced by Wolfgang Köhler in his experiments with anthropoid apes, the concept also was researched in experiments with humans. It continues to be studied by contemporary cognitive psychologists.

The Initial Experiment.   Assigned by the Prussian Academy to the Canary Islands in World War I, Köhler conducted several innovative experiments in learning. The basic experimental situation included two components: food placed out of the animal's reach and a type of mechanism placed nearby. If properly utilized, the mechanism would help the animal obtain the food. In the simplest experiment, food was hung from the roof near a scaffold. In other experiments food was placed outside the cage with a stick or dead branch nearby. In one complex situation, reaching the food required the fitting together of two separate sticks.

Köhler noted that when the animal perceived the stick, branch, or other mechanism as a tool, the problem was solved. This phenomenon is referred to in Gestalt psychology as insight. Köhler therefore maintained that the learning formula of "stimulus-response" should be replaced. Instead, he recommended that the learning formula should be "constellation of stimuli-organization-reaction to the results of the organization" (Köhler, 1929, p. 108). In other words, insightful behavior does not occur by following predetermined courses of action. Instead, it "presupposes the processes of organization and reorganization" (Koffka, 1935, p. 628).

Of importance is that the term *insight* refers to one type of behavior that cannot be reduced to another type (Koffka, 1935, p. 628). However, it is not an explanation; it is simply the name of a particular type of reorganization of the perceptual field. In addition, insight does not necessarily occur in a single step. Sometimes two or more steps are required, in which each is a case of partial insight (Koffka, 1935).

The Pendulum Problem.   In an experiment with human subjects, Norman R. F. Maier investigated the processes related to the discovery of a creative solution in the well-known pendulum problem. Sixty-one subjects, one at a time, were placed in a room in which two cords that reached the floor were hung from the ceiling. One hung near a wall and the other was near the center of the room. The task was to tie the ends of the two cords together. However, if one cord were held in either hand, the subject could not reach the other one (Maier, 1931, p. 182). The room also contained many other objects including poles, ringstands, clamps, pliers, extension cords, tables, and chairs.

Using the objects, four solutions to the problem were possible and all but one was obvious. Maier studied the difficult solution because it required originality and was least likely to be linked to prior experience. The three obvious solutions were (1) anchoring one cord with a heavy object near the other, (2) lengthening one cord with an extension cord so as to reach the other, (3) holding one cord and pulling the other in with a pole. The difficult solution was to tie a weight to the cord in the center of the room and set it in motion, thus making it a pendulum. The other cord is then brought near the center and the swinging cord catches it as it approaches the midpoint between the two cords (Maier, 1931, p. 183).

In the experiment, when subjects found one solution, they were directed to find another. If the subject did not discover solution 4 or was ready to give up after working conscientiously for 10 minutes, the experimenter walked to the window, passing the cord in the middle of the room and gently setting it in motion (hint 1). If, after a few minutes, solution 4 was not found, the experimenter gave the subject the pliers and said, "With the aid of this and no other object, there is another way to solve the problem" (Maier, 1931, p. 183).

Of the 61 college students in the study, 24 solved the problem without the hints, and 14 failed to solve it at all, even with assistance. Of the 23 subjects who solved the problem with assistance, 19 found the solution after one hint. Of interest, however, is that 16 students reported having the idea "all at once." In contrast, for 7 subjects, the idea of swinging the cord and that of attaching a weight occurred separately. They threw things at the cord, said they wished the wind would blow harder, or mentioned the need for a magnetic force to draw in the cord (Maier, 1931, p. 186). A little later the utilization of the weight occurred to the subject and the individual tied the pliers to the end of the rope. Maier concluded that insight may be either an "all or nothing" experience or a partial experience.

Factors Involved in Insight   Currently, some controversy exists as to the relationship of insight to other forms of problem solving (Schooler, Fallshore, & Fiore, 1995). The majority view, however, is that insight can be described within the framework of accepted psychological constructs, while differentiating it from other problem-solving situations (p. 580). Nevertheless, one of the difficulties in conducting research on insight is the lack of a clear definition. The two characteristics acknowledged by most cognitive researchers are that insight (1) represents seeing clearly into the heart or essence of a situation [the essential structural relationship (Wertheimer, 1945/1959)]; and (2) involves, at least partially, an automatic nonconscious process that does not include step-by-step reasoning (Gick & Lockhart, 1995).

Some researchers also identify the suddenness of a solution as a criterion, i.e., the "Aha! experience." References to anecdotes about the experiences of famous mathematicians and scientists appear to support this view. An example is the discovery of a particular type of mathematical function by Henri Poincaré as he was boarding a bus. Another is Alexander Fleming's discovery of penicillin following his accidental notice that bacteria flourishing in the laboratory dish did not grow near mold (Seifert, Meyer, Davidson, Patalano, & Yaniv, 1995, p. 93).

Some creative insights may indeed occur in this manner. However, research on introspective reports and interviews of creative individuals indicates that four phases often are involved. They are (1) hard work and research (mental preparation), (2) a period of idle time (incubation), (3) the moment of insight (illumination), and (4) work, including elaboration, to develop the idea (verification) (Csikszentmihalyi & Sawyer, 1995; Hadamard, 1949; Wallas, 1926). For example, by Poincaré's own account, his mathematical discovery involved several weeks of work with seemingly no progress, a brief seaside vacation in which an idea came to him, further work followed by an impasse, a second insight, and work to develop a finished product (Gruber, 1981; 1995).

Although insight is unpredictable, the long-term and short-term conditions most likely to lead to insight may be identified (Simonton, 1995). Long-term preparation includes (1) an early home environment that provides extensive culture and intellectual stimulation, including an appetite for reading, (2) development by the individual of a huge reservoir of discipline-relevant information interconnected into a complex network of meanings and unusual associations, (3) study with more than one mentor, and (4) keeping abreast of developments beyond the boundaries of a particular specialty area. Such a background makes possible the linkage of disparate ideas that become breakthroughs in a discipline.

In everyday life, preparation involves phases one and two of the four-stage process mentioned previously. That is, a favorable climate for insight involves preliminary work, including exploring possibilities and recognizing dead ends followed by a period of incubation in which the individual focuses on other activities (Simonton, 1995).

Summary

In the first half of the 20th century, Gestalt psychology served as the foil to behaviorism. Maintaining that molar rather than molecular behavior should be studied, the Gestalt psychologists focused on perception in learning. Specifically, organisms respond to sensory wholes rather than specific stimuli and the organization of the sensory environment influences the organism's perception. In addition to the laws of perceptual organization that indicate the factors influencing visual perception, Gestalt psychology introduced the concept of insight. In the early studies, animal and human subjects were presented problems that required a novel solution. Perceptual reorganization of the situation led to a solution.

Currently, insight is described as seeing clearly into the heart of a situation or problem through a nonconscious process. Suddenness of a solution sometimes is mentioned as a characteristic. However, research indicates the importance of preparatory work on a problem and an incubation period, followed by elaboration and other activities, to develop the idea.

OTHER GESTALT DEVELOPMENTS

Although concerned primarily with perceptual processes, the Gestalt psychologists also applied their concepts to other areas of interest in psychology. By the mid-1930s, Gestalt psychology had redefined the major issues in psychology in terms of a theory of form or structure (Murphy, 1949, p. 293). Not surprisingly, their work focused on the role of perception in learning and thinking. Major developments were the distinctions between arbitrary and meaningful learning, additional studies of problem solving, Edward Tolman's purposive behaviorism, and Kurt Lewin's theory of motivation.

Arbitrary and Meaningful Learning

In applying the concepts of structure and wholeness to the analysis of learning, Wertheimer differentiated between arbitrary or "senseless" learning and meaningful learning (Katona, 1967). This distinction was made in two ways. First, some simple connections are arbitrary or senseless. An example is the fact that John's telephone number is 782-9031. It is a senseless connection because the telephone number cannot be derived from the name or character of John.

Some simple connections, however, are meaningful. An example is $(a + b)^2 = a^2 + 2ab + b^2$. If one side of this equation is presented, the other may be derived from it. In other words, they are connected in a nonarbitrary, meaningful way.

The major focus for Wertheimer, however, was not the nature of particular connections. Instead, he was concerned primarily with the distinction between senseless and meaningful learning methods in the classroom. In other words, meaningful structures should not be learned in a senseless or rote manner.

Wertheimer (1945) reported a classroom visit in which students learned to determine the area of a parallelogram by dropping two perpendicular lines to the baseline. However, when faced with another form of the parallelogram, the students were at a loss as to an appropriate course of action. Their reaction was, "We haven't had that yet."

In working with another group of children, Wertheimer first showed them how to calculate the areas of rectangles. He then presented them a parallelogram and asked if they could make use of their knowledge of rectangles to determine the area. After some false starts, some children cut off the "triangle" at one end of the parallelogram and placed it on the other end, thereby forming a rectangle (see solution a, Figure 3.3). They then proceeded to solve for the area of the rectangle that they had just constructed. Others, however, perceived the rectangle formation in a different way. They cut the parallelogram in half, inverted one of the halves, and placed the

FIGURE 3.3
Children's solutions to the parallelogram problem

Solution a

Solution b

diagonal ends together to form a rectangle (see solution b, Figure 3.3). Solving the problem depended on the children's reorganization of the field and their reaction to the reorganization.

Wertheimer did not recommend specific teaching methods based on Gestalt theory. However, the implication from this example is that providing information that assists students to reorganize their view of the problem should be an integral component in teaching problem solving.

The relevance of Wertheimer's concern for meaningful learning is apparent in a discussion of the "Mathnet" segments of the public television program *Square One TV.* In the program, a problem-solving duo fashioned after the *Dragnet* detective series duo (with calculators in their holsters) act as sleuths to solve problems (Blau, 1990). Important in the program format is that the "detectives" use various ways of solving problems, such as drawing a picture of the situation or recalling the way a similar problem was solved.

Results of pre- and posttesting of viewers and a control group indicated differences in problem-solving skills. Viewers improved an average of 46% in the number and variety of techniques they used to solve problems and by an average of 56% in the sophistication and completeness of their answers. Also of interest is the rationale for developing the program. The developers had noted a tendency among 8- to 12-year-olds, when given a problem, either to see the solution instantly or to say, "We haven't had that yet."

Research on Problem Solving

Of continuing interest to the Gestalt theorists was a further analysis of factors that influenced perception in problem solving. Concepts identified by the researchers that are relevant to today's classrooms are **transfer of training, problem approach and functional fixedness,** and **problem set.**

Transfer of Training

The effects of different ways of demonstrating problem solutions on problem-solving skills were investigated by George Katona. He conducted a series of experiments on matchstick problems in which the task was to change the number of squares formed by the matchsticks by moving a minimal number of matches. A typical example is to move three matchsticks to make five squares, illustrated in Figure 3.4.

One experiment involved teaching two groups of students different approaches to the problems. In one group, the instructor illustrated the solutions to four variations of the same task that were all solved in the same way. In contrast, the method used with the second group was referred to by Katona (1940) as "guided discovery". The instructor illustrated six transitions in the matchstick configuration by moving only a few matches. For example, removing only three matchsticks created a "hole" in the center of the configuration. This method provided hints to solving other problems by illustrating that major changes could be made by moving only a few matchsticks. That is, the important structural principle in these problems is that a matchstick may serve as a side in two squares simultaneously. Results compar-

FIGURE 3.4

Matchstick problem

Note: From *Organizing and Memorizing* by G. Katona, 1940, New York: Columbia University Press. Reprinted by permission.

Problem: Solution:

Move three matchsticks to make five squares

ing the two groups of subjects indicated that the quantity and quality of the solutions to new problems were greater in the guided discovery group.

Problem Approach and Functional Fixedness

Karl Duncker (1926) noted that most theories seek to explain problem solving in terms of a "third factor". That is, they name some extraneous factor such as past experience or imitation to account for the connection between a problem situation and the solution.

Duncker analyzed the protocols of several subjects as they attempted to solve several unique problems. His analysis indicated that the first step taken by successful problem solvers is that of a "comprehended conflict." The next step, sometimes taken after some false steps and perhaps hints from the experimenter, is a clear identification of the basic difficulty. The final step is that of a problem solution that addresses the basic difficulty. Such solutions, in his view, are examples of productive thinking and they are therefore referred to as *solutions with functional value*.

One example, referred to as the "X-ray problem", is a situation in which a man cannot be cured of a tumor because the required concentrations of X-rays will kill healthy tissue. The key to solving the problem is to note that the rays are too "thick", i.e., too concentrated (felt difficulty). The solution as illustrated in Table 3.2 is to provide "thin" rays from various angles that converge on the tumor.

As indicated in Table 3.2, a key factor in a successful solution is getting to the heart of the problem, i.e., identifying the basic difficulty. Productive thinking, in other words, is distinguished by an inventory of the problem situation, and the recognition of a definite lack (Aufgabe) that is supplied by the thinking process (Duncker, 1926, p. 702).

Students who are unable to perceive the elements of the situation in a new way are said to suffer from **functional fixedness** (Duncker, 1945). Examples include the inability of some apes to see that a stick can be used as a tool and the subjects in Maier's pendulum experiment who failed to "see" a new use for the pliers.

Problem Set

Functional fixedness is one perceptual difficulty in problem solving. A related concept is **problem set** or **Einstellung**, identified by Abraham Luchins (1942). Briefly,

TABLE 3.2
Problem solutions with functional value

Problem	Comprehended Conflict	Difficulty	Solution with Functional Value
Ape wants the food outside the cage.	Ape cannot reach the food.	Ape's arm is too short.	Make use of something that extends the animal's reach.
Man needs X-ray treatment for tumor inside his body.	X-ray cannot cure man because surrounding tissue would be damaged.	Bundle of X-rays is too concentrated, too united (or too "thick").	Scatter out X-rays, send weak (thin, momentary) rays from various angles.

Note: Summarized from "A Qualitative (Experimental and Theoretical) Study of Productive Thinking (Solving of Comprehensible Problems)" by K. Duncker, 1926, *Pedagogical Seminary, 33,* 642–708.

problem set refers to rigidity in problem solving because the individual perceives that a series of problems are to be solved in the same way. Luchins devised the well-known water jar problems to investigate the effects of problem set. Subjects were given three jars of different capacities and then asked to measure a particular amount of water. The solution to each problem requires pouring certain amounts of water from one jar to another (Table 3.3).

In the experiment, problems 2 through 6 are the set-inducing or "E" problems. Problems 7 through 11 are the test problems because they can be solved by the simple A – C method. However, for problems 7, 8, 9, 10, and 11, the more cumbersome strategy used in problems 1 through 6 will also yield a correct solution. Problem 9 is referred to as the extinction problem because the strategy B – A – 2C will not produce 25 units. The subject who fails problem 9 is regarded as demonstrating rigid behavior because he or she adheres to a repeated strategy although it is completely inadequate (Luchins & Luchins, 1959, p. 111).

Luchins demonstrated that, in the series of problems, the strategy used for problems 1 through 6 was applied also by the subjects to problems 7 through 11. Of 1,039 subjects, 83% used the B – A – 2C in problems 7 and 8, and 64% failed problem 9 (Luchins & Luchins, 1959, p. 110).

In contrast, of 970 subjects who received only problems 7 through 11, less than 1% used B – A – 2C in 7 and 8, and only 5% failed problem 9. This phenomenon was named *"Einstellung"* to denote a certain kind of set that immediately predisposes one to a particular conscious act (Luchins & Luchins, 1959).

In one variation of the basic experiment, the solutions of elementary school children to the first six problems were collected prior to the distribution of problems 7 through 11. The children also were told not to use the same method on these problems.

Although the children heeded the warning, most of them failed problems 7 and 8 and others again used the earlier strategy on problems 10 and 11. Some of the children explained that the old method "kept 'popping up' in their minds and they could not help using it" (Luchins & Luchins, 1959, p. 134).

TABLE 3.3
Series of water jar problems on problem set

	Problem	Solution
1. Task: Given:	Measure 20 units of water Jug A = 29 units; B = 3 units	Fill Jar A and pour off into B three times: $29 - (3 \times 3) = 20$ $A - 3B$
2. Task: Given:	Measure 100 units Jug A = 21 units, B = 127, C = 3	Fill Jar B, pour into A, and then fill C twice from jar A $B - A - 2C$ or $127 - 21 - 6 = 100$
3. Task: Given:	Measure 99 units A = 14 units, B = 163, C = 25	Same as above: $B - A - 2C$
4. Task: Given:	Measure 5 units A = 18, B = 43, C = 10	$B - A - 2C$
5. Task: Given:	Measure 21 units A = 9, B = 42, C = 6	$B - A - 2C$
6. Task: Given:	Measure 31 units A = 20, B = 59, C = 4	$B - A - 2C$
7. Task: Given:	Measure 20 units A = 23, B = 49, C = 3	$A - C$*
8. Task: Given:	Measure 18 units A = 15, B = 39, C = 3	$A + C$*
9. Task: Given:	Measure 25 units A = 28, B = 76, C = 3	$A - C$ only
10. Task: Given:	Measure 22 units A = 18, B = 48, C = 4	$A + C$*
11. Task: Given:	Measure 6 units A = 14, B = 36, C = 8	$A - C$*

*Solvable also by $B - A - 2C$

Note: Summarized *from Rigidity of Behavior: A Variational Approach to the Effects of Einstellung* by A. S. Luchins and E. H. Luchins, 1959, Eugene, OR: University of Oregon Books.

Efforts to answer the question, What is learned? during the problem-solving activity revealed a variety of answers. Some subjects learned to generalize a rule, others learned to begin with the middle jar, and others learned to begin with the largest jar. Thus, problem rigidity appears to be not one factor, but many.

Summary

Gestalt psychologists also applied their views of structure and perception to issues in school learning. Wertheimer differentiated arbitrary (senseless) and meaningful learning in which the student learned the relevant structure of a situation or problem. Assisting students to reorganize their view of a problem can facilitate meaningful learning. Katona's experiments demonstrated the role of guided discovery in facilitating an understanding of structural principles in visual problems and transfer to new situations.

Other issues in problem solving are clearly identifying the problem goal to develop a solution with functional value, and avoiding the impasses referred to as functional fixedness and problem set. Functional fixedness refers to the inability to see elements of the problem in a new way and problem set refers to rigidity in problem-solving procedures.

Edward Tolman's Purposive Behaviorism

Tolman (1932) referred to his theory as a "subvariety of Gestalt psychology" (p. 230), and he, too, studied molar behavior. Examples included "a rat running a maze, a cat getting out of a puzzle box, a man driving home to dinner, and a pupil marking a test sheet" (Tolman, 1932, p. 8). Although the theory focused on goal-directed behavior, Tolman defined the term as behavior that is maintained by the environment. An example is the behavior of a rat moving through a maze that ends when the animal gets to the food. Although the animal appears to be seeking a goal, the behavior is governed by the stimuli of the turns in the maze and the food.

The Process of Learning
Instead of specific S–R connections, the subject learns the critical events that lead to some goal, referred to as a "sign-gestalt-expectation." For example, Pavlov's dogs learned that "waiting-in-the-presence-of-sound" leads to food. According to Tolman, learning occurs because the subjects bring certain expectancies to the learning situation, referred as a hypotheses. The expectations that are confirmed are the ones that survive. Confirmation, in other words, is similar to reinforcement in other theories.

Latent Learning
The term **latent learning** refers to knowledge that is acquired, but which is not necessarily enacted. In other words, learning and performance are not interchangeable. Albert Bandura later incorporated this distinction into his theory of learning.

Tolman and his associates designed several ingenious experiments that challenged the concepts in S–R theory. In one experiment, three different groups of rats ran a maze on 10 successive days. One group received food at the end of each run and another group received no food. The third group, however, received no food for the first 10 days, but were fed from the goalbox on the 11th day. For the remaining 6 days of the experiment, the error rate of this group fell dramatically and was not significantly different from that of the group rewarded daily with food (Tolman & Honzik, 1930).

Tolman (1932) maintained that this experiment demonstrated that the subjects in the third group "learned" from being fed from the goalbox on the 11th day. That is, running the maze (performance) and receiving the food reward for correct maze-running was not essential for learning. In other words, learning and performance are not synonymous.

Some behaviorists, however, suggested that reinforcement was present for the subjects that did not receive the food. Specifically, removal of the subject from the goalbox at the end of the run may act as a reinforcer for reaching the goalbox. This suggestion may also explain the slight improvement of the first group which never received food for a successful run.

Cognitive Learning

Tolman (1932) maintained that subjects learn "cognitive maps" of the environment. Behaviorists, in contrast, maintain that responses are learned. To address these different views, one study compared the performance of two groups of rats, labeled the "response learners" and the "place learners." The food reward for the response learners was located in different places on different days; however, they always had to turn in only one direction (right or left) to find the food. This group was the response learners. In contrast, the food reward for the place learners was always in the same place. However, they were started through the maze at different points; therefore, to find the reward they had to take different routes (Figure 3.5). The performance of the place learners was superior, supporting the hypothesis that learners acquire cognitive maps of the environment (Tolman, Ritchie, & Kalish, 1946).

Tolman defended the use of rats to demonstrate cognitive learning. Rats "do not go on binges the night before one has planned an experiment; they do not kill each other off in wars; . . . they avoid politics, economics, and papers on psychology. They are marvelous, pure, and delightful" (Tolman, 1949, p. 166).

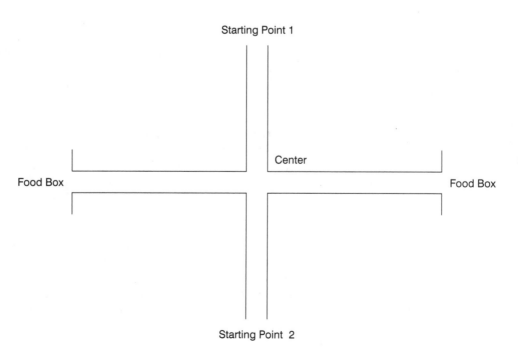

FIGURE 3.5
Maze with different starting points used in Tolman's latent learning experiments

Applications to Social Psychology

In the early 1930s, Gestalt psychologists began to apply the concept to the formation of social groups and motivation and personality. For example, Koffka (1935, p. 651) describes a psychological group as any group of individuals that meets the Gestalt criterion of "we." Examples include primitive societies and a weekly foursome of bridge players. According to Koffka, the principles of field organization that account for perception also apply to the formation of groups. Particularly important are similarity and closure.

In addition, Maier expanded his studies on problem solving to include the work setting. Working with employees and supervisors, he investigated the dynamics of group problem solving, the role and effects of group leaders on problem solving, and the perceptions of supervisors and employees toward work-related problems (see Maier, 1970).

Among his findings were that mixed-sex groups were superior to either all-male or all-female groups in the quality of their solutions. Also, a supervisor's perception of workers as PEs (problem employees) or IMs (idea men) influenced both the number and innovativeness of employee solutions. He also found that a group without adequate leadership tended either (1) to fail to explore a problem because they agreed on a solution at the outset or (2) to engage in irreversible interpersonal conflict as a result of their inability to deal with conflicts generated by emotional bias (Maier, 1970, p. 414).

Another theorist associated with the Gestaltists was Kurt Lewin. He primarily was interested in motivation. His ideas led to the work now referred to as group dynamics. The focus of Lewin's field theory was the interpretation of the changes that result from psychological forces. Analysis begins with the situation referred to as the individual's life space, and proceeds to identify the interacting psychological forces that influence behavior. The basic concept in his theory is that "to understand or predict the psychological behavior (B) one has to determine for every kind of psychological event (actions, emotions, expressions, etc.) the momentary whole situation, that is, the momentary structure and state of the person (P) and the state of the psychological environment (E). $B = f(P, E)$" (Lewin, 1933, p. 598). In other words, behavior is a function of the person and the psychological environment. Albert Bandura later used this formula in his analysis of learning in the social setting.

Lewin (1942) also distinguished between learning information and motivational learning. Saying that "the spastic child has to learn to relax" is quite different from "learning French vocabulary," which also has little in common with "learning to like broccoli." Therefore, we should not expect identical laws to hold for these different processes (Lewin, 1936, p. 220). Lewin also coined the term *cognitive structure* to differentiate knowledge learning from motivational learning. The term was then used by Tolman and later was adopted by cognitive psychology.

In summary, Tolman, Maier, and Lewin extended the concepts of Gestalt psychology beyond the focus on perception. Tolman identified the process referred to as latent learning and he also maintained that learners acquire cognitive maps of new learning. In contrast, Maier and Lewin applied the concept of a dynamic interrelated system to the study of social groups. Lewin's concepts led to the work now referred to as social dynamics. He also distinguished between learning information in a subject area and motivational learning.

SUMMARY

In the first half of the 20th century, Gestalt psychology served as the cognitive response to behaviorism, the dominant movement. The major focus on Gestalt writings and research was the dynamic nature of perception. Emphasizing the importance of sensory wholes in perception as the meaningful alternative to the discrete elements of behaviorism, the Gestalt psychologists first developed several laws that govern the dynamic nature of visual perception.

Creative problem situations in which the subject must develop a novel solution illustrated the importance of reorganizing one's perceptions in order to "see" the solution. Referred to as insight, the concept, from the Gestalt perspective, represented understanding the essence or key structural relationships in a situation. Currently, the term also refers to new discoveries in a subject discipline.

Other contributions of Gestalt psychology include the role of guided discovery in meaningful learning, types of problem impasses, and the work of Tolman and Lewin.

APPLICATIONS TO EDUCATION

Issues raised for education by the Gestalt perspective were meaning, understanding, and insight, which are distinctly human characteristics (Wertheimer, 1991). Computer programs, in contrast, can model human problem solving only after the relevant information about the problem has been extracted and fed into the program. In other words, the computer can address a problem once it has been understood (Wertheimer, 1991). The organizing, the thinking, and the understanding are, instead, in the mind of the programmer (p. 203). Therefore, education should address these issues, rather than the steps undertaken after understanding and reorganization have occurred. In other words, situations or problems include some elements that are structurally central and others that are peripheral. Of major importance in learning to solve problems is to grasp the structurally central elements and differentiate them from the peripheral or unimportant features (Wertheimer, 1945).

The difficulty in applying the Gestalt perspective in the classroom is the lack of a set of clearly defined principles of learning. Instead, Gestalt researchers developed general suggestions for problem-solving instruction. First, embed the problem or learning task in concrete, actual situations (Wertheimer, 1945). Finding the area of a rectangle, for example, may be embedded in the situation in which two farmers wish to exchange two plots of land (p. 272). In other words, the teacher should provide reasonable problem situations that the student attempts to address. Then cooperative help should be provided as needed.

Second, the assistance provided during problem solving should not be that of copying or repeating procedures. Instead, the teacher should provide guided discovery in the form of cues or hints to help learners reorganize their view of the problem and overcome inadequate or inaccurate views of the problem (referred to as functional fixedness). The goal is for students to discover a solution with functional value; that is, a solution that addresses the basic difficulty posed by the problem. The test of the occurrence of real learning is to determine if the individual can solve a related problem or task (the principle referred to as transfer) (Cox, 1997; Wertheimer, 1945). If the student has only memorized some steps, he or she will not be able to recognize the similarities of the two situations and will be unable to solve the situation.

Third, instruction should not present students with sets of trite problems that can be solved by learning a series of rote steps. This approach leads to the difficulty referred to as problem set.

Of interest is that two Gestalt concepts, problem set and insight, continue to be discussed by contemporary cognitive psychologists. Problem set (referred to as stereotypy) occurs with poor students who may have the appropriate skills, but stick to one strategy, even when it is not successful (Kaplan & Davidson, 1988). However, an incubation period sometimes permits the unproductive associations to weaken. Further, when students reach an impasse on problems that require creative solutions, researchers suggest that taking a break accompanied by hints and self-reflection can lead to insight (Seifert, Meyer, Davidson, Patalano, & Yaniv, 1995).

A COMPARISON OF BEHAVIORISM AND GESTALT THEORY

The early proponents of behaviorism and Gestalt theory differed in at least three ways from the philosophers who attempted to define learning. First, the psychologists based their theories on experimental observations of behavior. Second, they established, even if in rudimentary form, laws and principles that were testable. Third, they applied their principles to real-world situations. Thorndike applied his habit-formation theory to the analysis of school subjects, Watson conditioned Albert's fear reaction, and Wertheimer extended Gestalt theory to children's problem solving.

Among the contributions of this period were the applications of classical conditioning to emotional reactions, the key to effective punishments, the role of guided discovery in problem solving, and the importance of organization in perception. However, in the mid-1930s, both behaviorism and Gestalt theory became overextended. Each perspective attempted to develop the one comprehensive theory that would explain all learning. (See Table 3.4)

As early as the 1940s, the conflict between the S-R and Gestalt positions was criticized for nonproductivity. Two practices contributed to this problem (McConnell, 1942). First, the terms used by each perspective magnified the differences between them. For example, the terms "insight" and "connection" represent extreme descriptions of the learning process. Also, task difficulty may be a factor in the learning process ultimately described by the theorist. If the task is so difficult that the learner cannot establish relationships with the situation, the subject must resort to trial and error. In contrast, less difficult tasks, in which past experience may play a role, may be reacted to quickly and accurately. Therefore, the flashes of insight described by the Gestalt psychologists may, in some cases, be included under transfer through identical elements (McConnell, 1942, p. 26).

TABLE 3.4
A comparison of behaviorism and Gestalt theory

Major Characteristics	Behaviorism	Gestalt Theory
Basic assumption(s)	Learning is the formation of associations between elements.	Individuals react to unitary, meaningful wholes; therefore, learning is the organization and reorganization of a sensory field. The whole possesses emergent properties that differ from that of the elements. *Tolman:* Learning is essentially the acquisition of cognitive maps that direct behavior.
Typical experiments(s)	(a) *Trial and error*: Rats run mazes; animals escape from cages. (b) *Emotional or reflex responses*: Stimulus pairing.	(a) *Reorganization*: Subjects are placed in situations that require restructuring for solution. (b) Animals run mazes from different starting points and under different reward conditions.
Learning formula	(a) Stimulus-response-reward (b) Emotional responses: Stimulus 1 ⎤ ⎟ Response Stimulus 2 ⎦	Constellation of stimuli-organization-reaction

Second, different descriptions of learning arose, in part, from differences in the experimental context. Tasks can be classified according to the amount of discovery required to make a correct response. Rote learning, for example, is reflected in the simple conditioning experiments whereas complicated unstructured situations require the learner's reorganization of past experience and discovery of the appropriate behavior pattern (McConnell, 1942).

Of importance is that Thorndike's theory was not a strictly behaviorist perspective. In his view, connections between ideas accounted for a major portion of knowledge.

As the decade of the 1950s approached, interest in the development of all-encompassing theory declined. Hilgard (1964), in his review of the end of this period of theory development, noted that the "great debate" among comprehensive theories was now over.

CHAPTER QUESTIONS

1. Katona (1940) differentiated between arbitrary or "senseless" connections and meaningful connections. Describe an example of each.

2. Students in mathematics sometimes complain that they cannot solve word problems that have been rearranged or restated in some way. According to Wertheimer, what is the source of the student's difficulty?

3. Katona (1940) found that illustrating different ways that the matches may be rearranged

("guided discovery") was successful in assisting students to solve certain matchstick problems. According to Gestalt theory, why should this type of assistance be helpful?

4. The following problem on the National Assessment of Educational Progress (NAEP) is mishandled frequently. One hundred-thirty children are waiting to go on a field trip. How many buses are needed if each bus holds 50 students? Students often produce a fractional answer, not recognizing the absurdity. Silver (1986) maintains this error results in part from the division word problems in the curriculum that require partitioning a number into groups of a particular size. What is the Gestalt explanation for this phenomenon?

5. How do the insight problems used by the Gestalt psychologists differ from insight in a subject domain?

REFERENCES

Baars, B. J. (1986). *The cognitive revolution in psychology.* New York: Guilford.

Blau, E. (1990, March 26). Making math come alive on television. *New York Times,* p. C18.

Cox, B. D. (1997). The rediscovery of the active learner in adaptive contexts: A developmental-historical analysis of transfer of training. *Educational Psychologist, 32*(1), 41–55.

Csikszentmihalyi, M., & Sawyer, K. (1995). Creative insight: The social dimension of a solitary moment. In R. J. Sternberg & J. E. Davidson (Eds.), *The nature of insight* (pp. 329–363). Cambridge, MA: MIT Press.

Duncker, K. (1926). A qualitative (experimental and theoretical) study of productive thinking (solving of comprehensible problems). *Pedagogical Seminary, 33,* 642–708.

Duncker, K. (1945). On problem solving. *Psychological Monographs, 58* (Whole No. 270).

Gick, M. L., & Lockhart, R. S. (1995). Cognitive and affective components of insight. In R. J. Sternberg and J. E. Davidson (Eds.), *The nature of insight* (pp. 197-228). Cambridge, MA: MIT Press.

Gruber, H. E. (1981). On the relation between the "Aha!" experiences" and the construction of ideas. *History of Science, 19,* 41–59.

Gruber, H. E. (1995). Insight and affect in the history of science. In R. G. Sternberg and J. E. Davidson (Eds.), *The nature of insight* (pp. 397–432).

Hadamard, J. (1949). *The psychology of invention in the mathematical field.* Princeton, NJ: Princeton University Press.

Hartmann, G. W. (1942). The field theory of learning and its consequences. In N. B. Henry (Ed.), *The 41st yearbook of the National Society for Study of Learning Part II. The Psychology of Learning* (pp. 165–214). Chicago: University of Chicago Press.

Heider, F. (1973). Gestalt theory: Early history and reminiscences. In M. Henle, J. Jaynes, & J. Sullivan (Eds.), *Historical conceptions of psychology* (pp. 63–73). New York: Springer.

Hilgard, E. R. (1964). Postscript: Twenty years of learning theory in relation to education. In E. R. Hilgard (Ed.), *Theories of learning and instruction. The sixty-third yearbook of the National Society for the Study of Education* (pp. 416–481). Chicago: University of Chicago Press.

Hilgard, E. R. (1987). Perspectives on educational psychology. In J. A. Glover & R. R. Ronning (Eds.), *Historical foundations of educational psychology* (pp. 425–429). New York: Plenum.

Hilgard, E. R. (1996). History of educational psychology. In D. C. Berliner & R. C. Calfee (Eds.), *Handbook of educational psychology* (pp. 990–1004). New York: Macmillan Library References.

Kaplan, C. A., & Davidson, J. E. (1988). *Hatching a theory of incubation effects.* (Tech. Rep. No. C.I.P. 472). Pittsburgh: Carnegie Mellon University, Department of Psychology.

Katona, G. (1940). *Organizing and memorizing.* New York: Columbia University Press.

Katona, G. (1967). *Organizing and memorizing: Studies in the psychology of learning and teaching.* New York: Hafner.

Koffka, K. (1935). *Principles of Gestalt psychology.* New York: Harcourt Brace.

Köhler, W. (1928). Chapter VII. Intelligence in apes; Chapter VIII. An aspect of Gestalt psychology. In C. Murchison (Ed.), *Psychologies of 1925* (pp. 145–195). Worcester, MA: Clark University Press.

Köhler, W. (1929). *Gestalt psychology.* New York: Horace Liveright.

Lewin, K. (1933). Environmental influences. In C. Murchison (Ed.), *A handbook of child psychology* (2nd ed., pp. 590–625). Worchester, MA: Clark University Press.

Lewin, K. (1936). *Principles of topological psychology.* New York: McGraw-Hill.

Lewin, K. (1942). Field theory of learning. In N. B. Henry (Ed.), *The psychology of learning: The 41st yearbook of the National Society for the Study of Education, Part II* (pp. 215–242). Chicago: University of Chicago Press.

Luchins, A. S. (1942). Mechanization in problem solving: The effect of *Einstellung. Psychological Monographs, 54* (Whole No. 248).

Luchins, A. S., & Luchins, E. H. (1959). *Rigidity of behavior: A variational approach to the effects of Einstellung.* Eugene, OR: University of Oregon Books.

Maier, N. R. F. (1930). Reasoning in humans I. On direction. *Journal of Comparative Psychology, 10,* 115–143.

Maier, N. R. F. (1931). Reasoning in humans II. *Journal of Comparative Psychology, 12,* 181–194.

Maier, N. R. F. (1970). *Problem solving and creativity in individuals and groups.* Belmont, CA: Brooks/Cole.

McConnell, T. R. (1942). Reconciliation of learning theories. In N. B. Henry (Ed.), *The psychology of learning. The forty-first yearbook of the National Society for the Study of Education* (pp. 371–401). Chicago: University of Chicago Press.

Murphy, G. (1949). *Historical introduction to modern psychology.* New York: Harcourt, Brace, and World.

Schooler, J. W., Fallshore, M., & Fiore, S. (1995). Epilogue: Putting insight into perspective. In R. J. Sternberg & J. E. Davidson (Eds.), *The nature of insight* (pp. 559–587). Cambridge, MA: MIT Press.

Selfert, C. M., Meyer, D. E., Davidson, N., Patalano, A. L., & Yaniv, I. (1995). Demystification of cognitive insight: Opportunistic assimilation and the prepared-mind perspective. In R. J. Sternberg & J. E. Davidson (Eds.), *The nature of insight.* Cambridge, MA: MIT Press.

Silver, R. (1986). Using conceptual and procedural knowledge: A focus on relationships. In J. Hierbert (Ed.), *Conceptual and procedural knowledge: The case of mathematics* (pp. 181–198). Hillsdale, NJ: Erlbaum.

Simonton, D. K. (1995). Foresight in insight? A Darwinian answer. In R. J. Sternberg & J. E. Davidson (Eds.), *The nature of insight* (pp. 466–494). Cambridge, MA: MIT Press.

Tolman, E. C. (1932). *Purposive behavior in animals and men.* New York: Appleton-Century-Crofts.

Tolman, E. C. (1949). There is more than one kind of learning. *Psychological Review, 56,* 144–155.

Tolman, E. C., & Honzik, C. H. (1930). Introduction and removal of reward, and maze performance in rats. *University of California Publications in Psychology, 4,* 257–276.

Tolman, E. C., Ritchie, B. F., & Kalish, D. (1946). Studies in spatial learning, II. *Journal of Experimental Psychology, 36,* 221–229.

Wallas, G. (1926). *The art of thought.* New York: Harcourt Brace & Jovanavich.

Watson, R. I. (1963). *The great psychologists* (4th ed.). Philadelphia: Lippincott.

Wertheimer, M. (1938). Laws of organization in perceptual forms. In W. Ellis (Ed.), *A source book of Gestalt psychology* (pp. 71–88). New York: Harcourt Brace.

Wertheimer, M. (1945). *Productive thinking.* New York: Harper.

Wertheimer, M. (1991). Max Wertheimer: Modern cognitive psychology and the Gestalt problem. In G. A. Kimble, M. Wertheimer, & C. White (Eds.), *Portraits of pioneers of psychology* (pp. 189-207). Hillsdale, NJ: Lawrence Erlbaum Associates.

CHAPTER 4

Learning and Instruction

Theories are nets to catch what we call "the world"; to rationalize, to explain, and to master it. We endeavor to make the mesh ever finer and finer (Popper, 1968, p. 59).

The early behaviorist and Gestalt proponents each sought to build the one comprehensive theory that would explain all learning. By the 1940s, however, these efforts were reaching a dead end. More important, the need to solve pressing educational problems became a national priority and indicated the inadequacy of these approaches to explain complex learning. First came the need to design effective instruction for military training needs in World War II. This initial emphasis on instruction was followed by the curriculum redesign efforts after the Soviet Union's launch of *Sputnik* in the 1950s. These events redirected attention from learning in restricted laboratory settings to learning in the real world.

MAJOR TRENDS

The years from 1950 to the present may be described in terms of three trends. The first, from 1950 to approximately 1975, is the shift from laboratory research to instructionally relevant research. The second, from the mid-70s to approximately 1990 is the rise of cognitive psychology. Overlapping with this focus, from the mid-80s to the present, is the rise of social, cultural, and personal factors in learning. In addition, two recent developments have entered discussions of educational policy in the 1990s. They are the movement referred to as *constructivism* and interest in extrapolating classroom practices from research in neuroscience.

The Shift from the Laboratory to the Classroom (1950–1975)

The two major trends in this period are (1) the emergence of instructional psychology and (2) the influence of B. F. Skinner's behaviorism.

The Beginning of Instructional Psychology

The military training problems of World War II included complex tasks that challenged existing concepts of learning developed in the laboratory. Examples include training for aircraft gunners, radio operators, and troubleshooters (Gagné, 1962). Specifically, the recommended learning principles of reinforcement, distribution of practice, and response familiarity did not lead to successful instruction (Gagné, 1962). Instead, efforts to design effective instruction indicated that topic sequencing and providing instruction on component tasks enhanced learning (Gagné, 1962). These concepts were later developed by Robert Gagné into hierarchies of skills, the basis for his theory of conditions of learning (see chapter 6).

Although initiated by military training needs, instructional research did not become a priority until the late 1950s. The precipitating event was the successful launch of the space capsule *Sputnik* by the Soviet Union in 1957. This technological feat by a Cold War opponent was viewed by the American public as a failure of the country's educational system. The intensity of the international power struggle had magnified the role of education as the guardian of a free society's scholarship and technological achievements.

Curriculum Redesign.   The launch of *Sputnik* sparked a massively funded curriculum reform in the United States. In general, the new curricula were to produce disciplined thinkers through discovery learning and student involvement. The learning of isolated facts was to be discarded. Mathematics, science, and foreign languages—subjects identified as essential to national security—were targeted first for development.

Subsequent legislation extended the role of the federal government in education. Included were the Elementary and Secondary Education Act (ESEA) and the Economic Opportunity Act. Funds were provided for special programs for disadvantaged children, the development of innovative programs, 10 university research and development centers, and 19 regional laboratories (ESEA). The preschool compensatory program Head Start was funded by the Economic Opportunity Act. Later, Follow Through projects for disadvantaged children in the elementary grades were also established.

The new emphasis on curriculum development attracted subject matter experts, psychologists, social scientists, and educators. Research on classroom learning, formerly regarded as less prestigious than "pure" laboratory research, became legitimate.

The Need for Instructional Theory.   Faced with the problem of curriculum redesign for thinking skills and, perhaps influenced by the precision of space technology, researchers expressed the need for an instructional technology. Such a technology would translate learning theory into educational practice (see Bruner, 1964; Hilgard, 1980). Learning theory was described as no more capable of dictating instructional activities than the science of thermodynamics is of predicting whether a particular airplane will be jet propelled or propeller driven (Hilgard, 1980). That is, answers to the question How does learning occur? do not answer the question How does instruction facilitate learning?

Jerome Bruner (1960) called for an instructional theory that would describe principles for the design of effective classroom instruction. In Bruner's view (1964), a theory of learning is descriptive, whereas a theory of instruction is prescriptive. For example, learning theory may describe the optimum age at which addition is learned, and instructional theory prescribes the ways to teach addition.

The impact of the curriculum redesign effort was less than originally expected. However, the new focus on instructional research led to the identification of a new area in psychology. Introduced in 1969 as instructional psychology (see Gagné & Rohwer, 1969), the area includes the interests of educators, curriculum design teams, psychologists, sociologists, and others.

Four theoretical perspectives applicable to the classroom gained prominence in this period. The most well known is B. F. Skinner's operant conditioning (see chapter 5). The others are Jean Piaget's cognitive-development theory (see chapter 9), Robert Gagné's conditions of learning (chapter 6), and Jerome Bruner's cognitive approach to curriculum development.

Jerome Bruner's Curriculum-Development Model

Director of the Harvard Center for Cognitive Studies in the 1960s, Jerome Bruner (1964) recommended the cognitive-development approach to curriculum design. Like John Dewey, Bruner described the knowledgeable person as one who is a problem solver; that is, one who interacts with the environment in testing hypotheses and developing generalizations. The goal of education, therefore, should be intellectual development. Further, the curriculum should foster the development of problem-solving skills through the processes of inquiry and discovery.

Degree of cognitive development is described by Bruner in three levels or stages. The first stage, *enactive,* is the representation of knowledge in actions. An example is that of a child operating a balance beam by adjusting his or her position, although the child may be unable to describe the procedure. The second stage, *iconic,* is that of the visual summarization of images. The child at this stage can represent the balance beam in a drawing or diagram. The third and most advanced stage is that of *symbolic representation.* It is the use of words and other symbols to describe experience. The learner at this stage can explain the operation of the balance beam, using the concepts fulcrum, length of the beam, and weights to be balanced.

The subject matter, therefore, should be represented in terms of the child's way of viewing the world—enactive, iconic, or symbolic. The curriculum should be designed so that the mastery of skills leads to the mastery of still more powerful ones (Bruner, 1966, p. 35). Therefore, the fundamental structure of the subject matter, referred to as organizing concepts, should be identified and used as the basis for curriculum development. Such a practice, according to Bruner (1964, p. 33), permits the teaching of any subject effectively in an intellectually honest form to any learner at any stage of development. Referred to as a spiral curriculum, this organization is represented in the social studies curriculum developed by Bruner, "Man: A Course of Study."

The Influence of Skinner's Behaviorism

Unlike other psychologists, B. F. Skinner is well known outside the profession of psychology. The "controlled-environment" crib used with one of his daughters was featured in the popular magazines of the 1940s, and three of his books were written for the educated public. *Walden Two* describes life in a utopian society, *Beyond Freedom and Dignity* applies his behavioral management techniques to social engineering, and *Beyond Behaviorism* both responds to his critics and relates his concepts to everyday life.

Skinner is the only post-World War II psychologist to be featured on the cover of *Time* magazine, and a survey of American college students in 1975 indicated that he is the best-known American scientist (Gilgen, 1982, p. 97). A survey of psychologists in the late 1970s also indicated that Skinner's behavioral management techniques were considered one of the major developments in psychology.

By the late 1950s, Skinner's principles had surpassed Hull's theory in influence within psychology (Guttman, 1977). The initiation of two journals, *The Experimental Analysis of Behavior* and *The Journal of Applied Behavioral Analysis,* widened that influence.

Programmed Instruction.   At about the same time that the curriculum reform was getting under way, Skinner developed the teaching machine for classroom use. The teaching machine and the accompanying materials, programmed instruction, became a part of the "new technology" recommended for the classroom. The instruction consisted of self-paced "stand-alone" materials that did not require teacher intervention. The subject matter was sequenced from simple to complex, and students interacted with the materials by responding to a series of incomplete statements. The lesson on morphemes at the end of chapter 5 is an example. The programmed instruction movement lasted less than 10 years, from approximately 1957 to 1965. Poorly designed materials developed by individuals who did not understand the basic design principles and the clumsiness of the early machines contributed to the decline.

Behavioral Management.   The term *behavior modification* first appeared in *Psychological Abstracts* in 1967 (Gilgen, 1982). It refers primarily to behavioral management based on operant conditioning principles, specifically the manipulation of reinforcers for appropriate behaviors.

During the 1960s and 1970s, programs for behavioral change were implemented in a variety of clinical, institutional, and educational settings. Included were schools, businesses, hospitals, clinics, prisons, and governmental settings. The programs have been referred to as *applied behavioral analysis, behavioral modification,* and *contingency management.* Some programs used tokens to reinforce appropriate behaviors that later were exchanged for privileges and thus are known as *token economies.*

Publications in cognition currently dominate the major journals in psychology. However, behavior analysis continues to thrive, even in the absence of its mentor, B. F. Skinner (Pierce, 1966), and behavioral methods continue to be widely used by researchers and clinicians to describe and study human behavior (Robins, Gosling & Craik, 1999, p. 4)

The Rise of Cognitive Psychology (1975–1990)

During the height of behaviorism in psychology, research focused on the analysis of observable responses and their related environmental conditions. The basic learning paradigm, developed in laboratory research studies, revolved around the presentation of a task or stimulus to the learner. Redirection of the research began with the training needs of World War II and the 1960s curriculum reform. Gagné's conditions of learning describe the complexity of human learning in various settings from the classroom to the job site.

The goal of the cognitive revolution, as originally conceived, was to bring "mind" back into the human sciences (Bruner, 1990, p. 2). The intent was to discover and document the meanings that humans develop from their daily encounters (Bruner, 1990). The focus was on the symbolic activities used by humans in constructing and making sense of both their world and themselves (p. 2). However, developments soon shifted from "meaning" to "information" and from the construction of meaning to the processing of information (p. 4). Two key factors contributed to this shift. The first was the communications research initiated in World War II. This research led to the conclusion that the learner is a complex information-processing system. Training problems related to the sophisticated equipment included the perception, judgment, and decision-making processes of the human operators. The term *information,* already a foundation concept in the fundamental sciences, became a legitimate topic for psychology. In biology, for example, the genetic functions of DNA may be expressed as the transmission of information (Baars, 1986, p. 150).

The second major influence was the development of high-speed computers. Machines that followed a set of instructions (whether they involve logic, arithmetic, or natural language) placed internal processes in the realm of tangible events. Research on such processes thereby became legitimate. Moreover, computer capabilities in symbol manipulation, transformation and storage of information, and problem solving provided an analogy for the information-processing model of human memory. Proposed in 1958 by Donald Broadbent, this model of memory included (1) sensory registers, (2) a short-term memory, and (3) a long-term memory.

The application of computer operations to human problem-solving activities, initiated by Newell and Simon (1961), further supported the concept of complex mental functions. This work accelerated research into the use of computers to simulate problem-solving skills (referred to as artificial intelligence research). Less than 10 years later, in 1967, the study of cognitive processes acquired a formal identity with the publication of Ulric Neisser's text *Cognitive Psychology.*

One of the effects of the development of cognitive psychology is that it initiated the involvement of experimental psychologists in research on the essential cognitive processes in learning. A second effect of cognitive psychology is that research has expanded beyond investigating the basic steps involved in processing information from the environment. Current areas of interest include metacognition, novice and expert knowledge, and problem solving. Metacognition is often defined as "knowing about knowing." Metacognitive activities, for example, include strategies undertaken to monitor one's own learning and understanding and to redirect one's efforts if necessary.

The Rise of Social, Cultural, and Personal Factors in Learning (1980–present)

Early studies of learning presented a stimulus or task to the learner, often in a laboratory setting. Extrapolations from these studies were then made to classrooms and other settings. Other perspectives, however, began to focus on different aspects of the natural setting. Three such theories that gained prominence in the 1980s are Albert Bandura's social-cognitive theory, Bernard Weiner's attribution theory, and Lev Vygotsky's cultural-historical theory (see Table 4.1).

Bandura's theory (1977) began with his analysis of the importance of models of behavior in learning. That is, in the naturalistic setting, individuals learn new behaviors through the observation of models and the effects of their own actions. According to Bandura, modeling, whether by live models or symbol models (film and televi-

TABLE 4.1

Some major events in learning theory from 1950 to 1995

1950		
1956 Broadbent's model of human memory		
1957 Soviet Union launches *Sputnik*		
1958 NDEA legislation		1958 Newell and Simon's artificial intelligence
1960		
1960–1969 Curriculum redesign		1960 Bruner calls for a theory of instruction
1960–1963 Piagetian concepts introduced to American education		1961 Skinner described importance of teaching machines
1965 Gagné's conditions of learning		
1967 Publication of Neisser's *Cognitive Psychology*		
1968 Publication of Skinner's *Technology of Teaching*		
1969 The term *instructional psychology* is coined		
1970		
1970–1975 Various models of human memory proposed		1970 Piaget summarizes major concepts for psychologists
		1971 Bandura's social learning theory introduced
		1972 Weiner introduces attribution theory
1977 Gagné expands his theory to include information processing		
1980		
Dominance of research on cognitive processes		
1984 Application of Vygotsky's concepts in reciprocal teaching		
1985 Cognitive psychology emphasizes strategy instruction and metacognition		1985 Social, cultural, and personal factors in learning acquire prominence
1990		
1990–1994 Various constructivist curricula are implemented		
1995 Interest in neuroscience emerges		

sion), is a key influence in the acquisition of both prosocial and reprehensible behaviors. Bandura's (1986) later work explores the role in self-efficacy in learning. Specifically, perceived self-efficacy consists of the learner's belief that he or she can be successful in a particular endeavor.

In contrast, Bernard Weiner proposes a theoretical framework for understanding learners' perceived causes of achievement-related outcomes. Known as attribution theory, the framework focuses on the ways that individuals arrive at causal explanations and the implications of these beliefs. The importance of understanding the cause(s) of events is twofold. First, they have implications for strategies to alter misperceptions. Second, they provide a framework for understanding different classroom goal structures.

The theory developed by Lev S. Vygotsky in the early 20th century has been reintroduced in the United States in recent years. Referred to as cultural-historical, the theory describes two broad cultural processes that determine the nature of learning. One is the ways that the signs and symbols developed by a particular culture influence the thinking of its members. The other describes the role of social interaction with knowledgeable members of the culture in the individual's cognitive development.

According to Bruner (1990), culture should become a central concept in psychology. An individual's participation in culture and the realization of one's mental capabilities through culture make the development of a human psychology on the basis of the individual alone impossible (p. 12). Of particular importance is the crucial feature of culture that Bruner (1990) refers to as "folk psychology." Briefly, a folk psychology consists of the culturally shaped notions through which people organize their views of themselves, others, and the world in which they live (p. 137). Therefore, one cannot understand the individual without understanding his or her culture.

The Emergence of Constructivism (1985-Present)

In recent years interest in addressing the issue of meaning in learning has led to several developments. One is the current emphasis in cognitive views of learning on an active learner. The individual who incorporates knowledge into the mind through asking questions, developing answers, and interacting with and interpreting the environment. That is, the learner actively constructs new knowledge (Larkin, 1994). Other developments that address meaning and sense-making are Vygotsky's cultural-historical theory, constructivism, and current school reform efforts.

The philosophical position known as *constructivism* views knowledge as a human construction. The various perspectives within constructivism are based on the premise that knowledge is not part of an objective, external reality that is separate from the individual. Instead, human knowledge, whether the bodies of content in public disciplines (such as mathematics or sociology) or the knowledge of the individual learner, is a human construction.

Three factors primarily have contributed to the interest of educators and educational psychologists in constructivism. One is dissatisfaction with information-processing theory. Criticisms include (1) the "overselling" of the computer as a metaphor for learning which excludes the everyday capabilities of individuals, everyday problems, and the role of context (Bredo, 1994); and (2) the transmission model of learning (Marshall, 1996). That is, some constructivists maintain that information-processing theory views learners as passive receptacles that receive performed knowledge (O'Connor, 1998).

The other two factors contributing to interest in constructivism are (1) concerns that students are acquiring isolated, decontextualized skills and are unable to apply them in real-world situations, and (2) an interest in Vygotsky's cultural-historical theory. A basic premise of his theory is that the cultural context and other symbols shape a child's view of reality. Further, these symbols also serve as psychological tools that are important in developing higher cognitive functions, such as self-regulated attention and conceptual thinking (verbal and mathematical). [Because the source of knowledge is the continuing interactions and reciprocity between a developing child and a simultaneously changing world, Moshman (1982) refers to Vygotsky's perspective as *dialectical constructivism*.]

Currently, constructivism includes two major belief systems, referred to as *radical* and *social constructivism*. Both perspectives describe the learner as a constructor of knowledge who actively searches for meaning. This search involves the formation, elaboration, and testing of possible mental structures until a satisfactory structure emerges (Perkins, 1991). Information-processing theorists also describe learning as knowledge construction. Learners use strategies, such as elaboration and self-questioning as they actively seek to make sense of presented material (King, 1991, 1994; Mayer, 1992; Pressley et al., 1992) [Moshman (1982) refers to this perspective as *exogenous constructivism* that is expanding toward *endogenous constructivism* with the view of the learner as active and interacting with the environment (p. 235).] Constructivists, however, maintain that storing a relatively accurate representation of presented reality in one's mind is not part of "true" knowledge construction (Marshall, 1996).

Radical Constructivism

Radical constructivism is derived directly from Piaget's cognitive-development theory. One key difference, however, is that Piagetian theory maintains the existence of an external reality to which the learner must gradually accommodate his or her thinking. In contrast, radical constructivism maintains that all knowledge is a human construction and ontological reality is not accessible to rational human knowledge (von Glaserfeld, 1991). Therefore, an individually constructed viewpoint cannot be judged as less "correct" than another. However, individual perspectives can be judged partly according to their correspondence to consensually accepted norms (e.g., the Earth revolves around the sun; the Earth is not flat).

A second major difference is that the focus of radical constructivism is not logical thinking. Instead, the focus is the tasks involved in school learning. However, Piagetian principles advocated by radical constructivism in teaching school subjects include (1) learning is an internal process that occurs in the mind of the individual, and (2) cognitive conflict when one's thinking is challenged and reflection are essential learning processes (see chapter 9 for details). [Moshman (1982) refers to Piagetian theory as *endogenous constructivism* because it involves the internal construction of holistic knowledge structures (p. 234).]

The teacher's role, as in Piagetian theory, is to develop an adequate model of the students' ways of viewing an idea, devise situations that challenge the child's way of thinking, and help students examine the coherence in their current mode of thinking (Confrey, 1985; Prawat & Floden, 1994). In other words, student learning progresses through many internal reorganizations that become more encompassing and integrative (Prawat & Floden, 1994). However, the mental reorganizations refer to the specific information associated with particular topics, such as photosynthesis.

Radical constructivism alters the classroom configuration from teacher-directed instruction to problem-based learning. This focus is a major force in current educational reform efforts. For example, the National Council of Teachers of Mathematics (NCTM) (1989) stated that students in mathematics should make conjectures, abstract mathematical properties, explain their reasoning, validate their assertions, and discuss and question their own thinking and that of others (Lampert, 1990; NCTM, 1989). The teacher's role is (1) to choose problems that can be solved in different ways and which have the capacity to engage all the students in the class, and (2) to probe students' thinking as they discuss the problem approaches and their thinking (Lampert, 1990).

Social Constructivism

Social constructivist beliefs differ from radical constructivism in three major ways: (1) the definition of knowledge, (2) the definition of learning, and (3) the locus of learning (see Table 4.2). Social constructivists interpret Vygotsky's discussions of knowledge as constructed by cultures as a classroom requirement. That is, they view the classroom as a community charged with the task of developing knowledge. Further, they view knowledge as inseparable from the activities that produced it (Bredo, 1994; Dewey & Bentley, 1949). Therefore, knowledge is transactional, learning is socially constructed, and is distributed among the co-participants. The role of the learner in such situations is to participate in a system of practices that are themselves evolving (Cobb & Bowers,

TABLE 4.2
Shared beliefs of social constructivist philosophy

Definition of knowledge	A product of the particular classroom or participant setting to which the learner belongs; the endpoint or product of a particular line of inquiry that is inseparable from the occasions and activities that produced it (Bredo, 1994; Dewey & Bentley, 1949).
Definition of learning	Socially shared cognition that is a process of becoming a member of a sustained community of practice (Lave, 1991); social interaction that constructs and reconstructs contexts, knowledge, and meanings (Marshal, 1996).
Locus of learning	Not confined to the individual's mind (Marshall, 1996); occurs in a community of participants and is distributed among the co-participants (Bredo, 1994).

1999). Therefore, classroom learning over several months can be analyzed in terms of a sequence of evolving mathematical practices in a community of learners. For example, first-grade children early in the fall may be using counters in various ways to determine the number of days remaining in the week and, in the spring, discussing different ways to address three-digit problems (Cobb & Bowers, 1999).

Subvarieties within social constructivism vary on the precise relationship of the individual to the community, the exact nature of the learning goals, and the role of language. For example, the most fully articulated social constructivist view, referred to as *emergent*, was developed "to account for students' mathematical development *as it occurs in the social context of the classroom*" (Cobb & Yackel, 1996, p. 176). Described by Paul Cobb (1994), the emergent perspective is a coordination of radical and social constructivist theories. This view, therefore, permits analyses of learning from both the social (group) and the psychological (individual) perspective in situations in which neither is primary. For example, social norms (rules of discourse) jointly negotiated by a teacher and her second-grade pupils included explaining and justifying one's solutions, attempting to make sense of the explanations of others and questioning proposed alternatives (Cobb & Bowers, 1999). Analyses from the psychological perspective addressed the individual's mathematical beliefs and beliefs about one's role and that of others in general nature of school mathematical activity (p. 177).

A very different view, described by Bredo (1994) as neo-Marxist, is the apprenticeship perspective of Jean Lave (1991; Lave & Wenger, 1991). Citing the current alienated condition in capitalism, which lacks opportunities for individuals to develop deep knowledgeable skill and identities of mastery, Lave (1991) calls for research on situated social practice or situated learning. Examples include Mayan midwives and West African tailors. Essential characteristics of such situations are the seamless immersion of the learner into a community of practice with gradual movement from peripheral tasks to full participation. Further, learning proceeds with no didactic structuring (Lave, 1991).

In addition, situated social practice maintains that no strict knowledge boundary exists between the intra- and extracranial aspects of human cognition (Lave, 1991, p. 68). Instead, knowing is *located in relations among practitioners*, their practice, and the social organization and political economy of communities of practice in a world in which social practices themselves are in the process of reproduction, transformation, and change (Lave & Wenger, 1991, p. 122).

Although immersion in a community of expert mathematicians, for example, is not possible in the classroom setting, some educators have called for a "kinder, gentler" form of situated learning. Prawat & Floden (1994) note that students may acquire cognitive tools (skills and strategies) through participation in a community of learners in a hands-on project-based approach to instruction. Another approach, which avoids the narrowness of particular skills, is the development of big ideas in the discipline (e.g., photosynthesis in science) which can "enlarge a child's field of vision, and have the potential to transform thinking" (p. 40). The teachers' role in the discourse community in the classroom is to be actively involved in assisting students to overcome obstacles by probing the limits of their understanding with difficult cases and helping students manage uncertainty. (This description of classroom discourse, however, does not differ from that recommended by Piaget.)

School Reform Discussions

Discussions of mathematics and science education have suggested the implementation of both radical and social constructivism in public school classrooms (Lampert, 1990; Drive, Asoko, Leach, Mortimer, & Scott, 1994). In addition, a different type of constructivism is proposed in special education (Poplin & Stone, 1992) and in language literacy in the form of whole language (e.g., Au, Mason, & Scheu, 1995; Reid, 1993). Shared beliefs of these two perspectives, referred to as "holistic," are (1) the learner constructs meaning by integrating new and previous experiences into a whole, (2) the integration is a transformation (rather than incremental) experience, and (3) learning should be student-directed and should involve authentic tasks (Green & Gredler, submitted). The importance of providing whole experiences instead of teaching incremented skills is that "the properties of the parts can only be understood from the dynamics of the whole" (Heshusius, 1989).

Of interest is that this belief is a basic Gestalt tenet. Further, both perspectives rely on an overarching set of teacher beliefs as the source of instructional practices rather than already developed curricula or classroom practices.

Another central belief of whole language proponents is that all forms of language—oral speech, reading, and writing—are learned incidentally through immersion in a functional literacy community. Although Vygotsky is cited by some as the source of this belief, he maintained that teaching reading and writing is difficult because written speech (unlike oral speech) is abstract and deliberate (Vygotsky, 1934/1962).

Discussion

Like the Gestalt perspective and some current developments, constructivists emphasize the search for meaning in learning. However, unlike other perspectives on learning, the constructivist philosophical perspective does not acknowledge the existence of an external objective reality. Knowledge, instead, is a human construction, whether at the level of subject disciplines or the learning of the individual.

For most social constructivists, learning is the province of a community of participants. Learners may be experiencing the thinking engaged in by mathematicians, acquiring cognitive tools through participation in hands-on projects, or developing big ideas in the discipline. The key to learning is the discourse community in the classroom in which students develop shared meaning through their participation.

Constructivism also seeks to overcome the sterility of rote mechanized learning and to enrich the knowledge of students through experiences in thinking that reflect discipline-based practices. Implementing a constructivist perspective, however, is complicated by the lack of explicit principles of learning or prescribed instructional activities. Of interest is that Cobb & Bowers (1999) question the practice of translating constructivist tenets directly into instructional prescriptions. That is, they state that specific directives are not warranted, such as (1) because learning involves the negotiation of meaning, students should continually discuss their differing interpretations; (2) students should always work in groups; and (3) instructional tasks should always be grounded in an authentic real-world setting.

Further, constructivists and others have identified two major concerns about implementation. First, in social constructivist classrooms, learning opportunities vary across classes as a result of the requirement for social negotiation (Popkewitz, 1998). The extent of student learning is dependent on both student capabilities in developing knowledge from group discussions and teacher skills in establishing thoughtful and reflective dialogue. Classroom observations indicate that both learning opportunities and success vary across classes as a function of teacher skills (Cobb & Bowers, 1999; Palinscar, 1998).

A second concern is that the implicit nature of the constructivist curriculum can lead to mislearning (Green & Gredler, submitted). Brown and Campione (1994) note the inaccurate scientific deductions made by students. Classroom observations by MacKinnon and Scarff-Seatter (1997) found a classroom focus on children's exploration and sharing of explanations without teacher efforts to challenge incoherence and inconsistencies. Addressing these concerns is a challenge for constructivism.

The Interest in Neuroscience (1995–Present)

Current interest in the potential contributions of neuroscience to an understanding of learning includes two areas. One is the research in cognitive neuroscience and the other includes efforts to derive educational policy and practice prescriptions from research on neural development in the brain.

Cognitive Neuroscience.   Researchers who are cognitive neuroscientists seek to establish links between cognitive behaviors and neural activity in the brain. This research makes use of methods referred to as neuroimaging, which permit examination of the structure and/or function of the brain (Nelson & Bloom, 1997).

Two frequently used methods, positron emission topography (PET) and functional magnetic resonance imaging (FMRI), permit the visualization of memory processes in the brain (Gabrieli, 1998). However, a limitation of these methods is that they are only indirect measures of neural activity. That is, they derive their signals from local changes in blood flow or metabolism that are correlated with neural activity, not neural activity itself (p. 88). The PET procedure usually involves the injection of radioactive oxygen or glucose, which are fuels for the brain, because the region of the brain performing a particular function requires more fuel than other regions. The PET procedure analyzes the positrons emitted by the radioactive substance as it decays and thereby identifies the location of the brain activity (Nelson & Bloom, 1997). The FMRI procedure, in contrast, tracks subtle increases and decreases in the oxygen in the blood flow in the brain. The scanner records successive images that are slices of the brain in various orientations and which indicate the areas of brain activity.

Measures of glucose use and blood flow rates in the brain obtained during the performance of cognitive tasks can lead to information about the particular regions involved in regulating specific cognitive processes (Gur & Gur, 1991). One research finding is that the encoding and retrieval of episodic events and knowledge in any domain (e.g., pictures or words, living or manufactured objects) is distributed over a specific yet extensive network that spans several lobes (Gabrieli, 1998, p. 94). Other studies indicate, for example, that portions of the cerebellum may be important in problem solving (Kim, Uğurbik, & Strick, 1994), and areas of the prefrontal cortex are activated in 8 to 10-year-olds during spatial memory tasks (Truwit et al., 1996). Also, for left-handed individuals, use of the left hand activates both the left and right motor cortices (Kim et al., 1994). The latter finding questions the prevalent view that each side of the body is controlled by the opposite hemisphere for both right- and left-handed individuals.

These and other studies do provide information about brain activity. However, the mental processes associated with a particular activation have yet to be specified.

Educational Recommendations Extrapolated from Neurobiology. Research on neurobiology addresses biological changes in neural networks in the brain. Studies have investigated the development of synapses (the connections through which impulses travel from one neuron to another) in cats, monkeys, and rats.

Calls for linking educational policy to brain research that have emerged in the 1990s refer to research findings of the 1970s (Bruer, 1998a, 1998b). This research indicates three major findings. First, studies of cats and rhesus monkeys indicate an early postnatal period of the overproduction of the number of synapses per neuron (synaptic density) which, in monkeys, reaches maximum levels two to four months after birth. This overproduction is followed by a period of synapse pruning and elimination which reduces the number of synaptic connections to adult mature levels (Bruer, 1997).

The second finding refers to a critical period in the visual development of kittens. Early research indicated that visual deprivation (the lid suture of one eye for the first three months of life) resulted in functional blindness in that eye and the inability to use the eye to guide behavior when the sutures were removed (Bruer, 1997). Subsequent research, however, has indicated a period following sensory deprivation in which training and therapy led to near-normal functioning (Daw, 1995; Bruer, 1997).

The third finding concerns the effects of complex environments on synaptic development in rats (Turner & Greenough, 1985). Rats raised in complex environments similar to their natural wild environment developed 20 to 25 percent more synapses per neuron in the visual cortex than rats raised in isolation in bare cages (Bruer, 1997). Subsequent research indicated that the brains of mature adult rats also develop new synapses in response to new experiences (Greenough, Black, & Wallace, 1987).

Some policymakers, referring to the neuroscientific research, call for providing enriched environments to children prior to the age of three because (1) this age is the critical period in brain development, (2) enriched environments can influence brain development in uniquely beneficial ways, and (3) the most crucial learning opportunities occur before the age of five (Begley, 1996; Newman, 1997; Shore, 1997). Enriched environments include talking, reading, or singing to and playing with the infant or toddler.

Providing such experiences to infants and toddlers may be important for a variety of reasons, such as socialization. However, the impetus to focus educational efforts on the toddler and preschool years is not supported by the neurobiological data (Bruer, 1997, 1998a, 1998b, 1999; Schoenfeld, 1999). First, changes in synaptic density in humans vary among areas of the brain and, in the frontal cortex, for example, do not stabilize at adult levels until mid or late adolescence. This is long after the "critical" early childhood period.

Second, increases in synaptic density are correlated with the initial emergence of sensory, motor, and memory skills, such as brief visual memory in the infant. However, these skills continue to develop after the period of synaptic adulthood when synaptic density has decreased to the same level as that of early infancy (Bruer, 1998b).

Third, the plasticity of the human brain is not limited to the early years. The adult human brain also can reorganize in response to personal experience and this capability makes lifelong learning possible (Nelson & Bloom, 1997).

Fourth, the research on complex environments simply indicates that species raised in sensory-deprived isolation will not develop in expected ways. Complex, however, does not translate into "enriched" which typically refers to activities selected according to one's value system (Bruer, 1997). Examples include *Sesame Street* but not other programs, and Mozart rather than Hootie and the Blowfish. Neuroscience, in other words, does not provide support for such choices (Bruer, 1997; 1998a). In summary, neuroscience has yet to develop information that can guide the selection and organization of learning activities or the development of educational policy.

Summary

Three trends have guided theory development and research in the second half of the 20th century. The first, instructional psychology, emerged in response to the need to design training for complex tasks in World War II, and continued as a part of the post-Sputnik curriculum redesign. Developments during this period include Gagné's conditions of learning, Piaget's cognitive-development theory, Bruner's curriculum development model, and applications of operant conditioning to classroom instruction, and the management of behavior.

Dissatisfaction with behaviorist tenets contributed to the second trend, the rise of cognitive psychology, in the late 1970s. The original goal was to bring "mind" back into the human sciences. However, influenced by communications research and the development of high-speed computers, the focus of the movement shifted to information processing. In the 1980s, research began to address related issues. Included are novice and expert knowledge and metacognition.

Emerging in the early 1980s, the third trend introduced social, cultural, and personal factors into the study of learning. Three theories that address some of these issues are Bandura's social-cognitive theory, Weiner's attribution theory, and Vygotsky's cultural-historical theory.

In the late 1980s and 1990s, two developments which have entered discussions of educational policy have emerged. The philosophical perspective referred to as constructivism maintains that the process involves the construction of knowledge by the learner. Social constructivism further maintains that this construction occurs in a community of learners. The second development is a response to some of the brain research conducted by neuroscientists. Although current extrapolations from the research to educational practice are premature, future research may link neurological processes to behaviors.

INTRODUCTION TO SEVEN
CONTEMPORARY THEORIES

In the late 20th century, seven theories related to human learning provide new insights to researchers and educators. Three of these theories directly address the basic processes essential for learning and are referred to in this text as *learning-process theories* (Table 4.3). Of these three, Skinner's principles continue the behaviorist tradition of the primacy of environmental conditions and events in bringing about behavioral change. Cognitive theories continue the concern about mental events initiated by Gestalt psychology. In contrast, Gagné's conditions of learning is an interactionist theory. The learner's cognitive processes are integrated with particular environmental events essential for learning different kinds of skills.

In contrast to the learning-process theories, the *cognitive-development theories* developed by Piaget and Vygotsky do not address the ways that specific items are learned. Instead, each theorist defines the nature of human thinking in a particular way and then describes the essential requirements for developing the highest levels of human thought.

Finally, both Bandura's social-cognitive theory and Weiner's attribution theory are described as *social-context theories.* Each perspective describes different kinds of information abstracted from the social setting that influence perceptions and behavior. Bandura emphasizes the interaction of the environment, personal factors,

TABLE 4.3

Comparison of seven contemporary theories influential in learning

Theory	Type	Focus
Skinner's operant conditioning	Learning-process theory	The arrangement of consequences for learner behavior
Gagné's conditions of learning	Learning-process theory	The relationship of the phases of information processing to type of learning task and instruction
Cognitive theories	Learning-process theory	The processes of acquiring information, remembering, managing one's learning, and problem solving
Piaget's developmental epistemology	Cognitive-development theory	The growth of intelligence from infancy to adulthood
Vygotsky's cultural-historical theory	Cognitive-development theory	The role of the culture in the development of higher mental functions
Bandura's social-cognitive theory	Social-context theory	The observation of and internal processing of modeled behavior
Weiner's attribution theory	Social-context theory	The influence of learner beliefs about success and failure on achievement-related behavior

and behavior in learning. Weiner, in contrast, focuses on the individual's cognitive and emotional reactions to success and failure outcomes.

The Analysis of Learning Theory

The discussion of each theory in this text proceeds from the theoretical to the practical. Basic principles of learning (or development) are discussed first, followed by principles of instruction. The relationship of each theory to classroom issues and a classroom example are presented in a third section ("Educational Applications"). Table 4.4 illustrates the questions that are answered in each section.

The sections "Principles of Learning" and "Principles of Instruction" are parallel discussions. The fundamentals of each learning theory are explained in the former, and the ways in which these fundamentals are applied to classroom instruction are described in the latter. The purpose of this arrangement is to develop a clear understanding of each theory. Discussing the interpretation of a theory at the same time as the basic principles are being explained risks misunderstanding and confusion for the reader.

TABLE 4.4
Topic outline* for the analysis of each theory

Topic	Focus
Principles of learning (or development)	
Basic assumptions	What assumptions about learning are made by the theorist? How is learning defined? Is learning viewed as behavioral change, a change in cognitive structure, or as some internal process?
The components of learning (or development)	What are the essential elements that must be present in each act of learning? What are the interrelationships?
The nature of complex learning	How are the components of learning (described in the preceding section) arranged to account for complex learning, such as how to solve problems?
Principles of instruction	
Basic assumptions	What are the theorist's assumptions about school learning?
The components of instruction	How do the components of learning relate to classroom instruction?
Designing instruction for complex skills	How is instruction to be developed for skills such as learning to play tennis and learning to solve problems?
Educational applications	
Classroom issues	How does the theory explain individual differences, cognitive processes, and the social context for learning?
Developing a classroom strategy	What are the specific steps in the development of instruction?
Classroom example	

*Minor wording changes have been made in Piaget's cognitive-development theory, Vygotsky's cultural-historical theory, and Weiner's attribution theory.

The basic assumptions of each theory are presented as an introduction to the principles of learning and instruction. No set of principles about learning is developed in a vacuum. Instead, each theory is derived from basic beliefs about the nature of learning. Such beliefs establish the emphasis and focus of the theory. For example, a theory that defines learning as behavioral change will focus on factors that influence behavior. Mental states or cognitive structures are the emphasis of other theories that define learning in terms of qualitative processes.

The purpose of the two sections "The Components of Learning" and "The Nature of Complex Learning" is twofold. One is to present and to describe the fundamental elements that must be present in every act of learning separate from any other discussion. The components of learning are the core of each theory. In Skinner's operant conditioning, for example, the components of each learning act are (1) a discriminative stimulus, (2) a learner response, and (3) a consequence. In contrast, the essential components in Bandura's social-cognitive theory are (1) the modeled behavior, (2) the nature of the reinforcement, and (3) the learner's cognitive processes. Understanding the components of learning and the relationships among them is essential to the analysis of instructional applications of the theory.

The ways in which the basic learning components are arranged to acquire complex skills, such as learning to solve algebra problems, are often not intuitively obvious. Therefore, the section "The Nature of Complex Learning" (or development) is included to illustrate these situations. In operant conditioning, for instance, complex sequences of skills are acquired through the implementation of various patterns of subtle reinforcement contingencies.

The final section, "Educational Applications," first relates the theory to classroom issues. Included are the theory's position on individual differences, cognitive processes, and the social context for learning. The specific steps required to develop an instructional strategy according to the theory are presented next, followed by a classroom example in a particular subject area. Each theory is discussed in a particular chapter with the exception of the information-processing theories, which are discussed in two chapters.

The Epilogue first compares and contrasts the basic components and major contributions of the seven contemporary theories. Then current issues in learning are discussed.

CHAPTER QUESTIONS

1. What is Bruner's rationale for the centrality of culture in psychology?

2. What counterarguments might be offered by the theories that seek to establish universal principles of learning?

REFERENCES

Au, K., Mason, J., & Scheu, J. (1995). *Literacy instruction for today.* New York: HarperCollins.

Baars, B. J. (1986). *The cognitive revolution in psychology.* New York: Guilford.

Bandura, A. (1977). *Social learning theory.* Upper Saddle River, NJ: Prentice Hall.

Bandura, A. (1978). The self-system in reciprocal determinism. *American Psychologists, 33,* 344–358.

Bandura, A. (1986). *Social foundations of thought and action: A social cognitive theory.* Upper Saddle River, NJ: Prentice Hall.

Begley, S. (1996). Your child's brain. *Newsweek, 127*(8), 55–62.

Bredo, E. (1994). Reconstructing educational psychology: Situated cognition and Deweyian pragmatism. *Educational Psychologist, 29*(1), 23–25.

Broadbent, D. E. (1958). *Perception and communication.* London: Pergamon.

Brown, A. L., & Campione, J. C. (1994). Guided discovery in a community of learners. In K. McGilly (Ed.)., Classroom lessons: Integrating cognitive theory and classroom practice (pp. 229–272). Cambridge, MA: MIT Press.

Bruer, J. T. (1997). Education and the brain: A bridge too far. *Educational Researcher, 26*(8), 4–16.

Bruer, J. T. (1998a). Brain science, brain function. *Educational Leadership, 56*(3), 14–18.

Bruer, J. T. (1998b). The brain and child development: Time for some critical thinking. *Public Health Reports, 113,* 389–397.

Bruer, J. T. (1999). *The myth of the first three years: A new understanding of early brain development.* New York: The Free Press.

Bruner, J. S. (1960). *The process of education.* Cambridge, MA: Harvard University Press.

Bruner, J. S. (1964). Some theorems on instruction illustrated with references to mathematics. In E. R. Hilgard (Ed.), *Theories of learning and instruction. The sixty-third yearbook of the National Society for the Study of Education, Part I* (pp. 306–335). Chicago: University of Chicago Press.

Bruner, J. S. (1966). *Toward a theory of instruction.* Cambridge, MA: Harvard University Press.

Bruner, J. S. (1990). *Acts of meaning.* Cambridge, MA: Harvard University Press.

Cobb, P. (1994). Where is the mind? Constructivist and sociocultural perspectives on mathematics development. *Educational Researcher, 23,* 13–20.

Cobb, P., & Bowers, J. (1999). Cognitive and situated learning perspectives in theory and practice. *Educational Researcher, 28*(2), 4–15.

Cobb, P., & Yackel, E. (1996). Constructivist, emergent, and sociocultural perspectives in the context of developmental research. *Educational Psychologist, 31*(3/4), 175–190.

Confrey, J. (1985). Towards a framework for constructivist instruction. In L. Streefland (Ed.), *Proceedings of the Ninth International Conference for the Psychology of Mathematics Education* (Vol. 1, pp. 477–478, 483). Noorlwijkerhout: Psychology of Mathematics Education.

Daw, N. (1995). Visual development. New York: Plenum Press.

Dewey, J., & Bentley, A. (1949). *Knowing and the known.* Boston: Beacon Press.

Driver, R., Asoko, H., Leach, J., Mortimer, E., & Scott, P. (1994). Constructing scientific knowledge in the classroom. *Educational Researcher, 23*(7), 5–12.

Gabrieli, J. D. (1998). Cognitive neuroscience of memory. In J. T. Spence, J. M. Darley, & D. J. Foss (Eds.), *Annual Review of Psychology, 49* (pp. 87-115). Palo Alto, CA: Annual Reviews.

Gagné, R. M. (1962). The acquisition of knowledge. *Psychological Review, 69,* 355–365.

Gagné, R. M., & Rohwer W. (1969). Instructional psychology. *Annual Review of Psychology, 20,* 381–418.

Gilgen, A. R. (1982). *American psychology since World War II.* Westport, CT: Greenwood.

Green, S. K., & Gredler, M. E. (submitted). *A critique and analysis of constructivism.*

Greenough, W. T., Black, J. E., & Wallace, C. S. (1987). Experience and brain development. *Child Development, 58,* 539–559.

Gur, R. C., & Gur, E. R. (1991). The impact of neuroimaging on human neuropsychology. In R. G. Lister & H. J. Weingartener (Eds.), *Perspectives on cognitive neuroscience* (pp. 417–436). Oxford: Oxford University Press.

Guttman, N. (1977). On Skinner and Hull: A reminiscence and projection. *American Psychologist, 32,* 321–328.

Harding, S. (1993). Rethinking standpoint epistemology: "What is Strong Objectivity?" In L. Alcoff
& E. Potter (Eds.), *Feminist Epistemologies* (pp.
49–82). New York: Routledge.

Heshusius, L. (1989). The Newtonian mechanistic
paradigm, special education, and contours of
alternatives: An overview. *Journal of Learning
Disabilities, 22*(7), 403-415.

Hilgard, E. R. (1980). The trilogy of mind: Cognition, affection, and conation. *Journal of the History of the Behavioral Sciences, 16,* 107–117.

Kim, S. G., Ashe, K., Hendrick, J. M., Ellermann, H.,
Merkle, H., Ugurbik, K., & Georgopoulos, A. P.
(1993). Functional magnetic resonance imaging
of motor cortex: Hemispheric asymmetry and
handedness. *Science, 261,* 615–617.

Kim, S. G., Ugurbik, K., & Strick, P. L. (1994). Activation of a cerebellar output nucleus during cognitive processing. *Science, 265,* 949–951.

King, A. (1991). Effects of training in strategic questioning on children's problem-solving performance.
Journal of Educational Psychology, 83, 307–317.

King, A. (1994). Guiding knowledge construction in
the classroom: Effects of teaching children how
to question and how to explain. *American Educational Research Journal, 31*(2), 338–368.

Lakatos, I. (1978). History of science and its rational
reconstructions. In I. Lakatos (Ed.), *The methodology of scientific research programs* (pp.
102–138). New York: Cambridge University Press.

Lampert, M. (1990). When the problem is not the
question and the solution is not the answer:
Mathematical knowing and teaching. *American
Educational Research Journal, 27*(1), 29–63.

Larkin, J. H. (1994). Forward. In K. McGilly (Ed.),
*Classroom lessons: Integrating cognitive theory
and classroom practice* (pp. ix-xiv). Cambridge,
MA: MIT Press.

Lave, J., & Wenger, E. (1991). *Situated learning:
Legitimate peripheral participation.* New York:
Cambridge University Press.

MacKinnon, A., & Scarff-Seatter, C. (1997). Constructivism: Connections and confusions in
teacher education. In V. Richardson (Ed.), *Constructivist teacher education* (pp. 38–56). Washington, DC: Falmer Press.

Marshall, H. (1996). Clarifying and implementing
contemporary psychological processes. *Educational Psychologist, 31*(1), 29–34.

Moshman, D. (1992). Exogenous, endogenous, and
dialectical constructivism. *Developmental
Review, 2,* 371–384.

National Council of Teachers of Mathematics.
(1989). *Curriculum and evaluation standards
for school mathematics.* Reston, VA: Author.

Neisser, J. (1967). *Cognitive psychology.* New York:
Appleton-Century-Crofts.

Nelson, C. A., & Bloom, F. E. (1997). *Child Development and Neuroscience, 68*(5), 970–987.

Newell, A., & Simon, H. (1961). *Human problem
solving.* Santa Monica, CA: Rand.

Newman, F. (1997). Brain research has implications
for education: Is first grade too late? *State Educational Leader, 15,* 1–2.

O'Connor, M. G. (1998). Can we trace the "efficacy
of social constructivism"? In P. D. Pearson & A.
Iran-Nejad (Eds.), *Review of Research in Education, 23* (pp. 25–71). Washington, DC: American
Educational Research Association.

Palinscar, A. (1998). Social constructivist perspectives on teaching and learning. *Annual Review
of Psychology, 49,* 345–375.

Perkins, D. N. (1991). What constructivism demands
of the learner. *Educational Technology, 31,* 19–21.

Pierce, W. D. (1996). Behavior analysis is alive and
well. *Contemporary Psychology, 41,* 461.

Popkewitz, T. (1998). Dewey, Vygotsky, and the social
administration of the individual: Constructivist ped-
agogy as systems of ideas in historical spaces. *American Educational Research Journal, 35,* 535–570.

Poplin, M. M., & Stone, S. (1992). Paradigm shifts in
instructional strategies: From reductionism to
holistic constructivism. In W. Stainback & S.
Stainback (Eds.). *Controversial issues confronting special education* (pp. 153–180).
Boston: Allyn & Bacon.

Popper, K. (1968). *The logic of discovery.* New York:
Harper & Row.

Prawat, R. S., & Floden, R. E. (1994). Philosophical
perspectives on constructivist views of learning.
Educational Psychologist, 29(1), 37–48.

Pressley, M., Wood, E., Woloshyn, V., Martin, V., King, A., & Monke, D. (1992). Encouraging mindful use of prior knowledge: Attempting to construct explanatory answers facilitates learning. *Educational Psychologist, 27*(1), 91–109.

Reid, D. K. (1993). Another vision of "Visions and revisions." *Remedial and Special Education, 14*(4), 14–25.

Robins, R. W., Gosling, S. D., & Craik, K. H. (1999). An empirical analysis of trends in psychology. *American Psychologist, 54*(2), 117–128.

Schoenfeld, A. H. (1999). Looking toward the 21st century: Challenges of educational theory and practice. *Educational Researcher, 28*(7), 4–14.

Shore, R. (1997). *Rethinking the brain: New insights into early development.* New York: Families and Work Institute.

Truwit, C. L., Le, T. H., Lim, J. C., Hu, X., Carver, L., Thomas, K. M., Monk, C., & Nelson, C. A. (1996, June). Functional MR imaging of working memory task activation in children: Preliminary findings. Paper presented to the American Society of Neuroradiology, Seattle, WA.

Turner, A. M., & Greenough, W. T. (1985). Differential rearing effects on rat visual cortex synapsis. *Brain Research, 329,* 195–203.

von Glaserfield, E. (1987). Learning as a constructivist activity. In C. Janvier (Ed.), *Problems of representation in the teaching and learning of mathematics* (pp. 3–17). Hillsdale, NJ: Erlbaum.

von Glaserfield, E. (1991). *Radical constructivism in mathematics education.* Dordrecht, The Netherlands: Kluwer.

Vygotsky, L. S. (1962). *Thought and language.* Cambridge, MA: MIT Press.

PART II

Learning-Process Theories

Three theories address the particular events and conditions necessary for the learning of information and/or skills. Continuing the behaviorist tradition, B. F. Skinner's operant conditioning describes the environmental events and conditions responsible for complex patterns of voluntary behavior. Examples are pigeons learning to bowl and children learning to read. Skinner's analyses include the various types of consequences that influence behavioral change, the emotional by-products of aversive consequences, and a mechanism for individualizing classroom instruction.

Robert Gagné, in contrast, began with an analysis of the various tasks found in the range of human learning. He identified five major types of capabilities, each reflected in a particular performance. His theory details the cognitive processes and learner states essential for each type of task, as well as the essential steps for instruction.

The cognitive perspective began with a model for the ways that the learner receives, processes, and later recalls information. At present, cognitive theory and research also address problem-solving and learner strategies for the management of learning.

CHAPTER 5

B. F. Skinner's Operant Conditioning

A baby shakes a rattle, a child runs with a pinwheel, a scientist operates a cyclotron—and all are reinforced by the results. (Skinner, 1968b, p. 153)

The principles of B. F. Skinner initiated a new direction in the 1930s for a behaviorism that was dominated by Pavlov's model. Skinner disagreed with the S–R position that "cues" or "drive stimuli" trigger all behavior like some "inexorable force" (Skinner, 1966b). Instead, his research indicated that the important event in changing behavior, whether that of a baby or a scientist, is the outcome produced by the action (Skinner, 1953). The baby's accidental movement of a rattle produces a new sound, and soon the baby is shaking the toy for several minutes at a time. Similarly, a scientist discovers an efficient way to stain slides for cell analysis. He then begins to spend evenings and weekends in the laboratory perfecting the technique. The increased frequency of the baby's and scientist's actions is influenced by the outcome produced by each behavior.

Skinner's analysis led to more than 50 years of research on what seems, at first glance, to be a very simple principle. Consider, however, the situation in which a well-meaning teacher delays helping a student so that he can show what he can do (Skinner, 1968b). When the student shows discouragement, the teacher quickly comes to his aid. For the anxious or insecure student, giving up on a difficult problem has "produced" adult attention and assistance. The reaction of the careless teacher has strengthened an undesirable behavior, which is likely to be repeated.

Skinner's work began with an analysis of the differences between reflexes and other behaviors (Skinner, 1935), and his principles of operant conditioning soon followed (Skinner, 1938, 1953). He later turned his attention to the school setting with the development of the teaching machine (Skinner, 1961) and a technology of classroom teaching (Skinner, 1968a, 1968b, 1973). His later comments on education include recommendations for microcomputer instruction (Skinner in Green, 1984; Skinner, 1989b).

In the 1980s, Skinner continued to apply his concepts to various aspects of the human condition. His work encompassed an analysis of the similarities and differences in natural selection and operant conditioning (Skinner, 1981, 1987), an analysis of aging (Skinner & Vaughan, 1983), a description of cultures and their development (Skinner, 1981, 1987, 1989b), and a further analysis of rule-governed behavior (Skinner, 1987). His work has been described as including (1) a philosophy of science, (2) a theory of behavior, and (3) a system for applying the principles in the natural setting (Kratochwill & Bijou, 1987, p. 138).

PRINCIPLES OF LEARNING

Skinner agreed with the position taken earlier by John Watson (1913). That is, psychology can become a science only through the study of behavior.

Basic Assumptions

Like Clark Hull, B. F. Skinner established rigorous procedures for the study of behavior. Unlike Hull, however, he did not believe in the use of theory as a research framework. Instead, the cornerstone of operant conditioning is Skinner's beliefs about the nature of a behavioral science and the characteristics of learned behavior.

The Nature of a Behavioral Science

The goal of any science, according to Skinner (1953), is to discover the lawful relationships among natural events in the environment. Therefore, a science of behavior must discover the lawful or "functional" relationships among physical conditions or environmental events and behavior. The challenge is to determine which changes in independent variables (conditions or events) lead to changes in the dependent variable, behavior. For example, what are the conditions or events responsible for one student's attending to academic tasks and another's avoidance of homework? To refer to the one student as "motivated" and the other as "unmotivated" does not, in Skinner's view, answer the question.

The development of a science of behavior is difficult because behavior is both complex and varied (Skinner, 1953). In addition, it is a temporal, fluid, and changing process. The task for the scientist is to discover its order and uniformity (Skinner, 1953).

Of importance is that neither theories nor discussions of inner states should be used as a basis for behavioral research (Skinner, 1950, 1966b). Theories create an artificial world of order and lawfulness by explaining one statement in terms of another. The result is that the yet undiscovered lawful relationships are obscured. Moreover, theories may stifle the scientist's sense of curiosity, thereby ending the search for clarification (Skinner, 1950).

Problems with Internal States.
At least three problems result from describing behavior as "caused" by some mental state or set of feelings. First, such explanations simply raise another issue—that of explaining the states themselves (Skinner, 1963a). For example, if anxiety is proposed as an explanation for poor test-taking skills, then what causes the anxiety?

Second, the emphasis on states treats behavior as merely an indicator or "symptom" of an inner mental or physiological activity (Skinner, 1966b, p. 213). Behavior becomes a "second-class variable" when it is viewed as merely an indicator of a process (e.g., learning or maturation), a state (such as alertness), or a drive, emotion, or available psychic energy.

Third, attention is diverted from research that may identify both the sources of problems and the solutions. For example, the state referred to as "consumer lack of confidence" in the economy is described as a "problem" in the restoration of economic growth. However, people plan to buy less when their money does not go very far, and the decreased buying is described as lack of confidence. Thus governmental actions to "restore confidence" are, in reality, actions taken to restore consumer buying—that is, to change behavior.

A similar situation is the depression that one experiences when moving to a new city. The problem is that the old set of behaviors is now useless (Skinner, 1987, p. 155). The old stores, restaurants, theaters, and friends are no longer present, and a new set of behaviors must be acquired. When this is done, the depression is relieved.

In the classroom, a student who demonstrates poor reading skills also will perform poorly in his academic subjects. The student may be labeled as lacking in self-esteem, or as having a poor self-concept, which refers to his lack of initiative in school. However, the problem is not that of the student's internal state, but is, instead, a lack of reading skills (Belfiore & Hornyak, 1998, p. 186).

Experimental Analysis.   To study behavior, the researcher must manipulate observable events in a controlled setting. This procedure is referred to as the experimental analysis of behavior (Skinner, 1953, 1968b).

To control environmental conditions, Skinner designed an experimental space that was free of distractions. A soundproof darkened box was used that included one or more response devices, such as levers, keys, or discs. Mechanisms to provide reinforcers (e.g., food and water) were also included. Sometimes other stimuli were used, such as lights, loudspeakers, or mechanisms for the delivery of mild shock. The chamber was automated so that reinforcers were delivered immediately after an appropriate response, and automated devices recorded the frequency of responses.

In addition, the behavior of individual subjects rather than of groups was recorded. In Skinner's view, group averages do not provide a clear picture of behavior. For example, the average 68.33 provides little information about the three scores from which it was obtained: 55, 60, and 90.

The first subjects in Skinner's experiments were rats; later he used pigeons. The information collected on these subjects also reveals information about the interactions between all organisms and the environment. "The schedule of reinforcement which makes the pigeon a pathological gambler is to be found at the racetrack and the roulette table, where it has a comparable effect" (Skinner, 1969, p. 84). Thus the research on these processes in the laboratory is considered to be applicable to human behavior.

A Definition of Learning

In Skinner's view, learning is behavioral change. As the subject learns, responses increase, and when unlearning occurs, the rate of responding falls (Skinner, 1950).

Learning therefore is formally defined as a change in the likelihood or probability of a response.

Because the likelihood of responding is difficult to measure, the rate, or frequency, of responding is measured instead. Although not precisely the same as the probability of future performance, it is an initial step in the analysis of behavioral change (Skinner, 1963b). Also, response rate may be applied to a variety of behaviors, from the behavior of pigeons in the laboratory to student responses in the classroom.

In summary, six assumptions form the foundation of operant conditioning:

1. Learning is behavioral change.
2. Behavioral change (learning) is functionally related to changes in environmental events or conditions.
3. The lawful relationships between behavior and the environment can be determined only if behavioral properties and experimental conditions are defined in physical terms and observed under carefully controlled conditions.
4. Data from the experimental study of behavior are the only acceptable sources of information about the causes of behavior.
5. The behavior of the individual organism is the appropriate data source.
6. The dynamics of an organism's interaction with the environment is the same for all species.

Summary

Like John Watson, Skinner believed that psychology could become a science only through the study of behavior. The goal of any science is to discover the lawful relationships among natural events in the environment. Therefore, a science of behavior must discover the lawful relationships among environmental events and behavior.

Of importance in developing a science of behavior is that both theories and discussions of inner states should be excluded. Theories create an artificial world of orderliness, and the use of inner states as explanations simply raises other issues to be explained. In addition, behavior is treated merely as a symptom of some inner state, and it becomes a second-class variable. Third, a reliance on inner states diverts attention from research that may identify both problems and solutions.

To study behavior, the researcher must manipulate both behavior and observable events in a controlled setting. Behavioral properties and experimental conditions are defined in physical terms, and the behavior of the individual organism can assist the researcher in identifying the processes of behavioral change, that is, learning.

The Components of Learning

Development of the principles of operant conditioning began with the analysis of Pavlov's classical conditioning. According to Skinner (1938), Pavlov's model is restricted to those responses that are already associated with a particular stimulus, such as the leg jerk that follows a hammer tap to the knee. Skinner described these reflexes as **elicited responses** or respondent behavior. Because the method of conditioning these responses requires stimulus substitution, Skinner designated Pavlov's model as *Type S conditioning*.

Analysis of complex behaviors, such as painting a picture or singing a song, indicated that they are not elicited by particular stimuli (events or conditions) (Skinner, 1935). These behaviors were named **emitted responses**. In addition, emitted responses act on the environment to produce different kinds of consequences that affect the organism and thereby alter future behavior. Singing a song, for example, may "operate" on the environment to produce consequences such as praise, applause, or money. These behaviors were therefore named **operants** (Skinner, 1935).

The key to understanding operant behaviors, in Skinner's view (1953, 1963b), was Edward Thorndike's law of effect. Specifically, an animal's escape behavior resulted in food, and under similar confinement conditions, the escape response was repeated. The importance of Thorndike's research was that it included the effects of the subject's action among the causes of behavioral change. Therefore, concepts such as purpose, intention, and expectancy were not needed to explain future behavior (Skinner, 1963b, p. 503).

Although Thorndike used some terms that lead to misunderstandings, the law of effect identified the three essential components in behavioral change (Skinner, 1953). They are (1) the occasion on which the response occurs, (2) the subject's response, and (3) the reinforcing consequences. These three components of learning are described as the discriminative stimulus (S^D), the response (R), and the reinforcing stimulus ($S^{reinf.}$). The sequence of learning events is (S^D)–(R)–($S^{reinf.}$).

The Discriminative Stimulus

Any stimulus that is consistently present when a response is reinforced is a **discriminative stimulus**. For example, after repeated reinforcement for tripping the latch of a cage, a confined animal responds only to the fastener and ignores other parts of the cage. The latch is referred to as the discriminative stimulus. Through association with the reinforced response, the discriminative stimulus serves as a cue for behavior.

The process by which the stimulus becomes a behavioral cue was demonstrated in an experiment in which a pigeon's behavior of pecking a red key was reinforced several times (Skinner, 1953). When the color was changed to green in midstroke, the pigeon's head stopped and its beak did not strike the key. The process is typically referred to as discrimination; however, the organism is simply responding more often to settings with certain properties (Skinner, 1989a, p. 128).

Behavioral change can, of course, be explained without reference to the preceding stimulus (Skinner, 1953). An example is neck stretching in the pigeon, which typically occurs without an S^D. Like other behaviors, neck stretching will increase in rate as a result of continued reinforcement. However, if neck stretching is reinforced only when a signal light is on, then eventually the behavior will occur only in the presence of the light (Skinner, 1953, p. 107).

The Role of Discriminative Stimuli.   The probability that a response will be repeated is maximized by the presence of a discriminative stimulus. Examples that

exercise control over behavior in everyday life include red and green traffic lights, stop signs, and other signals (Skinner, 1953). Also included are countless verbal commands, such as "Take out your pencils" and "Please pass the salt." However, signals, verbal commands, and other discriminative stimuli do not automatically trigger (elicit) operant behaviors. Rather, they acquire behavioral control as a result of prior reinforcements for particular responses in their presence.

Discriminative stimuli for human behavior are not restricted to environmental events. In many situations, individuals construct discriminative stimuli to which they can respond. People construct such stimuli when they make resolutions, announce expectations or intentions, and develop plans (Skinner, 1963b, p. 513). However, to be most effective in controlling behavior, these self-generated stimuli must be visible in some durable form, such as drafting a written plan or posting the resolution on a bulletin board (Skinner, 1963b).

Two or more different stimuli that share a common feature may also acquire control over a particular response. A pigeon's pecking response to both a lighted bar and a lighted disc and a child's verbal identification of $\mathcal{p}$, P, and p are examples. This process is referred to by Skinner as induction (commonly known as **stimulus generalization**).

Summary

The key to understanding complex behaviors is to understand the events and processes responsible for emitted responses. These responses, unlike Pavlov's elicited responses, are not automatically associated with a particular stimulus. The key, in Skinner's view, was Thorndike's law of effect. That is, emitted responses act on the environment to produce different kinds of consequences that affect the organism and thereby alter future behavior. The three essential components of learning that Skinner derived from Thorndike's paradigm are the discriminative stimulus (S^D), the response (R), and the reinforcing stimulus ($S^{reinf.}$).

The discriminative stimulus is any stimulus that is consistently present when a response is reinforced. Through repeated association with the reinforced response, the discriminative stimulus becomes a behavioral cue for the response. Examples of discriminative stimuli that exercise control over behavior include "Take out your pencils" and "Please pass the salt." Discriminative stimuli often are environmental events and the verbal statements of others. However, individuals also construct discriminative stimuli for themselves, such as lists and written plans.

Essential Principles of Reinforcement

The essential principles of reinforcement include the dynamics of reinforcement and factors that influence the role of behavioral consequences.

The Dynamics of Reinforcement.   Thorndike's experiments illustrated that certain consequences influence behavioral change. However, Thorndike emphasized the terms rewarding, satisfying, and trial-and-error learning, and these terms do not describe behavioral properties. Furthermore, reward implies remuneration for services performed (Skinner, 1989b, p. 92) or compensation that offsets a loss or sacrifice of some kind (Skinner, 1963b, p. 505).

The terms reinforcing consequence and reinforcement were substituted for reward. **Reinforcement** is defined as any behavioral consequence that strengthens behavior (i.e., increases the frequency of responding). The particular response that occurs immediately prior to the reinforcement has passed into history. However, the organism is changed by the particular consequence and later responds as a changed organism (Skinner, 1989b, p. 64).

The two key processes in operant conditioning are *variation* (of behavior) and *selection by consequence*. In other words, different behaviors are executed, only some of which are strengthened by the outcomes. For example, the rat's behaviors of sniffing the corners of the cage and looking at the ceiling do not produce a food pellet. Because important outcomes do not follow these behaviors, they decrease in frequency.

Also important is that not every behavioral consequence is a reinforcer. If the rat has been fed recently, producing a food pellet will not lead to an increase in lever pressing. To determine whether a particular event is reinforcing, a direct test is needed (Skinner, 1953, p. 73). The frequency of a selected response is first observed, and then a particular event is made contingent on that response. The rate of responding with the added consequence is observed. If the response frequency increases, the selected event is reinforcing in the given condition.

To be effective in altering behavior in a particular way, reinforcement also must be immediately contingent on the execution of an appropriate response. In the laboratory, lever pressing produces a food pellet instantaneously. Similarly, when a baby moves an arm so as to shake the rattle vigorously, he or she is reinforced at once by the sound.

Sometimes behaviors are reinforced accidentally. Such contingencies lead to the development of superstitious behavior (Skinner, 1953, p. 85). That is, random behavior that is reinforced accidentally will increase in frequency and very likely receive accidental reinforcement again.

Superstitious behavior in the laboratory was demonstrated by providing food to a pigeon every 15 seconds. Behaviors that were strengthened were those actions that were occurring when the food was delivered. Examples include strutting, wing flapping, bowing and scraping, and others (Skinner, 1948).

Random behaviors also are reinforced in the natural setting. For example, a man waiting for a bus may look in the direction that the bus is to appear, then pace up and down and look at his watch several times. None of these actions makes the bus arrive, yet all are reinforced by the appearance of the vehicle (Skinner, 1989a). When the man waits for a bus again (or a train), he is likely to pace up and down and to check his watch repeatedly.

Reinforcement increases the rate of responding; however, elimination of the reinforcing consequence decreases the rate. This decreased rate in the absence of a reinforcing outcome is known as **extinction** (Skinner, 1938, 1963b). If reinforcement is withdrawn completely, behavior will gradually cease. Thus, an important function of reinforcement in everyday life is to prevent the extinction of behavior.

Factors That Influence the Role of Behavioral Consequences.   At least three factors influence the extent to which particular events may function as reinforcers.

They are (1) the individual's past reinforcement history, (2) the skills repertoire of the individual, and (3) the particular characteristics inherited by the individual.

As already indicated, food is not likely to strengthen the behavior of a rat that has eaten recently. However, food *is* a powerful reinforcer if the rat has been deprived of food. Similarly, consider the child who has been deprived of parental love and affection for a period of time. Almost any form of attention from the parent, even if abusive, is likely to be reinforcing.

The importance of the individual's behavioral repertoire is that as skills become more complex, new reinforcement contingencies begin to operate (Skinner, 1987, p. 59). For example, when a researcher, writer, or student learns to operate a microcomputer, another set of reinforcement contingencies comes into play. Examples include success in operating the equipment, solving problems, and editing text quickly.

Both the individual's past reinforcement history and particular skills repertoire are products of a person's daily life. However, inherited characteristics, such as differences in mental ability, also influence the types of consequences that are likely to be reinforcing.

In addition, the current generation has inherited susceptibilities to at least four kinds of reinforcement from early humans. They are susceptibilities to reinforcement from overeating, the tastes of sugar and salt, sexual contact, and the outcomes of aggressive behavior.

Early humans lived in a difficult and dangerous environment, and certain behaviors were powerfully reinforced by survival. Included were eating as much as possible at one time whenever food was found and eating the few foods that were sweet, which often were especially nutritious (Skinner, 1987, p. 174). Western civilization, however, has an abundant food supply, and many individuals today often face health problems from overeating as well as from consuming excessive amounts of salt and sugar.

In addition, sexual contact that led to procreation and aggressive behavior against predators also led to survival of the strong "breeders" and fighters. Problems currently faced by their descendants include overpopulation and a susceptibility to reinforcement by the outcomes of aggression.

Summary

A reinforcing event is any behavioral consequence that strengthens behavior. That is, it increases the frequency of responding. The two key processes involving reinforcement that result in complex behaviors are variation of behavior and selection by consequence. Many behaviors are executed, but only some are strengthened. That is, they are selected by the consequences of reinforcement.

For a behavioral consequence to be effective, it must increase the rate of responding under particular environmental conditions. Also, it must be immediately contingent on the execution of the appropriate response. If reinforcement for a particular response is withdrawn, extinction or cessation of the behavior will occur.

Three factors that influence the extent to which stimuli may function as reinforcers are the individual's past reinforcement history, the skills repertoire of the individual, and the particular characteristics inherited by the individual. Inherited characteristics include mental ability and susceptibilities to certain reinforcers, such as food and the taste of sugar and salt.

Categories of Reinforcement

Three broad classifications of reinforcement are primary or secondary reinforcers, generalized reinforcers, and positive or negative reinforcement.

Primary and Secondary (Conditioned) Reinforcers.   As societies grow more complex, a greater variety of events can function as reinforcers (Skinner, 1989a). Included are getting a key to the executive washroom, winning an Olympic medal, and finding information on the Internet.

How do such events become reinforcers? The process begins with a small group of stimuli known as **primary reinforcers** (Skinner, 1953, 1963b). Under appropriate conditions, primary reinforcers are the stimuli that can increase the frequency of behavior without training. They also are essential to the survival of the species. Primary reinforcers include food, drink, shelter, and sexual contact.

Other events that strengthen behavior are **conditioned** or **secondary reinforcers**. They acquire reinforcing power by association with events that already reinforce behavior. A typical example in the laboratory is the sound of the food mechanism that occurs just prior to the delivery of food. Through repeated association with food (the primary reinforcer), the click of the mechanism acquires reinforcing power. In the everyday world, smiles and being rocked or cuddled often accompany the feeding of the young infant. In this way, receiving affection and the approval of others become secondary reinforcers.

Events also may acquire reinforcing power by association with other well-established secondary reinforcers. For example, the different trophies and medals awarded for winning various kinds of contests are reinforcing through association with the secondary reinforcers of social approval and recognition.

Conditioned reinforcers play an important role in the development of complex human behaviors. First, if behavior were strengthened only by primary reinforcers, the human behavioral repertoire would be limited to those actions that produce food, drink, sleep, shelter, and sexual contact.

Second, conditioned reinforcers bridge the gap between early stages of complex behavior and some future consequence. For example, "people are said to write articles or books for money or acclaim. Those may be rewards, but they do not occur soon enough to be reinforcers. At one's desk the reinforcers are the appearances of sentences that make sense, clear up puzzles, answer questions, make points" (Skinner, 1986, p. 109). These conditioned reinforcers, rather than ultimate publication or acclaim, maintain the day-by-day behavior of writing.

Generalized Reinforcers.   Some secondary reinforcers are restricted to a particular setting because they are linked to only one primary reinforcer. The click of the food magazine, for example, functions only in the laboratory. Others, however, are found in a variety of situations; they are **generalized reinforcers**. Examples include the reinforcements that are provided by other individuals, such as attention, approval, and affection (Skinner, 1953). Smiles, commendations, and the agreement of peers are all expressions of approval that function as reinforcers in numerous social situations.

Money also has been referred to as a generalized reinforcer because it has been associated with the primary reinforcers of food, drink, and shelter. However, Skinner (1987, p. 18) notes that money becomes reinforcing only when exchanged for strongly reinforcing goods or services. More important, money strengthens specific work behaviors only when it is paid on commission or for piecework. In contrast, money paid for a specified amount of time worked (such as per hour or per week) does not strengthen particular behaviors (Skinner, 1987, p. 19). Instead, the real function of money is to establish a standard of living that the worker, under certain circumstances, may lose (Skinner, 1987).

One powerful generalized reinforcer that often is overlooked is the reinforcement provided by successful manipulation of the physical environment. Our tendency to participate in activities that depend on skill, such as crafts, artistic creations, and skill sports such as bowling and tennis, may be a function of this generalized reinforcer (Skinner, 1953, p. 79). Similarly, in playing video games, "No one really cares whether PacMan gobbles up all those little spots on the screen. Indeed, as soon as the screen is cleared, the player covers it again with more little spots to be gobbled up. What is reinforcing is successful play" (Skinner, 1984, p. 24).

Positive and Negative Reinforcement.   The categories of primary and secondary reinforcement refer to the ways that events acquire reinforcing power. However, reinforcers also may be categorized in terms of the nature of the reinforcing consequence. In the examples already discussed, certain behaviors are followed by the appearance of a new object or event. Lever pressing produces a food pellet, correctly identifying the primary colors produces approval, and so on. These situations, in which a new stimulus is added to the situation, are defined as positive reinforcement (Skinner, 1953, 1989b).

In contrast, some behaviors result in the removal of or escape from a situation. For example, a rat is exposed to mild shock through an electrified floor grid. Backing into or touching the wall terminates the shock. The response—touching the wall—increases in frequency (is strengthened) because it removes the electric shock. Any behavior that provides escape from or avoidance of a situation typically increases. However, this form of reinforcement is referred to as **negative reinforcement** (Skinner, 1953, 1989b). In other words, "a negative reinforcer is properly defined as 'a stimulus the *reduction* or *removal* of which strengthens behavior'" (Skinner, 1989b, p. 127).

An everyday example is the loud buzz in some cars when the ignition is turned on. The intent is that the driver's behavior of fastening the seat belt will increase because it removes the irritating buzz.

Negative reinforcement is also known as escape conditioning because it strengthens escape behaviors. Consider, for example, a boy who has not made friends and is not doing well in school. One day he says that his stomach hurts, and he is allowed to leave class. A few days later he avoids school by saying he has a stomachache. The next Monday morning, he insists he does not feel well enough to attend classes. This set of events, which has strengthened an escape behavior, is one of negative reinforcement. The learning sequence is (1) the school (discriminative stimulus), (2) feigning illness to avoid school (escape response), and (3) avoiding school (reinforcement).

The similarities and differences between positive and negative reinforcement are illustrated by the examples in Table 5.1. Notice that the consequence in positive reinforcement is the addition of a new stimulus. In contrast, the consequence in negative reinforcement is the removal of or escape from the discriminative stimulus.

In the analysis of behavior, the terms *pleasant* and *unpleasant* should not be used as a basis for differentiating positive and negative reinforcers. Such a classification can lead to errors in behavioral analysis. For example, praise, typically considered to be pleasant or satisfying, often is treated as a positive reinforcer. Consider, however, the situation of a teenage male in the classroom who is seeking status in the eyes of his peers. Teacher praise is an aversive stimulus that the student seeks to escape. Teacher attention and praise for such a student is a discriminative stimulus for any of a variety of behaviors from apathy to minor classroom disruptions.

Emotional By-Products.   The use of negative reinforcement to regulate behavior introduces undesirable emotional by-products that accompany the subject's escape or avoidance behavior (Skinner, 1953, 1989b). Included are the emotions referred to as "anxiety" and "fear." The set of reactions called anxiety, for example, includes conditioned reflexes of the intestinal muscles, such as gastric changes, a sudden loss of blood from the face, and possibly, increased blood pressure.

Because these emotional reactions accompany the escape response, they become conditioned to situational characteristics that accompany the aversive stimulus. A horse that has been whipped by a rider, for example, will roll its eyes, become restive, and possibly rear up at the sight of a riding crop. On a more subtle level, the

TABLE 5.1
Examples of positive and negative reinforcement

Discriminative Stimulus	Response	Consequence	Type of Consequence	Type of Reinforcement*
Coffee machine	Subject puts change in machine and pushes button.	Subject receives a cup of coffee.	Subject's behavior "produces" a new stimulus.	Positive
Parent nags teenager to clean up room.	Subject straightens up his room every day for two weeks.	Nagging stops.	Subject's behavior has been followed by the withdrawal of the discriminative stimulus.	Negative

*The assumption here is that the response increases in frequency; therefore, the described consequence is functioning as reinforcement.

child who has been scolded for not completing his or her chores may become agitated when the parent comes home.

Interactive Examples.   In many situations, both positive reinforcement and mild negative reinforcers function to strengthen the same behaviors. For example, the scientist's long hours of work in the laboratory may be reinforced positively by the conditioned reinforcers of manipulating the experimental situation and, intermittently, by identifying new facts. In addition, perhaps social "small talk" with other people is mildly aversive. If the scientist leaves a party to go to work in the laboratory, escaping from the party is functioning as a negative reinforcer.

In interactions between two or more people, a careful analysis is required to determine discriminative stimuli, responses, and reinforcers. For example, a child may begin to cry whenever the parents entertain guests. The parents may turn their attention momentarily to the disruptive child so that they can continue to enjoy the visit. In that situation, the child's interruption is the **aversive stimulus** for the parent's attention (Figure 5.1). Their attention terminates the interruption (withdrawal of the aversive stimulus). Terminating the child's interruption serves as a negative reinforcer for the parents. However, the attention of the adults, particularly if prolonged, serves as positive reinforcement for the child's crying and whining.

Summary

Three broad classifications of reinforcement may be identified. One is that of primary and secondary (conditioned) reinforcers. Primary reinforcers are those that, under appropriate conditions, can increase the frequency of behavior without training. They are food, shelter, drink, and sexual contact. Secondary or conditioned reinforcers acquire reinforcing power through association with events that already function as reinforcers. Examples are smiles and expressions of social approval that often are associated with the baby's first feedings.

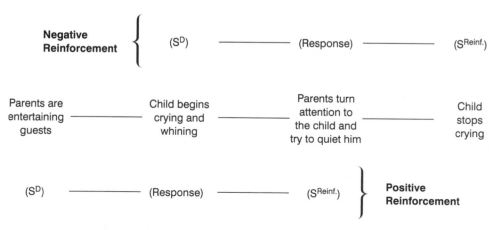

FIGURE 5.1
Behavioral analysis of parent–child interaction

The second category, generalized reinforcers, refers to reinforcers that function in a variety of settings. Examples are attention, approval, and affection. One powerful generalized reinforcer that often is overlooked is the successful manipulation of the physical environment. Participation in sports, skill activities, and hobbies may be a function of this generalized reinforcer.

The third category, positive or negative reinforcement, refers to the nature of the reinforcing consequence. In positive reinforcement, the response produces a new stimulus, for example, a lever press produces a food pellet. In contrast, negative reinforcement refers to the withdrawal or reduction of the discriminative stimulus. Fastening one's seat belt to terminate the annoying buzzing sound is an example. Another term for negative reinforcement is escape conditioning because behaviors that represent escape from aversive stimuli are reinforced. One problem associated with negative reinforcement is that undesirable emotional responses accompany the subject's escape or avoidance behavior. Included are the emotions referred to as anxiety and fear.

In many situations, both positive and mild negative reinforcement function to strengthen behavior. Also, both positive and negative reinforcement may be operating in interactions between individuals. A careful analysis is needed to determine the discriminative stimuli, responses, and reinforcers.

Punishment

The term *punishment,* like many commonly used words, is associated with a variety of meanings. Typically, **punishment** is viewed as imposing unwanted consequences on the individual to stop a particular behavior.

Behavior may be punished in either of two different ways. One form of punishment is the removal of a positive reinforcer (Skinner, 1953, 1968b). Withdrawing the privilege of watching television is an example. The other form of punishment is the addition of a negative reinforcer to a situation. Examples include being sent to one's room and writing 50 times "I will not talk in class."

Because both punishment and negative reinforcement involve aversive stimuli, they often are confused. However, two major differences may be identified. One is the relationship of the individual to the aversive stimulus. In negative reinforcement, the individual successfully escapes from or avoids the aversive situation. In contrast, in punishment, the individual is placed in an aversive situation. Second, the effects on behavior differ. Negative reinforcement (successful escape or avoidance of an aversive situation) strengthens a particular behavior. In contrast, punishment only temporarily suppresses behavior. For example, a child punished for scribbling on the furniture may decorate a bedroom wall a few days later.

Also, in terms of effect, punishment is not the opposite of reinforcement (Skinner, 1953). At least four undesirable effects of punishment may occur. First, as already mentioned, punishment only temporarily suppresses behavior; it is not a permanent solution. Second, punishment also produces undesirable emotional reactions, such as frustration, anger, and guilt. Third, actions other than the unwanted behavior also may be punished. Red marks on a term paper and a low grade for misspelled words punish the errors. Also punished, however, are the student's time and effort in writing the paper.

The major shortcoming associated with punishment, however, is that it does not generate positive behaviors (Skinner, 1953, 1968b). Interest in schoolwork does not result from the punishment of indifference (Skinner, 1968b, p. 149). Similarly, students do not learn correct speech by being punished for bad grammar.

If punishment should not be used, then what are some alternatives? First, avoid the conditions that make punishment necessary. For example, punishing students for shouting out in class can be avoided by eliminating events that ask for call-out behavior, such as "Who has their homework done?" Also, lessons with purpose that move briskly with clear signals to students leave few opportunities for misbehavior. Interruptions and confusion resulting from missing props, unclear directions, false starts, and backtracking do not occur.

Second, reinforce a behavior that is incompatible with the undesirable behavior. For example, we suppress competitive behavior when we reinforce cooperation (Skinner, 1968b). In other words, punishing a student for being out of his or her seat may be unnecessary if the student has tasks to complete that earn reinforcement (in-seat behavior).

In summary, both negative reinforcement and punishment involve aversive stimuli. However, negative reinforcement strengthens an escape behavior, whereas punishment temporarily suppresses behavior. The shortcomings of punishment are the negative emotional reactions, the punishment of behaviors associated with the punished behavior, the inability to generate positive behaviors, and the fact that the punished behavior is only temporarily suppressed.

Cultural Practices and Operant Conditioning

Skinner (1981) maintained that the essential processes in conditioning individual behavior also operate at two other levels. One, already discussed, is the biological evolution of the species. The other is the development of cultures.

Specifically, a culture or a set of social practices is defined as the contingencies that are maintained by a group (Skinner, 1989b, p. 52). An example is the American practice of joining family members or friends on Thanksgiving. Celebrating this holiday is positively reinforced by good food and social reinforcers such as affection, companionship, and the approval of others. It is also negatively reinforced through escape from work.

The reinforcement contingencies in cultural practices shape the behavior of each member of the group. Also, social practices are transmitted when members shape the behavior of new or younger members. Young parents, for example, reinforce the participation of their children when they continue the same rituals as their parents.

Cultures, and governments in particular, also often control their members through the use of aversive stimuli, either as negative reinforcers or as punishments for undesirable behavior. Citizens obey laws primarily to escape from or to avoid fines and imprisonment (Skinner, 1989b, p. 53).

Some cultural practices, however, erode the contingencies available through operant conditioning (Skinner, 1987). For example, families no longer must grow their own food or weave the material for their clothing. Although some aversive consequences are avoided by paying someone else for goods and services, opportunities for reinforcement, such as pride in the finished product, are also lost.

In addition, the degree of job specialization in contemporary society has reduced the opportunities for reinforcement. Although society gains from a division of work (more products are available), the assembly line worker who completes one part of the circuitry in a television set does not directly experience reinforcement from the final product.

Another problem in Western civilization is the abundance of things described as "interesting, beautiful, delicious, entertaining, and exciting" (Skinner, 1987, p. 231). Included are beautiful pictures, beautiful music, and exciting entertainments. However, the only behaviors reinforced by such easy access to beautiful and exciting things are the behaviors of looking and listening. However, this is only a very small sample of human behavior (compared with the vast range of behaviors that might receive reinforcement) (Skinner, 1987, p. 24). In other words, easy access to pleasing reinforcers creates a situation in which "the reinforcers are not contingent upon the kinds of behavior that sustain the individual or promote the survival of (either) the culture or the species" (Skinner, 1987, p. 24).

The Nature of Complex Learning

The law of effect specifies the temporal relationship between a response and a consequence (Skinner, 1953, 1963b). However, it does not explain the acquisition of complex behaviors such as pigeons playing ping-pong, or table tennis, and humans working with computers. Instead, the development of new and complex patterns or "topographies" of behavior results from complex and subtle contingencies of reinforcement. For example, a child learns to pull itself up, to stand, to walk, and to move about through the reinforcement of slightly exceptional instances of behavior (Skinner, 1953). Later, this same process is responsible for the individual's learning to sing, to dance, and to play games, as well as all the other behaviors found in the normal adult repertoire (Skinner, 1953, p. 93).

Shaping Behavior

The acquisition of complex behaviors is the result of the process referred to as shaping (Skinner, 1954, 1963b, 1989b). This process involves a carefully designed program of discriminative stimuli and reinforcements for subtle changes in responses. An example is that of teaching a pigeon to bowl (Skinner, 1958). The desired terminal behavior is that of swiping a wooden ball with a sideways movement of the beak so that the ball is sent down a miniature alley toward a set of toy pins.

The shaping process begins by providing reinforcement for responses that indicate approaches to the ball. Reinforcement is then withheld until the pigeon's beak makes contact with the ball. After initial reinforcements for contact, reinforcement is withheld again until further refinement in the behavior occurs (i.e., the pigeon sideswipes the ball). The procedure of first reinforcing responses that only remotely resemble the desired response and then reinforcing only refinements in the response is referred to as *reinforcing successive approximations* (Skinner, 1953, 1968b, 1989b) or differential reinforcement. Shaping is effective because it is sensitive to the continuous nature of a complex act, and it illustrates the utility of constructing complex behavior by a continual process of **differential reinforcement** (Skinner, 1953).

The importance of shaping is that it can generate complex behaviors that have an almost zero probability of occurring naturally in the final form (Skinner, 1963a). A complex behavior is shaped by a series of changing contingencies referred to as a **program** (Skinner, 1963b, p. 506). Each stage of the program evokes a response that also prepares the organism to take the next step in the behavioral sequence.

Shaping differs from the modification of behavior that occurs with puzzle boxes, mazes, and memory drums. In those situations, the organism is thrown into a problem situation and must discover the successful behaviors through trial and error. However, performance of the appropriate response has been left to chance, and random, incorrect responses also occur.

Contingencies of Reinforcement

Behavior that acts on the immediate physical environment, in general, is reinforced consistently (Skinner, 1953, p. 99). Standing and walking are examples. However, a large part of behavior generates only intermittent reinforcement, such as writing.

In the laboratory, intermittent reinforcement may be delivered precisely according to different schedules or combinations of schedules (see Ferster & Skinner, 1957). The schedule may be controlled by either (1) a system outside the organism or (2) the behavior itself (Skinner, 1953, p. 100). The former may be determined by the clock and is referred to as **interval reinforcement**. The latter, which is determined by the number of responses emitted by the organism, is known as **ratio reinforcement** (Table 5.2).

TABLE 5.2
Comparison of ratio and interval schedules of reinforcement

Ratio Reinforcement	Interval Reinforcement
Reinforcement delivery is based on number of responses emitted.	Reinforcement delivery is based on elapsed time. *Examples:* Reading books, going to the theatre, watching television (Skinner, 1966a)
Fixed: A constant number of responses generates reinforcement (e.g., every fifth response) *Examples:* Selling on commission; pay for piecework in industry	*Fixed:* Reinforcement for a correct response at a constant time interval (e.g., every 15 seconds)
Variable: Reinforcement delivered after a varying number of correct responses (e.g., every fifth, eighth, third, etc.) *Examples:* Payoffs from slot machines, roulette, horse races, and other games of chance	*Variable:* Reinforcement delivered for an appropriate response at varying time intervals (e.g., every 10 seconds, 4 seconds, 7 seconds, etc.)

When fixed schedules are used, ratio or interval, the timing of reinforcement is certain. Typically, responding slows down immediately after reinforcement and then gradually increases in rate. The slowdown in response rate can be avoided through the use of a variable schedule. The delivery of reinforcement is uncertain, and the rate of responding is more nearly constant.

Intermittent reinforcement for a particular response can sustain behavior for long periods of time. One particularly effective schedule is the **variable-ratio** schedule. Reinforcement is frequent at first, but then it is gradually reduced. For example, a television program may become less reinforcing as jokes or story lines become less interesting. Someone who has followed the program from the beginning, however, may continue to watch the program for a long time (Skinner, 1966a, p. 164).

The Concept of Negative Utility

The variable-ratio schedule is useful because it maintains behavior against extinction when reinforcement is infrequent (Skinner, 1989b, p. 77). The behavior of dedicated artists and scientists, for example, is sustained by occasional, unpredictable reinforcements.

In some situations, however, the variable-ratio schedule can lead to the long-term detriment of the subject. For instance, pigeons reinforced on a variable-ratio schedule for pecking a disc at a high rate will peck until the beak becomes inflamed. Similarly, the compulsive gambler is reinforced periodically for betting at the roulette table or playing the slot machine. Every winning play, of course, is reinforcing, but they do not occur often and eventually the gambler exhausts his or her resources. This situation, in which a stretched variable-ratio schedule leads to the long-term detriment of the subject, is one of **negative utility** (Skinner, 1987, p. 24).

Gambling sustained by a variable-ratio schedule to the point of negative utility is one form of addiction. Another form of addiction occurs when substances are used that initially are positively reinforcing but that subsequently are taken to escape from physical states known as "withdrawal symptoms" (Skinner, 1989b, p. 76). The long-term condition is one of negative utility; greater and greater amounts of the substance are required to provide escape from the physical symptoms, while the general physical and emotional states of the individual steadily deteriorate.

Rule-Governed Behavior

The process known as shaping exposes the subject to changing contingencies of reinforcement for the performance of progressively more accurate behaviors. This method is referred to as **contingency-governed behavior** (Skinner, 1969).

For the human learner, however, not all behaviors are acquired through direct exposure to response consequences. "Few people drive a car at a moderate speed and keep their seat belts fastened because they have actually avoided or escaped from serious accidents by doing so" (Skinner, 1953, p. 168). Instead, people often do what others tell them to do; that is, they follow advice (Skinner, 1987, p. 21). Typically, the advice is in the form of verbal suggestions or instructions, such as, "If you wish to avoid the gridlock near Sumner Tunnel on the way to Logan Airport, take McGrath Highway" (Vaughan, 1987, p. 260). The instructions are verbal stimuli that alter the listener's behavioral repertoire. Such behavior is known as *rule-governed* (Skinner, 1987).

In addition to informal advice, rule-governed behavior may be acquired through formal rules, such as maxims, proverbs, and the rules of grammar and spelling. Also included are the legal, ethical, and religious practices of a society that are compiled into laws and other codified procedures. These rules and laws are important to a culture in two ways. First, they help the individual benefit from the experience of others. Second, they also help the group to command and censure consistently (Skinner, 1989b).

Why do individuals follow advice or rules? The primary reason is that following advice in the past has produced particular consequences. For example, we follow the directions for assembling a piece of equipment if similar behavior has produced the outcome of properly assembled equipment (Skinner, 1987, p. 180). Also, when parents provide positive reinforcers for following directions and rules, children will do as they are told because positive reinforcers have followed (Skinner, 1989b, p. 80).

Rule-governed and contingency-governed behavior differ in two ways. One is that behavior is more effectively executed in the contingency-governed condition. When learning to drive a car, for example, the procedures executed by the learner in response to instructions are awkward and halting. Skilled behaviors are acquired in the contingency-governed condition when the novice driver experiences the consequences of his or her actions.

The second difference is that only the immediate response consequences alter the probability of future occurrence of the response. In the rule-governed condition, however, the probability of a response remains undetermined (Skinner, 1953, p. 147). "For example, having learned that 'procrastination is the thief of time,' we are probably no less likely to put off unpleasant tasks" (Skinner, 1989b, p. 41).

A particular problem in efforts to change behavior is advice based on probable adverse consequences, such as warnings about cigarette smoking. One does not stop smoking as a result of the statistical probabilities of dying from a heart attack or lung cancer. In other words, statistical predictions are ineffective in establishing rule-governed behavior.

Summary

The acquisition of a complex set of behaviors results from the process known as shaping. This process consists of a series of discriminative stimuli with reinforcement for subtle changes in responses. Shaping illustrates the development of complex behavior through differential reinforcement. It also generates behaviors that have an almost zero probability of occurring naturally in the final form. In the laboratory, reinforcement may be delivered according to different schedules. If determined by the clock, the schedule is referred to as interval reinforcement. However, if based on the number of responses emitted by the organism, the schedule type is ratio reinforcement. The timing for each schedule also may be fixed or varied.

One advantage of variable-ratio reinforcement is that it maintains behavior against extinction when reinforcement is infrequent. The behavior of dedicated artists and scientists is an example. However, when a variable-ratio schedule leads to long-term detriment of the organism, the process is referred to as negative utility. An addiction to gambling is an example.

When the execution of particular behaviors receives reinforcement, the learned responses are referred to as contingency-governed behavior. However, not all behaviors are acquired through direct exposure to response consequences. Instead, individuals often follow advice, instructions, or directions that constitute the discriminative stimulus. The instructions alter the listener's behavioral repertoire. This behavioral change occurs because individuals have been reinforced in the past for compliance with verbal directives. Such behavior, referred to as rule-governed, differs from contingency-governed behavior in two ways. One is that behavior is more effectively executed in the contingency-governed condition. The other is that the probability of a response in the rule-governed condition remains undetermined.

PRINCIPLES OF INSTRUCTION

Skinner became interested in education when his children entered school, and he began in the 1950s to apply operant conditioning to the classroom. He devised techniques for developing step-by-step instruction, mechanical devices for instruction referred to as teaching machines, and a technology of classroom teaching. He also wrote essays on the problems in education.

Basic Assumptions

Assumptions about the nature of learning and the nature of science established the parameters within which the principles of operant conditioning were developed in the laboratory. Similarly, B. F. Skinner's beliefs about the nature of schooling and classroom learning established the parameters for his technology of teaching.

The Nature of Education

The educational system is extremely important because the welfare of any culture depends on it. A culture is no stronger than its capacity to transmit its skills, beliefs, and practices to the next generation, and this responsibility belongs to education (Skinner, 1953).

Contemporary education, however, faces three major problems in fulfilling this mission. One is that it takes place in an artificial setting. That is, schools prepare students for a world that lies in the future (Skinner, 1989b, p. 87). Educators have tried to bring real life into the classroom, for example, by teaching botany with a few plants (Skinner, 1989b, p. 88). The problem is that so little of the world actually can be made available to the student during 12 years of schooling. Because the school has access to so few of the natural reinforcers found in the world, educators face the task of designing reinforcement contingencies to bridge the gap between initial learning and later real-world contingencies.

Second, the public school was established to provide the services of a private tutor to more than one student at a time (Skinner, 1989b, p. 85). However, by the time classes reach 25 or 30, personal attention is intermittent and brief, at best. "The larger the class or the school, the worse the problems faced by the teacher" (Skinner, 1989b, p. 86).

The third problem is an outgrowth of the other two. Because students are placed in groups to read and hear about events rather than experience them, the individual student seldom does anything that is immediately or visibly successful (Skinner, 1987, p. 91).

Faced with these three problems, the school has resorted to the use of aversive control. The result is that students complete their work primarily to avoid the consequences of not doing so (Skinner, 1968b, 1989b). Moreover, the educational system again is facing criticism much like the reaction to Russia's launching of *Sputnik*. Skinner (1987) notes that a report of the National Commission on Excellence in Education describes American schools as comparing poorly with those in other nations in several fields. Among the current suggested solutions are extending the school day, lengthening the school year, raising scholarship standards, and increasing teacher salaries.

These proposed solutions are like those recommended in the curriculum reform of the 1960s following Russia's launching of *Sputnik*. That is, a basic omission in all the suggestions is that they contain no indication that teaching should be improved (Skinner, 1987, p. 114). However, in Skinner's view, no institution can realize progress and improvement until it analyzes the basic processes for which it is responsible.

Learning in the Classroom Setting

The specific characteristics of the educational setting differ from those of the laboratory. The dynamics of behavioral change, nevertheless, are the same (Skinner, 1968b, 1987). In the laboratory, internal states such as "hunger" were redefined as observable conditions or events. In the classroom, the state referred to as "readiness" is defined as the set of skills already in the student's behavioral repertoire.

When a teacher is responsible for 20 to 30 students at one time, several problems for instruction arise. Included are (1) the infrequency of positive reinforcement, (2) the excessive lengths of time between behavior and reinforcement, and (3) the lack of programs that lead the child through a series of approximations to the final behavior (Skinner, 1954).

To correct these problems, programs of carefully selected stimuli and reinforcements are needed. In basic arithmetic alone, approximately 50,000 reinforcements for each student would be needed to ensure that the skills are acquired (Skinner, 1968b). Because the teacher cannot provide the needed reinforcements, machines such as computers and other current technology are necessary in the classroom. Appropriate applications of these aids would then free the teacher to spend more time listening and talking with individual students (Skinner, 1987).

In summary, three assumptions support Skinner's approach to a technology of teaching. First, the experimental analysis of behavior also applies to the classroom. Second, behavioral repertoires in the classroom may be shaped in the same manner as other behaviors. Third, technology is needed to provide the large number of reinforcements for behavioral responses.

The Components of Instruction

Skinner (1989a) emphasized that teaching is more than telling. Teaching occurs when a response is evoked for the first time and is then reinforced. Thus, the design of effective instruction requires careful attention to two important issues: the selection of the discriminative stimuli and the use of reinforcement.

Selecting the Stimulus

In classroom instruction, the selection of stimuli includes two major concerns. One is that stimulus discrimination and stimulus generalization are important prerequisites for the learning of more complex verbal behaviors. In discrimination, for example, the student must learn to respond verbally "p" to the *p*, but not to *r, d, b,* and so on. Then the response must be reinforced in the presence of different forms of the stimulus, such as *P*.

The other important consideration is the transfer of stimulus control. For example, when pictures are associated with words to assist the student in saying the correct word, the picture is the stimulus that controls the student's response. A picture of a flag, for example, induces the student to respond "flag" to the four-letter word. Inducing a response through prompting is not learning, however (Skinner, 1968b). The picture must be gradually withdrawn so that the word alone has control over the student's response. In other words, the transfer of stimulus control refers to the gradual withdrawal of contrived cues or hints that signal the correct response so that stimuli within the learner or other events are followed by appropriate responses.

The failure to provide for the transfer of stimulus control is one of the major errors found in microcomputer instruction (Vargas, 1986). For example, a program that consistently highlights words that students are to type teaches them to copy whatever is highlighted rather than to think about the content on the screen.

In the social environment of the classroom, a variety of verbal stimuli, such as "Look at this picture" and "Take out your pencils" may serve as discriminative stimuli to direct student attention. However, good classroom management can also make use of nonverbal stimuli and thus reduce the need for oral directions. In one classroom, for example, the teacher used colored name tags for the children. A particular color indicated the work or study group to which the child was to report that day. This technique permitted the teacher to rotate group membership easily and without confusion. In addition, any child who needed help with seatwork set up a little red tent provided in each work folder. The tent served as a discriminative stimulus for the teacher's behavior and eliminated hand and arm waving (Becker, 1973).

Providing Reinforcement

To be effective, reinforcement must be immediately contingent on the emission of the correct response. The two types of reinforcers available in the classroom are natural reinforcers and contrived reinforcers.

Natural Reinforcers.   The events available in the setting that provide nonaversive feedback are referred to as natural reinforcers (Skinner, 1954). Examples include playing with mechanical toys, painting, and cutting with scissors. Others include finding the right word to describe something, resolving a temporary confusion, and having the opportunity to advance to the next stage of an activity (Skinner, 1958, p. 380). Further, a child learning to read is reinforced when the material "makes sense."

The research conducted by David Premack (1959) indicates that children's preferred activities will reinforce their participation in their less preferred activities. For the child who prefers playing with mechanical toys to painting, time with the toys may be used to reinforce participation in art activities.

In two studies, high-priority academic activities were used to strengthen other academic behaviors. Gallant, Sargeant, and Van Houten (1980) made access to a highly preferred subject area, a science lab activity, contingent on accurately completing assignments in reading and mathematics. Moreno and Hovell (1980) used access to a language laboratory to reinforce a Spanish-speaking teenager for answering questions in English. However, care should be exercised in the use of academic activities so that students are not denied access to important methods of instruction.

Contrived Reinforcers.   In many situations, the use of natural reinforcers alone is insufficient to change behavior. For example, people should consume lesser amounts of certain kinds of goods because the by-products of those goods irreversibly foul the environment (Skinner, 1989b, p. 118). However, such a consequence is too remote to have an immediate effect on behavior. Contrived contingencies are needed to alter behaviors of overconsumption.

In education, contrived reinforcers also are often needed to bridge the gap between the early stages of learning and the setting in which natural reinforcers can function. Teaching reading and writing are examples in which the behavior is too much a product of an advanced culture to rely on natural reinforcers, such as reading for information or for pleasure.

In some of the learning centers in the United States, students listen to instructions on cassette recorders and respond on work sheets. A magic-ink effect immediately indicates whether their behavior is correct or incorrect. Although no natural contingency exists between correct responses to a word or a passage and the appearance of a reaction, children, nevertheless, learn to read quickly (Skinner, 1987, p. 176).

Contrived reinforcers also include verbal comments, gold stars, early dismissal, and free time. They must be used judiciously, however, with careful attention both to effectiveness and to the transfer of control to natural reinforcers.

The Timing of Reinforcement.   Particularly important in the effectiveness of reinforcement is timing the delivery of reinforcing stimuli. "A fatal principle is 'letting well enough alone'—giving no attention to a student so long as he behaves well and turning to him only when he begins to cause trouble" (Skinner, 1968b, p. 180). Because the attention of the teacher often is reinforcing in the classroom, the careless teacher unintentionally will reinforce the attention-getter and the show-off. Further, at-risk students in a class who are not receiving attention for their academic behaviors will engage in nonacademic behaviors because nonacademic behaviors are producing reinforcement (Belfiore & Hornyak, 1990, p. 187).

Another example is that of dismissing the class early. If the class is dismissed when the students are loud or disruptive, the early dismissal reinforces inappropriate behavior. The teacher must time the dismissal to occur when the class is quiet and busy.

The mistiming of reinforcement also occurs with brightly colored and attractive learning materials. Bright colors, animated sequences, and other innovations have a temporary effect—they induce the student to look at the materials (Skinner, 1968b, p. 105). Computers also have used such techniques to attract the attention of students (Vargas, 1986).

The problem is that the student is not taught to look and listen. In effective instruction, the student should attend to the situation because previous encounters were reinforcing. Similarly, an attractive school building reinforces the behavior of coming in view of it, and a colorful classroom reinforces only the behavior of entering it (Skinner, 1968, p. 105). Although attending is important, good instruction reinforces the student *after* he or she has read the page, listened to the explanation, solved the problem, and so on.

Equally important in planning reinforcement is to avoid the overuse of reinforcers. For example, research data indicate that excessive praise for right answers to teacher questions is both intrusive and counterproductive (Brophy, 1981).

Problems with Aversive Control.   Classroom control often includes both the use of aversive stimuli and the withdrawal of positive reinforcement. Governments use punishment to suppress the behavior of troublesome individuals. Punishing students for such things as "not studying," however, is different (Skinner, 1989b, p. 88). First, the aim of education is to strengthen behavior, not suppress it. Second, the use of aversive stimuli as negative reinforcers and punishments leads to unwanted by-products. Specifically, this practice generates unwanted emotional reactions and escape behaviors. Escape behaviors include forgetting, inattention, truancy, and vandalism, as well as subtle forms of behavior, such as looking at the teacher while not paying attention (Skinner, 1968b, p. 97). The emotional side effects include reactions typically described as apathy, anxiety, anger, and resentment, all of which inhibit learning.

The third problem associated with the use of aversive control is that punishment does not generate positive behaviors. "We do not strengthen good pronunciation by punishing bad, or skillful movements by punishing awkward" (Skinner, 1968b, p. 149).

Reprimands can be used effectively, if they are in the form of "gentle admonitions" for small units of behavior (Skinner, 1968b, p. 101). Slight reprimands to the child who is learning to tie a shoelace for holding the lace wrong or moving it in the wrong direction, for example, are acceptable. They provide the opportunity for the learner to select the correct response from a small number of possibilities.

Summary

Effective instruction requires the careful selection of discriminative stimuli and reinforcement for changes in responding. An important classroom consideration in the selection of stimuli is that stimulus discrimination and stimulus generalization are important prerequisites for learning complex verbal behaviors. Another important issue is the transfer of stimulus control. Cues and other events that signal the appropriate response must be gradually withdrawn so that stimuli within the learner or other events are followed by appropriate responses. In other words, prompting responses does not ensure learning. In the classroom, discriminative stimuli range from teacher directions and signals to color-coded materials and printed text.

The teacher must rely often on contrived reinforcers because natural reinforcers are either unavailable or are remote consequences for expert performance. Success in the form of confirmation of a correct answer is an example. Important in implementing reinforcement is the judicious use of contrived reinforcers, avoidance of the overuse of reinforcement, and ensuring that reinforcement is contingent on appropriate behavior. Aversive control should be avoided if possible because it is accompanied by negative emotional reactions and escape behaviors. Moreover, punishment does not generate appropriate behavior.

Designing Instruction for Complex Skills

The development of complex skills should not be left to chance. One of the problems with Thorndike's experiment is that the animal was placed in the cage and left to "discover" the correct method of escape (Skinner, 1953). Similar situations occur in the school setting with the practice of "assign and test" or asking students to write a term paper without teaching them the subordinate skills. Skinner refers to these situations as placing the learner in a set of **terminal contingencies**. The situation is one in which the learner is left, through trial and error, to discover the complex skill or series of skills required for success.

Shaping Human Behavior
Developing complex skills in the classroom involves the key ingredients identified in teaching pigeons to play ping-pong and to bowl. The key ingredients are: (1) inducing a response, (2) reinforcing subtle improvements or refinements in the behavior, (3) providing for the transfer of stimulus control by gradually withdrawing the prompts or cues, and (4) scheduling reinforcements so that the ratio of reinforcements to responses gradually increases and natural reinforcers can maintain the behavior.

Consider learning to pronounce new words in a foreign language. For instance, the teacher typically holds up an object or picture, pronounces the words or phrases, and the student is induced to repeat the words. Reinforcement is provided initially for sounds that only remotely resemble correct pronunciation. Then reinforcement is withheld briefly until the pronunciation improves slightly. The teacher continues to prompt the pronunciation of difficult syllables or sounds and to provide reinforcement for improved pronunciation. The prompts then are gradually withdrawn. Instruction is complete when the student can identify the new objects or pictures correctly without assistance.

In the classroom, the first step in shaping behavior is to clearly specify the behavior that is to be learned (Skinner, 1989b, p. 122). For example, one mathematics teacher wanted the students to learn to follow a course of logical reasoning. This expectation is too vague to be of assistance in planning instruction. However, examples of specific expectations (subskills) include identifying the "givens" in a word problem, determining what the problem is asking, and so on.

The second step is to identify the entry skills of the learners (Skinner, 1987). This step is important because any missing skills should be included in the instruction. The third step is to program the subject matter in carefully graded steps and teach first things first (Skinner, 1987). One temptation is to move too quickly to the final product (i.e., the terminal contingency). However, a well-designed program takes small steps and guarantees a great deal of successful action (Skinner, 1987, p. 125).

The purpose of the step-by-step instruction is to provide a series of reinforcements, contrived if necessary, for increasingly refined or complex behavior. However, the reinforcements are programmed so that eventually natural reinforcers in the environment come into play and/or the activity itself becomes reinforcing for the learner. In learning to read, for example, a magic-ink effect may indicate initial success, whereas later the student is reinforced when a sentence makes sense, answers a question, or solves a problem. The activity of reading becomes reinforcing when the individual reaches the stage of reading for pleasure.

Shaping often has been viewed as limited to highly specific skills, such as discriminating sounds, words, or colors. However, Glaser (1990) identifi   'ements of shaping in representative instructional programs for developing self-   ory skills. All of the programs incorporate features to ensure student success   ninimize student errors. In addition, Brown (1994) notes that operant condit   veloped fading and scaffolding. Currently, the program referred to as recipro   ng uses successive approximations and the gradual fading of support (desc   detail in chapter 10). The goal is for students to learn to monitor their own   comprehension. First, the teacher structures the situation so that students .   ent only what they are able to do. Supporting cues from the teacher, close m   .oring, and frequent feedback improve students' skills. As the students become more proficient, the teacher relinquishes control of parts of the comprehension monitoring process, that is, withdraws the supporting cues. (The process is referred to as "vanishing" in programmed learning.) After a few weeks, the students are monitoring their reading comprehension without assistance and are being reinforced by their success in extracting meaning from printed text.

The techniques of teaching new routines and procedures at the beginning of the school year that effective classroom managers use in elementary school classrooms also incorporate elements of shaping. Such teachers spend considerable time in the early weeks of school teaching the routines for use of storage areas, the pencil sharpener, and the bathroom, step by step with encouragement for each step (Doyle, 1986; Emmer, Evertson, & Anderson, 1980). Effective classroom managers consistently use cues to signal appropriate behavior, carefully monitor the classroom, provide reinforcement for appropriate behaviors, and redirect student behavior when small errors occur.

Teaching Machines and Computers

Teaching machines were designed to provide sequenced instruction and the reinforcing power of immediate consequences (Skinner, 1989b). The importance of a mechanical device is that it gives reinforcement only for correct responses. When programmed instruction is implemented in a book format, students may look ahead, skip frames, or lose their places. The first teaching machine was developed in 1954, and Skinner (1989b) described it as a mechanical anticipation of the computer.

The early mechanical teaching machines provided contingent reinforcement for right answers in the form of (1) confirmation for correct answers, (2) the opportunity to move forward to new material, and (3) the opportunity to operate the equipment. The machine functioned as a patient tutor with no reprimands for errors, and a student moved forward at his or her own pace.

Current versions of the teaching machine include desktop models that are equipped with earphones and voice feedback Currently, some 400 Skinnerian learning centers around the country are providing remedial work in reading and mathematics. They use an advanced version of the original teaching machine (Skinner in Green, 1984).

Skinner (1989b) considers the computer as the ideal teaching machine. He notes, however, that it tends to be used to provide drill or to teach in the same way as teachers in large classes. In contrast, computers can bring aspects of "real life" into the classroom. In industry, for example, meltdowns in nuclear power plants can be simulated on computers.

Another advantage of computers is that they expand the range of potential reinforcers and can be programmed to provide appropriate feedback for a variety of responses. Included in the potential reinforcers are opportunities (1) to change the screen display, (2) to play simple games, and (3) to develop one's own games. One group of games to teach math skills embeds the games in fantasy themes, (e.g., a scavenger hunt theme in San Francisco) and allows the children to choose the problem type, game piece, and level of game. The games use the contrived reinforcers of verbal praise and an item needed in the scavenger hunt for helping a game character solve a problem (Azar, 1998).

Skinner cautions, however, that computer programs that try to "jazz up" the material with fancy graphics often are doing the students a disservice. When programs seek to attract students' attention through animation or color graphics, they may actually be distracting the student from learning (Skinner, in Green, 1984). According to Skinner, there is no substitute for discovering that one can learn and for experiencing increasing levels of success.

Summary

Shaping behavior in the classroom first requires the clear specification of the behaviors to be learned. Second, entry skills of the learner must be identified. Then the subject matter should be programmed carefully in graded steps so that the instruction guarantees a great deal of successful action. Programs that initially provide instructional support, gradually fade or withdraw the support, and use successive approximations are using operant conditioning techniques. Effective classroom managers also use the methods to teach appropriate classroom behavior.

Mechanical devices known as teaching machines were developed by Skinner to teach programmed subject matter. Computers are improvements over teaching machines because they can bring aspects of real life into the classroom and also expand the range of potential reinforcers that may be used. However, computer programs should not be overloaded with animation or fancy graphics to attract student attention because they may distract the student from learning.

Operant Analysis of the Intrinsic and Extrinsic Motivation Discussion.

In the early 1970s, two experiments tested the effect of giving a reward to nursery school children for engaging in an activity that they had previously engaged in spontaneously (Lepper & Greene, 1973, 1974). Children who had drawn pictures with magic markers during free-choice time were divided into three groups for the experiment: (1) expected reward, (2) unexpected reward, and (3) no reward. Each child, brought to the experimental room individually, was asked if he or she would like to draw some pictures for an important person who was to visit the school the next week. Children assigned to the expected reward condition also were told that, for drawing some pictures, they would receive a Good Player certificate decorated with a gold star and a red ribbon. Children assigned to the unexpected reward condition received the Good Player certificate at the end of the 6 minutes of coloring. Children in the no reward group were thanked by the experimenter at the end of 6 minutes.

After 6 minutes, the assistant thanked each child who then returned to the class. Post-session observations indicated that the mean percentage of free-choice time spent by children in the reward condition on drawing with magic markers was significantly less than that of the other two groups.

The researchers stated three conclusions. First, one effect of providing extrinsic incentives (the certificates) seemed to be the undermining of the children's intrinsic interest in the activity. Second, the studies did not deal with the learning of new skills, and in other situations with learning goals, the acquisition of new skills should enhance intrinsic motivation (Lepper & Greene, 1975). Third, schools should avoid the use of extrinsic rewards, such as gold stars or special privileges, for an entire class because some of the activities children are asked to do are intrinsically interesting to some of them (Lepper & Greene, 1973, p. 136).

In subsequent years, some discussions in the literature (1) equated the term "extrinsic motivation" with the use of contrived reinforcers, and (2) urged school personnel to focus on intrinsic motivation. These suggestions seem to stem from a theory of intrinsic motivation (i.e., an internal wellspring for action) in which three psychological needs can precipitate learning. They are need for competency, autonomy, and relatedness (Deci & Ryan, 1990).

An analysis of the prior experiment, from the operant conditioning perspective, is that the offer and acceptance of the certificate for the activity of drawing constituted a pre-activity contract between the assistant and the child. Reinforcement, in contrast, whether contrived or natural, is produced (often spontaneously) by an appropriate response. Second, the imposition of some type of reward for behaviors that already are producing reinforcers (such as the children's drawing activity) violates the basic principles of operant conditioning.

Third, in operant conditioning, contrived reinforcers fulfill an important but limited goal. The purpose is to bridge the gap between early stages of complex behavior (which do not generate "natural" reinforcers of success or accomplishment, resolving a difficulty, or other reinforcers) and the future consequence. Reinforcing oneself, for example, with a special treat for diligently working on a manuscript for an hour a day, particularly when paired every few days with the verbal reinforcer of noting the number of pages completed, can sustain early writing efforts while the individual is developing writing fluency and competency.

Also important is to withdraw or fade the special treat as the appearance of paragraphs that make sense, answer questions, or clarify important points begin to strengthen behavior (natural reinforcers). When these and other nonobservable reinforcers are functioning, the person is said by some to be "intrinsically motivated." However, the behavior is simply being observed after the behavioral change has occurred.

The key to using contrived reinforcers effectively is (1) to restrict their use to early stages of developing complex behavior, (2) plan the use of discriminative stimuli to include transfer to internal or non-arbitrary stimuli, (3) plan for the emergence of natural reinforcers, and (4) gradually fade the contrived reinforcers as the behavior develops and natural reinforcers are functioning. Step three can be aided by a respected teacher, for example, who reads several paragraphs when the student completes them and verbally confirms good points made or improvement in fluency or expression.

EDUCATIONAL APPLICATIONS

Like Watson's behaviorism in the 1920s, Skinner's methodology has enjoyed wide popularity. Its rapid popularization, however, has led to a variety of misapplications of the principles. Many of the behavioral management programs that emerged in the 1950s were a combination of operant conditioning and other methods (Kazdin, 1989). (See Belfiore & Hornyak (1998) for a discussion of self-monitoring programs that combine operant and other principles.) For example, many programs use time-out and response cost procedures. *Time-out* is a brief period of removal of the individual from a setting that provides reinforcement. *Response cost* is the loss of a reinforcer for misbehavior and requires paying a penalty. Because both techniques involve loss of reinforcers, they are a form of punishment (Becker, 1973; Kazdin, 1989). According to Skinner, punishment is to be avoided.

In addition, many of the individualized materials for verbal behaviors copied the stimulus–response–feedback format of programmed instruction but not the substance. Textbook materials subdivided into sentences with blanks do not shape verbal behaviors. The disillusionment of educators with these poorly developed programs and the clumsiness of the original teaching machines contributed to the rapid decline of the programmed instruction movement. Also, the token-economy programs developed for behavioral management in the classroom often focused on trivial behaviors, contributing to the view that the methodology has only limited applications.

A commercial program developed in the 1960s to teach reading, DISTAR, continues to be successful with at-risk children. Now known as SRA Reading Mastery, the program is a highly structured, scripted program in which children are taught according to skill level (Foorman et al., 1998).

Classroom Issues

B. F. Skinner's approach to learning is in terms of the factors responsible for behavioral change. Therefore, the issues of importance to education are discussed either as behaviors or as stimuli that lead to behavioral change.

Learner Characteristics
In the Skinnerian framework, learner characteristics are particular behaviors that students bring to the learning situation, and they may influence the acquisition of new behaviors.

Individual Differences.   According to Skinner (1953), individual differences in student behaviors result from (1) the organism's genetic endowment and (2) a particular history of reinforcement. The behavior of mentally retarded individuals, for example, is primarily the product of a defective genetic endowment. However, planned programs can develop new skills (Skinner, 1968b).

In Skinner's view (1968b), defective reinforcement contingencies in the individual's experience result in the failure to acquire a variety of skilled behaviors. An example is "rhythm" (Skinner, 1958). Some individuals, such as skilled typists and musicians, are under the influence of reinforcers that generate subtle timing. However, the development of this and other skills that influence career choices, artistic interests, and participation in sports is typically unplanned. Yet, important skills that presently contribute to such individual differences can be taught. A simple machine can teach a child first to tap in unison and then to echo more and more subtle rhythmic patterns that constitute "a sense of rhythm."

Mechanical devices that present instruction (Skinner, 1968b) can both provide the necessary individual reinforcement and correct the problems caused by multi-track systems and ungraded classes. In these situations, large groups of students move forward at the same speed and are required to meet the same criteria, usually those of the mediocre or average student. However, no teacher can teach 30 to 40 students at one time and allow each one to progress at an optimal speed (Skinner, 1987, p. 124). In contrast, new technologies such as microcomputers can accommodate different entry skills and also may present self-paced instruction.

Readiness for Learning.   In the operant conditioning framework, "readiness" is the behavioral repertoire that the student brings to the learning situation. Deficiencies in particular entry skills may be corrected through the use of carefully designed programs.

The concept of readiness interpreted as age or maturational level is unacceptable in the Skinnerian concept of designing instruction. Chronological age is of little help in determining the presence or absence of important skills (Skinner, 1953, p. 156). Also, developmental studies may indicate the amount usually learned by a child of a given age; however, such studies do not indicate the extent of a child's intellectual development under an appropriate schedule of events (Homme, deBaca, Cottingham, & Homme, 1968). For example, once a child can discriminatively respond to objects, planned contingency management can advance the child's reading levels in a systematic way independent of age.

Motivation.   Behaviors that illustrate interest, enthusiasm, appreciation, or dedication are included in descriptions of motivation. The diligent and eager student, the individual who enjoys "reading good books," and the scientist who works long hours in the laboratory are all said to be motivated (Skinner, 1968b).

Such sustained activity in the absence of observable reinforcement is the result of a particular history of reinforcement. It is not the result of natural contingencies. No child really learns to plant seed because he or she is reinforced by the resulting harvest, nor do we learn to read because we enjoy interesting books (Skinner, 1968b, p. 154). Such long-range natural contingencies are insufficient to develop and maintain "dedicated" behavior. Instead, dedication is the result of exposure to a gradually increasing variable-ratio schedule of reinforcements. The individual first receives an immediate payoff for engaging in the activity (Skinner, 1968b). Then the reinforcements are gradually extended (referred to as stretching the ratio) until the activity itself acquires secondary reinforcing power. Ironically, the same reinforcement schedule produces both the compulsive gambler and the dedicated scientist (i.e., a variable-ratio schedule). However, only the scientist is considered by society to be "dedicated" (Skinner, 1963b).

Cognitive Processes and Instruction

Internal or mental events are included in the operant conditioning paradigm only to the extent that they can be translated into identified behaviors. Therefore, transfer of learning is excluded from Skinner's formulations, but learning "how-to-learn" skills and problem solving, defined behaviorally, are included.

Transfer of Learning.   Thorndike and Woodworth's (1901) experiments explained students' performance on learning tasks as caused in part by the degree of similarity between those tasks and prior learning tasks. Therefore, training in particular skills, such as playing the piano, is said to improve performance in playing other instruments. According to Skinner (1953), however, transfer merely appears to strengthen behavior without reinforcing it directly. Many responses, in fact, possess common elements, such as the use of the same musculature. Skill in manipulating tools and instruments, for example, may be a part of a number of different responses. "Transfer," then, is simply the reinforcement of "common elements wherever they occur" (Skinner, 1953, p. 94).

Learning "How-to-Learn" Skills.   According to Skinner (1953, 1968b), the process commonly referred to as "thinking" often means behaving in a particular way with regard to certain stimuli. When a child responds to certain stimulus properties, the child's response has come under the control of those stimuli. An example is a child's identification of a closed three-sided plane figure as a triangle. The child's identification is under the control of the figure. Little is gained in such situations by describing the learning as that of "forming an abstraction."

Certain activities typically identified with thinking, however, should be analyzed and taught (Skinner, 1968b). Such behaviors are called precurrent responses because they either change the environment or change the learner so that an effective response becomes possible. Thus, precurrent responses are defined as "behavior which affects behavior" (Skinner, 1966b, p. 216). Precurrent responses are covert; that is, they are private events that are not observable.

Also, they are the self-management behaviors that increase the probability of an effective response to a stimulus. Included are (1) reviewing the characteristics of a particular problem or calculating a mathematical answer by speaking silently to oneself and (2) visualizing a problem or situation in the "mind's eye" (i.e., covert seeing) (Skinner, 1968b).

Other self-management behaviors that are precurrent responses are (1) attending to stimuli, (2) underlining important ideas in textual material, (3) using mnemonic devices or other cues to remember important ideas, and (4) rearranging the elements in a problem situation so that a solution is more likely.

Teaching Problem Solving.   In the true "problem situation," the subject has no response immediately available that will reduce the deprivation or remove the aversive stimulus (Skinner, 1953, p. 246). If the room is too warm, for example, a problem exists if we cannot open the window (Skinner, 1968b). The problem is solved when we change the situation so that either the available response can occur or the deprivation or aversive stimulation is reduced in some other way. We find either some way to get the window open or some other means to cool the room (Skinner, 1968b).

Formally defined, problem solving is "any behavior which, through the manipulation of variables, makes the appearance of a solution more probable" (Skinner, 1953, p. 247). The "difficulty" of a problem depends on the availability of a response in the subject's repertoire that solves the problem. If no response is immediately available, the problem is difficult. To maximize the likelihood of a response (solution), the individual must change the situation so that he or she can respond appropriately. Steps that may be taken include (1) reviewing the problem carefully and clarifying the problem, (2) rearranging or regrouping the components of the problem, and (3) searching for similarities between the problem and others that have been solved. In anagrams, for example, the player maximizes the chances of forming a word from the set of letters by regrouping the letters in logical sequences (i.e., vowels separated by consonants).

Individuals learn to solve problems effectively by manipulating stimuli and receiving reinforcement for the behavior. Reinforcement for the effective manipulation of the problem situation will reduce the occurrence of haphazard or trial-and-error responses to problems.

The Social Context for Learning

Reinforcers that require the mediation of another person are referred to as *social reinforcers.* This group includes the positive reinforcers of attention, approval, and affection (typically, positive reinforcers) and the negative reinforcers of disapproval, insult, contempt, and ridicule (typically, negative reinforcers).

Social reinforcers, both positive and negative, have been used in group settings for the modification and maintenance of behavior. However, the relationships between stimuli, responses, and reinforcers in a social setting are both dynamic and reciprocal. For example, two children alone in a room with few toys provide an ideal situation for the shaping of selfish behavior (Skinner, 1958).

Behavior in the classroom is also a product of ongoing and complex contingencies that include teacher and students reinforcing each other both positively and negatively (Skinner, 1968a, p. 252). If a student is not punished by his or her peers for answering the teacher's questions and is reinforced by the teacher, he or she will answer as often as possible. If the teacher calls only on students whose hands are raised, the student will raise his or her hand. Similarly, teachers who are reinforced by right answers will call on students whose hands are raised. However, teachers who are reinforced by wrong answers are exercising aversive control, and they typically call on students who do not raise their hands (Skinner, 1968a).

Therefore, designing a classroom environment to modify behavior must take into account the reciprocal reinforcement characteristics of a social setting. Brigham (1978, p. 266) describes one study in which special education children were taught to reinforce the positive comments of other children and teachers. As their behavior changed, so did the environment, and they became skillful at manipulating the environment. Furthermore, the children's behaviors changed the teacher's environment as well because the children became the source of social reinforcement for their teachers.

Relationships to Other Perspectives

Unlike cognitive approaches to learning, operant conditioning addresses behavior rather than knowledge or internal states. That is, evidence of learning is behavioral change. Moreover, student actions such as contributing verbally to classroom discourse (constructivism), manipulating objects (Piagetian theory), or observing the reinforcement received by others (Bandura's social-cognitive theory) are not indicators of learning unless they are new behaviors.

The application of operant conditioning to the priorities of other theoretical perspectives lies in the implementation of reinforcement to develop complex behaviors. Examples include reinforcing children's explanations of their problem-solving steps and listening respectively to the strategies of others (radical constructivism and cognitive theory), developing persistence in academic tasks (Weiner's attribution theory) and monitoring one's own learning (cognitive theory). Further, reciprocal teaching makes use of reinforcing successive approximations and the gradual fading of cues for student responses.

Operant conditioning would not support presenting open-ended problems or tasks to groups of children in the absence of prior teaching of required behaviors. This practice is conducive to trial-and-error learning, does not ensure the acquisition of essential behaviors, and can precipitate the learning of incorrect responses. Further, not all children in the group situation may receive reinforcement for appropriate responses.

Developing a Classroom Strategy

The classroom teacher can make use of Skinner's technology in two ways. One is the appropriate use of reinforcement in classroom interactions, and the other is the development of individualized instructional materials.

Developing a Positive Classroom Climate

An important application of Skinner's technology is that of developing a positive classroom climate. This goal differs from that of implementing an extensive behavior modification program. Skinner (1973) notes that an obvious approach, such as a token economy, may indeed be necessary in a totally disruptive classroom. However, a teacher can make the transition from punishment to positive reinforcement with one simple change—merely by responding to student successes rather than to student failures (Skinner, 1973, p. 15). Instead of pointing out what students are doing wrong, point out what they are doing right. The result, in Skinner's view, will be an improved classroom atmosphere and more efficient instruction.

Applying the technology developed by Skinner in the classroom can make use of the following steps:

Step 1: Analyze the current classroom environment.

1.1 What are the positive student behaviors currently receiving reinforcement in the classroom? What are the undesirable behaviors that are receiving reinforcement? For example, withholding help so that the child has an opportunity to demonstrate his or her knowledge and then providing help when the child shows discouragement may be reinforcing behavior that indicates discouragement (Skinner, 1968b, p. 252).

1.2 For which behaviors is punishment currently dispensed in the classroom? (Recall Skinner's definition of punishment: removal of a positive reinforcer or introduction of an aversive stimulus from which the individual seeks escape.)

1.3 What is the frequency of punishment? Have the punished behaviors been suppressed but other, related behaviors appeared?

Step 2: Develop a list of potential positive reinforcers.

2.1 What are the students' preferred activities? (Students can rank their preferences on a list; young children can identify pictures.)

2.2 Which of the punished behaviors identified in step 1.2 may be used as reinforcers? For example, if talking with peers currently is punished, consider incorporating it occasionally as a reinforcer for less preferred activities, such as completing seatwork assignments quietly.

2.3 Which activities that you have observed in the natural setting may serve as positive reinforcers for other behaviors? One reading teacher, for example, expressed difficulty in keeping children on task because they constantly interrupted to discuss the progress of their favorite TV shows that aired the previous evening. Discussing the TV programs for 10 to 15 minutes is a potential reinforcer in that setting.

Step 3: Select the behavioral sequences to be initially implemented in the classroom. Include discriminative stimuli and reinforcers.

3.1 Which of the punished behaviors identified in step 1.2 may be restructured in the form of positive behaviors? For example, use positive reinforcement for promptness instead of punishment for tardiness. Becker (1973) suggests that instead of punishment for fighting, a student may earn 1 minute of recess for no fighting.

3.2 Which of the positive student behaviors from the list in step 1.1 are occurring infrequently? Examples may include demonstrating independence in learning by getting and putting away needed materials on time, attending to relevant characteristics of stimuli during instruction, and so on.

3.3 What are the initial discriminative stimuli to be used? To which stimuli is the transfer of behavioral control to be made? For example, the verbal statement "Time to begin" may be replaced by a signal, such as a bell, and then by the students' observations of the clock time.

Step 4: Implement the behavioral sequences, maintaining anecdotal records and making changes when necessary.

4.1 Are the rules for classroom behavior clear and consistent?

4.2 Is the method for earning reinforcement clear, and is reinforcement provided for improved behavior?

4.3 Does every child have the opportunity to earn reinforcement for behavioral change? If reinforcement is provided only for one or two behaviors that must meet a high standard, some children have no means of earning reinforcement in the classroom and are likely to seek attention in disruptive ways (Resnick, 1971).

4.4 Following initial behavioral change, are reinforcements provided after longer intervals (stretching the ratio), and are other reinforcers also implemented?

Programming Instruction

Programs to develop verbal behaviors should be designed to lead the student from a state of no knowledge to proficiency in one or more skills. The following steps are recommended in the development of a Skinnerian or constructed-response program:

Step 1: Identify the terminal skill to be acquired and analyze the subject matter to be learned.

1.1 What is the nature of the terminal behavior? Is it a discrimination skill, such as learning color names, or is it the application of a rule, such as carrying in addition?

1.2 What terms or definitions must be learned to acquire the skill?

1.3 What types of examples should the student respond to during learning (e.g., color bands, simple and complex addition problems)?

Step 2: Develop the initial sequence of frames and response confirmations.

2.1 What information should be placed in the first frame to induce a response (referred to as a *copying frame*)?

2.2 What is a logical sequence of responses (behaviors) that can be expected of the student?

2.3 What sequence of discriminative stimuli that progress from simple to complex can provide for the transfer of stimulus control?

Step 3: Review the sequence of frames, reordering if necessary.

3.1 Does the sequence progress from simple to complex?

3.2 Are the prompts gradually vanished in the sequence?

3.3 Does the student respond to meaningful rather than trivial content?

Step 4: Implement the instruction with a few students and revise if necessary.

4.1 Do any students experience difficulty with any of the frames? Such frames may need to be rewritten.

4.2 Do the students race through any of the frames, getting the right answer by only reading part of the frame? The frame may be superfluous or it may be asking trivial information.

4.3 Does the program lead to mastery performance on the criterion posttest?

Classroom Example

The following frames were developed to teach the concept "morpheme" to advanced high school students or college freshmen. The terminal skills are that (1) the student can define *morpheme* and (2) the student can identify examples of free morphemes and bound morphemes.

Discussion of Classroom Example

Skinner originally developed programmed instruction for mechanical devices known as teaching machines. However, Skinner (1984) recommended that microcomputers be utilized to present the instruction. A partial program for teaching the student to discriminate morphemes is illustrated in Figure 5.2. The style of programming is referred to as *constructed response* because the student writes or constructs the answer. After a brief introduction to the lesson on morphemes (including lesson objectives), the next screen and the computer feedback is programmed as follows:

One aspect of linguistics is the analysis of words into the smallest units that carry meaning. The study of such word parts is an area of study in l_ _ _ _ _ _ _ _ _.

Computer feedback for correct answer: The correct answer is linguistics. Good. Continue with the program. When you enter the correct answer, the program will display it on the screen. For a wrong answer, you will be asked to try again.

Computer feedback for wrong answer: Sorry your answer is not correct. Try the question again.

The first frame is referred to as a copying frame because essentially it involves the student's copying or repeating basic information in the stimulus. Each frame includes one item of information to which the student responds. The cues, or

1. One aspect of linguistics is the analysis of words into the smallest units that carry meaning. The study of such word parts is an area of study in l_ _ _ _ _ _ _ _ _ _ . (linguistics)

2. The smallest word parts that carry meaning are *morphemes*. In the word "unhappy," the part "un-" means "not." Therefore, "un-" is a m_ _ _ _ _ _ _ . (morpheme)

3. Some words are composed of only one morpheme or unit of meaning. An example is *cat*. In this case, the morpheme making up the word is _ _ _ . (cat)

4. Sometimes morphemes may be added to existing words, for example, the letter "s." When added to some words, "s" means "more than one." In such a situation, the "s" is a _ _ _ _ _ _ _ _ _ _ . (morpheme)

5. Of course, some letters do not carry any meaning in words, such as the "s" in "slide." In this case, "s" is _ _ _ a morpheme. (not)

6. Some words are composed of two or more morphemes. An example is "biology," which includes "bio-" (life) and "-logy" (study of). Biology, therefore, is composed of _ _ _ _ _ _ _ _ _ _ _ _ . (two morphemes)

7. The word "morpheme" itself may be analyzed as follows: "Morph-" = unit or form and "-eme" = "small." The complete word is composed of _ _ _ _ _ _ _ _ _ _ _ _ . (two morphemes)

8. Prefixes and suffixes are word parts that frequently function as units of meaning. An example is "pre-" (before or prior) as in "preview." In this example, the prefix is also a _ _ _ _ _ _ _ _ _ _ . (morpheme)

9. In the earlier example, "un-" in "unhappy" was identified as a morpheme. This prefix is a morpheme because it is a u_ _ _ _ _ _ _ _ _ _ _ . (unit of meaning)

10. Language includes two kinds of morphemes, one of which is "free morphemes." They are the smallest unit of meaning that can stand alone. For example, in the word "cats," the word part "cat" is a _ _ _ _ _ _ _ _ _ _ _ _ . (free morpheme)

11. Some words are composed only of free morphemes. The word "cowboy" is composed of two free morphemes. They are _ _ _ and _ _ _ . (cow, boy)

12. The other type of morpheme is a "bound morpheme." It is a unit of meaning that cannot stand alone. For example, the morpheme "s" in the word "cats" is a _ _ _ _ _ _ _ _ _ _ _ _ _ . (bound morpheme)

13. The letter "s" in the word "cats" is a bound morpheme because it is a unit of meaning that can/cannot stand alone. (cannot)

14. Some words may be composed of only bound morphemes. An example is the word "biology," composed of "bio-" and "-logy." This word includes two _ _ _ _ _ _ _ _ _ _ _ _ . (bound morphemes)

15. Still other words, like "cats," may be composed of both bound and free morphemes. Another example is the word "unhappy," which includes _ _ _ _ _ _ _ _ _ _ free morpheme and _ _ _ _ _ _ _ _ _ _ bound morpheme. (one, one)

16. The study of morphemes can be a means for building vocabulary. We have learned, for example, that "-logy" means "study of." Further, "psycho-" is a morpheme that means mind or mental life. Therefore, "psychology" means "study of the mind or mental life," based on the two _ _ _ _ _ _ _ _ _ _ _ _ _ . (bound morphemes)

FIGURE 5.2
Introductory frames on morphemes
Source: Terry L. Norton, Winthrop College

prompts, for the correct answers are gradually withdrawn so that stimuli within the learner or other textual stimuli are generating appropriate responses (see frame 15).

Care should be taken in the design of programmed instruction to lead the students from no knowledge to skill proficiency. Notice the examples in the unit on morphemes shown in Figure 5.2. Frames 2 and 3 present the definition, later followed by the definition of bound and free morphemes.

The advantage of several short units of programmed instruction on specific skills is twofold. Remediation is provided that is targeted to specific deficiencies. Often students are unable to participate in ongoing instruction because they lack a particular skill. Continuation of the deficiency, however, only compounds the problem. In this example, students will be unable to analyze complex word meanings unless they first are able to differentiate commonly used morphemes.

The second advantage is that such materials can assist the teacher in individualizing instruction. Students who enter a grade lacking some essential skills or students who experience difficulty with the initial instruction for a topic may be given the material while the teacher works with other students on other problems.

Review of the Theory

B. F. Skinner's principles of operant conditioning continued the tradition established by John Watson. That is, for psychology to become a science, the study of behavior must become the focus of psychological research. Unlike the other S–R theorists, Skinner avoided the contradiction posed by Pavlov's classical conditioning model and Thorndike's instrumental conditioning. He proposed a paradigm that includes both types of responses and analyzed the conditions responsible for emitted responses or operant behavior (Table 5.3).

Skinner's analyses yielded a parsimonious system that was applied to the dynamics of behavioral change in both the laboratory and the classroom. Learning, represented by increased response rate, was described as a function of the three-component sequence $(S^D)–(R)–(S^{reinf.})$. Skinner described the typical practice of placing experimental animals in puzzle boxes and mazes as that of placing the subject in a "terminal contingency"; that is, the animal must either sink or swim in the search for escape or food. Instead, the appropriate procedure is to shape the animal's behavior through carefully established stimulus-response-reinforcement sequences. Approximations to appropriate responses are reinforced on intermittent schedules until the behavioral repertoire is acquired, such as pigeons playing ping-pong.

In the classroom, Skinner cited the practice of "assign-and-test" as one example of placing the human learner in a terminal contingency. Instead, Skinner recommended the practice of reinforcing the component behaviors, such as attending to stimuli and executing appropriate study behaviors. Punishment should be avoided because it produces unwanted emotional side effects and does not generate the desired positive behaviors.

Included in Skinner's analyses are the role of conditioned and natural reinforcers, positive and negative reinforcers, and generalized reinforcers. Also included is the development of programmed learning for verbal behaviors. Individual differences in entry skills and rates of learning may be accommodated by such materials.

TABLE 5.3
Summary of Skinner's technology

Basic Elements	Definition
Assumptions	Behavioral change is a function of environmental conditions and events.
Learning	A change in behavior represented by increased response frequency
Learning outcomes	New responses (behaviors)
Components of learning	(S^D)-(R)-$(S^{reinf.})$
Designing instruction for complex learning	Design sequences of stimuli-responses-reinforcements to develop sets of complex responses
Major issues in designing instruction	Transfer of stimulus control, timing of reinforcement; avoidance of punishment

ANALYSIS OF THE TECHNOLOGY

Disadvantages	1. Technology for complex situations is incomplete; successful analysis depends on the skill of the technologist.
	2. Response frequency is difficult to apply to complex behaviors as a measure of probability.
Applications to classroom practice	1. Analysis of states such as "readiness" and "motivation"
	2. Analysis of aversive classroom practices and interactive classroom situations
	3. Individualized learning materials: teaching machines, microcomputers

Disadvantages

Two major problems in the application of Skinner's recommendations may be identified. One is that the technology for the experimental analysis of complex human behaviors is incomplete. Some students respond well in highly structured situations in which objectives and the steps to be taken are clearly specified. Others, however, are reinforced by the opportunity to explore on their own and to relate ideas without external directives. The procedures for identifying these and other differences in the variety of potential reinforcements is yet to be developed.

Second, in the classroom, response frequency as a measure of learning may be applied to simple behaviors, such as naming colors or adding two-digit numbers. Complex behaviors, however, such as diagnosing an illness or calculating one's taxes, are not conducive to response frequency as a measure of learning.

Contributions to Classroom Practice

Three major contributions to educational practice are illustrated in Table 5.3. First, the search for conditions and behaviors that represent states such as "unmotivated" is an important step in the identification of an appropriate course of action. Second, observations of contemporary classrooms reveal many inconsistent and noncontingent uses of reinforcement that contribute to classroom discipline problems. An analysis of these interactive situations in terms of discriminative stimuli, responses, and reinforcements is an important step in correcting the problems. Third, programmed learning materials, if properly designed, can provide for individual differences in the classroom.

CHAPTER QUESTIONS

1. Skinner (1989b) stated that governments make use of aversive situations both as punishment and as negative reinforcers. His examples are having to pay a fine for parking in a "no parking" zone and the directive "Pay your taxes and avoid a fine." Identify the type of consequence in each example.

2. Which reinforcement concept is most likely to explain a person's involvement with the Sunday crossword puzzle?

3. Good and Power (1976) have identified five types of students in the classroom. Three are briefly described below. Name some potential reinforcers that may be effective for each type.

   _____ a. *successful*—does not require structure or praise from the teacher

   _____ b. *social*—is more person-oriented than task-oriented

   _____ c. *dependent*—seeks teacher structure and teacher support

4. For the dependent student, which behaviors should the teacher seek to reinforce? What problems should be avoided in the use of reinforcement with this type of student?

5. One of the concerns about Internet use is that of individuals spending hours and days in computer chat rooms to the exclusion of eating and sleeping regularly and no engagement in face-to-face interactions. Which concept in operant conditioning describes this phenomenon?

REFERENCES

Azar, B. (1998). Research-based games enhance children's learning. *APA Monitor, 29*(8), 18, 20.

Becker, W. D. (1973). Application of behavior principles in typical classrooms. In C. E. Thoresen (Ed.), *Behavior modification in education: The seventy-second yearbook of the National Society for the Study of Education, Part I* (pp. 77–106). Chicago: University of Chicago Press.

Belfiore, P. J., & Hornyak, R. S. (1998). Operant theory and application to self-monitoring in adolescents. In D. Schunk & B. J. Zimmerman (Eds.), *Self-regulated learning: From teaching to self-reflective practice* (pp. 184–202). New York: The Guilford Press.

Brigham, T. A. (1978). Self-control: Part II. In A. C. Catania & T. A. Brigham (Eds.), *Handbook of applied behavioral analysis* (pp. 259–274). New York: Irvington.

Brophy, J. (1981). Teacher praise: A functional analysis. *Review of Educational Research, 51,* 5–32.

Brown, A. L. (1994). The advancement of learning. *Educational Researcher, 23*(4), 4–11.

Deci, E. L., & Ryan, R. M. (1990). A motivational approach to self: Integration in personality. In D. Diensthier (Ed.), *Nebraska Symposium on Motivation* (pp. 237–288). Lincoln, NE: University of Nebraska Press.

Doyle, W. (1986). Classroom organization and management. In M. C. Wittrock (Ed.), *Handbook of research on teaching* (3rd ed. pp. 392–431). Upper Saddle River, NJ: Merrill/Prentice Hall.

Emmer, E., Evertson, C., & Anderson, L. (1980). Effective classroom management at the beginning of the school year. *The Elementary School Journal, 80*(5), 219–231.

Ferster, C. B., & Skinner, B. F. (1957). *Schedules of reinforcement.* New York: Appleton-Century-Crofts.

Foorman, B. R., Francis, D. J., Fletcher, J. M., Schatschneider, C., & Mehta, P. (1998). The role of instruction in learning to read: Preventing reading failure in at-risk children. *Journal of Educational Psychology, 90*(1), 37–55.

Gallant, J., Sargeant, M., & Van Houten, R. (1980). Teacher-determined and self-determined access to science activities as a reinforcer for task completion in other curriculum areas. *Education and Treatment of Children, 3*(2), 101–111.

Glaser, R. (1990). The reemergence of learning theory within instructional research. *American Psychologist, 45*(1), 29–39.

Good, T., & Power, C. (1976). Designing successful classroom environments for different types of students. *Journal of Curriculum Studies, 8,* 1–16.

Homme, L. E., deBaca, R., Cottingham, L., & Homme, A. (1968). What behavioral engineering is. *The Psychological Record, 18,* 424–434.

Kazdin, A. (1989). *Behavior modification in applied settings* (4th ed.). Pacific Grove, CA: Brooks/Cole.

Kratochwill, T., & Bijou, S. (1987). The impact of behaviorism on educational psychology. In J. Glover & R. Ronning (Eds.), *Historical foundations of educational psychology* (pp. 131–157). New York: Plenum.

Lepper, M. R., & Greene, D. (1973). Undermining children's intrinsic interest with extrinsic reward: A test of the "overjustification" hypothesis. *Journal of Personality and Social Psychology, 28*(1), 129–137.

Lepper, M. R., & Greene, D. (1974). Effects of extrinsic rewards on children's subsequent intrinsic interest. *Child Development, 45*(4), 1141–1145.

Lepper, M. R., & Greene, D. (1975). When two rewards are worse than one: Effects of extrinsic reward on intrinsic motivation. *Phi Delta Kappan, 56*(8), 565–566.

Moreno, R., & Hovell, M. (1980). Teaching survival English skills and assessment of collateral behavior. *Behavior Modification, 6*(3), 375–388.

Premack, D. (1959). Toward empirical behavior laws. I. Positive reinforcement. *Psychological Review, 66*(4), 219–233.

Resnick, L. (1971). Applying applied reinforcement. In R. Glaser (Ed.), *The nature of reinforcement* (pp. 326–333). New York: Academic Press.

Skinner, B. F. (1935). Two types of conditioned reflex and a pseudotype. *Journal of General Psychology, 12,* 66–77.

Skinner, B. F. (1938). *The behavior of organisms.* New York: Appleton-Century-Crofts.

Skinner, B. F. (1948). "Superstition" in the pigeon. *Journal of Experimental Psychology, 38,* 168–172.

Skinner, B. F. (1950). Are theories of learning necessary? *Psychological Review, 57,* 193–216.

Skinner, B. F. (1953). *Science and human behavior.* New York: Macmillan.

Skinner, B. F. (1954). The science of learning and the art of teaching. *Harvard Educational Review, 24*(2), 86–97.

Skinner, B. F. (1958). Reinforcement today. *American Psychologist, 13,* 94–99.

Skinner, B. F. (1961). Why we need teaching machines. *Harvard Educational Review, 31*(4), 377–398.

Skinner, B. F. (1963a). Behaviorism at fifty. *Science, 140,* 951–958.

Skinner, B. F. (1963b). Operant behavior. *American Psychologist, 18,* 503–515.

Skinner, B. F. (1966a). Contingencies of reinforcement in the design of a culture. *Behavioral Science, 11,* 159–166.

Skinner, B. F. (1966b). What is the experimental analysis of behavior? *Journal of the Experimental Analysis of Behavior, 9*(3), 213–218.

Skinner, B. F. (1968a). Teaching science in high school—What is wrong? *Science, 159,* 704–710.

Skinner, B. F. (1968b). *The technology of teaching.* New York: Appleton-Century-Crofts.

Skinner, B. F. (1969). *Contingencies of reinforcement.* New York: Appleton-Century-Crofts.

Skinner, B. F. (1973). The free and happy student. *Phi Delta Kappan, 55,* 13–16.

Skinner, B. F. (1981). Selection by consequence. *Science, 213,* 501–504.

Skinner, B. F. (1984, February). In J. O. Green, Skinner's technology of teaching. *Classroom Computer Learning,* pp. 23–29.

Skinner, B. F. (1986). Programmed instruction revisited. *Phi Delta Kappan,* 103–110.

Skinner, B. F. (1987). *Upon further reflection.* Upper Saddle River, NJ: Merrill/Prentice Hall.

Skinner, B. F. (1989a). The origins of cognitive thought. *American Psychologist, 44*(1), 13–18.

Skinner, B. F. (1989b). *Recent issues in the analysis of behavior.* Upper Saddle River, NJ: Merrill/Prentice Hall.

Skinner, B. F., & Vaughan, M. (1983). *Enjoy old age.* New York: Norton.

Thorndike, E. L., & Woodworth, R. S. (1901). The influence of improvement in one mental function upon the efficiency of other functions: I, II, and III. *Psychological Review, 8,* 247–261, 384–395, 553–564.

Vargas, J. S. (1986). Instructional design flaws in computer-assisted instruction. *Phi Delta Kappan, 64,* 738–744.

Vaughan, M. (1987). Rule-governed behavior and higher mental processes. In S. Modgil & C. Modgil (Eds.), *B. F. Skinner: Consensus and controversy* (pp. 257–264). New York: Falmer.

Watson, J. B. (1913). Psychology as the behaviorist sees it. *Psychological Bulletin, 20,* 158–177.

CHAPTER 6

Robert Gagné's
Conditions of Learning

Human skills, appreciations, and reasonings in all their great variety, as well as human hopes, aspirations, attitudes, and values, are generally recognized to depend for their development largely on the events called learning (Gagné, 1985, p. 1).

Robert Gagné's conditions of learning shifted the focus in theory development from the laboratory to the classroom. Beginning with the training needs of the armed forces in World War II, he addressed the question, What are the conditions essential to developing expertise in real-world tasks?

Assigned to the Aviation Psychology Program, Gagné worked to develop realistic analyses of a broad class of human skills, including those of radar operators, pilots, and bombardiers. Later tasks, which were part of the weapons system planning of the air force, included analyzing man-machine systems and forecasting training requirements for weapons systems yet to be built (Gagné, 1987b, 1989).

Three principles of instruction identified by Gagné in the analysis of training tasks were (1) providing instruction on the set of component tasks that build toward the final task, (2) ensuring that each component task is mastered, and (3) sequencing the component tasks to ensure optimal transfer to the final task (Gagné, 1962a, 1962b).

Convinced that the analysis procedures that were successful for the armed forces also were applicable to school learning, Gagné began to analyze problem solving in mathematics. Incidental observations of students indicated that the lack of success experienced by some students was the result of apparent gaps in their knowledge of procedures, such as simplifying fractions (Gagné, 1987b, p. 398). Identification of subcomponents of the final task led to the concept of a **learning hierarchy**, or a progression of prerequisite skills (Gagné, 1968a, 1968b). Various research technologies applied in the verification of learning hierarchies (see Airasian & Bart, 1975; White, 1974), indicate that properly identified prerequisite skills contribute to the learning of more complex capabilities.

Continued research in classrooms and other educational settings on the question, What kinds of things are learned in school? led to several developments. These developments included the identification of five distinct domains or varieties of learned capabilities, the internal states and information-processing steps required for learning in each domain, and the supporting requirements for instruction. Included in the guidelines for designing instruction are media selection guidelines.

Currently, his concepts of analyzing tasks into component tasks and identifying needed prerequisite skills are incorporated into the development of an instructional program in a variety of areas (see, e.g., Griffin, Chase & Siegler, 1994; Jonassen, Tessmer, & Hannum, 1999).

PRINCIPLES OF LEARNING

The key to the development of a comprehensive learning theory, according to Gagné (1974a, 1977a), is to identify the factors that account for the complex nature of human learning. This view contrasts with earlier approaches that typically began with an explanation of the learning process based on laboratory research and then attempted to fit the conclusions to human learning. Instead, the principles developed by Gagné are derived from the analysis of the variety of performances and skills executed by human beings.

Basic Assumptions

The basic assumptions of Gagné's theory address the unique characteristics of human learning and the diversity of learning.

The Nature of Human Learning

Several elements are included in Gagné's conception of learning. Key factors are the relationship of learning to development, and the cumulative nature of learning.

A major task for psychologists interested in learning is that of separating the changes that result from learning from those that result from maturation or growth. According to the growth-readiness model (often referred to as the Gesellian model), certain growth patterns must occur before learning can be beneficial. This model maintains that body growth is closely related to mental growth. One suggestion, for example, is that the acquisition of permanent teeth is an indicator of the appropriate developmental age to begin reading instruction (see Gredler, 1992, for a review).

In contrast, the model described by Gagné assigns a primary role to learning. According to Gagné (1968a), learning is an important causal factor in the individual's development. Within the broad parameters established by growth, *"behavioral development results from the cumulative effects of learning"* (Gagné, 1968a, p. 178).

Two characteristics of learning account for its importance in development. One is that human learning is not simply acquiring isolated bits of information. Instead, much of human learning generalizes to a variety of situations. Addition, for example, applies to situations such as computing wages and deductions, constructing a family budget, calculating taxes, and many others.

The other important contribution of learning to development is that complex skills that are learned build on prior learning. In other words, human learning is *cumulative*. Again, addition serves as an example. The skill of adding numbers contributes to the learning of long division. The child does not need to learn to add all over again when learning to divide. Instead, addition merely is incorporated into the new skill.

In summary, intellectual development "may be conceived as the building of increasingly complex and interesting structures of learned capabilities" (Gagné, 1968a, p. 190). These learned capabilities contribute to the learning of more complex skills, and they also generalize to other situations. The result is that an ever-increasing intellectual competence is generated.

The Diversity of Learning

According to Gagné, prior theories presented limited views of the nature of human learning. For the most part, the ideas presented by the early theories are tied to specific situations, such as dogs salivating at the sight of food or people recalling words or syllables that have been paired with other words (Gagné, 1984, p. 388).

One group of theories includes those derived from laboratory studies of learning; examples are the theories of Pavlov, Thorndike, Hull, and Skinner. However, these models do not account for the human capacity to learn complex skills and abilities, according to Gagné (1977a). Some of them do describe the subcomponents of human learning, but these subskills are not the major objectives of learning. Examples are signal learning (Pavlov's model), S–R associations, and chainlike skills. Signal learning involves feelings of well-being generated by a favorite stuffed toy or a favorite melody. Chainlike skills include buttoning, fastening, printing, and writing, and verbal sequences, such as the "Pledge of Allegiance."

Although the S–R model has been used to characterize human learning, Gagné (1977a) observes that "pure" examples of S–R learning are difficult to find. Such learnings rapidly are incorporated into longer sequences. Letters of the alphabet, for example, soon become a part of decoding words.

Like the S–R model, the "insight" experience identified by Gestalt psychologists also attempted to explain the "true" nature of learning. However, although Gestalt theorists maintained that learning occurs when a subject "sees" a new relationship, the process of insight is not a spontaneous occurrence (Gagné, 1977a). Instead, it is influenced by transfer from prior learnings to new situations. In the school setting, children may display insight when they are led to understand relationships. An example is the relationship between weight and the pull of gravity (Gagné, 1977a, p. 14). The major problem with the Gestalt explanation, however, is that it, too, does not explain all learning. For example, learning to speak a foreign language and learning to read are not the result of insight.

This analysis indicates that learning is not a single process (Gagné, 1970, 1972). Neither the learning of word associations nor the problem solving described by the Gestalt theorists can be reduced one to the other. The learning of associations cannot be explained by insight, nor can problem-solving behavior be explained by the pairing of stimulus elements (Gagné, 1977a). Therefore, no one set of characteristics can be applied to all learning.

Efforts to force-fit all learning into a single description is one error in the development of learning principles. Equally erroneous is the view that psychology should develop principles of specific subject-matter learning, such as principles of mathematics learning, science learning, and computer-repair learning (Gagné, 1984). Important general principles are overlooked unless one searches for the similarities in learning outcomes between reading and mathematics, for example, or between the procedures of office management and those of aircraft maintenance (Gagné, 1984, p. 333).

In addition, an adequate conception of human learning must not be restricted to the learning found only in the laboratory or the school. Instead, an adequate perspective should apply also to, for example, masons, carpenters, astronauts, politicians, housewives, and word-processing operators (Gagné, 1984, p. 378). Thus, the task is to identify principles of learning that generalize to the various situations and circumstances in which learning occurs.

A Definition of Learning

The human capacity for learning makes possible an almost infinite variety of behavioral patterns (Gagné, 1977a). Given this diversity, no one set of characteristics can account for such varied activities as learning to define a word, to write an essay, or to lace a shoe (Gagné, 1972, p. 2). Therefore, the task for learning theory is to identify a set of principles that accommodates both the complexity and the variety of human learning.

If human learning is indeed a complex, multifaceted process, how is it to be defined? First, learning is the mechanism by which an individual becomes a competently functioning member of society (Gagné, 1977a). The importance of learning is that it is responsible for all the skills, knowledge, attitudes, and values that are acquired by human beings. Learning, therefore, results in a variety of different kinds of behaviors, referred to by Gagné (1972, 1977a) as **capabilities**. They are the outcomes of learning.

Second, these capabilities are acquired by human beings from (1) the stimulation from the environment and (2) the cognitive processing undertaken by the learner. In other words, the learner is not passive. Formally defined, learning is the set of cognitive processes that transforms the stimulation from the environment into the several phases of information processing necessary for acquiring a new capability (Gagné & Briggs, 1979, p. 43).

Summary

The key to the development of a comprehensive learning theory, according to Gagné, is to account for the complex nature of human learning. First, unlike the growth-readiness model, in which maturation governs learning, Gagné maintains that learning is an important causal factor in development. Second, human learning is cumulative. That is, the learning of certain skills contributes to the learning of more complex skills. The result is an ever-increasing intellectual competence.

Third, human learning is both complex and diverse. That is, human learning cannot be reduced to either S–R associations or the insight experiences described by the Gestalt theorists. Instead, an adequate description of human learning must apply to, for example, masons, carpenters, astronauts, politicians, housewives, and word-processing operators. That is, the principles must generalize to the various situations and circumstances in which learning occurs. Learning, in other words, results in a variety of different behaviors, referred to as capabilities. Learning is the set of cognitive processes that transforms the stimulation from the environment into capabilities.

The Components of Learning

The essential components in a theory of learning, according to Gagné, must account for the diversity of human capabilities. In addition, theory must describe the processes by which the capabilities are acquired.

The Learning Framework

A major focus in Gagné's principles is the identification of categories or varieties of learning that reflect the range and complexity of human experience. According to Gagné (1984, p. 2), any set of categories that purports to describe human learning should meet at least four major criteria:

1. Each category should represent a formal and unique class of human performance that occurs through learning.

2. Each category should apply to a widely diverse set of human activities and be independent of intelligence, age, race, socioeconomic status, classroom, grade level, and so on.

3. Each category should require different instructional treatments, prerequisites, and processing requirements by the learner.

4. Factors identified as affecting the learning of each category should generalize to tasks *within* the category but not across categories (with the exception of reinforcement).

The five varieties of learning identified by Gagné meet the foregoing criteria. They are verbal information, intellectual skills, motor skills, attitudes, and cognitive strategies (Gagné, 1972, 1977a, 1985). Like the S–R associations and the insight experience, none of these categories may be reduced to the other. However, unlike associations and insight, they represent the range of human learning.

The five varieties represent the outcomes of learning. That is, they reflect the distinct types of skills or capabilities that individuals acquire as a result of learning. In addition, Gagné (1977a, 1985) has identified the internal states required in the learner to acquire the new skills. These states are referred to as the **internal conditions of learning**.

However, the conditions for acquiring new skills or capabilities are not all within the individual. Also important are the particular kinds of interactions between the learner and the external environment. Therefore, the third component in learning includes the types of environmental stimuli that are required to support the internal learning processes. These environmental supports are referred to as the **external conditions of learning**. (Gagné, 1974b, 1977a, 1985). They also are referred to as the events of instruction, and they are designed to support learning (Gagné 1977a, 1977b, 1985) (Figure 6.1). They are described further in the Principles of Instruction section. Discussed here are the five varieties of learning outcomes and the essential internal conditions for each category.

The Varieties of Learning

In the 1960s, attempts to identify instructional objectives led to an awareness that different classes of behaviors are acquired through learning. Efforts began with the identification of behavioral categories that consistently would indicate particular requirements for instruction (Gagné, 1965a, 1965b). However, accounting for the diversity of human learning in a systematic and comprehensive way is a difficult task. Some approaches attempted to reconcile laboratory learning descriptions and the behaviors taught in the classroom (Melton, 1964). For school subjects, Gagné (1972) noted that categories such as "cognitive learning," "rote learning," "discovery learning," and "concrete versus symbolic learning" often were used. The difficulty, however, is that these learning categories do not generalize to different settings. Examples may be classified as rote learning in one context and as conceptual in another (Gagné, 1972).

The five **varieties of learning** are summarized in Table 6.1. They are referred to as capabilities because they make possible the prediction of many instances of performance by the learner (Gagné & Briggs, 1979, p. 51). An individual who has acquired an intellectual skill, for example, can interact with the environment using symbols. Composing sentences, adding two-digit numbers, and identifying colors are all intellectual skills. In contrast, the student who has learned verbal information can restate or paraphrase definitions and major points in bodies of knowledge. Examples

FIGURE 6.1
Essential components of learning and instruction

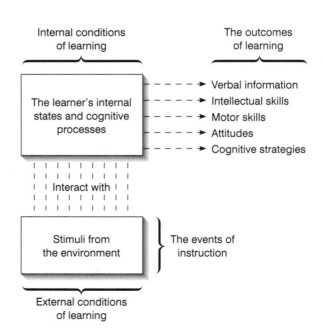

TABLE 6.1
Overview of the five varieties of learning

Category of Learning	Capability	Performance	Example
Verbal information	Retrieval of stored information (facts, labels, discourse)	Stating or communicating the information in some way	Paraphrasing a definition of patriotism
Intellectual skills	Mental operations that permit individuals to respond to conceptualizations of the environment	Interacting with the environment using symbols	Discriminating between red and blue; calculating the area of a triangle
Cognitive strategies	Executive control processes that govern the learner's thinking and learning	Efficiently managing one's remembering, thinking, and learning	Developing a set of note cards for writing a term paper
Motor skills	Capability and "executive plan" for performing a sequence of physical movements	Demonstrating a physical sequence or action	Tying a shoelace; demonstrating the butterfly stroke
Attitudes	Predisposition for positive or negative actions toward persons, objects, and events	Choosing personal actions toward or away from objects events, or people	Electing to visit art museums; avoiding rock concerts

include stating the formula for salt and defining *fulcrum*. However, the capability of stating information does not in itself imply that the individual can apply the information in new ways. In other words, the capability of defining *fulcrum* does not imply that one can identify different examples of fulcrums or use them in any way.

Verbal Information.   The capability represented by this category is that of acquiring (1) labels and facts, (2) meaningfully connected selections of prose or poetry, and (3) organized bodies of knowledge. *Declarative knowledge* is another term that also may be used, implying the capability to "declare" or "state" something (Gagné, 1984, 1985). In learning labels, for example, a consistent verbal response or "name" is applied to an object or an object class, such as "rose" or "tiger."

When a fact has been learned, the response is an oral or written statement of the relationships between two or more objects or events. "Columbus discovered America in 1492" and "Rectangles have four sides" are examples. Recalling selections such as the salute to the flag or Hamlet's soliloquy are longer verbatim reinstatements of particular words and phrases than the recall of a fact.

Larger bodies of knowledge also are learned as information. Examples include the biblical story of creation and the contents of a local ordinance on littering. The performance is slightly different from other forms of verbal information. Typically, the performance is that of paraphrasing or reporting a summary of learned information.

In summary, the nature of the learning outcome for verbal information may be defined as (1) the reinstatement in speech or writing of a word or series of words in the order presented or (2) the reconstruction of the organized presentation of a verbal passage, including the main and subordinate ideas (Gagné, 1984). Internal conditions for learning verbal information include a preexisting set of organized knowledge (referred to as a "cognitive structure" by David Ausubel) and strategies for processing (encoding) the new information.

Intellectual Skills.   The essential characteristic of intellectual skills is that they involve interacting with the environment using symbols. Instead of simply stating or paraphrasing information, the learner is making decisions about a variety of events. The range of capabilities that are intellectual skills includes everyday skills such as analyzing the evening news as well as applying the rules that govern speaking, writing, and reading. In mathematics, such skills are using the rules for computation, interpreting word problems, and verifying problem solutions (Gagné, 1984). Intellectual skills may be described as "the basic and, at the same time, the most pervasive structures of formal education" (Gagné & Briggs, 1974, p. 24).

Intellectual skills also are found in a host of occupations, such as a technician in a nuclear power plant or a computer programmer. In other words, intellectual skills are the capabilities that make human beings competently functioning members of society.

Unlike factual information, however, intellectual skills cannot be learned by simply hearing them or looking them up (Gagné, 1977a, p. 11). The major difference between information and intellectual skills is the difference between knowing *that* and knowing *how* (Gagné, 1974b, p. 55). The student learns how to add integers, how to make the verbs and subjects of sentences agree, and countless other skills (Gagné, 1974b). Each skill is that of interacting with the environment using a variety of symbols. Such symbols include numbers, letters, words, and pictorial diagrams.

Unlike the other four varieties of learning, intellectual skills include four discrete skills. From simple to complex, they are discrimination learning, the learning of concrete and defined concepts, rule learning, and higher-order rule learning (problem solving). These skills are discussed in the Learning Hierarchies section and are summarized in Table 6.3 (p. 145). Internal conditions of learning for any of the intellectual skills include (1) recalling prerequisite skills, (2) interacting in a variety of ways with the new learning, and (3) applying the new skills to a range and variety of different situations and contexts.

Motor Skills.   To a certain extent, all performances are "motor" (i.e., stating something, pushing a button, or pointing at something) (Gagné, 1984). Identifying a category that represents new learning, however, refers to activities such as fly casting, lariat twirling, using a typewriter, or others that have not been previously executed. Included are simple skills learned early in life, such as fastening clothing and executing communicable speech sounds (Gagné, 1977a). In the early years of schooling, important motor skills include printing and writing letters and symbols, skipping rope, and balancing on a beam. Later, motor skills include learning the separate skills involved in playing tennis, basketball, and other sports.

The common characteristic of all these skills is the requirement to develop smoothness of action, precision, and timing (Gagné, 1977a, 1985). Novice and expert performances differ in these qualities.

Three major phases may be identified in the learning of motor skills. First is the learning of the sequence of the movements in the skill, referred to as the executive routine (Gagné, 1984). Then practice enables all the parts of the skill to be fitted together. Finally, continued practice results in improved timing and smoothness of performance. Practice continued over long periods of time eventually leads to automatization of the skill. In other words, the skill can be executed in the presence of potentially interfering activities, such as the roar of the crowd at an athletic event.

The feature of motor skills that sets this category apart from the others is that such skills improve through practice. Repetition of the basic movements with feedback from the environment is essential for learning. It leads to the identification of the kinesthetic cues that signal the differences between inaccurate and error-free performance (Gagné, 1977a, p. 19).

Attitudes.   Capabilities that influence an individual's choice about the kinds of actions to take are attitudes. In other words, they are inferred internal states that appear to modulate behavior (Gagné, 1984). In general, attitudes are considered to include three different aspects. One is a cognitive aspect, that is, an idea or a proposition. The second is an affective aspect, the feelings that accompany the idea. The third is a behavioral aspect that pertains to the readiness or predisposition for action (Gagné, 1985, p. 222).

An important characteristic, however, is that attitudes do not determine specific acts. Rather, they only make classes of individual actions more or less likely to be engaged in (Gagné, 1977a, p. 231). For example, the student develops attitudes toward reading books or constructing art objects (Gagné & Briggs, 1979, p. 86).

In contemporary society, various institutions and individuals attempt to establish and modify attitudes. The most pervasive medium in this effort is television. Both commercials and other aspects of television, such as soap operas, influence attitudes toward the various problems of everyday life (Gagné, 1984).

In contrast to the other categories of learning, the specific conditions for learning attitudes are yet to be identified. One clear requirement, however, is that being told what to do does not facilitate learning (Gagné, 1984). Reading a printed message, such as "Avoid harmful drugs," is not expected to have any effect on a learner's attitude (Gagné, 1974a).

Efforts to establish attitudes directly, such as through emotional appeal or persuasive logic, also have been found to be ineffective. However, one essential component appears to be Bandura's (1977) concept of the human model of behavior (Gagné, 1984, 1986). When the model is perceived as admirable, powerful, and credible, learning is most effective (Gagné, 1986). Imitation of the model's actions is most likely to occur when the model receives reinforcement for his or her choices of action.

Important considerations for future research on technology include the precise effects of modeling via television (Gagné, 1986). Examples are the relation of the model to different viewers, the importance of the context in which the model appears, and the nature of the messages that are being sent to viewers (Gagné, 1986, p. 4).

Cognitive Strategies.   Prior to the extensive development in information-processing theories and cognitive theory, Gagné (1972) identified another category of skills essential for learning. Referred to as cognitive strategies, this category includes the capabilities that control the management of learning, remembering, and thinking. Other terms for these skills include *strategic knowledge* (Greeno, 1978) and *executive control processes.* Cognitive strategies also are similar to Skinner's (1968) self-management behaviors and Rothkopf's (1970) mathemagenic behaviors (Gagné, 1977a, 1985). Currently, cognitive theory uses the term *metacognition* to refer to these strategies. Metacognition, however, also includes one's knowledge about learning tasks and one's learning capabilities. Gagné's cognitive strategies, in contrast, describes skills.

Unlike verbal information and intellectual skills, which are directly content related, the object of cognitive strategies is the learner's own thought processes. Cognitive strategies influence the learner's attending to stimuli, the ways that learners encode information for memory storage, and the size of the "chunks" of information that are stored. They also influence the learner's search and retrieval strategies and the organization of the learner's responses. In addition, they enable the learner to choose the relevant verbal information and intellectual skills to apply during learning and thinking (Gagné, 1984).

Three levels of cognitive strategies may be identified. One is that of task-specific strategies. An example is telling children to remember a set of pictures by putting them into categories (Gagné, 1984). In some situations, such as troubleshooting equipment, specific strategies are particularly important. One is to weigh the difficulties and potential benefits of tests prior to their use (Gagné in Twitchell, 1991).

The second level includes general strategies that are applicable to a variety of tasks. An example is the general problem-approach strategy described by Greeno (1978). The strategy includes constructive search, limiting the problem space, and dividing a problem into parts.

A third level of cognitive strategy is that of a "strategy to select strategies" or an executive strategy (Gagné, 1980a). Success in problem solving, for example, has been found to be related to the learner's ability to shift strategies and even to consider each strategy in rapid succession to reach a solution. Current research has yet to determine whether learners can readily or quickly acquire strategies that enable them to review, select, and reject their available cognitive strategies and to persist in the search for the best strategy for a given stage of problem solving (Gagné, 1980a, p. 89). General observation indicates that a period of time, a variety of situations, and reflective thought are essential in the development of an efficient executive strategy.

Research indicates that the disadvantaged students in Chapter One programs, in particular, are most likely to need extensive strategy training (Brophy, 1988). Low-achieving students tend to rely primarily on rote memorization and other inefficient strategies. They also fail to organize their learning and tend to skip over material they do not understand (p. 262).

Summary

The framework of learning described by Gagné consists of (1) the five varieties of learning, (2) the cognitive processing phases, referred to as internal conditions, and

(3) the environmental supports for learning, referred to as external conditions of learning. The five varieties of learning are verbal information, intellectual skills, motor skills, attitudes, and cognitive strategies. Each category represents a unique class of performance that is learned, is independent of individual characteristics, generalizes across situations, and requires different instructional treatments.

Verbal information refers to the acquisition of labels, facts, meaningfully connected selections of text, and organized passages. Intellectual skills, in contrast, involve interacting with the environment using symbols. Motor skills consist of both simple skills, such as fastening clothing, and complex skills, such as those involved in playing tennis, basketball, and other sports. Attitudes, in contrast, are the states that influence an individual's choices about the kinds of actions to take in a situation. The fifth category, cognitive strategies, consists of the capabilities that control the management of learning, remembering, and thinking.

Internal Conditions of Learning

The five varieties of human capability are one component of Gagné's framework of learning. The other key component consists of the internal prerequisites for each type of learning and the set of internal learning processes. These cognitive processes are executed in somewhat different ways for each of the five varieties of learning.

Internal learning conditions are composed of (1) the learner's internal states that are required for the particular capability to be acquired and (2) the set of cognitive processes involved in learning. Internal states consist of the prerequisite skills and attitudes that influence the new learning.

Internal Prerequisites.   The two types of internal states required for learning are *essential* and *supportive prerequisites* (Gagné & Briggs, 1979; Gagné, Briggs, & Wager, 1988). Supportive prerequisites are the capabilities that facilitate learning, regardless of the type of outcome. An attitude of confidence in learning is an example. Verbal information, for example, requires a context of meaningful information for the new associations to be learned.

In contrast, essential prerequisites are particular skills that become an integral part of the new learning (Gagné & Briggs, 1979, p. 106). In other words, essential prerequisites are "folded into" the more complex skill when it is learned. An example is learning to discriminate between three-cornered geometric figures and those with four or more corners. This discrimination skill later becomes a part of the skill of classifying and labeling triangles. In contrast, learning a motor skill requires knowledge of the steps in the sequence and, if a complex skill, the related part-skills.

The essential prerequisites for a capability to be learned are obtained by analyzing the skill into the subskills that must be learned first (Gagné et al., 1988). For example, the task of "supplying the definite article" for writing a noun in German requires the skills of identifying gender and identifying number (singular or plural). They are component skills that become a part of the final task.

The Nine Phases of Learning.   Developments in cognitive psychology indicate that the learner's cognitive processes interact with the environment in several ways during learning. Included in these processes are the individual's perception of stimuli in the environment, the transformation of stimuli into codes to be remembered, and the later recall of stored information. Also important are the concepts "long-term memory" and "working memory." The memory system in which all our memories and learning are stored is long-term memory. In contrast, **working memory** is responsible for processing stimuli from the environment. It also is referred to as **short-term memory** because it has a limited capacity for holding information.

Gagné (1977a, 1985) has applied the cognitive processing concepts to his analysis of learning. He has identified nine stages of processing that are essential to learning and that must be executed in sequential order. The nine stages are referred to as **phases of learning** (Gagné, 1985). In this text, for the purposes of understanding the functions of the learning phases, the nine phases are categorized into three stages: (1) preparation for learning, (2) acquisition and performance, and (3) transfer of learning. The importance of these stages is that they are enacted in different ways for the different varieties of learning (see Table 6.2).

TABLE 6.2
Summary of the nine phases of learning

Description	Phase	Function
Preparation for learning	1. Attending	Alerts the learner to the stimulus
	2. Expectancy	Orients the learner to the learning goal
	3. Retrieval (of relevant information and/or skills) to working memory	Provides recall of prerequisite capabilities
Acquisition and performance	4. Selective perception of stimulus features	Permits temporary storage of important stimulus features in working memory
	5. Semantic encoding	Transfers stimulus features and related information to long-term memory
	6. Retrieval and responding	Returns stored information to the individual's response generator and activates response
	7. Reinforcement	Confirms learner's expectancy about learning goal
Transfer of learning	8. Cueing retrieval	Provides additional cues for later recall of the capability
	9. Generalizability	Enhances transfer of learning to new situations

Implementing the Phases of Learning

Preparation for learning sets the stage for the learning task, and these steps typically require only a few minutes. Acquisition and performance, however, are the "core events" that are responsible for the learning of the new capability. Depending on the complexity of the skill to be learned, these phases may require from one to several sessions. Finally, transfer of learning provides for retrieval of the new skill from long-term memory and generalizability of the skill to new contexts. Transfer of learning may take place a few days after acquisition of the new skill.

Preparation for Learning.   The initial phases of learning are attending, expectancy, and retrieval of relevant information and/or skills from long-term memory. These activities set the stage for learning. The learner first "takes in," or apprehends, the relevant stimulus, and an expectancy for learning is established. The stimulus may be the spoken or printed word, a still or moving picture, an object, or a human model. (Selection of stimuli to support learning is discussed later in the Selecting Instructional Events section.)

The importance of the learner's expectancy is that it represents the specific motivation of the learner to attain the learning goal (either set by others or self-selected) (Gagné, 1985, p. 78). Expectancy orients the learner toward goal accomplishment; thus, it enables the learner to select appropriate output at each subsequent stage of processing information. For example, if the learner has the expectancy of learning ways to find the resistances of electric circuits, certain characteristics of the circuit relevant to that goal will be processed and others will be ignored (Gagné, 1985, p. 78).

Expectancy is followed by the retrieval from long-term memory of previously learned capabilities essential to the new learning. In learning the concept "triangle," for example, the child first must recall that three-sided figures differ from other geometric shapes (discrimination learning).

Acquisition and Performance.   The four phases known as selective perception, semantic encoding, retrieval and responding, and reinforcement are here referred to as the core phases of learning. The first phase, *selective perception,* requires only a few seconds. In this phase, the learner transforms physical stimuli into recognizable features and permits the brief retention of those features in working memory so that encoding may occur.

The next phase, encoding, is the process whereby the stimulus features are given a conceptual or meaningful framework and then stored in long-term memory. This process is the central and critical stage in learning (Gagné, 1977a, p. 66). Without it, learning has not occurred.

The stored code may be a concept, proposition, or some other meaningful organization (see Gagné & White, 1978). In learning the concept "triangle," for example, the child encodes typical examples of triangles. For motor skills, however, the learner encodes a visual image of the skill and the executive routine required to enact the component performances.

The core events of learning conclude with performance and confirmation of the new learning. The learner *retrieves* the newly stored code from long-term memory and executes a *response*. If the child is learning the concept "triangle," he or she identifies examples of triangles that include various sizes, colors, and materials. For a motor skill, the student demonstrates the physical performance.

Feedback about the achievement of the learning goal is the next step. The feedback may be provided by the environment, or it may result from the learner's observation of his or her performance (Gagné, 1977a). The importance of the feedback, according to Gagné (1985, p. 79), is derived from Estes's (1972) concept of *reinforcement*. That is, feedback is reinforcing to the learner when it confirms that the goal has been attained or is close to being accomplished. In other words, feedback acquires reinforcing power by confirming the learner's expectancy.

Transfer of Learning. Providing for transfer of learning is important for two reasons. One is that the new learning should not be limited to one or two examples or situations. Instead, the learner should be able to generalize the capability to several new situations. This generalizability is known as *lateral transfer* (Gagné, 1985). For example, the learner should be able to pick out the triangles in a geometric painting, as well as those drawn on a sheet of paper.

Second, the importance of applying the new learning in several contexts also provides the learner with additional cues that later can be used in searching long-term memory for the new capability.

Acquiring additional cues for retrieval and generalizability may not immediately follow the other phases of learning. Short delays of a day or two may intervene between the initial learning and opportunities for transfer (Gagné, 1974b).

In summary, the cognitive processes required for learning include nine phases that translate physical stimuli from the environment into new capabilities. The set of nine learning phases is executed in different ways for each of the five varieties of learning.

Summary

The internal conditions of learning consist of the learner's internal states required to learn particular capabilities and the set of cognitive processes involved in learning. The two types of internal states are essential and supportive prerequisites. Supportive prerequisites facilitate learning whereas essential prerequisites are particular skills that become integral parts of the new learning.

The cognitive processes in learning consist of the nine phases of information processing that may be categorized into three general stages. They are preparation for learning, acquisition and performance, and transfer of learning. Each of these stages is important in learning new capabilities.

The Nature of Complex Learning

Gagné's analysis of learning includes two organizations of capabilities that represent complex learning. The two organizations are *procedures* and *learning hierarchies*.

Procedures

A set of different actions that must be executed in a sequential or steplike fashion is referred to as a procedure (Gagné, 1985, p. 262). Examples of procedures include writing a check, balancing a checkbook, parking a car, and changing a tire.

Procedures are organizations of skills that include both motor and intellectual skills. The motor skills in parallel parking, for example, include positioning the vehicle appropriately, backing at low speed in a certain direction, and turning the wheels straight from the turn (Gagné, 1977a, 1985). The intellectual skills include identifying the correct angle of approach, identifying alignment with the other car, and so forth. Learning the procedure involves learning to perform the discrete motor skills as well as learning the essential concepts and rules.

Some procedures, such as parking a car or changing a tire, require learning the step-by-step actions that constitute the total sequence. Others, however, require decisions about alternative steps at certain points in the procedure. This type is sometimes referred to as a **conditional procedure**. In such a procedure, the outcome of one step provides clues to the choice to be made in the next step (Gagné, 1977a, p. 271). When balancing a checkbook, for example, an individual first must determine if the checks are in numerical order. If not, the next step is to arrange the checks in sequence by date of issue.

Learning Hierarchies

Procedures are organizations of both motor and intellectual skills. Learning hierarchies, in contrast, are organized sets of intellectual skills only. The concept of cumulative learning is represented in the set of skills referred to as a **learning hierarchy**. Briefly summarized, a learning hierarchy is a set of subordinate skills or capabilities, such that each skill is essential to the learning of the next-higher skill. Figure 6.2 illustrates the subordinate skills for learning to subtract whole numbers. Subtracting when a single borrowing is required—skill VII, for example—is prerequisite to skills VIII, IX, and X, which involve several or successive borrowings across columns. In other words, in a valid hierarchy, a connection exists between two skills if the higher element cannot be learned without first learning the lower element (Gagné, 1977a, 1985).

Of importance in understanding learning hierarchies is that they are *psychological organizations of skills*. In other words, a learning hierarchy is neither a logical ordering of information nor a description of the ways in which verbalized knowledge is acquired (Gagné, 1968b). Within intellectual skills, four kinds of discrete psychological capabilities have been identified. They are **discrimination learning, concept learning** (both concrete and defined concepts), **rule learning**, and **higher-order rule learning** (problem solving). Each of these skills is an essential prerequisite to the next higher-order skill. They are summarized in Table 6.3.

At least two major implications for curriculum may be derived from learning hierarchies. One is that curricula may be designed to reflect "process" as opposed to content. In the development of "Science—A Process Approach," emphasis was on the skills involved in classifying, measuring, and predicting, rather than that of verbalizing the accomplishments of science (Gagné, 1968b).

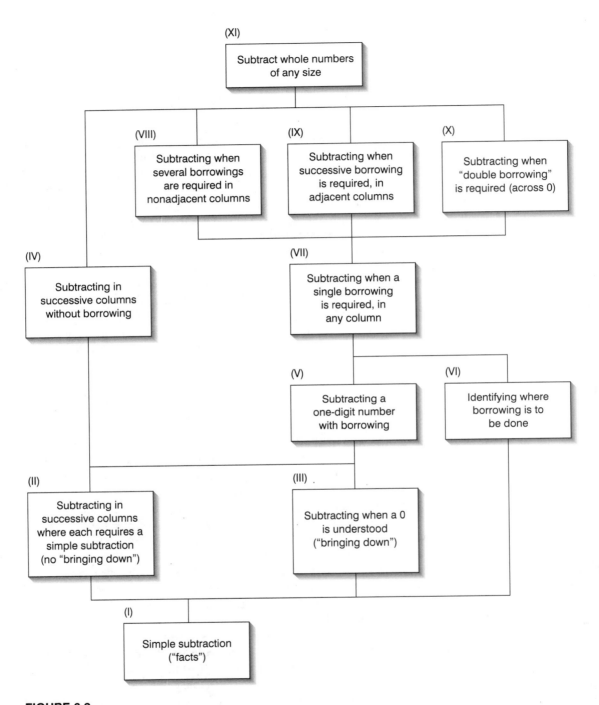

FIGURE 6.2

A learning hierarchy for subtracting whole numbers

Note: From *Principles of Instructional Design* by R. M. Gagné, 1974, New York: Holt, Rinehart and Winston. Copyright 1974 by Holt, Rinehart and Winston. Reprinted with permission.

TABLE 6.3
Summary of intellectual skills from simple to complex

Type of Skill	Description
Discrimination learning	Child responds differentially to characteristics that distinguish objects, such as shape, size, color
Concept learning	
Concrete concepts	Child identifies object or event as a member of a concept class; learned through direct encounters with concrete example, such as triangles
Defined concepts	Cannot be learned through concrete examples; acquired by learning a classifying rule, such as "liberty," "patriotism"
Rule learning	Student can respond to a class of situations with a class of performances that represents a relationship; for example, student responds to 5 + 2, 6 + 1, and 9 + 4 by adding each set of integers
Higher-order rule learning (problem solving)	Student combines subordinate rules in order to solve a problem; most effective learning strategy is guided discovery

The second implication is that careful attention to prerequisite skills may reduce greatly the need for remedial education. When remedial education is necessary, the case often is that some basic skill or set of skills has not been learned. When remedial students attempt problems using basic math operations, they typically make use of rules they have developed themselves—the wrong rules. Similarly, one of the major differences between good and poor readers is the lack of essential prerequisite skills (Gagné, 1982).

In summary, the two organizations of capabilities that represent complex learning are procedures and learning hierarchies. Procedures are sets of actions that must be executed sequentially, and they consist of both motor skills and intellectual skills. Learning hierarchies, in contrast, are organized sets of intellectual skills in which each skill is an essential prerequisite to the next higher skill. The intellectual skills are discrimination learning, concept learning, rule learning, and higher order rule learning or problem solving.

PRINCIPLES OF INSTRUCTION

Robert Gagné framed his analysis of the conditions that affect human learning from the perspective of the question, "What factors really can make a difference in instruction?" (Gagné, 1985, p. xiii). This view derives from the realization that children's experiences play a major role in their development. This heavy dependence of learning on environmental circumstances implies a great responsibility for society because the situations in which learners are placed have great effects on them (Gagné, 1985,

p. 1). These situations may encourage the development of great artists and scientists, or they may inhibit the development of the human intellect (Gagné, 1977a, p. iv).

As a result of the perspective from which the theory was developed, the transition from the principles of learning to the principles of instruction requires no translation. The five varieties of learning as outlined in Table 6.3 are capabilities that are the outcomes of school learning. Similarly, the essential internal states for each of the five varieties are important prerequisites for school learning. Finally, each of the nine phases of learning is supported by a particular type of event during classroom instruction.

Basic Assumptions

The importance of instruction is a major consideration in Gagné's discussions of learning. His assumptions about classroom learning therefore include the nature of instruction and the process referred to as instructional design.

A Definition of Instruction

Learning can occur whether or not instruction is present (Gagné, 1987a, p. 400). However, each of the learning processes may be influenced in some way by events external to the learner. When these events are deliberately planned to support learning, they are referred to as *instructional events.* An important characteristic of instruction is that these external events occur in the context of the learner's internal control processes. Therefore, the external events do not *produce* learning; instead, they can only support the learner's internal processing (Gagné, 1974a).

A second characteristic of instruction is that it does not have a single unitary purpose. Instead, instruction has several functions that correspond to the different information-processing phases of learning. That is, an external event appropriate for one phase may be inappropriate or irrelevant for another phase (Gagné, 1974a). An instructional event to arouse attention, for example, is different from one to provide transfer of learning.

Third, decisions about instruction must be made in the context of the skill or skills to be learned. Instruction for information, for example, is not the same as instruction for motor skills. Therefore, the question, Is this example of instruction good? cannot be answered. Instead, the relevant question is, Is this instruction good for learning (information, intellectual skills, motor skills, attitudes, cognitive strategies)? (Gagné, 1974a).

The Nature of Instructional Design

The focus in Gagné's principles is on instruction rather than simply teaching. The intent is to address all the events that may directly influence an individual's learning (Gagné & Briggs, 1979). In addition to teaching, instruction may be delivered by print materials, pictures, television, computers, and other media. The design and development of instruction in such detail is an essential element of the larger enterprise known as **instructional systems design** (Gagné, 1987a, p. 400).

Five assumptions support Gagné's recommendations for designing instruction (Gagné & Briggs, 1979). First, instruction should be planned to facilitate the learning of an individual student. Although students often are grouped for instruction, learning takes place within the individual. Therefore, the needs of the learner are placed in the planning sequence prior to grouping.

Second, both immediate and long-range phases are included in the design of instruction. The teacher or instructional designer plans daily lessons, but the lessons occur within the larger segments of units and courses, which also must be planned. Third, instructional planning should not be haphazard or provide merely a nurturing environment. Such a course of action can lead to the development of individuals who are not competent. In other words, to influence human development as much as possible, instruction should be designed systematically (Gagné & Briggs, 1979, p. 5).

Fourth, instruction should be designed using the systems approach. The systems approach to planning is defined as the organized, sequential selection of components that makes use of information, data, and theoretical principles as input at each planning stage (Gagné et al., 1988, p. 15). At each step in the development process, the prospective outcomes are checked against the goals originally established by those who will implement the final product. In the last step, the product is tested in real-world situations both during development and at the completion of the development process.

In designing curriculum and instruction, the application of the systems approach should begin with the analysis of needs, continue with the development of goal statements, and then proceed step by step to develop the instruction. Empirical evidence is then obtained about the effectiveness of the instruction in order to revise the materials. Tryout and revision continue until the standards established for the instruction are met.

Finally, instructional design should be developed from knowledge about how human beings learn (Gagné & Briggs, 1979, p. 5). These five assumptions are consistent with Gagné's definition of instruction. Specifically, instruction has several functions that correspond to the different information-processing phases of learning. Equally important, decisions about instruction should be made in terms of the skills to be learned.

The Components of Instruction

The various kinds of capabilities and the ways of analyzing the different learning requirements are combined by Gagné (1985) in a theory of instruction. The cornerstone of the theory is the designation of the five varieties of learning. They serve as a frame of reference to identify the capability or capabilities to be learned for a particular lesson. Instructional outcomes in the form of performance objectives are developed first. Then instruction is planned using the set of nine instructional events that support the nine phases of learning.

Designing Performance Objectives

All five varieties of learning reflect important outcomes for school learning. Motor skills are found in physical education and dance and also are subcomponents of other school subjects. Examples include the physical skills in printing and writing. In contrast, cognitive strategies and attitudes include hoped-for outcomes. Specifically, they are developing the learner's management strategies and fostering positive, self-confident attitudes toward learning.

The content of the curriculum is for the most part represented by the learning of information and the acquisition of intellectual skills, regardless of the subject area. Performance objectives for these two varieties of learning are found in all courses in the curriculum.

The function of performance objectives for instruction is that they are unambiguous statements of the capabilities to be learned. Terms such as *understand, comprehend,* and *appreciate* should be replaced with more precise terms that clearly communicate the skill or attitude to be acquired. An example of a performance objective is "The student demonstrates, by solving verbally stated examples, the addition of positive and negative numbers" (rule learning) (Gagné et al., 1988, p. 124).

Because each of the five learning varieties represents a different class of performances, the verbs used also will differ. For example, *states* or *defines* are appropriate verbs for information objectives. However, they are not appropriate for intellectual skills that require learner decision making and interaction with the subject matter. Instead, depending on the level of intellectual skill, verbs such as *selects, classifies, demonstrates,* or *solves* are needed. (See Table 6.4 for a listing of sample verbs.)

Stating capabilities to be learned as performance objectives fulfills two important functions in the school setting: (1) the needs of instruction are identified, and (2) the method of testing is determined. That is, different capabilities are both taught for and tested in different ways. Specifically, verbal information may be tested by asking the student to define or state the particular item of information. The testing of intellectual skills, however, requires that the student (1) interact with the stimulus situations using symbols and (2) respond to a new set of situations that are not the same as those used in instruction.

TABLE 6.4
Suggested verbs for the varieties of learning

Capability	Verbs
Information	States, defines, paraphrases
Motor skill	Executes, performs, enacts, pronounces
Attitude	Chooses to . . . , freely elects to . . . , selects (a preferred activity)
Cognitive strategy	Originates (a strategy)
Intellectual skills	
Discriminate	Selects (same and different)
Concept	Identifies (examples), classifies (into categories)
Rule	Demonstrates, predicts, derives
Higher-order rule	Generates (a problem solution), solves

Selecting Instructional Events

As a guideline for planning instruction, nine instructional events have been identified. Their function is to support the learner's cognitive processes during learning. For example, saying "Today we are going to learn to figure earned run averages of baseball players" (stating the objective) assists the student to establish the purpose and key elements of the events that are to follow (expectancy for learning). Similarly, providing hints or cues can facilitate the encoding and storage of the new learning in long-term memory. Table 6.5 lists the instructional events for each of the nine learning phases.

Preparation for Learning.   Gaining attention, informing the learner of the objective, and stimulating the recall of prior learning are three instructional events that set the stage for new learning. Gaining the learner's attention may be accomplished by asking a provoking question, depicting an unusual event, or appealing to a child's particular interests. For example, a lesson on the Earth's atmosphere may begin with a question, such as "Did you know that one of the things we breathe every day is sulfuric acid?" (Gagné & Driscoll, 1988, p. 73). The teacher may say, "Today we are going to learn why leaves change colors and fall from the trees" or "Let's find out why the liquid changes colors when certain drops are added." The answer to the initial question or the response to the unusual event provides closure and informs the learner of the new objective (event 2).

The importance of informing students of the objective should not be underestimated, particularly for elementary school children. Research reported by Peterson (1988) indicated that most of them are unable to determine the skills and concepts

TABLE 6.5
Relationships between learning phases and instructional events

Description		Learning Phase	Instructional Event
Preparation for learning	1.	Attending	Gain learner's attention through unusual event, question, or change of stimulus
	2.	Expectancy	Inform the learner of the objective
	3.	Retrieval (of relevant information and/or skills) to working memory	Stimulate recall of prior learning
Acquisition and performance	4.	Selective perception of stimulus features	Present distinctive stimulus features
	5.	Semantic encoding	Provide learning guidance
	6.	Retrieval and responding	Elicit performance
	7.	Reinforcement	Provide informative feedback
Transfer of learning	8.	Cueing retrieval	Assess performance
	9.	Generalizing	

to be learned from their academic tasks. Typically, they report that the goal, particularly for seatwork, is to get the task finished (p. 323).

Next, to prepare the student for a new level of learning, the instruction should stimulate the recall of important prerequisites (event 3). Relevant information, concepts, and rules, such as how plants make food, may be needed. Recall is stimulated through the use of questions such as Do you remember . . . ? or What did we do yesterday that might help us answer this question?

Materials and objects also may stimulate recall. In a unit on linear measurement, children were given sticks of different lengths. Then they were asked to think about using the sticks to measure the height of a box (Gagné & Briggs, 1979, p. 167). Recall of the skill of counting numbers was initiated as each of the children used a particular length of stick to determine height.

Acquisition and Performance.   The core phases of learning are selective perception, semantic encoding, retrieval and responding, and reinforcement. Each of these four phases also is supported by a particular instructional event. Specifically, the four events are presenting distinctive stimulus features, providing learning guidance, eliciting performance, and providing feedback.

The stimulus characteristics, or situations with which the learner is to interact during instruction, are presented first. Next, specific situations accompanied by hints or prompts as needed are presented to the learner. This activity is that of providing learning guidance. The communications to the learner should stimulate a particular direction of thought and therefore prevent the learning from getting off the track (Gagné & Briggs, 1974, p. 129).

Providing learning guidance is a critical event in instruction (Gagné, 1980b). First, it helps the learner transform the new capability into a code for later recall. Second, it "makes the difference between learning that is facile and learning that is hard; and also between learning that is relatively effective and learning that is ineffective" (Gagné, 1980b, p. 61).

To determine the effectiveness of encoding, the learner's performance of the new skill is elicited. Feedback is then provided that indicates either necessary corrections or provides reinforcement by confirming that the objective has been achieved.

The core events, in particular, should be flexibly implemented for different kinds of learning. For example, instruction for the concept "circle" may include a variety of circles of different colors or sizes (presenting the stimulus). Examples made of string or rope also may be used (Gagné & Briggs, 1974, p. 129). In addition, the children might be asked to join hands and form a circle.

Then the children may be presented with a variety of pictures and other examples that include different geometric figures. They may be asked to look carefully at each picture in the set and to decide which ones represent circles. Hints or prompts concerning the characteristics of circles may be provided by the teacher as each picture is introduced and included in the set (providing learning guidance).

After identification with teacher assistance of several circles, the children may be asked to point to examples in a new set of geometric figures or pictures (eliciting performance). Incorrect identifications are followed by reminders about the characteristics of circles and comparisons with the examples already identified (providing informative feedback).

In contrast, if the objective is that the students are to discover a rule, the core instructional events are executed somewhat differently. For example, the task may be to discover the rule of prime numbers. The rule is that these numbers are divisible only by one set of factors (the number itself and the number 1).

The student first may be asked to recall that any number can be expressed as the product of various factors (e.g., $4 = 2 \times 2$; 4×1). Then the student may be presented with a succession of numbers from 1 to 15 and asked to write out all the various factors for the set of numbers (presenting distinctive stimulus features). The learner is asked next if the factors for any of the numbers vary in any way (learning guidance). However, this suggestion may not be sufficient for the student to discover that certain numbers are divisible only by themselves and 1. The student then may be asked the differences between the numbers 3, 5, 7, and 4, 8, 10 (Gagné & Briggs, 1974, p. 129). Learning guidance in the form of questions and prompts continues in this way until the learner discovers the prime numbers.

Retrieval and Transfer.   The concluding segment of instruction provides for assessment of the new learning followed by cues for retrieval and transfer. For assessment, new situations or examples should be presented to students to be certain that learning is not restricted to only a few examples.

Then instruction should conclude with stimuli specifically designed to enhance retention and transfer. This phase may take the form of spaced reviews after a reasonable delay of a day or more following the initial learning (Gagné, 1974b). For example, if the student has learned to define *legislative* with regard to the U.S. Congress, the spaced reviews may include the meaning of *legislative* with regard to state and city lawmaking bodies (Gagné, 1974b, p. 116).

In summary, teachers and instructional designers select verbal statements, questions, objects, diagrams, and other stimuli to stimulate the learner's internal processing. These stimuli are selected to meet the requirements of the nine instructional events.

Applicability to the Learning Varieties.   Each of the nine instructional events supports a particular phase in the learning process. However, these events are executed in somewhat different ways for each of the five varieties of learning. Table 6.6 illustrates the unique external conditions (requirements for instructional events) for the five learning varieties.

As indicated, specific requirements for instructional events vary for preparation for learning, the core events, and learning transfer. For example, in introducing instruction for attitudes, the teacher does not inform students of the objective but must first establish respect for the model who is to execute the desired behavior. In contrast, introducing instruction for intellectual skills requires stimulating the recall of the prerequisite discriminations, concepts, or rules that are subcomponents of the new skills to be learned.

Also important is that the instructional events should not be treated as an ironclad sequence. Learning a complex concept, for example, may require cycling through the

TABLE 6.6
Unique external conditions of learning for the five varieties

	Preparation for Learning	Core Instructional Events	Transfer of Learning
Verbal information	Relate new content to learner's framework of information.	Provide meaningful context of information for encoding. Provide elaborations, imagery, or other encoding cues. For bodies of knowledge, present information so that it can be learned in chunks.	Give cues for effective retrieval and generalization.
Intellectual skills	Stimulate recall of prerequisite skills.	Provide varied concrete examples and rules. Provide opportunities for interacting with examples in different ways. Assess in new situations.	Use a variety of contexts and novel situations to promote transfer.
Cognitive strategies	Elicit recall of necessary intellectual skills.	If task-specific, describe the strategy; if general, demonstrate the strategy. Provide opportunities for strategy practice with support and feedback.	Provide unfamiliar problems for strategy use.
Motor skills	Show performance of skill to be learned. Stimulate recall of part-skills, if appropriate.	Establish executive subroutine and provide for mental rehearsal. Arrange several repetitions of skill with corrective feedback.	Supply opportunities for performing skill in new physical setting.
Attitudes	Learner is *not* directly informed of the objective. Establish that learner respects the model.	Provide respected model(s) who enact positive behavior and reinforce the model. When learner enacts the behavior, provide reinforcement.	Provide opportunities for learner to continue to enact behavior, and provide reinforcement.

core events two or three times, given the number of criteria essential for identifying concept examples. The instructional plan presented later in this chapter is an example.

Although the instructional events were developed for teacher and other media-directed instruction, Flynn (1992) observed them in a fourth-grade cooperative learning environment. The teacher set the stage (preparation for learning), and the core events of instruction occurred in peer interactions in small groups. Flynn (1992) suggests that these events contribute to the effectiveness of the cooperative learning model over large-group instruction because the group interactions provide enhanced opportunities for their occurrence.

In summary, instructional events are selected for performance objectives based in large measure on the variety of learning represented by the objective. However, events are included as needed for the types of students and complexity of the information, skill, strategy, or attitude to be learned.

The Role of Media in Instruction

The term *media* typically conjures up images of computer-assisted instruction, instructional television, videocassette recordings, and similar mechanized delivery systems. However, instructional media also include the teacher's voice, printed text, and real objects; in short, any physical means that communicates an instructional message (Gagné & Briggs, 1979; Reiser & Gagné, 1983).

The typical approach to media selection is to choose a media form and then plan the instruction. However, this approach is deficient in two ways. First, research on media utilization indicates that no one medium is universally superior to all others for every type of learning outcome for all learners (Gagné et al., 1988, p. 204). Therefore, to choose arbitrarily a computer, television, or some other medium for a lesson is to ignore factors such as learner characteristics and task variables that can influence the effectiveness of a particular delivery system. Computer-assisted instruction, for example, can provide the interactive tutoring capability for the core events in intellectual skills for some learners. For example, it can provide the practice in basic skills that is essential for children in grades K–3 (Gagné in Twitchell, 1991). Further, interactive videodiscs can provide instruction on intellectual skills and cognitive strategies. Harvard Law School, for example, has developed interactive videodiscs in which students learn direct and cross-examination skills in a tenant–landlord case, applications of search and seizure law, and so on (Miller, 1990). Television or film, however, does not include this capability but can provide the meaningful context required for verbal information.

Second, the arbitrary selection of media can result in the omission of essential instructional events. A film or audiotape, for instance, may provide content but exclude instructional events such as providing learning guidance or pauses for student responding and feedback (Gagné et al., 1988, p. 199). Also, with a few notable exceptions, many of the computer materials developed for the public school classroom are inadequate examples of instruction. For example, the majority of computer exercises labeled "simulations" are either competitive games or drill-and-practice exercises accompanied by animated graphics (Gredler, 1986). Like other models of media selection, the model developed by Reiser and Gagné (1983) first provides for the identification of a range of appropriate choices and then narrows the choices to one or two.

Criteria to be considered first are the nature of the learning outcome and the characteristics of the learners. For example, computer instruction, interactive television, and interactive videodisc instruction are three possible choices for an intellectual skill. Then important learner characteristics, such as age and extent of reading comprehension, are considered. Interactive television may be selected for nonreaders, for example.

The next step is to review the choices for the capability of providing the required instructional events. The final selection is based on practical factors, such as cost, size of the group to be accommodated at one time, and ease of implementation.

The media selection model is useful for expanding one's thinking about the various types of media for instruction. It is particularly useful when the same unit of instruction will be replicated several times with similar groups of students.

Summary

Application of the nine instructional events to the five varieties of learning leads to differences in instruction for the different learning outcomes. Elaboration, imagery, and methods for encoding chunks of information are sufficient core events for verbal information. However, they are not appropriate for intellectual skills. Instead, students must interact with situations and examples in a variety of ways. Attitude change, in contrast, depends on respected models and reinforcement for positive behaviors.

Also important in the use of instructional events to plan instruction is that they are not an ironclad sequence. Once the instructional events are identified, media may be selected. In other words, one does not first select media, such as television or the computer, and then design instruction. Instead, media are selected to fit the requirements of particular instructional events.

Designing Instruction for Complex Skills

Defining each capability to be learned in the form of a performance objective and selecting the appropriate instructional events are important steps in the design of instruction. Also important, however, is providing for the cumulative nature of human learning. Thus, Gagné (1977a) describes the methods by which instruction is to be developed for organizations of complex skills. As described earlier, the two types of capabilities organized from simple to complex are procedures and learning hierarchies. Instructional planning for these two different organizations of skills occurs in somewhat different ways.

Instructional Design for Procedures

The first step in developing instruction for complex skills is to determine the set of skills to be taught. For a procedure, each separate step is identified first. For example, for the procedure of changing a tire, the identified sequential skills include removing the wheel cover, placing a block under the other wheel, using the jack to raise the wheel, and so on (Gagné, 1977a, p. 360).

The motor skills in the sequence are then analyzed into part-skills that also may need to be taught. An example is the skill of backing up a car, which is an essential step in parallel parking. Stopping the car at the right point so that it is neither too close nor to far away from the curb is a part-skill in backing up a car.

For some procedures, choices between alternative steps may be required. For example, one step in reconciling a bank statement with check records is to determine if the checks are numbered. If the answer is yes, the checks are arranged in numerical order. If the answer is no, the checks are arranged by date of issue (Gagné, 1977a, p. 262). Both alternatives must be included in the instruction.

After the skills and part-skills are identified, the type of capability of each skill is identified. Performance objectives then are written for the skills and part-skills, and instruction is planned for the set of objectives.

Instructional Design for Learning Hierarchies

The task of deriving a learning hierarchy is not necessarily an easy one (Gagné & Briggs, 1974, p. 112). Correct identification of subordinate skills requires the identification of component mental operations, not the identification of items of information (p. 113).

Essential prerequisites for the intellectual skills are determined by the method referred to as **learning task analysis** (Gagné & Briggs, 1979). This method, essentially a questioning approach, is first applied to the most complex skill to be taught; it asks What simpler skill is essential to the learning of the present skill? The key to the identification of the immediate prerequisite is the word *essential*. Many simpler skills may be identified that are not integral components of the skill to be learned. The prerequisite skill is the one that must be recalled by the student if the learning is to proceed rapidly and without difficulties.

An example is the skill "subtracting a one-digit number with borrowing" in Figure 6.2 (p. 144). An immediate prerequisite skill is "subtracting when a zero is understood (bringing down)." Learning to subtract zero from a one-digit number is essential to learning to subtract one-digit numbers that do not require borrowing.

The importance of learning task analysis is illustrated by the objective "converting Fahrenheit to Celsius temperature readings" (Gagné & Briggs, 1974, p. 113). One might be tempted to identify a prerequisite as "knowing that $C = \frac{5}{9}(F - 32)$." This statement, however, is an item of information. In contrast, the prerequisite skills include "finding numerical values of an unknown variable by solving equations" and "substituting numerical values of variables in equations to yield a single numerical value for a variable" (p. 113).

Each skill identified by the questioning procedure also is subjected to the same question to determine the next simpler set of prerequisites. This analysis by questioning is repeated until a logical endpoint is reached for the particular group of learners. The logical endpoint is the set of prerequisite skills that the students already have learned. These skills are identified as the entry capabilities for the unit or course of instruction.

Each skill to be taught then is categorized as to type of capability and is written in the form of a performance objective. The relevant verbal information and attitudes also are identified and written as performance objectives. Instruction is developed for each objective, using the instructional events described earlier.

EDUCATIONAL APPLICATIONS

Programs in several areas have implemented the concepts of component subtasks and prerequisite skills. For example, Reading Recovery, a program for the poorest readers, has found that understanding basic concepts about print is essential to success in reading instruction. Among the basic concepts are identifying the front of the book, indicating that print (not pictures) carries the message, identifying the purpose of the spaces between words, and so on (Clay, 1999). In arithmetic, Griffin, Case, & Siegler (1994) found that a significant number of low-income inner-city children lack central essential prerequisites for beginning formal arithmetic. They also use maladaptive strategies, such as counting up from neither addend in a simple addition problem. The essential capabilities, which most middle-income children acquire prior to school, include counting reliably, quantifying sets, matching sets of numbers, and correctly identifying the larger and smaller numbers in a pair (p. 37).

Classroom Issues

Gagné's approach to the analysis of learning is from the perspective of the needs of instruction. As a result, his work addresses several issues of importance in the classroom.

Learner Characteristics

Individual differences, readiness, and motivation are issues for both the systems approach to designing instruction and the classroom teacher. Gagné (1974b, 1980a) and Gagné and Briggs (1979) discuss these issues with regard to both instructional design and the delivery of instruction.

Individual Differences.   The effectiveness of instruction is influenced by several kinds of individual differences among students. Included are differences in cognitive strategies and rate of learning. Particularly important, however, are differences in student entry capabilities (Gagné, 1974b) (see the Readiness section). Entry capabilities are "the raw materials with which instruction must work" (Gagné, 1974b, p. 125). They may be assessed at several beginning points within the curriculum, such as the beginning of a school year or the start of a new course or unit.

Methods of compensating for individual differences in the delivery of instruction include small-group instruction, the tutorial mode, independent learning (Gagné, 1974b), and individualized instructional systems (Gagné & Briggs, 1979). The advantage of individualized systems is that they are delivery systems for adjusting instruction to the individual student in a group of 25 or more (Gagné & Briggs, 1979, p. 261).

Readiness.   For Gagné (1968a, 1977a), developmental readiness is viewed as the individual's relevant capabilities. Readiness is not a matter of maturation in which certain growth changes must take place before learning can occur (referred to as the growth-readiness model; Gagné, 1968a). Nor is readiness a matter of the gradual internalization of logical forms of thought as Piaget (1970) suggested. Both of these models, Gagné notes, have assigned a secondary role to the influence of learning in human development. However, because learning is cumulative, readiness for new learning refers to the availability of essential prerequisite capabilities. As discussed earlier, readiness includes the lower skills in the hierarchy of intellectual skills and the essential rules, concepts, and part-skills in procedures.

Motivation.   Designing effective instruction includes the identification of student motives and the channeling of those motives into productive activities that accomplish educational goals (Gagné, 1977a, p. 287).

Although often treated as a single characteristic, motivation includes both general and specific types. General motivational states include David McClelland's achievement motivation (1965) and R. W. White's competence motivation (1950) (Gagné,

1977a). More specific types include incentive motivation and task motivation, both of which may be developed through the careful use of reinforcement contingencies. That is, reinforcement for the activities of working with other children, relating to school tasks, and for mastery and accuracy can establish incentive motivation (Gagné, 1977a).

Cognitive Processes and Instruction

Gagné's analysis of learning is conducted from the perspective of the factors that make a difference in instruction. Therefore, the issues of transfer of learning, the students' self-management skills, and the teaching of problem solving are integral components of the conditions of learning.

Transfer of Learning.   The concept of learning transfer is the heart of Gagné's model of cumulative learning. First, Gagné describes essential prerequisites for each of the five varieties of learning. Second, the essential prerequisites within intellectual skills provide for transfer in two ways. They contribute to the learning of the next higher-order skill, and they also generalize to other situations. Examples include the skills of adding, subtracting, multiplying, and dividing whole numbers and fractions.

    The sequence of nine instructional events also includes attention to transfer of learning. At the conclusion of learning, cues are provided for retrieval of the capability, and new situations are introduced to which the student applies the skill.

Learning "How-to-Learn" Skills.   These skills are the cognitive strategies identified by Gagné (1972, 1977a). They are the ways that the individual manages his or her learning, remembering, and thinking. Gagné notes that improving students' how-to-learn skills so that each student is "working up to potential" is one of the challenging problems for education (Gagné, 1977a, p. 36).

Teaching Problem Solving.   According to Gagné (1977a, p. 34), the process of problem solving is one in which the learner discovers how to combine some previously learned rules to generate a solution to a problem that is new to the learner. Teaching problem solving requires that (1) the necessary rules are already acquired by the learner, and (2) a problem situation is presented to the learner that he or she has not encountered before (Gagné & Briggs, 1979, p. 71). The learner, in generating the solution, engages in "discovery learning" in that he or she must select from memory the appropriate rules and combine them.

    Problem solving, although it includes discovery learning, differs from the solving of novel problems suggested for cognitive strategies. In cognitive strategies, the learner is *originating* a solution that may require the selection of information from a variety of sources and the combining of information in novel ways. In the problem solving included in intellectual skills, the learner is *generating* a solution that requires the recombination of previously learned related rules. The result is a higher-order rule.

The Social Context for Learning

The methods recommended by Gagné (1977a) and Gagné and Briggs (1979) focus on the design of instructional systems rather than on the development of models of teaching. A major difference between the two is that models of teaching place the teacher or other individual in the role of conducting and/or managing instruction for some identified group of learners. Instructional systems, in contrast, often include sets of materials and activities for which the pacing and management of instruction may reside in the learner. As a result, the context for learning with regard to instructional design is discussed in terms of the effects on the management of instruction (Gagné & Briggs, 1979). That is, the differences in the implementation of instructional events among the tutoring situation, small-group instruction, and large-group instruction are described. Gagné and Briggs also discuss the implications of different entry capabilities of students for each of these contexts.

Relationships to Other Perspectives

Unlike prior theorists, Gagné began his analysis with the various skills and capabilities that humans enact in diverse situations. Noting that some theories had identified at least part of the complex picture of human learning, his conditions of learning incorporate the Gestalt concept of partial insights and guided discovery in the description of intellectual skills, and the modeling plus reinforcement component from Bandura's theory in the description of attitudes.

Gagné's conditions of learning also is a bridge between the behavioral focus of operant conditioning and the cognitive approaches to learning. That is, learners acquire responses and environmental events (the events of instruction) are essential to learning (behavioral principles). However, the responses reflect different kinds of internal capabilities and require different internal states (mental events). Further, the variety of learning referred to as cognitive strategies is also reflected in the information-processing concept referred to as metacognition.

Like operant conditioning, the sequence of instruction in the conditions of learning is teacher-directed and managed, and moves toward a predetermined outcome for learners. Thus, it differs from social constructivism in which the community of learners, with input from the teacher, largely determines the direction and depth of learning. It also differs from the cognitive perspectives which, although discussing internal processing activities of the learner and instructional supports, often do not specify the learning outcome.

Developing a Classroom Strategy

According to the systems approach, the design of a classroom lesson is one component of a total process that includes both curriculum and instruction. Therefore, ideally, developing particular lessons is preceded by design at the curriculum and course levels.

The Systems Design Model

Systems models for instructional design are characterized by three major features. First, instruction is designed for specified goals and objectives. Second, the development of instruction utilizes media and other instructional technologies. Third, pilot tryouts, materials revision, and field testing of the materials are an integral part of the design process. In other words, systems models specify objectives, design the instruction, and try out the materials with students, revising the instruction until the desired achievement is produced. The design, tryout, and revision process is the major characteristic of systems models; the development is a "closed loop" process.

The systems model described by Gagné and Briggs (1979) includes all the stages in the design of curriculum and instruction (Figure 6.3). It begins with needs assessment and the development of goal statements. The model also entails the development of end-of-course objectives, specific performance objectives, instructional events, selection of media, and field testing of the final product.

One important feature of the model is that it places lesson development within the total context of curriculum design. In so doing, it extends the concept of cumulative learning beyond instruction to the curriculum level. The relationship between learning at the instructional and course levels is illustrated by the following set of objectives:

1. *Course objective.* The student can critically analyze events and situations in a country's judicial, governmental, economic, and political systems, consistent with that country's identified priorities.

2. *Unit objective.* The student can demonstrate the relationships between political and economic systems.

3. *Specific subskill.* The student can classify systems as "political" or "economic."

FIGURE 6.3
Summary of the phases in the Gagné–Briggs systems design model

In the design model, the term *formative evaluation* (step 11) refers to materials tryout with small groups of students. The purpose is to identify areas in the instruction that are not working effectively and to revise them. After these changes are made, field testing is undertaken with a large group. Minor changes in the materials may be required after the field test. Finally, summative evaluation (step 13) assesses the materials with a typical population. This evaluation certifies the objectives that are met by the instruction and identifies the population for which the materials are effective.

Designing the Lesson.   The complete systems model is designed for curriculum development that includes both courses and units of instruction. However, the principles are applicable to the design of individual lessons.

Step 1: Write or select performance objectives.

> **1.1** What is/are the culminating skill(s) to be learned at the end of the lesson?
>
> **1.2** What are the related subordinate skills? If learning to use a rule is the end-of-lesson skill, what are the supporting concepts? If a cognitive strategy is to be learned, what are the related intellectual skills?
>
> **1.3** Determine which of the supporting skills are entry skills to the lesson and which are to be taught as part of the lesson.
>
> **1.4** Select appropriate verbs for the skills to be taught and write in the form of performance objectives.

Step 2: Select instructional events for each of the performance objectives.

> **2.1** Identify the variety of learning for each objective. If intellectual skills, identify as to discrimination skill, concept learning, rule learning, or higher-order rule learning.
>
> **2.2** Identify entry skills and particular characteristics of the group to be taught (e.g., average or poor reading ability).
>
> **2.3** Given 2.1 and 2.2, select instructional events to meet the unique learning conditions for each objective (see Table 6.6).

Step 3: Select media for instructional events.

> **3.1** Identify several choices that meet the requirements for the particular learning outcome.
>
> **3.2** Eliminate media inappropriate for the age and/or reading level of the learners.
>
> **3.3** Make final media choices for instructional events based on cost, size of the group, and ease of implementation.

Step 4: Develop tests for the objectives.

> **4.1** Write 4 to 8 items per objective that reflect the performance stated in the objective. For example, for "identifying the main idea," select several short paragraphs with a set of possible choices for each.
>
> **4.2** Assemble the items for each objective into a test and check for length and item difficulty.

Classroom Example

The lesson in Table 6.7 is an example of instruction designed for the objective of identifying the main idea. The lesson builds on a concept learned previously, that of topic. The lesson illustrates the use of the nine instructional events in specific classroom activities.

Note that in step 4, presenting distinctive stimulus features, the teacher presents core information that illustrates the defining rule of the concept of main idea. This information is applied first by the teacher and then by the students in the identification of concept examples.

The use of the game in step 4 provides a chance for the children to try out their new skills prior to assessment of their performance. The game thus provides a source of feedback other than the teacher.

During the lesson, instructional events 5, 6, and 7 are repeated to give the children experience with two types of statements often confused with the main idea. The two types are general statements that do not describe the topic and specific details. Each type is contrasted separately with examples of the main idea so that the children may clearly understand the differences.

Retention and transfer is provided a few days after the initial instruction using a discussion of the children's favorite television programs. The children receive additional cues for later recall at this time.

This lesson illustrates an important characteristic of effective instruction. Too often, too much information is presented to the learner too quickly. Confusion and mislearning often result. In this lesson, one new feature of the concept is presented at a time, with practice by the learner at each stage.

The lesson also demonstrates the major requirements for intellectual skills. Specifically, they are the integration with prior information and the learner's interaction with symbols.

Review of the Theory

Prior learning theorists developed explanations of the learning process in the laboratory and extended the findings to the human situation. Robert Gagné, in contrast, began with the complexity and variety that characterizes human learning and developed a system to account for that variety.

Gagné's analysis yielded five categories or varieties of learning that are distinguished by different performances and different requirements for learning. The five varieties are verbal information, intellectual skills, cognitive strategies, attitudes, and motor skills. In addition, intellectual skills include four discrete skills that form a hierarchy from discrimination learning to higher-order rule learning (problem solving). Unlike other designations, such as "rote learning" or "conceptual learning," the five varieties cut across school subjects, ages of learners, and grade levels.

Each learning variety requires a different set of internal and external conditions for acquisition of the particular capability. Internal conditions include (1) the necessary prerequisite skills and (2) the nine phases of cognitive processing required for learning. External conditions are the events of instruction that support the learner's cognitive processes.

TABLE 6.7

Classroom example

Capability to be learned: The students can identify statements that represent the main idea for short selections (fourth- and fifth-graders).

	Instructional Event	Medium for Instruction	Classroom Activity
1.	Gaining attention	Teacher communication	Teacher asks students to name their favorite TV show or story.
2.	Informing learner of the objective	Teacher communication	Teacher asks the children if they know how to tell someone what the show (story) is about without retelling the story. Teacher explains that they are going to learn how to find the main idea of story so they can tell a friend what the story is about.
3.	Stimulate recall of prior learning	Teacher communication	Learners asked to recall the term *topic* (who or what a story is about).
4.	Present distinctive stimulus features	Transparency and teacher communication	*Transparency:* TOPIC + SOMETHING SPECIAL ABOUT THE TOPIC = MAIN IDEA Example: Three Little Pigs Main idea: The three pigs (topic) built houses, and the wolf blew down all except the brick house. Teacher explains why the statement is the main idea.
5.	Provide learning guidance	Transparencies and group discussion	*Transparencies:* Brief situations plus set of three statements about each. In each set, one choice is the main idea; others are specific details. Teacher and student discuss options and reasons for correct choices. Students are divided into groups and play the game "Natural Topics" (Bell & Weikert, 1985, pp. 78–83). Students take turns drawing game cards, each of which has three statements, and select the main idea. Tokens are moved on a game board—one space for easy answers, two for more difficult choices.
		Academic game	

6.	Elicit performance	Print material	Children are given brief situations, each with several choices from which they select the main idea.
			Example: Movie *E.T.*
			Choices: The main idea is:
			  A. E.T. rode on the handlebars of Elliott's bicycle.
			  B. E.T. was left on Earth and wanted to go home, although he had friends on Earth.
			  C. E.T. hid in a closet full of toys in Elliott's house and was hard to tell apart from the toys.

7. Provide feedback	Group discussion and teacher communication	Class discusses the answers

Instructional events 5, 6, and 7 are then repeated, with the difference that the other statements about the story are not details; they are general statements. However, they do not describe "something special" about the topic.

Example: A short selection describes edible grasses and includes wheat, rice, hay, and their uses as food.

Choices: The story is about:
A. how to eat grass.
B. how grass grows.
C. the uses of grass.

Instructional events 5, 6, and 7 are then repeated, using a wide selection of statements that may represent the main idea.

Example: A short selection describes three rings (topic), how they are formed, and what they tell us about a tree's growth.

Choices: The story as a whole is about:
A. tree rings that are close together.
B. how rain makes trees grow.
C. how tree rings tell about trees.

8. Assess performance	Print material	Children are given several short reading selections with choices for main ideas (general and specific), and they select the sentence that tells what the whole story is about.
9. Provide retention and transfer	Group discussion	Children talk about the stories and the TV shows mentioned in instructional event 1. The teacher introduces several choices for the main idea of each, and the children as a group make a decision about the main idea during a class discussion.

A major goal of Gagné's theory is the planning of effective classroom instruction. The skills to be learned are written in the form of performance objectives and the variety of learning is identified. Task analysis is then used to identify prerequisite skills, and instructional events are selected for each objective to be taught.

Disadvantages

The theory was developed to account for the range of psychological processes observed in prior research on learning and to specify precisely the sequence of instructional events for the identified processes. Thus the theory is easier for a curriculum design team to implement than for the classroom teacher to use (Table 6.8).

TABLE 6.8
Summary of Gagné's conditions of learning

Basic Elements	Definition
Assumptions	Within the parameters established by growth, development is the result of the cumulative effects of learning.
	Learning is characterized by more than a single process, and these processes cannot be reduced or collapsed into one.
Learning	The phases of information processing supported by stimulation from the environment executed for the different kinds of learning.
Learning outcome	An internal capability manifested in a particular performance for each of the kinds of learning.
Components of learning	*Five varieties of learning:* verbal information, intellectual skills, cognitive strategies, attitudes, and motor skills
	Internal conditions of learning: prerequisite skills and the nine phases of information processing
	External conditions of learning: the events of instruction
Designing instruction for complex skills	Provide instructional events for the sequences of skills in procedures and learning hierarchies
Major issues in designing instruction	Identification of capabilities to be learned; task analysis of objectives; selection of appropriate instructional events
ANALYSIS OF THE THEORY	
Disadvantage	Difficult for the classroom teacher to implement without special training
Contributions to classroom practice	Provides a mechanism for designing instruction from simple to complex; identifies the psychological processes in cumulative human learning
	Accounts for the diversity of human learning
	Links instructional events to specific phases in information processing

Contributions to Classroom Practice

The best-known contribution of the theory is that it operationalizes the concept of cumulative learning and provides a mechanism for designing instruction from simple to complex. The concepts of cumulative learning, task analysis, and the identification of component skills have become accepted curriculum components.

CHAPTER QUESTIONS

1. A classroom teacher is developing a unit on solving for the areas of plane geometric figures. She presents two formulas, $A = lw$ and $A = w \times \frac{1}{2} l$. She then uses the formulas to solve for the area of two rectangles and two triangles. The students are given several problems to complete for homework. According to Gagné's theory, what are some of the things that the teacher has done wrong?

2. Classify the following objectives as to the variety of learning. If the objective is an intellectual skill, identify the type.

   _____ a. The learner can classify paintings as examples of cubism, impressionism, or realism.

   _____ b. The computer analyst can debug computer programs for errors in program commands.

   _____ c. The suburbanite voluntarily takes recyclable garbage to a community reclamation site.

   _____ d. The student can develop a set of logical arguments to support U.S. trade restrictions to other civilized countries.

3. Identify at least two prerequisites for skills (b) and (d).

4. Discussions continue as to whether Head Start and other preschool programs are successful in reducing subsequent school failure. From Gagné's perspective, what key question should be asked in this debate?

REFERENCES

Airasian, P. W., & Bart, W. M. (1975). Validating a priori instructional hierarchies. *Journal of Educational Measurement, 12,* 163–173.

Bandura, A. (1977). *Social learning theory.* Upper Saddle River, NJ: Prentice Hall.

Bell, I. W., & Wieckert, J. E. (1985). *Basic media skills through games* (Vol. 1, 2nd ed.). Littleton, CO: Libraries Unlimited.

Brophy, J. (1988). Research linking teacher behavior to student achievement: Potential implications for instruction of Chapter One students. *Educational Psychologist, 23*(3), 235–276.

Clay, M. M. (1999). An observation survey of early literacy achievement. Portsmouth, NH: Heinemann.

Estes, W. K. (1972). Reinforcement in human behavior. *American Scientist, 60,* 723–729.

Flynn, J. L. (1992). Cooperative learning and Gagné's events of instruction. *Educational Technology, 32*(10), 53–60.

Gagné, R. M. (1962a). The acquisition of knowledge. *Psychological Review, 69*(4), 355–365.

Gagné, R. M. (1962b). Military training and principles of learning. *American Psychologist, 17,* 83–91.

Gagné, R. M. (1965a). The analysis of objectives. In R. Glaser (Ed.), *Teaching machines and programmed learning: II. Data and directions* (pp. 21–65). Washington, DC: National Education Association.

Gagné, R. M. (1965b). *The conditions of learning.* New York: Holt, Rinehart & Winston.

Gagné, R. M. (1968a). Contributions of learning to human development. *Psychological Review, 75*(3), 177–191.

Gagné, R. M. (1968b). Learning hierarchies. *Educational Psychologist, 6,* 1–9.

Gagné, R. M. (1970). Some new views of learning and instruction. *Phi Delta Kappan, 51,* 486–472.

Gagné, R. M. (1972). Domains of learning. *Interchange, 3*(1), 1–8.

Gagné, R. M. (1974a). *Expectations for school learning.* Bloomington, IN: Phi Delta Kappa.

Gagné, R. M. (1974b). *Essentials of learning for instruction.* Hinsdale, IL: Dryden.

Gagné, R. M. (1977a). *The conditions of learning* (3rd ed.). New York: Holt, Rinehart & Winston.

Gagné, R. M. (1977b). Instructional programs. In M. H. Marx & M. E. Bunch (Eds.), *Fundamentals and applications of learning.* New York: Macmillan.

Gagné, R. M. (1980a). Learnable aspects of problem solving. *Educational Psychologist, 15*(2), 84–92.

Gagné, R. M. (1980b). Preparing the learner for new learning. *Theory into Practice, 19*(1), 6–9.

Gagné, R. M. (1982). Learning from the top down and the bottom up. *Florida Educational Research Journal, 24,* 1–10.

Gagné, R. M. (1984). Learning outcomes and their effects: Useful categories of human performance. *American Psychologist, 37*(4), 377–385.

Gagné, R. M. (1985). *The conditions of learning* (4th ed.). New York: Holt, Rinehart & Winston.

Gagné, R. M. (1986). Instructional technology: The research field. *Journal of Instructional Development, 8*(3), 7–14.

Gagné, R. M. (Ed). (1987a). *Instructional technology: Foundations.* Hillsdale, NJ: Erlbaum.

Gagné, R. M. (1987b). Peaks and valleys of educational psychology. In J. A. Glover & R. R. Ronning (Eds.), *Historical foundations of educational psychology* (pp. 395–402). New York: Plenum.

Gagné, R. M. (1989). *Studies of learning: Fifty years of research.* Tallahassee, FL: Learning Systems Institute.

Gagné, R. M., & Briggs, L. J. (1974). *Principles of instructional design.* New York: Holt, Rinehart & Winston.

Gagné, R. M., & Briggs, L. J. (1979). *Principles of instructional design* (2nd ed.). New York: Holt, Rinehart & Winston.

Gagné, R. M., & Driscoll, M. P. (1988). *Essentials of learning for instruction.* Upper Saddle River, NJ: Prentice Hall.

Gagné, R. M., & White, R. T. (1978). Memory structures and learning outcomes. *Review of Educational Research, 48*(2), 187–222.

Gagné, R. M., Briggs, L. J., & Wager, W. W. (1988). *Principles of instructional design* (3rd ed.). New York: Holt, Rinehart & Winston.

Gredler, G. R. (1992). *School readiness: Assessment and educational issues.* Brandon, VT: Clinical Psychology Publishing Company.

Gredler, M. B. (1986). A taxonomy of microcomputer simulations. *Educational Technology, 26*(3), 36–40.

Greeno, J. (1978). Nature of problem-solving abilities. In W. Estes (Ed.), *Handbook of learning and cognitive processes* (pp. 239–270). Hillsdale, NJ: Erlbaum.

Griffin, S. A., Case, R., & Siegler, R. S. (1994). Rightstart: Providing the central conceptual prerequisites for first formal learning of arithmetic to students at risk for school failure. In K. McGilly (Ed.), *Classroom lessons: Integrating cognitive theory and classroom practice* (pp. 25–49). Cambridge, MA: MIT Press.

Jonassen, D. H., Tessmer, M., & Hannum W. H. (1999). *Task analysis methods for instructional design.* Mahwah, NJ: Lawrence Erlbaum.

McClelland, D. C. (1965). Toward a theory of motive acquisition. *American Psychologist, 20,* 321–323.

Melton, A. W. (Ed.). (1964). *Categories of human learning.* New York: Academic.

Miller, E. J. (1990). In videodisc veritas: Interactive video at Harvard Law School. *T.H.E. Journal,* March, 78–80.

Peterson, P. (1988). Selecting students and services for compensatory education: Lessons from aptitude-treatment interaction research. *Educational Psychologist, 23*(4), 313–352.

Piaget, J. (1970). Piaget's theory. In P. H. Mussen (Ed.), *Carmichael's manual of psychology* (pp. 703–722). New York: Wiley.

Reiser, R. A., & Gagné, R. M. (1983). *Selecting media for instruction.* Englewood Cliffs, NJ: Educational Technology.

Rothkopf, E. Z. (1970). The concept of mathemagenic activities. *Review of Educational Research, 40,* 325–336.

Skinner, B. F. (1968). *The technology of teaching.* New York: Appleton-Century-Crofts.

Twitchell, D. (Ed.) (1991). Robert M. Gagné and M. David Merrill in conversation. *Educational Technology, 31*(1), 34–40.

White, R. T. (1974). A model for validation of learning hierarchies. *Journal of Research in Science Teaching, 11,* 1–3.

White, R. W. (1950). Motivation reconsidered. The concept of competence. *Psychological Review, 66,* 297–333.

CHAPTER 7
Cognitive Perspectives:
I. The Processing of Information

The brain is not a passive consumer of information. . . . The stored memories and information-processing strategies of our cognitive system interact with the sensory information received from the environment, selectively attend to this information, relate it to memory, and actively construct meaning for it (Wittrock, 1990, p. 348).

Development of the digital computer illustrated the ways a complex machine uses a set of instructions to engage in complex tasks, such as playing chess. This development led to the view of the mind as a set of processes for operating on symbols. Early research, based on computer-related models of memory structures, addressed the sequence of mental operations and the products (information) in the performance of a cognitive task (Anderson, 1990).

Criticisms of the computer-related models, which did not adequately address the human capabilities involved in constructing meaning, led to new research directions. The view of learners as active constructors of knowledge who can understand and control the learning process has led to a gradual shift toward studying learning in educational settings (Brown & Campione, 1994, p. 231). Current research includes the ways that individuals develop meaning from text and other information sources, and the ways that learners organize knowledge.

Theorists and researchers also address the development of metacognition and problem solving. These capabilities are the complex skills addressed by the cognitive perspective and they are discussed in Chapter 8.

PRINCIPLES OF LEARNING

Information-processing theory, which addresses the basic steps in the ways individuals obtain, code, and remember information, is the central theory of the cognitive perspective. However, unlike Skinner's operant conditioning and Gagné's conditions of learning, information-processing does include some variations. Nevertheless, researchers who adopt this perspective share the broad assumption that individuals transform much of the information impinging on the senses from the environment into memory codes that are stored for later use. From this foundation, researchers developed particular assumptions about the nature of human memory and the ways that knowledge is represented in memory. Essential components of learning are the organization of information to be learned, the learners' prior knowledge, and the processes involved in perceiving, comprehending, and storing information.

Basic Assumptions

Two key assumptions support information-processing research. They are (1) the memory system is an active organized processor of information and (2) prior knowledge plays an important role in learning. Related to these basic assumptions are beliefs about (1) the nature of the human memory system, (2) the ways that specific knowledge items are represented in long-term memory, and (3) the organization of bodies of knowledge in long-term memory.

The Nature of Human Memory

The early conception of human memory was that it served simply as a repository or passive collector of information over long periods of time. In the 1960s, however, researchers began to view human memory as a complex system that processes and organizes all our knowledge. It is not a passive repository; instead, it is a system that is both organized and active. That is, human memory actively selects the sensory data that are to be processed, transforms the data into meaningful information, and stores much of that information for later use. Four different perspectives on the nature of human memory are (1) the multistage model, (2) the state concept, (3) levels of processing, and (4) the connectionist perspectives. The dominant perspective, however, is the multistage concept.

The Multistage Concept.

The conceptualization of an active memory system was influenced by Broadbent's (1958) initial description of a multistage memory. The current general model, derived from a computer metaphor, assumes that information is processed in sequential stages that are linked to particular memory systems. The structures described in the multistage concept, however, are functional, not neurophysiological. That is, they are not locations in the brain where processing activities occur. These structures are the sensory registers, short-term memory, and long-term memory (see Figure 7.1). The various processing steps are managed by an executive control that keeps track of information, determines the activities to be undertaken, and monitors the allocation of resources to the processing components.

A vast array of physical signals impinges on the sensory system, which is primarily visual and auditory. Many of these signals are not processed, some are retained only briefly in the sensory registers (0.5–2.0 seconds), and some are selected for further processing. Information that is selected for further processing then enters **short-term** or **working memory**. Here much of the information is encoded into some meaningful form and transferred to **long-term memory** for per-

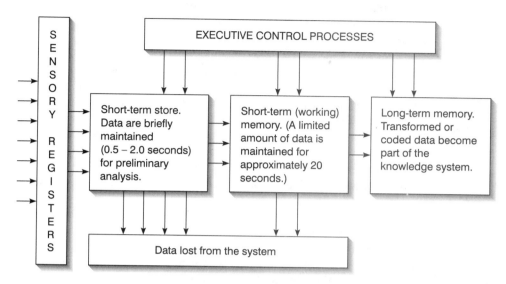

FIGURE 7.1
Early conceptualization of the human memory as a structural system

manent storage. Some information in short-term memory, however, is present only for immediate utilization and is not processed further. An example is a little-used telephone number that is looked up and retained only until the call is completed.

Criticisms of the model include (1) the lack of research confirmation of the capacity of the structures and (2) the portrayal of brain functioning in terms of constancy, rather than incorporating the wide variations that occur. (Edelman, 1987). That is, the processes illustrated in Figure 7.1 do not adequately capture the range and variety of the ways the brain functions. Also, another view is that mindful procedures are brain products, not processes (Iran-Nejad, Marsh, & Clements, 1992). Nevertheless, the processes associated with these systems, which are discussed in this chapter, are useful in addressing issues involved in learning.

The multistage model describes a single, long-term store for human memories. In contrast, Tulving (1985) describes memory as composed of a number of systems, each of which serves a different purpose and operates with different principles. The three major types of memory identified by Tulving are episodic, semantic, and procedural. Semantic memory includes general knowledge, such as the words of a poem, telephone numbers, concepts, and definitions. Semantic memory makes possible the construction of mental models of the world by the individual. Procedural memory enables the organism to respond adaptively to the environment (Tulving, 1985, p. 387).

In contrast, personal or autobiographical information (i.e., events experienced by the individual) are stored in episodic memory. Included are childhood memories, the hurricane one survived last year, and the movie that was seen last week. The unique characteristic of items in episodic memory is that each is identified by a personal "tag." Typically, such memories are recalled through association with a particular time or place.

Applied to education, the identification of episodic memory directs attention to the individual, subjective characteristics of students' learning experiences in the classroom (Martin, 1993, p. 177). Mundane classroom experiences may merge together so that later episodes are indistinguishable from earlier ones. However, the learning of procedures or concepts that are particularly difficult have the potential to be mediated by particularly memorable classroom episodes (Martin, 1993).

The State Concept.   Other current models of human memory also address the differences between short-term and long-term memory. However, the focus has shifted from that of storage bins to the nature of the process. In the model illustrated in Figure 7.2, information is either in an inactive or active state. (In other words, short-term memory is a temporary active state rather than a structure).

The concept of working memory as the active state of information accounts for such activities as looking up a telephone number and memorizing a poem. The digits of the telephone number have already been learned, and looking up and repeating the number establishes new connections among the digits. This information is active until the call is completed, then the sequence is forgotten. The digits, however, remain in long-term memory, while only the particular set of connections between them is lost.

Memorizing a poem also establishes new connections, and this activity is accomplished in working or short-term memory. However, the new connections are established between many already-learned words that typically are new expressions of thoughts, ideas, or images. In contrast to the telephone number, both the words and their new connections are retained in an inactive state from which they may be later recalled.

The conceptualization of short-term memory as the active state of information also permits the accommodation of qualitatively different processes. Included are the activation of automatic processes involved in skills learned to a high degree of proficiency as well as the events that require selective attention. Carrying on a conversation with a friend while driving to work is the activation of information in memory that requires selective attention (the conversation) as well as the activation of an automatic process (operating the car). Because the automatic process does not

FIGURE 7.2
Activation of information from long-term memory to short-term memory

require conscious attention, short-term memory can also accommodate the ongoing conversation with friends.

Levels of Processing.   Craik and Lockhart (1972) proposed levels of processing as an alternative to the multistage model. Basically, a memory is a by-product of perceptual analysis that occurs in a series of sequential, hierarchical stages or levels. They are sensory analysis, pattern recognition, and semantic association. For example, the lines of the letters may be processed in a word first, then the pronunciation of the word, and finally, the meaning (Neath, 1998). However, Craik (1979) subsequently concluded that the suggestion of a fixed, linear series of analytic levels was not supported by research. Instead, subjects often engage in both bottom-up (beginning with details) and top-down (conceptual framework) processing in no particular sequence.

One problem with the levels of processing perspective is that the term "depth" has been interpreted in more than one way. Craik (1979) defined the term as referring to *qualitative* changes in processing, not quantitative differences (such as number of associations with other information). However, the term has been viewed in the literature in various ways, including effort expended in processing, order of processing, and greater expertise in developing meanings (Craik, 1979). A related problem with the concept is differentiating sensory or "shallow" processing from deep processing. For example, is pictorial information sensory or does it convey meaning?

The major problem, however, is that a key assumption of the model is circular (Neath, 1998). Specifically, the assumption is that deeper levels of processing lead to better memory. When researchers document better memory, they credit it to a deeper level of processing (p. 115). The problem is that depth of processing cannot be measured independently from the amount of information that is remembered. The importance of the levels of processing perspective, however, like the Gestalt perspective before it, is that it directed attention to the perceptual actions of the subject during learning.

Connectionist Networks.   *Connectionist networks* are also known as neural networks or parallel distributed processing (PDP). Briefly, connectionist networks consist of simple processing units (nodes) and the links between the nodes. (These networks differ from Thorndike's connectionism, which consists of stimulus-response pairs). The concept of such networks, in which nodes (thoughts) fire impulses through the connections to other nodes was first proposed by William James (1890; Neath, 1998). James was intrigued by the "restless flight" of one idea before another and conceptualized a network to account for the rapid generation of different thoughts.

Current connectionist models for the structure of cognition approximate the networklike appearance of the brain. Memory consists of interacting connection nets composed of elements (units) and links referred to as connection weights. Knowledge is stored in the connection weights that also modulate the transfer of activity from one unit to the next (Schneider & Graham, 1992). Also, unlike the multistage concept discussed earlier, connectionist models do not include an executive controller or processor.

One way to think of connectionism is the Frisbee/rubber band analogy described by Bereiter (1991). Imagine a hundred or more Frisbees connected to each other by rubber bands of various lengths and thicknesses piled in the middle of a bare room. Each wall contains a clamp that can hold a Frisbee. If any four Frisbees are each clamped to one wall, an oscillation goes through the system as the four Frisbees pull on each other and all the other Frisbees (p. 12). When the oscillations cease, some of the Frisbees will be high off the floor, some will be on the floor, and some will sag limply. The distance of each Frisbee above the floor is its level of activation, and the resulting pattern is referred to as the output pattern.

Three defining characteristics of connectionist models are (1) processing occurs in populations of simple elements (the Frisbees), (2) all knowledge is stored in the connection weights between the elements (the rubber bands), and (3) all the elements perform simple computations on their inputs and compute a nonlinear transformation on the inputs to produce outputs. This process contrasts with symbolic perspectives of cognition (such as the procedural knowledge discussed in the following section), which typically involve rules and elaborate algorithms (Schneider & Graham, 1992, p. 516). Learning, in the connectionist view, involves modifying the connection weights among certain units to produce a different output pattern, in other words, knowledge is stored in the connections.

Developers of connectionist models (e.g., McClelland & Rumelhart, 1986) note that many activities, such as interpreting language, require the processing of information from several sources at once. Further, only the connectionist models account for such events. That is, multiple processing occurs simultaneously because information is stored in the strengths between the connections instead of in the form of static patterns. The models maintain that, in reading, for example, letter and word recognition and recognition of constraints are occurring and interacting simultaneously. Referred to as *parallel distributed processing,* this activity, according to the models, accounts for the instant recognition of **THE CAT** as "the cat."

Bereiter (1991) notes that some models, referred to as "symbolic connectionist" models, use elements (Frisbees) that represent concepts or propositions (Holyoak, 1991; Thagard, 1989). Although these models sidestep the issue of how the symbolic representations are acquired, the models function as people often do. That is, they illustrate the gradual change from vagueness (or imprecise impressions) to clarity that is found in much of human thought (Bereiter, 1991, p. 13).

Nevertheless, some limitations of connectionist models should be noted. First, the need for a physical agent to alter the connection weights (rubber bands) disqualifies them as explanations for autonomous learning by the brain (Bereiter, 1991). Computer simulation programs of connectionist models have "learned" the past tense of verbs and to pronounce text. However, the initial random connection weights in these simulations must be mechanically changed by the designer (Iran-Nejad, Marsh, & Clements, 1992). Second, connectionism uses the networklike appearance of the brain as a basis for representing cognition. However, there is no evidence that indicates the brain's physical network is the key to complex thinking (p. 481).

The Representation of Knowledge

The mechanisms with which the human memory system functions are a major issue in the information-processing perspective. Another and equally important issue is the nature of the symbolic form in which information is stored in memory. Early views described the representation of specific items of information in memory. Later perspectives address the organization of larger bodies of knowledge.

Representation of Specific Items. The record of information that is stored is not a literal copy of the stimulus input because the physical signals received by the senses are not perfect representations of the world. Therefore, to be remembered, the physical signals must be transformed in some way.

Two major views on the form of stored information have been proposed. One is the dual-code model proposed by Paivio (1971, 1983, 1986). The other perspective maintains that information is stored in verbal form only.

The Dual-Code Model. The essential characteristic of the **dual-code model** is that information may be stored in long-term memory in nonverbal as well as verbal form. The model describes two functionally independent, although interconnected, systems for the processing and storing of information. Abstract objects and events that do not refer to concrete, tangible objects or events are stored in verbal form. Examples are "success," "soul," "truth," and "ability." In contrast, nonverbal representations include environmental sounds, actions, visceral sensations, and other nonlinguistic objects and events. Examples include the sound of church bells, drawing lines, or pressing keys, and a clenched jaw or racing heart (Clark & Paivio, 1991).

Some events and objects, such as "house," that have both concrete and abstract characteristics may be coded in both systems. The overall likelihood of the activation of verbal or nonverbal representations depends upon the combined effects of the presented stimulus (verbal or objects/pictures), instructions, and other contextual stimuli and individual differences in abilities to process visually or verbally (Paivio, 1986, p. 69).

The importance of nonverbal encoding is reflected in the greater recall of concrete over abstract text and items in list memory tasks (Paivio, 1983; Clark & Paivio, 1991). The explanation of the dual-code model for imagery effects is the additive effects of imagery and verbal codes. Moreover, when separate elements are integrated into a compound image, a partial cue can later reactivate the total representation (Clark & Paivio, 1991).

Critics of visual imagery maintain that information storage in picture form would exceed the storage capacity of the brain and also would require a "perceiver" in the brain to "read" the pictures (Pylyshyn, 1973). However, the visual encoding theorists maintain that the stored codes are not pictures but rather are analog representations or analog memories. That is, the images are structurally related to the real objects in the same sense that keys and locks are related (Shepard, 1978). Physically, keys and locks are quite different; however, only the correct key will open a particular lock. Similarly, only particular objects will activate the neural processes with which the object is represented.

Verbal Representations. The theorists who advocate verbal representations in long-term memory do not question the importance of imagery in the processing of information for later recall. However, they maintain that the ultimate representation of information is in verbal form and that images are reconstructed from verbal codes.

Two types of knowledge are represented in verbal form. One, declarative knowledge, is stored in the form of verbal networks. The other, procedural knowledge, is stored in the form of condition–action pairs.

Declarative Knowledge.   Influenced by Noam Chomsky's work in linguistics, the early models describe stored information as base strings (Tom is tall) plus related comparative information. An early network model developed by Quillian (1968; Collins & Quillian, 1968) used nodes to portray concepts and superordinate concepts. Properties of each concept, such as "has four legs," "has fur," and "is a predator," were attached to the concept by links or pointers. Deficiencies in Quillian's model in accounting for retrieval times as well as other problems led to the development of other network models.

The common dimensions of currently accepted structural networks are "nodes" and "links." The nodes represent central conceptual components joined (linked) to various relationships that may include features, properties, functions, other concepts, and facts (DiVesta, 1987, p. 212). The critical feature of these representations is that knowledge is composed of ideas linked by relations.

The network organization proposed by John R. Anderson (1983; 1990) is composed of propositions. Formally defined, a proposition is "the smallest unit of knowledge that can stand as a separate assertion; that is, the smallest unit about which it makes sense to make the judgment true or false" (Anderson, 1990, p. 123). Examples include "Mary is my sister" and "The Cadillac is beautiful." In other words, propositions are "atomic units of meaning" (Anderson, 1990, p. 143). Other proposed models of human memory describe a fixed architecture (as does Anderson) whereas others differ on the processing components (unitary or multicomponent) (see Miyake & Shah, 1999).

Procedural Knowledge.   Briefly, *procedural knowledge* is knowing how to execute a particular task or activity, such as parallel parking a car. Procedural knowledge may range from simple tasks, such as unlocking a door, to complex activities, such as using word processing software on a computer. According to the theorists, procedural knowledge is encoded in the form of condition–action pairs that are if–then statements (Anderson, 1993; Newell & Simon, 1972). For example, *if* a plural subject, *then* the present tense of the verb "to be" takes the form of "are."

Organizations of Knowledge

The dual-code concept, verbal representations, and condition–action pairs describe hypothesized representations of specific information in long-term memory. Researchers, particularly those investigating school learning, often are interested in the ways that individuals acquire and make use of bodies of information or knowledge. Among the terms used in the research literature are prior knowledge, domain knowledge, schema, content-specific knowledge, and topic knowledge. Reviews of the uses of the terminology in the literature indicated that explicit definitions of terms typically are missing (Alexander, 1992; Alexander, Schallert, & Hare, 1991). However, analyses of implicit uses, by Alexander et al. (1991), clarified the relationships among some of the various terms. The analysis first identifies two broad categories of knowledge, tacit and explicit. Then the components of explicit knowledge, referred to as conceptual and metacognitive, are described.

Tacit and Explicit Knowledge.

A large part of an individual's knowledge is tacit (Alexander, 1992; Alexander et al., 1991). Specifically, tacit knowledge is implicit and typically operates below the level of conscious awareness. Sociocultural knowledge, such as the appropriate ways to treat one's elders, are an example.

Another form of tacit knowledge is scripts. First described by Schank and Abelson (1977), scripts contain the general information found in familiar frequently experienced events. For example, included in a "going to the movies" script are going to the theater, buying the ticket, buying refreshments, finding a seat, seeing the movie, leaving the theater, and going home. In the school setting, the first few weeks of the fall term in elementary school address the socialization of the children according to the scripts for the major events in the school day.

Research indicates that babies, by 7 months of age, show recall of caretaking scripts, such as teeth brushing and bath and peek-a-boo games (Ashmead & Perlmutter, 1980). Further, individuals tend to name the same major events when asked to state the important events in an episode such as going to a restaurant (Anderson, 1990). However, once learned, scripts tend to operate below the individual's level of conscious awareness, that is, as tacit knowledge.

Explicit knowledge, in contrast, is easily available to consciousness and is the object of thought (Prawat, 1989). One broad type of explicit knowledge is referred to as conceptual (see the following section).

The other broad type of explicit knowledge is referred to as *metacognitive*. Included in metacognitive knowledge are knowledge of specific and general strategies for learning new information; knowledge of plans, goals, and specific tasks; and knowledge of oneself as a learner (Alexander et al., 1991). An example is the knowledge that encountering words or sentences one does not understand in a text passage is a signal to initiate a "fix-it" strategy to aid comprehension (Dole, Duffy, Roehler, & Pearson, 1991). Metacognitive knowledge contributes to the ways that the executive control processes illustrated in Figure 7.1 (p. 171) function.

Conceptual Knowledge.

Conceptual knowledge includes subject-related knowledge and knowledge about the communication of information, and both are essential to learning. The two types of conceptual knowledge described by Alexander et al. (1991) are content knowledge and discourse knowledge (see Table 7.1). Content knowledge consists of information about the individual's physical, mental, and social world (Alexander et al., 1991). Discourse or linguistic knowledge consists of knowledge of text, syntax, and rhetoric of language. This category is important because discourse knowledge interacts with content knowledge. For example, the learner's knowledge of signal words, such as "on the other hand," "nevertheless," and "exceptions are," alert the learner to important points that qualify or run counter to the concepts previously discussed.

TABLE 7.1
Two broad categories of explicit conceptual knowledge

Content knowledge*—information about some aspect of one's physical, social, or mental world (corresponds roughly to the abstract structure referred to in the literature as content schemata)	*Discourse knowledge**—information about language and its use (linguistic knowledge) (corresponds roughly to the abstract structure referred to in the literature as textual schemata)
May be informal or formal	May be informal or formal
May be organized and integrated at either of the following two levels:	Formal organization consists of the following types:
Domain knowledge—organized knowledge about (1) a defined area (such as baseball or computer programming) or (2) related to a discipline (such as biology)	*Text-structure knowledge*—understanding of the forms or frames of expository texts; the story schema or grammar activated by the learner during reading; and learner construction of hierarchies within the text
Discipline knowledge—extensive academic knowledge that is organized around the fundamental principles defining a particular field that is a discipline (such as biology and chemistry)	*Syntactic knowledge*—knowledge of the conventions of language; linguistic connections and ties
	Rhetorical knowledge—sense of audience style, or tone or register of language that can be used

Note: Summarized from "Domain Knowledge; Evolving Themes and Emerging Concerns," by P. A. Alexander, 1992, *Educational Psychologist, 27*(11), 33–51 and Alexander et al., 1991.
*This category and the subtypes consist of declarative and procedural knowledge.

Domain Knowledge and Discipline Knowledge.   As concepts become central to a defined area or a discipline, they contribute to the construction of formal organizations of content. The two major types are domain knowledge and discipline knowledge. Domain knowledge is less extensive and less comprehensive than discipline knowledge for one of two reasons. First, it may involve an area of study that is not a discipline, for example, baseball and computer programming. Second, the individual may be developing knowledge in a discipline, but that knowledge is limited. Examples are the extent of knowledge of first-semester students in biology or chemistry.

Discipline knowledge, in contrast, consists of extensive academic knowledge in a particular field designated as a discipline. Specifically, a discipline is an extensive field of study that is defined by sets of rules or generalizations, and has a history of knowledge construction. Examples are physics, biology, and chemistry. A senior who is majoring in biology and a third-year medical student, for example, are acquiring discipline knowledge.

Schemas.   The term **schema** was first defined by Frederick Bartlett (1932) as an "active organization of past reactions" which is assumed always to be operating in an individual's response (p. 201). In a now-classic experiment to illustrate the influence of schemas, Bartlett (1932) gave the first subject a folk story from an unfamiliar culture to read. The individual then reproduced the events, and gave this accounting to the second subject. The second subject read the first subject's version, laid it aside, reproduced the events, and handed that account to the third subject, and so on. By the time the story reached the tenth subject, it was no longer a folk story about mythical visitors ("The War of the Ghosts"). Instead, it had become a fishing trip. Unfamiliar information was dropped in the repeated stories, a few details were retained, and each story became more like the reader's expectations.

A recent definition of **schema** describes it as an "organized structure that reflects an individual's knowledge, experience, and expectations about some aspect of the world" (Neath, 1998, p. 328). Further, schemas represent knowledge at any of a variety of levels, from a schema of an office to a schema of social structure.

Three functions identified for schemas are (1) to provide a framework into which new data must fit in order to be comprehended, (2) to serve as a guide for goal-directed activities and to undertake searches of the environment, and (3) to fill in gaps in information received from the environment (Alba & Hasher, 1983; Neisser, 1967). An experiment on the influence of schemas on visual perception and memory used a room designed as a graduate student's office (Brewer & Treyens, 1981). However, items were included that did not fit in that setting, such as a skull, a toy top, and a picnic basket. Each subject on arrival was asked by the graduate assistant to wait in his office while he checked on the prior subject. After 35 seconds, the subject was escorted to a conference room and asked to write his or her recollections of the room. Of interest is that 88 objects were recalled by one or more subjects, of which 19 were objects not found in the room. Among the nonpresent items named by the subjects were books, a filing cabinet, coffee cup (a coffee pot was in the room), pens, and a lamp. These objects were highly relevant to the schema "office"; thus, the researchers concluded that schema knowledge became integrated with actual information about the room (p. 228). In other words, although schemas can aid in recall, as indicated by the prior study, they also can introduce errors (Neath, 1998).

The term schema is not included in the essential types of knowledge identified by Alexander et al. (1991) because the term has been interpreted in different ways over the years and has no fixed definition (Alba & Hasher, 1983; Hampson & Morris, 1996). For example, two of the problems are (1) knowing how much information to include in a schema and (2) deciding how much information should be designated as optional (Hampson & Morris, 1996). For example, the schema of a room would include walls, floor, and a ceiling. Then the question arises, should minimum dimensions be included (to differentiate "room" from "closet")? Further, should the schema of a room include windows as an option?

The most common criticism of the concept of schema is that it is too vague to be of use. That is, it explains everything, but predicts nothing (Neath, 1998, p. 331). Also the functions of schemas are met by the types of conceptual and tacit knowledge discussed earlier in this chapter.

Summary

Current models of human memory and concepts on the representation of knowledge are based on two key assumptions. They are (1) human memory is actively involved in the construction of knowledge and (2) the learner's prior knowledge plays an important role in learning. Four different views of the nature of human memory are the multistage concept, the state concept, levels of processing, and the connectionist perspectives.

The multistage model of memory identifies three structures involved in the processing of information and their associated processes. The structures are the sensory registers, short-term or working memory, and long-term memory. The associated processes are perception, encoding and the construction of meaning, and the storage and later recall of reconstructed information. The state concept, in contrast, specifies that working memory is simply an active state of information whereas long-term memory is inactive information. Tulving (1985) further describes long-term memory as composed of three distinct memory systems. They are episodic, semantic, and procedural. Personal events experienced by the individual are stored in episodic memory, and general knowledge is found in semantic memory. Procedural memory enables the individual to respond adaptively to the environment. Similar to the state concept of memory is the levels of processing perspective. Specifically, a memory results from perceptual analysis that occurs in a series of sequential, hierarchical levels.

Connectionist models, in contrast, approximate the neural networks found in the brain. Memory consists of interacting connection nets composed of elements or units and links known as connection weights. Learning involves modifying the connection weights among certain units to produce output patterns.

Theorists also have proposed different forms of knowledge representation in long-term memory. (The exception is the connectionist models, which exclude the processing of symbols.) The dual-code model maintains that abstract objects and events are stored in verbal form. Environmental sounds, actions, and sensations are stored in nonverbal form. Some events and objects that have both abstract and concrete characteristics may be coded both verbally and nonverbally.

The verbal perspective, in contrast, identifies two major types of knowledge representation: declarative and procedural. Declarative knowledge is stored in the form of propositional networks, and procedural knowledge is stored in the form of if–then statements or condition–action pairs.

Larger bodies of knowledge also have been organized as to type. Tacit knowledge refers to knowledge that is implicit. Social knowledge about everyday events is an example. Included in tacit knowledge are scripts which consist of general information about the activities in frequently experienced events.

In contrast to tacit knowledge, explicit knowledge is easily available to consciousness and is the object of thought. Explicit knowledge consists of both conceptual and metacognitive knowledge. Conceptual knowledge includes both specific content, and larger organizations at either the domain or discipline level. Knowledge of text structure and syntax (discourse knowledge) also is included in conceptual knowledge. Finally, metacognitive knowledge comprises the information that is essential in acquiring conceptual knowledge. Included are knowledge of oneself as a learner, task knowledge, knowledge of plans and goals, and strategy knowledge.

Another organization, schema, refers to organized knowledge, experience, and expectations about some aspect of the world. Although useful for educators, the vagueness of the concept limits its use in research.

The Components of Learning

The multistage concept of information processing identified particular processes that occur at each stage in the model. These processes are perception (short-term store), encoding (working memory), storage (long-term memory), and retrieval (long-term and working memory). Similar to computer processing, these human processes refer to activities in relation to specific items of information. Human cognition, however, often involves broader tasks, such as developing expertise in knowledge domains and disciplines. Moreover, cognitive processes do not occur in a vacuum. Instead, the information that is learned is strongly influenced by the learning framework. Included are the learner's prior knowledge and the nature of the information to be learned. In other words, learning is a product of the interactions between the learning framework and the individual's activities during learning.

The Learning Framework

The framework for learning consists of both internal and external factors. The internal factors are the types of knowledge in the individual's cognitive framework (tacit, conceptual, and metacognitive knowledge). The external factors consist of the nature and organization of the knowledge to be learned.

The Role of Learner Knowledge.   The extent and variety of knowledge that the individual brings to the learning situation influences all aspects of processing. First, the learner's tacit and content knowledge base serves as the framework for identifying incoming information. This knowledge functions at the level of perception as the individual recognizes familiar objects, symbols, faces, and events. For example, a child may recognize a tall, leaf-bearing plant as a tree, whereas an adult perceives it as a willow, a poplar, and so on.

Second, both tacit and content knowledge are major determinants of the inferences that individuals make about new information. For example, if your friend tells you she has a big dog named Brutus, you infer that the animal has four legs and hair, barks, and is likely to be protective of his home territory (Adams, 1989). Prior knowledge also serves as the framework to minimize the potential confusion among similar types of information. For example, in reading about John Dean in *All the President's Men,* one does not confuse him with King John, Pope John, or a former classmate John (Adams, 1989).

More important, research indicates that individuals' prior knowledge predicts both rate of learning and retention scores for factual learning, general topics, and word meanings (Bors & McLeod, 1996). In other words, extent of prior knowledge has serious implications for learning.

Third, an extensive knowledge base can enhance the capacity of short-term memory by making it possible to chunk new information into large units (see the section on encoding). Fourth, prior knowledge also influences the speed of processing. For example, an art historian reading a detailed description of a particular type of Chinese porcelain can rapidly process the technical terms in the discussion because they were previously learned by the expert.

Organization of Information to Be Learned.   Two formal organizations of information to be learned are teacher presentations, including lectures, and text passages. Research on the nature of texts indicates that the ambiguity or complexity of the text influences the extent and nature of the learning. For example, expert readers briefly experience the same difficulties in constructing meaning as novice readers when faced with obscure or ambiguous text (Alexander et al., 1991).

An analysis by Garner (1992) indicates that many textbooks are difficult to read, include information that is irrelevant to the topic, seldom focus learner attention on important information, and contain long digressions (p. 53). This situation is particularly a problem for younger or less-skilled students with inadequate text-structure knowledge (a component of discourse knowledge). They are likely to acquire trivial details instead of important generalizations (p. 54). The inclusion of highly interesting details tangential to important concepts may interfere with the recall of key generalizations (Garner, 1992). However, early studies on the so-called seductive detail effect are flawed (Goetz & Sadoski, 1995). More recent studies with college students report that pictures as seductive details interfered with text recall (Harp & Mayer, 1998), but the effect was not found for all print text (Schraw, 1998). However, further research is needed with younger students.

In summary, the learner's tacit and content knowledge interact with text and other sources of information to influence learning. When the match between learner knowledge and complexity of text is poor or when learner knowledge is inaccurate or incomplete, faulty learning is likely to occur.

Perception

Both the internal and external organizations of knowledge are important components of learning. Equally important are the processing steps undertaken by the learner. Perception, the first step in comprehending information, is the process whereby information impinging on the senses is selected and recognized. Information from the environment is first detected in the form of physical energy by the sensory system (vision, hearing, touch, smell, and taste). Receptor cells in the senses transform the physical energy into neural signals that are then sent to the sensory register in the central nervous system.

However, we do not have a use for much of the environmental stimuli impinging on the senses. Thus, the sensory register serves as a brief temporary store so that some of the information may be selected for further processing. The brief availability of visual images is referred to as *iconic memory,* and the brief auditory store is known as *echoic memory.*

Information that is not attended to in the sensory registers is lost. The remaining information is rapidly compared with one's knowledge and assigned a preliminary meaning. This process, referred to as pattern recognition, is responsible for the identification of thousands of specific sensations and images, from the scent of a rose to the faces of one's friends.

Two important factors in the determination of the information that is perceived are learner attention and the learner's knowledge. **Attention** plays a key role because the individual must selectively address particular events, objects, symbols, and other stimuli if they are to be learned. Attention, however, is not an unlimited resource. Instead, it is similar to energy, fuel, or other resources that must be allocated among competing alternatives (see Grabe, 1986). As indicated earlier, for example, when vivid details in text distract learner attention, important generalizations in the material may not be attended to. Thus, learner attention may be described as a "front-line manager" that is instrumental in determining the information that will be available for encoding (Kulhavey, Schwartz, & Peterson, 1986).

One solution to the problem of the limited capacity of attention is to practice some essential tasks until they become *automatic*. Then they can be executed with little or no conscious attention. For example, the child's task of learning the shapes and names of letters requires concentration and effort. At this stage the task is described as dependent on *deliberate* or *controlled processing*. However, after extended practice and use, letter identification becomes an automatic perceptual task. Later, for good readers, word identification also becomes largely automatic, freeing attention for the tasks of comprehending meaning and developing relations among major concepts in the material.

In addition to attention, the individual's knowledge plays an important role in perception. Someone who has lived in the city all of his life, for example, may identify a large plant with a central trunk as a tree. In contrast, another individual who has lived in the country and majored in forestry in college may indicate that she has seen a hybrid American elm grafted onto a Chinese elm stock (Bruning, Schraw, & Ronning, 1995). Similarly, comparisons of the recall of chess pieces on a board viewed for 20 seconds indicated large differences between chess masters and novices (Chase & Simon, 1973). The chess masters perceived the arrangements as configurations while the beginners perceived them in terms of individual pieces.

Encoding and Constructing Meaning

In the information-processing model, **encoding** is the process whereby information is prepared so that it will be remembered. That is, perceived information is acted on in some way so that it is retained in long-term memory in an inactive state and can be retrieved later.

The process of encoding occurs in the state referred to as short-term or working memory. The capacity of working memory originally was described as "seven plus or minus two" (Miller, 1956). However, this analysis refers only to the number of items or "chunks" that can be held in short-term memory at any one time unless action is taken by the learner to retain the information. Also, a chunk varies in the amount of information it contains. For example, the letters *bkj* may be three chunks, but the three letters in *cow* are only one chunk for a fluent reader (DiVesta, 1987, p. 210).

Maintaining information in working memory is similar to the circus act of spinning plates on a reed (Anderson, 1990, p. 153). The performer must get each plate spinning in turn and then get back to the first one before it slows down and falls off. If we try to keep too many items in working memory, the first item, like the spinning plate, will fall off.

Types of Encoding Strategies.   Information can be retained in short-term memory and also remembered for later recall through various encoding strategies. These

strategies are important because the accessibility of an item at a later time depends on (1) the ways the item is encoded, and (2) the more ways of encoding, the greater the chances of later retrieval (Hampson & Morris, 1996).

The two major types of encoding strategies are maintenance, or **primary rehearsal**, and **elaborative rehearsal**. Reciting information over and over—such as names, dates, and definitions—is maintenance rehearsal. The problem, however, is that the effects usually are only temporary (McKeown & Curtis, 1987). In other words, studying for an examination by reciting information over and over may, on a recognition or verbatim recall test, facilitate performance. However, maintenance rehearsal does not relate the information to the student's knowledge, and the information is quickly forgotten.

In contrast, elaborative rehearsal transforms the information in some way. The information may be (1) modified so that it relates to the learner's prior knowledge, (2) replaced by another symbol (referred to as stimulus substitution by Tulving & Madigan, 1970), or (3) supplemented by additional information to aid in recall. Elaborative rehearsal makes use of associations and images and relates new information to the learner's existing knowledge. These additional connections to material already learned and additional cues to aid in recall lead to the construction of elaborated structures in memory. One perspective about the effectiveness of elaboration is that alternate routes are developed for later retrieval of the information (Anderson, 1990, p. 182). In other words, such elaborations increase the redundancy of the information that is stored in memory.

Different methods of elaborative encoding are appropriate for different kinds of information. Content knowledge that is specific and factual, such as dates of events, the spelling of words, or state capitals, requires linking the information to images or other cues that convey meaning. In contrast, concepts, principles, and ideas are related to each other in different ways. Elaborations should make use of the meaningful relationships among concepts and principles and establish connections to the student's prior knowledge.

Encoding Specific Items.   Depending on the nature of the encoding process, specific items and facts may be forgotten, stored as isolated fragments, or integrated into a larger framework. One method that enhances the encoding of specific items so that they may be remembered is additional assessment. Research on the learning of word lists indicates that a test prior to the final test increases the number of words recalled. Tests, in other words, are not merely neutral events that provide evidence of the person's knowledge (Dempster, 1996). Instead, they require individuals to retrieve information from long-term memory and interact with it again (Roediger & Guynn, 1996).

The best-known methods of encoding specific items are referred to as *mnemonics*. A mnemonic technique is "any mental strategy that facilitates the learning of material by using other, initially extraneous material as an aid" (Turnure & Lane, 1987, p. 331). Thus, mnemonic devices are one type of elaboration (Turnure & Lane, 1987). Mnemonic methods include both images and verbal cues. An example of imagery is associating the technical term for German measles, roseola, with the image of a spray of red rosebuds. An example of a verbal mnemonic is the acronym ROY G BIV for the seven primary colors (red, orange, yellow, green, blue, indigo, and violet).

Some advocates of imagery maintain that bizarre and vivid images are more effective than mundane images in enhancing recall (e.g., Bower, 1970). However, a review of 44 studies of normal versus bizarre images indicated that most bizarre images are effective only under certain conditions and in tests administered after only short delays (Einstein & McDaniel, 1987). Moreover, the use of bizarre images is counter to the traditional view that new information should fit into one's scheme of reality in some way (Bellezza, 1996, p. 365).

Some mnemonic methods serve as organizing frameworks for the information to be learned. A well-known organizing system that includes imagery is the **method of loci**. The method supposedly originated with the Greek poet Simonides, and it was used by the early Greek and Roman orators to remember the main points in their lengthy speeches. To use the method of loci, one should select a familiar setting, such as the rooms in a house or the pathway of a customary walk. Then, using mental images, each of the items to be remembered is associated with a particular location.

A variation of the method of loci appropriate for collections of important facts is to visualize a course of study or an area of content as a filing cabinet. Each drawer is mentally labeled by major topics, periods of time, or some similar designation. Each folder in a drawer may represent a subtopic, a major event, a person, or some other important designation. During learning, the student visualizes the label on a particular drawer, the opening of the drawer, and the insertion of particular information in the relevant folder. For example, for a course in human development, a student may visualize the drawer labeled *early childhood* and mentally place information about children's types of play experiences in a folder labeled *play*.

To be effective as mental cues for the retrieval of information, mnemonic devices should meet three criteria. They are (1) constructibility, (2) associability, and (3) discriminability (Bellezza, 1996). Constructibility refers to the reliability that the cue can be generated from memory at the time of recall as well as at the time of learning. For example, the method of loci will not be effective if one or more of the locations cannot be generated at a later time.

The second criterion, associability, means that the mnemonic must be linked easily to the new information to be learned (p. 353). Typically, visual images are more readily associated with new information than abstract words.

Third, discriminability refers to the requirement that mnemonic devices must be dissimilar and easily identified as different. If they cannot be easily differentiated from each other, then more than one item of new information will become attached to basically the same cue. The result is confusion or forgetting (p. 354).

Encoding Concepts, Principles, and Ideas.   Two methods address the encoding of content knowledge that consists of concepts, principles, and ideas. They are (1) additional spaced presentations or reviews of the material, and (2) Wittrock's (1990, 1992) generative learning model.

Research indicates that presentations spaced over a period of time are almost twice as effective as two massed presentations separated by only a few hours (see

Dempster, 1996, for a review). This phenomenon, referred to as "spacing effect", has been found for verbal learning tasks, addition facts, science concepts, and the processing of text materials (Dempster, 1996).

Spaced readings or reviews provide the learner with an opportunity to retrieve the information from long-term memory and to encode additional facts or details on the second reading. In contrast, the generative model, developed by Wittrock (1990, 1992), maintains that comprehension and understanding are the result of generating two types of relations. They are relations among concepts and between the student's prior experiences or knowledge base and the new information. Teaching for comprehension, according to the generative model, involves leading students to construct these two types of relations (Wittrock, 1992, p. 532). The importance of establishing relationships within the new information is supported in a study by Benton, Glover, & Bruning (1983). They found that students who answered one to three inferential questions after reading paragraphs recalled a greater number of idea units than students who read declarative versions of the question. Further, Spires and Donley (1998) found that ninth-grade students taught a prior knowledge activation strategy had higher comprehension scores than students taught a strategy for identifying the main idea.

Retrieval

The term *retrieval* refers to accessing information that has been stored in long-term memory. Although computer models may imply that retrieval is rapid and effortless, it is often reconstructive and effortful. For example, if asked to recall when a particular chair in one's living room was purchased, the owner searches her memory and recalls that it was when she lived in apartment X in town Y. This information assists in recalling that she saw it in a sale at store W (Conway, 1996).

Until the 1970s, the failure to produce information when needed was viewed as either an encoding problem or the result of the deterioration of the memory of the event (Roediger & Guynn, 1996). Tulving (1974), however, introduced the possibility that encoding and memory storage may be successful, but failure to recall an item of information occurs as a result of retrieval failure. In other words, recall of an event is a product of both (1) the encoding process and (2) the retrieval cue, which is the information in the individual's cognitive environment at the time of retrieval (p. 74). According to Tulving (1974), remembering is similar to other familiar psychological events. For example, a star in the sky can be seen if its light reaches our eyes *and* if no light is reflected from the sky around it. Similarly, we recall an event if encoding developed a memory trace *and* if something reminds us of the event (Tulving, 1974, p. 74). According to this view, information may be available in long-term memory, but may be inaccessible through lack of a retrieval cue.

The stimulus for retrieval may be an external cue, an internal cue, or a combination. In the prior example, the purchase date of the chair, the friend's question is an external cue that leads to the recall of the town and apartment lived in (internal cue), which then leads to the recall of the sale at store W.

Subsequent testing also suggests that learners develop internal cues. Experiments on the recall of categorized words, states, and other information indicate that subjects demonstrate a different pattern of recall when tested a second time. That is, they may forget some items, but recall others that were not remembered on the first test. Roediger and Guynn (1996) suggest that individuals use cues they generate themselves to guide retrieval.

Although individuals can generate mental cues that aid in recall, the encoding process is a critical step in the retrieval process. The rationale for using mnemonics for information that may be low in imagery or meaningfulness, for example, is to establish an internal mental cue that may be easily accessed at a later time.

Summary

The essential components of learning are the learning framework and the processes of perception, encoding, and retrieving the learned information from long-term memory when needed. The learning framework consists of (1) the learner's prior knowledge, both tacit and conceptual (content and discourse knowledge), and (2) the nature and organization of the information to be learned. The learner's knowledge serves as the framework for identifying incoming information and also influences the inferences made by the learner about new information. Extensive knowledge also can enhance the capacity of short-term memory to encode information in large chunks as well as the speed of processing.

Two formal organizations of material to be learned are teacher presentations and text passages. However, many textbooks are difficult to read and often include irrelevant information. Some texts use irrelevant vivid details, which can distract student attention from important information.

Perception, the first step in comprehending information, selects and recognizes information impinging on the senses. Two factors that influence perception are the learner's knowledge and learner attention. Learner attention functions as a front-line manager that determines which information will be selected for further processing while the learner's knowledge assists in the identification of incoming information.

Encoding is the process that prepares selected information for storage in long-term memory and later recall. Reciting information over and over (maintenance rehearsal) is only effective for recall within a short time period. Instead, elaborative rehearsal, which transforms information in some way and establishes links with previously learned knowledge, is an effective encoding approach. Two effective methods of elaboration for specific items of information are additional testing and mnemonics. Also important is to select a mnemonic device that can also serve as a retrieval cue. Encoding concepts, principles, and ideas, in contrast, requires the construction of meaningful links between the new concepts or ideas and between the new material and the learner's prior knowledge.

PRINCIPLES OF INSTRUCTION

Information processing is a particular perspective within the larger domain of cognitive perspectives. Currently, instructional guidelines have been derived from classroom research in this area.

Basic Assumptions

The basic assumptions that underlie the information-processing view describe the nature of the human memory system and the representation of knowledge in memory. Classroom applications are derived from the assumption that human memory is an active system that selects, organizes, and encodes for storage the new information or skills to be learned. Another important goal is to develop in the learner a rich store of knowledge and effective strategies for understanding and comprehending information. In particular subject domains, such as mathematics, physics, and computer programming, the goal of instruction is to facilitate the learner's construction of new domains of knowledge that differ from the student's prior experiences.

The Components of Instruction

Major components in instruction are (1) structuring the framework for learning, (2) facilitating learner perception and encoding of information, and (3) teaching students strategies for constructing meaning.

The Learning Framework

The learning framework, in the information-processing view, consists of learner knowledge and the organization of the information to be learned. The role of instruction is (1) to contribute to the ways that learner knowledge interacts with new learning and (2) to structure the information to be learned in meaningful ways.

Enhancing the Learner's Prior Knowledge.   Both discourse knowledge, particularly text-structure knowledge, and the student's domain knowledge are important in the student's comprehension of teacher presentations and text materials.

Knowledge of Text Structure.   Garner (1990) suggests that students' lack of text knowledge hampers their ability to invoke and apply useful comprehension strategies, such as summarizing. Specifically, knowledge of text structure, particularly organization, is important in assisting readers to differentiate important from unimportant information (Dole et al., 1991; Garner, 1990). Lack of understanding of text structure is illustrated in two studies in which 20% of the seventh graders were unable to logically sequence seven randomly organized sentences into a coherent paragraph. Further, one-third of the third and fifth graders were unable to identify the topic sentence in the set of randomly ordered sentences (Garner et al., 1986).

Instruction on text structure can enhance students' comprehension of reading materials (Mayer, 1984). In addition to the organization of text, instruction on the recognition and understanding of signal words also is important. Signal words are non-content words that emphasize the conceptual structure of the material. Examples include preview sentences, paragraph headings, and connectives such as "the problem is. . . . " Also included are "pointer words," such as *unfortunately* and *more important.*

Domain Knowledge.   Across all ages and ability levels, readers use their knowledge base as a filter to interpret and construct meaning from text passages (Dole et al.,

1991). When learner knowledge is incomplete, naïve or misleading interpretations will be incomplete or faulty (p. 24). Further, when the material to be learned is in conflict with or contradicts the learner's knowledge base, learner knowledge typically prevails (see Dochy, Segers, & Buehl, 1999, for a discussion).

Inaccurate knowledge can be a major problem because the relationship between the learner's domain knowledge and text material becomes increasingly important as the student moves through the educational system (Alexander, Kulikowich, & Jetton, 1994). One reason is that texts become more important as information sources in the middle and high school grades. Thus, texts become a primary mechanism for increasing the student's domain knowledge. Paradoxically, however, the student's subject matter knowledge is an important factor in interpreting texts, which become lengthier and more complex in middle and high school (Alexander et al., 1991).

The relationship between the learner's domain knowledge and text comprehension is described by Stanovich (1986) as *Matthew effects*. The term is derived from the biblical passage in Matthew XXV:29, which states that those who have shall have abundance, but those who have not shall lose the little they have. Applied to school learning, those with more subject-matter knowledge are better able to process information from text and, therefore, acquire more domain-related information as they move from grade to grade. In contrast, students with weak domain knowledge become less able to address the more demanding texts and, thus, fall further and further behind (Alexander et al., 1994, p. 215).

One classroom strategy to address this problem is the use of classroom discussions following reading assignments. The purpose is to clarify difficult or unfamiliar concepts. For example, statements in one elementary school passage were "Plains Indians lived mainly in tepees; some California tribes lived in simple earth-covered shelters," and so forth. For children who did not know or who were unable to activate knowledge about the relationship of house style to lifestyle, climate, and availability of raw materials, the information is simply a list of arbitrary statements (Bransford, Vye, Adams, & Perfetto, 1989, p. 216). Classroom discussions in which students explore possible reasons for differences described in general statements provide experience in elaborating text and altering their prior knowledge about the topic.

Organizing the Information To Be Learned. As indicated earlier in the chapter, textbooks often are not well organized and are difficult to read. In a few studies, text material was restructured to illustrate key concepts within and between domains. The restructured material enhanced both learning and interest in the subject matter (Alexander et al., 1994). However, given that textbooks, for the most part, are unlikely to be restructured, teachers are faced with the responsibility of providing a meaningful organization for the text material. One suggested strategy is the use of **advance organizers**. As discussed in the following section, advance organizers serve as umbrellas into which the student can fit more detailed information as he or she reads. Advance organizers can assist in countering the seductive detail effect in which the reader misses the main point through focusing on vivid details.

Another possible strategy is the development of materials using nonlinear or hypercard computer materials. In such an arrangement, the learner can access portions of the information as he or she chooses. However, many of the initial hyper-card texts that have been researched to date are quite lengthy (Alexander et al., 1991). Such texts can pose a problem for readers with poor processing strategies.

One hypercard development used as supplementary material in coordinated English and history high school courses addressed a key difficulty in designing an appropriate conceptual structure in the humanities and social sciences. That is, items of information often are multiply linked to different topics and the meaning of an abstract concept depends, in part, on the ways it relates to other concepts (Spoehr, 1994). The modules (hypercard stacks) were organized into three "conceptual neighborhoods" (themes): (1) historical periods, (2) literary movements/individual authors, and (3) themes in American culture (e.g., popular music, war and revolution). Initial entry generates a choice of one of three "neighborhoods." A choice typically provides the learner with a finer-grain subdivision of options. Of importance is that, when the learner selects an option, the program first displays an overview screen that diagrammatically illustrates the major relationships between the conceptual themes and the types of information on the topic.

Also, as the learner, in exploring the topic, "descends" into more detailed levels of information, the program also provides suboverviews of relationships at those levels (p. 895). In addition to assisting the learner to develop a conceptual organization of information, the overviews are intended to avoid the problems of learners wandering through the material in inefficient and disorganized ways, missing sections of relevant information, or getting lost. In other words, the information within the three major themes is organized hierarchically and laterally (Spoehr, 1994).

Facilitating Learner Attention

Of major importance in planning instruction is that the learner does not respond to instruction as presented. Instead, the learner responds to the instruction that he or she actively apprehends (Shulman, 1986). Thus, an important aspect of instruction is to first structure the environment so that student attention is focused on important tasks (Bruning et al., 1995) and then to informally assess learner perceptions. One approach is to introduce preteaching activities that activate students' relevant knowledge. For example, prior to a lesson on heat conduction and the relationship of an object's density to its heat conduction, students generate examples of objects that conduct heat. One girl named the handle of the metal frying pan on a hot stove burner, another the outside-facing wall of a room on a cold day, and so on. A carefully controlled experiment in which several different materials of the same size were placed in a flame led to a discussion as to why some of the materials became warm quickly while others seemed to remain cool (Bruning et al., 1995).

Advance Organizers.

The concept of advance organizers, introduced by Ausubel (1968), refers to highly inclusive concepts that would serve as "ideational scaffolding." Presented prior to instruction, the purpose is to serve as an "umbrella" into which more detailed information is incorporated as learning progresses. The material must be carefully selected to serve as a link between the student's present store of information and the new learning. According to Ausubel (1968), advance organizers provide a conceptual framework and also facilitate encoding. More recently, theorists have suggested that advance organizers are effective because they activate the learner's prior knowledge.

The two types of organizers identified by Ausubel (1968) are expository (used with unfamiliar material) and comparative (used to facilitate the integration of new ideas in relatively familiar material with similar, previously learned concepts).

Although some of the early research indicated no effects, Corkill (1992) notes that a variety of materials, such as prereading activities, paragraph headings, study objectives, and outlines, were mislabeled as advance organizers. Subsequent research indicates that written organizers should be concrete and contain an example that illustrates the analogous relationship between ideas in the advance organizer and ideas in the new material (Corkill, 1992, p. 63). Also important is that the advance organizer must be at the appropriate reading level for the student and assist the student in accessing relevant knowledge. Thus, different students may require different advance organizers, depending on their prior knowledge and reading levels.

Teaching Selective Attention Strategies. The second major task for teachers in facilitating learner attention is to teach students to be strategic processors of information. The initial key step is focusing attention on important ideas, facts, concepts, and generalizations to be learned. However, researchers note that, particularly when reading text materials, the attention of both children and adults often is not strategic, conscious, or selective (Garner, 1992, p. 58). That is, when individuals process meaningful materials, they often do so superficially (Pressley et al., 1992).

Teachers can provide instruction on focusing attention, using questions first to direct students' attention to important material and then observing their use of these questions on their own. Appropriate questions to begin with are, Where should we look first for important information? (first or second sentence in the paragraph) and What other information do we need to include? (Garner, 1992).

Facilitating the Encoding of Specific Items

Laboratory research on the encoding of word lists indicates that a test prior to the final assessment enhances recall. In the classroom, this practice can apply to spelling and vocabulary in the elementary grades. A practice test administered on Wednesday, for example, can indicate learning problems prior to the weekly graded test on Friday.

The method referred to as mnemonics is appropriate for arbitrary associations in different subject areas that must be learned. Sentences and acronyms, for example, are organizational mnemonics that assist in learning the information and they also serve as retrieval cues for later recall. They are most effective for items that must be recalled in a certain order (Snowman, 1986). For example, a useful mnemonic for music students is the sentence, "Every good boy does fine." The initial letters of the words *(e, g, b, d, f)* are the notes printed on the lines of the treble clef. Similarly, the word *face* represents the notes printed in the spaces *(f, a, c, e)*.

Acronyms, rhymes, and sentences are most effective for items that must be recalled in a certain order (Snowman, 1986). An example useful for anatomy students is the rhyme, "On old Olympia's towering top, a Finn, Visigoth, and German vault, skip, and hop" (Solso, 1988, p. 227). The initial letter of each word of the first line represents the cranial nerves (olfactory, optic, oculomotor, trochlear, trigeminal, and so on).

Both visual and verbal learner-generated cues can enhance encoding. A flexible mnemonic technique, originally developed for foreign-language learning, is the keyword method. The method divides vocabulary learning into two major steps. The first step is for the learner to select an English word that sounds like some part of the foreign language word. This step is the acoustical link (Atkinson, 1975, p. 821). The second step is to form a mental image of the keyword interacting with the English equivalent of the foreign language word, referred to as an imagery link. For example, the Spanish word for *duck* sounds like "pot-o" (acoustical link). An interactive image is that of a duck hiding under an overturned flower pot. Another example (Jones & Hall, 1982) is the use of the keyword *wave* for the Spanish word *huevo* (wave-o), which means "egg." The visual image is that of a giant egg riding the crest of a wave.

Although designed for foreign language learning, the keyword method is applicable also to other learning tasks. It has been used in learning medical definitions, linking explorers with discoveries (Jones & Hall, 1982), enhancing memory for facts (Levin, 1986), and increasing learning from text (McCormick & Levin, 1984). Mnemonic imagery is also useful for learning information about totally unfamiliar concepts, such as information about unknown countries (Pressley, Johnson, Symons, McGoldrick, & Kurita, 1989, p. 12).

Several studies indicate that both mentally retarded and learning disabled students can learn imagery-based strategies to enhance learning and recall in several areas (see Mastropieri & Fulk, 1990, and Turnure & Lane, 1987). In some studies, regular classroom teachers implemented the methods over time and reported increased recall on both immediate and delayed posttests. However, Turnure and Lane (1987) caution that educators must not succumb to the illusion that installing an array of monolithic information-processing mnemonics can rescue students from all their learning, memory, and thinking problems (p. 330). To be effective, mnemonic techniques must be explained, demonstrated, and applied in many, many situations in which they are to be used. However, this method and other elaborative techniques can serve as mental cues to recall items that are low in imagery or meaningfulness (Bellezza, 1996).

In addition to enhancing the recall of specific items, mnemonic methods also may be useful in conveying both meaning and structure when terms are hierarchically organized. Levin and Levin (1990) developed a mnemonic system for plant classification terms in which (1) the particular terms were recoded into acoustically or orthographically similar concrete proxies (keywords), and (2) links between the terms were represented as pictorial semantic relationships. For example, angiosperm became an angel who is holding a pet leash attached to a monkey (for monocotylan) and the monkey is shooting an arrow (for arales) at a frying pan (for pandanales) (p. 302). The subordinate relationships were illustrated in the picture by placing the images in sequence from the top to the bottom of the picture beginning with the angel at the top. Results indicated that the system, when compared to a taxonomy chart, significantly increased recall on both immediate and delayed tests (2 months later) for college students. Also important is that the mnemonic group was more fluent in accurately placing the plant terms within the taxonomy.

Strategies Instruction

Teaching processes and strategies for learning concepts, principles, and ideas is important because many students fail to use effective strategies. Specifically, strategies are operations over and above the processes that are involved in a task (Pressley, Borkowski, & Schneider, 1987). Important issues in strategy instruction are the types of strategies for constructing meaning and the steps in strategy instruction.

Types of Strategies for Constructing Meaning. Two specific strategies shown

to be effective for constructing meaning from both text and orally presented material are summarizing and self-questioning. The purpose of these strategies is to assist students to construct a model of meaning from their prior knowledge, cues noted in the material, and the instructional context (Dole et al., 1991).

Summarizing. The purpose of summarization is to capture the gist of instruction while, at the same time, reducing the material. Effective summarization requires that the learner sift through large organizations of information, distinguish important from unimportant ideas, and then synthesize the key ideas into a new coherent organization that represents the original (Dole et al., 1991). Brown and Day (1983) identified several rules for developing useful summaries. They are (1) delete unnecessary material, (2) eliminate redundancy, (3) substitute a superordinate term for groups of terms and/or lists of events, and (4) invent a topic sentence if none appears in the text.

Summarization often is recommended as a strategy for enhancing the meaning of reading passages. In addition, King (1992) found that the strategies enhanced the comprehension of orally presented material. She taught students a summarization strategy following notetaking during lectures. The strategy involved (1) turning the topic into a sentence that reflected the main idea and (2) successively linking subtopics (or main idea) and related ideas together.

The effectiveness of summarization, however, depends on the student's ability to differentiate important from unimportant information (Dole et al., 1991). In reading, for example, research indicates that good readers use their general knowledge and domain knowledge as well as their knowledge of text structure to help them determine importance (Dole et al., 1991). Garner (1990) differentiates strategically inefficient from strategically efficient summarizers on the basis of this capability. That is, inefficient summarizers copy ideas verbatim from text and do not paraphrase or combine ideas. In contrast, efficient summarizers select only the most important text, use rules for condensing text, and produce coherent summaries (p. 263).

Self-Questioning. Teacher-generated questions are a traditional practice in the teaching of reading. Current research, however, indicates that teaching students to generate their own questions stimulates their inferences and explanations about the material and, therefore, their understanding (Dole et al., 1991; King, 1991, 1992; Pressley et al., 1992).

The product generated in self-questioning is a set of questions and answers about the instruction. When the questions require inferences by the learner, that is, when they are high-level questions, they can assist the learner to organize the new material and to integrate the information with existing knowledge. In addition, self-questioning also is a metacognitive strategy because it is a way for learners to check their level of comprehension and understanding (King, 1992).

Asking high-level questions is particularly important in facilitating understanding. Pressley et al. (1992) note that questions that affect only selective attention or maintenance rehearsal do not require transformation of the material. The result is small, if any, learning gains.

One role of self-questioning is useful in relation to facts. Referred to as elaborative interrogation, the method involves asking "why" questions about factual statements in text passages. For example, for statements on Canadian provinces, Canadian university students asked questions such as, "Why would it make sense that the first radio stations were in Alberta?" (Pressley et al., 1992). For the students, the researchers hypothesized that the "why" questions activated the students' prior knowledge related to the new facts (p. 98).

One approach to generating thought-provoking questions is to teach specific stems (King, 1990, 1991, 1992). This strategy is appropriate for high school and college students. Examples are How would you use . . . to . . . ? What is a new example of . . . ? Explain why. . . . How does . . . affect . . . ? and What do you think would happen if . . . ? (King, 1992, p. 114). Formulating such questions forces students to identify main ideas and the ways the ideas relate to each other and to the students' prior knowledge and experience. These two levels of elaborations are the essential components in Wittrock's (1990) model.

A strategy recommended by King (1994) is referred to as guided cooperative questioning. In small groups or pairs, students ask each other specific thought-provoking questions on the material presented in teacher-led presentations and lessons. Students were taught two types of specific stems: lesson-based questions and experience-based questions. Examples of lesson-based questions include What . . . mean? Why is . . . important? How . . . and . . . similar? What are strengths and weaknesses of . . . ? (p. 341). Examples of experience-based questions are What would happen if . . . ? How could . . . be used to . . . ? How does . . . tie in with . . . that we learned before? (p. 341). Combining the two types of questions for a science lesson was more effective than either lesson-based questions or learner construction of cognitive maps of science concepts.

Recommendations for Strategy Instruction. A frequent criticism of strategy instruction is that students do not continue using the strategies without specific directions to do so (Pressley & El-Dinary, 1992, p. 86). However, implementing particular steps along with strategy instruction does promote transfer to other similar tasks. A first step in strategy instruction is to determine the particular activities undertaken by students and the underlying rationales for their actions. To the extent that students are skimming a passage merely to get through it suggests an avoidance of school tasks and/or a sense that such tasks have no inherent meaning for life in the world outside of school.

Next, demonstrate the benefits of strategy use in both school assignments and other activities. For example, demonstrate the role of strategies in reading to construct a model of meaning from one's prior knowledge and cues noted in the text and the situational context (Dole, et al., 1991). Another activity is for students to compare their performance before and after using the particular strategy (Pressley & El-Dinary, 1992).

Other essential steps in strategy instruction are (1) to describe and then model the strategy and (2) to provide teacher-guided practice accompanied by praise and corrective feedback. Practice should begin with simple materials and progress to grade-level tasks (Pressley et al., 1989, p. 25). Also important is to teach students when and where to use particular strategies. This information is an important component of the student's metacognitive knowledge (see chapter 8).

Strategy instruction is not a "quick fix." Strategies such as paraphrasing, summarizing, and self-questioning require time and practice to develop. Therefore, only one strategy should be taught at a time, and it should be learned well prior to the introduction of another strategy.

In summary, successful strategy instruction should not be viewed as remediation. Instead, the goal is to develop sophisticated comprehension skills in all students (Pressley et al., 1989).

Summary

Major components in instruction from the information-processing perspective are enhancing prior learner knowledge, organizing the material to be learned, facilitating learner attention, encoding and the construction of meaning, and teaching students strategies to enhance their understanding of text and oral presentations.

Both discourse knowledge and the student's domain knowledge are important in the comprehension of text materials and teacher presentation. Teachers can assist students in developing text-structure knowledge by teaching them to recognize signals such as preview sentences, paragraph headings, and signal words. For students with poor background knowledge or for texts that are poorly written, small group and class discussions can develop some of the missing links.

Of major importance in planning instruction is the realization that the student responds only to the instruction that he or she actively apprehends. Therefore, instruction should focus learner attention on important tasks and informally assess learner perceptions. One approach is to implement preteaching activities that activate prior knowledge and/or link prior knowledge to key concepts. Another approach is to use advance organizers. They are highly inclusive concepts that serve as a link between the student's present store of information and the new learning. Their purpose is to serve as a conceptual framework and also to facilitate encoding. Another instructional strategy is to teach students ways to find important information in text and other materials.

Methods for encoding specific items of information such as vocabulary words, dates, and facts include prior testing and various mnemonic techniques. Examples are rhymes, acronyms, sayings, and learner-generated cues, such as the keyword method. Designed for foreign language learning, the student first selects an English word that sounds like some part of the foreign word. Then the student forms a mental image of the keyword interacting with the English equivalent. Imagery-based strategies can also aid mentally retarded students and learning-disabled students with learning and recall.

Two strategies for the construction of meaning for complex information are summarizing and self-questioning. One summarization strategy involves turning the topic into a sentence that reflects the main idea and successively linking subtopics and related ideas together.

Self-questioning can be useful both for facts and other types of information. When used for facts, the method involves asking "why" questions about factual statements in text passages. The purpose is to activate students' prior knowledge related to the new facts. Self-questioning to generate the meanings in a passage should involve application questions in which the learner generates new examples, explains how the key concepts are used, and identifies relationships between major ideas. Use of such strategies also depends on the student's metacognitive strategies, which are discussed in chapter 8.

EDUCATIONAL APPLICATIONS

Information-processing theories began as a research effort to understand the cognitive operations undertaken by humans. Investigations of the ways that students process information in various subject areas are increasing (Lampert, 1990; Rohrer & Thomas, 1989; Schoenfeld, 1985). In addition, methods for developing students' understanding and use of strategies to facilitate processing also are being developed (see King, 1992, 1994; Pressley et al., 1992).

Classroom Issues

Classroom issues addressed by information-processing theory are those that are directly related to cognitive processes.

Learner Characteristics

The student characteristics that are important in the management of classroom learning are individual differences, readiness for learning, and motivation. Of these three, the concept of individual differences is addressed directly in relation to problem solving, which is discussed in chapter 8.

Cognitive Processes and Instruction

The focus in information-processing theories is the variety of processes whereby individuals perceive, encode, remember, recall, and apply information or knowledge. The issue of transfer of learning and learning how-to-learn skills are also addressed.

Transfer of Learning.   Typically, transfer of learning refers to skills or knowledge learned in one context or situation that later are applied in new contexts. Mnemonic techniques and other mechanisms to assist encoding are generalizable to a variety of settings as are text comprehension strategies and others.

However, transfer will not occur unless the appropriate prior knowledge is activated. This failure to activate relevant knowledge that has been learned is referred to as *inert knowledge* (Bransford et al., 1989; Whitehead, 1929). The problem of inert knowledge (i.e., lack of transfer) may be the result of (1) memorizing rather than learning the significance of new information, (2) acquiring concepts in a limited context, or (3) being unable to access acquired knowledge efficiently with minimal effort (Bransford et al., 1989, p. 214). Important in facilitating the transfer of strategies for specific tasks, such as comprehending text, are the student's skills in managing and directing his or her own learning.

Learning "How-to-Learn" Skills.   The term *metacognition* refers to the capabilities required to direct one's learning, remembering, and thinking, discussed in chapter 8.

Teaching Problem Solving.   This topic is discussed in chapter 8.

The Social Context for Learning

Information-processing theories focus on the cognitive mechanisms involved in the comprehension and retention of sensory data from the environment, as well as the application of learned information to solving problems. Although much of this learning occurs in a social environment, the theories have yet to address the influence of that environment on cognitive processing.

Relationships to Other Perspectives

Like Gestalt psychology, information-processing theory also assesses perception. However, the Gestalt psychologists discussed perception only in problem-solving situations that require a reorganization of visual stimuli. In contrast, information-processing theory treats perception as one of the major steps in acquiring and remembering information.

Information-processing theory also discusses strategies for constructing meaning that operate within a context of pre-determined knowledge to be learned. Constructivists, however, maintain that such constraints prevent the "true" construction of knowledge which, instead, must begin with the learner and does not build toward a performed outcome.

The comprehension of knowledge in a subject-matter area or domain is the focus of information-processing. Unlike Gagné's conditions of learning, the theory does not address the different types of cognitive operations that may be developed in relation to knowledge.

Developing a Classroom Strategy

The importance of designing instruction for information processing is that logical meaning of the knowledge is transformed into psychological meaning. Logical meaning is the relationship of the symbols, concepts, and rules of the subject area. Psychological meaning is the relationship of the symbols, concepts, and rules to the student's cognitive structure (Ausubel, 1968). Developing psychological meaning in the comprehension of knowledge and in solving problems depends on student interaction with the subject matter.

Comprehension

Step 1: Develop cues to guide the reception of the new learning.

1.1 What informal questions will access the learner's existing cognitive structure?

1.2 Does the lesson include broadly written objectives or a statement of purpose that can direct the learner's attention?

1.3 How will the new knowledge or skills enhance or build on the learner's existing knowledge?

Step 2: Select or develop conceptual supports that facilitate the encoding of information.

2.1 What information should be included in advance organizers so that they bridge the student's knowledge and the new learning?

2.2 What concepts, episodes, and images already acquired by the student may be used to illustrate the new terms, definitions, or concepts?

2.3 Are there adjunct questions in the text or major points in the text that can be used as a basis for secondary rehearsal by the students?

2.4 What are the logical points in the instruction for students to engage in secondary rehearsal (i.e., visual and/or verbal elaboration)? What are some examples of associative images and verbal codes that can be provided to students?

Step 3: Develop cues that aid in the retrieval of learned information.

3.1 What are some comparisons with related concepts, terms, or ideas that may be made? For example, if the concept is *morpheme,* it may be contrasted with *phoneme* and compared with the term *word.*

3.2 What inference questions may be used to conclude the lesson?

Comprehension Strategies

Step 1: Teach attention-focusing strategies.

1.1 Use questions first to direct students' attention to important material.

1.2 Provide opportunities for students to apply the questions.

Step 2: Teach summarization and self-questioning strategies.

2.1 Demonstrate turning topic sentences into a statement of the main idea.

2.2 Demonstrate linking the main idea to subtopics.

2.3 Provide opportunities for student application, feedback, and further opportunities for application.

2.4 Demonstrate the use of generic question stems to generate information from text.

2.5 Provide opportunities for student application, feedback, and further opportunities for application.

Classroom Example

The following strategy is a component of the story grammar strategy developed to assist students with learning and/or writing problems to write better stories. The strategy is a component in a program developed by Graham and Harris (1994) to teach writing and self-regulation skills to students with learning problems. The purpose is to provide students with an explicit, context-based strategy.

Initial conference: The purpose of instruction is explained. Teacher and students then discuss the common parts of a story and the goal for learning the story grammar strategy.

Pre-skill development: Teacher and students discuss the common story parts (characters, place, time, setting) and story episodes (precipitating event, characters' goals, action to achieve goals, resolution, and characters' reactions).

Story grammar strategy: The following steps to help the students write stories are taught by the teacher:

1. Think of a story you would like to share with others.
2. Let your mind be free.
3. Write down the reminders of the story parts (W-W-W; What = 2; How = 2).

    W — Who is the main character? Who else is in the story?
    W — When does the story take place?
    W — Where does the story take place?
    What does the main character do or want to do and what do the other characters do?
    What happens with other characters?
    How does the story end?
    How do the main character and the other characters feel? (Graham & Harris, 1994, p. 219)

4. Make notes of your ideas for the story parts.
5. Write the story. Use some parts, add, expand, or revise as you go (summarized from Graham & Harris, 1994).

Review of the Theory

The communications research of World War II and computer simulations of human intellectual capabilities introduced a new paradigm to the study of mental operations. This paradigm is reflected in the information-processing descriptions of mental operations. According to this paradigm, the human memory is an active orga-

TABLE 7.2
Summary of information-processing theory

Basic Elements	Definition
Assumptions	Human memory is a complex and active organizer of information; the memory system transforms information for storage (and later retrieval) in long-term memory.
Learning	The processes by which information from the environment is transformed into cognitive structures
Learning outcome	Some form of cognitive structure; the prevalent view is that of semantic networks.
Components of learning	The processes of perception, encoding, and storage in long-term memory
Designing instruction for complex skills	See Chapter 8
Major issues in designing instruction	Relating new learning to existing knowledge; teaching students to monitor comprehension; and structuring learning to facilitate processing
ANALYSIS OF THE THEORY	
Disadvantages	Information-processing theory lacks a coordinated theoretical foundation; various perspectives are somewhat disjointed.
	Computer model of cognitive processes may or may not be valid.
Contribution to classroom practice	Identification of the importance of designing instruction for the cognitive processes in learning

nized system that selects the information to be processed and then transforms that information into meaningful codes for later use (see Table 7.2).

The core of the theory comprises the processes by which individuals perceive, encode, and then store information in long-term memory for later use. The theorists agree that codes are stored internally in some type of cognitive structure. The prevalent view is that this structure takes the form of semantic networks, in which verbal elements are linked to each other. Large bodies of knowledge are categorized as tacit and explicit. Included in explicit knowledge are domain and discipline knowledge (content knowledge), discourse knowledge, and metacognitive knowledge.

Key components in learning include (1) the learning framework, which consists of the learner's knowledge and the organization of the information to be learned, and (2) the learner's cognitive processes, learning strategies, and metacognitive decisions. Applications to education include specific recommendations for enhancing the learner's prior knowledge, the use of advance organizers, and the use of learner-generated cues for encoding and constructing meaning. Included are the use of images, combinations of images and words, and students' summarization and self-questioning strategies.

Disadvantages

Information-processing theory is a collection of various approaches to the study of cognitive functions. Thus, the theory lacks an overarching framework for integrating the various research studies.

Contributions to Classroom Practice

Information-processing theory has described in detail the processes that the Gestalt theorists were attempting to identify. For classroom learning, the processes identified in encoding and constructing meaning indicate the importance of structuring lessons to support these processes and to teach strategies to enhance comprehension. Table 7.2 summarizes information-processing theory.

CHAPTER QUESTIONS

1. A student is faced with the task of learning the following information stated in a biology textbook: Arteries are thick, elastic, and carry blood rich in oxygen from the heart. Veins are thinner, less elastic, and carry blood rich in carbon dioxide from the body to the heart.

    _____ a. What are some visual imagery and/or mnemonic elaborations that the student may generate to facilitate learning this information?

    _____ b. What information can the teacher provide about the significance or relevance of these facts that may assist the student in remembering the information?

2. Why are the sentences in Set A below easier to remember than the sentences in Set B?

    _____ Set A: Benjamin Franklin flew the kite. George Washington hid the ax. Santa Claus walked on the roof. Noah built a boat.

    _____ Set B: Jim flew the kite. John hid the ax. Ted walked on the roof. Malcolm built a boat (Bransford et al., 1989, p. 204).

REFERENCES

Adams, M. J. (1989). Thinking skills curricula. *Educational Psychologist, 24*(1), 25–77.

Alba, J. W., & Hasher, L. (1983). Is memory schematic? *Psychological Bulletin, 93,* 203–231.

Alexander, P. A. (1992). Domain knowledge: Evolving themes and emerging concerns. *Educational Psychologist, 27*(1), 33–51.

Alexander, P. A., Kulikowich, J. M., & Jetton, J. (1994). The role of subject-matter knowledge and interest in the processing of linear and nonlinear texts. *Review of Educational Research, 64*(2), 201–252.

Alexander, P. A., Schallert, D. A., & Hare, V. C. (1991). Coming to terms: How researchers in learning and literacy talk about knowledge. *Review of Educational Research, 61*(3), 315–343.

Anderson, J. R. (1983). *The architecture of cognition.* Cambridge: MA: Harvard University Press.

Anderson, J. R. (1990). *Cognitive psychology and its implications* (3rd ed.). New York: Freeman.

Anderson, J. R. (1993). Problem solving and learning. *American Psychologist, 48*(1), 35–44.

Ashmead, D. H., & Perlmutter, M. (1980). Infant memory in everyday life. In M. Perlmutter (Ed.), *New directions for child development: Children's memory* (Vol. 10, pp. 1–16). San Francisco: Jossey-Bass.

Atkinson, R. C. (1975). Mnemotechnics in second-language learning. *American Psychologist, 30,* 821–825.

Ausubel, D. P. (1968). *Educational psychology: A cognitive view.* New York: Holt, Rinehart & Winston.

Bartlett, F. C. (1932). *Remembering.* New York: Cambridge University Press.

Bellezza, F. S. (1996). Mnemonic methods to enhance storage and retrieval. In E. L. Bjork & R. A. Bjork (Eds.), *Memory: Handbook of Perception and Cognition* (2nd ed.) (pp. 345–380). San Diego, CA: Academic Press.

Benton, S. L., Glover, J. A., & Bruning, R. H. (1983). The effect of number of decisions on prose recall. *Journal of Educational Psychology, 75,* 382–390.

Bereiter, C. (1991). Implication of connectionism for thinking about rules. *Educational Researcher, 20*(3), 10–16.

Bors, D. A., & McLeod, C. M. (1996). Individual differences in memory. In E. L. Bjork & R. A. Bjork (Eds.), *Memory: Handbook of perception and cognition* (2nd ed.) (pp. 411–441). San Diego, CA: Academic Press.

Bower, G. H. (1970). Imagery as a relational organizer in associative learning. *Journal of Verbal Learning and Verbal Behavior, 9,* 529–533.

Bransford, J. D., Vye, N., Adams, L. T., & Perfetto, G. (1989). Learning skills and the acquisition of strategies. In A. Lesgold & R. Glaser (Eds.), *Foundations for a Psychology of Education* (pp. 199–249). Hillsdale, NJ: Erlbaum.

Brewer, W. F., Treyens, J. T. (1981). Role of schemata in memory for places. *Cognitive Psychology, 13,* 207–230.

Broadbent, D. E. (1958). *Perception and communication.* London: Pergamon.

Brown, A. L., & Campione, J. C. (1994). Guided discovery in a community of learners. In K. McGilly (Ed.), *Classroom lessons: Integrating cognitive theory and classroom practice* (pp. 229–274). Cambridge, MA: MIT Press.

Brown, A. L., & Day, D. (1983). Macrorules for summarizing texts: The development of expertise. *Journal of Verbal Learning and Verbal Behavior, 22,* 1–14.

Bruning, R. H., Schraw, G. S., & Ronning, R. R. (1995). *Cognitive psychology and instructions.* Upper Saddle River, NJ: Merrill/Prentice Hall.

Chase, W. G., & Simon, H. A. (1973). The mind's eye in chess. In W. G. Chase & H. A. Simon (Eds.), *Visual information-processing* (pp. 215–281). New York: Academic.

Clark, J. M., & Paivio, A. (1991). Dual coding theory and education. *Educational Psychology Review, 3*(3), 149–210.

Collins, A. M., & Quillian, M. R. (1969). Retrieval time from semantic memory. *Journal of Verbal Learning and Verbal Behavior, 8,* 240–247.

Conway, M. A. (1996). Autobiographical memory. In E. L. Bjork and R. A. Bjork (Eds.), *Memory: Handbook of perception and cognition* (2nd ed.) (pp. 165–194). San Diego, CA: Academic Press.

Corkill, A. J. (1992). Advance organizers: Facilitators of recall. *Educational Psychology Review, 4*(1), 33–68.

Craik, F. I. M. (1979). Levels of processing: Overview and closing comments. In L. S. Cermak & F. I. M. Clark (Eds.), *Levels of processing human memory.* Hillsdale, NJ: Lawrence Erlbaum.

Craik, F. I. M., & Lockhart, R. S. (1972). Levels of processing: A framework for memory research. *Journal of Verbal Learning and Verbal Behavior, 11,* 671–684.

Dempster, F. N. (1996). Distributing and managing the conditions of encoding and practice. In E. L. Bjork & R. A. Bjork (Eds.), *Memory: Handbook of perception and cognition,* 2nd ed. (pp. 317–344). San Diego: Academic Press.

DiVesta, F. J. (1987). The cognitive movement and education. In J. Glover & R. Ronnings (Eds.), *Historical foundations of educational psychology* (pp. 203–233). New York: Plenum.

Dochy, F., Segers, M., & Buehl, M. (1999). The relation between assessment practices and outcomes of studies: The case of research on prior knowledge. *Review of Educational Research, 69*(2), 145–186.

Dole, J. A., Duffy, G., Roehler, L. R., & Pearson, P. D. (1991). Moving from the old to the new: Research on reading comprehension instruction. *Review of Educational Research, 61*(2), 239–264.

Edelman, G. M. (1987). *Neural Darwinism: The theory of neuronal group selection.* New York: Basic Books.

Epstein, G. O., & McDaniel, M. A. (1987). Distinctiveness and the mnemonic benefits of bizarre images. In M. A. McDaniel & M. Pressley (Eds.), *Imagery and related mnemonic processes: Theories, individual differences, and applications.* New York: Springer-Verlag.

Garner, R. (1990). Children's use of strategies in reading. In D. Bjorklund (Ed.), *Children's strategies: Contemporary views of cognitive development* (pp. 245–268). Hillsdale, NJ: Erlbaum.

Garner, R. (1992). Learning from school texts. *Educational Psychologist, 27*(1), 53–64.

Garner, R., Alexander, P., Slater, W., Hare, V. C., Smith, T., & Reis, R. (1986). Children's knowledge of structural properties of expository text. *Journal of Educational Psychology, 78,* 411–416.

Goetz, E. T., & Sadoski, M. (1995). The perils of seduction: Distracting details or incomprehensible abstractions? *Reading Research Quarterly, 30,* 500–511.

Grabe, M. (1986). Attentional processes in education. In G. Phye & T. Andre (Eds.), *Cognitive classroom learning* (pp. 49–82). Orlando, FL: Academic.

Graham, S., & Harris, K. R. (1994). The role and development of self-regulation in the writing process. In D. Schunk & B. J. Zimmerman (Eds.), *Self-regulation of learning and performance.* Hillsdale, NJ: Lawrence Erlbaum.

Hampson, P. J., & Morris, P. E. (1996). *Understanding cognition.* Cambridge, MA: Blackwell.

Harp, S. F., & Mayer, R. E. (1998). How seductive details do their damage: A theory of cognitive interest in science learning. *Journal of Educational Psychology, 90*(3), 414–434.

Holyoak, M. (1991). Symbolic connectionism: A paradigm for third-generation theory of expertise. In K. A. Ericsson & J. Smith (Eds.), *Toward a general theory of expertise.* NY: Cambridge University Press.

Iran-Nejad, A., Marsh, G. E., & Clements, A. C. (1992). The figure and the ground of constructive brain functioning: Beyond explicit memory processes. *Educational Psychologist, 7*(4), 473–492.

James, W. (1890). *The principles of psychology.* New York: Henry Holt.

Jones, B. F., & Hall, J. W. (1982). School applications of the mnemonic keyword method as a study strategy for eighth graders. *Journal of Educational Psychology, 74,* 230–237.

King, A. (1990). Reciprocal peer-questioning: A strategy for teaching students how to learn from lectures. *The Clearing House, 64,* 131–135.

King, A. (1991). Effects of training in strategic questioning on children's problem-solving performance. *Journal of Educational Psychology, 83,* 307–317.

King, A. (1992). Comparison of self-questioning, summarizing, and notetaking review as strategies for learning from lectures. *American Educational Research Journal, 29*(2), 311–323.

King, A. (1994). Guiding knowledge construction in the classroom: Effects of teaching children how to question and how to explain. *American Educational Research Journal, 31*(2), 338–368.

Kulhavey, R. W., Schwartz, N. H., & Peterson, S. (1986). Working memory: The encoding process. In G. Phye & T. Andre (Eds.), *Cognitive classroom learning* (pp. 115–140). Orlando, FL: Academic.

Lampert, M. (1990). When the problem is not the question and the solution is not the answer: Mathematical knowing and teaching. *American Educational Research Journal, 27*(1), 29–63.

Levin, J. R. (1986). Educational applications of mnemonic pictures: Possibilities beyond your wildest imagination. In A. A. Sheikh (Ed.), *Imagery in the educational process* (pp. 202–265). Farmingdale, NY: Baywood.

Levin, M. E., & Levin, J. R. (1990). Scientific mnemonics: Methods for maximizing more than memory. *American Educational Research Journal, 27*(2), 301–321.

Martin, J. (1993). Episodic memory: A neglected phenomenon in the psychology of education. *Educational Psychologist, 28*(2), 169–183.

Mastropieri, M. A., & Fulk, B. J. M. (1990). Enhancing academic performance with mnemonic instruction. In T. E. Scruggs & B. Y. L. Wong (Eds.), *Inter-*

vention research in learning disabilities (pp. 102–112). New York: Springer-Verlag.

Mayer, R. E. (1984). Aids to text comprehension. *Educational Psychologist, 19,* 30–42.

McClelland, J. L., & Rumelhart, D. E. (1986). A distributed model of human learning and memory. In J. L. McClelland & D. E. Rumelhart (Eds.), *Parallel distributed processing: Explanations in the microstructure of cognition, Vol. 2: Psychological and biological models.* Cambridge, MA: MIT Press.

McCormick, C. B., & Levin, J. (1984). A comparison of three different prose-learning variations of the mnemonic keyword. *American Educational Research Journal, 21,* 379–398.

McKeown, M. G., & Curtis, M. E. (1987). *The nature of vocabulary acquisition.* Hillsdale, NJ: Erlbaum.

Miller, G. A. (1956). The magic number seven, plus-or-minus two: Some limits on our capacity for processing information. *Psychological Review, 63,* 81–97.

Miyake, A., & Shah, P. (Eds.). (1999). *Models of working memory.* New York: Cambridge University Press.

Neath, I. (1998). *Human memory.* Pacific Grove, CA: Brooks-Cole.

Newell, A., & Simon, H. A. (1972). *Human problem solving.* Upper Saddle River, NJ: Prentice Hall.

Niesser, U. (1967). *Cognitive psychology:* Appleton-Century-Crofts.

Paivio, A. (1971). *Imagery and verbal processes.* New York: Holt, Rinehart & Winston.

Paivio, A. (1983). The empirical case for dual coding. In J. C. Yuille (Ed.), *Imagery, memory, and cognition* (pp. 307–332). Hillsdale, NJ: Erlbaum.

Paivio, A. (1986). *Mental representations: A dual coding approach.* New York: Oxford University Press.

Prawat, R. S. (1989). Promoting access to knowledge, strategy, and disposition to students: A research synthesis. *Review of Educational Research, 59,* 1–41.

Pressley, M., & El-Dinary, P. B. (1992). Memory strategy instruction. In D. J. Hermann, H. Weingartner, A. Searleman, & C. McEvoy (Eds.), *Memory improvement: Explications for memory theory* (pp. 79–100). New York: Springer-Verlag.

Pressley, M., Borkowski, J., & Schneider, W. (1987). Cognitive strategies: Good strategy users coordinate metacognition and knowledge. *Annals of Child Development, 4,* 89–129.

Pressley, M., Johnson, C. J., Symons, S., McGoldrick, J. A., & Kurita, J. A. (1989). Strategies that improve children's memory and comprehension of text. *The Elementary School Journal, 90*(11), 3–32.

Pressley, M., Wood, E., Woloshyn, V., Martin, V., King, A., & Menke, D. (1992). Encouraging mindful use of prior knowledge: Attempting to construct explanatory answers facilitates learning. *Educational Psychologist, 27*(1), 91–109.

Pylyshyn, L. (1973). What the mind's eye tells the mind's brain: A critique of mental imagery. *Psychological Bulletin, 80,* 1–24.

Quillian, M. R. (1968). Semantic memory. In M. Minsky (Ed.), *Semantic information processing* (pp. 216–270). Cambridge, MA: MIT Press.

Roediger, H. L., III, & Guynn, M. J. (1996). Retrieval processes. In E. L. Bjork & R. A. Bjork (Eds.), *Memory: Handbook of perception and cognition* (2nd ed.) (pp. 197–236). San Diego, CA: Academic Press.

Rohrer, W. D., & Thomas, J. W. (1989). Domain-specific knowledge, metacognition and the promise of instructional reform. In C. B. McCormick, G. E. Miller, & M. Pressley (Eds.), *Cognitive strategy research* (pp. 104–132). New York: Springer-Verlag.

Schank, R. E., & Abelson, R. (1977). *Scripts, plans, goals, and understanding.* Hillsdale, NJ: Erlbaum.

Schneider, W., & Graham, D. J. (1992). Introduction to connectionist modeling in education. *Educational Psychologist, 27*(4), 513–530.

Schoenfeld, A. H. (1985). Metacognition and epistemological issues in mathematical understanding. In E. A. Silver (Ed.), *Teaching and learning mathematical problem solving: Multiple research perspectives* (pp. 361–379). Hillsdale, NJ: Erlbaum.

Schraw, G. (1998). Processing and recall differences among seductive details. *Journal of Educational Psychology, 90*(1), 3–12.

Shulman, L. (1986). Paradigms and research programs in the study of teaching: A contemporary perspective. In M. C. Wittrock (Ed.), *Handbook of research on teaching* (pp. 1–36). New York: Macmillan.

Snowman, J. (1986). Learning tactics and strategies. In G. F. Phye & T. Andre (Eds.), *Cognitive classroom learning: Understanding, thinking, and problem solving* (pp. 243–275). Orlando, FL: Academic.

Solso, R. L. (1988). *Cognitive psychology* (2nd ed.). New York: Allyn & Bacon.

Spires, H. A., & Donley, J. (1998). Prior knowledge activation: Inducing engagement with informational tests. *Journal of Educational Psychology, 90*(2), 249–260.

Spoehr, K. T. (1994). Enhancing the acquisition of conceptual structures through Hypermedia. In K. McGilly (Ed.), *Classroom lessons: Integrating cognitive theory and classroom practice* (pp. 75–101). Cambridge, MA: MIT Press.

Stanovich, K. E. (1986). Matthew effects in reading: Some consequences of individual differences in the acquisition of literacy. *Reading Research Quarterly, 21,* 360–406.

Thagard, R. (1989). Explanatory coherence. *Behavioral and Brain Sciences, 12*(3), 435–502.

Tulving, E. (1974). Cue-dependent forgetting. *American Scientist, 62,* 74–82.

Tulving, E. (1985). How many memory systems are there? *American Psychologist, 40,* 385–398.

Tulving, E., & Madigan, S. A. (1970). Memory and verbal learning. *Annual Review of Psychology, 21,* 437–484.

Turnure, J. E., & Lane, J. F. (1987). Special education applications of mnemonics. In M. A. McDaniel & M. Pressley (Eds.), *Imagery and related mnemonic processes* (pp. 329–357). New York: Springer-Verlag.

Wittrock, M. C. (1990). Generating processes of comprehension. *Educational Psychologist, 24*(4), 345–376.

Wittrock, M. C. (1992). Generative learning processes of the brain. *Educational Psychologist, 27*(4), 531–541.

CHAPTER 8
Cognitive Perspectives:
II. Metacognition and Problem Solving

The reconceptualization of thinking and learning that is emerging suggests that becoming a good thinker in any domain may be as much a matter of acquiring the habits and dispositions of interpretation and sense-making as of acquiring any particular set of skills (Resnick, 1988, p. 58).

In the preschool years, most situations that require learning or remembering are part of the child's daily experiences, and the reasons for learning are fairly obvious (Howe, 1988). Young children learn to feed and dress themselves, and they acquire a lexicon of terms for the people and objects in their daily environment.

In contrast, in the school setting, the reasons for learning are less obvious. As the child progresses through school, learning tasks become more complex and abstract. Some middle-school textbooks in mathematics, for example, introduce the concepts of probability and statistics. In addition, students are responsible for tasks such as learning from text and applying their learning to solve problems in various knowledge domains.

The need for self-directed learning does not end with formal schooling. Rapid increases in knowledge in several disciplines, the explosion of technology into daily affairs, and technological advances are changing the workplace and placing new demands on individuals. Managing one's learning and learning to solve new problems are important capabilities in a variety of settings.

THE NATURE OF COMPLEX LEARNING

The basic learning processes studied by cognitive theorists are perception, encoding, and storage and retrieval. Also researched are comprehension-related strategies that can facilitate these processes (e.g., focusing attention, elaboration, and summarizing text).

Initially, the complex processes addressed by cognitive researchers were those involved in solving problems that were not related to school subjects. Examples include Katona's matchstick problems and so-called "move" problems. An example of a move problem is the Tower of Hanoi where the goal is to transfer a stack of different-size discs from one peg to another without placing a larger disc on top of a smaller one. The rationale for studying these problems was that simple domains permitted a focus on the development of strategies and this work could then be expanded into semantic-rich domains (Schoenfeld, 1992).

Since the early years, research on complex cognitive processes has expanded in two ways. One is the extension of research on problem solving to issues in subject-matter disciplines. Also included are the differences between novices and experts in areas such as physics and historical document analysis.

The second body of research addresses the knowledge of higher order processes involved in the selection and management of specific activities in learning and thinking. An example is knowing that the skimming strategy used to read the newspaper is inadequate for obtaining information from a difficult text.

The concept of a particular knowledge base that addresses the organization and management of learning is relatively new. In the early 1970s, learning to use comprehension strategies, such as self-questioning and summarizing text, was viewed as moving from non-use to the spontaneous production of the effective strategy (Harnishfeger & Bjorklund, 1990). Spontaneous strategy production was attributed to increasing planning capabilities and acquisition of the component skills in the particular strategy (p. 9).

In the later 1970s and 1980s, an alternative view of strategy use emerged. This view introduced the concept of higher order processes that control the use of specific strategies. An early development was the concept of metamemory (Flavell, 1971). Specifically, metamemory referred to one's verbalizable knowledge about memory storage and the person, task and strategy variables that influence the performance of memory (Flavell & Wellman, 1977). In the late 1970s, research interests expanded to include knowledge about one's cognitive functioning in general (in addition to memory) (Harnishfeger & Bjorklund, 1990). The term **metacognition** was applied to this broad focus.

Metacognition

Important issues are the basic definitions of metacognition and differences between younger and older learners and between experts and novices in the use of metacognitive strategies.

Components

The terms *metacognition* and *metacognitive knowledge* have been defined in somewhat different ways by different researchers. In general, metacognition involves thinking about thinking. Some perspectives emphasize the individual's knowledge about cognition and strategy use. Others emphasize both the knowledge and regulation of cognition (Brown, 1987).

Knowledge of Cognition.   Key components of metacognition are (1) knowledge about and awareness of one's own thinking and (2) knowledge of when and where to use acquired strategies (Pressley & McCormick, 1995, p. 2). Knowledge about one's thinking includes information about one's own capacities and limitations and aware-ness of difficulties as they arise during learning so that remedial action may be taken.

Knowledge of when and where to use acquired strategies includes knowledge about the task and situations for which particular goal-specific strategies are appro-priate. For example, students are sometimes unaware that a difficult text for which they have little background knowledge should be read differently than a text on familiar topics. The students lack important metacognitive knowledge about reading. In other words, metacognitive knowledge is important because simply learning par-ticular goal-specific strategies, such as summarizing, underlining, and note taking, is insufficient to be a good strategy user (Pressley, Borkowski, & Schneider, 1987).

Alexander, Schallert, and Hare (1991) also consider knowledge of plans and goals to be a component of metacognition. For example, young children sometimes believe that the purpose of reading is to pronounce all the words without mistakes. They also believe that good reading involves verbatim recall of the text. These chil-dren lack sufficient metacognitive knowledge about the purposes of reading.

Regulation of Cognition.   One issue in the regulation of cognition is the differ-ence between metacognitive and cognitive strategies. The major difference is that they fulfill different goals. Cognitive strategies are applied to content or information whereas metacognitive strategies are applied to one's thinking. For example, a reader who is familiar with the Louisiana Purchase reads the chapter and takes notes on the major points. These activities are cognitive strategies that are undertaken to facilitate comprehension and learning. The goal is to improve the student's knowl-edge (Flavell, 1979).

Later, the reader is concerned about being prepared for an upcoming test. She then quizzes herself to evaluate her level of preparedness using the end-of-chapter questions and her own self-generated questions. As indicated in chapter 7, this strat-egy both assists the learner in constructing meaning and is a metacognitive strategy for checking one's level of learning (evaluation). An example of metacognitive evalu-ation methods in mathematics is the way in which students can judge the reason-ableness of their answers (van Haneghan & Baker, 1989).

Researchers have proposed somewhat different models of metacognition for different tasks. One model includes the three components of planning, evaluation, and monitoring (Jacobs & Paris, 1987). Planning consists of setting goals, activating relevant resources (including budgeting time), and selecting appropriate strategies. Evaluation involves determining one's level of understanding.

Monitoring, the third component, involves checking one's progress and select-ing appropriate repair strategies when originally selected strategies are not working. Developing meaning from text while reading, which involves evaluation and moni-toring, is referred to as *comprehension monitoring*. The term refers to one's aware-ness of the quality and degree of comprehension and knowing what to do and how to do it when one discovers comprehension failures (Dole, Duffy, Roehler, & Pear-son, 1991). For example, readers may proceed through a relatively easy reading assignment with rapid construction of meaning until a confusion or other comprehension problem occurs and is detected. Garner (1990, p. 251) describes this situation as cognitive failure (information processing is impaired), but a metacognitive success (the reader notices the problem and addresses it).

Research indicates that active monitoring and control of comprehension during reading increases the likelihood of one's understanding of text and one's knowledge that he or she understands (Hacker, 1998). When readers fail to monitor and control comprehension, "triggering events" that can alert them to comprehension failure (such as realizing they do not know the meaning of one or more of the words) simply do not occur. The result is that the reader erroneously believes he or she has comprehended the text.

A model of the metacognitive activities in studying describes four stages in which these activities occur (see Table 8.1). They are defining the task, goal setting and planning, enacting study tactics and strategies, and adapting studying (Winne & Hadwin, 1998). If the study task is very familiar, stage one may be skipped.

Each stage generates a product that is evaluated (a metacognitive activity) and updates the conditions of work in the next stage. The student's perception of the learning task, for example, is the basis for setting goals in stage two.

Important in the model is the student's personal standards, which influence the actions at each stage. For example, students with an orientation to "just get by"

TABLE 8.1
A model of the metacognitive activities in studying[1]

Stage	Description	Example
Defining the task	Generate a perception of the nature of the studying task, available resources and constraints.	Complete an assigned reading on volcanoes from *National Geographic;* language is complex for middle school students, but student has $1\frac{1}{2}$ hours to complete assignment.
Goal setting and planning	Select or generate goals and a plan for addressing the study task.	Read the article for deep processing to prepare for unit test; personal note taking and self-questioning are needed.
Enacting study tactics and strategies	Implement the activities selected in stage two, and fine-tune, if necessary.	Difficult vocabulary encountered during reading leads to pauses to look up term definitions and rereading.
Adapting studying	(1) Make large-scale adjustments to the task, goals, plans, and engagement.	Major difficulties in understanding the article lead to searching for basic information about volcanoes on the Internet.
	or	or
	(2) Alter one's conditions for future studying (knowledge, skills, beliefs, dispositions, and motivational factors).	Lower one's standard of proficiency for difficult material to shallow processing.

[1] Stages and definitions are summarized from Winne & Hadwin (1998).

may, in stage two, select simplistic tasks, such as paraphrasing headings and noting boldface terms in the text.

In stage three, the internal feedback generated by monitoring the enactment of study strategies may lead to adjustments. However, if the student perceives no tactics are available to achieve the goals, the task may be abandoned. Stage four, a broad metacognitive activity, does not refer to fine-tuning ongoing strategies. Instead, one of two adaptive decisions is made. One is to make large-scale adjustments to the student's understandings of the task, goals, plans, and strategies. The second is to make relatively permanent changes in future study conditions. An example is lowering one's personal standards for success (Winne & Hadwin, 1998, p. 285).

As indicated by these examples, metacognitive strategies are considered to be conscious and intentional. They involve an awareness of one's thinking processes and decisions about the actions to be taken if progress is unsatisfactory. In some cases, however, metacognitive processes can be highly automatized. For example, some studying tasks may be so familiar that defining the task (stage one in the model) is bypassed (Winne & Hadwin, 1998). Further, expert readers process text fluidly and rapidly without conscious attention allocated to their level of comprehension until a contradiction or other difficulty occurs. They then take steps to resolve the difficulty.

Relationship of Metacognition to Other Internal States

At least three internal learner states interact with or influence the implementation of the individual's metacognitive skills. They are the learner's knowledge about a topic or domain, achievement goal orientation, and beliefs about oneself as a learner [referred to as personal agency formulations (Zimmerman, 1995)].

The Learner's Topic or Domain Knowledge. The cognitive resources available for processing and evaluation are limited. Therefore, detailed knowledge about a topic or in a domain allows an individual to process information about the domain efficiently and with little effort (Bjorklund, Muir-Broaddus, & Schneider, 1990, p. 95). In other words, metacognitive strategies play minor roles in comprehension and recall when an individual is well-informed on a topic. For example, a biology professor rarely has to monitor comprehension when reading about the effects of acid rain on the environment (Garner, 1990). However, when reading about Renaissance art, a domain in which he has little knowledge, he must use metacognitive strategies to generate knowledge from the text.

Metacognitive strategies can enhance learning when domain knowledge is weak. In one study, novices in knowledge about soccer with greater metacognitive knowledge of study tactics recalled more than novices with less metacognitive knowledge (Winne & Hadwin, 1998).

Achievement Goal Orientation. An achievement goal orientation refers to different conceptions of success with accompanying reasons for engaging in academic tasks. Three types of goal orientation are mastery, performance, and failure-avoidance (see chapter 12 for a discussion). Students with a mastery goal orientation, for example, seek to demonstrate their ability through developing new skills (Ames,

1992). These students, given the opportunity, also develop effective and sophisti-cated metacognitive skills.

In contrast, a performance goal orientation involves a focus on score attainment or counting the tasks to be completed (Ames, 1992; Elliott & Dweck, 1988). In one study, individuals who studied more each week on glossary terms had lower final examination scores than students who prepared for frequent quizzes (Tuckman, 1996). The lower scores were attributed to a performance goal of adding terms to their glossary rather than a goal of expanding one's knowledge.

A third orientation, referred to as failure avoidance, involves a preoccupation with one's image in the class (Midgley, Kaplan, Middleton, & Maeke, 1998). Student attention is focused on avoiding such actions as responding in class and volunteering for difficult subtasks in small group work. In terms of learning, this orientation fosters nonproductive strategies.

Personal Agency Formulations.   Metacognitive models of the management and control of learning emphasize knowledge states and reasoning about tasks, goals, resources, and learning progress. Factors that influence decision making include personal agency formulations—beliefs and judgment about one's competence that often are formed intuitively and are applied in particular contexts (Zimmerman, 1995). An example is believing that one "is terrible" at solving mathematical word problems. As a result, the individual is not motivated to attempt a solution or to monitor one's efforts (Hacker, 1998, p. 10). Such views, referred to as *self-efficacy,* are defined as beliefs in one's capabilities to organize and execute the actions necessary to manage and be successful in particular situations (Bandura, 1995, p. 2). Included are tasks in the academic sphere (Zimmerman, 1995). Individuals with high self-efficacy engage in challenging tasks, persist, even when confronted with difficulties, and flexibly alter their strategies when initial steps or strategies are ineffective.

Models of effective learners that incorporate the motivational construct of self-efficacy along with goal setting and monitoring and evaluating learning, are referred as models of self-regulated learning (see chapter 11; Schunk & Zimmerman, 1998). These perspectives address issues such as effort, persistence, and task choice. Whereas metacognitive models focus on the particular metacognitive skills enacted by individuals during learning, the self-regulated learning models focus on the relationship of self-efficacy to goal setting and other metacognitive activities.

In summary, the enactment of metacognitive capabilities is influenced by at three types of internal learner states. They are the topic or domain knowledge of the individual, the individual's achievement goal orientation, and one's personal beliefs about his or her capabilities to be successful in particular situations.

Differences in Metacognitive Capabilities

Differences in metacognitive capabilities, in general, are found in two types of comparisons. They are (1) the differences between younger and older children and (2) the differences between experts and novices.

The differences between younger and older children, on occasion, have been referred to as developmental differences. However, in large measure, they are the result of an increasing knowledge as the child has more experience with formal schooling.

Differences Between Younger and Older Children.   Several differences in metacognition between younger and older students have been identified. Among them are the extent of awareness of the purposes of instruction and different task demands, monitoring one's comprehension and understanding, detection of mathematical errors, and awareness of strategy flexibility.

Awareness of Instructional Purposes and Task Demands.   School curricula and classroom lessons often reflect multiple purposes. For example, the general purpose of a mathematics exercise may be for students to learn to apply a particular procedure. In addition, the teacher expects the students' papers to be neat and handed in at the end of the class period. Young children typically are aware of the peripheral lesson requirements, but they often are unaware of the broader purposes of instruction. Thus, they may report that the goal of instruction is to finish seatwork on time. Or, as mentioned earlier, they may believe that the goal of reading is to pronounce all the words correctly (Alexander et al., 1991).

Lack of awareness of task performance is not universal, however. Fang and Cox (1999) found that some preschool children, when asked to dictate their favorite experience so that other children may read it, monitored and self-corrected their ongoing oral speech. Comments included, "What do I want to do here?" and "I wanna change that word."

Recognition of the need to remember as a purpose for working through instructional materials is a capability that develops slowly throughout childhood. One study asked young children what they would do to remember information (Jacobs & Paris, 1987). Options such as to think hard and try to remember and to ask yourself questions about the ideas were provided. Many of the children, however, selected the option that stated they would skip the parts they did not understand.

A second difference between younger and older children is that younger children often are unaware of task demands. They are likely to believe, for example, that reading a story for fun and reading for science or social studies do not differ. In other words, children often have only a rough idea about the factors that influence task difficulty (Bruning, Schraw, & Ronning, 1995). Karmiloff-Smith (1979) documented differences in children ages 4 to 9 who were to construct a railroad track in the form of a complete loop. The 4- and 5-year-olds picked up pieces at random and arranged them in that order. The 8- and 9-year-olds, however, first sorted the pieces into straight and curved and then chose systematically from each stack to complete the loop.

Monitoring One's Comprehension and Understanding.   Research indicates that children show little indication of monitoring their comprehension to determine whether it is successful (Kuhn, 1999, p. 21). Further, although improvement accompanies development, mastery often is not attained even by adulthood.

Evidence indicates that younger and older children differ in their ability to accurately monitor their comprehension (e.g., Garner, 1987, 1990; Jacobs & Paris, 1987). One measure of comprehension monitoring used in research studies is the error detection task. Subjects read or listen to a text that contains inconsistencies with either the text or world knowledge. Vosniadou, Pearson, and Rogers (1988) found that first graders were able to detect inconsistencies in texts that were read to them when the topic was a familiar one. However, they were unable to recognize anomalies in unfamiliar material they listened to, even if the contradiction appeared later in the text. In contrast, third and fifth graders were able to detect inconsistencies in texts on unfamiliar topics.

Other studies report similar differences in error detection, but note that both younger and older children read the contradictory statements more slowly than other lines in the story (for a discussion, see Garner, 1990). One explanation for the observed discrepancies between reading times and reported contradictions is that younger children have only a momentary awareness of comprehension difficulties, which they dismiss as unimportant (Garner, 1990).

Detecting Mathematical Errors and Other Problems.   Related to the concept of error detection in text is the detection of mathematical errors. One application is the use of strategies to check one's work at the completion of a problem. The other is the detection of logical inconsistencies in word problems.

A study by Van Haneghan (1986) found that first-, third-, and fifth-grade children differed in their strategies for checking their answers to grade-appropriate open-sentence problems. First graders typically used memorized addition and subtraction facts or counted on their fingers or with objects. In contrast, the older children checked their work against a computational standard, such as adding the column up in the opposite direction. Of interest is that most of the children who originally arrived at wrong answers were not led to change their answers on the basis of the checking.

In another study, children were presented with several problems that required dealing with "more than" and "less than" relations among quantities (Van Haneghan & Baker, 1989). The tasks included the problem text, an algorithmic form of the problem, and another child's answer. Problems ranged from correctly solved, to computational or operational error, to unanswerable, but "solved" anyway. (An example of an unsolvable problem is stating that Matt has 22 cents and Ken has 69 cents and asking how many more cents Matt has than Ken.) Results indicated that the fifth graders found more of the errors than the third graders. Of the various problem errors, calculational errors were most likely to be found, and unanswerable problems were least likely to be identified (p. 229).

One reason for the lack of identification of the unsolvable problems is that children develop a "word problem" schema in which word problems are divorced from real-world problems. Also, children often develop limited expectations for the structure of word problems. One group of third- and fifth-grade children, for example, stated that a legitimate problem was unsolvable because it differed from typical problems (Van Haneghan, 1986). The misjudged problem stated that Sam had 28 cookies and he had 13 more than John. The problem asked how many cookies John had. The two reasons given by the children as to the unsolvability of the problem were (1) the problem does not tell you how many John has, and (2) the problem says first that Sam has 28 cookies and then he has 13, and this does not make sense (Van Haneghan, 1986, p. 225).

A somewhat different problem detection skill is essential in writing. Specifically, revising one's writing depends on detecting sentences or passages that do not communicate clearly. However, students often fail to revise their writing because they assume the text is clear and understandable (Graham & Harris, 1994). Beal (1989) found that third-grade children revised more ambiguous messages than younger children. The performance differences were largely the result of the level of skill in finding the problem in the passage.

Awareness of Strategy Flexibility. A fourth characteristic of children is that they often lack the knowledge about when and where to make use of different strategies. This component of metacognition is described by Paris, Lipson, and Wilson (1983) as *conditional knowledge.* The lack of conditional knowledge is indicated by children's inability to transfer learned strategies to new situations.

The development of conditional knowledge is related, in part, to children's reliance on primitive strategies that they have developed. These strategies, such as copying selected text sentences verbatim (used as a summarization strategy), hinder their development of more appropriate strategies. Moreover, these primitive strategies hinder their awareness of strategy flexibility.

Although the lack of conditional knowledge is most noticeable in young children, it is found in other age groups as well. For example, beginning graduate students may focus on memorizing content from textbooks instead of integrating information and ideas (Garner, 1990).

The Development of Cognitive Maturity. Coming to cognitive maturity in complex societies is not an easy task, and it involves several factors. First, it depends on developing knowledge about the internal mental world. Basic information about this world includes the fact that people possess minds, mental processes are distinct from feelings and emotions, and a person can understand and react to his or her mental states (Wellman, 1985). Young children, however, have little knowledge of beliefs, certainties, illusions, mistakes, or deceptions (Garner, 1990). Thus, they are not skilled in identifying inconsistencies in text passages or monitoring their thinking. Older children, in contrast, have a more sophisticated theory of mind and also are able to treat language itself as an object of thinking. Thus, older children can use this knowledge to direct and manage their thinking.

Second, developing cognitive maturity also involves mastering tasks that may not be of interest to the child. Kindergarten children can differentiate classroom activities into work and play and can state that "work" activities are more important to the teacher than play activities (Garner, 1990). However, they may expend less cognitive effort on tasks that represent work. The often-cited example is the student who can cite earned run averages, runs batted in, and other baseball statistics of major players, past and present. The student, however, has difficulty in history and other fact-loaded subjects.

Expert–Novice Differences. Several differences have been identified between experts and novices in metacognitive skills. For example, in contrast to novices, experts in diagnosing X-rays tested and revised their diagnoses until they accounted for all the characteristics of a particular situation (Lesgold et al., 1988).

In reading, the metacognitive skills of experts and novices differ in four major ways. First, experts are aware of the general goals of reading and studying and of the specific objectives of a particular task (Rohrer & Thomas, 1989). As a result, they allocate their time and effort differently to different tasks and typically expend greater time and effort on more difficult tasks. Also, in the rapid pace of the classroom, which often has an emphasis on task completion, experts weigh the costs of using different strategies against the benefits of the goals to be achieved (Garner, 1990).

In contrast, novices tend not to read for meaning. They do not adjust their reading behavior to different kinds of content or reading situations. Further, they do not slow down for difficult passages (Rohrer & Thomas, 1989).

Second, experts are aware of and use "fix-it" strategies when problems occur (Dole et al., 1991). In this way, difficulties are addressed before they become major problems. Third, experts are more likely to use available resources, such as the strategy of looking back at prior text when a difficulty occurs and the pause-and-reflect strategy.

Finally, the strategy use of experts is more flexible than that of novices in at least two important ways. They are more likely to use different strategies in different circumstances, and they also adapt question-asking strategies to different kinds of texts and task demands (p. 248). Novices, in contrast, tend to apply a single strategy across contexts. Moreover, although they may use strategies, such as context clues, when directed to do so, they do not apply them spontaneously (Rohrer & Thomas, 1989).

In one study, social science professors were asked to read aloud a text in their area of expertise that was important to them (Wyatt et al., 1993). The readers applied strategies that assisted them in abstracting important information from the articles. These strategies included anticipating and predicting information, testing predictions as they read, searching for information related to their reading purpose, looking backward and forward in the text to find particular information, and developing summary interpretations of the articles.

Pressley and Afflerbach (1995) developed a comprehensive catalog of the processes reported in verbal protocols of reading. They found 15 common processes, which included overviewing before reading, searching for and paying more attention to important information, and relating important points in the text to each other to understand the text as a whole. The authors concluded that skilled reading is constructively responsive reading. That is, the reader exploits text clues, reflects on the text after reading, and monitors his or reading extensively (Pressley & Afflerbach, 1995; Pressley, 1995).

Summary

In the 1970s, the spontaneous production of effective strategies was thought to result from increases in planning skills and the learning of subskills in a strategy. The revised view of the 1980s is that higher order processes control the use of cognitive strategies. Referred to as metacognition, this knowledge base includes two broad components. They are the knowledge of and regulation of cognition. Knowledge of cognition includes knowledge about tasks, strategies, instructional plans, and goals. Regulation of cognition involves setting goals, activating relevant resources, selecting appropriate strategies, evaluating one's understanding, checking one's progress, and redirecting effort, if necessary. Although conscious and internal, metacognitive processes can become highly automatized. Also, the greater the learner's knowledge base, the less need for metacognitive strategies.

Individual differences that can influence and interact with the execution of metacognitive strategies include the learner's topic or domain knowledge, achievement goal orientation, and beliefs about personal agency. Individuals with a mastery goal orientation seek to develop new skills and typically develop effective and complex metacognitive strategies. A performance goal orientation, in contrast, typically leads to simplistic or surface strategies whereas failure avoidance generates nonproductive monitoring and evaluation activities. Beliefs about personal agency—specifically, self-efficacy—influence goal setting and learner persistence and flexibility during learning.

Several developmental differences in metacognition between younger and older children have been identified. They are awareness of instructional purposes and changing task demands, the capability of monitoring one's comprehension and mathematical errors, and awareness of strategy flexibility. These differences result, in part, from increasing cognitive maturity in which children begin to recognize and react to their mental processes. Further, experts in metacognitive thinking allocate their time and effort differently for different tasks, use "fix-it" strategies when problems occur, and are more flexible in strategy use than novices.

Problem Solving

Problem solving, in general, involves dealing with new and unfamiliar tasks when the relevant solution methods (even if partly mastered) are not known (Schoenfeld, 1992, p. 354). Initially, research on problem solving focused on the strategies used by problem solvers to research the correct solution (see the section on prior research). However, various interpretations of the definition and the role of problem solving in the school curriculum have led to a re-examination of problem solving in the 1990s. That is, the focus is the learner's interpretation, structuring, and adaptation of knowledge (both content and strategic) to new situations (Resnick, 1989). Important topics are the different types of problems, the major subprocesses in problem solving, and the differences between expert and novice problem solvers.

Types of Problems

Formally defined, a problem consists of three components: givens, a goal, and allowable operators. The givens include the elements, the relations among them, and conditions or constraints that constitute the initial form of the problem (Anderson, 1985; Davidson & Sternberg, 1998). The goal is the desired outcome or solution and the allowable operators are the steps or procedures that will transform the givens into the goal (Mayer & Wittrock, 1996).

In addition, the problem situation also may include obstacles (Davidson & Sternberg, 1998). They are the characteristics of either the problem and/or the student that make it difficult for the student to transform the initial form of the problem in the desired outcome. The situations referred to as functional fixedness and problem set by the Gestalt researchers are examples.

Two types of problems mentioned in the literature are well-defined and ill-defined. In well-defined problems, the givens, desired goal, and allowable operators are explicit. Computation problems, such as 2.69 × .078 = _____, are examples. Well-defined problems are the type that Edward Thorndike addressed in his research on the applications of connectionism to school learning.

In ill-defined problems, the givens, desired goal, and allowable operators (procedures) are not immediately clear to the problem solver (Mayer & Wittrock, 1996). The problems investigated by the Gestalt researchers are examples. An example in the school setting is "Write a computer program that can serve as a teacher's grade book" (p. 48). Although most educational materials address well-defined problems, most problems in the real world are ill-defined.

Problems also may be categorized as routine and nonroutine (Mayer, 1992; Mayer & Wittrock, 1996). Routine problems are those that the individual has solved in the past and he or she instantly recognizes a solution. Nonroutine problems, in contrast, are those that the individual has not solved previously and for which he or she cannot generate a preexisting solution (Mayer, 1992, p. 4). These designations are analogous to the processes identified by the Gestalt researchers as reproductive and productive thinking (Katona, 1940; Wertheimer, 1945/1959). Reproductive thinking is the application of procedures used to solve similar problems whereas productive thinking is the construction of a novel solution.

These categories, however, actually identify the endpoints of a continuum. Between these two extremes lie problems for which the individual does not have a ready solution but which also do not require a novel solution. Instead, they require the application of prior strategies in new ways or the restructuring of prior strategies for different goals. Examples include the problems devised by first-grade children who are learning to solve various types of simple word problems in mathematics. Among them are finding out how much older a book they are reading is than they are and how old the book is this year (Fennema, Franke, Carpenter, & Carey, 1993).

Prior Cognitive Research

Prior developments in the 1970s include the General Problem Solver (GPS), discussions of heuristics, and artificial intelligence research.

The GPS. Developed from tasks such as the Tower of Hanoi problems, the GPS identifies three main steps in problem solving. First, represent the problem, the givens, and the legal operators. Second, establish goals and subgoals and begin solving for the subgoals. Three, use means–ends analysis to assess progress; redefine subgoals, if necessary (Newell & Simon, 1972). Means–ends analysis involves assessing the differences between a present state and a desired state, searching for an appropriate operator to reduce the differences, and evaluating the results (Simon, 1980).

GPS is particularly appropriate for well-defined problems for which subgoals can be clearly defined and which are solved in sequential steps. Many problems, however, do not fit this category. Another difficulty is that most problems require domain-specific information to solve them. However, individuals cannot derive domain-specific strategies from general problem-solving approaches.

Heuristics.   A focus on well-defined problems led to discussions of heuristics, which typically refer to a rule of thumb for reducing uncertainty about a problem. In addition to means–ends analysis, examples are working backward from the goal state, hill climbing, and dividing the problem into subproblems. Hill climbing involves taking any step that moves the problem solver closer to the goal. One difficulty with such strategies is that they may or may not result in a solution. For example, the rule of thumb "Always take the smaller number from the larger number" in subtraction will result in errors some of the time (e.g., $3 - 7 = -4$, not $+4$).

In addition to the prior examples, Polya (1973) also included general heuristic strategies used to match conceptual and procedural knowledge to a particular problem. Examples are searching one's memory for similar problems for special cases and analogies.

In a pair of studies, Gick and Holyoak (1980, 1983) used the medical problem developed by Duncker (1945) discussed in chapter 3. Subjects were asked to solve the problem immediately after reading a brief analogous episode of a general dispersing his forces to invade a town. However, the results indicated that the presence of an analogous situation is insufficient for subjects to solve the target problem. Spontaneous transfer occurred in the majority of subjects (62%) only when they were given two priming stories, asked to write a summary of them, and then were given an explicit statement of the solution principle.

Like the GPS, one difficulty with heuristics is that most problems require domain-specific information in order to solve them. Another is that heuristics do not address the key thinking processes required by the problem.

Artificial Intelligence Research.   This research involves programming computers with humanlike rules inferred from think-aloud protocols of human subjects. A dramatic example of the artificial intelligence research is PARRY, a program that simulated a paranoid patient so well that psychiatrists communicating by computer terminal were unable to determine whether the "patient" was real or a computer program (Bereiter, 1991). The rules incorporated into PARRY included rules for reacting emotionally to the psychiatrist's language in addition to rules for interpreting the psychiatrist's words.

Despite the success of PARRY and other programs, some concerns about this approach to analyzing problem solving have emerged (Bereiter, 1991). One major concern is that the easiest tasks to simulate on the computer are those that are most difficult for humans, that is, extended chains of reasoning (p. 11). Conversely, the tasks that humans complete easily are extremely difficult to program with rule-based systems. Examples are associative memory retrieval and pattern recognition (Bereiter, 1991, p. 11). A second major concern is that human problem solving is not as neat and orderly as portrayed in the computer programs.

Subprocesses in Problem Solving

Research on problem solving in the 1970s primarily addressed move problems that require the physical movement and recombination of objects to fulfill a specific goal. In recent years, the shift in research focus to learner construction, interpretation, and adaptation of knowledge to new situations places primary importance on the thinking strategies of students. Further, expertise requires knowledge of principles in a domain rather than general heuristic strategies (Chi, Glaser, & Farr, 1991). Important in these activities is the metacognitive skills of planning and monitoring and evaluating one's decisions.

Table 8.2 illustrates the four major subprocesses of problem solving, all of which require metacognition. The major subprocesses are described as representing the problem, planning strategies, overcoming obstacles, and executing plans (Mayer & Wittrock, 1996; Davidson & Sternberg, 1998). Further, in addition to planning, the metacognitive skills of monitoring and evaluating one's decisions also are important.

Representing the Problem.   This phase, often overlooked by students, is essential to successful problem solving for both well-defined and open-ended situations. Important in identifying the key features of the problems and creating a mental map of the relationships is the related information in the learner's long-term memory. Included are informal and intuitive knowledge about the domain (tacit knowledge in the Alexander, Schallert, & Hare model), content knowledge, and metacognitive knowledge about problem approaches and strategies for similar problems.

Some problem solvers, however, possess inaccurate metacognitive knowledge about problems. For example, some schoolchildren thought that they need not read

TABLE 8.2
Subprocesses in problem solving and the role of metacognitive skills

Subprocesses	Role of metacognitive skills
1. Representing the problem (identify the most relevant features and create a mental map of the components.)	1a) Assist in accessing relevant information from long-term memory that can contribute to the identification of key problem components. b) Assist in creating a "mental map" of the givens, the relations among them, the goal, and the constraints (Davidson & Sternberg, 1998). c) Assist in selective recoding, selective combination, and selective comparison, when necessary (Davidson & Sternberg, 1998).
2. Planning	2a) Review and select plans and strategies, perhaps engaging in structured exploration (Schoenfeld, 1992). b) Initiate 1a above, when necessary.
3. Overcoming obstacles	3a) Assist in searching LTM for new information. b) Initiate 1c above.
4. Executing plans (and overcoming obstaces)	4a) Monitor progress and modify plans when necessary. b) Return to 3, if necessary.

an entire math problem because the critical information was always in the last sentence (Briars & Larkin, 1994).

After identifying the key relevant information in the problem, creating a mental map of the relationships is important. This process assists the individual to organize the conditions, decide on appropriate steps, and keep track of his or her progress (Davidson & Sternberg, 1998).

Difficulties in constructing a mental map of the problem may require the processes of selective recoding, selective combination, and selective comparison. Selective recoding involves seeing elements that previously were unnoticed and selective combination involves putting the problem elements together in a new way. The result is a new mental representation of the problem and the goal. Selective comparison is the discovery of a nonobvious relationship between problem elements and already-acquired information (Davidson & Sternberg, 1998, p. 53).

These processes reflect the components of problem solving identified earlier by the Gestalt researchers. Specifically, they include "the restructuring of the given material" (Köhler, 1969, p. 146), mentally redefining and clarifying the problem, such as redefining the goal (Duncker, 1945), or reformulating the functions of the givens (Maier, 1930).

Planning.   Effective problem solvers review strategies and tactics prior to implementing them [the structured exploration identified by Schoenfeld (1992)]. The importance of this phase is that it helps the problem solver anticipate the consequences of particular approaches and helps to avoid costly mistakes (Holyoak, 1995). Unsuccessful identification of a viable strategy may require the review and possible reorganization of the learner's mental map of the problem (1 in Table 8.2).

The importance of representing the problem and planning is indicated in the differences in the problem-solving behavior of a faculty member and a group of students faced with a difficult two-part problem. The faculty member spent more than half his allotted time in analyzing and structured exploring before beginning to implement a solution (Schoenfeld, 1992). Students, however, began to work immediately on the problem. Also, although they had more of the facts and procedures readily accessible to them than the faculty member, few solved the problem. The faculty member generated a number of potential wild-goose chases, but he abandoned paths that did not bear fruit and solved the problem (p. 356). (See the following section on the differences between expert and novice problem solvers.)

Overcoming Obstacles.   One major obstacle that can occur during planning is the state referred to as stereotypy (Davidson & Sternberg, 1998), which consists of the problem set and functional fixedness identified by the Gestalt researchers. The other is the inability to generate any plans or procedures, which occurs most often in insight problems. One strategy is to search long-term memory for models, analogies and metaphors that may provide a new perspective on the problem. Another is to take a break from the problem to allow one's thoughts to incubate (Davidson & Sternberg, 1998).

Executing Plans.   Students often fail to correctly solve problems because they do not monitor their execution of the selected strategy. Monitoring is important to keep track of the steps already executed and the actions yet to be completed. It also can prevent misapplication of routine steps in a strategy. For example, Vye et al. (1997) found that, in solving a complex multistage problem, use of inappropriate data and calculation errors accounted for 13 and 2 percent of the errors, respectively, of sixth-grade students. Further, Declos and Harrington (1991) found that requiring middle-school students to monitor their strategies in solving computer-based problems reduced errors and decreased problem-solving time.

Summary
The formal components of a problem are the givens, the goal, and the allowable operators or procedures that transform the given information. The situation also may include obstacles that impede progress in solving the problem.

Two categorizations of problems are well-defined (information is explicit) and ill-defined (information is implicit). From the learner's perspective, problems also may be described as routine (has an instantly recognizable solution) and nonroutine (involves developing a novel solution). However, between these two designations are problems that require the restructuring of prior strategies to fit a new goal.

Cognitive research in the 1970s primarily included development of the General Problem Solver (GPS), discussions of heuristics, and artificial intelligence research. A limitation of GPS and heuristics is that they do not provide for domain-specific knowledge. Currently, research is beginning to focus on the subprocesses of problem solving and the related metacognitive skills. Identified subprocesses are representing the problem, which includes identifying key elements and creating a mental map, planning, overcoming obstacles, and executing the plans. Overcoming obstacles often requires taking account of previously unnoticed elements, combining them in new ways, and discovering new relationships between problem elements and learner knowledge. In addition to metacognitive knowledge about problems and strategies, the skills of planning, monitoring, and evaluation are essential in successful problem solving.

Expert and Novice Problem Solvers
Efforts to simulate human capabilities in computer programs in the 1960s have led to increased interest in expertise as a subject for investigation (Glaser & Chi, 1988, p. xv). Research in the ensuing period has identified several key characteristics of expert performance that are generalizable across knowledge domains (Glaser & Chi, 1988). First, expertise is developed over a lengthy period of time in a particular domain. Research indicates that around 5 years or approximately 10,000 hours are required (Hayes, 1988). Second, experts and novices differ both in the nature of their knowledge and their problem-solving strategies.

Knowledge Differences.   The knowledge differences between novices and experts are substantial. They are found both in the amount of knowledge and the organization and accessibility of that knowledge. Specifically, the knowledge structures of novices are organized around the main phenomena in a domain, such as the behavior of objects on inclined planes in physics. In contrast, the knowledge struc-

tures of experts represent the phenomena in a domain in relation to higher-order principles, such as Newton's laws of force (Chi, Glaser, & Rees, 1982).

The organization of the expert's domain or discipline knowledge has implications for problem solving. Experts in the sciences use a different "problem schema" than novices to encode and represent problems (Glaser & Chi, 1988). That is, with experience, experts have encoded procedures for solving relevant problems and the conditions under which they are applied, along with representations of higher-order principles. Over time, problem and solution become entwined in the problem schema so that the activation of problem–solution strategies becomes more automatic. Thus, for the expert, strategies become one component of the knowledge base.

Knowledge differences also contribute to the more efficient use of short-term and long-term memory by experts. They are more efficient at searching a solution space because their recall is chunked (Bruning, Schraw, & Ronning, 1995). For example, in pattern recognition tasks using a chessboard, the knowledge base of the master chess player greatly simplifies recall. Both experts and novices were shown mid-game positions for a few seconds and were asked to replicate the configurations. Chess masters were able to construct 80% to 90% of the board positions of pieces after a few seconds' exposure. However, beginners were able to place only a few pieces. The chess expert has stored some 50,000 configurations in long-term memory, and new information is encoded in the form of these configurations. The beginner, however, depends on rote memory for the location of individual pieces (Chase & Simon, 1973).

As indicated in chapter 7, the extent of the individual's knowledge base also influences his or her capability to process verbal information in large chunks. For example, the expression $(a + b)$ may be one chunk for a mathematics teacher and several chunks for the beginning student in algebra. Also, experts in physics recall the equations linked with a particular physics principle in a single configuration or "bundle" (Bruning et al., 1995, p. 352). Thus, although the short-term memory capacity of experts is no larger than that of other individuals, their chunking of information makes efficient use of short-term memory.

Strategy Differences.   As discussed earlier in the chapter, experts and novices differ in their metacognitive skills. In the area of problem solving, the metacognitive skills of experts and novices differ in three ways. They are (1) problem representation, (2) problem approach, and (3) self-monitoring skills (Glaser & Chi, 1988).

Problem Representation.   For difficult or ambiguous problems, experts in mathematics and in the sciences often spend time in constructing representations of the problem (Rohrer & Thomas, 1989; Schoenfeld, 1992). The differences between the faculty member and students working on a difficult two-part problem is an example. Further, Voss (1989, p. 274) notes that when Michael Faraday was attempting to solve the problem of electromagnetic induction, he spent considerable time in developing a representation of the problem and subsequently proposed two possible solutions. Deductions then were made from these solutions and tested in the laboratory.

Similar processes were observed in a study of expert radiologists diagnosing difficult X-ray films (Lesgold et al., 1988). Experts viewed each film, constructed a tentative mental representation of the problem, and then proceeded to test this schema. If disconfirmed, the schema was set aside and the film was examined for clues to another representation of the problem. Medical residents, in contrast, were more likely to go with their initial perspective of the problem. They also tended to force-fit film features that should have signaled abnormality into their schemata for normal anatomy.

Experts also represent problems at deep structural levels in terms of basic principles in the domains, such as conservation of energy. Novices, in contrast, represent problems in terms of surface or superficial characteristics or objects stated in the problem. Examples include rotating discs on inclined planes.

Problem Approach.   For easy or moderately difficult problems, experts in mathematics and in the sciences apply their well-developed problem schema. They also work forward from information given in the problem. The expert has solved many such problems in the past, and similar problems and their solutions are recalled with little effort.

Novices, on the other hand, typically use "working backward" strategies and, sometimes, trial and error. As already indicated, because they lack sophisticated problem schema, they must begin with the unknown in the problem. In science, for example, novices often begin with an equation that contains the unknown and work backward in hopes of finding the variable they need (Anzai, 1991). See Table 8.3 for a comparison of novice and expert problem solvers.

Expertise in mathematics and science typically involves bringing the appropriate problem schema to the task of solving well-structured problems. In contrast, expertise in the humanities depends more on constructing a context-specific schema tailored to specific events (Spoehr, 1994; Wineburg, 1991). That is, expertise requires searching for patterns of knowledge in the construction of explanations at abstract levels (Spoehr, 1994, p. 79). In one study, trained historians working with a group of fragmented and contradictory historical documents (1) looked first to the source of the document as a framework for reviewing the text, (2) carefully validated and rejected various details by checking and crosschecking the documents (corroboration), and (3) constructed sequences and locales of events as a means to verify witness accounts (Wineburg, 1991). Novices, in contrast, tended to not notice discrepancies and rarely looked back at previous documents. They also struggled with interpreting accounts, in part through failure to identify the writer or to construct sequences of events.

Metacognitive Skills.   Experts and novices also differ in their metacognitive skills. First, experts spend more time in planning and they routinely self-monitor their decisions. As already stated, experts in diagnosing X-rays, for example, test and fine-tune their tentative diagnoses until all the characteristics of a particular film are accounted for (Lesgold et al., 1988). Novices, however, test and self-monitor their conclusions less often and are often unaware of their errors.

Particularly interesting in the study of radiologists is that third- and fourth-year radiology residents, in general, perform worse than either the experts or the first- and second-year residents. One explanation is that the schemata of the "true"

TABLE 8.3

A comparison of novice and expert problem solvers in mathematics and science

Novices	Experts
1. Knowledge structures are organized around the main phenomena in a domain	1 a. Knowledge structures of experts represent phenomena in the domain in relation to higher-order principles
	b. Knowledge is organized in the form of problem schema that include procedures for solving relevant problems
2. Inefficient use of short-term and long-term memory because knowledge often is stored in unrelated items	2 a. Efficient use of short-term and long-term memory because recall occurs in chunks of related information
	b. Automatization of sequences of steps within problem strategies
3. Little or no time spent constructing representations of problems; represent problems at surface or superficial levels	3. Considerable time spent constructing representations of problems; represent problems at deep structural levels
4. Reliance on working backward strategies and, sometimes, trial and error	4. Reliance on working forward from information given in the problem
5. Frequent lack of awareness of errors and the need to check solutions	5. Use of strong self-monitoring skills that include testing and fine-tuning solutions

Note: Summarized from "Expertise in Problem Solving" by M. T. H. Chi, R. Glaser, and E. Rees, 1982. In R. J. Sternberg (Ed.), *Advances in the Psychology of Human Intelligence* (Vol. 1, pp. 7–75). Hillsdale, NJ: Lawrence Erlbaum; Greeno (1980); Glaser & Chi (1988); Larkin (1980); Sternberg (1998).

novices are bound tightly to the perceptual data, while the expert rigorously tests possible schemata. The third- and fourth-year residents, in contrast, are beginning to replace perceptual decision making with cognitive reasoning, and rigorous testing is not possible in early stages of this process. In other words, the development of certain complex problem-solving skills is not linear.

Summary.   Research on the differences between experts and novices in problem solving indicates the role of knowledge and metacognition skills in thinking. The extensive knowledge base of experts also makes possible the efficient use of short-term and long-term memory.

In addition to a greater store of knowledge, experts in science and mathematics encode problems and procedures/solutions in schema organized around higher-order principles in the domain. They also spend time in constructing a representation of the problem, apply well-developed schema, and test and monitor their strategies through the process. In the humanities, experts construct explanations of situations or events that reflect the search for and identification of patterns of knowledge and they also check and crosscheck their emerging deductions.

PRINCIPLES OF INSTRUCTION

Metacognition and problem solving are the complex higher-order capabilities described by cognitive theorists. However, a set of definitive learning principles related to these constructs has yet to be developed. Therefore, instructional principles may only be inferred from current developments.

Metacognition

Research on metacognition suggests areas that may be addressed by metacognitive instruction in the classroom. Among them are essential instructional conditions for any metacognitive instruction; knowledge of strategy applications, conditions, and cues; and self-monitoring and evaluation.

General Instructional Conditions

Four general conditions are essential for successful instruction for metacognition. First, any instruction on cognitive strategies should be "cognitive training with awareness" or "informed training" as opposed to "blind training" (Brown, Armbruster, & Baker, 1986; Rohrer & Thomas, 1989). For example, transfer of comprehension strategists to new tasks is far from automatic. Extensive teaching about when and where to use them is essential (Pressley, El-Dinary, Wharten-McDonald, & Brown, 1998).

Second, the performance criteria used to evaluate student achievement should require the kinds of metacognitive activities addressed in the instruction. If testing only includes low-level performances, students will have little incentive to engage in evaluating task demands, allocating resources carefully, evaluating performance, and monitoring progress. For example, students are unlikely to relinquish a summarization strategy that emphasizes rote recall if tests require only factual information. Instead, test items should be included that require the integration of disparate information to answer a novel question or solve a novel problem (Rohrer & Thomas, 1989, p. 113).

Third, instruction should provide supports for engaging in metacognitive activities. That is, instruction should present tasks that require cognitive strategies while providing training in the monitoring and evaluation of strategy use (Rohrer & Thomas, 1989, p. 113).

Of major importance is that instruction should avoid providing compensations, which are the conditions that decrease the demand for cognitive and metacognitive activities (Rohrer & Thomas, 1989). For example, a problem occurs when test items appear to require integrative processing, but students have received review materials that contain the integrated propositions needed for the test (p. 113). In other words, handouts and other aids should not provide the end product of metacognitive activities. Instead, they should facilitate students' constructions of such products.

Fourth, instruction should provide extensive practice in a variety of contexts with reinforcement. Teaching comprehension strategies with the accompanying metacognitive skills is a long-term process and, ideally, should continue across school years (Pressley et al., 1998). Also of importance, in addition to teacher reinforcement for student improvement, is that the teacher should demonstrate the use of self-reinforcement as he or she works through a strategy (e.g., "Great, this is a good reason") (Graham, Harris, & Troia, 1998, p. 28).

Knowledge of Strategy Applications.   A key component of metacognitive knowledge is knowledge about the learning task and when and where to use particular learning strategies. For example, the initial steps in one program to teach writing skills are (1) develop background knowledge about the criteria for good writing and (2) introduce the strategy to be learned, the purpose, and when to use it (Graham et al., 1998). In addition to providing explanations, teachers introducing reading comprehension strategies should model them in a variety of naturally occurring contexts (Pressley et al., 1998). In addition, practice and adaptation of the strategies by the students is essential in helping students construct knowledge about when and where to use them. Then, as implementation of the strategy continues, learner driven discussions about the ways students are adapting the strategies they know to new contexts and situations help develop reflective knowledge about strategy use (p. 53).

Three typical problems related to the execution of strategies for students have been identified by Butler and Winne (1995). One is the failure to recognize task conditions that should cue strategy use, referred to as the lack of conditional knowledge. The second problem is the misperception of task conditions (cues), which leads to selection of the wrong strategies and the selection of inappropriate criteria for judging performance. The third is the failure to recognize the relationships between task conditions and performance.

A fourth problem in the failure to make strategic use of new knowledge. One reason is that new concepts and strategies compete with old and, very likely, deeply ingrained procedures (Pressley, 1995). In addition, applying newly learned information requires more effort than relying on prior concepts. Finally, many more connections exist in knowledge between old strategies and misconceptions than to newly learned concepts (p. 209). Therefore, a few experiences with new concepts or new knowledge about tasks, conditions, and strategies are insufficient to develop use of the information. Instead, the self-monitoring use of newly learned strategies requires many experiences, and sophisticated use typically requires years (Pressley, 1995, p. 209).

Self-Monitoring and Evaluation.   Students often do not realize the importance of monitoring and evaluating their learning. Research on computer-based instruction indicates that when students are given control over their involvement in instruction, they often exit prematurely (Steinberg, 1989). These findings indicate that the students were not adequately monitoring their understanding.

Further, one student in a program to teach strategies believed that admitting he did not know something meant that he was admitting he was dumb (Gaskins, 1994, p. 151). To illustrate the importance of explicitly noting lack of understanding, the teacher modeled monitoring as she solved a problem or wrote an essay. Self-talk demonstrated by the teacher included comments such as, "There's a lot of information in that last paragraph and I'm not sure I understand it. I'd better see if I can say it in my own words" (p. 151).

Because monitoring and evaluation activities require effort, instruction should include (1) teacher modeling and remodeling when necessary, (2) opportunities to practice strategies in pairs and in groups, and (3) teacher reinforcement. These steps are particularly important until the skills become less effortful for students and they begin to see the benefits of using them (Pressley, et al., 1998).

Summary.   Explicit principles of instruction cannot yet be derived from the early work on metacognition. However, instructional guidelines may be suggested in three broad areas. They are essential conditions for metacognitive instruction, analyzing task purposes and conditions, and self-monitoring and evaluation.

The three general conditions that are essential for successful instruction in metacognition are (1) cognitive training should be implemented with awareness of applications, (2) performance criteria and test situations require metacognitive activities, and (3) instructional support should be provided for metacognitive activities. Of importance is that classroom handouts and other learning aids should not substitute or compensate for metacognitive strategies.

During instruction, brief class discussions can explore the purposes of key activities, such as reading and seatwork. Classroom activities can also be developed that make use of the learning from reading, seatwork, and other instructional activities. Discussions also can explore the relationships between task conditions, strategies, and the products from different tasks.

Self-monitoring and evaluation, according to some researchers, requires goal setting by students. Thus, instruction on setting subgoals may be helpful. Particularly important is teaching students to ask themselves questions during an activity, such as Do I understand this information? and evaluating the products of their efforts. However, learning appropriate metacognitive strategies involves the unlearning of inappropriate management behaviors.

Problem Solving

The terms *problem* and *problem solving* in the school curriculum have had multiple and contradictory meanings over the years (Schoenfeld, 1992). Stanic and Kilpatrick (1988) note that problem solving has become a catchall term for different views of education and schooling in general and mathematics in particular. Beginning in the late 1980s, however, the nature and role of problem solving in the curriculum is undergoing examination and revision.

Traditional Curriculum Approaches

College courses described as problem solving range across several perspectives. Among them are teaching students to think creatively and preparing students for competitions (e.g., the international Olympiads); providing instruction to potential teachers on some heuristic strategies; and providing a new approach in remedial mathematics (Schoenfeld, 1992, p. 237). Of interest is that thinking skills programs aimed at general improvement in intellectual ability have not presented convincing evidence of general transfer (Mayer & Wittrock, 1996, p. 51).

In elementary and secondary education, problems traditionally have been viewed as routine exercises. In mathematics, they serve to provide practice on a particular mathematical technique that has been demonstrated to the students (Schoenfeld, 1992, p. 337). Moreover, the word problems typically are highly artificial decontextualized tasks about cookies in jars or birds on wires (Bruer, 1994, p. 278). Given the stated goal and needed numbers, the only task for students is to pick a suitable computation to apply to the situation. Often the problems or tasks are devised to introduce a technique, which is illustrated by the teacher and/or the text, and more problems or tasks are completed by the students for practice. This conventional mathematics, however, undermines reflective thinking (Pressley & McCormick, 1995, p. 415).

Lampert (1990) notes that the cultural assumption in mathematics is that doing math means following the teacher's rules. Further, mathematical truth is determined when the right answer is verified by the teacher. Similarly, typical student beliefs about mathematics identified by Schoenfeld (1985, p. 43) include "Problems are always solved in 10 minutes if they are solved at all," and "Only geniuses are capable of discovering mathematics."

In science, problems are often in the form of laboratory exercises. An analysis by Mergandoller, Mitman, Marchman, & Packer (1987) revealed three types. Explicit exercises pose the questions, prescribe the procedures, and specify the solution to be obtained. Implicit exercises pose the questions and prescribe the methods. Integrative exercises pose only the problem. An analysis of the laboratory exercises in seventh-grade science, however, revealed no integrative exercises. Instead, 45% of the assigned exercises were explicit and 55% were implicit (Mergandoller et al., 1987). In addition, 84% of the worksheet questions and 82% of the test questions required only verbatim recall.

In other words, instruction has traditionally focused on the content in the domain. Students are expected to master, in a preordained sequence, sets of facts and procedures that represent the content domain. Thus, the emphasis is on getting the right answer for problems and experiments.

Current Approaches

Explication of the subprocesses involved in problem solving and the associated metacognitive skills leads one to expect programs and classroom-based curricula targeted to these strategies. At present, however, some curricula continue to be text-based accompanied by specific routine problems. That is, these materials do not include problems that can challenge student thinking.

Some curricula that focus on developing dispositions to use mathematics in the real world and mathematical understanding address children's strategies in the context of "doing mathematics" (Lester, Garafola, & Kroll, 1989). Required are exploring various ways to address problems, showing and discussing solutions, and discussing alternative solutions. Also required are developing rich knowledge structures and integrated understandings by all students. Thus, a key focus in such curricula is the various strategies that children engage in to solve problems. Lester et al. (1989) suggest using whole-class discussions to elicit ideas for possible ways to solve the problem. During team or small-group problem solving, early finishers can be challenged to generalize their strategies. As a concluding activity, children can present and discuss their different strategies and the approaches can be extended or generalized to other situations. The teacher's role is to serve as a facilitator to provide hints when students experience difficulties.

One curriculum approach derives the content of problems from other activities that the children are involved in. For example, when discussing a book or an author, the children determine how old the author's book would be this year, how much older the book is than the child, and so on (Fennema et al., 1993, p. 565). Children also construct their own problems that they then solve, work in small groups, and discuss their strategies with each other, the class, and the teacher. Results indicate that all of the children solved problems that are more difficult than those typically found in first-grade textbooks (Fennema et al., 1993). Strategies ranged from representing the problem concretely (with manipulables) and counting to standard algorithms and complex invented algorithms (used by children in the middle and high performance ranges).

Implementing curricula that emphasize developing rich knowledge structures and integrated understandings by all students requires a reorganization of teacher beliefs and practices. The teacher must have an extensive knowledge structure of both mathematics and the ways that children think and learn. He or she also must be willing to permit children to work through their difficulties with hints or assistance from peers. That is, when the child becomes confused, the teacher's role is not to persuade the child of the "right" procedure.

Summary.   The terms *problem* and *problem solving* have been interpreted in various ways in the curriculum. In the elementary and secondary school curriculum, problems traditionally have been viewed as routine exercises. They represent the organization of the content in the domain in terms of facts and procedures. Problems are introduced because they reflect a particular mathematical technique, and students then practice on additional problems so that they become proficient in the procedure. Thus, the cultural assumption of mathematics, for example, is that one must follow the teacher's rules and that the goal is the right answer. In science, the focus is on explicit exercises that pose the questions, prescribe the procedures, and specify the solution to be obtained.

Currently, the emphasis is on "doing mathematics" and mathematical understanding. This focus involves developing rich, integrated knowledge structures that result from an emphasis on the various strategies that may be used to solve basic representational problems. Implementing such curricula, however, requires a reorganization of teacher beliefs and practices and teachers with both mathematics knowledge and knowledge about how children think.

EDUCATIONAL APPLICATIONS

Classroom Issues

The basic issues related to cognitive perspectives of learning are discussed in chapter 7. Issues addressed by the research on complex cognitive processes are learning "how-to-learn" skills, learner differences, and teaching problem solving.

Learning "How-to-Learn" Skills

The term *metacognition* refers to the capabilities required to direct one's learning, remembering, and thinking. Included are knowledge about and awareness of one's own thinking and awareness of difficulties as they arise during learning so that remedial action may be taken.

Learner Differences

Differences in metacognitive capabilities between younger and older children have been identified. They include the extent of awareness of the purposes of instruction and different task demands, skills in monitoring one's understanding and applying new strategies, and awareness of strategy flexibility. In problem solving, differences in both knowledge base and strategy use have been identified between novice and expert problem solvers.

Teaching Problem Solving

Current perspectives on problem solving are addressing a new priority. Specifically, it is that students should acquire the same habits and dispositions to interpretations as experts in the domain. Therefore, problem solving in mathematics means "doing mathematics" and in viewing real-world situations as opportunities to model and quantify variables and/or types of data.

Relationships to Other Perspectives

Metacognition includes (1) knowledge about and awareness of one's thinking, (2) knowledge about the application of strategies to monitor, evaluate, and adjust one's learning activities, and (3) the execution of these strategies. The capabilities that control the management of learning, remembering, and thinking are described by Gagné as cognitive strategies. The goal setting, monitoring, and evaluation of one's learning also are components of models of self-regulation (see chapter 11). A key difference is that these models also address the motivational characteristics that influence the implementation of metacognitive strategies. Also of interest is that Vygotsky's cultural-historical theory addressed the self-regulation of attention and the conscious awareness and mastery of one's thinking processes in the school years (see chapter 10).

Prior theories and research typically conceptualized problem solving in terms of moves or changes in given conditions required to research a solution. Gagné's conditions of learning described problem solving as the search for and application of relevant rules. Current developments in cognitive theory describe the learner's internal subprocesses during the problem-solving process. This focus, particularly the emphasis on the individual's conceptualization of the problem, addresses the issues of problem organization and understanding raised by the Gestalt psychologists.

Developing a Classroom Strategy

Step 1: Select or develop meaningful problems.

      1.1 What real-world situations can serve as the basis for problems to be solved?

      1.2 Do the problems reflect broad operations or principles in the domain?

1.3 Are there situations for which the students can construct problems?

Step 2: Focus classroom discussion on alternative strategies.

2.1 Which problems are to be solved by teams and which ones by small groups?

2.2 What manipulations or other materials are needed to assist students in developing their strategies?

2.3 Will training be needed to refocus students on providing rationales for their work and listening to the rationales of others?

Classroom Example

Subject: Addition and subtraction in first-grade mathematics.

Organization of subject matter: Problems are organized by the following problem types: join, separate, part-part-whole, and compare.

Example of a "join" problem: Connie has 5 marbles. How many more marbles does she need to make 13 marbles altogether?

Example of a "compare" problem: Jim has 5 marbles. Connie has 8 more than Jim. How many marbles does Connie have?

The curriculum is an example of children learning to "do" mathematics. Beginning the first few days of school, children are asked to solve word problems that the teacher constructed. Later, children also construct and solve their own problems.

Content of the problems is derived from other activities that the children are involved in. For example, when discussing a book or an author, the children determine how old the author or book would be this year, how much older the book is than the child, and so on.

A key focus in the curriculum is the various strategies that children use to solve problems. Children are expected to be engaged in mathematics—solving problems they, their peers, or the teacher has written. They also are expected to persist in their work, and to report how they solved the problem. In addition, they are expected to reflect on their own thinking by comparing it with someone else's approach or on the difficulty of a particular problem for them (Fennema et al., 1993, p. 565). Finally, they are expected to listen to the solutions of others and to respect other solutions. The teacher encourages the use of multiple solution strategies and emphasizes the importance of children using a strategy that is most appropriate for them (p. 578).

Children often work in small groups, and they also present and discuss their work individually with the teacher and participate in whole-class sessions. In class discussions, the teacher often calls on children with less mature strategies first, challenging those with more mature strategies to think of alternative ways to solve the problem. For example, in response to the question, How many ways can you make 3?, strategies ranged from $6 - 3$ and $1 + 1 + 1$ to $3 + 3 + 3 - 3 - 3$.

CHAPTER QUESTIONS

1. What are some likely reasons for children's lack of implementation of metacognitive strategies following instruction on such strategies?

2. What are the major differences between the Gestalt view of problem solving and the information-processing perspective?

3. What are some of the potential advantages and disadvantages of having children construct their own problems?

4. Children often approach writing tasks as simply writing down somewhat appropriate information with each new sentence stimulating the next idea. What type of metacognitive deficiency do they have?

REFERENCES

Ames, C. (1992). Achievement goals and the motivational climate. In D. Schunk & J. Meece (Eds.) *Student perceptions in the classroom* (pp. 327–348). Hillsdale, NJ: Lawrence Erlbaum.

Anderson, J. R. (1985). *Cognitive psychology and its implications* (2nd ed.), New York: W. H. Freeman.

Anzai, Y. (1991). Learning and use of representations for physics expertise. In K. A. Anders & J. Smith (Eds.), *Toward a general theory of expertise* (pp. 64–92). NY: Cambridge University Press.

Bandura, A. (Ed.) (1995). *Self-efficacy in changing societies*. New York: Cambridge University Press.

Beal, C. (1989). Children's communication skills: Implications for the development of writing strategies. In C. McCormick, G. Miller, & M. Pressley (Eds.), *Cognitive strategy research: From basic research to educational applications* (pp. 191–214). New York: Springer-Verlag.

Bjorklund, D. F., Muir-Broaddus, J. E., & Schneider, W. (1990). Knowledge and strategy development. In D. J. Bjorklund (Ed.), *Children's strategies: Contemporary views of cognitive development*. Hillsdale, NJ: Erlbaum.

Briars, D. J., & Larkin, J. M. (1984). An integrated model of skills in solving elementary school problems. *Cognition and Instruction, 1,* 245–296.

Brown, A. L., Armbruster, B. B., & Baker, L. (1986). The role of metacognition in reading and studying. In J. Orsanu (Ed.), *Teaching comprehension: From research to practice* (pp. 49–75). Hillsdale, NJ: Erlbaum.

Butler, D. L., & Winne, P. H. (1995). Feedback and self-regulated learning. *Review of Educational Research, 65*(3), 245–281.

Chi, M. T. H., Glaser, R., & Farr, M. (1991). *The nature of expertise*. Hillsdale, NJ: Lawrence Erlbaum Associates.

Chi, M. T. H., Glaser, R., & Rees, E. (1982). Expertise in problem solving. In R. J. Sternberg (Ed.), *Advances in the psychology of human intelligence* (Vol. 1: pp. 7–75). Hillsdale, NJ: Erlbaum.

Davidson, J., & Sternberg, R. (1998). Smart problem solving: How metacognition helps. In D. J. Hacker, J. Dunlosky & A. C. Graesser (Eds.), *Metacognition in educational theory and practice* (pp. 47–68). Mahwah, NJ: Lawrence Erlbaum Associates.

Declos, V. R. & Harrington, C. (1991). Effects of strategy monitoring and proactive instruction on children's problem-solving performance. *Journal of Educational Psychology, 83,* 35–42.

Duncker, K. (1945). On problem solving. *Psychological Monographs 68*(5), Whole no. 270.

Elliott, E. E., & Dweck, C. S. (1988). Goals: An approach to motivation and achievement. *Journal of Personality and Social Psychology, 54*(1), 5–12.

Fang, Z., & Cox, B. E. (1999). Emergent metacognition: A study of preschoolers' literate behavior.

Journal of Research in Childhood Education, 13(2), 175–185.

Fennema, E., Franke, M. L., Carpenter, T. P., & Carey, D. A. (1993). Using children's mathematical knowledge in instruction. *American Educational Research Journal, 30*(3), 555–563.

Flavell, J. H. (1971). First discussant's comments: What is memory development the development of? *Human Development, 14,* 272–278.

Flavell, J. H. (1979). Metacognition and cognitive monitoring: A new area of cognitive development inquiry. *American Psychologist, 34,* 906–911.

Flavell, J. H., & Wellman, H. M. (1977). Metamemory. In R. V. Kalil, Jr., & J. W. Hagen (Eds.), *Perspectives on the development of memory and cognition* (pp. 3–33). Hillsdale, NJ: Erlbaum.

Gaskins, I. W. (1994). Classroom applications of cognitive science: Teaching poor readers how to learn, think, and problem solve. In K. McGilly (Ed.), *Classroom lessons: Integrating cognitive theory and classroom practice* (pp. 129–154). Cambridge, MA: MIT Press.

Graham, S., Harris, K. R., & Troia, G. A. (1998). Writing and self-regulation: Cases from the self-regulated strategy development model. In D. J. Schunk & B. J. Zimmerman (Eds.), *Self-regulated learning: From teaching to self-reflective practice* (pp. 20–41). New York: Guilford Press.

Hacker, D. J. (1998). Self-regulated comprehension during normal reading. In D. J. Hacker, J. Dunlosky, & A. C. Gaesser (Eds.), *Metacognition in educational theory and practice* (pp. 165–191). Mahwah, NJ: Lawrence Erlbaum.

Harnishfeger, K. K., & Bjorklund, D. F. (1990). Children's strategies: A brief history. In D. Bjorklund (Ed.), *Children's strategies* (pp. 1–22). Hillsdale, NJ: Erlbaum.

Hayes, J. R. (1988). *The complete problem solver* (2nd ed.). Hillsdale, NJ: Erlbaum.

Holyoak, K. J. (1995). Problem solving. In E. E. Smith & D. N. Osherman (Eds.), *Thinking.* Cambridge, MA: MIT Press.

Howe, M. J. A. (1988). Context, memory, and education. In G. M. Davies & D. M. Thomson (Eds.), *Memory in context: Context in memory* (pp. 267–280), New York: John Wiley.

Jacobs, J. E., & Paris, S. G. (1987). Children's metacognition about reading: Issues in definition, measurement, and instruction. *Educational Psychologist 22*(2 & 4), 255–278.

Katona, G. (1940). *Organizing and memorizing.* New York: Columbia University Press.

Köhler, W. (1969). *The Task of Gestalt psychology.* Princeton, NJ: Princeton University Press.

Kuhn, D. (1999). A developmental model of critical thinking. *Educational Researcher, 28*(2), 16–25.

Lesgold, A., Robinson, H., Feltovich, P., Glaser, R., Klopfer, D., & Wang, Y. (1988). Expertise in a complex skill: Diagnosing X-ray pictures. In M. Chi, R. Glaser, & M. Farr (Eds.), *The nature of expertise* (pp. 311–342). Hillsdale, NJ: Erlbaum.

Lester, F., Garofolo, J., & Kroll, D. (1989). *The role of metacognition in mathematical problem solving: A study of two grade seven classes.* Final report to the National Science Foundation of NSF project MDR 85-50346.

Maier, N. R. F. (1930). Reasoning in humans I. On direction. *Journal of Comparative Psychology,* 10, 115–143.

Mayer, R. E. (1992). *Thinking, problem solving, cognition* (2nd ed.). New York: Freeman.

Mayer, R. E. (1995). The search for insight: Grappling with Gestalt psychology's unanswered questions. In R. J. Sternberg & J. E. Davidson (Eds.), *The nature of insight* (pp. 3–32). Cambridge, MA: MIT Press.

Mayer, R. E., & Wittrock, M. (1996). Problem-solving transfer. In D. C. Berliner & R. C. Calfee (Eds.), *Handbook of educational psychology* (pp. 47–62). New York: Macmillan Library References.

Mergandoller, J., Mitman, A. J., Marchman, V. A., & Packer, M. J. (1987). Task demands and accountability in middle-grade science classes. *The Elementary School Journal, 3,* 251–265.

Midgley, C., Kaplan, A., Middleton, M., & Maeke, M. (1998). The development and validation of scales assessing students' goal orientation. *Contemporary Educational Psychology, 23,* 113–131.

Paris, S. G., Lipson, M. Y., & Wilson, K. K. (1983). Becoming a strategic reader. *Contemporary Educational Psychology, 8,* 293–316.

Pressley, M., El-Dinary, P. B., Wharton-McDonald, R., & Brown, R. (1998). Transactional instruction of comprehension strategies in the elementary grades. In D. Schunk & B. J. Zimmerman (Eds.), *Self-regulated learning: From teaching to self-reflective practice* (pp. 42–56). New York: Guilford Press.

Resnick, L. B. (1989). Developing mathematical knowledge. *American Psychologist, 44,* 162–169.

Schunk, D., & Zimmerman, B. J. (Eds.) (1998). *Self-regulated learning: From teaching to self-reflective practice.* New York: Guilford Press.

Spoehr, K. T. (1994). Enhancing the acquisition of conceptual structures through hypermedia. In K. McGilly (Ed.), *Classroom lessons: Integrating cognitive theory and classroom practice* (pp. 75–101). Cambridge, MA: MIT Press.

Stanic, G., & Kilpatrick, J. (1988). Historical perspectives on problem solving in the mathematics curriculum. In R. Charles & E. Silver (Eds.), *The teaching and assessing of mathematical problem solving* (pp. 1–22). Reston, VA: National Council of Teachers of Mathematics.

Sternberg, R. (1998). Abilities are forms of developing expertise. *Educational Researcher 27*(3), 11–20.

Tuckman, B. W. (1996). The relative effectiveness of incentive motivation and prescribed learning strategy in improving college students' course performance. *Journal of Experimental Education, 64,* 197–210.

Van Haneghan, J. P., & Baker, L. (1989). Cognitive monitoring in mathematics. In C. B. McCormick, G. Miller, & M. Pressley (Eds.), *Cognitive strategy research* (pp. 215–238). New York: Springer-Verlag.

Vosniadou, S., Pearson, P. D., & Rogers, T. (1988). What causes children's failures to detect inconsistencies in text? Representation vs. comparison difficulties. *Journal of Educational Psychology, 80,* 27–39.

Vye, N. J., Goldman, S. R., Voss, J. F., Hmelo, C., Williams, S., and The Cognition and Technology Group at Vanderbilt (1997). Complex mathematical problem solving by individuals and dyads. *Cognition and Instruction, 15*(4), 435–484.

Vye, N. J., Schwartz, D. L., Bransford, J. D., Barron, B. J., Zech, L., and the Cognition and Technology Group at Vanderbilt (1998). SMART environments that support monitoring reflection, and revision. In D. J. Hacker, J. Dunlosky, & A. C. Graeser (Eds.), *Metacognition in educational theory and practice* (pp. 305–346). Cambridge, MA: MIT Press.

Wertheimer, M. (1945). *Productive thinking.* New York: Harper.

Wineburg, S. (1991). Historical problem solving: A study of the cognitive processes used in the evaluation of documentary and pictorial evidence. *Journal of Educational Psychology, 81*(1), 73–87.

Winne, P. H., & Hadwin, A. F. (1998). Studying as self-regulated learning. In D. J. Hacker, J. Dunlosky, & A. C. Graesser (Eds.) *Metacognition in educational theory and practice* (pp. 277–305). Mahwah, NJ: Lawrence Erlbaum Associates.

Wyatt, D., Pressley, M., El-Dinary, R. B., Stein, S., Evans, P., & Brown, R. (1993). Comprehension strategies, worth and credibility monitoring, and evaluations: Cold and hot cognition when experts read professional articles that are important to them. *Learning and Individual Differences, 5,* 49–72.

Zimmerman, B. J. (1995). Self-regulation involves more than metacognition: A social cognitive perspective. *Educational Psychologist, 30*(4), 217–221.

PART III

Cognitive-Development Theories

Theories of learning address the particular events and conditions essential in the acquisition of knowledge and specific skills. In contrast, cognitive-development theories first identify the capabilities that represent the highest levels of human thought. Then they describe the events and conditions necessary to attain these levels of thinking. Although schooling, properly designed, may facilitate such development, the implication is that higher levels of human thinking cannot be taught directly.

The two cognitive-development theorists, Jean Piaget and Lev S. Vygotsky, described thinking in different ways. Jean Piaget, a Swiss psychologist, described logical thinking and reasoning about complex situations as the highest form of cognitive development. He grounded his investigations in the individual child's manipulation of and interaction with objects in his or her particular environment.

Lev Vygotsky, in contrast, viewed cognitive development as culturally based in that the signs and symbols essential for cognitive development are products of one's culture. Vygotsky identified logical memory, voluntary attention, categorical perception, and the self-regulation of behavior as the highest forms of psychological functioning. He grounded his analyses in the cultural history of the human race and the child's interactions with knowledgeable adults in his or her particular culture.

CHAPTER 9
Jean Piaget's Cognitive-Development Theory

To present an adequate notion of learning one must first explain how the individual manages to construct and invent, not merely how he repeats and copies (Piaget, 1970b).

The work of Jean Piaget is a major contribution to developmental psychology in several ways. First, prior to his research, young children were viewed simply as miniature adults. However, Piaget's theory and research clearly demonstrated the novel message that young children's thinking and ways of organizing experience differ qualitatively from adult thinking (Chandler & Chapman, 1991).

Second, the aim of Piaget's work was not to investigate changes in problem solving or cognitive skills. Instead, his purpose was to discover the characteristics of natural logic—the logic of the acting, speaking, reasoning individual in all of its various forms (Inhelder & deCaprona, 1990, p. 39). For example, at a certain point in development, the child knows *without looking at a concrete set of examples,* that A is greater than C if he knows that A is greater than B and B is greater than C. He also knows that this conclusion must be true. Similarly, the child also knows that there are more Bs than As when A is included in B, and she does not waiver in her belief. This is the essence of Piaget's natural logic (Borel, 1987, p. 68). Discovering the characteristics of natural logic involved discovering the origins of knowledge and reasoning and the transitions from one form of reasoning to another. This goal requires the investigation of the roots of logical thinking in infancy, the kinds of reasoning that young children engage in, and the reasoning processes used by adolescents and adults.

Third, Piaget's approach to studying the development of natural logic was itself an innovation. He formed the framework for his research and theory from the disciplines of philosophy, biology, and psychology. From philosophy came the initial questions to be answered: What is the nature of knowledge? and What is the relationship between the knower and reality? For Piaget, the term *knowledge* refers to natural logic. Thus, the study of knowledge is the study of intelligence.

Biology, the second component in the framework of Piaget's work, is the source of his basic assumptions about the nature of intelligence. In Piaget's view, the adaptation and growth of organisms explain the problems and processes involved in the adaptation of intelligence to the environment (Piaget, 1980) (see section titled A Constructivist View of Intelligence). The role of psychology in Piaget's framework was to provide the method of study. Questions about the ways that intelligence grows and adapts to the environment can only be answered through psychological research (Piaget, 1972b, p. 9).

The fourth contribution of Piaget's work is that it consists of richly detailed analyses of thinking and reasoning, which Beilin (1992a) maintains is unrivaled in developmental psychology in both scope and depth. The areas addressed by Piaget include children's language and thought, children's understanding of causality and the world, moral development, arithmetic reasoning, stages in infant cognitive development, a theory of adaptation, the components of logical thinking, and analyses of prelogical thinking. Works published after Piaget's death address the role of possibility and necessity in logical thinking, analyses of the forms of knowledge in each of the sciences, and a theory of meaning. In addition, the group who collaborated with Piaget in Geneva at the Center for Genetic (developmental) Epistemology conducted hundreds of experiments on various aspects of children's reasoning and thinking.

Unfortunately, misinterpretations were made of Piaget's action-oriented model when it was assimilated in to the English and American empiricist tradition (Beilin, 1992b; Birkhard, 1997; Chandler & Chapman, 1991; Chapman, 1988; Dean & Youniss, 1991; Lorenço & Machado, 1996; Smith, 1991). First, his descriptions of the stages of reasoning were used to develop curricula in mathematics, science, and early childhood. In Piaget's view, however, the stages are not explanatory. Their purpose simply is to distinguish the various kinds of reasoning that were to be explained (Chapman, 1988, p. 338). Second, some researchers incorporated Piaget's concepts into their framework of questions while excluding issues the theory was intended to address. The result was a distorted version of the theory (Chapman, 1988; Chandler & Chapman, 1991; Dean & Youniss, 1991; Lorenço & Machado, 1996). Others, in efforts to remove extraneous factors from experiments on children's reasoning, developed tasks that required different and less complex forms of thinking than the Piagetian tasks (Chapman, 1988; Chandler & Chapman, 1991; Montangero, 1991). Thus, conclusions that some complex forms of reasoning were developed at earlier ages were in error. Further, some interpretations of Piaget's theory were so distorted that he was criticized for positions he had never taken (Birkhard, 1997; Chapman, 1988; Lorenço & Machado, 1996).

Understanding Piaget's work is hindered by at least three factors. One is that only some of his writings and the Genevan research is available in English. Second, Piaget, in his later writings, often did not restate the purpose and broad aims of his work, thus making it easier to misapply the theory to inappropriate questions (Chapman, 1988). Third, Piaget continued to revise and rework the theory based on continuing experimentation; he once described himself as its chief revisionist (Piaget, 1970b). For example, Piaget originally used the term *logico–mathematical* to refer to the child's construction of classes and relations involving number and quantity (Piaget, 1952). He later (Piaget, 1971) expanded the category to include all the organism's intercoordinations of its activities.

One of Piaget's last writings revisited the issues of the construction of the structures of logical thinking, specifically the role of possibility and necessity (Piaget, 1987a, 1987b). His last work on the logic of meaning (Piaget & Garcia, 1991) identified implications among actions as the basis for the later development of logical thinking.

PRINCIPLES OF COGNITIVE DEVELOPMENT

The focus of Jean Piaget's theory is the development of natural logic from birth to adulthood. Understanding the theory depends on understanding the biological assumptions from which it is derived and the implications for defining knowledge (Piaget, 1970b, p. 703).

Basic Assumptions

The basic assumptions of the theory are Piaget's conception of the nature of intelligence and the essential factors in cognitive development.

A Constructivist View of Intelligence

The introduction of Piaget's theory to the English-speaking community after World War II created a near-sensation with its bold theoretical claims and counterintuitive experimental data (Beilin, 1992a, p. 191). One of his counterintuitive claims was that intelligence and knowledge are not static quantities or things. Instead, intelligence and knowledge are ever-changing processes, and the role of the psychologist is to study the nature of the changes.

The Nature of Intelligence.   The basic assumption of Piaget's theory is that human intelligence and biological organisms function in similar ways. Both are organized systems that constantly interact with the environment. They also construct the structures they need in order to adapt to the environment (Piaget, in Bringuier, 1980, p. 3).

Piaget's view that the organism is not a passive agent in genetic development is supported by his research on mollusks. He found that certain mollusks, transported from their calm-water habitat to turbulent wind-driven waters, grew an extra "foot" to maintain a hold on the rocks in the fast current. Furthermore, these biological changes, constructed in response to an environmental change, were inherited by some descendants of the mollusks. For some of the organisms, this change persisted even when they were transported back to calmer waters (Piaget, 1980).

Piaget (1980) concluded that intelligence constructs the cognitive structures that it needs in the process of adaptation to the environment. Cognitive structures, like biological structures, "are not given in advance, neither in the human mind nor in the external world as we perceive and organize it" (Piaget, in Bringuier, 1980, p. 37). An example is the infant's coordination of her actions into the reaching-grasping-pulling scheme. This new structure enables her to pull a string to reach the object at the end of it (Piaget, 1967), to pull a blanket to get an out-of-reach toy, and so on. Other examples throughout childhood involve the gradual construction of logical ways of interacting with objects and events, instead of acting on the basis of perceptual cues. Therefore, intelligence is not a static trait that can be quantitatively assessed. Instead, intelligence is active, dynamic, and changing, for it seeks explanations and understandings both to construct itself and to function effectively.

The Relationship Between Knowledge and Intelligence.   The traditional view that learning involves acquiring static objective knowledge about a "real" world is based on two erroneous assumptions (Piaget, 1970b). One is that objective knowledge is some entity "out there" in objects and events that can be identified. The second erroneous belief is that the external environment and the individual can be separated into two entities in any definition of knowledge.

According to Piaget, knowledge is a process that is created by the activity of the learner. "To know is to act, and, in the absence of action, the question of knowledge becomes mute within Piaget's system" (Pufall, 1988, p. 16). Moreover, in the creation of knowledge, the individual and the object are fused and cannot be separated. Knowledge also contains many subjective components; therefore, it is a relationship and not some a priori given.

More important, the relationship between the learner and the object is always undergoing transformation. "The relationship between subject (knower) and objects is in no way determined beforehand, and what is more important, it is not stable" (Piaget, 1970b, p. 704). The infant, for example, first learns about the environment by putting all objects into its mouth and later by shaking, dropping, pushing, or pulling them. At the most sophisticated level of intelligence, however, scientists and scholars build theories using abstract symbols that may have no concrete counterparts in the environment. Between the activities of the infant and the theoretical scientist lies a continuum of ever-changing development.

In summary, genetic epistemology "above all sees knowledge as a continuous construction" (Piaget, 1972b, p. 17). Since knowledge is constructed through the individual's interactions with the environment and intelligence is also so constructed, the issues in understanding knowledge and intelligence are reduced to the same question. In other words, to answer the question about how the individual progresses from a state of less sufficient to more sufficient knowledge is to determine the ways in which intelligence is interacting with the environment.

Essential Factors in Cognitive Development

Four factors are necessary for the developmental transitions from one form of reasoning to another. They are the physical environment, maturation, social influences, and the processes referred to as equilibration (Piaget, 1977).

Contact with the physical environment is indispensable because the interaction between the individual and the world is the source of new knowledge. However, such contact is insufficient for developing knowledge unless the individual's intelligence can make use of the experience. Maturation of the nervous system is, therefore, important because it permits the child to realize maximum benefit from physical experience. In other words, maturation opens up possibilities for development, whereas the lack of it establishes broad limits on cognitive achievement. The emergence of hand–eye coordination in the infant, for example, is essential for the construction of the infant's action schemes, such as reaching-grasping-pulling.

Although maturation is an important condition for cognitive development, the particular events are not predetermined. Development proceeds at different rates, depending on the nature of the contact with the environment and the learner's own activity.

The third factor, the social environment, includes the role of language and education and, particularly, contact with others. In the absence of social interactions, the child, subjectively certain in his or her beliefs, would be unlikely to initiate the actions required to change inaccurate ideas. Piaget (1926) states, "Never without the shock of contact with the thought of others and the effort of reflection which this shock entails would thought as such come to consciousness" (p. 144). Also, differences in social experiences, like physical experience, can accelerate or retard the development of cognitive structures (Inhelder, Sinclair, & Bovet, 1974).

The foregoing three factors are the classical factors described by other theorists that influence development. Piaget maintained, however, that these three factors (either singly or in combination) were insufficient to explain the emergence of new forms of thinking (Chapman, 1988, p. 388). Also essential is the fourth factor, equilibration. This factor consists of the set of processes that maintain a steady state in intellectual functioning in the midst of transformation and change. Equilibration (described in the following section) regulates the individual's interactions with the environment and permits cognitive development to proceed in a coherent and organized fashion.

Summary

The purpose of Piaget's work was to discover the characteristics of natural logic, that is, the reasoning processes used at various phases during development.

The framework for Piaget's research and theory was formed from the disciplines of philosophy, psychology, and biology. The basic issues, the nature of knowledge and the relationship between the knower and reality, came from philosophy. The methodology for answering the questions came from psychology, and biology was the source of Piaget's assumptions about the nature of intelligence. Specifically, intelligence, like biological organisms, is an organized system that constantly interacts with the environment and constructs the structures essential for adaptation to the environment. Therefore, intelligence is an ongoing and changing process, and knowing is created by the activity of the learner. The key question for psychology thus becomes the ways that the learner progresses from one stage of knowledge construction to another.

The transition from one form of reasoning to another depends on four essential factors. They are the physical environment, maturation, social influences, and the processes referred to as equilibration. The role of equilibration is to maintain the functioning of intelligence while it undergoes major transformations.

The Components of Cognitive Development

The focal point of the theory is the processes that account for progress from one level of reasoning and thinking to a higher level. Two major topics in Piaget's theory illustrate these processes. They are the psychological nature of logical thinking and the fundamental processes involved in interactions with the environment.

The Psychological Nature of Logical Thinking

Three key concepts are important in understanding the nature of logical thinking in Piaget's theory. They are the psychological structure of operations, the role of possibility and necessity, and the logic of meaning.

Psychological Structure.   The basic units of logical thinking are particular kinds of cognitive activity that Piaget (1928, 1970b) refers to as *operations*. They are the cognitive structures that govern logical reasoning in the broad sense (Piaget, 1970a, 1970b). However, operations are not static structures of information. Instead, operations are transformations performed on data or objects that form a particular psychological structure. They are actions that are internalizable, reversible, and coordinated into systems.

Essential Characteristics.   Three key characteristics differentiate operations from other kinds of actions. First, the data or object transformation is one in which a change in one feature of the situation is exactly compensated by a change in another characteristic. For example, if a pile of 40 pennies is subdivided into four equal piles (transformation), the number of piles *increases* (from 1 to 4) while the number per pile *decreases* (from 40 to 10). Second, as a result of these balancing compensations, the essential nature of the object(s) or the data remains invariant or constant. In the prior example, the total number of pennies (40) does not change. Recognition of the unchanging feature of the situation by the child is referred to as *conservation*. When a ball of clay is flattened into the shape of a pancake, for example, the amount of clay remains invariant; the quantity is conserved.

The third important characteristic of operations is that the transformation in the data or the object can be restored to the original by an inverse operation. The four piles of pennies, for example, can be recombined into the whole of 40 pennies.

The capability of a child to simultaneously coordinate an operation and its inverse is referred to as **reversibility**. When a child develops the understanding that a transformation *simultaneously* and necessarily implies its inverse, he or she can manipulate the situation and analyze it correctly without becoming confused. At that point, the child has constructed an operational structure (see the example in the following section).

In other words, both the data transformation and its inverse are essential elements of an operational structure. The inverse of adding $2 + 3 = 5$, for example, is subtraction (i.e., $5 - 3 = 2$). However, simply demonstrating the capability of adding numbers does not imply that operational thinking has been attained. The child must view addition as the inverse of subtraction and vice versa; that is, the existence of one requires the presence of the other (Murray, 1990, p. 199).

Example of a Psychological Structure.   Experiments on the conservation of quantity illustrate the phases involved in the child's invention of an operational structure.

Children were shown little balls of clay that were then rolled into sausage shapes. When asked if the amount of clay was the same, three levels of development were found prior to operational thinking. Children focused only on the lengths of the sausage shape (Level I), began to notice that rolling out the clay makes it thinner (Level II), and then understood that rolling out the clay makes it simultaneously longer and thinner (Level III). Children at Level III also may understand that the sausage shape can be returned to the ball. However, they do not yet comprehend reversibility in terms of the compensatory relations between transformations of length and width (Chapman, 1988, p. 299).

Construction of the operational structure of conservation of quantity (Level IV) means that children can predict in advance the compensatory changes in length and thickness that result from rolling out the clay. In addition, they are able to identify the constant or invariant in the process.

Figure 9.1 illustrates the set of affirmations and compensatory negations that compose the structure referred to as conservation of quantity. The diagram illustrates the totalities of an operational structure that is identified by its own transformational rules about relations (Inhelder & deCaprona, 1990, p. 53).

To create an operational structure, the child must invent the opposite of factors x and y. Further, the child must determine exactly what non-x and non-y are, such that existence of one (x, y) requires the existence of the other (non-x, non-y) (Murray, 1990, p. 199). For example, when the child sequentially orders a dozen sticks of different lengths, she must realize simultaneously that "big" means "not little" and vice versa. Also, "bigger" means "less little," and a stick can be bigger or smaller than another depending on the comparison that is being made (Piaget, 1985, p. 104). Another is the late development of the concepts of possibility and necessity.

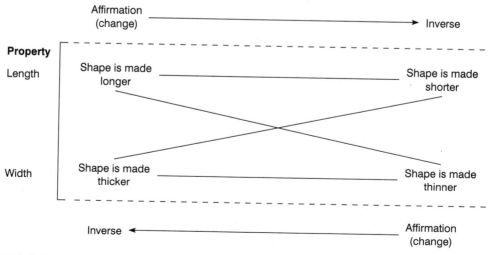

FIGURE 9.1
Illustration of the psychological structure of conservation of quantity

Operational structures develop slowly, over months and years, and their development requires reorganizations of prior thinking. One factor in this lengthy process is that only positive observables are registered perceptually. In contrast, negations are neglected or constructed slowly and laboriously after the development of positive observable characteristics (Piaget, 1985, p. 13). Another is the late development of the concepts of possibility and necessity.

The Role of Possibility and Necessity. The interdependence of the factors and their inverses in Figure 9.1 illustrates a key concept in the construction of operational structures: necessity. That is, the child realizes that certain things he or she knows are true also *must* be true. Young children, and even adults, often are slow to appreciate the necessity that is inherent in situations (Murray, 1990, p. 192). For example, in two studies, children were able to accurately add numbers from 1 to 3. However, from 30% to 70% of the children thought the answer also could be a different number (Cauley, Murray, & Smith, 1983; Murray, 1990).

The importance of distinguishing between necessary knowledge and "simply true" knowledge is that they differ in key characteristics. "Simply true" knowledge may be developed through induction, noting observable facts, probability, and contingent relations among events. In contrast, necessary knowledge (for example, conservation of number), depends on deduction, universality (can be acquired by any individual), certainty, and necessary relations between states and affairs.

Research by Piaget in his later years revealed the lengthy development by the child of possibility and necessity (Piaget, 1987a, 1987b). The child's understanding of these concepts in problem-solving situations emerges late in the concrete operational period (Acredolo, 1997; Piaget, 1987a, 1987b). Beilin (1992a) views this work as one of the most important redirections of the theory.

At the preoperational level of thinking, children cannot differentiate between reality, possibility, and necessity. Shown a partially hidden box, young children stated that the hidden sides must be the same color as the visible portion (Chapman, 1988). This phase, in which only one possibility is viewed as valid, is referred to by Piaget (1987a) as "pseudonecessity."

At Level IIA, children think of a few concrete co-possibilities such as the hidden sides could be "green, blue, violet, yellow, white—and that's all" (Piaget, 1987a, p. 44). At Level IIB, when concrete operations are firmly established, each possibility is treated as one among many others that are conceivable (Beilin, 1989, p. 115) (see Table 9.1).

Children at Level II also make some effort to rule out false possibilities on the basis of the data. In one experiment, the task was to arrange three animals in the same sequence as three animals hidden behind a screen. The six possible sequences of the sheep (S), the rabbit (R), and the chicken (C), are SRC, SCR, RSC, RCS, CSR, and CRS. The children were told the number of their correct positions after each attempt. This information can lead to the systematic elimination of certain possibilities until only one remains (the "necessarily" correct solution) (Chapman, 1988, p. 320). However, Level II children were able to eliminate only a few possibilities after feedback; none recognized that getting only two of the three animals correctly positioned is impossible.

TABLE 9.1
Levels of reasoning about possibility and necessity

Level of Thinking	Possibility	Necessity
Level I (preoperations)	(a) Recognition of only a single possibility; (b) Later recognition of at least one other possibility	(a) Reality as perceived or manipulated appears to be necessarily so (Piaget, 1986a, p. 148) (b) Lack of cumulative accounting of possibilities eliminated on successive trials of a problem (5–7 years)
Level IIA (onset of concrete operations)	Formation of concrete co-possibilities; limited to those the child can imagine	Some systematic exclusion of possibilities that proved to be false in previous trials. However, children sometimes forget the possibilities already excluded over an extended series of trials.
Level III (hypothetico-deductive operations)	Indeterminate unlimited possibilities are completely deducible	Systematic exclusion of possibilities; recognition that more than one series of trials is possible and leads inevitably to the correct solution

Level III children recognize unlimited possibilities and also systematically exclude possibilities until they arrive at the one that is necessary. In the animal sequence problem, for example, children at Level III systematically solved both the three-animal and four-animal sequences.

These transitions indicate that testing the development of operational thinking involves more than obtaining a correct answer to particular tasks. Genuine tests of operational thinking also must certify that the child's response is a necessary conclusion (Murray, 1990). Children may be asked, for example, if the outcome can be different, or if this outcome occurs only sometimes (p. 188). Equally important is eliciting the child's reasons for his or her conclusions.

The Logic of Meaning.   The logic of operational thinking is referred to as extensional logic. It involves the truth or falsity of a term or a statement based on its extensions or links to other terms or statements. Examples are part/whole and inclusion relations. For example, given a collection of both brown and white wooden beads, the statement, "There are more white beads than wooden beads" is false. The relative quantity of the white beads is determined by the other types of beads in the total collection.

Piaget's last work, *A Logic of Meaning* (Piaget & Garcia, 1991), laid the foundation for his theory of intensional logic, or a logic of shared meaning. In Piaget's view, the shared meanings in actions are the roots of operational or extensional logic. The major principles are as follows:

1. **Knowledge always involves inference.** That is, a relation between actions is a logical implication. For example, some infants at 9 to 10 months, when given empty cubes, sticks, and small plasticine balls, will insert an object into a cube. However, the infants first put the object into their mouths. According to Piaget and Garcia (1991, p. 5), they have constructed the content-container action scheme from the "insert into the mouth" scheme, and these schemes have, as a result, shared meaning. The infants then extend the content-container scheme to new schemes or subschemes, such as to insert and take out, to fill and to empty, and so on.

2. **The meaning of an object includes what can be done with the object as well as descriptions of it** (Piaget & Garcia, 1991, p. 119). Therefore, meaning is an assimilation to an action scheme (whether overt or mental). For example, the meanings of objects for an infant include pushing, opening, pulling, closing, and so on.

3. **Logic begins at the moment a child is able to anticipate a relation between actions**, referred to as *meaning implications* or *implications between actions* (Piaget & Garcia, 1991, p. 155). When the infant's action, such as inserting, is followed by the reverse action, emptying, the infant has begun to construct an implication between actions. In this example, the implication is that "action implies the possibility of the reverse action" (Piaget & Garcia, 1991, p. 6).

With the appearance of language, children can express action implications as statements and begin to construct logical links that represent "and" and "or." In one problem, two tunnels *(A1* and *A2)* each branch into two *B* tunnels, which in turn each branch into two *C* tunnels. The task is to open as few windows as possible on the tunnels to determine the path taken by the car, which is indicated by a ribbon. (The problem consists of 12 branched tunnels, but is solved by opening three windows in the correct sequences). One 6-year-old first opened a window on an *A* tunnel, correctly inferring that the ribbon must be in either *A1* or *A2* and that the absence of the ribbon implies the car's path was through the other tunnel.

Although children can form logical connections that reflect "and" and "or" as well as negations of the combinations, their constructions do not yet represent operational thinking. Their constructions are context-bound fragments that later will become operational structures. Unlike the extensive research on concrete operations by Piaget and his colleagues, only a few experiments have been conducted on meaning implications (see Piaget & Garcia, 1991). Thus, this aspect of the theory remains incomplete. However, one analysis of this work by Ricco (1990) maintains that it provides a foundation for explaining necessity in operational settings.

Summary. Three essential characteristics differentiate operational (logical) thinking from other kinds of actions. First, a transformation is exactly compensated by a change in another characteristic. Second, the essential nature of the object(s) or data remains invariant. Recognition of the unchanging feature of the situation and being able to explain why it does not change is referred to as conservation. Third, the transformation or change can be restored to the original by an inverse operation. When a child understands that a transformation simultaneously and necessarily implies its inverse, the child has developed the concept of reversibility. The child has constructed an internal operational structure and can analyze the situation accurately without becoming confused.

Essential to operational thinking is the child's construction of the concept of necessity. Young children cannot differentiate between reality, possibility, and necessity. At the onset of concrete operations, the child forms limited concrete co-possibilities but is only able to limit some of them in a systematic way. Eventually, the child is able to conceive of unlimited possibilities and to systematically exclude them.

Piaget's last work sketched the roots of operational thinking, which are found in the early actions of the infant and then the child. The basic principles are that knowledge always involves inference, the meaning of an object includes actions that can be carried out with it, and logic begins when a child is able to anticipate a relation between actions. Children's early logical connections, however, are context-bound fragments that later will become operational thinking.

The Fundamental Processes

Like biological systems, intelligence interacts with the environment, adapts to it, develops new structures as needed, and maintains a steady state while change and growth are occurring. Piaget, therefore, used terms derived from biological concepts to describe the essential nature of the interactions between intelligence and the environment. They are the processes referred to as *assimilation, accommodation,* and *equilibration.*

Assimilation and Accommodation.

The integration of external elements into the organism's structures is referred to as **assimilation**. Examples include the digestion of food and the incorporation of chlorophyllian in a plant's growth (Piaget, 1970b, p. 307). In intellectual life, assimilation is "the incorporation of an external element, for example, an object or event, into a sensorimotor or conceptual scheme of the subject" (Piaget, 1985, p. 5). An infant grasping a toy, a child weighing an object in his hand, and a scientist reviewing experiments in light of a particular theory are examples.

Assimilation is not the process of passively registering a copy of reality, nor is it an association between some environmental stimulus and a response (S ⇔ R). Instead, it is the filtering of the stimulus through an action structure so that the structures are themselves enriched (i.e., S=R) (Piaget & Inhelder, 1969, p. 6).

An important requirement for assimilation is an internal structure that can make use of the information. Young children, for example, base many of their decisions about the environment on perceptual cues alone. Often they do not integrate new information because they lack an appropriate assimilatory structure. For example, when asked to draw a picture of a half-full bottle that is tipped to one side, young children typically draw the water line as always parallel to the bottom of the bottle (Figure 9.2).

When confronted with the physical situation, young children fail to see the discrepancy between their drawings and reality (Piaget, 1977, p. 4). They have not developed a coordinate spatial system that enables them to place the water in a frame of reference outside the bottle.

Accommodation is the adjustment of internal structures to the particular characteristics of specific situations. For example, biological structures accommodate to the type and quantity of food at the same time that the food is being assimilated.

Similarly, in cognitive functioning, internal structures adjust to the particular characteristics of new objects and events. The child assimilates the familiar characteristics of a green felt triangle (closed, three-sided) while accommodating to its particular features (in this case, color and material).

Assimilation and accommodation function together in encounters with the environment at all levels of cognitive functioning. When the infant has discovered that he or she can grasp everything he or she sees, everything becomes an object to grasp (i.e., assimilation) (Piaget, in Bringuier, 1980, p. 43). For a large object, however, both hands may be needed, and for a small object, the fingers may need to be tightened (accommodation). Similarly, the theories of the scientist and the scholar are assimilatory schemes that are then adapted to diverse situations (Piaget, in Bringuier, 1980, p. 43).

In cognitive development, accommodation also refers to the modification of the individual's internal cognitive structures. When the learner realizes that his or her ways of thinking are contradicted by events in the environment, the prior ways of thinking are reorganized. This reorganization, which results in a higher level of thinking, is also a form of accommodation.

Equilibration.   The processes involved in maintaining a steady state while undergoing continuous change is referred to as **equilibration**. However, equilibration is

FIGURE 9.2
Young child's conception of the water line in containers placed at different angles

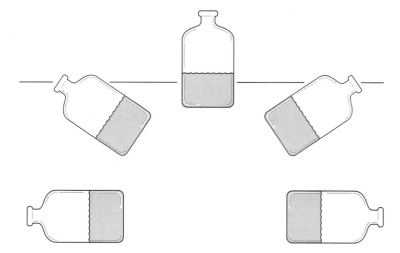

not a balance of forces (which would be an immobile state). Instead, it is the complex and dynamic processes that continuously regulate behavior (Piaget, in Bringuier, 1980, p. 41).

The three general forms of equilibrium identified by Piaget (1985) are (1) between assimilation and accommodation, (2) between schemes or subsystems, and (3) between the whole and its parts. Equilibrium between assimilation and accommodation is essential for the child's comparisons about the properties of objects. Equilibration balances assimilation and accommodation almost equally in most situations. However, the brief dominance of one or the other is sometimes necessary. Examples include symbolic play (the dominance of assimilation) and imitation (the dominance of accommodation). Equilibration, however, regulates these two types of childhood activities so that each occurs when appropriate (Piaget & Inhelder, 1969, p. 58).

Equilibration and the Construction of Operational Structures.   One of the sources of progress in the construction of both the action schemes of the infant and later logical operations is found in disequilibria (contradictions). Such events can force the individual to go beyond his or her current state and strike out in new directions (Piaget, 1985, p. 10). However, disequilibria do not always lead to progress. The various reactions to disequilibria described by Piaget (1985) are alpha, beta, and gamma reactions. Another important aspect of equilibration is the processes by which thinking is reorganized on a higher level. These processes are referred to as reflective abstraction.

Alpha, Beta, and Gamma Reactions.   The two types of alpha reactions are (1) ignoring or removing the disturbance, and (2) incorporating the conflict into one's beliefs without changing them. Examples of ignoring conflict involve failing to recognize (1) the true water line in a tilted bottle and (2) the changes in width when a ball of clay is lengthened into a cylinder (Level I thinking in the example discussed earlier in this chapter). An example of fitting a disturbance into core beliefs is the child who believes the earth is flat and, when told the Earth is round, concludes that it is shaped like a disc (Vosniadou & Brewer, 1992).

In contrast, beta reactions involve a modification of thinking in order to accommodate the disturbance. For example, the child incorporates the thinning of the ball as it becomes longer into his or her thinking (Level III thinking). However, the child has not constructed a new cognitive structure that permits him or her to predict all the transformations in advance. Such a reorganization of thinking is a gamma reaction (Level IV thinking). That is, the child can predict *in advance* that rolling out balls of clay into sausage shapes involves changes in both length and thickness and that the changes are compensatory. That is, the thinning of the ball as it is lengthened becomes logically necessary (Piaget, 1985, p. 100).

Reflective Abstraction.   The equilibration process that accounts for the transition between relatively impoverished to richer cognitive structures is **reflective abstraction** (Piaget, 1986b, p. 142). This process consists of (1) projecting (reflecting) something borrowed from a lower level to a higher level and (2) cognitively reconstructing ("reflexion") of what is transferred (Piaget, 1985, p. 29). An example is raising the step-by-step set of sensorimotor actions used to rotate an object, such as a cube, to the representational level (Piaget, 1980, p. 98). This process, although developed slowly over time, makes possible the visualization of the reverse side of the cube when only one aspect can be seen. Reflective abstraction is important because it is essential for the construction of concrete operations.

The subject matter in reflective abstraction is the individual's thought process. (In contrast, **empirical abstraction** refers to focusing on the observable characteristics of objects.) At the level of formal operations, thought processes are independent of any reference to physical manipulation (unlike concrete operations). This pure form of developing rich cognitive structures is referred to as reflected abstraction (Piaget, 1980).

Summary

The components of cognitive development consist of (1) the psychological structure of logical thinking and (2) the fundamental processes involved in interactions with the environment. Logical thinking in a particular domain has been achieved when the learner can simultaneously coordinate an operation and its inverse, can predict in advance the types of changes that will occur, and can support his/her decision on the basis of necessity.

The fundamental processes in the development of logical thinking are assimilation, accommodation, and equilibration. Assimilation is the integration of external elements into the learner's internal structures. Accommodation, in contrast, includes both adjustments in the learner's internal structures and qualitative transformations in thinking. Equilibration is the set of processes that maintains cognitive organization during the learner's changes in thinking. A major role for equilibration is that of maintaining intellectual functioning when disequilibria or cognitive conflicts occur. The alpha reaction involves either disregarding the disturbance or distorting the new information to maintain one's core beliefs. The beta reaction involves a modification of thinking in order to accommodate the disturbance. In contrast, a gamma reaction is the anticipation in advance of possible disturbances and the treatment of them as potential transformations. A gamma reaction indicates that the individual has constructed a new cognitive structure.

The processes responsible for the reorganization of thinking are referred to as reflective abstraction. The key characteristic is that the subject matter is the individual's thought processes. At the level of formal operations, the reorganization is referred to as reflected abstraction.

The Levels of Complex Reasoning

The early research conducted by Piaget (1967, 1970a) established the framework for his analyses of thinking processes. The framework consists of four broad periods or stages of cognitive development: sensorimotor, preoperational, concrete operational, and formal operational stages (see Table 9.2). Each one "extends the preceding period, reconstructs it on a new level, and later surpasses it to an even greater degree" (Piaget & Inhelder, 1969, p. 152). Contrary to early beliefs about Piaget's the-

TABLE 9.2
Summary of the qualitative changes in reasoning processes

Stage	Reasoning Processes
Sensorimotor period (birth–1½ years)	Presymbolic and preverbal intelligence involves the development of action schemes. Inference begins when the infant develops relations among actions. An example is constructing the container-content scheme from the "insert-in-the-mouth" scheme.
Preoperational period (2–3 to 7–8 years)	Partially logical thought begins; e.g., water poured into another container is the same water: a=a. However, the child reasons from one particular to another and decisions are made on the basis of perceptual cues. Young child does not differentiate between reality, possibility, and necessity in problem-solving situations.
Concrete operational period (7–8 to 12–14)	Logical ways of thinking linked to concrete objects are developed. Child comes to understand that a given operation simultaneously and necessarily implies its inverse. Child begins to develop co-possibilities in problem-solving situations and ways to systematically exclude them.
Formal operational period (older than 14)	The capability of dealing logically with multifactor situations begins. Individuals can deduce multiple possibilities and systematically exclude them. Reasoning proceeds from the hypothetical situation to the concrete.

ory, the stages were not the goal of his work. Instead, they represent the kinds of logical issues the child can deal with at a particular phase in his or her development.

Of the four stages, concrete and formal operational thinking represent complex reasoning. Both are logical forms of thinking, but they differ in qualitative ways.

Concrete Operations

Concrete operations are linked to the direct manipulation of objects. The common characteristic of concrete operational structures is that they consist of an equilibrium between "affirmations" (direct operations) and their inverses (opposites) (Piaget, 1985). The child has invented a "closed" concrete operational structure when he or she has constructed both the set of affirmations and their corresponding inverses.

Concrete operational structures are constructs in the domains of (1) numerical operations; (2) conservation (number, length, weight, area, mass, and volume); (3) classification and categorization (the addition and multiplication of classes); and (4) ordering relations (seriation). However, each is acquired independently of the others. For example, conservation associated with discontinuous quantities is acquired prior to the conservation of continuous quantities (e.g., weight and mass).

Unlike concrete operational thinkers, young children (preoperational thinkers) combine a sense of quantity, weight, and volume into a fuzzy concept of size (Smith,

1991, p. 85). They also use circular reasoning and the inconsistent application of criteria to justify their answers.

An earlier section in this chapter (Psychological Structure) describes an example of concrete operational thinking in relation to number and one on conservation of matter. Two other types of concrete operational thinking involve class inclusion operations and seriation. Class inclusion operations involve the separation of a collection into subclasses, such as subdividing a group of flowers into roses and tulips. The concrete operational child also can "double classify," that is, she can divide the flowers into red roses, red tulips, white roses, and white tulips. Preoperational children, in contrast, can only focus on one feature at a time. When asked to identify the red roses, they will choose either all the red roses or all the red flowers.

Seriation is characterized by transitivity or the "transfer" of relations. If $A = B$ and $B = C$, then $A = C$ and $C = B = A$ (the inverse). Seriation also includes asymmetric relations ["greater than" ($>$) and "less than" ($<$)], such as $A > B > C$. Concrete operational children understand that some element B is both longer and shorter than some other elements. Unlike preoperational thinkers who proceed haphazardly to form a series, concrete operational children systematically search for the longest (or shortest) stick, then the next one in length, and so on. They also can demonstrate that the reverse of $A > B > C$ is $C < B < A$.

Of interest are the differences between the original Piagetian transitivity task and the task used by subsequent researchers who maintained that younger children also were proficient at seriation. In the original task, the child sees and compares two sticks at a time (A and B; B and C). The third stick is out of sight (Lorenço & Machedo, 1996, p. 145). With this procedure, the inference that A is smaller than C is not based on any perceptual cues.

In contrast, other researchers began with all three sticks on the table in the order of increasing size. The sticks were separated so that length differences could not be perceived directly. The experimenter first placed A and B in front of the child, returned them to their original places, and then used the same procedure with A and C. The child then was asked to compare A with C. The problem with this procedure is that the child need only know the direction (right or left) in which the sticks increased in size (Lorenço and Machado, 1996). Chapman and McGrade (1992) implemented both the standard and altered versions of the task with 6- to 9-year-old children. Performance was better on the altered version, but the children's justifications were that the bigger stick was on the right.

Formal Operations

The concrete operational thinker can only reason from empirical data in developing an explanation (Inhelder & Piaget, 1958, p. 251) and is limited to pairing characteristics two by two. This approach, however, does not take into account the possibilities that the variables are mixed. That is, one effect may be caused by several factors, or a single causal factor may be accompanied or masked by several varying factors that are not causes (Inhelder & Piaget, 1958, p. 282). Efforts in such a situation to classify or order events on the basis of covariation are inadequate.

Formal operational thinkers, in contrast, can solve multifactor situations (as opposed to only two-factor situations) because they have developed new ways of thinking. The formal operational thinker is able to conceptualize all combinations of the factors in a particular situation. For example, given four characteristics, such as red and white and tulips and roses, the formal operational thinker can generate the 16 possible combinations of these characteristics. Among the possibilities are white tulips + red roses, red roses + red tulips, and so on. The concrete operational thinker, however, can only generate the four subclasses (red roses, red tulips, white roses, white tulips).

Piaget (1970a) refers to the capability of generating the 16 possibilities as *combinatorial operations.* According to Piaget (Inhelder & Piaget, 1958, p. 313), this capability is essential for formal operational thinking because it makes possible the analysis of relationships in multifactor situations.

However, the individual, when faced with a complex situation, does not actually construct the table of combinations. Instead, he or she begins by conceptualizing some of the possible combinations and systematically testing hypotheses in order to isolate the correct explanation. The important characteristic that distinguishes formal operations from concrete operations is that the individual begins with a theoretical synthesis that implies certain relationships and then proceeds to test the hypothesized relationships (Karmiloff-Smith & Inhelder, 1975).

An example is the colorless liquids experiment (Inhelder & Piaget, 1958). The experimenter adds a substance *g* to each of two beakers of colorless liquid(s). In one case, the new substance produces no change; however, in the other, the color *yellow* appears. The task for the student is to identify which of four colorless liquids, singly or in combination, produces the yellow color (Figure 9.3).

Formal operational thinkers will figure out the possible combinations, often jotting them down, and then proceed to test them. Individuals who are at the concrete level of thinking will proceed to test combinations, two by two. However, this approach results in omissions and errors.

Piaget (1972a, p. 10) noted that his research into formal operations had utilized situations likely to be understood by children in an academic setting. However, the applicability of such situations to professional environments is questionable. In other words, carpenters, locksmiths, or mechanics may well reason hypothetically in their specialty. Their unfamiliarity with structured school subjects, however, would hinder them from reasoning in a formal way with the experimental situations used in the research.

Similarly, research conducted by DeLisi and Stewart (1980) indicates that college students reason hypothetically in the area of their college majors. However, formal operational reasoning was not observed in other areas.

Other Interpretations

Research summarized by Berk (1989) indicates that infants attain some accomplishments in the sensorimotor stage, such as object permanence, earlier than Piaget indicated. However, some researchers have used the reaction of surprise on the disappearance of an object (rather than a search for the hidden object) as evidence of the concept of object permanence (Lorenço & Machado, 1996). The difficulty is that

FIGURE 9.3
The colorless liquids experiment

infants often display surprise at a change in a perceptual array of objects. Thus, the reaction is not a reliable indicator of object permanence. Further, as Piaget indicated, mental representations of hidden objects are rarely error-free until 18 months of age.

One line of theoretical development undertaken by Case (1985, 1992, 1993) has retained the broad perspective of Piaget's theory and introduced new concepts. This perspective, referred to as neo-Piagetian, has, according to Case (1992, p. 61), altered the Piagetian framework substantially. Further, the work is not a simple extension of Piaget's concepts nor a revision that he would have sanctioned (p. 62).

The broad concepts retained from classic Piagetian theory are that children create their own cognitive structures, assimilate experience to existing cognitive structures, pass through a universal sequence of structures, and incorporate earlier structures in later ones. Elements developed by Case (1985, 1992, 1993) are that (1) the general factor in children's development is their attentional or information-processing capacity (Case, 1992, p. 72) and (2) analysis of task performance should include children's goals and strategies and the information load required for the strategies.

Analyses of children's actions in different tasks led Case (1993) to conclude that children younger than 5 years approach computational tasks, such as telling time and making change with money, in a global fashion. In contrast, 5- to 7-year-olds have an integrated structure for such problems that includes counting and comparison. This integrated structure becomes automatic as children apply it in various situations and as functional working memory increases (p. 225).

Summary

The theory developed by Piaget traces the development of natural logic and reasoning from birth to adulthood. The transition from one form of reasoning to another depends on the physical environment, maturation, social influences, and the processes referred to as equilibration.

Two major concepts in Piaget's theory are the psychological nature of logical thinking and the fundamental processes in the functioning of intelligence. Three essential characteristics differentiate operational or logical thinking from other kinds of actions. They are that (1) each transformation in the data or object is exactly compensated by a change in another characteristic, (2) the essential nature of the data or object remains invariant, and (3) the transformation can be restored to the original by an inverse operation. A key concept in the construction of operational structures is that of necessity. That is, the individual is able to conceive of unlimited possibilities coupled with ways to exclude them and arrive at the necessary solution.

The three fundamental processes in intellectual functioning are assimilation, accommodation, and equilibration. Assimilation and accommodation are the basic processes in interactions with the environment, whereas equilibration maintains a steady state during growth and change. The three types of reactions to disturbances or cognitive conflicts are alpha, beta, and gamma reactions. When a gamma reaction occurs, the individual has reorganized his or her thinking into a more logical structure, a process referred to as reflective abstraction.

The qualitative differences in children's thinking form four broad periods or stages of development. They are the sensorimotor, preoperational, concrete operational, and formal operational periods. Presymbolic intelligence in the form of action schemes develops in the sensorimotor period while partially logical or transductive thought develops in the preoperational period.

At the level of concrete operations, the child develops logical structures in four domains. In addition to numerical operations, they are the conservation of number, length, weight, area, mass, and volume; classification and categorization; and ordering relations, or seriation. Concrete operations are linked to the manipulation of physical objects. Formal operational thinkers, in contrast, can solve multifactor situations because they are able to begin with a theoretical synthesis, and they then can test the hypothesized relationships in systematic ways.

PRINCIPLES OF INSTRUCTION

The derivation of instructional principles from Piaget's developmental theory requires careful and thoughtful analysis and interpretation. The primary reason is that the theory describes the qualitative changes in thought processes that lead to logical thinking. It does not address the learning of specific facts, such as state capitals. Early efforts to fit Piaget's developmental theory to curricula organized around specific objectives and goal-based evaluation resulted in misinterpretations. In recent years, some curricula based on the principle that children construct cognitive structures have been developed.

Basic Assumptions

One's perspective of the nature of the child's thinking has important implications for education (Piaget, 1970c). If childhood is believed to be simply a period that the child goes through to become an adult, then the relationship between the educational system and the child will be unilateral. The child will receive already finished products of adult knowledge and morality. Educational experiences will be organized and directed by the teacher and transmitted to the child. In such an educational climate, even individual tasks such as writing an essay will be directed toward obedience rather than autonomy (Piaget, 1970c).

However, if childhood is accepted as a necessary and important phase in the development of logical thinking, education will be viewed differently. The child's thought patterns undergo qualitative changes essential to the development of logical hypothetical thought. Therefore, the relationship between the educational system and the child must be a reciprocal one (Piaget, 1970c).

Piaget recommended the use of active methods that require the student to rediscover or reconstruct the truths to be learned. However, a highly industrialized and technological society presents problems in that it is not an ideal setting for exploration and spontaneous activity (Furth, 1980). How can a child apply his spontaneous curiosity to a television set, when only an expert knows how it works? Or to vegetables in a can when he has never seen them growing? The problem is that these children enter school with an intelligence that has not been well nourished. Thus, a "high-tech" society faces particular problems in developing individuals who are capable of constructing new knowledge.

The Components of Instruction

Instead of the verbal transmission of knowledge, education should be characterized by the use of methods that support the spontaneous research of the child or adolescent (Piaget, 1973). Such an approach is particularly important in the teaching of mathematics and science. Mathematics, for example, is composed of actions and operations, and therefore understanding mathematics should begin with action (Piaget, 1973). Such instruction should begin in nursery school with concrete exercises related to lengths, surfaces, numbers, and so on, progressing to physical and mechanical experiments in secondary school (Piaget, 1973, p. 104).

The basic need for education, according to Piaget (1973), is "to introduce both liberal arts and science students to experimental procedures and the free activity such training implies" (Piaget, 1973, p. 35). The solution he recommended is to provide mixed curricula—science classes that focus on self-directed experimentation and courses that use experimentation where possible. Some psychology classes, for example, could be devoted to individual experimentation in psycholinguistics.

Of course, subjects such as history or Latin cannot be "reinvented" by the students. That is, individuals cannot verify explanatory hypotheses with regard to Greek civilization (Piaget, 1973, p. 47). However, when research reveals some understanding of the ways in which students acquire spontaneous operational thought in historical understanding, methods may change.

A requirement that must accompany experimentation is that of collaboration and interchange among the students themselves (Piaget, 1973, p. 108). The traditional school often excludes this interchange, recognizing only the social exchange between teacher and student. However, both independent and collaborative student activity should be included. Using one's intelligence, according to Piaget (1973), assumes the exercise of a critical spirit. Such objectivity, however, can be developed only in the group situation in which give-and-take with one's peers occurs. Therefore, spontaneous activity, with small groups of students brought together by means of their mutual interest in a particular activity, should be a major feature of classroom learning. The classroom should be "a center of real (and experimental) activities carried out in common, so that logical intelligence may be elaborated through action and social exchange" (Piaget, 1973, p. 47).

Facilitating the Young Child's Construction of Knowledge

Organizing education around the child's spontaneous research implies an educational goal to develop the child's intelligence as an organized whole (Kamii, 1975). Important issues in preschool curricula are the problems with direct teaching, the role of make-believe play, the use of activities, sensorimotor activities, and the teacher's role.

Problems with "Direct Teaching".   Children do not learn by internalizing knowledge in ready-made form (Kamii & Kamii, 1990). Therefore, abstract ideas or principles should not be taught through verbal transmission (Kamii & DeVries, 1978). First, a logical rule contradicts the child's spontaneous beliefs and therefore confuses the child. The preoperational child does not notice the contradictions in his or her own explanations. One child, for example, stated that a wooden blade floats because it is thick, and copper wire sinks because it is long (Kamii & DeVries, 1978, p. 32). The fact that the wooden blade also was long was irrelevant to the child. Therefore, because the child is unaware of the contradictions, a logical rule to fit all contingencies at this point is only a verbalization that introduces confusion.

In addition, direct teaching of ideas stifles children's initiative in the construction of knowledge (Kamii & DeVries, 1978). Children may lose confidence in their ability to figure things out and focus instead on picking up cues from the teacher that indicate the desired right answer.

Make-Believe Play.   A key characteristic of preschool children, according to Piaget (1951), is that they manage to live in a world where the adult distinction between fiction and reality does not apply. This feat is accomplished in part through make-believe or symbolic play.

The importance of make-believe play is that it provides the child a temporary escape from the strange outside world. The child is free to accept from the environment what appeals to her or him and to ignore what is beyond immediate interest or understanding. For example, the child can "bake a cake" without having to be careful about breaking or burning. Also, the anger of an adult about some misbehavior can be reenacted using rules that the child understands. In other words, make-believe play provides a world of actions, symbols, and images where the child can feel free because it is under his or her own intellectual control (Furth, 1980, p. 67).

One of the current concerns about the use of VCRs and television as baby-sitters is the lost opportunities for creative play. The child is passive, instead of creating roles, actions, and thoughts through symbolic play. An important element in developing new ideas and ways of thinking is lost through reliance on these passive activities (Berk, 1989). Thus, an important activity to include in the preschool curriculum is some time in which children are free to engage in make-believe actions.

Use of Activities.   Many activities customarily included in preschool curricula can provide opportunities for cognitive development (Kamii & DeVries, 1978). Block painting, finger painting, musical games, cooking, dramatic play, and others are easily adaptable to a Piagetian curriculum. The first step is to evaluate the activities during preplanning for their potential to engage the children in the processes of empirical and logico–mathematical abstraction. That is, the activities should include problems that cannot be solved on the basis of perceptual cues only. Any activity, of course, can be inappropriate if used in the wrong way. Cuisinaire rods, for example, are inappropriate if the teacher demonstrates their uses and the outcomes that may be achieved (Piaget, 1973).

Some early curriculum developments advocated the diagnosis of the child's level of cognitive functioning and the provision of particular activities appropriate for the different levels in the classroom. In any one class of 30 children, however, various levels of development and breadth of understanding will be represented. Tailoring narrow exercises for individual children, though, is both impractical and unnecessary (Duckworth, 1979). First, the time required to test the children's level of cognitive development for different subsystems (number, space, length, etc.) is prohibitive. Second, logistical problems are generated by efforts to provide continuously a variety of activities and experiences for several different levels.

Third, activities or exercises that isolate and present one form of reasoning should not be used. They lack the element essential for progress, which is the dynamics of the conflict among modes of thinking (Inhelder et al., 1974, p. 265). Therefore, classroom activities should maximize the child's opportunities to construct and coordinate many relationships that he or she is capable of exercising (DeVries, 1978, p. 85).

Planning activities for classroom use should include consideration of two important factors: (1) the nature of the sensorimotor activities and (2) the use of teacher questions (i.e., the teacher's role).

Sensorimotor Activities.   For preschool children, Kamii and DeVries (1978, p. 49) identify four criteria for physical activities. Objects should be included that can be acted on directly by the child and for which different actions by the child will produce different effects. In addition, the effects of the child's actions on the object should be both immediate and observable.

Activities that meet these criteria can provide opportunities for the enrichment and clarification of the child's awareness of object characteristics, actions, and reactions (i.e., assimilation). Many such activities can also facilitate the process of accommodation that occurs when a cognitive structure adjusts to particular object characteristics and to the development of inferences about one's actions (meanings) (Piaget & Garcia, 1991).

Table 9.3 summarizes an activity for 4- and 5-year-olds that is appropriate for different developmental levels. The nature of the activity is such that it provides numerous opportunities for children to determine the physical properties of objects in the water. The interaction between blowing and speed of the objects contributes to the development of implications between actions.

The Teacher's Role.   Piaget (1973) indicated that no more difficult task exists for the teacher than that of becoming attuned to the spontaneous mental activity of the child or adolescent. Yet intellectual development depends on that constructive activity with all its errors and all the extra time that it seems to consume (Piaget, 1973, p. 107).

The use of active methods does not mean that students are left to their own devices. Instead, the teacher's role is first to create and organize classroom experiences. Second, the teacher's responsibility is to provide examples that cause students to rethink hastily developed ideas.

TABLE 9.3

Summary of classroom activity for young children

Activity	Blowing objects with a straw across the water surface in a water table
Objects	A drinking straw for each child; assorted objects, including ping-pong balls, cotton balls, crayons, Ivory soap, paper cups, styrofoam bits, a round Tinker toy, and others
Follow-up activity	Suggest a race with some objects or a hockey game with the ping-pong balls
Potential logicomathematical knowledge	"Lighter than," "heavier than," "faster than;" relationship between angle of straw, blowing effort, and speed
Sample follow-up questions	"What happened when you used two straws?" and "What would you like to try next time?" (Kamii & DeVries, 1978, p. 60)

Note: Summarized from *Physical Knowledge in Preschool Education* by C. Kamii and R. DeVries, 1978, Upper Saddle River, NJ: Prentice Hall.

Furthermore, children's "errors" that result from their experimentation must not be eliminated by coercion. The information that children use in reaching their conclusions may be inadequate for a correct solution of a specific problem. However, the choice is representative of a certain developmental stage that cannot be bypassed (Inhelder et al., 1974, p. 25). Therefore, games and activities should be reevaluated after implementation since children often take unexpected directions in pursuing their own questions.

In the implementation of activities, teacher questions can play an important role, but they must be carefully planned. Any questions that are used should be simply stated and should be real questions designed to provoke thinking; they should not be rhetorical statements in question form (Copple, Sigel, & Saunders, 1979, p. 213). Children's ideas, however, may be elicited through indirect questions, such as "Can you tell me about this?" or "What else feels [tastes, looks] like this?" (Copple et al., 1979, pp. 231–232). Examples of questions that keep children engaged are, "Can you find any more like that?" and "What did you do that was different from what she did?" (Duckworth, 1990, p. 46).

Prediction questions such as "What would happen if . . . " also may be used (Kamii & DeVries, 1978). These types of questions facilitate assimilation and accommodation and encourage children to go beyond physical reality in the construction of new knowledge. Questions such as "How did you know that the pudding was hot?" focus the child's attention on his or her strategy for reaching a conclusion.

However, with regard to direct actions on physical objects, young children often are unaware of which of their own actions produced a particular effect. For example, 4-year-olds can twirl an object on a string and time its release to land it in a box several feet away. Until the age of 9 or 10, their descriptions of the ways to accomplish this goal differ from their actions (Piaget, 1976). Thus explanations of such effects by 4- and 5-year-olds, and their accompanying understanding of such causes, will be inaccurate.

In summary, rich opportunities to act on objects and to observe the resulting reactions develop the foundation for logical thinking. The major requirements for the curriculum therefore are opportunities for children to interact with the physical world in a variety of ways, to make their own mistakes, and to develop answers to their questions in interaction with their peers.

Facilitating Operational Thinking

True logical thinking, in the Piagetian view, is constructed by the learner in self-directed or peer-collaborative research on topics of interest to the students (Duckworth, 1978, 1990). As Piaget (1973) indicated, self-directed experimentation is particularly important in science and mathematics.

Applications in Science.   In elementary school science, the material world should be the starting point (Duckworth, 1990). The material world is both accessible and contains complexities children have never dreamed of (p. 25). For example, in one second-grade classroom, some children were interested in crystals. The children made a "crystal" museum of examples they collected, grew crystals, examined them under a microscope, and read books about them. One snowflake picture led to their building a 12-sided polygon with their pattern blocks. Some children were fascinated to discover that, within such a shape, patterns were found 1, 2, 3, 6, or 12 times. Their explorations to determine the basis for these numbers led to the factors of 12. Other children appreciated most the beauty of the patterns (Duckworth, 1990, p. 22).

Research in science education indicates that both children and older students hold a variety of intuitive beliefs about scientific concepts (Champagne, Gunstone, & Klopfer, 1985; Gilbert, Watts, & Osborne, 1985). Furthermore, these views are not merely isolated ideas. Instead, they are incorporated in conceptual structures that provide a coherent understanding of the world from the child's perspective. Judgments often are based on appearances, such as, "It has evaporated, but it has not gone into the steam form, because you can't see it" (Gilbert, Osborne, & Fresham, 1982). In one study, students as old as 19 held contradictory beliefs without being aware of their contradictions (Osborne & Gilbert, 1980). One student, for example, when asked if any force was acting on a man standing on the moon, replied, "There is no air up there, so there is no gravity" (p. 379). Later, in the same interview, the student indicated that there was some gravity, but no air.

The first step in altering the curriculum, suggested by Osborne and Gilbert (1980), is to determine the student's current level of thinking. They developed pictures of different events (e.g., a boy riding a bicycle, a man hitting a golf ball, and others) to use in determining students' concepts of force. Using interviews to determine the students' rationales for their answers provides the information for an assessment of students' thinking. Once the intuitive beliefs are identified, experimental activities may be implemented that produce cognitive conflict between the intuitive ideas and scientific thinking. For example, confronting student misconceptions about Newtonian mechanics is the goal of several process simulations in physical science (Flick, 1990; White, 1984). In one set of exercises, students perform several actions on a "spaceship" in a frictionless environment (space). In this way, they confront their misconceptions about force, velocity, and speed.

Constructivism in Mathematics. As indicated in chapter 4, some developers have incorporated some of Piaget's concepts in curricula that also make use of classroom discourse. One perspective, referred to as radical constructivism, is derived directly from Piagetian principles. That is, essential learning processes are assimilation and accommodation following cognitive conflict and reflective abstraction. Another perspective, referred to as emergent (Cobb, 1995), advocates the Piagetian views that (1) knowledge is actively created by learners, (2) learners create new knowledge by reflecting on their physical and mental actions, (3) substantive learning occurs in periods of conflict and confusion, surprise, and over long periods of time, and (4) opportunities for learning occur during social interaction (Wood, Cobb, & Yaeckel, 1991, p. 591).

In one second-grade classroom, an example of this perspective, pairs of children first solve problems that may be resolved in more than one way. In the subsequent whole-class discussion, children are expected to justify and explain their answers and also to listen to other children's explanations (Wood et al., 1991).

Important in this and similar implementations is the reconstruction of classroom social norms so that the children feel "psychologically safe" to explain their solutions to each other and the class (Wood et al., 1991, p. 598). Also important is that the teacher must be able to accept the students' incorrect answers unconditionally. In this second-grade classroom, the teacher learned, however, that letting children struggle to resolve conflicts in their thinking provided occasions for the children to learn. That is, the children's responses were not aimless, and her role was to create circumstances in which conflicts and confusions could be resolved through students' procedures (p. 699).

Role of the Computer.   Used appropriately, the computer can provide opportunities for children to exercise logic in action, a key concept in Piagetian theory. In the nonverbal computer program Symbol–Picture–Logic (SPL), for example, children discover the rules represented by symbols, complete symbol–logic statements, and, thereby, develop insights into logical necessity (Furth, 1986a, 1986b). The computer also can assist students to manipulate and construct objects that are impossible or impractical to use in the classroom. One computer environment is the Turtle Geometry and LOGO created by Seymour Papert (1980). The "turtle" in LOGO is a computer-controlled triangular symbol (Δ). Simple commands direct the turtle to move forward and backward as well as to change direction at any angle from 1 to 359 degrees. The turtle's movement leaves a trace (line) as though the student is drawing with pen or pencil. Any number of geometric figures may be designed, restricted only by the creativity and imagination of the student.

In creating a geometric figure, the student decides the kind of task that the turtle is to complete and sets about giving the turtle the computer commands (i.e., developing a computer program). When the turtle goes in an unexpected direction after receiving a particular command, the student must readjust his or her thinking and correct the command.

In this way, the student experiments with designing rectangles, triangles, squares, and circles, altering his or her strategy according to the performance of the turtle. Thus, students learn strategies for designing geometric figures without being directly taught (Clements & Gullo, 1984; Gallini & Gredler, 1989).

Such an environment is referred to as a microworld (Pufall, 1988, p. 27). It is an environment that does not prescribe what the child should know. Instead, a microworld is a context within which the child can construct knowledge. The developer of computer software, however, must not confuse *interactive* with *constructive*. This message is important because creating interactive environments is educationally appealing (Pufall, 1988). Interacting with the computer, however, is a necessary but not sufficient condition for the child's construction of knowledge.

Facilitating Formal Operational Thinking

The problems associated with placing students in multivariate problems before they have developed the conceptual structures to address such complex situations is illustrated in a study by Lavoie and Good (1988). Students were presented with a simulation in which some combination of five variables (temperature, waste type, dumping rate, type of treatment, and type of body of water) affected oxygen and waste concentration of the water. Problem-solving ability on prediction problems was related to high or moderate initial knowledge and performance at the Piagetian stage of formal operational thinking. Unsuccessful students tended to have both low initial knowledge and to be at the stage of concrete operational thinking.

Obviously, formal operational thinking cannot be acquired through "prepackaged experiments" or by solving end-of-chapter problems for a predetermined answer. Any experiment that is not carried out by the individual with complete freedom is not an exercise; it is simply drill with no educational worth (Piaget, 1973, p. 20).

Changes in thinking have been achieved in science and physics through situations that require the students to confront their inaccurate ideas through exploration (Champagne et al., 1985; Kuhn & Phelps, 1979). An essential characteristic of one intervention was described as "ideational confrontation." It is, of course, the disequilibrium described by Piaget.

In one study, students who showed no evidence of formal reasoning strategies were provided with a rich problem environment with opportunities to explore the causes of different events (Kuhn & Phelps, 1979). After 3 months of weekly problem-solving sessions, both fifth graders and adolescents showed changes in their reasoning strategies. However, the process was slow and uneven with setbacks along the way. "Conflicts and contradictions are encountered and resolved, not once, but many times over" (Kuhn & Phelps, 1979, p. 54). Similar to another study conducted by Kuhn (1979), the most common difficulty seemed to be not the mastery of new strategies but the inability to relinquish inadequate strategies.

Some students began by conducting experiments in such a way that their hypotheses could not be disproved (Champagne, Klopfer, & Anderson, 1980; Kuhn & Phelps, 1979). Other students, faced with findings that contradicted their hypotheses, simply ignored the conflicting data. Thus, open-ended exploration by itself is not sufficient to develop hypothetical reasoning. Probing questions and challenges to the student's thinking are essential.

Progress also requires that the instructor push students to formulate explanatory hypotheses and to test them repeatedly. Even so, "reconceptualization will be a slow tortuous process. It will come only after many alternative ideas and explanations have been tried and failed" (Champagne et al., 1980, p. 1078).

Summary

The focus of Piaget's theory is the development of logical thinking; therefore, it does not include specific guidelines for instruction. However, general guidelines for instruction to facilitate student thinking may be derived from the theory. First, knowledge, particularly in mathematics and science, should not be taught as though it were a set of truths that can be relayed through abstract language. Knowledge is constructed by the learner through self-directed and peer-collaborative research. The teacher's role is that of organizing and creating situations that present meaningful problems. Collaboration and interchange among the students also should accompany experimentation.

Many activities in the preschool curriculum can provide opportunities for cognitive development. Examples include block painting, finger painting, and musical games. Objects should be provided in the classroom that can be acted on directly by the child, and the child's actions should produce different effects that are immediate and observable. The teacher's role is that of asking thoughtful questions that provoke children's thinking.

At the elementary school level, a variety of materials for measurement and experimentation can provide children with opportunities to use their developing subsystems. Experimentation in science also is important to help children confront their intuitive beliefs about scientific concepts. In addition, used appropriately, computer environments can provide opportunities for students to construct and manipulate objects and thereby confront their intuitive beliefs.

Formal operational thinking also requires self-directed exploration. Students should be encouraged to formulate explanatory hypotheses, to test them, and to address conflicting data. However, reconceptualization will be a slow process.

EDUCATIONAL APPLICATIONS

The concepts developed by Piaget can be implemented in preschool and elementary school classrooms by providing rich activities for children's exploration. In mathematics and science, Piaget's concepts, combined with other concerns, such as developing a community of learners, have been implemented to develop curricula. Students are encouraged to solve problems in ways that make sense to them, to be able to justify and explain their answers, and to participate in class discussions to resolve conflicts and confusion.

Some of the curriculum misapplications resulted from the failure to coordinate a developmental curriculum with the academic curriculum. Kamii (1981) suggests three general objectives compatible with the school curriculum. Briefly summarized, they are (1) the development of children's autonomy through interactive situations; (2) the decentering and coordination of various points of view by children; and (3) the development of alertness, curiosity, initiative, and confidence in learning (Kamii, 1981, p. 24). These objectives may be integrated into the school curriculum without displacing it. Further, policies of the National Council of Teachers of Mathematics (NCTM) (1989) that advocate questioning others' thinking and supporting one's views are consistent with Piaget's theory.

Classroom Issues

Piaget's theory is neither a theory of academic learning nor a teaching theory. Nevertheless, it does address several educational issues.

Learner Characteristics

Jean Piaget's theory addresses the broad issues involved in cognitive development. Individual differences, readiness, and motivation are therefore viewed in terms of their relationship to long-term cognitive development.

Individual Differences.   The theory has been criticized by some educators for omitting specific references to individual differences. However, such a concern is simply outside the realm of the theory; the goal was to identify and to study the universal laws of cognitive development.

Nevertheless, cultural differences in the rate of attainment of cognitive structures have been observed. Children in some rural settings are slower than urban children in the attainment of concrete operations. Furthermore, formal operations are not attained by all individuals, nor are they acquired in all areas of expertise (e.g., physics, law, and engineering) (Piaget, 1972a).

Readiness.   Readiness has two meanings in the interpretation of Piaget's theory. One is that of the individual's capacity to assimilate new information; a requirement is a cognitive framework that can make use of the new information.

The second way in which readiness is manifested is in relation to the construction of logical cognitive structures, or operations. Specifically, logical constructions do not result until the subject experiences cognitive conflict and seeks to resolve it on a higher plane. Readiness therefore is the acknowledgment of conflicting statements coupled with the felt need to resolve two subsystems—for example, number and space.

Piaget has mistakenly been viewed at times as a maturationist because he identified four sequential stages of development. However, only the ordering of the stages is invariant; attainment requires learner experience with the environment, learner activity, and interaction with the social environment.

Motivation.   Two sources of motivation are identified by Piaget (1973). One is a general motivating factor that functions at all levels of development—that of need. As in other theories, needs may be physiological, affective, or intellectual. Since intelligence seeks both to understand and to explain, an intellectual need often appears in the form of a question or a problem (Piaget, 1967, p. 5). In Piaget's view, all action, whether movement, thought, or emotion, is in response to a need. In the theory, need is described as a manifestation of disequilibrium (Piaget, 1967). When the need is satisfied, equilibrium is restored.

Disequilibrium represents the general factor of need at all levels of development. The second source of motivation is the specifics or content of need at a particular age or period of development. These specific needs depend on the system of ideas that a child has developed plus his or her affective inclinations. For example, a young child may engage in behavior to gain the approval of a parent, but a teenager is more likely to seek the approval of peers.

Cognitive Processes and Instruction

Three important classroom issues are developing "how-to-learn skills," providing transfer of learning, and teaching problem solving. In the context of Piaget's theory, these issues take on a different meaning.

Developing "How-to-Learn" Skills.   The individual's ability to organize his or her own behavior efficiently in order to extract meaning from a situation or to initiate steps to solve some predetermined problem are typically defined as how-to-learn skills. In the context of genetic epistemology, however, manipulating and experiencing concrete objects in the environment is the foundation for knowledge construction. Children learn how to learn by generating problems, investigating questions, and examining their answers.

Transfer of Learning.   The facilitation of new learning that results from similarities to prior learning is an important classroom issue. Transfer of learning implies some sequencing of learning tasks in order to take advantage of their common properties.

Cognitive development, however, differs from specific learning. The attainment of particular cognitive structures do not "transfer" to the development of the next stage in the sense of isomorphic elements. The cognitive structures attained in any period of development do, however, prepare the learner to undertake the next stage.

Teaching Problem Solving.   According to Piaget (1973), the skill of problem solving cannot be directly taught. Instead, the rules of experimentation and, therefore, the rules for problem solution must be discovered or reinvented by each student. This experimentation and reinvention is essential to the development of problem-solving skills. In addition, Piaget maintains that the rules or theories that operate in any particular subject area must be reinvented by the individual; they cannot be conveyed verbally.

The Social Context for Learning

Unlike educational approaches that focus on teacher–student interaction, Piaget (1973) emphasizes the importance of peer interactions in the context of self-directed experimentation. Only through this type of interaction does the student acquire the capability of viewing issues from other perspectives. Furthermore, in exchanges with others, students examine their own thinking, explore other alternatives, and reorganize their views and conclusions. The teacher, however, must create situations that promote exploration.

Relationships to Other Perspectives

Unlike operant conditioning, the conditions of learning, and the information-processing perspective, Piaget's theory does not address the factual and conceptual information that constitutes subject domains. Instead, his principles address the characteristics involved in thinking and reasoning about events, i.e., natural logic, and the various changes across the lifespan. The activities and strategies recommended by Piaget for the classroom, therefore, target children's spontaneous research in the development of reasoning and thinking skills.

Although Piaget identified questioning and interaction among peers in the classroom as important, the teacher must create classroom situations conducive to a variety of student actions. Thus, in his view, the goal is not to become a community of learners, as is recommended by social constructivism. Further, the individual student, not the group, is the locus of learning.

Piaget's view of the role of make-believe play and children's egocentric speech also differed from that of Lev Vygotsky. These differences are discussed in chapter 10.

Developing a Classroom Strategy

The implementation of Piaget's concepts at any level of the curriculum can be accomplished using the following four general steps and the subquestions for each step:

Step 1: Determine which principles in a course or curriculum typically taught by verbal means may be replaced by student-directed research.

1.1 Which aspects of the curriculum are conducive to experimentation?

1.2 Which principles are conducive to problem-solving activity in a group situation?

1.3 Which topics (or concepts) can be introduced at a manipulable level using physical objects prior to verbal treatment?

Step 2: Select or develop classroom activities for the identified topics. Evaluate the selected activities using the following list of questions:

2.1 Does the activity provide opportunities for a variety of methods of experimentation?

2.2 Can the activity lead to a variety of questions by the students?

2.3 Can the student compare various modes of reasoning in working through the activity?

2.4 Is the problem one that *cannot* be solved on the basis of perceptual cues alone?

2.5 Is the activity one that generates both physical activity and opportunities for cognitive activity? (Inappropriate activities include constructing a picture or diagram or building objects prespecified by the teacher.)

2.6 Can the activity enrich an already learned construct?

Step 3: Identify opportunities for teacher questions that support the problem-solving process.

3.1 What probing follow-up questions may be used (e.g., predictions, "what if" questions)?

3.2 What potential comparisons can be identified within the material that are conducive to spontaneous questions?

Step 4: Evaluate the implementation of each activity, noting successes and needed revisions.

4.1 What aspect of the activity generated the most intense interest and involvement? Are there ways that this may be capitalized on in the future?

4.2 What aspect of the activity, if any, "fell flat"? Did the activity fail to engage the efforts of one or more learners? What are some alternatives to try next time?

4.3 Did the activity provide opportunities to develop new strategies of investigation or to enhance already learned strategies?

In summary, maximize the opportunities for students to construct knowledge for themselves through student-directed research. Discussions about research findings in which answers were developed through group interaction and that require consideration of a number of variables will enhance the student's construction of knowledge. Finally, whenever possible, provide direct student experience with constructs, rules, and theories prior to any verbalization. Otherwise, the information remains only verbalization and does not become knowledge.

Classroom Example

The following classroom lesson emerged as part of a research and development project in teaching conducted by Magdalene Lampert (1990). The goal was to determine in what ways the practice of knowing mathematics in the classroom could be brought closer to what it means to know mathematics within the discipline. The primary mechanism in this process is to alter the roles and responsibilities of both students and teacher during classroom discourse (Lampert, 1990, p. 29).

The goal was not to create a Piagetian curriculum. However, the construction of knowledge undertaken by the fifth-grade students, the role of the teacher, and the nature of the peer interaction reflect classroom characteristics described by Piaget as essential for cognitive development.

Basic premise: "Doing" mathematics is not a matter of finding a right answer that is ratified by the teacher. Instead, mathematics develops as a process of "conscious guessing" about relationships that are examined and then tested through the use of counterexamples (Lakatos, 1976; Lampert, 1990).

Content: Exponents, fifth-grade class

Purpose: One can determine aspects of the characteristics of unknown quantities by studying patterns in numbers one can observe (Lampert, 1990; Polya, 1954). Also, students can acquire the attitudes and skills to participate in a disciplinary discourse that is knowledge *about* mathematics (Lampert, 1990; Schoenfeld, 1985).

Prior activities: The use of mathematical discourse, and the rules for interchange, were already in use in the classroom (Lampert, 1990). When a problem was posed to the class, student conjectures and their names were written on the board. When students wanted to change a conjecture, they had learned to say, "I want to revise my thinking." When proposing a possible answer (conjecture), they were expected to provide a rationale. All the students had prepared their own tables of squares from 1^2 to 100^2 using calculators.

Constructing knowledge: The teacher challenged the students to find patterns in their tables of numbers by examining the last digits of the numbers. They actively participated in this investigation for three 45-minute class periods. The key to the lesson was that "the mathematical content embedded in inventing the strategies that can be used to assert the answers without doing the calculations is mathematically significant and engages students in arguing about the key ideas behind how exponents work" (Lampert, 1990, p. 46).

The first assertion made by the students was that the last digits of the squares alternated between odd and even just as the base numbers did. Other assertions were that multiples of 10 would always end in 0, and the square of a number ending in 5 always ends in 5. They then began to explore further the hypothesis that "if the last digit is always n when you raise n to some power, the last two digits will always be n^2" (Lampert, 1990, p. 49). Two students asserted that the powers of 6 should end in 36, but other students quickly identified a counterexample.

Students also determined that the strings of last digits always will be symmetrical around both 0 and 5. A chart was used to work out the symmetrical pattern of last digits. The students also proved that the pattern would go on forever because numbers ending in 9 or 1 have squares that end in 1, numbers ending in 2 or 8 have squares that end in 4, and so on.

The final segment of the lesson shifted to strategies for figuring out the last digit in a number raised to the 5th power. In the discussion of 7^5, several digits were proposed along with the accompanying rationale. One student thought the pattern of last digits would be 1, 7, 9, 1, 7, 9, and so on. However, after several assertions and discussions of each, the students determined that the pattern of last digits would be 7, 9, 3, 1, 7; therefore, 7^5 ends in 7.

During the discussion, one of the students stated that 7^5 should end in 1. The teacher's role was to ask him to explain, to assert what some of the student's assumptions might have been, and, later, to ask him to articulate the revision in thinking he had made. The purpose is not simply for the student to rethink his assumptions, but to help the other students to see why those assumptions had led him to the conclusion that the last digit was 1. In other words, in this type of lesson, both students and teacher have a different relation to the subject matter than they would in a "knowledge telling exchange" (Lampert, 1990, p. 53).

Review of the Theory

Jean Piaget's theory of cognitive development redefines intelligence, knowledge, and the relationship of the learner to the environment. Intelligence, like a biological system, is a continuing process that creates the structures it needs in continuing interactions with the environment.

The essential characteristic of logical thinking is the construction of a psychological structure with particular characteristics. Specifically, the learner (1) clearly recognizes the changing (transformation) and unchanging (conservation) features of a situation, (2) understands the inverse operation for each transformation (reversibility), and (3) identifies the problem solution as logically necessary.

The development of the individual's different ways of thinking from infancy to adulthood include the action schemes of the infant, preoperations, concrete operations, and formal operations. The process by which each of these more complex structures is constructed are assimilation and accommodation, regulated by equilibration (Table 9.4).

TABLE 9.4
Summary of Jean Piaget's cognitive-development theory

Basic Element	Definition
Assumptions	Intelligence, like a biological system, constructs the structures it needs to function. Knowledge is the interaction between the individual and the environment. The growth of intelligence is influenced by four factors (physical and social environment, maturation, and equilibration).
Cognitive development	The growth of logical thinking from infancy to adulthood
Outcomes of cognitive development	The construction of new structures from prior structures (i.e., action schemes, concrete and formal operations)
Components of cognitive development	Assimilation and accommodation, regulated by equilibration Physical experience and logicomathematical experience
Facilitating logical thinking	Providing rich opportunities for experimentation with physical objects supported by peer interaction and teacher questions
Major issues in designing instruction	Maintenance of reciprocal relationship between child and education; avoidance of direct teaching and correction of children's "errors"
ANALYSIS OF THE THEORY	
Disadvantages	Understanding of basic terms and definitions is difficult. Piagetian curriculum is difficult to implement and maintain. Perspective excludes the relationship between logical thinking and basic learning, such as reading.
Applications to classroom practice	Provides a rich description of the world through the child's eye Identifies problems in curricula, particularly the teaching of mathematics and science as "socialized knowledge" Operationalizes the often-cited concept, "discovery learning"

The role of education, in Piaget's view, is to support the spontaneous research of the child. Experimentation with real objects and interaction with peers, supported by the teacher's insightful questions, permits the child to construct both physical and logico–mathematical knowledge. The major requirements for the curriculum are rich opportunities for children to interact with the physical world in a variety of ways, to make their own mistakes, and to develop answers through interaction with their peers.

Disadvantages

A major problem in the implementation of Piaget's ideas arises from the different perspective he casts on intelligence, knowledge, and learning. Considerable effort is required to alter one's perspective from intelligence and knowledge as products to treating these concepts totally as process.

The development of curriculum, according to Piagetian concepts, requires, as Piaget himself indicated, considerable work and effort. Implementation of a Piagetian curriculum is also complicated by the fact that his theory excludes the relationships between logical thinking and curriculum basics, such as reading and writing.

Contributions to Educational Practice

A major contribution of Piaget's work is that he changed the view of a child from that of a little adult to one with distinctive and changing patterns of thinking. Another is that he identified the shortcomings of directly taught curricula. He clearly delineates the problems and effects of teaching mathematics and science, for example, as "socialized knowledge." In addition to providing us a rich description of the world from the child's eye, he has operationalized the often-cited concept "discovery learning." Table 9.4 summarizes Piaget's cognitive-development theory.

CHAPTER QUESTIONS

1. A student is using a computer software program to write an essay. She is required to use certain symbol keys to direct the computer to double-space, number the pages, and so on. In Piaget's view, what is this process?

2. A child feels the rush of air on his face made by fanning a paper. Later, on a windy day, he feels the wind and decides it is caused by the swaying trees (Wolfgang & Sanders, 1981, p. 117). Which stage of thinking does this notion of causality represent? Why?

3. A group of middle school students are asked to predict which of two objects, dropped at the same time, will fall faster. Most of the students predict that the heavier object will reach the floor first. When given several objects to experiment with, they are puzzled that they cannot determine any difference in the rate of descent. Some of the students conclude, in error, that the heavier object falls faster but that the difference is too small for them to observe. According to Piaget, what has happened in this situation?

4. How would the Gestalt psychologists describe the child's drawings of the water in Figure 9.2?

REFERENCES

Acredolo, C. (1997). Understanding Piaget's new theory requires assimilation and accommodation. *Human Development, 40,* 235–237.

Bickhard, M. H. (1997). Piaget and active cognition. *Human Development, 40,* 238–243.

Beilin, H. (1989). Piagetian theory. In *Six theories of child development: Annals of child development 6* (pp. 85–131). Greenwich, CN: JAI Press.

Beilin, H. (1992a). Piaget's enduring contribution to developmental psychology. *Developmental Psychology, 20*(2), 191–204.

Beilin, H. (1992b). Piaget's new theory. In H. Beilin & P. Pufall (Eds.), *Piaget's theory: Prospects and possibilities* (pp. 1–20). Hillsdale, NJ: Erlbaum.

Berk, L. E. (1989). *Child development.* Boston: Allyn & Bacon.

Borel, M. (1987). Piaget's natural logic. In B. Inhelder, D. deCaprona, & A. Cornu-Wells (Eds.), *Piaget today* (pp. 65–75). Hillsdale, NJ: Erlbaum.

Bringuier, J. C. (1980). *Conversations with Jean Piaget* (B. M. Gulati, Trans.). Chicago: University of Chicago Press.

Case, R. (1985). *Intellectual development: Birth to adulthood.* New York: Academic.

Case, R. (1992). Neo-Piagetian theories of cognitive development. In H. Beilin & P. Pufall (Eds.), *Piaget's theory: Prospects and possibilities* (pp. 61–104). Hillsdale, NJ: Erlbaum.

Case, R. (1993). Theories of learning and theories of development. *Educational Psychologist, 28*(3), 219–233.

Cauley, K., Murray, F., & Smith, D. (1983). Necessity in children's reasoning: Criteria for conservation and operativity. Paper presented at the Eastern Educational Research Association, Baltimore, MD.

Champagne, A. B., Gunstone, R. F., & Klopfer, L. E. (1985). Effecting changes in cognitive structures among physics students. In L. H. J. West & A. L. Pines (Eds.), *Cognitive structure and conceptual change* (pp. 163–188). Orlando, FL: Academic.

Champagne, A. B., Klopfer, L. E., & Anderson, J. H. (1980). Factors influencing the learning of classical mechanics. *American Journal of Physics, 48*(2), 1074–1079.

Chandler, M., & Chapman, M. (1991). *Criteria for competence.* Hillsdale, NJ: Erlbaum.

Chapman, M. (1988). *Constructive evolution.* New York: Cambridge University Press.

Chapman, M., & McBride, M. (1992). Beyond competence and performance: Children's class inclusion strategies, superordinate class cues, and verbal justifications. *Developmental Psychology, 28*, 319–327.

Clements, D. H., & Gullo, D. F. (1984). Effects of computer programming in young children's cognition. *Journal of Educational Psychology, 76*, 1054–1058.

Cobb, P. (1995). Continuing the conversation: A response to Smith. *Educational Researcher, 24*(6), 25–27.

Copple, C., Sigel, E., & Saunders, R. (1979). *Educating the young thinker: Classroom strategies for cognitive growth.* New York: Van Nostrand.

Dean, A. L., & Youniss, J. (1991). The transformation of Piagetian theory by American psychology: The early competence issue. In M. Chandler & M. Chapman (Eds.), *Criteria for competence* (pp. 92–100). Hillsdale, NJ: Erlbaum.

DeLisi, R., & Stewart, J. (1980). Individual differences in college students' performance on formal operational tasks. *Journal of Applied Developmental Psychology, 1*, 201–208.

DeVries, R. (1978). Early education and Piagetian theory. In J. M. Gallagher & J. A. Easley, Jr. (Eds.), *Knowledge and development: Vol. 2. Piaget and education* (pp. 75–91). New York: Plenum.

Duckworth, E. (1978). The having of wonderful ideas. *Harvard Educational Review, 42*, 217–231.

Duckworth, E. (1979). Either we're too early and they can't learn it or we're too late and they know it already: The dilemma of "applying Piaget." *Harvard Educational Review, 49*, 297–312.

Duckworth, E. (1990). Opening the world. In E. Duckworth, J. Easley, D. Hawkins, & A. Henriques (Eds.), *Science education: A minds-on approach for the elementary years* (pp. 21–59). Hillsdale, NJ: Erlbaum.

Flick, L. B. (1990). Interaction of intuitive physics with computer simulated physics. *Journal of Research in Science Teaching, 27*(3), 219–231.

Furth, H. (1980). *The world of grownups: Children's conceptions of society.* New York: Elsevier North Holland.

Furth, H. (1986a). Piaget's logic of assimilation and logic for the classroom. In G. Forman & P. Pufall (Eds.), *Constructivism in the computer age* (pp. 37–46). Hillsdale, NJ: Erlbaum.

Furth, H. (1986b). *Symbol-picture logic (SPL)* (Vol. 2). Washington, DC: Computer Age Education.

Gallini, J., & Gredler, M. (1989). *Instructional design for computers: Cognitive applications in BASIC and LOGO.* Glenview, IL: Scott, Foresman.

Gilbert, J. K., Watts, D. M., & Osborne, R. J. (1985). Eliciting student views using an interview technique. In L. H. T. West & A. L. Pines (Eds.), *Cognitive structure and conceptual change* (pp. 11–27). Orlando, FL: Academic.

Gilbert, J. K., Osborne, R. J., & Fresham, P. J. (1982). Children's science and its consequences for teaching. *Science Education, 6*, 623–633.

Inhelder, B., & deCaprona, E. (1990). The role and meaning of structures in genetic epistemology.

In W. F. Overton (Ed.), *Reasoning, necessity, and logic: Developmental perspectives* (pp. 333–344). Hillsdale, NJ: Erlbaum.

Inhelder, B., & Piaget, J. (1958). *The growth of logical thinking from childhood to adolescence* (A. Parsons & S. Milgram, Trans.). New York: Basic.

Inhelder, B., Sinclair, H., & Bovet, M. (1974). *Learning and the process of cognition.* Cambridge, MA: Harvard University Press.

Kamii, C. (1975). One intelligence indivisible. *Young Children, 30*(4), 228–238.

Kamii, C. (1981). Application of Piaget's theory to education: The pre-operational level. In I. Sigel, D. A. Brodzinsky, & R. M. Golinkoff (Eds.), *New directions in Piagetian theory and practice* (pp. 231–265). Hillsdale, NJ: Erlbaum.

Kamii, C., & DeVries, R. (1978). *Physical knowledge in preschool education.* Upper Saddle River, NJ: Prentice Hall.

Kamii, C., & Kamii, M. (1990). Why achievement testing should stop. In C. Kamii (Ed.), *Achievement testing in the early grades* (pp. 15–38). Washington, DC: National Association for the Education of Young Children.

Karmiloff-Smith, A., & Inhelder, B. (1975). If you want to get ahead, get a theory. *Cognition, 3,* 195–212.

Kuhn, D. (1979). The application of Piaget's theory of cognitive development to education. *Harvard Educational Review, 49,* 340–360.

Kuhn, D., & Phelps, E. (1979). A methodology for observing development of a formal reasoning strategy. *New Directions for Child Development, 5,* 45–57.

Lakatos, I. (1976). *Proofs and refutations: The logic of mathematical discovery.* New York: Cambridge University Press.

Lampert, M. (1990). When the problem is not the question and the solution is not the answer: Mathematical knowing and teaching. *American Educational Research Journal, 27*(1), 29–63.

Lavoie, D. R., & Good, R. (1988). The nature and use of prediction skills in a biological computer simulation. *Journal of Research in Science Teaching, 25*(5), 335–360.

Lorenço, O., and Machado, A. (1996). In defense of Piaget's theory; A reply to 10 common criticisms, *Psychology Review, 103 (1),* 143–164.

Montangero, J. (1991). A constructivist framework for understanding early and late-developing psychological competencies. In M. Chandler and M. Chapman (Eds.), *Criteria for competence: Controversies in the conceptualization and assessment of children's abilities* (pp. 111–129). Hillsdale, NJ: Erlbaum.

Murray, F. B. (1990). The conversion of truth into necessity. In W. F. Overton (Ed.), *Reasoning, necessity, and logic: Developmental perspectives* (pp. 183–204). Hillsdale, NJ: Erlbaum.

National Council of Teachers of Mathematics (NCTM) (1989). *Curriculum and evaluation standards for school mathematics,* Reston, VA: Author.

Osborne, R. J., & Gilbert, J. J. (1980). A technique for exploring students' views of the world. *Physics Education, 15,* 376–379.

Papert, S. (1980). *Mindstorms.* New York: Basic.

Piaget, J. (1926). *Judgment and reasoning in the child.* New York: Harcourt.

Piaget, J. (1928). *Judgment and reasoning in the child.* London: Routledge & Kegan Paul.

Piaget, J. (1951). *Play, dreams and imitation in children.* New York: Norton.

Piaget, J. (1952). *The child's conception of number.* London: Routledge & Kegan Paul.

Piaget, J. (1965). *The moral judgment of the child.* New York: Free Press.

Piaget, J. (1967). *Six psychological studies* (A. Tenzer, Trans.). New York: Random House.

Piaget, J. (1970a). *Genetic epistemology* (E. Duckworth, Trans.). New York: Columbia University Press.

Piaget, J. (1970b). Piaget's theory. In P. H. Mussen (Ed.), *Carmichael's manual of psychology* (Chap. 9, pp. 703–732). New York: Wiley.

Piaget, J. (1970c). *Science of education and the psychology of the child.* New York: Orion.

Piaget, J. (1971). *The construction of reality in the child.* New York: Ballantine.

Piaget, J. (1972a). Intellectual evolution from adolescence to adulthood. *Human Development, 15,* 1–12.

Piaget, J. (1972b). *The principles of genetic epistemology* (W. Mays, Trans.). New York: Basic.

Piaget, J. (1973). *To understand is to invent: The future of education.* New York: Grossman.

Piaget, J. (1976). *The grasp of consciousness: Action and concept in the young child.* Cambridge, MA: Harvard University Press.

Piaget, J. (1977). Problems in equilibration. In M. Appel & S. Goldberg (Eds.), *Topics in cognitive development: Vol. I. Equilibration: Theory, research, and application* (pp. 3–13). New York: Plenum.

Piaget, J. (1980). *Adaptation and intelligence: Organic selection and phenocopy* (S. Eames, Trans.). Chicago: University of Chicago Press.

Piaget, J. (1985). *The equilibration of cognitive structures.* Chicago: University of Chicago Press.

Piaget, J. (1987a). *Possibility and necessity* (Vol. 1). Minneapolis, MN: University of Minnesota Press.

Piaget, J. (1987b). *Possibility and necessity* (Vol. 2). Minneapolis, MN: University of Minnesota Press.

Piaget, J., & Garcia, R. (1991). *The logic of meanings.* Hillsdale, NJ: Erlbaum.

Piaget, J., & Inhelder, B. (1969). *The psychology of the child* (H. Weaver, Trans.). New York: Basic Books.

Polya, G. (1954). *Induction and analogy in mathematics.* Princeton, NJ: Princeton University Press.

Pufall, P. B. (1988). *Function in Piaget's system: Some notes for constructors of microworlds.* In G. Forman & P. B. Pufall (Eds.), *Constructivism in the computer age* (pp. 15–35). Hillsdale, NJ: Erlbaum.

Ricco, R. B. (1990). Necessity and the logic of entailment. In W. F. Overton (Ed.), *Reasoning, necessity, and logic: Developmental perspectives* (pp. 45–66). Hillsdale, NJ: Erlbaum.

Schoenfeld, A. H. (1985). Metacognitive and epistemological issues in mathematical understanding. In E. A. Silver (Ed.), *Teaching and learning mathematical problem solving: Multiple research perspectives* (pp. 361–379), Hillsdale, NJ: Erlbaum.

Smith, L. (1991). Age, ability, and intellectual development. In M. Chandler & M. Chapman (Eds.), *Criteria for competence* (pp. 69–91). Hillsdale, NJ: Erlbaum.

Vosniadou, S., & Brewer, W. F. (1992). Mental models of the Earth: A study of conceptual change in childhood. *Cognitive Psychology, 24,* 535–585.

White, B. Y. (1984). Designing computer games to help physics students understand Newton's laws of motion. *Cognition and Instruction, 1*(1), 69–108.

Wood, T., Cobb, P., & Yaeckel, E. (1991). Change in teaching mathematics: A case study. *American Educational Research Journal, 28*(3), 587–616.

CHAPTER 10

Lev S. Vygotsky's Cultural-Historical Theory of Psychological Development

Culture creates special forms of behavior. . . . In the process of historical development social man changes the ways and means of his behavior, transforms the natural instincts and functions, [and] elaborates and creates new forms of behavior (Vygotsky, 1930/1966, p. 19).

The work of Lev Vygotsky, which spanned the brief period from 1924 to 1934, has steadily grown in influence in the United States since the early 1980s. Unfortunately, however, misconceptions about his work have entered the mainstream of Western discourse, complicating the analysis of his contributions to educational psychology. Some scholars note that Vygotsky is credited with being 50 years ahead of his time for ideas that he himself credited to others (Cole, 1996; Valsiner, 1988; Van der Veer & Valsiner, 1991). For example, some Westerners, unfamiliar with history, sometimes credit Vygotsky with the view that culture is a major influence on human cognitive development. However, the concept was introduced by two German academics, Moritz Lazarus and Hijam Steinthal, 60 years prior to Vygotsky's work and it became the cornerstone of Wundt's "second psychology" (discussed in chapter 1). At the time Vygotsky entered psychology, anthropologists were debating various issues about the relationship between culture and individual development. Among them were the nature of the cultural influence on the individual, the relationship of different cultures to different forms of thinking (Van der Veer & Valsiner, 1991), and whether different cultures form a continuum from "primitive" to "advanced" (Cole, 1996).

The broad focus of Vygotsky's theory was to explain the qualitative changes that account for the emergence of higher psychological (cognitive) functions from lower (or primitive) functions at both the species (phylogeny) and individual (ontogeny) levels and to explain the role of culture in these changes. Although a novice in psychology, Vygotsky was in a unique position to influence the discipline in the USSR. With the dominance of the Bolsheviks, the task was to recast the discipline in a Marxist framework. In his work, Vygotsky drew on many concepts in the work of anthropologists, psychologists, and sociologists. Some he modified and supplemented with additional work and he integrated this broad range of ideas into a theory that went beyond the disciplinary boundaries of the social sciences, humanities, and historical sciences (Wertsch, 1985).

Initial misconceptions about Vygotsky's work are the result of several factors. One is the rapid acceptance and popularity of the theory which, Valsiner (1988) suggests, is inversely related to the depth of understanding. Others are translation difficulties of some Russian words which do not have an English equivalent, lack of accessibility to many of his writings, and initial reliance on limited translations. Specifically, Vygotsky's writings were banned in the USSR from 1936 until the 1950s (Cole & Scribner, 1978; Valsiner, 1988). Then, in the 1970s and early 1980s, as U.S. interest in the theory emerged, 82.2% of the citations in English-language journals (1969 to 1985) were to only two abridged translations of some of his work (Valsiner, 1988).

Among the misconceptions about Vygotsky are (1) the often-repeated story about his entry into psychology, (2) the belief that the zone of proximal development, the genetic law of cognitive development and other concepts originated with him, and (3) omissions of the role of the teacher and formal schooling, particularly concept learning, in the development of higher cognitive functions. Clarification of these issues is facilitated by the detailed 10-year research and translation of many of Vygotsky's unpublished works, archival documents, and family correspondence by Rene Van der Veer and Jean Valsiner (1991) and careful reading of recent translations of some of Vygotsky's work.

Vygotsky was born in Orsha, a town in western Russia near Minsk, in 1896, the same year that Jean Piaget was born. His intellectual bent emerged in adolescence when, with a circle of friends, he debated ideas such as Hegel's philosophy of history and the role of the individual in society (Van der Veer & Valsiner, 1991).

Graduating with a law degree in 1917 from Moscow University, Vygotsky had also studied philosophy, psychology, and literature at the Shanyavaskii People's University. He later completed a Master's degree with a thesis on the psychology of Hamlet. In addition, he read extensively in a variety of fields, including political science and history. Later, when he became interested in learning disabilities and similar problems, he entered medical school, focusing on neurophysiological studies.

In 1917, he returned to his native province as an instructor at a teacher's college and at various other institutes until 1924. The standard account of Vygotsky's entry into psychology is that this provincial teacher delivered an electrifying presentation critical of Pavlov's reflexology at the Second All-Russian Psychoneurological Congress in Leningrad in 1924. As a result, he was invited to join the staff at the Institute of Experimental Psychology in Moscow.

First, Vygotsky was no ordinary schoolteacher. He had established his own psychological laboratory while teaching, had begun to read the available psychological and educational literature, and had published articles in various journals and newspapers (Van der Veer & Valsiner, 1991, p. 39). Second, audience reaction to his Leningrad presentation seems to have been moderately enthusiastic.

Third, personnel needs at the Institute of Experimental Psychology provided an opportunity for his appointment. The prior director (along with many of his staff) had been dismissed for "idealism." The new director, Konstantin Kornilov, was reorganizing the institute and welcoming those who would support his battle against

Pavlovian reflexology. Vygotsky's presentation was compatible with his position. In addition, they shared the view that dialectical synthesis (discussed in this chapter) was an appropriate approach to the construction of a Marxist psychology (Van der Veer & Valsiner, 1991).

Vygotsky then began to read the writings of the Gestalt psychologists which provided support for the Institute's anti-reductionist view of psychology. These writings and those of other Western psychologists and sociologists were translated into Russian by Vygotsky and his colleagues (Cole, 1996). Of interest is that Wolfgang Köhler's experiments served as the model for Vygotsky's "double stimulation" experiments (Vygotsky, 1929). However, he criticized the Gestalt psychologists for failing to address development and the ways that novel structures can contribute to even newer structures.

In Vygotsky's view, given the unique characteristics of humans (described in chapter 1), psychology should address the ways that human abilities and accomplishments develop. To be successful, this focus requires an analysis of human consciousness in all its dimensions. Vygotsky (1924/1979a) cautioned that psychology would fail in its major task if it could not explain the formation of uniquely human behaviors.

Vygotsky's primary goal was to reformulate psychology as a part of a unified social science and to create a comprehensive analysis of psychological functions. His other goals were to develop answers to practical problems facing the USSR, and conduct research. He lectured extensively at universities and institutes in Moscow, Leningrad and Bolova, conducted clinical work, organized research activities, and began his medical studies (Wertsch, 1985a, p. 12). Interested in physical and medical problems, Vygotsky also participated in the founding of the Institute of Defectology in Moscow and became the first director. He was also involved in organizing child study in the Soviet Union (Valsiner & Van der Veer, 1991). Further, he organized medico–pedagogical conferences in which doctors, psychologists, special education teachers, and others observed him examining special needs children with their parents and teachers (Vygodskaia, 1998).

Although ill with tuberculosis, Vygotsky mustered a Herculean effort to accomplish his goals. Living in one room in a crowded apartment with his wife and two daughters, he often wrote after 2 a.m., the only time when he had a few quiet hours to himself (Wertsch, 1985a). Some of his writings were begun in the crowded, noisy barracks atmosphere of the sanatoriums where he was periodically hospitalized with tuberculosis (see excerpts from Vygotsky's correspondence translated in Van der Veer & Valsiner, 1991).

In the last three years of his life, Vygotsky completed manuscripts, articles, and books at an almost frenetic pace. Needless to say, his tuberculosis worsened and, in June 1934, he died at the age of 37.

A few of Vygotsky's writings were published after his death. However, his theory was receiving criticism for "bourgeois thinking" and in 1936 the intellectual climate changed. The Central Committee of the Communist Party banned all psychological testing in the USSR At the same time the leading psychological journals ceased publication for nearly 20 years (Cole & Scribner, 1978, p. 10). Later, some of Vygotsky's views were found to conflict with Stalin's 1950 essay on linguistics and thus were not published until 1956 (Wertsch, 1985a).

Vygotsky's concept of the cultural and historical development of cognitive functions remained incomplete at his death. Among the issues he had begun to address at that time were the possible hierarchical relationships among mental functions and the development of affect and its role in intellectual processes (Bozhovitch, 1977, p. 15).

PRINCIPLES OF PSYCHOLOGICAL DEVELOPMENT

Vygotsky's goal was to create a psychology that was theoretically and methodologically equal to the task of investigating uniquely human characteristics.

Basic Assumptions

The framework for the analysis of human cognitive functions constructed by Vygotsky rests on four assumptions. They are (1) the nature of human intelligence, (2) the delineation of two different lines of psychological development, referred to as biological and cultural–historical, (3) the nature of psychological processes, and (4) the design of an experimental method for the investigation of dynamic psychological processes.

The Nature of Human Intelligence

Vygotsky's description of the nature of human intelligence includes four related topics. They are (1) the differences between animals and humans, (2) the philosophy of G. W. F. Hegel as extended by Marxism, which formed the overarching framework of his theory, (3) the designation referred to as *psychological tools,* and (4) the influence of culture on human cognitive development.

Animal/Human Differences in Mental Activities.   Vygotsky first contrasted the key mental processes of animal and humans. Specifically, the primitive mental processes of animals, such as perception and simple memory, are governed by the recognition of co-occurring stimuli in the environment. For example, the young gazelle learns to recognize the appearance of a lion as an indicator of danger.

This process, referred to as *signalization*, is part of the biological heritage of both animals and humans (Vygotsky, 1977). For example, a child puts his hand on a hot stove and feels pain. On approaching the stove again, the child recalls the pain and exercises caution.

The essential difference between animal and human behavior is that humans progressed beyond their biological heritage. Vygotsky (1977), drawing on Koffka, maintained that, early in evolutionary history, humanlike apes developed simple tools. This development set the stage for the emergence of early humans.

Hegelian Philosophy as Extended by Marxism.   The overarching framework for Vygotsky's theory was the philosophy of G. W. F. Hegel and the ideas of Marxism. According to Hegel, humans create diverse worlds (cultures) that differ from the natural world. Further, work is a social rather than a natural activity. Work provides the means through which humans perceive the world as independent objects and acting subjects. Marxism built on these concepts in that the tools created in the process of work lead to particular production systems and social organizations. Further, tool invention by pre-humans led to (1) the emergence of humans because it led to labor, the need for cooperation, and speech (Engles, 1925/1978); (2) through tool use, humans transform both nature and themselves; and (3) the particular social organizations that result from tool use determine human mental life (Engles, 1940). Thus, human labor transforms both nature and human experience. The discovery of fire, the invention of simple agricultural tools, and the discovery of electricity are examples.

The Role of "Psychological Tools".   Like Karl Marx, Vygotsky believed that human mental abilities develop through the individual's interactions with the world. That is, cognitive development is rooted in social interaction and social experiences. The difficult questions for psychology left unanswered by the Marxist framework were, How does a relatively simple activity, tool use, account for such sweeping developments as the emergence of the human species and advanced cognitive development? and What are the relationships among tool use, social organizations, and differences in cognitive development?

Essential to bridging the gap between tool use and cognitive development was Vygotsky's designation of signs and symbols as *psychological tools*. Likely sources for this concept were (1) Wolfgang Köhler's references to "the priceless tool of speech," and (2) Emile Durkheim's discussions of the collective representations of a society as "clever instruments of thought" (Van der Veer & Valsiner, 1991, pp. 302, 206).

According to Vygotsky, the importance of these psychological tools (signs and symbols) is that they, rather than the tools of work, bring about the transformation of human consciousness and are the instruments essential to the development of higher cognitive functions. In other words, the essential difference between technical tools and psychological tools is that technical tools change an external situation but psychological tools direct the mind and change the process of thinking. Moreover, these psychological tools differ throughout human history and across cultures. The theory developed from this foundation was referred to by Vygotsky as the *cultural-historical theory of the psyche* (Leont'ev & Luria, 1968).

The Influence of Culture on Human Development.   Relationships among the use of signs and symbols (psychological tools), social organizations, and cognitive development at the species level discussed by contemporary anthropologists are found in Vygotsky's untranslated work (Van der Veer & Valsiner, 1991). Among them are (1) thought and language are more well developed in contemporary cultures (Levy-Bruhl, 1910/1922, 1923/1976), and (2) different cultures imply different kinds of cognitive growth through their various developments in law, music, art, language, religion, writing, and counting systems (Thurnwald, 1922). However, Vygotsky (1966) retained only symbol systems from Thurnwald's list because they can serve as psychological tools to self-regulate cognitive processes and therefore transform behavior (Van der Veer & Valsiner, 1991).

An early example is the so-called "messenger's wands" found in Australia (Leont'ev, 1959). Messenger's wands are large sticks or rectangular wooden slabs marked by a series of cuts. The sticks or slabs were given to messengers as they were sent out to deliver communications to distant tribes.

The notches were not arbitrary symbols of syllables or words, however. Instead they were memory aids designed for the messengers. The notches designated certain persons and objects and their number and localities to the extent that they occurred in the given message. With the aid of this simple device, the messenger reconstructed the message at the time of delivery.

The uniquely human events associated with the use of these wands is that (1) new connections are established in the brain through the act of perceiving the external reminder and returning to the ideas they represent, and (2) the construction of the process of memorizing by externally forcing an external object to remind the individual of something (Vygotsky, 1929/1977, p. 69).

That is, human behavior is determined not by the stimuli given in the environment but by a man-made psychological situation (Vygotsky, 1930/1966, p. 27). That is, humans are "*constructing* the process of memorizing by externally forcing an external object to remind them of something" (Vygotsky, 1929/1977, p. 69). The operation of memory is thereby extended beyond the given biological level and becomes a qualitatively different process.

Biological and Cultural-Historical Lines of Development
Analysis of the differences between animal and human behavior led to the identification of two qualitatively different lines of psychological development (Figure 10.1).

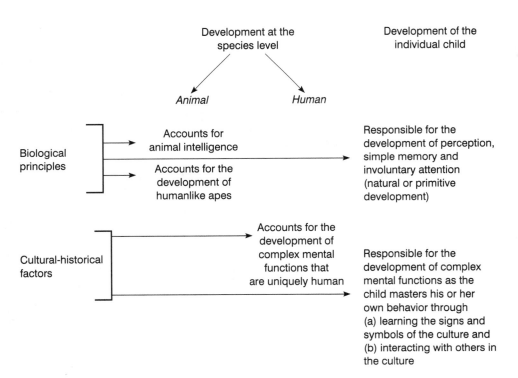

FIGURE 10.1
The influence of biological and cultural-historical lines of development

One line is that of the biological factors that were a part of the evolutionary process. These biological factors include the development of the central nervous system and physical growth and maturation. In the human species, biological factors dominate the early months of life, accounting for the development of perception, simple memory, and involuntary attention. The emergence of these primitive mental functions also is referred to as natural or primitive development (Vygotsky, 1929/1977).

The second line of development is cultural-historical. It began with the creation and use of the culturally based signs and symbol systems of the early humans. They are the symbols created to organize and regulate social existence, such as speech and written language.

Cultural-historical development is the process that differentiates human behavior from that of other animal species. It also plays a key role in the cognitive growth of the individual child. The child inherits the symbol systems of his or her culture, and, depending on their complexity, these systems may lead to the development of rudimentary thinking skills (e.g., counting, simple addition and subtraction) or complex thinking skills (e.g., operating with differential functions and advanced probability systems).

In other words, psychological development involves the transformation of primitive (or natural) mental functions to higher mental forms. Further, agreeing with Thurnwald (1922), Vygotsky (1929/1977) maintained that cultural diversity in symbols leads to differences in the level of mental functions. For example, in one village in Papua New Guinea, counting is accomplished by using body parts (Saxe, 1981). Counting begins with the right thumb, progresses around the hand, arm, shoulder, right ear, eyes, and then down the left side to the left forearm and fingers. Because the maximum number that may be counted using this method is 29, villagers have great difficulty with even simple addition and subtraction problems. Furthermore, the counting system limits the quantities that can be added and subtracted.

In contrast, cultures with advanced mathematical systems can produce individuals who think about differential equations in calculus. In other words, different historical eras produce different levels of individual psychological development (Davydov, 1995, p. 15). Therefore, the complexity of symbol use in a culture sets broad parameters for individual development.

Although cultural-historical factors influence both the development of the species and of the child, three important differences may be identified. First, childhood does not repeat the stages that occurred in the development of civilization. (One early psychologist, G. Stanley Hall, maintained that childhood included the same stages as civilization, i.e., ontogeny recapitulates phylogeny. The theory, however, was found to be scientifically unsound.)

Second, in the development of the culture, humans are the creators and elaborators of sign systems. In contrast, the child is involved in the activity of mastering and internalizing the available sign systems and the associated reasoning processes. The two processes of creation and mastery, however, are psychologically different (Scribner, 1985, p. 130).

Third, when cultural development began for the human species, biological factors, in terms of influencing species development, were displaced. However, in the cognitive development of the individual child, biological factors become subordinated to cultural development in a complex transformative process.

The identification of two lines of development reflects Vygotsky's position that no one single set of principles can explain human cognitive development. For example, single factors such as S–R bonds and maturation are insufficient explanations. Early in the child's life, cognitive functions begin a major transformation, and the goal of psychology should be to explain these qualitative changes by identifying the various responsible factors.

In summary, the behavior of a modern cultured adult is the result of two different processes of mental development. One is the biological evolution of the animal species that gave rise to the species *homo sapiens*. The second is the process of historical development that transformed primitive humans into humans who use signs and symbols to change their mental functioning (Vygotsky, 1930/1966).

The Nature of Psychological Processes

A key aspect of Hegelian and Marxist ideology described the processes of change. Referred to as dialectical materialism, this concept maintains that (1) a thesis is negated by its oppositive, antithesis, and (2) the resolution emerging from their interaction is a synthesis, that is, a qualitatively new phenomenon. For example, matter, which is the foundation of existence, is not viewed as absolute and unchanging. Instead, the world or matter is "a combination of processes, eternally changing or developing" (Kornilov, 1930, p. 250). Light, heat, electricity, magnetic currents, chemical transformations, life, and psychological processes are examples. Specifically, psychological processes are simply the properties of the most highly organized forms of matter—the human brain and the nervous system.

Like other processes, psychological processes are undergoing a process of dialectical change in which primitive cognitive functions are qualitatively transformed into higher cognitive processes. Therefore, to understand the dynamics of human cognitive development implies the study of processes in all their changes and phases—from birth to death (Vygotsky, 1934/1978). In this way, the very nature of psychological processes and the essence may be discovered, for it is only in movement that a body shows what it is (Vygotsky, 1934/1978, p. 65).

However, the problem with experimental research is that process has not been studied (Vygotsky, 1930/1966, p. 21). Instead, psychological research has made use of only one model, that of stimulus–response. Regardless of the process under study, the psychologist exerts some action on the individual or exposes him or her to particular stimuli and analyzes the individual's reaction. Different constellations of stimuli and various reactions have been studied. However, not one fundamental step has been made beyond this basic model (Vygotsky, 1930/1966, p. 21). Until psychology bases its studies on the premise that psychological functions change under the influence of sociocultural experience, it will not discover the laws of human behavior (Leont'ev, 1977, p. 61).

The Experimental–Genetic (Developmental) Method

To discover the dynamics of the development of human mental functions, Vygotsky (1929/1979b) and his co-workers devised experiments referred to as the *experimen-*

tal-genetic method. The researchers modeled their experiments after the experiments that Köhler conducted with anthropoid apes (Vygotsky, 1929). In those studies, Köhler placed the apes in a problem-solving situation with a means to the solution nearby, and observed their actions.

Similarly, Vygotsky and his colleagues placed a task before a child that usually was above his or her natural capacities. That is, the task could not be completed using processes that had already become automatized. Some object or objects were available nearby, such as pictures. The experimenter then studied whether the child used the materials and, if so, in what way. Changes in the child's activity and modifications in mental functions also were observed. By implementing the task with children of different ages as well as with adults, the researchers identified differences in cognitive functioning (Vygotsky, 1934/1978, p. 74).

This particular approach is referred to as the **functional method of double stimulation** (Vygotsky, 1934/1978), and it is illustrated in the experiments conducted by A. N. Leont'ev. The child participates in a question-and-answer game in which points are forfeited for forbidden answers, such as naming the color *red* and naming any color more than once. Examples of the 18 questions (the first stimulus set) include "Do you go to school? What color are the desks in school? Do you like to play? Have you been to a hospital? What color is grass?" (Vygotsky, 1929/1979b). The child also was given a set of cards, each a different color (the second stimulus set), to use in any way.

Observations indicated that preschoolers did not use the cards effectively, often looking at them at inappropriate times. However, the older children (1) set aside the cards with the forbidden colors; and (2) once a "nonforbidden" color was named, they added the corresponding card to the stack.

Another technique was to introduce obstacles into an ongoing task to observe the resulting disruptions in the process. For example, in studying communication and children's egocentric speech, children were placed in a cooperative task situation with other children who did not speak their language (Cole & Scribner, 1978, p. 12).

A major concern in the study of behavior, Vygotsky (1934/1978) cautions, is the problem of **fossilized behaviors**. They are the processes that have undergone a long period of historical development and are the so-called automated or mechanized processes. Owing to their ancient origins, they are being repeated for the millionth time and have lost their original appearance (Vygotsky, 1934/1978, pp. 63–64). The problem is that their outer appearance indicates nothing about their internal nature.

An example is voluntary (selective) attention that is controlled by the individual. In its final form, attention is self-directed internally using self-generated stimuli. Because the process is unobservable and in adults has become automated, self-regulated attention in surface appearance is indistinguishable from involuntary attention. However, the two processes differ greatly; involuntary attention is neither self-directed nor self-monitored.

Summary of Basic Assumptions

Vygotsky maintained that psychology should study humans, rather than animals, to discover the unique aspects of human cognition. Unlike animals, humans progress beyond their biological heritage and develop complex ways of thinking. Important in this development was the invention of simple tools by pre-humans, which led to the emergence of the human species. Marxism maintained that tool use transforms both nature and human experience. Vygotsky, however, modified this view to include only psychological tools, which are the sign and symbol systems of the individual's culture. Humans, through **active adaptation** of the environment to fit their goals and the need to communicate with and regulate human groups, developed complex symbol systems. Included are speech, written language, mathematical systems, musical notation, and others. Through the creation and use of these arbitrary stimuli, humans create new ways of thinking.

However, both biological and cultural factors contribute to human cognitive development. Biological factors, such as maturation, are responsible for the development of primitive mental functions (involuntary attention, simple perception, and simple memory). Then the particular culture to which the child belongs sets broad limits on the level of higher cognitive thinking that the child can attain. That is, a culture restricted to a simple counting system lacks the tools for individuals to develop conceptual manipulations of abstract symbols.

In addition, the process of change as described by Marxism, reflected the processes whereby primitive cognitive functions were transformed into complex ways of thinking. Specifically, a thesis is negated by its opposite, antithesis, and the resolution of this conflict is a synthesis that is a qualitatively new phenomenon. Cognitive development involves the qualitative transformation of some forms into others and a complex process of overcoming difficulties and of adaptation. Therefore, because cognitive processes are dynamic and ever-changing, they must be studied using research methods that reveal their dynamic nature. The aim of psychological research is (1) process analysis rather than object analysis; (2) an accounting that reveals real, causal, or dynamic relations, rather than a tabulation of external features; and (3) a reconstruction of all the points in the development of a particular structure (Vygotsky, 1934/1978, p. 65).

The Components of Cognitive Development

When Karl Marx (1850) wrote his analysis of capitalism, he began by describing the basic living "cell" of capitalist society—value. He then proceeded to construct the major principles and structure of the socioeconomic system from this one concept (Vygotsky, 1934/1978, p. 8). Vygotsky's goal was to identify the basic functional unit from which the structure of consciousness could be unfolded. He noted that "anyone who could discover what a 'psychological cell' is—the mechanism producing even a single response—would thereby find the key to psychology as a whole" (p. 8). Vygotsky determined that the basic psychological cell is word meaning. Specifically, the word is a microcosm of consciousness as a living cell is related to an organism (Vygotsky, 1982/1987, p. 285).

Key principles describe the transformation of primitive mental functions, such as involuntary attention and simple memory, into complex functions such as logical memory. Two principles are the two branches of cultural cognitive development and the **general law of genetic development**. The other major principle of human behavior is that of signification. This principle describes the ways that signs and symbols that are learned for the purpose of communication also contribute to the construction of new psychological structures of behavior.

The Two Branches of Cultural Cognitive Development

Rarely mentioned by Vygotsky (1930/1966), but important in the differentiation between the two major uses of language and other symbol systems, is the two branches of cultural cognitive development. That is, the development of higher cognitive functions consists of

> . . . two inseparably connected but never confluent streams of development of the higher forms of behavior. These are, first, the processes of mastering the external means of cultural development and thinking—language, writing, counting and drawing, and secondly, the processes of development of the special higher mental functions (Vygotsky, 1930/1966, p. 16).

Stated another way, "in the process of development, the child not only masters the items of cultural experience, but the cultural forms of reasoning" (Vygotsky, 1929, p. 415). That is, complex cognitive functions are developed in the process of subordinating symbol systems to human control to carry out cognitive tasks (Vygotsky, 1929/1979b). Using colored cards to monitor the color names one has used in a game is an example. Constructing a hierarchy of related concepts in a subject area is another.

The inference that may be made from these statements is that learning to communicate with language is a necessary, but not sufficient condition for the development of higher cognitive functions (Gredler & Shields, in preparation). This inference is supported by Vygotsky's description of signs and symbols as only *potential* psychological tools. Specifically, "a stimulus becomes a psychological tool not by virtue of its physical qualities . . . (but) by virtue of its use as a means of influencing the mind and behavior" (Vygotsky, 1920/1981, p. 141). An example is the child who uses a geographical map, a plan, scheme, or summary as a means of remembering (Vygotsky, 1929, p. 416).

The General Law of Genetic Development

Central issues to understanding a basic principle of Vygotsky's theory are the components of the law of genetic development, applications of the law, and the role of peers, teachers, and the learner (discussed in the section "Principles of Instruction").

The basis for Vygotsky's law of genetic development is the social–behavioral relationship described by the French psychologist Pierre Janet (Van der Veer & Valsiner, 1988). Specifically, all higher psychological processes develop through the application of aspects of social relationships to oneself and words are the most powerful social stimuli because they originated as commands (Janet, 1926, 1929, cited in Van der Veer & Valsiner, 1988; Vygotsky, 1930/1966, 1981).

Vygotsky emphasized the importance of signs and symbols, particularly speech, in the social relationship. He stated the genetic law as "every function in the child's cultural development appears twice: first on the social level, and later on the individual level; first, *between* people (interpsychological), and then *inside* the child (*intrapsychological*)" (Vygotsky, 1934/1978, p. 57). An example is speech, which originally is a means of communication with other people and later, in the form of inner speech, becomes a means of thinking (Vygotsky, 1930/1966, p. 40).

The process of the internal acquisition of the use of signs is not automatic. Instead, the transition from the external social plane to the internal psychological plane is one in which the child begins to practice with respect to himself the same forms of behavior that others formerly practiced with respect to him (Vygotsky, 1930/1966, p. 40).

Applications.   The law of genetic development applies to learning both the functions (meanings) of words, signs, and symbols, and developing the higher cognitive functions. Included in the higher functions are categorical perception, conceptual verbal and mathematical thinking, logical memory, and self-regulation (see the section "The Nature of Complex Thought").

Given that cultural development is based on the use of signs, their inclusion in a general system of behavior initially occurs in a social external form (Vygotsky, 1930/1966, p. 41). For example, children often begin to learn about counting through simple games with an adult (e.g., "This little piggy went to market") and by interacting with others in simple counting activities. Later the child is able to use the process of counting in relation to his or her own activities and the mechanism becomes a tool for thinking.

Learning word meaning involves three general steps (Vygotsky, 1960, 1981). They are (1) the word (or phrase) and its meaning must form an objective bond, (2) the bond between the word and the object must be used functionally by the adult as a means of social interaction with the child, and (3) then the word acquires significance for the child (p. 162). Learning word meaning, however, is only the first step in a series of qualitative changes in thinking that lead to the development of higher cognitive functions (Vygotsky, 1928–31/1988b).

An example of the mediation of another's behavior is the child's learning the gesture of pointing (Vygotsky, 1930/1966; 1978, p. 56). First, when the child tries to grasp an object that is out of reach, his hands are stretched out toward the object, often in a grasping movement (a natural unmediated impulse). When the mother or other adult comes to the child's aid and comprehends the movement as indicating an object, the situation changes. The child's gesture originally is directed toward the *object*; however, it leads to a reaction from another person, not the object (Vygotsky, 1930/1966).

Later, the child is able to link his grasping movement to the total situation (including the adult) and he understands his actions as a pointing gesture. Here the function of the movement changes. Instead of a movement directed toward an object, it becomes a form of communication, a movement directed toward another person. The child then uses the gesture as a signal or indicator to others. In other words, the conscious use of the gesture is late in its development. The child is the last person to realize its meaning.

The Processes of Signification

Psychologists often view the learning of speech, written language, and other symbols as simply acquiring information passed down by adults (Vygotsky, 1930–35/1978).

Others view it as the result of pure logic or a sudden insightful discovery by the child (Vygotsky, 1934/1978, p. 45). However, learning the meaning of signs and symbols and their role in directing and regulating one's behavior is a lengthy one that includes many qualitative changes. The young child, for example, is unable to use pictures as cues to recall a set of words. Adults, in contrast, often construct complex verbal relationships as memory aids. A grocery list, for example, may contain only the words *bread, milk,* and *tomatoes.* To the writer of the list, however, the three words are cues to buy San Francisco soda bread, one quart of 2% milk, three large tomatoes, and half a dozen cherry tomatoes.

The semantics of word meaning also are extremely complex (Luria, 1971, p. 262). A word potentially can evoke an entire system of associations. For example, the word *oak* implies the image of a powerful tree and the wooded area where it grows, a sign of hardness (perhaps of stubbornness), and hard material. Furthermore, the word may evoke any of several abstract linkages (e.g., birch, pine, maple), the category of green growing things, and contrasts with other categories, such as shrubs and animals. The task of a fully developed consciousness, therefore, is to choose from the set of equally likely associations the meaning appropriate for a given situation (p. 262).

The importance of learning to attach meaning to symbols (signification) is that such learning changes the thinking process. The difference between primitive and complex mental functions lies not only in the fact that humans are able to use pictures, record books, and other memory aids. Of importance is that turning to their use changes the very nature of the cognitive process.

At the highest level of development, individuals internalize the process of directing memory and attention through the use of self-generated stimuli. In one experiment, for example, one subject remembered the words *beach, hail,* and *dress* by creating the sentence, "A lady walked on the beach; it began to hail and ruined her dress" (Leont'ev, 1959, p. 94). In other words, the development of higher mental processes is dependent on a lengthy process in which the child learns to use auxiliary stimuli first to control behavior externally and later to control it by more complex inner symbols and operations (Vygotsky, 1934/1978, p. 73).

The Role of Auxiliary Stimuli.   The primitive mental functions—simple perception, natural memory, and involuntary attention—are linked to concrete experience. These functions are represented by the S–R model.

In contrast, other stimuli such as notched sticks or a few brief notes for a lecture used as guides for thinking and action are auxiliary stimuli generated by the individual. They are the intermediate links that appear between the stimulus toward which one's behavior is directed and the person's reaction. The direct S-R model of behavior is changed to include both "object stimuli" and "means stimuli," and the process of thinking thereby changes (Vygotsky, 1930/1966, p. 32).

The auxiliary stimuli available to a child include (1) the tools of the culture into which he or she is born, (2) the language of the family and other adults who relate to the child, and (3) ingenious examples devised by the child. For example, poor children do not possess manufactured toys, but they are able to play "house" or "train" with available resources (Vygotsky, 1934/1978, p. 73).

The successful use of an auxiliary stimulus meets at least three major criteria. First, the individual must establish the link between the task and the auxiliary stimulus. Second, the link must create a new relationship between the stimulus and the response. Third, and most important, the link possesses the characteristics of reverse action (Vygotsky, 1934/1978, p. 39) (Figure 10.2). That is, *it operates on the individual* and permits him or her to control behavior *from the outside.*

Of importance is that the process of using auxiliary stimuli is not acquired through one-time insight nor by imitating adult actions (Kozulin, 1990). In a series of experiments on word recall, Leont'ev (1959) found qualitative differences among different age groups in the ability to make use of an auxiliary stimulus (Table 10.1). A series of 15 words was read to each subject, one at a time, and the subjects were permitted to select a picture from a group for each word to assist them in later recall.

The preschool children either selected pictures randomly and were unable to use them, or they made associations between the pictures and words that did not facilitate word recall. In other words, the mere presence of an association is insufficient to guide the child's memory. This level of functioning is analogous to the performance of a man who is able to press on a lever but who is unable to use the skill to move a heavy rock (Leont'ev, 1959, p. 141).

A qualitative change was found in the behavior of the school children. They formed word–picture links that indicated "an adaptation to the future conceived of *as a future*" (Leont'ev, 1959, p. 147). In this action, word and picture are combined into a complex integrated structure. This operation indicates that primitive or natural memory has been converted into an intellectual operation (i.e., a new form of memory).

In contrast, the adults formed complex verbal links between word and picture and often did not use the pictures during recall. Memory had become self-directed in that the created verbal association served as the cue. These phases in the development of mediated memorization indicate that intermediate forms of thinking appear between primitive mental processes and higher mental processes (Kozulin, 1990).

A similar developmental sequence was found in the experiments (described earlier) in which children were given colored cards to help them answer a series of questions. The young children often looked at the cards at inappropriate times or, when setting aside the forbidden colors, named that very color (Vygotsky, 1929/1979b). Older children, however, used the cards successfully to direct their

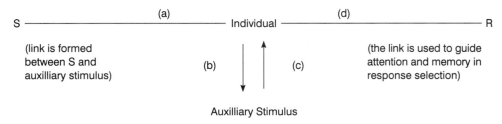

FIGURE 10.2
The role of the auxiliary stimulus

TABLE 10.1
Age differences in the use of auxiliary stimuli

Age	Picture Use	Example of Associations	Words Recalled (N = 15)
4- to 6-year-olds	Some children chose pictures randomly; when pictures were taken away, they were unable to identify their choices. Others established links with the pictures but not in terms of the task of future recall.	"Notebooks" selected for the word "study"; later recall was "one goes to school." "Tree" selected for the word "night" because 'naughty' children climb trees at night; word not recalled later.	1–4
School-age children	Majority selected pictures carefully, sometimes rejecting first choice for another. Pictures were selected in terms of future task of recall.	"Bird" selected for "butterfly" because "a butterfly is a little bird." "Chair" selected to represent "house" because "A house is where one can sit."	8–14
Adults	Pictures were selected quickly; complex verbal links were established with words. Subjects often used only the verbal associations to later recall the words.	"Candle" selected to represent "fire" with verbal association "Moscow burned up from a candle worth a kopeck."	Not reported

Note: Summarized from *Problems of Mental Development* by A. N. Leont'ev, 1959, Moscow: Publishing House of the Academy of Pedagogical Sciences RSFSR.

attention and to assist their recall of acceptable colors. Also, the quality of their answers changed. For example, when the forbidden color was "green," grass was described as "In the fall, it is yellow" (Vygotsky, 1929/1979b).

In other words, sign-using activity "arises from something that is originally not a sign operation and becomes one only after a series of *qualitative* transformations" (Vygotsky, 1934/1978, p. 46). The transitions that occur between the biologically given functions (primitive mental functions) and those that are culturally acquired are referred to as the natural history (law) of the sign (Vygotsky, 1934/1978, p. 47). These transitions are summarized in Table 10.2.

The Development of Speech

Of the signal systems developed by the human species, the most far reaching in terms of its effects is human speech. However, Vygotsky noted that psychologists viewed the detailed study of the development of speech and other forms of sign use as unnecessary. Instead, the assumption was that the child's mind contained all the stages of future intellectual functioning. All that was required was the proper moment for them to emerge (Vygotsky, 1934/1978, p. 24).

The development of human speech, however, is a lengthy process with several stages that are analogous to the stages in learning to use other signs. Also, develop-

TABLE 10.2
Natural history of the sign

Stage in sign use	Characteristics
1. Preintellectual	Child is not capable of mastering his or her behavior by organizing special stimuli.
2. Intellectual: "naively" psychological	Child uses pictures but in the form of "direct" representation, and the formation of the association is not sufficient to guarantee recall.
3. Dominance of external sign use	The auxiliary stimulus is a psychological instrument acting from the outside.
4. "Ingrowth" or internalization	External sign becomes transformed into a self-generated internal sign as a means of remembering.

Note: Summarized from *Mind in Society: The Development of Higher Psychological Processes* by L. S. Vygotsky, 1934/1978, Cambridge, MA: Harvard University Press.

ment is not a linear path of quantitative accumulations. Instead, development is a series of qualitative transformations. Each stage is a complex disintegration and re-integration in the form of a particular organization of psychological activity.

In the preintellectual stage, speech is essentially a form of contact with the parent. The next stage is the lowest level of intellectual speech, that of labeling. This phase occurs when the child discovers the "instructional function" of a word; that is, every thing has a name (Vygotsky, 1929, p. 429). Vygotsky agreed with Koffka that the child's discovery of the functional role of a word as a sign is analogous to the discovery by the ape of the functional importance of a stick as a tool (p. 429). The child's discovery leads to the active search for new words with the incessant question "What is this?" Also, through speech, the child also is able to direct his or her attention, to separate an object from the environment, and to organize his or her visual field (Table 10.3).

The most significant activity in the child's cognitive development also occurs at this time. It is the joining of speech and the child's practical activity that makes possible the subsequent development of abstract intelligence (Vygotsky, 1934/1978, p. 24). When the child, using speech, begins to make a plan, his practical thinking rises to a new level. Behavior is no longer determined by the structure of the visual field (Vygotsky, 1928–31/1998a, p. 115).

The beginnings of the intellectual use of speech, however, are referred to as "naively psychological." That is, the child can use words correctly in grammatical structure long before grasping their true meaning. However, at the third stage, the child uses external signs to assist in the solution of internal problems. During this period, the child's use of speech to organize his or her own behavior is referred to as "egocentric."

Experiments in which children are confronted with problems slightly too complicated for them to solve indicate the importance of egocentric speech. Efforts to solve the problem were accompanied by direct appeals to the experimenter, com-

TABLE 10.3
Stages in the child's development of speech

Stage	Characteristics
1. Preintellectual	Babbling; crying; use of first words primarily as an emotional form of behavior
2. Intellectual: "naively" psychological	Child realizes importance of language at about the age of 2 and feels the need for words; speech fulfills a labeling function through which the child begins to organize her world. Speech is joined to practical intelligence. Many words are used without grasping true meaning (e.g., "because, but, when").
3. Dominance of external sign use	Counting on one's fingers is an example. Speech first merely *accompanies* the child's actions. Later it moves gradually to the begin- ning of the problem-solving process and pre- cedes action. Speech is then used to synthesize events and to plan problem-solving activities.
4. "Ingrowth" or internalization	Child begins to count in his head and to use logical memory, i.e., to operate with inherent relationships and inner signs. Egocentric speech becomes inner speech, which becomes the basis for the child's thinking.

Note: Summarized from *Thought and Language* by L. S. Vygotsky, 1934/1962, Cambridge, MA: Massachusetts Institute of Technology.

ments on their own actions, and direct verbal appeals to objects in the problem itself (Vygotsky, 1934/1978, p. 30).

Naturalistic observations of low-income Appalachian children conducted by Berk and Garvin (1984) support Vygotsky's views. The researchers found that the major function of private speech is self-guidance and that it is greater during cogni- tively demanding academic tasks. Research also indicates that children who use pri- vate speech in conjunction with challenging tasks are more attentive and show greater improvement than their peers (Berk, 2000; Berk & Spuhl, 1995). Also, the rates of private speech are higher over a longer developmental period for children with learning problems (Berk, 2000).

Vygotsky (1934/1978, p. 28) also points out that words can shape activity into a structure in the same way a mold gives shape to a substance. That is, the child can evaluate proposed actions in terms of both future goals and past activities. However, this accomplishment represents only an early phase in the development of higher cognitive functions.

The final stage of intellectual development is the "ingrowth" stage. External operations turn inward and undergo a transformation. The child begins to operate with inner signs (i.e., to use logical memory). Egocentric speech becomes inner speech as well as the basic structure of the child's thinking. Inner speech, however, is speech carried out almost without words because it is speech for oneself, not for communication (Vygotsky, 1982/1987, p. 277).

In summary, the child's intellectual growth requires that the child master the social means of thought, which is language. In other words, verbal thought is not an innate or natural form of behavior. Instead, it is determined by a historical-cultural process with characteristics that differ from natural (primitive) forms of thought.

Both Piaget and Vygotsky consider the acquisition of speech to be a major activity in cognitive development. They differ in their view of the child's egocentric speech. For Piaget, egocentric speech is a characteristic of preoperational thinking, and this form of speech disappears as the child moves into concrete operations.

In contrast, Vygotsky views egocentric speech as an important transitional stage between external and inner speech. It is a significant phase in the child's learning to solve problems and to manage his or her own cognitive activity. Thus, egocentric speech is a transitional stage between social speech and advanced thinking.

Development in Children with Disabilities

The basic principles in Vygotsky's cultural-historical theory apply to children with disabilities as well. That is, cognitive development occurs in the context of the social activities of children with adults. The prevailing view at the time Vygotsky was writing was that a sensory defect or a mental weakness was regarded as a biological problem. The then-current belief was that a defect could be compensated for by a heightened sensitivity in another sensory function. Kozulin (1990) notes that examples are the senses of hearing and touch in the blind and vision in the deaf.

In contrast, Vygotsky viewed the problem of the disabling condition as primarily social (Gindis, 1995). That is, society's response to those with disabilities leads to social deprivation that results in defective development (Vygotsky, 1993). The disability, in other words, alters the child's relationship with the world and affects his or her interactions with people. Thus, "the blindness of an American farmer's daughter, of a Ukrainian landowner's son, of a German duchess, of a Russian peasant—are all psychologically different facts" (Vygotsky, 1983, p. 50).

Physical disabilities, such as blindness or deafness, alter the child's relationship with the world and affect his or her interactions with people. Vygotsky noted that self-reports from individuals with these disabilities indicated that the defects are not perceived as "abnormalities" until they are brought into the social context (Gindis, 1995, p. 78).

The disabilities prevent the children from mastering social skills and acquiring knowledge in the same ways and at the same rate as other children. Also, deafness is a more serious disability than blindness because it prevents the mastery of speech, blocks verbal communication, and limits entry to the world of culture (p. 780).

Vygotsky described disabilities in terms of primary and secondary defects. A primary defect is an impairment of biological origin. Secondary defects are the distortion of higher psychological functions that result from social factors. For example, many symptoms of disabling conditions, such as immature behavior and primitive emotional reactions, are secondary defects that are acquired in the process of social interaction.

Therefore, instead of training other sensory functions, such as acuteness of hearing, Vygotsky maintained that physical or mental defects can be compensated for through alternative, yet equivalent means of cultural development (Gindis, 1995). Where necessary, symbolic systems should be changed, while preserving the basic meaning of social communication. Examples are the Braille system, sign language, lip-reading, and finger spelling. Further, societies should continue developing special psychological tools that can provide the social and cultural interactions essential for development. Many of today's computer developments, such as activating a keyboard through a breathing apparatus for paralyzed individuals, are examples.

Summary

The basic functional unit which forms the structure of consciousness, according to Vygotsky, is the word. It functions in three general principles that are the components of cognitive development. First, Vygotsky (1930/1966) described two branches of cognitive development. One involves mastering the symbol systems of the culture and the other involves developing the cultural forms of reasoning.

Second, the law of genetic development states that all complex functions begin as social interactions between individuals and gradually acquire meaning and are internalized by the learner. However, also required is practice by the learner of the behaviors that adults used with him or her.

The third principle describes the process whereby speech and other artificial symbols are first mastered as a form of communication and then become instrumental in structuring and managing the child's thinking. The young child, for example, is unable to use pictures as cues to recall a set of words. However, adults often construct complex verbal relationships as memory aids. The lengthy process of learning to use artificial symbols to structure one's thinking begins with learning to use auxiliary stimuli to mediate one's memory. Gradually, over an extended period of time, the individual acquires the capability to construct symbols to aid in thinking. This process is referred to as the natural history (law) of the sign.

The use of speech also changes throughout childhood and follows the same four stages as the use of symbols in thinking. These stages are (1) preintellectual, (2) "naively" psychological, (3) dominance of external sign use, and (4) "ingrowth" or internalization.

The Nature of Complex Thought

Two descriptions developed by Vygotsky indicate the nature and development of complex thought. They are the characteristics of higher mental functions and the role of the zone of proximal development.

Characteristics of Higher Mental Functions

According to Vygotsky (1934/1978), the higher mental functions include categorical perception, logical memory, abstract thought, and voluntary (selective) attention. They are the uniquely human capabilities that are the products of cultural-historical development. They differ in a variety of ways from the primitive functions (involuntary attention, simple perception, and natural memory) that are biological in origin.

Table 10.4 illustrates the major characteristics of both types of functions. Primitive functions are the natural inborn psychological structures conditioned primarily by biological characteristics (Vygotsky, 1929/1966, p. 31). They are represented by the S-R model and are characterized by immediacy and a reliance on concrete experience. For example, a child's definition of grandmother may be "a soft lap" (Vygotsky, 1934/1978). In other words, the memory of the small child is manifested as recognition, thinking is linked to action. Further, the school-age child, when asked what to do on missing a train, relies on concrete experience for the answer (Vygotsky, 1928–31/1998a).

The transformations that lead from primitive to higher mental functions are a shift in control from that of the environment to that of the individual. That is, the child's thinking gradually becomes less dependent on perception and, instead, involves thinking with abstract symbols. Like Piaget, Vygotsky (1928–31/1998a, 1998b) maintained that true logical thinking does not develop prior to adolescence. For Vygotsky, the higher cognitive functions reflect logical verbal thinking. In adolescence, verbal thinking makes a transition to abstract thinking with the development of (1) categorical perception, (2) thinking in concepts, (3) memory based on connections and relations among concepts, and (4) focused self-regulated attention. Stated another way, *the sign (languages and other symbols) and the method of its use are the focus of the entire process* (Vygotsky, 1930/1966, p. 32).

In other words, the most important factor underlying these structures is a new organization constructed by drawing in well-known artificial stimuli that play the part of signs (Vygotsky, 1930/1966, p. 32). The importance of this reconstruction is that it

TABLE 10.4
A comparison of primitive and higher mental functions

		Primitive Functions	**Higher Mental Functions**
1.	Processes	Simple perception, natural memory, involuntary attention	Categorical perception, logical memory, conceptual thinking, self-regulated attention
2.	Source of control	Stimulation from the environment	The use of both "object stimuli" and "means stimuli" by the individual to master and control his or her own behavior
3.	Dynamics	Co-occurrence of two stimuli	Creation of new links through the individual's artificial combination of stimuli
4.	Defining characteristics	Immediacy; bounded by concrete experience	Characterized by conscious awareness (of the processes), abstraction, and control
5.	Thinking and reasoning	Determined by natural memory; limited to reproducing established practical situations	Abstract, conceptual; makes use of logical relations and generalizations
6.	Origin	Biological factors	Cultural-historical development

involves the *mastery of one's own process of behavior* (Vygotsky, 1930/1966, p. 33). Thus, memory becomes "logicalized"; that is, it becomes a task of remembering and finding logical relations. Similarly, higher levels of recognition consist of discovering the element that the task indicates must be found (Vygotsky, 1934/1978, p. 51).

Thus, unlike the primitive functions, in which natural memory dominates thought, the relationship is reversed in the higher mental functions. *"For the young child, to think means to recall; but for the adolescent, to recall means to think"* (Vygotsky, 1934/1978, p. 51, 1928–31/1998a).

The Zone of Proximal Development

Two topics of importance in understanding the conditions that contribute to the development of higher cognitive functions are Vygotsky's conceptualization of development and the ways that progress in development may occur.

The relationship between learning and cognitive development was a key concern for Vygotsky. Using the dialectical approach (thesis—antithesis—resolution in the form of synthesis), Vygotsky (1929) analyzed contemporary proposals of the relationship. One perspective maintained that learning lags behind development (thesis) in the manner of a shadow falling behind an object. From this perspective, learning is an external process that somehow is congruent with child development and does not actively change it. Vygotsky placed Piaget's conception in this category (p. 21).

An opposing view maintained that learning is synonymous with development (antithesis), symbolized by two concentric circles. In this view, development is viewed as merely the accumulation of reactions, which does not differ from learning.

A third set of theories, a proposed synthesis, maintained that each particular acquired skill improves all acquired abilities. An example is the formal discipline concept discussed in chapter 2. This perspective is reflected by a small circle (learning) embedded in a larger circle (development) (p. 24).

However, Vygotsky (1963), agreeing with Thorndike, argued that the proposed synthesis was inaccurate. Further, any resolution of the relationship between learning and development first requires an adequate description of development itself. Referring to the work of Ernest Meumann, Vygotsky described development in terms of two levels. One is actual or completed development and the other is potential development (p. 29). The former refers to tasks or problems that the child can work through independently. Potential development, in contrast, refers to abilities that are just beginning to emerge and this level should be the focus of attention. Specifically, the zone of potential development refers to the higher cognitions, not the learning of specific content items.

Vygotsky described three different situations that exemplified the concepts of actual and potential development. Perhaps the most familiar is the standard testing situation which documents the level at which a child can complete problems or tasks independently. Suppose, for example, that two children test at the same level using an I.Q. test (Vygotsky, 1934/1962; 1934/1978). However, suppose that each child is shown various ways of addressing the problems. If, under these circumstances, one child can deal with problems up to a 12-year-old level and the other with problems up to a 9-year-old level, these children differ in their potential development.

Specifically, in this situation the zone of potential (or proximal) development consists of the capabilities the child demonstrates with adult assistance.

Two other situations that can call emerging capabilities to life are the play of preschool children and a child's independent problem solving at home. Play creates a zone of proximal development in that "a child is always above his average age, above his daily behavior; in play, it is as though he were a head taller than himself" (Vygotsky, 1933/1967, p. 16). An example is a child caring for a sick doll by imitating her mother's actions of giving medicine, and so on. The rationale for this effect of play is that creating an imaginary situation can be viewed as a means of developing abstract thought. Specifically, it creates a new relationship between the semantic (thinking) and visible (real) situations (p. 17). When the child gallops with a stick and calls it a horse, for example, he or she is following a self-initiated purpose and is moving in an abstract field.

An independent problem-solving situation at home can (but may not) create a zone of proximal development. The key is whether the learner is implementing (1) actions of the teacher implemented with the student in class and (2) imitating the teacher through a process of recreating previous classroom collaborations with the teacher (Vygotsky, 1934/1978).

The activity in each of these examples that brings out emerging capabilities and creates the zone of proximal development is that of imitation. The process of imitation in these cases, however, is not mechanical copying. Instead, it is the constructive application in a new situation (Valsiner & Van der Veer, 1993). Thus, the child can imitate only processes that are within the limits set by the state of his development (Vygotsky, 1934/1962, p. 103). For example, a child cannot win a chess game even if shown how to do it. Similarly, if an adult demonstrates the solutions to algebraic equations to the young child, he will not be able to understand them. The key to instruction that is effective in influencing development is that it "awakens and rouses to life functions which are in a stage of maturing, which lie in the zone of proximal development" (Vygotsky, 1956, p. 273).

In contrast, if an adult uses leading questions and examples and demonstrates the solution to a subtraction problem, the child may be able to solve the problem. The important point is that, in order to imitate, the child must have some means of crossing from what he or she does know to what is new knowledge for the child.

Summary

The higher cognitive functions are the uniquely human capabilities that are the products of cultural-historical development. Unlike the primitive psychological functions, the higher cognitive functions are characterized by conscious awareness (of the processes), abstraction, and control, and permit the individual to make use of logical relations and generalizations.

A key factor in the emergence of higher cognitive functions is the concept referred to as the zone of proximal development. Prior theories described instruction as lagging behind development, synonymous with development, or addressing a particular skill and thereby improving all acquired abilities. Instead, development should be described in terms of two levels: actual and potential. Three situations that reflect potential or proximal development are the problems that the child can solve in collaboration with an adult, the imaginative play of preschool children, and independent problem solving in which the student recreates prior interactions with the teacher. The key to the development of emerging (potential) capabilities in each of these situations is imitation that recreates adult actions.

PRINCIPLES OF INSTRUCTION

Like Piaget, Vygotsky analyzed particular developmental processes responsible for complex cognitive functioning. Piaget emphasized the growth of logical thinking as the goal of cognitive development. Vygotsky, in contrast, described the transformation of simple perception, involuntary attention, and simple memory into categorical perception, conceptual thinking, logical memory, and self-regulated attention.

Neither Piaget nor Vygotsky developed explicit principles of instruction. Although both theorists commented on certain aspects of the teaching process, instructional principles may be inferred only indirectly from their writings.

Basic Assumptions

The role of the culture in learning and the relationship between instruction and development provide the foundation for inferring basic assumptions about instruction.

Role of the Culture
According to Vygotsky, the culture does more than provide the setting in which learning occurs. Instead, the very structure of social functioning determines the structure of individual psychological functioning. That is, major concepts and ideas as well as the means of communication and ways of viewing the world are created by the culture. Thus, the child learns to think in ways that are directly fostered and developed by his or her particular culture.

Therefore, the basic structures of perception, representation, and self-awareness are likely to differ across different historical conditions. Vygotsky and Luria developed a research plan to analyze the cultural-historical shaping of mental processes. The research was conducted in the early 1930s in remote parts of the Soviet Union that had been faced with a radical restructuring of their economic system and culture (Luria, 1976). The research was conducted in the villages and mountain pasture lands of Uzbekistan and Kirghizia. The groups compared on various tasks were (1) Ichkari women in remote villages whose lives were controlled by strict Islamic codes; (2) peasants in remote villages who were not involved in socialized labor; (3) collective farm workers who had experience in planning, distributing labor, and monitoring work output; and (4) women students in a teacher's school.

The tasks, which were accompanied by in-depth interviews, involved perceptual and memory strategies, classification, and problem solving. In one task, the subjects were shown 27 different hues of skeins of wool. When asked to name the colors, the collective farm workers and women students used categorical names (red, blue, yellow) with occasional designations (light yellow, dark blue) (Luria, 1976). In contrast, the Ichkari women used graphic names, such as fruit-drop iris and spoiled cotton (p. 26).

When asked to group the different skeins, the collective farm workers and students usually arranged all the colors in seven or eight groups. In contrast, some of the Ichkari women maintained that the task could not be done while others arranged the skeins of yarn into series of colors according to increasing brightness. One series, for example, included pale pink, pale yellow, and pale blue. In other words, attempts by the experimenter to obtain a color grouping with only one primary color in a group led to failure to perform the task (Luria, 1976, p. 30).

Relationship Between Instruction and Development

According to Vygotsky (1934/1962; 1934/1978), instruction influences development in two ways. One is that good learning precedes and leads development. That is, the tasks that the child can accomplish in collaboration with the teacher today, she can accomplish alone tomorrow (Vygotsky, 1934/1962, p. 104). Thus, both instruction and imitation play a major role in the child's development. "They bring out the specifically human qualities of the mind and lead the child to new developmental levels" (Vygotsky, 1934/1962, p. 104).

Planning instruction, therefore, includes determining the lowest threshold at which instruction may begin, since only a certain minimal development of cognitive functioning is required (Vygotsky, 1934/1962, p. 104). Like Montessori, Vygotsky believed that each subject of instruction is most influential at a certain period because the child is most receptive at that time. Therefore, important qualities for teachers include a sensitivity to the actions and words of the child and the ability to structure tasks so that the child may exercise his or her emerging capabilities.

The second way that instruction influences development is in the learning of school subjects, such as reading and mathematics. These subjects include operations that require awareness and deliberate control. Learning to master and consciously control operations (such as addition and multiplication) and to think in subject matter concepts furthers the development of complex mental functions (Vygotsky, 1982/1987).

In summary, two basic assumptions related to instruction may be inferred from Vygotsky's theory. The first is that the structure of social relations in the cultural setting determines the individual's psychological structure. The second is that instruction should precede and thereby maximally influence development.

Components of Instruction

The two major components of instruction include (1) implementing the general law of genetic development and (2) structuring the processes of signification to gain control of the symbol system.

Implementing the Law of Genetic Development

According to Vygotsky, internal psychological functions begin as interactions between the child and a knowledgeable member of the culture. However, the assumption should not be made that a sudden clean shift occurs from social to individual functioning. That is, a child does not simply work with someone on a task and then begin to carry it out independently (Wertsch, 1985b, p. 158). Instead, contemporary research indicates that several changes take place on the interpersonal level, and each is accompanied by a change on the intrapersonal level. Studies of mother-child dyads in which the task is that of constructing a puzzle to match a completed model indicate five important factors in the transition from inter- to intrapsychological functioning (see Wertsch, 1985b). They are (1) the cognitive readiness of the child, (2) a willingness by the adult to transfer responsibility to the child, (3) the adult's use of "reflective assessments" as feedback to the child on the significance of particular behaviors, (4) the explicitness of the adult's directives, and (5) the construction of a joint definition of the task that gradually moves toward a culturally appropriate definition (Wertsch, 1985b, p. 166).

Establishing a joint definition of the task initially is particularly important because the adult and the child likely bring different concepts to a task setting. Therefore, the challenge to the adult is to find a way to communicate with the child so that he or she can participate in the task with the adult. This communication is the foundation for the transition to interpsychological functioning (Wertsch, 1985b, p. 161).

Establishing an initial task definition between teacher and student is referred to by Wertsch (1985b, p. 161) as intersubjectivity. Of importance is that this factor is not limited to simply facilitating the adult–child interaction in a task. It is also critical to the psychological transitions described by Vygotsky in any learning situation.

One term applied to the situation in which a tutor enables a child or novice to solve a problem that is beyond his or her individual efforts is *scaffolding*. Introduced by Wood, Bruner, and Ross (1976), it refers to the process of controlling task elements that are initially beyond the learner's capability. In this way, the learner can concentrate on and complete those elements within his or her immediate capability (p. 90). Of importance in understanding Vygotsky's theory is that he did not advocate this practice. In his view, higher cognitive functions, such as monitoring one's attention, develop when the child is capable of applying to himself the earlier attention-focusing directives applied by others to his actions.

Also important is that social interaction is only the first step. The learner's subsequent activities are also essential. The student must imitate, invent, and practice with respect to himself, the same forms of behavior that others formerly practiced with respect to him (Vygotsky, 1930/1966, p. 157).

An example is the teaching of composition to older Brazilian women in the College of the Bahamas (Fiore & Elsasser, 1982). Teaching began with the use of "generative themes," which are themes drawn from the students' daily lives. These themes were important because they allowed the students to explore the larger cultural and historical implications of personal experience. One generative theme, for example, was marriage. The students gradually moved from personal anecdotes to more sophisticated forms of expression, such as cause and effect, definition, and comparison and contrast. The increasing sophistication of the women's writing was accompanied by a more analytical approach to the issues.

Vygotsky (1982/1987) cautions that the relationship between instruction and development is not a one-to-one correspondence. For example, "the first, second, third, and fourth components of arithmetic instruction may be inconsequential for the development of arithmetic thinking, but some fifth dimension may be decisive" (p. 207). That is, the child, at that point, may finally have learned a general principle that was clarified in this "aha experience" (p. 207).

The Processes of Signification

A major premise in Vygotsky's theory is that the signs and symbols used for communication in a culture are also the mechanisms for cognitive development. However, the teaching of symbol systems, such as writing and mathematics, will not bring about the development of complex mental functions if the educational goal is the transmission of knowledge (Elsasser & John–Steiner, 1977, p. 363). However, if the expectation is that the student is to internalize existing knowledge, thought processes are not required to change, grow, and develop. Also important is that the direct teaching of concepts is "impossible and fruitless" (Vygotsky, 1934/1962, p. 83). All that is accomplished is empty verbalization and a parrotlike repetition of words that is usually disguising a vacuum.

The research conducted by Vygotsky and his colleagues indicated that children gradually move from external sign use, such as counting on their fingers, to inner speech, such as counting in one's head and developing logical memory. School tasks can assist children in making these transitions as well as help them use speech for planning.

In summary, the two major components of instruction include (1) implementing the general law of genetic development and (2) structuring the processes of signification to gain control of the symbol system. Required are the cognitive readiness of the child, a joint definition of the task, and gradual transfer of responsibility to the child, based on the adult's ongoing reflective assessments. Also important are the applications and inventions of the learner in working with new situations.

Designing Instruction to Develop Complex Cognitive Functions

Important issues in developing complex cognitive functions are (1) the "foundational" psychological functions, (2) teaching writing, (3) the role of scientific (subject-matter) concepts, and (4) the role of peers, the teacher, and the learner.

The Foundational Psychological Functions

Vygotsky (1982/1987) identified two broad psychological functions that form the foundation of the higher cognitive functions. These two functions are conscious awareness of and mastery (volitional control) of one's mental activities (p. 208). These functions are components of categorical perception, self-regulated attention, logical memory, and conceptual thinking (verbal and mathematical).

The importance of the foundational functions is that they begin to emerge at school age and school instruction is essential in their development. That is, consciousness of and self-regulatory control of one's thinking are in the child's zone of proximal development and school subjects play a major role in their development. For example, the preschool child can use the correct case and verb form in oral speech, but is unaware that such forms exist and he or she cannot conjugate a verb fully (p. 206). An important effect of school learning is developing conscious awareness and control of such activities. For example, the child becomes aware of different verb forms and tenses, and can choose the correct form when writing.

Teaching Writing.   Oral speech is learned and used unconsciously. In contrast, the cognitive functions required for writing are quite different (Vygotsky, 1982/1987, p. 204). First, written speech lacks the expressive intonational qualities of oral speech. Thus, a major problem in learning to write is that the child must disengage himself from the sensory aspect of speech and must replace the sound images by written symbols. (Vygotsky, 1934/1962, p. 99). Thus, it is analytical.

A second problem is that, unlike speech, writing is often a message addressed to no one in particular. To the child, this is a confusing and strange situation because writing is not linked to immediate needs (Vygotsky, 1934/1962, p. 99).

Third, thought or inner speech, which is compact and abbreviated, must be expanded into intelligible written form. These characteristics explain the lag in development between oral and written speech.

However, the deliberateness and analysis required in writing depend on the foundational psychological functions of conscious awareness and control of one's cognitive activities. Instruction in writing is one of the most important subjects in the child's early school years because it requires that the child begin to develop these basic cognitive functions that have not yet matured (Vygotsky, 1982/1987, p. 211).

An important factor in teaching reading and writing is that instruction should be organized so that these activities are necessary for a goal important to the child (Vygotsky, 1934/1978, p. 117). If they are used for some task determined by the teacher, the exercise will be both mechanical and boring to the child. In other words, writing should be taught as being relevant to life (Vygotsky, 1934/1978). An example is the "Writing to Read" program developed by John Martin. Kindergarten and first grade children learn letters of the alphabet and words in order to type their own stories on manual typewriters. Thus, both reading and writing are essential components in the child's expression of his or her own thoughts.

The Role of Subject-Matter Concepts.   The learning of subject-matter concepts (referred to as *scientific concepts* by Vygotsky, 1982/1987) also is important in developing complex mental functions. One reason is that simply learning the meaning of a word is only a beginning (Vygotsky, 1934/1978). Learning the definition does not mean that the learner can complete the difficult task of *thinking* in concepts.

Another is that learning subject-matter concepts differs from learning spontaneous (every day) concepts, which are learned through experience. The weakness of spontaneous concepts is in the child's incapacity for abstraction (Vygotsky, 1982/1987, p. 69). That is, the child is aware of the object represented in a concept, but is not consciously aware of the act or thought that would allow him or her to abstractly represent the object (p. 217).

Further, unlike spontaneous or everyday concepts, concepts in a subject-matter domain typically are abstract in that they are removed from the object or event they represent and they form a system. That is, concepts in the domain can be represented in terms of other concepts in a number of ways. Important features of subject-matter concepts with implications for thinking are the processes of abstraction required to identify the concept's defining characteristics, and those of generalizing the relevant defining characteristics to other concepts in the system. Thus, the learning of subject-matter concepts is important in that it leads to the child's conscious awareness of the processes of generalization and abstraction. When the child has mastered a subject-matter concept, he or she can define it easily, implement it in various logical operations, and identify relationships between it and other concepts (Vygotsky, 1982/1987, p. 218). Thus, the strength of the subject-matter concept *"lies in the higher characteristics of concepts, in conscious awareness and volition"* (p. 220).

The Role of Peers, the Teacher, and the Learner.   Many writings on instruction describe the primacy of large and small-group discussions as an instructional approach, often citing Vygotsky as the source. O'Connor (1996) notes "These beliefs about classroom discussions are generally buttressed by reference to Vygotskyan theory, in that collaboration or joint reasoning, the 'intermental' plane of cognition, is viewed as the genesis of a child's individual 'intramental' functioning" (p. 495). However, the term *collaboration,* when used by Vygotsky in reference to the school setting, refers to collaboration between teacher and student (Gredler & Shields, in preparation). Examples include " . . . the entire process of their (concepts) formation is worked out by the child in collaboration with the adult in instruction (Vygotsky, 1934/1978, p. 78), and "the teacher, working with the school child on a given question, explains, informs, inquires, corrects, and forces the child himself to explain; [and] when the child solves a problem, although the teacher is not present, he or she must make independent use of the earlier collaboration" (Vygotsky, 1982/1987, p. 216).

Further, on occasion, the general law of genetic development is described in some secondary sources as referring to the relations *among* people instead of the relations *between* people. This subtle change confuses the concept of adult–child collaboration described in the school setting by Vygotsky.

Vygotsky does name one situation in which a particular type of peer interaction can contribute to cognitive development. The situation is that of children contesting the statements of other children, the argumentation described by Piaget (Vygotsky, 1930/1966, p. 40). Specifically, argumentation among children becomes the process of reflection for the individual child. That is, these interactions provide the basis for the child's subsequent development and weighing of alternative perspectives on an issue.

Vygotsky's (1982/1987) references to learning in the subject areas, in contrast, describe the teacher modeling, explaining, and asking the student for explanations. The importance of the verbalizations by the teacher is that they are the basis for the student's self-questioning and explaining concepts when studying and reviewing materials.

Important Concerns

One issue in planning instruction is that English-speaking scholars interpret the zone of proximal development more narrowly than Vygotsky intended (Griffin & Cole, 1984, p. 45). However, it should be conceptualized as a total problem-solving activity and not as the teaching of discrete separable skills and subskills (Moll, 1990, p. 7). When viewed as teaching specific skills, the zone of proximal development is reduced to skills transfer from more knowledgeable individuals to those who know less. Thus, any task in which a challenging performance level is set, followed by assisted performance, fits the transfer-of-skills view but would not reflect the zone of proximal development.

Two issues confronting psychological analysis arise from the concept of the zone of proximal development. One is to describe the ways in which school learning awakens new relations in internal intellectual processes. The second is to reexamine the significance of each particular subject in the curriculum from the perspective of overall mental development (Vygotsky, 1934/1978, p. 91). The second issue, however, only can be resolved through research based on the concept of the zone of proximal development.

In summary, designing instruction for complex cognitive functions includes attention to developing the child's conscious awareness and control of his or her own mental activities. These capabilities are the foundation for the higher cognitive functions and they are beginning to emerge at school age.

Important in the development of the two foundational capabilities is the teaching of writing. The relationship of writing to these capabilities is that it is abstract. That is, sound images must be replaced by symbols, the message often is not addressed to a particular audience, and abbreviated inner speech must be expanded into intelligible form. Of importance is that both reading and writing should be organized for goals important to the child.

Subject-matter ("scientific") concepts also play an important role in the development of higher cognitive functions. Unlike everyday (spontaneous) concepts, subject-matter concepts are removed from the object or event they represent and they also form a system. That is, concepts may be expressed in terms of other concepts. Thus, subject-matter concepts foster development of the processes of abstraction and generalization.

Essential in classroom instruction to develop higher cognitive functions is the collaboration between teacher and student. Although some individuals cite Vygotsky as the source for relying on small- and large-group discussions in the classroom, Vygotsky identified the specific activities that teacher–student collaboration should include.

EDUCATIONAL APPLICATIONS

Vygotsky's cultural-historical theory has received considerable attention in the United States in recent years. Two programs to teach reading to poor readers reflect Vygotsky's concepts of teacher–student collaboration, teacher modeling and imitation, and the abstraction of meaning from symbols. One is Reading Recovery designed by Marie Clay (1985) for first-grade children who have been unable to master the reading process in regular classrooms (the lowest 10%). The shared collaboration between teacher and child helps children monitor and integrate information from many sources. That is, they learn to use four types of cues (semantic, syntactic, visual, and phonological [oral language sounds]) and also develop meaning from reading (Clay &

Cazden, 1990). The other is reciprocal teaching developed by Palinscar and Brown, to teach comprehension strategies to older children with reading problems. Reciprocal teaching in reading helps the children develop the subjective judgment essential in monitoring whether they have understood the text (Brown, 1994, p. 6).

Vygotsky's principles have at least two other important implications for several areas of the curriculum. First, the meaning of signs and symbols used in the culture cannot be left to chance. Second, Vygotsky (1934/1978) suggests that each subject in the curriculum should be examined from the perspective of overall mental development. In other words, the content should contribute to the development of complex mental functions in order to remain in the curriculum.

Moreover, the theory also speaks to society in general as cultures attempt to understand the implications of a media-based society. In past history, thinking and new discoveries produced by civilizations increased as their symbol systems became more advanced. The implications of Vygotsky's theory, however, are profound for a civilization in which the major symbol system is one that makes use of co-occurring stimuli (images) and thus requires of the individual only primitive mental functions. Thinking, in other words, can regress in society as well as show progress from one generation to another.

Classroom Issues

The theory establishes the sociocultural setting as the genesis for cognitive development and learning. Therefore, learner characteristics, cognitive processes, and the context for learning are all viewed from that perspective.

Learner Characteristics
Individual differences and readiness are two issues that are specifically addressed by Vygotsky's theory.

Individual Differences.   One of the incomplete concepts in Vygotsky's theory is that of individual differences. However, Vygotsky (1930/1977a) noted that differences in the quality of memory are not the major differences between individuals. Instead, the power of attention and the force of one's drives are the critical differences. In other words, the way that the individual makes use of his or her own capacities, that is, their role in the personality, is the important factor in determining individual differences.

Readiness.   The zone of proximal development, in which cognitive functions are beginning to emerge, represents readiness. Because readiness refers to potential development, it cannot be determined by a standardized test.

Motivation.   One of Vygotsky's major interests that remained uncompleted at his death was the issue of affect. He believed that primitive emotions developed in the same general cycle and became moral, ethical feelings in the way that primitive mental functions are transformed into complex mental functions (Vygotsky, 1930/1977).

Also, he believed that subjective feelings regulated behavior, but the mechanisms of this regulation remain to be developed.

Cognitive Processes and Instruction

Transfer of learning, developing "how-to-learn" skills, and teaching problem solving are addressed by the theory in terms of the social nature of learning.

Transfer of Learning.   All higher mental functions first appear as interactions between a knowledgeable member of society and the child. "Transfer," then, in Vygotsky's view, involves the qualitative shift between interindividual actions and the internalization of these actions as complex intellectual functions. This process, however, is a lengthy one that first involves three major stages. They are (1) the use of the symbol system as communication, (2) the use of the symbol system to guide developing mental abilities, and (3) the development of internal cues and signs to monitor and regulate one's remembering and thinking.

Developing "How-to-Learn" Skills.   This issue is not addressed in the terminology familiar to American psychologists. However, Vygotsky does describe the highest level of symbol use—that of creating internal cues to monitor and regulate one's behavior. This activity involves the control of logical memory and thinking through symbol use and is one aspect of learning how to learn.

Teaching Problem Solving.   Like the learning of signs and symbols, learning to solve problems occurs in a social context. The teacher models the appropriate behaviors and then provides guidance as the learner works through the task.

The Social Context for Learning

Two aspects of the social setting determine the nature and extent of the child's learning. One is the historical developments inherited by the child as a member of a particular culture. That is, the culture may employ a primitive counting system, as in Papua New Guinea, or it may rely extensively on complex symbol systems, such as algebra, calculus, and complex probability systems. The nature of the symbol system inherited by the child sets broad parameters on the higher cognitive functions the child can develop.

The second crucial element is the nature of the child's social interaction with knowledgeable members of the society. Only through this interaction does the child acquire both meaning and utilization of important symbols and thereby develop his or her thinking abilities.

The implication in Vygotsky's theory is that the culture that teaches its children symbols as communication only is omitting the most important function of artificial signs, that of mastering and developing one's thought processes.

Relationships to Other Perspectives

Like Piaget, Vygotsky focused on the mechanisms by which individuals develop higher cognitive processes. However, cultural–historical theory defines them as self-regulated attention, categorical perception, logical memory, and conceptual thinking (instead of as logical reasoning processes). Other differences with Piagetian theory are the role of culture in cognitive development, the role of egocentric speech, and the pivotal role of school subjects. Egocentric speech does not disappear, but becomes inner speech. Vygotsky also placed greater emphasis on the role of make-believe play in that it provides opportunities for the child to extend his or her behavior beyond that of his or her average age.

Also of interest is that Vygotsky discussed the importance of developing the cognitive processes of abstraction and generalization through learning concepts some 40 years prior to their discussion in Gagné's conditions of learning and the instructional design literature. Further, particularly relevant, given the current interest in self-regulated learning, is Vygotsky's identification of (1) the importance of self-regulated attention, (2) the role of signs and symbols in directing and managing one's learning, and (3) the identification of two key foundational processes in self-regulated learning. They are the learner's conscious awareness of the cognitive process to be developed and voluntary control (mastery) of one's actions. Further, he emphasized the importance of imitation prior to the introduction of modeling in American psychology. Finally, his focus on signification and learner development of meaning identifies Vygotsky (along with Piaget) as an early constructivist.

Developing a Classroom Strategy

Implementing Vygotsky's theory in the classroom changes the roles of both teacher and students. Ideally, one teacher would be working with one or two students; at most, the group should be limited to five or six. The steps for planning instruction inferred from Vygotsky's broad outline are as follows:

Step 1: Identify the concepts or principles to be taught.

   1.1 What connections and relations to other concepts are students to learn?

   1.2 How will the concepts to be taught facilitate the student's mastery of his or her own thinking?

Step 2: Structure the learning task as a collaborative teacher–student activity.

   2.1 What is the level of shared meaning required to initiate learning?

   2.2 What aspects of the task are to be modeled by the teacher?

   2.3 What self-regulatory skills are to be modeled by the teacher?

   2.4 In what ways is the student to use signs and symbols to regulate his or her own behavior?

   2.5 What teacher suggestions and feedback to students are needed to assist learning?

Step 3: Implement instruction and evaluate the results.

   3.1 Did the teacher gradually add other concepts as the students acquired mastery?

3.2 Were the students able to function independently at the conclusion of instruction?

3.3 Are the students thinking in concepts after instruction?

3.4 Do the students' skills generalize to other settings and situations?

Classroom Example

The following lessons are taken from day 1 and day 4 of a Reciprocal Teaching Lesson (Palinscar & Brown, 1984, p. 138) with a student who met the minimal decoding standards but failed on comprehension. The lessons illustrate the concepts of scaffolding and the gradual ceding of responsibility to the student.

> *Day 1:* The teacher and student have read one paragraph silently together, and the teacher has modeled the self-review questions one would ask to check comprehension. The second paragraph, also read silently, mentions several poisonous snakes called pit vipers. The paragraph explains the reason for the name and describes some characteristics of one pit viper known as the water moccasin, or "cottonmouth."

Teacher: This paragraph talks about several different kinds of poisonous snakes called pit vipers. What would be a good question to ask about pit vipers that begins with the word *why*?

Student: (no response)

Teacher: How about "Why are the snakes called pit vipers?"

Student: Why do they, uh, pit vipers in a pit?

Teacher: Try it again. "Why are the snakes called . . . ?"

Student: Why are the snakes called pit vipers?

Teacher: Good for you. Now what would be a good question to ask about the water moccasin?

Student: The name?

Teacher: What about the name?

Student: Why is it called a moccasin?

Teacher: That's close; try again. What about the name "cottonmouth"?

Student: Why is it called a cottonmouth?

Teacher: Good. But we need to know which snake is called a cottonmouth.

Student: How about "Why is the moccasin called a cottonmouth?"

Teacher: Good. Now let's answer the questions to be sure we understand the paragraph. (Teacher and student review the questions and the answers in the same manner.)

> *Day 4:* The brief paragraph is about a spinner's mate and his characteristics.

Student: (no question)

Teacher: What is this paragraph about?

Student: Spinner's mate. How do spinner's mate . . .

Teacher: Good. Keep going.

Student: How do spinner's mate is smaller than. . . . How am I going to say that?
Teacher: Take your time. You want to ask about spinner's mate and what he does, using the word *how*.
Student: How do they spend most of their time sitting?
Teacher: That's almost it. Sitting is the answer to the question. Can you ask the question without using *sitting*?
Student: How do they spend most of their time?
Teacher: Good, but we should name spinner's mate in the question. "How does a spinner's. . . . " Now you finish it.
Student: How does a spinner's mate spend most of his time?
Teacher: Good job.

Review of the Theory

Lev Vygotsky, like Jean Piaget, analyzed particular aspects of human cognitive development. Their approach to this task shares four major characteristics. They are (1) the establishment of a theoretical framework for the study of psychological processes, (2) the identification of different psychological structures constructed during development, (3) the analysis of the psychological processes required to attain the highest levels of cognitive development, and (4) an assertion that cognitive development does not proceed through small incremental changes. Instead, it undergoes qualitative transformations.

Vygotsky emphasized the complex mental functions of categorical perception, logical memory, conceptual thinking, and self-regulated attention. The potential for development of these capabilities is determined by the cultural-historical heritage of the child's culture and the child's social experience.

The key to the development of complex mental functions is mastering the signs and symbols of the culture and learning to use them to direct and regulate one's own behavior. The creation and use of arbitrary signs changes the psychological nature of processes such as perception, memory, and attention into more complex forms. However, because the meanings assigned to symbols are a product of a particular culture, the nature of the child's cognitive functioning is socially determined.

Three basic principles in cognitive development were identified by Vygotsky. They are the two branches of cultural cognitive development, the general law of genetic development, and the processes of signification. Essential in the development of higher cognitive function is interactions with knowledgeable adults to develop both the meanings of cultural symbols and the ways of thinking of the culture. Also important in this process are the imitation and intervention of the learner in applying actions modeled during adult–teacher interactions. (See Table 10.5.)

The major disadvantage of the theory is that Vygotsky was unable to complete his ideas before his death. Thus, educators are left with a broad outline, but with few details on implementation.

Major contributions of the theory include the role of culture in learning and development, recognition of the psychological contributions of signs and symbols in psychological functions, and the importance of social interaction during learning.

TABLE 10.5
Summary of Vygotsky's cultural–historical theory of psychological development

Element	Definition
Assumptions	Human behavior differs from the behavior of animals in the same way as the adaptation and historical development of humans differs from the evolution of animals. The distinguishing feature of human psychological development is the presence of created stimuli in addition to given stimuli. Psychological processes are not static and should be studied as processes in transition or change.
Cognitive development	The development of complex mental functions that make use of both given stimuli and created stimuli
Components of development	The internalization of actions that first appear on an interpsychological plane; the mastery of the signs and symbols of the culture and learning to use them to master one's own behavior
Outcomes of cognitive development	Complex mental functions, including self-regulated attention, categorical perception, conceptual thinking, and logical memory
Designing instruction for complex skills	Develop conscious awareness of and mastery of one's thinking through teaching concepts, and the use of writing for thinking.
ANALYSIS OF THE THEORY	
Disadvantages	The incompleteness of the system and the lack of specific guidelines for implementation
Contributions	Recognition of the psychological contribution of created stimuli in cognitive development; the importance of social interaction and the social nature of learning

CHAPTER QUESTIONS

1. Low SES children typically are viewed as having a disadvantage in school because their homes lack magazines and other reading material and reading is not a regular activity for the parents. How would Vygotsky explain the children's disadvantage?

2. Why would Vygotsky not advocate the use of mechanized devices such as computers to provide remedial instruction?

3. What do you think Vygotsky meant when he said that written language is the algebra of language?

4. Schoenfeld (1985) and others express concern that individuals approach mathematical problems as mechanical exercises and seem to possess little awareness of what they are doing (see discussion in chapter 8). How would Vygotsky explain the problem, and what should instruction include to correct the problem?

5. How might writing be used to develop one's thinking?

REFERENCES

Berk, L. E. (2000). *Child development* (5th ed.). Boston: Allyn & Bacon.

Berk, L. E., & Garvin, R. A. (1984). Development of private speech among low-income Appalachian children. *Developmental Psychology, 20,* 271–286.

Berk, L. E., & Stuhl, S. T. (1995). Maternal interactions, private speech, and task performance in preschool children. *Early Childhood Research Quarterly, 10,* 145–169.

Bozhovitch, L. I. (1977). The cultural-historical development of the mind. *Soviet Psychology, 16*(1), 5–22.

Brown, A. L. (1994). The advancement of learning. *Educational Researcher 23*(8), 4–12.

Clay, M. (1985). *The early detection of reading difficulties* (3rd ed.). Portsmouth, NH: Heinemann.

Clay, M. C., & Cazden, C. B. (1990). A Vygotskian interpretation of Reading Recovery. In L. C. Moll (Ed.), *Vygotsky and education* (pp. 206–222). New York: Cambridge University Press.

Cole, M. (1996). *Cultural psychology*. Cambridge, MA: The Belknap Press of Harvard University Press.

Cole, M., & Scribner, S. (1978). Introduction. In L. S. Vygotsky (Ed.), *Mind in society* (pp. 1–14). Cambridge, MA: Harvard University Press.

Davydov, V. V. (1995). The influence of L. S. Vygotsky on education theory, research and practice (S. Kerr, Trans.), *Educational Researcher,* 12–21.

Elsasser, N., & John-Steiner, V. P. (1977). An interactionist approach to advancing literacy. *Harvard Educational Review, 47*(3), 355–369.

Engels, F. (1940). *Dialectics of nature*. New York: International.

Engels, F. (1925/1978). *Dialectic on culture*. Berlin: Dietz Verlag.

Fiore, K., & Elsasser, N. (1982). Strangers no more: A laboratory literacy curriculum. *College English, 44,* 115–128.

Gindis, B. (1995). The social/cultural implications of disability: Vygotsky's paradigm for special education. *Educational Psychologist, 30*(2), 77–81.

Gredler, M., & Shields, C. (in preparation). *A re-examination of Vygotsky in the classroom.*

Jahoda, G. (1993). *Crossroads between culture and mind*. Cambridge, MA: Harvard University Press.

Janet, P. (1926). De l'angoisse a l'extase. Vol. I. Paris: Alcan.

Janet, P. (1929). De l'angoisse a l'extrase. Vol. II. Paris: Alcan.

Kornilov, K. N. (1930). Psychology in the light of dialectical materialism. In C. Murchison (Ed.), *Psychologies of 1930* (pp. 243–278). Worcester, MA: Clark University Press.

Kozulin, A. (1990). *Vygotsky's psychology: A biography of ideas.* Cambridge, MA: Harvard University Press.

Leont'ev, A. N. (1959). *Problems of mental development.* Moscow: Publishing House of the Academy of Pedagogical Sciences RSFSR.

Leont'ev, A. N. (1977). The dialectical method in the psychology of memory. *Soviet Psychology, 16*(1), 53–69.

Leont'ev, A. N., & Luria, A. R. (1968). The psychological ideas of L. S. Vygotsky. In B. B. Wolman (Ed.), *Historical roots of contemporary psychology* (pp. 338–367). New York: Harper & Row.

Levy-Bruhl, L. (1910/1922). *Les onctions mentales dans les societes inferieures*. Paris: Alcan.

Levy-Bruhl, L. (1922/1976). *La mentalite primitive*. Paris: Retz.

Luria, A. R. (1971). Towards the problem of the historical nature of psychological processes. *International Journal of Psychology, 6*(4), 259–272.

Luria, A. R. (1976). *Cognitive development: Its cultural and social foundations.* Cambridge, MA: Harvard University Press.

Luria, A. R. (1979). *The making of mind: A personal account of Soviet psychology.* Cambridge, MA: Harvard University Press. (Edited by M. Cole & S. Cole).

Marx, K. (1850). *Captital. Vol. 1.* Moscow: Gospolitizdat.

Moll, L. C. (1990). Introduction. In L. C. Moll (Ed.), *Vygotsky and education* (pp. 1–27). New York: Cambridge University Press.

O'Connor, M. C. (1996). Managing the intermental: Classroom group discussion and the social context of learning. In D. I. Slobin, J. Gerhardt, A. Kyratzis, & J. Guo (Eds.). *Social interaction, social context, and language*. Mahwah, NJ: Lawrence Erlbaum.

Palinscar, A. S. (1989). Less chartered waters. *Educational Researcher, 18*(4), 5–7.

Palinscar, A. S., & Brown, A. L. (1984). Reciprocal teaching of comprehension-fostering and comprehension-monitoring activities. *Cognition and Instruction, 1*(2), 117–175.

Saxe, G. B. (1981). Body parts as numerals: A developmental analysis of numeration among the Oksapmin in Papua New Guinea. *Child Development, 52*, 306–316.

Schoenfeld, A. H. (1985). Metacognitive and epistemological issues in mathematical understanding. In E. A. Silver (Ed.), *Teaching and learning mathematical problem solving: Multiple research perspectives* (pp. 361–379). Hillsdale, NJ: Erlbaum.

Scribner, S. (1985). Vygotsky's uses of history. In J. V. Wertsch (Ed.), *Culture, communication, and cognition: Vygotskian perspectives* (pp. 119–145). Cambridge, MA: Cambridge University Press.

Thurnwald, R. (1922). Psychologie des primitiven Menschen. In G. Kafka (Ed.), *Handbuck der vergleichenden Psychologie Band 1.* (pp. 147-320). Munchen: Verlag von Ernst Reinhardt.

Valsiner, J. (1988). *Developmental psychology in the Soviet Union*. Brighton: Harvester Press.

Valsiner, J., & Van der Veer, R. (1993). The encoding of distance: The concept of the zone of proximal development. In R. R. Cocking & K. A. Rehninger (Eds.), *The development and meaning of psychological distance* (p. 35–62). Hillsdale, NJ: Lawrence Erlbaum.

Van der Veer, R., & Valsiner, J. (1988). Lev Vygotsky and Pierre Janet. *Developmental Review, 8,* 52–65.

Van der Veer, R., & Valsiner, J. (1991). *Understanding Vygotsky: A quest for synthesis*. Cambridge, MA: Blackwell.

Vygodskaia, G. (1995). Remembering father. *Educational Psychologist, 30*(2), 57–59.

Vygotskaia, G. (1998). Afterword. In K. Topping & S. Ehly (Eds.), *Peer-assisted learning* (pp. 329–332). Mahwah, NJ: Lawrence Erlbaum.

Vygotsky, L. S. (1929). The problem of the cultural development of the child. *Journal of Genetic Psychology, 36,* 415–434.

Vygotsky, L. S. (1930). Foreword. In W. Köhler, *Isseldovanie intellekka chelovekopodobnykh obez'jan* (pp. I–XXIX). Moscow: Izdatel'stvo Kommunisticheskoj Akademii.

Vygotsky, L. S. (1956). *Selected psychological investigations*. Moscow: Izdtel'stp Academii Pedagogicheskikh Nauk SSSR.

Vygotsky, L. S. (1960/1981). The instrumental method in psychology. In J. Wertsch (Ed.), *The concept of activity in Soviet psychology* (pp. 134–143). Armonk, NY: M. E. Sharpe.

Vygotsky, L. S. (1962). *Thought and language*. Cambridge: Massachusetts Institute of Technology. (Original work published 1934)

Vygotsky, L. S. (1963). The problem of learning and mental development at school age. In B. Simon & J. Simon (Eds.), *Educational psychology in the U.S.S.R.* (pp. 21–34). London: Routledge & Kegan Paul.

Vygotsky, L.S. (1966). Development of the higher mental functions. In A. N. Leont'ev, A. R. Luria, & A. Smirnol (Eds.), *Psychological research in the U.S.S.R. Vol. I* (pp. 11-45). Moscow: Progress. (original work published 1930)

Vygotsky, L. S. (1967). Play and its role in the mental development of the child. *Soviet Psychology, 5*(3), 6–18. (Original work published 1933.)

Vygotsky, L. S. (1977a). *Talks on psychological systems, notes*. Cited in L. I. Bozhovitch, The cultural-historical development of the mind. *Soviet Psychology, 16*(1), 5–22. (Original work published 1930)

Vygotsky, L. S. (1977b). The development of higher psychological functions. *Soviet Psychology, 16,* 60–73. (Original work published 1929)

Vygotsky, L. S. (1978). *Mind in society: The development of higher psychological processes*. Cambridge, MA: Harvard University Press. (Original work published 1934)

Vygotsky, L. S. (1979a). Consciousness as a problem in the psychology of behavior. *Soviet Psychology 17*(4), 3–35. (Original work published 1924).

Vygotsky, L. S. (1979b). The development of higher forms of attention in childhood. *Soviet Psychology, 18*(1), 67–115. (Original work published 1929)

Vygotsky, L. S. (1982/1987). *The collected works of L. S. Vygotsky: Vol. 1. Thinking and speech* (N. Minick, Trans.). New York: Plenum.

Vygotsky, L. S. (1983). *Collected Works* (Vol. 5). Moscow: Pedagogika.

Vygotsky, L. S. (1993). *The collected works of L. S. Vygotsky: Vol. 2. The fundamentals of defectology (abnormal psychology and learning disabilities)* (J.E. Knox & C. B. Stevens, Trans.). New York: Plenum.

Vygotsky, L. S. (1998a). Development of higher mental functions during the transitional age. In R. W. Rieber (Ed.), *The collected works of L. S. Vygotsky* (pp. 83–149). (M. J. Hall, Trans.). New York: Plenum. (Original work published 1928–31)

Vygotsky, L. S. (1998b). Development of thinking and formation of concepts in the adolescent. In R. W. Rieber (Ed.), *The collected works of L. S. Vygotsky* (pp. 29–81). (M. J. Hall, Trans.). New York: Plenum. (Original work published 1928–31)

Wertsch, J. V. (1985b). Introduction. In J. V. Wertsch (Ed.), *Culture, communication, and cognition: Vygotskian perspectives* (pp. 1–18). Cambridge, U.K.: Cambridge University Press.

Wertsch, J. V. (1985b). *Vygotsky and the social formation of the mind*. Cambridge, MA: Harvard University Press.

Wertsch, J. V. (1992). L. S. Vygotsky and contemporary developmental psychology. *Developmental Psychology, 28*(4), 548–557.

Wertsch, J. V. (Ed.) (1985a). *Culture and cognition: Vygotskian perspectives*. Cambridge, U.K.: Cambridge University Press.

Wood, D., Bruner, J. S., & Ross, G. (1976). The role of tutoring in problem-solving. *Journal of Child Psychology and Psychiatry*, 17, 89–100.

PART IV

Social-Context Theories

As indicated by Vygotsky's cultural-historical theory, the social setting is a powerful influence on cognitive development. Other aspects of social influences on the individual are addressed by Albert Bandura's social–cognitive theory and Bernard Weiner's attribution theory.

The primary mechanism in social–cognitive theory is that individuals learn from observing the behaviors of others and the social consequences of those actions. Both live models and the symbolic models portrayed in the mass media are sources for learning. Factors that influence learning are the characteristics of the model and the learner's ability to process the observed events. The acquisition of skilled or accomplished performance, however, depends also on the learner's belief that he or she can execute the complex skill, referred to as perceived self-efficacy.

In contrast, attribution theory addresses individuals' perceived causes of events or outcomes. Attribution research analyzes the ways that individuals arrive at causal explanations and the implications of those beliefs. Focusing on achievement outcomes, Weiner identified the major causes cited for success and failure and the conceptual and emotional links to subsequent behavior. The influence of teacher reactions to success and failure and the effects of learning-oriented and performance-oriented classrooms on students also are discussed.

CHAPTER 11

Albert Bandura's Social–Cognitive Learning Theory

A major function of thought is to enable people to predict events and to develop ways to control those (events) that affect their lives (Bandura, 1995, p. 6).

Social–cognitive theory began with Albert Bandura's clinical work with snake-phobic patients. Their observations of former patients handing snakes was a more effective therapy technique than persuasion and observations of others. The patients observed relevant peers (former patients), abstracted information from their behavior, made decisions about which behaviors to implement (such as stroking a snake), and enacted them.

Early works identified the role of behavioral models in the learning of both prosocial and antisocial behaviors (Bandura, 1969, 1971a; Bandura & Walters, 1963) and the role of models in the modification of behavior (Bandura, 1965, 1971b). The theory then identified several social and cognitive factors that influence learning. Included are the capabilities of using symbols and engaging in intentional and purposive actions. Also included in the theory are the influences of the media on the values, attitudes, and behavior styles of the observers (Bandura, 1986).

Since the 1980s, the concepts of perceived self-efficacy and self-regulated learning have become a major focus of the theory. Self-efficacy refers to personal beliefs about one's capabilities to be successful in tasks with novel or ambiguous elements (Bandura, 1977a, 1997). Self-regulated learning refers to (1) students' proactive efforts to mobilize emotional, cognitive, and environmental resources during learning and (2) self-observation, judgment, and reaction to one's progress (Bandura, 1986; Schunk & Zimmerman, 1998).

PRINCIPLES OF LEARNING

Albert Bandura's social–cognitive theory seeks to explain learning in the naturalistic setting. Unlike the laboratory setting, the social milieu provides numerous opportunities for individuals to acquire complex skills and abilities through the observation of modeled behaviors and the behavioral consequences.

Basic Assumptions

The assumptions of social–cognitive theory address the nature of the learning process and the outcomes of learning.

The Nature of the Learning Process

The definition of observational learning in social–cognitive theory is based on identified weaknesses in prior views of imitative learning.

Other Views of Imitative Learning.   Some theories maintained that the learner imitates a modeled behavior and is reinforced for the imitation, and later repeats the behavior. Other theories maintained that behavior imitation was the result of a particular relationship between the child and the adult. Examples include the child's identification with the same-sex parent, nurturance, power, envy, and others.

However, Bandura (1969) notes that these mechanisms are insufficient to explain much of the child's imitative behavior. For example, the learning of sex-role behaviors is facilitated by a variety of events. Included are the pink or blue treatment of the nursery, parental selection of particular clothing and toys, and parental reinforcement for sex-appropriate activities (Bandura, 1969, p. 215).

Early studies of observational learning also indicated that a nurturant relationship is not a prerequisite for imitation. Furthermore, fear of an aggressor is not a sufficient condition for imitation of aggressive behaviors. Instead, the appeal for imitating an aggressor is that dominance through physical and verbal force leads to possession of material resources and control over others.

Like prosocial behaviors, theories have proposed a variety of mechanisms to account for antisocial behavior. One belief is that frustration activates a frustration drive that then produces aggression. However, the term *frustration* is not a unidimensional state. Instead, it includes a variety of aversive conditions such as physical assault, insult, deprivation, harassment, goal blocking, and defeat (Bandura, 1979, p. 329).

More important, the aversive stimulation from these conditions leads to a variety of responses. Examples include withdrawal and resignation, achievement, self-anesthetization with drugs and alcohol, and aggression. Further, millions of people live in a state of deprivation. Yet comparatively few of those deprived engage in civil disturbances. The important question for social scientists, therefore, is not why aggression occurs in such conditions but why a majority of the ghetto population is resigned to dismal living conditions in the midst of affluence (Bandura, 1979, p. 333).

Other views of learning also assumed a unidimensional relationship between the individual and the environment. That is, either the environment or the individual is a controlling factor in learning. However, Bandura maintained that this simple relationship did not account for the development of complex behaviors.

Assumptions about Learning.   Prior theories have proposed a variety of mechanisms to account for the learning of prosocial and antisocial behaviors. Excluded from these explanations, however, is that the learner can (1) abstract a range of information from observing the behavior of others, and (2) make decisions about which behaviors to adopt and enact. A basic assumption of social–cognitive theory is that this observational and decision-making process is a key mechanism in the acquisition of both prosocial and antisocial behaviors.

Further, the acquisition of complex behaviors is not explained by a simple bidirectional relationship between the environment and the individual. Instead, most environmental influences on behavior are mediated by a variety of internal personal factors. Therefore, Bandura (1978) includes in his explanation of learning the three factors first proposed by Kurt Lewin. They are behavior (B), the environment (E), and the internal events that influence perceptions and actions (P). In Bandura's view, a three-way interlocking relationship, referred to as **reciprocal determinism**, exists among these three factors. For example, after assertiveness training, an individual's behavior activates new environmental reactions (Bandura, 1977b). These reactions, in turn, generate self-confidence in the individual, which then mediates future behavior.

The relationships between the environment, internal events, and behaviors are often complex and subtle. Certain personal attributes, such as sex or race, often activate differential social treatment. The individual's self-conception, in turn, is influenced by the treatment such that biases are either altered or maintained. Also, the relative influence exerted by each of the factors will vary across individuals and situations. For example, behavior and its intrinsic feedback is a major influence for people who play the piano for their own enjoyment. In contrast, when deciding which book to check out of the library, cognitive factors are dominant (Bandura, 1986, p. 24).

The Outcomes of Learning

Most theories equate learning and performance or accept performance as an indicator that learning had in fact occurred. In contrast, Bandura believes that individuals acquire internal codes of behavior that may or may not be performed later. Therefore, learning and performance are regarded as two separate events. Learning is defined as the acquisition of symbolic representations in the form of verbal or visual codes that serve as guidelines for future behavior. An example is a child who sees an older boy in a fight with the class bully. Admiration from classmates may lead the observer to conclude that fighting in certain circumstances is both acceptable and rewarding. The younger child acquires both a set of behaviors and a tendency to enact the behaviors at a later point in time.

Visual codes consist of abstractions of the distinctive features of events instead of merely mental copies (Bandura, 1986). Included are activities, places, and objects. Examples are tennis, New Orleans, and the Eiffel Tower. Verbal codes include language symbols, numbers, musical notations, Morse code, and others (Bandura, 1971b). The importance of symbolic codes, both visual and verbal, is that they include a great deal of information in an easily stored form (Bandura, 1977b, p. 26).

In summary, three assumptions support social learning theory. First, the learning process requires both the cognitive processing and decision making skills of the learner. Second, learning is a three-way interlocking relationship between the environment, personal factors, and behavior. Third, learning results in the acquisition of verbal and visual codes of behavior that may or may not later be performed.

The Components of Learning

In the naturalistic setting, individuals learn new behaviors through the observation of models and through the effects of their own actions. The components of learning are (1) the behavioral model, (2) the consequences of the modeled behavior, (3) the learner's internal processes, and (4) perceived self-efficacy.

Behavior, however, is demonstrated and observed in a variety of settings and under different conditions. For learning to occur, the modeled behavior, the reinforcement, and the learner's cognitive processing must meet certain requirements.

The Behavioral Model

Key issues in the role of the behavioral model are the effects of models, the types of modeling stimuli, the model characteristics, and the characteristics of observers.

The Effects of Models.   The primary function of the modeled behavior is to transmit information to the observer. This function may occur in any one of three different ways. One is that modeled behavior serves as a social prompt to initiate similar behavior in others. For example, a guest at an elaborate dinner party may observe the hostess in order to select the piece of silver appropriate for each course.

On the darker side, sensational crimes also serve as cues for copycat acts that erupt after the publicized event. For example, after the first airplane hijacking to Cuba in 1961, subsequent hijackings eventually involved 71 different countries over the next 14 years (Bandura, 1979, p. 325). A current concern about the extensive media coverage of school shootings is that repetitions of video reports of the incidents accompanied by national attention is a powerful cue to individuals who may feel disenfranchised by society.

The second effect of modeling is to strengthen or weaken the learner's existing restraints against the performance of particular behaviors. Individuals' restraints typically are strengthened if the model receives punishment or other aversive consequences for the behavior.

The weakening of the learner's restraints toward the performance of particular behaviors can occur in two ways. One is the lack of punishment for reprehensible behavior (discussed in detail later in this chapter). The other is the modeling of defensible violence, which adds legitimacy to the use of violence as a solution to problems (Bandura, 1973, p. 33). Verbal and physical abuse by authority figures to restrain rioters is an example. Repeated exposure to such models results in a weakening of the individual's restraints on the use of aggressive solutions.

The third influence of modeling is to demonstrate new patterns of behavior. Models are particularly important in the socialization process of both children and adults. Language, mores, familial customs, as well as educational, social, and political practices are modeled in countless situations.

Types of Modeling Stimuli.   Defined functionally, a model consists of an organized stimulus array such that an observer can extract and act on the main information. The two principal types of modeling stimuli are live and symbolic models. Live models include family members, friends, work associates, and others with whom the individual has direct contact.

Symbolic models, in contrast, are pictorial representations of behavior. In contemporary American society, the greatest range of exposure to models is through the mass media. Symbolic models have supplanted the role of direct experience in learning about different aspects of the world (Bandura, 1982a, 1986). For example, the individual's only knowledge of an operating room, a criminal courtroom, a jail, and other settings may be from the mass media. Further, one report indicates that, by school age, a child will have spent more time watching television than would be spent in a college classroom (Gerbner & Gross, 1976, p. 176). Other reports indicate that children engage in more television viewing than in any other activity except sleeping (Berk, 1989; Carpenter, Huston, & Spear, 1989; Huston, Watkins, & Kunkel, 1989). Another report states that a typical adult spends three hours each day watching television (Robinson & Godbey, 1997).

Television, however, is not real life. The cultural view often fostered by the mass media is one in which family problems are resolved in less than an hour, the criminal is always brought to justice, and the criminal's victims experience little pain or suffering. These "facts of life" are the hidden curriculum that no one teaches but that everyone learns (Gerbner, 1974). Thus, the viewer's knowledge about many settings is based on a symbolic fictional reality, and may be distorted.

Characteristics of Models.   An important factor in the learning process is the degree to which the model is attended to by the learner. Some models, such as regular associates and peers, are more effective than others in attracting the learner's attention. For young children, both peer and adult models play an important role in the socialization process.

Responsiveness to models is influenced by three situational characteristics (Bandura, 1986, p. 207). One is the particular attributes or characteristics of the model. Important model characteristics are relevance and credibility for the observers. Models who have an impact on observers may be prestigious, appear to deserve trust, portray consensus in a group, offer believable standards to guide observers' aspirations, or provide realistic reference figures for observer comparison (Rosenthal & Bandura, 1978, p. 636).

In the classroom, observing success on school tasks achieved by those who are similar in age and competence should enhance the likelihood of observational learning (Schunk, 1987). In one study, children deficient in subtraction skills improved their performance after observing both the teacher and peer models solve problems (Schunk & Hanson, 1985).

The second factor that influences responsiveness to a model is uncertainty about a particular course of action. In such situations, the observer is likely to attend to the behavior of a prestigious model. Cues such as general appearance, speech, style, age, and signs of expertise are interpreted as indicators of past successes (Bandura, 1986, p. 208). Of importance, however, is that these characteristics exert the greatest influence when the consequences of the modeled action are unknown (Bandura, 1986).

The third stimulus characteristic that influences learning is the degree of intrinsic reward already present in the situation. Watching television is an example. The activity itself is satisfying to the observer (Bandura, 1971c).

Observer Characteristics.   In addition to situational characteristics, the nature of the observer also affects responsiveness to modeling influences (Bandura, 1986). Some research indicates that those who lack self-confidence and have low self-esteem are especially prone to adopt the behavior of successful models. Such characteristics may in part explain tendencies of teenagers to emulate the dress and hairstyles of rock stars, for example.

However, when modeling is used explicitly to develop competencies, those who are more talented and venturesome are likely to derive the greatest benefit from observing proficient models (Bandura, 1986, p. 208). In other words, individuals with clear goals select models that are examples of valued skills. These observers differ greatly from insecure observers who turn to others because they lack confidence in their own abilities (Bandura, 1986, p. 208).

Summary.   Behaviors performed by models are an essential component of learning in the naturalistic setting. The primary function of the modeled behavior is to transmit information to the observer in any of three different ways. They are (1) to serve as a cue for similar behavior in others, (2) to strengthen or weaken the learner's existing restraints against the performance of particular behaviors, and (3) to demonstrate new patterns of behavior.

The two principal types of models are live and symbolic. Live models are family members, teachers, friends, work associates, and others in the immediate social setting. Symbolic models are pictorial examples of behavior, such as the mass media. However, media often present fictional views of the world. Thus, the observer may obtain distorted views of various settings.

Three situational characteristics influence observer reactions to models. They are the attributes of the model, the extent of uncertainty about a particular course of action, and the degree of intrinsic reward present in the situation.

Responsiveness to models is also influenced by observer characteristics. Some research indicates that observers who lack self-confidence are likely to adopt the behaviors of successful models. However, when modeling is used to develop particular competencies, the talented and adventuresome observers are most likely to derive the greatest benefit from the modeling.

The Consequences of Behavior

Operant conditioning includes only consequences that impinge directly on the learner for behavior that he or she has executed. In contrast, social–cognitive theory also includes two other types. They are vicarious consequences and self-imposed consequences. Vicarious consequences are associated with the observed behaviors of others. That is, a model receives reinforcement or punishment for a particular behavior, and the consequence to the model generates emotional effects in the observer. The two types of such consequences are vicarious reinforcement and vicarious punishment. Also important in learning are the interactions of vicarious and self-imposed consequences with the direct consequences that the environment delivers for performance.

Vicarious Reinforcement. For vicarious reinforcement to occur, (1) a model must be reinforced for the execution of particular behavior, and (2) positive emotional reactions must be aroused in the observer. This effect is used extensively by television commercials. For example, a well-known actress eats a particular low-calorie food and demonstrates her weight loss. A handsome actor dressed in a tuxedo demonstrates the features of a luxury car and then joins other expensively dressed people going to a party. In these situations, the vicarious reinforcement for a particular group of viewers is the positive feelings associated with being slim or acquiring social status.

Similarly, when playing a slot machine, for example, one sees and hears the other players win (Kazdin, 1989, p. 197). The loud noises and flashing lights announce the winners to others. Similarly, advertisements of contests often include reports of happy previous winners that may elicit positive emotional reactions in certain readers.

In addition to emotional reactions, vicarious reinforcement also conveys information about which behaviors are appropriate in which settings. A third effect occurs when the modeled behavior is repeatedly reinforced. When outcomes are viewed as personally attainable, seeing others reinforced for successful behaviors arouses expectations of similar results in observers. The observer anticipates the same reinforcement consequences for enactment of the same or similar behaviors. In other words, the model's continued reinforcement for a behavior predicts success for the observer. Such behaviors are described as having acquired *functional value* (Bandura, 1971b). (See Table 11.1 for a summary of the three effects.)

In one semester-long observational study of a third-grade classroom (Goetz, 1976), the children indicated that finishing on time, getting the right answers, and

TABLE 11.1
Primary effects of vicarious consequences

Vicarious Reinforcement	Vicarious Punishment
Conveys information about which behaviors are appropriate in which settings	Conveys information about which behaviors are inappropriate in which settings
Arousal of the emotional responses of pleasure and satisfaction in the observer	Tends to exert restraining influence on imitation of modeled behavior (inhibitory effect)
After repeated reinforcements, incentive-motivational effects are generated; behavior acquires functional value.	Tends to devalue the model's status since a functional behavior was not transmitted

mastering the subject were important. These behaviors earned time for fun activities and had acquired functional value for the children.

Vicarious Punishment.   Like vicarious reinforcement, punishment received by a model tends to convey three primary effects. First, information is conveyed about behaviors that are likely to be punished and are therefore inappropriate. Second, a restraining influence on imitative aggressive actions is also likely to occur (inhibitory effect).

Finally, because the behavior transmitted to the observers was unsuccessful, the model's status is likely to be devalued. If the model enacts a behavior highly prized by a peer group, such as challenging unfair treatment, punishment may enhance the model's status.[1] Usually, however, the model's status is devalued.

Other outcomes may occur as the result of the presence or absence of punishment. One outcome is that of altering the observer's valuation of reinforcing agents (Bandura, 1977b, p. 51). The misuse of power generates resentment in observers and undermines the legitimacy of the agent's power. The observation of inequitable punishment may release angry observers from self-censure of their own behavior. The result is increased transgression rather than compliance. An example is that of excessive police reaction to crimes committed in certain urban neighborhoods or by members of particular subgroups in society. Outbreaks of vandalism and riots by other members of the subgroup often follow (Figure 11.1).

The Absence of Punishment.   The anticipation of punishment usually restrains the imitation of forbidden actions. However, when individuals are not punished for transgressions, the information conveyed is that of implicit acceptance. An example is a classroom in which the teacher is careless about monitoring examinations and cheating occurs. If the cheating goes unpunished, others are more inclined to cheat on the next examination. The behavior has acquired functional value through the omission of punishment.

---

[1] Status is most likely to be enhanced by punishment for principled conduct. Personal communication from Albert Bandura, July 27, 1983.

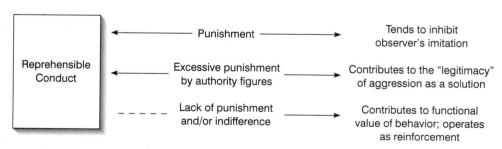

FIGURE 11.1
Some effects of consequences for reprehensible conduct

Similarly, when aggressive actions go unpunished or when people respond approvingly or indifferently, aggression is viewed as both acceptable and expected in similar circumstances (Bandura, 1973, p. 129). Aggression acquires functional value for the observer.

The lack of punishment for forbidden actions has important implications for the classroom. In one group of junior high classrooms, for example, some of the new teachers ignored students' initial disruptive actions and continued to teach or to wait until the situation was out of hand before trying to get order (Moskowitz-Hayman, 1976, p. 288). By the end of the school year, in one class, students were throwing chairs, pencils, and books; walking around the room; slapping each other; and humming, singing, and talking out loud. The importance of addressing disruptive actions early and consistently also is supported by a number of other classroom studies (see Doyle, 1986; Good & Brophy, 1987).

The absence of adverse consequences to the model fulfills a useful purpose in situations such as the treatment of phobic patients. Snake-phobic patients, for example, experienced reduced fear and anxiety after observing models handle snakes who did not incur adverse consequences.

The influence of vicarious consequences, however, is relative rather than absolute. The extent of the influence varies with the observer's valuation of the type of outcome and the type of behavior (Bandura, 1977b, p. 119). In addition, observed consequences are of minimal influence if observers believe that the model's contingencies do not apply to them. For example, the physical aggression of a soldier is unlikely to enhance imitative aggression in the average citizen (Bandura, 1971b). Moreover, both vicarious and direct reinforcement are operating together in most situations. Therefore, the separate effects of either type are difficult to determine.

Self-Reinforcement.   Both direct and vicarious reinforcement involve consequences delivered by the environment. Gold stars awarded for attendance, prizes won on television quiz shows, and minimal prison terms imposed for heinous crimes are dispensed to individuals by some member or agent of society, and they may influence the behavior of others. Self-reinforcement, on the other hand, is independent of the consequences delivered by society. Furthermore, it must be consciously cultivated by the individual. Young children respond to immediate physical consequences (food and physical contact) and other material rewards. Then, symbolic consequences, including social reactions of approval and disapproval, followed by social contracting arrangements, become reinforcing or punishing. Finally, individuals become capable of establishing self-evaluative and self-produced consequences (Bandura, 1978, p. 103).

Self-reinforcement involves three subsidiary elements. They are (1) a self-prescribed standard of behavior, (2) reinforcing events under the control of the individual, and (3) the individual as his or her own reinforcing agent.

In general, individuals establish performance standards for themselves and tend to respond to their behavior in self-rewarding ways if their performance matches or exceeds the standard. Similarly, they respond in self-criticizing ways if their performance fails to meet the standard. Thus, although humans—like rats and chimpanzees—respond to reinforcement, the human capacity for thought and self-direction sets the species apart. Unlike human beings, "rats and chimpanzees are disinclined to pat themselves on the back for commendable performances, or to berate themselves for getting lost in the cul-de-sacs" (Bandura, 1971b, p. 249).

Interactions with External Consequences.   An important characteristic of self-imposed consequences is that they often operate together with external consequences (Bandura, 1974). These two sources of reinforcement either conflict with or supplement each other. When external rewards are outweighed by self-condemnation, external rewards are relatively ineffective. An example is the student who seeks to earn an *A* grade in every course. Earning a *B* in a particular course in which others earn *C*s and *D*s does not meet the individual's standards. Earning the highest grade is small consolation.

A second type of conflict that can occur is that of external punishment delivered by the environment for behaviors that the individual values highly (and therefore believes are worthy of reward). Nonconformists, dissenters, and, at the extreme, martyrs are in this category. For the latter group, their sense of self-worth is so strongly linked to particular beliefs that they suffer pain and even death rather than relinquish their values.

Summary.   Like operant conditioning, the consequences of behavior are essential to learning in social–cognitive theory. However, unlike operant conditioning, the theory incorporates other consequences in addition to reinforcement for behaviors that the learner executes. They are vicarious and self-imposed consequences. In vicarious reinforcement, the model is reinforced for a particular behavior, and positive emotional reactions are aroused in the observer. Vicarious reinforcement also conveys information about appropriate behaviors. Further, repeated reinforcements to the model for behaviors that the observer views as personally attainable raise expectations of similar results for the observer. Such behaviors have functional value for the observer.

Similarly, vicarious punishment delivered to a model also conveys three primary effects. First, information is conveyed about behaviors that are inappropriate. Second, punishment to the model exerts an inhibitory effect on imitation for the observer. Third, the model's status is devalued. Excessive punishment, however, can release observers from the self-censure of their own behavior.

In contrast to punishment for inappropriate behaviors, the absence of punishment implies implicit acceptance for those behaviors. For example, when aggression goes unpunished or is responded to indifferently, it is viewed as acceptable and expected in similar circumstances. The implication for the classroom is that disruptive actions should be addressed early and consistently.

Although important, the influences of vicarious consequences on observers are relative rather than absolute. The extent of influence varies with the observer's valuation of the outcome and the behavior and the importance of the model.

Unlike direct and vicarious reinforcement, self-reinforcement is delivered by the individual for his or her own behavior. In general, individuals establish performance standards for themselves and tend to respond to their behavior in self-rewarding ways if their performance matches or exceeds the standard. They also tend to respond in self-critical ways if the performance fails to meet the standard.

Self-imposed consequences also often operate in conjunction with external consequences. When external rewards are outweighed by self-censure, external rewards are relatively ineffective. Also, when external punishment is delivered for behaviors the individual values highly, it has little effect.

The Learner's Internal Processes

In social–cognitive theory, cognitive processes play a central role in learning. The learner's ability to code and store transitory experiences in symbolic form and to represent future consequences in thought are essential to the acquisition and modification of human behavior.

The cognitive processing of events and potential consequences guide the learner's behavior. For example, homeowners do not wait until their houses are burning to buy insurance. Instead, knowledge of the potential loss that can be the consequence of no insurance is the stimulus that prompts individuals to invest in homeowner's protection (Bandura, 1971b).

Four component processes are responsible for learning and performance. They are attention, retention, motor production, and motivational processes (Bandura, 1971a, 1977b). The relationships between the behavioral model, the learner's cognitive processes, and learning and performance are illustrated in Figure 11.2.

Attentional Processes.   New behaviors cannot be acquired unless they are attended to and accurately perceived (Bandura, 1977b). The learner's attentional

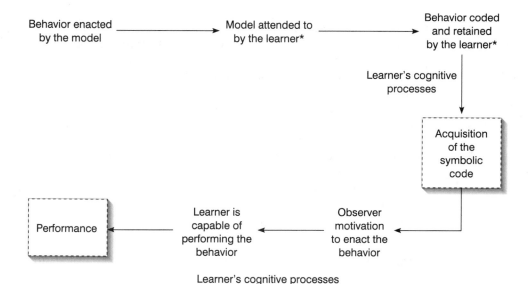

*Facilitated by reinforcement to the model

FIGURE 11.2
Sequence of steps in observational learning according to social–cognitive theory

processes, however, are influenced by a variety of factors. Included are the model's characteristics, characteristics and functional value of the behavior, and observer characteristics. Behavior that is successful for the model tends to be attended to and coded by the observer.

Characteristics of the behaviors that influence attention include complexity and relevance. For example, long verbal sequences are too complex for young children to process. However, they are able to process visually presented models that are accompanied by a high degree of verbal repetition. The animal characters and dialogue in "Sesame Street" are an example.

Relevance, in general, refers to the importance of the behavior to the observer. Learning to drive a car, for example, is relevant for a teenager but not for a 2-year-old child.

Among the observer characteristics that influence attentional processes are perceptual set, observational skills, arousal level, past performance, and sensory capacities (Bandura, 1977b, p. 23). The learner's arousal level and perceptual set influence the selection of activities to be observed, whereas observational skills influence the accuracy of processing.

Learning from models also depends on the observer's skill in monitoring and interpreting ongoing events. Preschool children, for example, typically believe that an instant replay on television is a new example of the same event (Rice, Huston, & Wright, 1986). Also, Huston et al. (1989, p. 426) note that preschool children typically do not differentiate between program content and commercials. Thus, developmental differences in abstracting information from symbolic models influence the interpretation of events.

Retention Processes.   These processes are responsible for the symbolic coding of the behavior and the storage of the visual or verbal codes in memory. These processes are important because the learner cannot benefit from the observed behaviors in the model's absence unless they are coded and retained for later use (Bandura, 1977b).

An important retention process is rehearsal. Both mental rehearsal, in which individuals imagine themselves enacting the behavior, and motor rehearsal (overt action) serve as important memory aids. Mental rehearsal requires that the learner internally represent the absent events. These representations can then guide the motor rehearsal.

Retention processes are, of course, influenced by the learner's development. The ability to represent behaviors in the form of labels and to generate verbal and visual cues enhance retention.

Motor Reproduction Processes.   After the observer has acquired a symbolic code, performance of the acquired behaviors depends on the learner's motor reproduction and motivational processes. Motor reproduction includes the selection and organization of responses at the cognitive level, followed by their execution (Bandura, 1977b). Like the processes of retention, motor reproduction is influenced by the developmental level of the individual.

Motivational Processes.   The three processes that function in observational learning as motivators are direct (external) reinforcement, vicarious reinforcement, and self-reinforcement. During the modeling of behavior, reinforcement to the model (vicarious reinforcement for the observer) is important in motivating the learner to attend to and code the observed behavior.

The Role of Self-Efficacy

The construct labeled self-efficacy refers to beliefs about one's capabilities and these beliefs also motivate learners in particular ways. Important issues in self-efficacy are the essential characteristics, the sources of efficacy beliefs, and the effects on psychological processes.

Definition.   Perceived self-efficacy refers to a belief in one's capabilities to organize and execute the actions necessary to manage particular situations (Bandura, 1995, p. 2). Such judgments typically apply to situations that may include novel, unpredictable, or often stressful elements (Bandura, 1986; Bandura & Schunk, 1981).

Self-efficacy differs from self-concept in that self-concept is a general assessment. It is a global construct that includes several self-reactions (such as one's perceptions of popularity) (see Bong & Clark, 1999, for a discussion of the differences). Self-efficacy, in contrast, is a content-related judgment and, in the academic sphere, it refers to the belief that one can perform particularly academic tasks successfully (Zimmerman, 1995a, p. 218).

Efficacy expectations should not be confused with response–outcome expectations. A response–outcome expectancy is the belief that a particular behavior will lead to certain outcomes. However, an efficacy expectation is the belief in one's capability to execute the required behavior successfully (Bandura, 1977b, p. 193). For example, the anticipated social recognition, applause, trophies, and self-satisfaction for the highest broad jump are outcome expectations. The belief that one can successfully high jump 6 feet is an efficacy judgment (Bandura, 1986, p. 391).

Perceived self-efficacy involves self-appraisal; it is not a fixed act, and it involves more than simply knowing what to do (Bandura, 1982b). Included in the self-appraisal are both personal and situational factors. For example, students who are capable of mastering a situation often make judgments that indicate they consider themselves to be inadequate (Zimmerman, 1986). University students often find their career options limited because they fear taking courses that involve quantitative methods (Henderson, 1986).

Faulty self-appraisal can, on occasion, lead to high self-efficacy that may be inaccurate. For example, in mathematics, children sometimes rely on "buggy algorithms." They are the systematic, but inaccurate strategies that children often use in solving arithmetic problems. Knowledge of such strategies and being able to apply them well (they sometimes lead to correct answers) lead to a false sense of self-efficacy (Schunk, 1995, p. 214).

Sources of Efficacy Beliefs.   Four types of influence contribute to individuals' beliefs about their personal efficacy (Bandura, 1986; 1995). They are mastery experiences, vicarious experiences, social persuasion, and physiological and emotional states.

Mastery experiences provide the most authentic evidence about the individual's capabilities of mustering the resources required for success (Bandura, 1982a; 1995). Success tends to raise the judgment of efficacy, whereas repeated failures lower the judgment. For the individual who has a strong sense of efficacy, occasional failure will affect judgment very little. In contrast, failure is influential for individuals who are unsure of their abilities.

Mastery experiences designed to enhance students' self-efficacy should not consist of easy successes. Individuals who experience only easy successes are easily discouraged by failure because they tend to expect quick results (Bandura, 1995). Also, developing a sense of efficacy through mastery experiences must involve acquiring the cognitive and behavioral capabilities for executing appropriate courses of action (p. 3). Then after individuals are convinced that they have the capabilities required to succeed, they are able to persevere in the face of setbacks.

Vicarious experiences provided by social models also contribute to self-efficacy. Observing similar individuals perform successfully can raise one's appraisals of efficacy. Vicarious experiences are particularly influential when people have had little or no direct experience in a situation. The models also demonstrate effective strategies for managing environmental demands and positive attitudes (Bandura, 1995, p. 4).

The third source of efficacy beliefs, verbal persuasion, can help counter an individual's mild self-doubts. Persuasion can assist individuals to avoid a focus on their personal deficiencies and to measure success in terms of improvement rather than outperforming others. However, persuasion cannot, in the absence of other influences, develop high beliefs of personal efficacy.

Physiological and emotional states also provide information about efficacy. Individuals tend to interpret stress reactions and tension as indicators of vulnerability to poor performance (Bandura, 1995, p. 4). Therefore, one way to alter personal efficacy is to reduce stress and negative emotional tendencies. In addition, individuals should learn to interpret the first signs of tension as an indicator that more focused effort is needed. Individuals with high self-efficacy tend to perceive heightened tension as a signal to energize one's efforts.

Effects on Psychological Processes.   Self-efficacy beliefs influence human functioning indirectly through four major processes. They are cognitive, motivational, affective, and selection processes (Bandura, 1995). Those with high self-efficacy construct success scenarios, whereas individuals with low self-efficacy do not. In specific, demanding situations, high self-efficacy contributes to continued analytical thinking, whereas low self-efficacy is accompanied by erratic strategies and thought processes (Wood & Bandura, 1989).

Efficacy beliefs enhance or limit motivation by influencing the types of goals that individuals set for themselves, the extent of effort they expend, and their persistence in the face of difficulties. A low sense of efficacy contributes to a slackening of effort and the tendency to give up easily.

Affective processes that are influenced by personal efficacy include anxiety, frustration, and depression (Bandura, 1993; 1995). A sense of efficacy assists in controlling disturbing thoughts and by supporting coping behaviors in difficult situations. For smokers, for example, research indicates that perceived self-efficacy in resisting smoking in stressful situations is related to relapses and the reinstitution of self-control after a relapse. Those with low self-efficacy relapse completely (Bandura, 1982b, p. 131). In other words, high self-efficacy contributes to the creation of a positive psychological environment for individuals that enables them to manage difficult situations.

Finally, efficacy beliefs influence the types of activities and environments that individuals choose (Bandura, 1995). Specifically, people avoid activities and environments that they believe are beyond their coping capabilities (p. 10). In contrast, individuals with a strong sense of efficacy approach difficult tasks as challenges to be mastered. Such an outlook, in turn, fosters personal accomplishment (Bandura, 1986).

Table 11.2 summarizes the task-related and long-term effects of high and low self-efficacy. As indicated, individuals with low self-efficacy focus attention on their deficiencies, set lower aspirations, and avoid the particular enriching environments that can enhance their competencies. Also of interest is that self-efficacy beliefs contribute to predictions of mathematics performance (Pajares, 1996; Pajares & Graham,

TABLE 11.2

Comparison of the effects of perceived high and low efficacy

	High Self-efficacy	**Low Self-efficacy**
Task-related behavior	1. Effort is strengthened in the face of difficulties	1. Efforts slacken.
	2. Already-acquired skills are intensified and strengthened in the face of difficulties.	2. Task may be given up altogether in the face of difficulties.
	3. Effort and attention are focused on the demands of the situation.	3. Attention is focused on personal deficiencies and difficulties; these problems are magnified.
Long-term effects	4. Aids self-development through precipitating involvement in a variety of activities and experiences.	4. Hinders development by facilitating the avoidance of enriching environments and activities
	5. Individual experiences little stress in taxing situations.	5. Individual suffers anxiety and stress in a variety of performance situations
	6. Typically leads to lack of effort rather than lack of ability as the cause for failure	6. Undermines the effective use of one's skills by directing attention to personal shortcomings
	7. Leads to goals that are challenging that sustain interest and involvement	7. Leads to lowered aspirations as a mechanism for avoiding stress

Note: Summarized from *Social Foundations of Thought and Action: A Social–Cognitive Theory* by A. Bandura, 1986, Upper Saddle River, NJ: Prentice Hall.

1996), writing achievement (Pajares, Miller, & Johnson 1999; Zimmerman & Bandura, 1994), and differentiate between high and low achievers in high school (Zimmerman & Martinez-Pons 1986).

Summary.   Perceived self-efficacy is the learner's belief in his or her capabilities to successfully manage situations that may include novel or unpredictable elements. Perceived self-efficacy involves self-appraisal and it is not a fixed act. Students with similar academic abilities may differ in their sense of efficacy for particular subjects.

The four types of influence that contribute to efficacy beliefs are mastery experiences, vicarious experiences, social persuasion, and physiological and emotional states. Mastery experiences in which individuals acquire essential cognitive and behavioral skills for the situation and experience success are the most authentic evidence about capabilities. Vicarious experiences can be helpful when the observer can identify with the model and verbal persuasion can help counter mild self-doubts. Physiological and emotional states that signal vulnerability to poor performance to the individual should be reduced or interpreted as a signal for increased effort.

Self-efficacy beliefs affect human functioning indirectly by influencing individuals' cognitive, motivational, affective, and selection processes. Individuals with high self-efficacy construct success scenarios, set challenging goals, persist in the face of difficulties, and control disturbing thoughts. Also, choices of activities, tasks, and even career choices are influenced by self-efficacy. Individuals avoid situations that they believe are beyond their coping abilities.

The Nature of Complex Learning

Unlike other theories, social–cognitive theory does not describe the forms of thinking and/or behavior that represent complex learning. Instead, the theory describes the factors essential to the attainment of superior performance in any domain or discipline. According to Bandura (1986), the essential factor in achieving complex capabilities is the individual's self-regulatory system. Important topics are the components of the system and the ways in which the self-regulatory system develops.

Personal, Behavioral, and Environmental Influences.   A major goal of the self-regulatory system is to regulate the sources of personal, behavioral, and environmental influences that affect learning and performance. In addition to strategy knowledge and metacognitive knowledge, personal influences include perceived self-efficacy, learner goals, learner values and interests, perceptions of others (parents, teachers, and peers), and perceptions of learning environments (classrooms, libraries, and homes) (Zimmerman & Martinez-Pons, 1992; Schunk, 1995). Self-regulated learners view learning as a proactive enterprise. They set goals for themselves, are accurate self-monitors, and are resourceful in selecting learning strategies (Zimmerman, 1998).

Self-efficacy is important in self-regulation because it influences both the level at which goals are set and one's responses to failure to meet the preset goals. Goal setting and self-evaluation are critical for superior accomplishments in any area and particularly in the development of innovations. Self-generated standards and reinforcements sustain developments that often are resisted initially by society. In the absence of public recognition, self-reinforcement for meeting one's own standards maintains the artist's or innovator's creative efforts. Highly stringent standards, however, lead to self-created distress (Bandura, 1986). For example, the violinist in the second chair likely began as a prodigy with every expectation of dazzling the world. At 45 and balding, he is the most disappointed man on Earth (Bandura, 1986, p. 357).

The three major behavioral influences are self-observation, self-judgment, and self-reaction. Self-observation requires deliberate attention to one's behavior; whereas self-judgment refers to comparisons of one's present performance with pre-established goals (Schunk, 1995, p. 77). Graham and Harris (1994) describe an anecdote about Ernest Hemingway in terms of these three processes. The author recorded his daily production of words (self-observation) on a mounted chart. If the amount was less than originally planned (self-judgment), Hemingway curtailed his time spent fishing (self-reaction) (p. 206).

Self-observation can be aided by recording key aspects of learning-related behavior. One course designed to help college students required that the students keep an activity log with 30-minute intervals for 1 week. Students often expressed surprise at the data, which indicated the amount of procrastination and non-productive time (Zimmerman, Greenberg, & Weinstein, 1994).

A key environmental influence on self-regulation processes is achievement outcomes. Individuals receive information about achievement, determine whether it meets their goals, and alter their behavior accordingly. If the achievement does not meet the preset goal, the individual may alter his or her strategies, increase effort, or lower the goals.

Measurement Issues. The measurement of any unobservable construct, such as motivation, self-efficacy, or self-regulation, poses problems. Such constructs are not directly observable, and their presence must be inferred from behaviors that have been identified to occur only if individuals possess the particular construct. Measurement typically consists of observations of behavior in experimental or naturalistic settings (using checklists or other instruments) or self-reports of one's thoughts and typical behaviors.

The measurement of self-efficacy and self-regulation faces particular problems. First, although self-efficacy is described as dynamic and not a fixed act, it typically is measured as a fixed set of beliefs. Another problem is that the items on present instruments often consist primarily of cognitive and metacognitive strategies, such as how well the student remembers information.

A third measurement issue is that of separating individuals' assessments of their basic competencies from assessments of their beliefs that they can successfully manage and master situations with novel and ambiguous elements. For example, a study of self-efficacy in relation to writing uses items such as, "When I have written a long or complex paper, I can find and correct all my grammatical errors," "I can rewrite my wordy or confusing sentences clearly," and "I can locate and use appropriate reference sources when I need to document an important point." The differentiation between assessment of one's level of competency with regard to a particular task and beliefs in one's capability to mobilize, direct, and sustain necessary resources, including effort, is not clear. Initial research on the constructs assessed in student self-reports of their self-regulatory capabilities indicate from 3 to 5 subcomponents, depending on the instrument (Gredler & Garavalia, 2000a; Gredler & Schwartz, 1997; Pintrich & DeGroot, 1990).

Fourth, some students tend to overestimate their self-regulatory skills (Pajares, 1996). In one study, 8 entering graduate students with the highest scores on a measure of perceived self-regulatory skills had the lowest Graduate Record Examination and Miller Analogy Test scores (Schwartz & Gredler, 1998). Also, of 225 entering freshmen, provisionally admitted students (with insufficient SAT scores or high school grades) did not differ in their beliefs about their self-regulatory capabilities from fully admitted (qualified) freshmen (Gredler & Garavalia, 2000b).

Further, the measurement of goals in self-efficacy studies typically has been restricted to short-term performance standards. Examples include number of subtraction problems to be solved (Bandura & Schunk, 1981), surpassing customary employee productivity standards by 20% to 25% (Wood & Bandura, 1989), and expected course grade (Zimmerman, Bandura, & Martinez-Pons, 1992). The relationship of these short-term performance standards to intermediate or long-range goals is not clear. Recently, researchers have begun to include process goals (completion of task components) (see Schunk & Ertmer, 1999).

The Development of the Self-Regulatory System

The three-way interaction between personal factors, behavior, and the environment described by Bandura (1977a, 1978, 1986) contributes to the development of the self-regulatory system. A variety of models—teachers, parents, work associates, peers, and others—function as sources of information for standard setting and self-management of behavior. However, people do not passively incorporate everything they hear or see (Bandura, 1986). Instead, personal factors influence the development of generic standards from the behaviors of models in a variety of settings. In early childhood, for example, the approvals and punishments handed out by children to each other and to dolls or stuffed animals indicate the standards acquired by the children through modeling and direct experience (Bandura, 1986, p. 372).

The individual's self-regulated behavior influences the environment. In turn, however, environmental influences contribute to the development of self-monitoring and evaluative skills. They also provide support for the maintenance of internal standards (Bandura, 1986) (Figure 11.3).

Included in external reinforcements are rewards for excellence and negative sanctions for individuals who provide themselves with undeserved self-reward (Bandura, 1977b, 1978; Bandura, Mahoney, & Dirks, 1976). Examples include scholarships and other awards for outstanding academic achievements. Prizes, public acclaim, and monetary rewards reinforce winners of arduous sports events (e.g., the Indianapolis 500, the Wimbledon tennis tournament, and the Olympic Games). Negative sanctions also include public dishonor for cheating performances, such as that of the marathon runner who faked a victory.

FIGURE 11.3
Reciprocal determinism in the development of self-regulatory systems

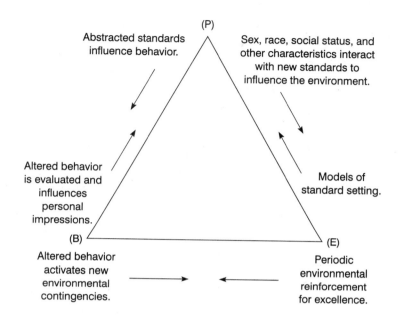

(P)

Abstracted standards influence behavior.

Sex, race, social status, and other characteristics interact with new standards to influence the environment.

Altered behavior is evaluated and influences personal impressions.

Models of standard setting.

(B)

Altered behavior activates new environmental contingencies.

(E)

Periodic environmental reinforcement for excellence.

The behavioral standards used by the individual and the delivery of self-reinforcement depend on the relationship between the particular task and the individual's expertise. A mathematician, for example, would not consider that solving elementary arithmetic problems is deserving of self-reward. On the other hand, a humanities scholar would not devalue his or her poor performance on a test of engineering skills (Bandura, 1971b). Particularly important are the self-reinforcements for engaging in difficult tasks or aversive activities, such as completing homework or speaking up in social situations. Arranged self-reward bridges the gap between initiation of the new behavior and the environmental contingencies that will be activated by competent performance.

Development of Reprehensible Conduct. The three-way interaction between personal factors, environmental factors, and behavior, given different sets of circumstances, also can lead to the disengagement of self-evaluative capabilities. The result is the development and maintenance of reprehensible conduct and inhumane activities (Bandura, 1977a, 1979, 1986). Prior theories have proposed different internal "watchdogs" that are responsible for moral behavior, such as a conscience, a superego, or an internalized moral code. Such theories, however, encounter difficulties when they attempt to explain inhumane conduct by otherwise humane moral persons (Bandura, 1982a, p. 351).

In the social–cognitive analysis, such acts are performed through processes that disengage the behavior from a self-evaluative reaction. Eight types of dissociative practices have been identified that are responsible for this disengagement (Table 11.3). Moral justification renders the behavior honorable by applying the view that the end justifies the means. Euphemistic labels "sanitize" the negative action, and advantageous comparisons attempt to downgrade the deplorable acts. They also create the impression that the behavior is the work of nameless forces. These three practices are applied to the behavior itself. They are effective because they (1) disengage morality from culpable behavior and (2) engage self-approval for doing it well (Bandura, in Evans, 1989, p. 44).

Euphemisms also are extensively used in everyday affairs when people do things for personal benefit that harm others. The extensive 1985 decline in the stock market was described in a memo by one brokerage house as "fourth quarter equity retreat" (Evans, 1989, p. 43).

Two practices, however, are efforts to avoid personal responsibility. Specifically, these tactics involve blaming those in charge or viewing oneself as only one among many. In contrast, three practices focus on the victim. The consequences to the victim may be minimized, or the victim may be viewed as subhuman and therefore incapable of feeling pain. The victim also may be viewed as a partial cause of the reprehensible act.

These practices, of course, do not quickly transform a gentle, law-abiding individual into an aggressor (Bandura, 1982a). Rather, the process is gradual, beginning with the performance of acts that do not lead to excessive self-censure. Then the individual's discomfort and self-reproach are gradually diminished through repeated performances until brutal acts are committed with little distress (Bandura, 1982a, p. 354).

The importance of these analyses is twofold. First, the self system is a critical factor in the development of accomplished skills and capabilities in any field of endeavor. Second, neither the development of self-evaluative reactions nor their disengagement is an automatic process. Rather, a series of particular types of reciprocal interactions between the individual and the environment is required.

Summary.   The self-regulatory system consists of informational cognitive structures on goals, outcomes, and behavior, and cognitive processes that perceive, evaluate, and regulate behavior. The self-system includes standards for one's behavior, self-observation, self-judgment, and self-reaction. The goal of self-regulated learning is to regulate sources of personal, behavioral, and social-environmental sources of influence. Individuals set goals for themselves, pay deliberate attention to their behavior (self-observation), and compare their performance with preset goals (self-judgment). Depending on the comparison, they may reward themselves and set higher goals, exert further effort to meet the goals, or lower the goals.

Achieving accomplished performance in any field requires goal setting and self-evaluation. Familiar examples are concert pianists and other artists. Self-generated standards and reinforcements are particularly important in the development of innovations that often are initially resisted by society. Self-efficacy is important in self-regulation because it influences the individual's choice of activities, effort and persistence, and toleration of failure.

Measurement issues related to self-efficacy and self-regulation include a clear specification of the constructs to be measured and instruments that differentiate between the self-assessment of one's competencies and self-efficacy.

The development of the self-regulatory system depends on the reciprocal three-way interaction between the environment, personal influences, and behavior.

TABLE 11.3
A comparison of disengagement practices for reprehensible conduct

	Practice	Definition	Examples
1.	Moral justification	A practice construed to support moral aims (the end justifies the means)	(a) Killing in warfare is necessary to protect one's way of life, to save humanity from an evil ideology, to preserve world peace, etc. (b) Religious persecution of unbelievers is essential to stamping out evil.
2.	Euphemistic labeling	Rendering pernicious conduct benign by using convoluted verbiage; includes (a) using palliative expressions and (b) attaching legitimate words to illegitimate activities	(a) A corporation is "downsizing" rather than firing employees; mercenaries "fulfill a contract" (rather than kill); in the nuclear industry, a "normal aberration" occurs instead of a nuclear accident. (b) In Watergate, criminal conspiracy was a "game plan," and the conspirators were "team players."
3.	Advantageous comparison	Contrasting deplorable acts with flagrant inhumanities	The slaying of people in Vietnam was compared to the alternative of commitment to enslavement.
4.	Displacement of responsibility	Actions are viewed as springing from the dictates of authorities.	Nazi prison commandants justified unprecedented inhumanities by insisting they were only following orders.
5.	Diffusion of responsibility	The use of division of labor or group decision making to provide anonymity for responsible agents	A CEO's decision to lay off workers is presented to and approved by vice presidents and division heads in a "management decision-making session."
6.	Disregard or distortion of consequences	Includes changing the major issues and/or "whitewashing" data or evidence	(a) The tobacco industry hires scientists to discredit evidence that heavy smoking includes health risks. (b) Rapists convince themselves that the victim "asked for it."
7.	Dehumanization	The portrayal of others in derogatory terms so as to depersonalize them and make them subhuman	The reliance on stereotypes and terms such as "gooks" and "wetbacks."
8.	Attribution of blame	Blaming the victim for the action or consequence	Nazi propaganda included the view that Jews were taking financial success away from "Aryan Germans," therefore they deserved to be punished.

Note: Summarized from *Social Foundations of Thought and Action: A Social–Cognitive Theory* (pp. 376–386) by A. Bandura, 1986, Upper Saddle River, NJ: Prentice Hall.

Individuals abstract information from the behavior of others, and personal factors influence the development of generic standards from those behaviors. The individual's behavior influences both the environment and one's personal reactions. The consequences in the environment, in turn, influence both personal perceptions and subsequent behavior. In some situations, the three-way interaction can lead to the disengagement of self-evaluative capabilities and the development of reprehensible conduct that is sanctioned by some in the environment.

PRINCIPLES OF INSTRUCTION

A theory of instruction has yet to be derived from social–cognitive theory. However, the principles of the theory have major implications for the classroom.

The theory has been implemented successfully in the acquisition of both motor and cognitive skills. Early applications of cognitive skills included linguistic rules, concept formation, and problem solving (see Rosenthal & Zimmerman, 1973, 1976, 1978). In recent years, modeling has been used to teach learning strategies. Examples include finding the main idea in paragraphs, setting up word problems, and monitoring one's own learning. Recall the references to teacher modeling in chapters 7 and 8.

Basic Assumptions

The three major assumptions that support the principles of social–cognitive theory also are applicable to classroom instruction. They are (1) the learner's cognitive processes and decision making are important factors in learning; (2) the three-way interaction between the environment, personal factors, and behavior are responsible for learning; and (3) the outcomes of learning are visual and verbal codes of behavior.

The Components of Instruction

In social–cognitive theory, the essential components of learning are a behavioral model, reinforcement to the model, and the learner's cognitive processing of the modeled behaviors. The components of instruction, therefore, are (1) identifying appropriate models in the classroom, (2) establishing the functional value of behaviors, and (3) guiding the learner's internal processing, which includes facilitating the learner's sense of self-efficacy.

Identifying Appropriate Models
In the classroom, both teachers and students can serve as live models for a variety of academic and social behaviors. For adolescents, the influence of peer models often is emphasized. However, the teacher is responsible for the classroom and is important as a model of responsibility, integrity, sincerity, and concern for both the individual and collective welfare of the students (Brophy & Putnam, 1979, p. 196). At any level of education, the teacher or faculty member should model emotional maturity, ratio-

nality, "common sense," and consistent follow-through on commitments (Brophy & Putnam, 1979).

Community members, such as firefighters, police, doctors, nurses, and other models who are interesting to young children, can be invited to spend some time in the classroom. To be maximally effective, however, a planned program of community involvement is needed. Visits or talks that appear to fill up time or give everyone a break on Friday will be ineffective. They also may convey the message that being a responsible adult is not important and does not contribute to self-worth.

Symbolic models also are effective influences in the development of prosocial behaviors. Research on "Sesame Street" and "Mister Rogers' Neighborhood," for example, indicates that the modeled prosocial behaviors enhance children's cooperativeness and friendliness (see Leifer, 1976).

Both live and symbolic models can teach abstract cognitive rules, problem-solving strategies, and sequences of integrated motor behaviors (see Carroll & Bandura, 1982; Rosenthal & Bandura, 1978; Rosenthal & Zimmerman, 1978).

The selection of a live or symbolic model often depends on practical considerations. For cognitive and motor skills, the advantages of the live model are (1) the physical demonstration of the behavior in front of the students and (2) the opportunities for student questions. The chemistry class in which the use of laboratory equipment often is demonstrated by the teacher is an example.

The major advantage of symbolic modeling is that the models may be viewed more than once by students. In one study, for example, a videotape was used to teach toothbrushing skills to children in Head Start classrooms (Murray & Epstein, 1981). In a project supervised by this author, videotapes of classroom teachers with their classes were made available to undergraduates about to undertake their own student teaching. The undergraduates returned to the tapes several times, reporting that they found something informative and interesting on each viewing.

In addition to the selection of the model, another important consideration is the selection of the behaviors to be modeled. They should be interesting to the observer and portrayed at a level of complexity to be understood by the learner. Also significant are the type and status of the model. Some research indicates that children are more likely to remember the actions of a friendly, powerful person than those of a cold, neutral person (Baldwin, 1973).

Nurturance of the model, however, must be implemented with care in powerful models. Since the young child seeks feedback from nurturant authority figures, expressive features can detract the child's attention away from modeled behaviors. This potential problem can be counteracted by the use of verbal directives focused on the relevant behavior as well as the display of minimal expressive reactions during modeling.

Establishing the Functional Value of the Behavior

According to social–cognitive theory, individuals pay attention to events in the environment that predict reinforcement (Bandura, 1977b, p. 85). They tend to ignore events that do not include reinforcement predictions. Therefore, Bandura (1977b) recommends that instruction should attempt to establish an expectancy for positive outcomes. Such an expectancy increases task attention.

Events that predict reinforcement have acquired functional value for the student and will be attended to. In the classroom, establishing the usefulness of new learning for the students is important. First-grade children, for example, frequently view the purpose of assignments as content coverage rather than content mastery (Anderson, 1981).

Also, in teaching learning strategies, students must learn when to use them and why they are used (the metacognitive knowledge described in chapter 8). For example, skimming is a strategy for previewing the information in a text passage. (It is dysfunctional if used merely to skip difficult words or sentences.) For a student to sense the need to use skimming and to spend effort in executing it, skimming must have utility (Paris, Lipscom, & Wilson, 1985, p. 304). Otherwise, it will be used only to comply with a teacher's request.

Establishing the functional value of social behaviors is also important in the classroom. Reinforcement to peer models for working quietly, proceeding in an orderly manner to recess, and so on, can influence the adoption of those behaviors by classmates.

Two cautions, however, must be observed in the use of reinforcement. First, vicarious reinforcement differs from **implicit reinforcement**. Exemplary behavior that is praised in one individual and disregarded in others may to the teacher imply reinforcement to all the students who behaved well. To the slighted individuals, the direct consequences of their behavior (i.e., no reinforcement) may be perceived as punishment.

The second caution is that reinforcement, like beauty, is in the eye of the beholder. The same compliment, when given to two different individuals, can have different effects. Similarly, the omission of expected punishment conveys the impression of permissiveness. Behavioral restraints are reduced, and the formerly forbidden behaviors are performed with greater freedom (Bandura, 1971a). Therefore, clearly stated rules in the classroom must be maintained when transgressions occur.

Guiding the Learner's Internal Processes

The recommended instructional activities vary somewhat, depending on the type of skill to be learned. Different emphases are required for cognitive and motor skills. However, for both types of skills, instruction should provide opportunities (1) to code the observed behavior into visual images or word symbols and (2) to mentally rehearse the modeled behaviors. Unless imitative performances are symbolized in memory codes and then stabilized through rehearsal, neither the memory codes nor the behaviors can be retrieved later (Bandura & Jeffrey, 1973). Also important is facilitating the learners' sense of personal efficacy.

Motor Skills. Successful performance of complex motor skills such as golf, skiing, and tennis depends on the individual's internal monitoring of kinesthetic feedback. A recommended strategy consists of (1) the presentation of a videotaped model, (2) the opportunity to develop a conceptual representation, and finally, (3) practice with concurrent visual feedback via a monitor (Carroll & Bandura, 1982). The strategy can be successful in teaching a new motor skill that is outside the learner's visual field, such as executing the backstroke.

Of primary importance is that mental rehearsal by the learner should precede physical execution of the skill (Jeffrey, 1976). Mental rehearsal fulfills an organizational function for the subsequent performance. Also, too early an emphasis on motor performance can jeopardize retention at a time when memory codes are unstable.

Delayed self-observation following modeling is also very useful for social and communication skills. Students in speech and debate, for example, can acquire essential information about needed changes in posture, voice level, gestures, and presentation and response styles.

Conceptual Behavior.   Initial studies indicated that children can infer judgmental rules from models when instructed to find consistencies across presented situations (Rosenthal & Zimmerman, 1978; Zimmerman & Rosenthal, 1974). However, in the classroom, the use of modeling alone appears to be less effective than when combined with some form of verbal instruction (Schunk, 1986). Verbalization during modeling should be carefully selected, however, so that it conveys important information. In addition, overt responding by the learner should not be required. Organizing and producing verbal responses appears to interfere with the observation of the behavioral sequence (Zimmerman & Rosenthal, 1974).

Facilitating Learner Efficacy.   Important for impulsive children is to exercise self-control when faced with new or ambiguous tasks. A plan developed by Meichenbaum and Goodman (1971) to teach impulsive children to manage their own behavior uses modeling combined with verbalized self-instruction. The method has been used for the self-regulatory training of underachieving children (see Fox & Kendall, 1983; Loper & Murphy, 1985).

An adult first models self-talk in three aspects of monitoring one's own learning. They are (1) problem definition ("What is it that I have to do?"), (2) self-instructions that focus on the task ("Now stop and repeat the instruction"), and (3) self-reinforcement and self-evaluation ("Good, I'm doing fine"; "That's OK, I can take my time until I get it right") (Meichenbaum & Goodman, 1971).

After observing the model, the students undertake four practice phases. The phases are (1) imitation of the model with guidance, (2) performance of the task while verbalizing aloud, (3) practice while whispering, and (4) practice using silent speech.

Student self-efficacy in the classroom also may be enhanced by observing the success of peers who are perceived to be similar in competence. Children with difficulties in subtraction who observed both the teacher and a peer model scored higher on self-efficacy, persistence, and achievement than those who observed only the teacher or no model (Schunk & Hanson, 1985).

Designing Instruction for Complex Skills

Social–cognitive theory addresses the learning of complex skills in three ways. One is that of modeling and teaching effective strategies for success in complex tasks. Examples in reading include analyzing word parts and using context to determine word meaning. The second application is that of modeling strategies for directing and monitoring one's own learning. The third application is that of developing the learner's self-regulatory system. Also essential in the classroom is a knowledgeable teacher with high self-efficacy.

Learning strategies are systematic plans that assist the comprehension of information and task performance (Schunk, 1989). Important in the learning of these strategies is the modeling that includes talking through unobservable processes. In this way, the cognitive and metacognitive processes are made explicit for students. Recall the example in chapter 8 in which the teacher verbalized her uncertainty in understanding a paragraph and noting she would reread it and summarize it in her own words.

Research indicates that such instruction is essential for low-achieving students. Unlike other students, low achievers do not develop these skills spontaneously (Brophy, 1988; Corno, 1986). Even if motivated to learn, low-achieving students tend to depend on rote memorization and other inefficient learning skills. Recall from chapter 10 the method referred to as reciprocal teaching, which teaches four strategies to enhance students' comprehension of text (Palinscar & Brown, 1984). Initially, the teacher models these strategies. Then, as students become more proficient, they become peer models for other students.

Self-regulation of learning includes goal-setting, a sense of personal efficacy for the task at hand, self-observation, self-judgment, and self-response. Both modeling and the suggestion of specific performance standards, *when accompanied by explicit instruction targeted to particular subskills,* are effective in enhancing self-efficacy for children with serious deficits in mathematics. For example, Bandura and Schunk (1981) implemented individualized targeted instruction in subtraction skills accompanied by either the performance standard of trying to complete 6 pages per session or 42 pages by the end of the seventh session. The targeted instruction plus the daily performance standard resulted in higher self-efficacy.

In the area of writing, Graham and Harris (1994) derive suggestions for developing self-regulation based on prior research. The suggestions are to (1) make writing an enjoyable and interesting activity, (2) provide opportunities for students to initiate and direct their own efforts, (3) use writing tasks that require self-regulation (narrating a personal experience is not one), and (4) model self-regulation and provide strategy assistance to students as they write (p. 223).

An essential factor in the development of self-efficacy in the classroom is the teacher's sense of efficacy (McLaughlin & Marsh, 1978). Teacher efficacy refers to the extent that the teacher believes he or she has the capabilities to affect student performance (p. 84). Several studies report that teacher efficacy is related to student gains and that teachers in effective schools have a strong sense of efficacy (see Guskey, 1987, and Tschannen-Moran, Hoy, & Hoy, 1998, for a discussion).

Teachers with a strong sense of efficacy are nonauthoritarian and change strategies when students are having difficulty. They also devote more time to classroom learning, provide students with help they need to be successful, and praise students for their accomplishments (Gibson & Dembo, 1984). In addition, they also support the development of students' intrinsic interests and academic self-directions (Woolfolk & Hoy, 1990).

In contrast, teachers with a low sense of instructional efficacy tend to use a custodial orientation that relies primarily on external inducements and negative sanctions to promote academic work. These teachers also spend more time in nonacademic activities and quickly give up on students if they do not get results (Gibson & Dembo, 1984; Woolfolk & Hoy, 1990). Further, recent research indicates that teachers' sense of efficacy is related to their behavior in the classroom and to student achievement (see review by Tschannen-Moran et al., 1998).

EDUCATIONAL APPLICATIONS

Social–cognitive theory has two major implications for education. First, modeling is a primary source of information for learners. The theory identifies situations in which children acquire information from the models in the mass media as well as from family models and others. Second is the importance of a sense of personal efficacy and self-regulatory skills in becoming a successful learner.

Classroom Issues

Social–cognitive theory addresses some of the issues of concern in the classroom setting. It also addresses some learner characteristics and aspects of the social setting for learning.

Learner Characteristics

Individual differences, readiness, and motivation for learning are the student characteristics that interact with instruction. Both individual differences and readiness are discussed in social–cognitive theory in terms of their relationship to learning through observation.

Individual Differences.   Learners differ in their ability to abstract, code, remember, and enact the behaviors that they see. They also differ in their receptivity to models. Behaviors watched intently by nature lovers, for example, will be considered dull and boring by others. Receptivity to a particular model varies along the dimensions of (1) the valuation of the behavior for the observer and (2) the degree of similarity between the observed model/context of the behavior and the observer's status and situation.

In the classroom, after the early school years, students also will differ on the functional value of the learning outcomes established by the school or the teacher. Some students will enthusiastically engage in learning activities, many will be more or less passively compliant, and others who perceive no social value in the outcomes may engage in antisocial behavior.

Readiness.   The developmental level of the learner and receptivity to particular models are the two major factors that determine the individual's capability for observational learning. The learner's perceptual set and the degree of anticipated reinforcement influence the decision to attend to or to ignore the model. The ability to abstract the important features of the modeled behaviors and to recall them later without error also influences the extent and accuracy of the learning. Young children, for example, cannot process complex sequences of behaviors. Instead, they require short explicit visual sequences with repetition.

Motivation.   Although some activities are initiated for direct reinforcement (e.g., activities prompted by thirst, hunger, pain, and so on), the primary source of motivation is cognitively based (Bandura, 1977b, p. 161). Two types of cognitive motivators are included. One is the cognitive representation of future consequences for particular behaviors. "Past experiences create expectations that certain actions will bring valued benefits, that others will have no appreciable effects, and that still others will avert future trouble" (Bandura, 1977b, p. 18).

The second type of cognitive motivator may be referred to as self-motivation because it involves the standard setting and self-evaluative mechanisms of the learner. This type of motivation develops as part of the individual's self-regulatory system, discussed earlier.

Cognitive Processes and Instruction

Transfer of learning, developing the individual's learning-how-to-learn skills, and teaching problem solving are cognitive issues of importance to education. Of the three, social–cognitive theory discusses the first issue.

Transfer of Learning.   The concept of transfer has been researched in the social–cognitive context in two ways. One is the investigation of different treatments for phobic patients. Self-directed mastery experiences were found to be more effective in providing transfer to generalized threat situations than participant modeling alone (Bandura, 1976; Bandura, Adams, & Beyer, 1977).

Modeling of cognitive behaviors has provided both immediate and delayed transfer to similar tasks. Concept attainment, linguistic rule learning, and problem solution strategies were generalized to similar situations (Schunk, 1981; Zimmerman & Rosenthal, 1974).

The Social Context for Learning

Social–cognitive theory addresses the issue of learning in the naturalistic setting. Thus it describes specifically the mechanisms by which individuals learn from each other as they go about their daily lives. The observation of a variety of models (family members, regular associates, films, television) and the reinforcements delivered to peers and others are all important influences on learning. In particular, social–cognitive theory reminds the educational system that learning in a media-oriented society extends beyond the classroom in subtle and pervasive ways.

Relationships to Other Perspectives

Bandura's social–cognitive theory describes learning in the naturalistic setting. Observing peers and others (models), learners abstract behaviors relevant for them and later execute these actions. Bandura's concept of modeling plus reinforcement to the model are key features of Gagné's attitudinal domain. Further, cognitive theorists recommend teacher modeling and verbalization of learning and metacognitive strategies. Although the theory refers to the learners' attentional and retention processes, these processes are not prescribed in detail (unlike Gagné's internal conditions or the phases of information processing).

Like operant conditioning, social–cognitive theory incorporates both direct and self-reinforcement. A key difference is the inclusion of vicarious reinforcement, the physiological effects of observing reinforcement accorded the model.

The self-regulatory system, essential for complex learning, includes the metacognitive skills of monitoring and evaluation. However, descriptions of the self-regulatory system also include goal setting, learner values and interests, perceptions of the learning environment, and learner self-efficacy.

In the classroom setting, social–cognitive theory assumes that instruction is teacher managed and directed and the individual student is the locus of learning. Thus, it differs from social constructivist perspectives in which a community of learners is primary.

Developing a Classroom Strategy

The design of instruction for observational learning includes a careful analysis of the behaviors to be modeled and the processing requirements for learning.

Step 1: Analyze the behaviors to be modeled.

   1.1 What is the nature of the behavior? Is it primarily conceptual, motor, or affective, or is it a learning strategy (such as rereading difficult paragraphs and making notes)?

   1.2 What are the sequential steps in the behavior?

   1.3 What are the critical points in the sequence, such as the steps that may be difficult to observe and those for which alternative incorrect actions are likely?

Step 2: Establish the functional value of the behavior and select the behavioral model.

   2.1 Does the behavior or strategy carry a "success prediction," such as learning to operate equipment essential for a job promotion?

   2.2 If the behavior is a weak success predictor, which potential model is most likely to predict success? Examples include peers, the teacher, and status models that appeal to the target group.

   2.3 Should the model be live or symbolic? Consider cost, the need to repeat the experience for more than one group, and the opportunity for portraying the functional value of the behavior.

   2.4 What reinforcement(s) is the model to receive for the behavior?

Step 3: Develop the instructional sequence.

   3.1 For motor skills, what are the "do this" but "not this" verbal codes to be used?

   3.2 Which steps in the sequence are to be presented slowly? What are the verbal codes that supplement but do not supplant these steps?

3.3 For a learning strategy, what unobservable processes and self-talk are to be modeled?

Step 4: Implement the instruction to guide the learner's cognitive and motor reproduction processes.

Motor skills:

4.1 Present the model.

4.2 Provide students the opportunity for symbolic rehearsal.

4.3 Provide student practice with visual feedback.

Conceptual behavior:

4.1 Present the model with supporting verbalization.

4.2 If a concept or a rule, provide students with opportunities to summarize the model behaviors.

4.3 If the learning is a problem-solving or strategy application, provide opportunities for participant modeling.

4.4 Provide opportunities to generalize to other situations.

4.5 Assist the students in analyzing their applications and setting goals.

Classroom Example

The behaviors modeled in the following example are note-taking skills. The identified population is middle school students (ages 10 to 14, grades 6 to 8).[2]

The teacher first models the strategy of note taking from written text. Important in this exercise is that the teacher model the process in which a particular recall cue is chosen over another. The teacher should "talk aloud" the cues that come to mind and the reasons for rejection of poor cues. After the teacher's demonstration, the students suggest the notes to be taken in the next two exercises. This activity provides for corrective feedback early in the learning. The students then complete a note-taking exercise on their own. This activity provides the symbolic coding and mental rehearsal necessary for conceptual behavior.

The follow-up exercise that demonstrates note taking from audiotaped material should be initiated only after the students have applied their skills for written materials in a variety of situations. Taking notes from an ongoing oral presentation is a difficult skill to learn. It is dependent on good listening skills and practice in the use of temporary auditory memory. In teaching this skill, exercises in listening and recall of oral material may be required prior to the note-taking exercise.

The teacher explains the importance of note taking in helping the students to remember material that they have heard or read. Also, good note-taking strategies should help them remember important information for tests.

---

[2] Example designed by Sharon Cohn, University of South Carolina.

Before beginning the actual classroom exercise, the teacher and students determine an initial goal for the skills to be learned. For example, they may decide that the goal should be to develop good recall cues for three important points in a short reading passage.

The teacher then distributes a four-paragraph reading selection and asks the students to read the first paragraph silently while the teacher reads it aloud.

A transparency that illustrates the note-taking format is placed on the overhead projector. It is divided into two columns, headed "recall cues" and "notes."[3] The teacher talks through the first paragraph in terms of its important points. Then under the "notes" column, two summary sentences for the paragraph and associated cues in the "recall cues" column are entered. The teacher verbalizes the ways in which these sentences and the recall words will help students to remember the paragraph.

The teacher then carries out the same procedure with the other two paragraphs. After reading each one aloud, the teacher talks though several alternatives for notes, selects one or two, and enters them in the appropriate column with associated cues. The importance of the exercise is that the students observe the ways in which the teacher analyzes the paragraph and selects summary sentences.

The students and the teacher then work through two or three exercises together, with the students suggesting the study notes. This activity is followed by independent note taking by the students on short passages that they have selected from other sources.

The teacher reviews the notes developed independently by the students on short passages they have selected and gives each student feedback on progress toward the initial goal. Suggested changes are made to students who are having difficulty with the assignment.

Reading Passage for Note-Taking Exercise[4]

A land grant of 10 million acres was given to George Calvert, a prominent nobleman from England known as Lord Baltimore. The land given by the king, Charles I, was located near Chesapeake Bay, and this gift enabled George Calvert to exert tremendous power. He was capable of establishing manors that resembled those of the feudal era, and of treating the inhabitants as serfs. He also functioned as a prosecutor and a judge of inhabitants charged with law breaking. George Calvert was called a proprietor, or an owner of landholdings, and his colony was known as a proprietary colony.

Prior to the king's seal being affixed to the charter describing the land grant, George Calvert died and his son served as the first proprietor. The colony was known as Maryland, named after the wife of Charles I, Queen Henrietta Maria. Since the Calvert family was Catholic, they intended to establish a Catholic colony in Maryland.

In 1634 the first settlers arrived and established the town of St. Mary's. The settlers could obtain food and other provisions from the adjacent and prosperous colony of Virginia. They did not have to wait for ships from England. They did not waste time looking for gold; instead, they immediately began to grow tobacco.

---

[3] Suggested by W. Pauk, *How to Study in College* (New York: Houghton Mifflin, 1962).

[4] Paraphrased from J. A. Garraty et al., *American History* (New York: Harcourt, 1982).

Recall Cues	Notes
Calvert	George Calvert, Lord Baltimore, was the proprietor of a large land area near the Chesapeake Bay.
Proprietary colony	He had a great deal of power, and his land was a proprietary colony.
Maryland	Calvert's son was the first proprietor of the colony called Maryland. Because Calvert's family was Catholic, they wanted Maryland to be a Catholic colony.
Tobacco	Early settlers in Maryland began to grow tobacco.

Note-Taking Exercise II

In this exercise, the teacher has previously recorded a script on audiotape. The speech is recorded with short pauses, much as one might give a talk to a group. In the modeling, the teacher plays each paragraph of the recorded tape and demonstrates how to take notes while the tape is playing. She writes recall cues and sentence fragments on the transparency during the brief pauses in the tape. The tape is stopped at the end of each paragraph, and the teacher completes the sentence fragments.

After the demonstration, the students and the teacher complete several short paragraphs together. This exercise is usually quite difficult for students because it involves listening and jotting down notes at the same time. Therefore, only very short paragraphs should be used until the students' skills are acquired; this may require several exercises over a period of time.

Taped Paragraph[5]

In the 17th century a cluster of religious reformers resided in England. These reformers were critical of the Church of England. However, they did not want to separate from the church. They wished to reform and to purify the church from the inside. These reformers were called Puritans.

Recall Cues	Sentence Fragments	Completed Sentence
Reform	the Church of England	The Puritans wanted to reform and purify the Church of England.
Purify		

Review of the Theory

Albert Bandura's social–cognitive theory began with his analyses of prior approaches to the learning of imitative behavior. Prior theories proposed a variety of mecha-

---

[5] Paraphrased from J. A. Garraty et al., *American History* (New York: Harcourt, 1982).

nisms to account for the adoption of prosocial and antisocial behaviors. Included were reinforcement for imitation, nurturance, power, envy, and frustration.

In contrast, Bandura proposes a single paradigm to account for the acquisition of both prosocial and antisocial behaviors. The components are (1) the modeled behaviors, (2) the consequences of the model, and (3) the learner's cognitive processes (Table 11.4). The consequences received by the model that contribute to the observer's learning the behavior include vicarious reinforcement, vicarious punishment, and the absence of anticipated punishment. These consequences signal behaviors that have functional value and therefore may be useful to the observer. Later successful performance by the observer depends in part on the learner's cognitive processes (attention, retention, motor reproduction, and motivation).

Learning, according to Bandura, is represented by a three-way interaction among the environment, the individual's internal events, and the individual's behavior (reciprocal determinism). Also included in the theory is the development of the self-regulatory system, a necessary component in the development of outstanding performance in any area. Included in the system are a sense of personal efficacy, goal setting, self-evaluation, and self-directed rewards or punishments.

TABLE 11.4
Summary of Bandura's social–cognitive theory

Basic Elements	Definition
Assumptions	Learning is a three-way interaction between the environment, personal factors, and behavior that also involves the learner's cognitive processes
Components of learning	Modeled behaviors, consequences to the model, and the learner's cognitive processes
Learning outcomes	Verbal and visual codes that may or may not later be performed
Designing instruction for complex skills	In addition to component skills, develop the learner's sense of efficacy and self-regulation
Major issues in designing instruction	Provide for mental rehearsal prior to practice; avoid omission of reinforcement or punishment when needed; avoid excessive use of punishment
ANALYSIS OF THE THEORY	
Disadvantages	Difficult to implement the requirements for self-efficacy and self-regulation along with other classroom priorities
Contributions	Description of the variety of attitudes and behaviors acquired from the mass media
	Provides a detailed description of the mechanisms of reinforcement and punishment in the group setting
	Identifies the importance of self-efficacy in learning

Disadvantages

Bandura identifies the importance of the learner's self-direction and sense of efficacy in interacting with the environment. However, in the limited classroom setting, developing the learner's self-regulatory system and sense of efficacy is a difficult task.

Contributions to Educational Practice

An important contribution is the detailed descriptions of the role of models and reinforcement and punishment in the classroom setting. That is, punishment or lack of it delivered to others as well as vicarious reinforcement are both operating in the classroom setting. Another contribution is the identification of the role of personal efficacy in learning.

CHAPTER QUESTIONS

1. In chapter 3, one technique for unconditioning children's fears made use of other children's acceptance of the feared object. According to social–cognitive theory, why was this technique successful?

2. Which types of reinforcement or punishment are likely to be operating in the following situations?

   _____ a. Three classmates are allowed to go to the library early for completing assignments quietly.

   _____ b. A student studying for a difficult final exam promises herself a day at the beach if she does well on the test.

   _____ c. Kazdin (1989) indicates that when brief time-outs are given to disruptive students the number of similar incidents in the classroom tends to decrease.

3. Describe a television commercial in which an action or belief demonstrated by a model earns positive consequences for the model.

4. What are the meanings of the euphemisms "termination with extreme prejudice" and "uncontained engine failure"? What other euphemisms have you read and/or heard via the media?

REFERENCES

Anderson, L. M. (1981). *Student responses to seatwork: Implications for the study of students' cognitive processing* (Research Series No. 102). East Lansing, MI: The Institute for Research on Teaching, Michigan State University.

Baldwin, A. L. (1973). Social learning. In F. Kerlinger (Ed.), *Review of research in education* (Vol. 1, pp. 34–57). Itasca, IL: Peacock.

Bandura, A. (1965). Behavioral modification through modeling practices. In L. Krasner & L. Ullman (Eds.), *Research in behavior modification* (pp. 310–340). New York: Holt, Rinehart & Winston.

Bandura, A. (1969). Social-learning theory of identificatory processes. In D. A. Goslin (Ed.), *Handbook of socialization theory and research* (pp. 213–262). Chicago: Rand McNally.

Bandura, A. (1971a). *Psychological modeling: Conflicting theories.* Chicago: Aldine–Atherton.

Bandura, A. (1971b). *Social learning theory.* Upper Saddle River, NJ: Prentice Hall.

Bandura, A. (1971c). Vicarious and self-reinforcement processes. In R. Glaser (Ed.), *The nature of reinforcement* (pp. 228–278). New York: Academic.

Bandura, A. (1973). *Aggression: A social learning analysis.* Upper Saddle River, NJ: Prentice Hall.

Bandura, A. (1974). Behavior theory and the models of man. *American Psychologist, 29,* 859–869.

Bandura, A. (1976). Social learning perspective on behavior change. In A. Burton (Ed.), *What makes behavior change possible?* (pp. 34–57). New York: Brunner/Mazel.

Bandura, A. (1977a). Self-efficacy: Toward a unifying theory of behavioral change. *Psychological Review, 84*(2), 191–215.

Bandura, A. (1977b). *Social learning theory.* Upper Saddle River, NJ: Prentice Hall.

Bandura, A. (1978). The self-system in reciprocal determinism. *American Psychologist, 33,* 344–358.

Bandura, A. (1979). Psychological mechanisms of aggression. In M. von Cranach, K. Foppa, W. Lepenies, & D. Ploog (Eds.), *Human ethology: Claims and limits of a new discipline* (pp. 316–379). New York: Cambridge University Press.

Bandura, A. (1982a). The self and mechanisms of agency. In J. Suls (Ed.), *Psychological perspectives on the self* (Vol. 1). Hillsdale, NJ: Erlbaum.

Bandura, A. (1982b). Self-efficacy mechanism in human agency. *American Psychologist, 37,* 122–147.

Bandura, A. (1986). *Social foundations of thought and action: A social-cognitive theory.* Upper Saddle River, NJ: Prentice Hall.

Bandura A. (1993). Perceived self-efficacy in cognitive development and functioning. *Educational Psychologist, 28*(2), 117–148.

Bandura, A. (1995). Exercise of personal and collective self-efficacy in changing societies. In A. Bandura (Ed.), *Self-efficacy in changing societies* (pp. 1–45). New York: Cambridge University Press.

Bandura, A., Adams, N., & Beyer, J. (1977). Cognitive processes mediating behavioral change. *Journal of Personality and Social Psychology, 35,* 125–138.

Bandura, A., & Jeffrey, R. W. (1973). Role of symbolic coding and rehearsal processes in observational learning. *Journal of Personality and Social Psychology, 26,* 122–130.

Bandura, A., Mahoney, M. J., & Dirks, S. J. (1976). Discriminative activities and maintenance of contingent self-reinforcement. *Behavior Research and Therapy, 14,* 1–6.

Bandura, A., & Schunk, D. H. (1981). Cultivating competence, self-efficacy, and intrinsic interest through proximal self-motivation. *Journal of Personality and Social Psychology, 41,* 586–598.

Bandura, A., & Walters, R. H. (1963). *Social learning theory and personality development.* New York: Holt, Rinehart & Winston.

Berk, L. E. (1989). *Child development.* Boston: Allyn & Bacon.

Bong, M., & Clark, R. E. (1999). Comparison between self-concept and self-efficacy in academic motivation research. *Educational Psychologist, 34*(3), 139–154.

Brophy, J. (1988). Research linking teacher behavior to student achievement: Potential implications for instruction of Chapter 1 students. *Educational Psychologist, 23*(3), 235–286.

Brophy, J., & Putnam, J. (1979). Classroom management in the elementary grades. *Classroom management. The eightieth yearbook of the National Society for the Study of Education* (pp. 182–216). Chicago: University of Chicago Press.

Carpenter, C., Huston, A., & Spear, L. (1989). Children's use of time in their everyday activities during middle childhood. In M. Block & A. Pellegrini (Eds.), *The ecological content of children's play.* Norwood, NJ: Ablex.

Carroll, W., & Bandura, A. (1982). The role of visual monitoring in observation learning of action patterns: Making the unobservable observable. *Journal of Motor Behavior, 14,* 153–167.

Corno, L. (1986). The metacognitive control components of self-regulated learning. *Contemporary Educational Psychology, 11,* 333–346.

Doyle, W. (1986). Classroom organization and management. In M. C. Wittrock (Ed.), *Handbook of research on teaching* (3rd ed., pp. 392–431). New York: Macmillan.

Evans, R. I. (1989). *Albert Bandura, the man and his ideas—a dialogue.* New York: Praeger.

Fox, D., & Kendall, P. (1983). Thinking through academic problems: Applications of cognitive–behavior therapy to learning. In T. Kratochwill (Ed.),

Advances in school psychology (Vol. 3, pp. 269–301). Hillsdale, NJ: Erlbaum.

Gerbner, G. (1974). Teacher image in mass culture: Symbolic functions of the "hidden curriculum." In D. R. Olson (Ed.), *The form of expression: Communication and education. The seventy-third yearbook of the National Society for the Study of Education* (pp. 470–497). Chicago: University of Chicago Press.

Gerbner, G., & Gross, L. (1976). Living with television: The violence profile. *Journal of Communication, 26*(2), 173–199.

Gibson, S., & Dembo, M. H. (1984). Teacher efficacy: A construct validation. *Journal of Educational Psychology 76,* 569–582.

Goetz, J. (1976). Behavioral configurations in the classroom: A case study. *Journal of Research and Development in Education, 9*(4), 36–49.

Good, T. L., & Brophy, J. E. (1987). *Looking in classrooms* (4th ed.). New York: Harper & Row.

Graham, S., & Harris, K. (1994). The role and development of self-regulation in the writing process. In D. Schunk & B. Zimmerman (Eds.), *Self-regulation of learning and performance: Issues and educational applications.* Hillsdale, NJ: Erlbaum.

Gredler, M., & Garavalia, L. (2000a). Students' perceptions of their self-regulatory and other-directed study strategies: A factor analysis. *Psychological Reports, 86,* 102–108.

Gredler, M., & Garavalia, L. (2000b, April). *The role of components of student regulation of learning, aptitude, and prior grades in explaining achievement.* Paper presented at American Educational Research Association, New Orleans.

Gredler, M., & Schwartz, D. (1997). Factorial structure of the self-efficacy for self-regulated learning scales. *Psychological Reports, 81,* 51–57.

Greenfield, P. (1984). *Mind and media: The effects of television, video games, and computers.* Cambridge, MA: Harvard University Press.

Guskey, T. R. (1987). Context variables that affect measures of teacher efficacy. *Journal of Educational Research, 81,* 41–47.

Henderson, R. (1986). Self-regulated learning: Implications for the design of instructional media. *Contemporary Educational Psychology, 11,* 405–407.

Huston, A., Watkins, B., & Kunkel, D. (1989). Public policy and children's television. *American Psychologist,* 424–433.

Jeffrey, R. S. (1976). The influence of symbolic and motor rehearsal in observational learning. *Journal of Research in Personality, 10,* 117–126.

Kazdin, A. (1989). *Behavior modification in applied settings* (4th ed.). Pacific Grove, CA: Brooks/Cole.

Leifer, A. D. (1976). Teaching with television and film. In N. L. Gagné (Ed.), *The seventy-fifth yearbook of the National Society for the Study of Education* (pp. 302–334). Chicago: University of Chicago Press.

Loper, A. B., & Murphy, D. M. (1985). Cognitive self-regulatory training for underachieving children. In D. L. Forrest-Pressley, G. E. MacKinnon, & T. G. Waller (Eds.), *Metacognition, cognition, and human performance* (pp. 223–265). Orlando, FL: Academic Press.

McLaughlin, M. W., & Marsh, D. D. (1978). Staff development and school change. *Teachers College Record, 80,* 70–94.

Meichenbaum, D. H., & Goodman, J. (1971). Training impulsive children to talk to themselves: A means of developing self-control. *Journal of Abnormal Psychology, 77,* 115–126.

Moskowitz-Hayman, G. (1976). Success strategies of inner-city teachers: A year-long study. *Journal of Educational Research, 69,* 683–689.

Murray, J., & Epstein, L. (1981). Improving oral hygiene with videotape modeling. *Behavior Modification, 5*(3), 360–371.

Pajares, F., Miller, M. D., & Johnson, M. J. (1997). Gender differences in writing, self-beliefs of elementary school subjects. *Journal of Educational Psychology, 91*(1), 30–61.

Pajaras, F., (1996). Self-efficacy beliefs in academic settings. *Review of Educational Research, 66*(4), 543–578.

Pajares, F., & Graham, D. (1999). Self-efficacy motivation constructs and mathematics performance of entering middle school students. *Contemporary Educational Psychology, 24*(2), 124–139.

Palinscar, A. S., & Brown, A. L. (1984). Reciprocal teaching of comprehension-fostering and comprehension-monitoring activities. *Cognition and Instruction, 1*(2), 117–175.

Paris, S., Lipscom, M., & Wilson, K. (1985). Becoming a strategic reader. *Contemporary Educational Psychology, 8,* 293–316.

Pintrich, P., & DeGroot, E. (1990). Motivational and self-regulated learning components of classroom academic performance. *Journal of Educational Psychology, 82*(1), 33–40.

Rice, M. C., Huston, A. C., & Wright, J. C. (1986). Replays as repetitions: Young children's misinterpretations of television forms. *Journal of Applied Developmental Psychology, 7,* 61–76.

Robinson, J. P., & Godbey, G. (1997). *Time for life: The surprising ways Americans use their time.* University Park: The Pennsylvania State University Press.

Rosenthal, T. L., & Bandura, A. (1978). Psychological modeling: Theory and practice. In S. L. Garfield & A. E. Begia (Eds.), *Handbook of psychotherapy and behavior change: An empirical analysis* (2nd ed., pp. 621–658). New York: Wiley.

Rosenthal, T. L., & Zimmerman, B. J. (1973). Organization, observation, and guided practice in concept attainment and generalization. *Child Development, 44,* 606–613 (LB 1101.C4).

Rosenthal, T. L., & Zimmerman, B. J. (1976). Organization and stability of transfer in vicarious concept attainment. *Child Development, 47,* 110–117.

Rosenthal, T. L., & Zimmerman, B. J. (1978). *Social learning theory and cognition.* New York: Academic.

Schunk, D. H. (1981). Modeling and attributional effects on children's achievement: A self-efficacy analysis. *Journal of Educational Psychology, 73,* 93–105.

Schunk, D. H. (1986). Verbalization and children's self-regulated learning. *Contemporary Educational Psychology, 11,* 347–369.

Schunk, D. H. (1987). Peer models and children's behavioral change. *Review of Educational Research, 57*(2), 149–174.

Schunk, D. (1989). Self-efficacy and achievement behaviors. *Educational Psychology Review, 1*(3), 173–208.

Schunk D. (1994). Self-regulation of self-efficacy and attributions in academic settings. In D. Schunk & B. Zimmerman (Eds.), *Self-regulation of learning and performance: A conceptual framework for education* (p. 75–99). Hillsdale, NJ: Erlbaum.

Schunk, D. (1995). Inherent details of self-regulated learning include student perceptions. *Educational Psychologist, 30*(4), 213–216.

Schunk, D. H., & Hanson, A. (1985). Peer models: Influence on children's self-efficacy and achievement. *Journal of Educational Psychology, 77*(3), 313–322.

Schunk, D. H., & Ertmer, P. (1999). Self-regulatory process during computer skill acquisition. *Journal of Educational Psychology, 91*(2), 251–260.

Schunk, D., & Zimmerman, B. (Eds.). (1998). *Self-regulated learning: From teaching to self-reflective practice.* New York: Guilford Press.

Schwartz, L., & Gredler, M. (1998). The effects of self-instructional materials on goal setting. *Journal of Research and Development in Education, 31*(2), 83–89.

Tschannen-Moran, M., Hoy, A. W., & Hoy, W. K. (1998). Teacher efficacy: Its meaning and measure. *Review of Educational Research, 68*(2), 202–248.

Wood, R. E., & Bandura, A. (1989). Impact of conceptions of ability on self-regulatory mechanism and complex decision making. *Journal of Personality and Social Psychology, 56,* 407–415.

Woolfolk, A., & Hoy, W. (1990). Prospective teachers' sense of efficacy and beliefs about control. *Journal of Educational Psychology, 82,* 81–91.

Zimmerman, B. (1986). Becoming a self-regulated learner: What are the key subprocesses? *Contemporary Educational Psychology, 11,* 370–404.

Zimmerman, B. (1995a). Self-efficacy and educational development. In A. Bandura (Ed.), *Self-efficacy in changing societies* (pp. 202–231). Hillsdale, NJ: Erlbaum.

Zimmerman, B. (1995b). Self-regulation involves more than metacognition: A social cognitive perspective. *Educational Psychologist, 30*(4), 217–221.

Zimmerman, B. J. (1998). Developing self-fulfilling cycles of academic regulation: An analysis of exemplary instructional models. In D. H. Schunk

& B. J. Zimmerman (Eds.) *Self-regulated learning: From teaching to self-reflective practice* (pp. 1–19). New York: Guilford Press.

Zimmerman, B., & Bandura, A. (1994). Impact of self-regulatory influences on writing course attainment. *American Educational Research Journal, 31*(4), 845–862.

Zimmerman, B. J., Bandura, A., & Martinez-Pons, M. (1992). Self-motivation for academic attainment: The role of self-efficacy beliefs and personal goal setting. *American Educational Research Journal, 29,* 663–676.

Zimmerman, B. J., Greenberg, D., & Weinstein, C. E. (1994). Self-regulating academic study time: A strategy approach. In D. H. Schunk & B. J Zimmerman (Eds.), *Self-regulation of learning and performance: Issues and educational applications* (pp. 181–199). Hillsdale, NJ: Erlbaum.

Zimmerman, B. J. & Martinez-Pons, M. (1986). Development of a structured interview for assessing student use of self-regulated learning strategies. *American Educational Research Journal, 23,* 614–628.

Zimmerman, B. J., & Martinez-Pons, M. (1992). Perceptions of efficacy and strategy use in the self-regulation of learning. In D. Schunk & J. Meece (Eds.), *Student perceptions in the classroom* (pp. 185–207). Hillsdale, NJ: Erlbaum.

Zimmerman, B. J., & Rosenthal, T. L. (1974). Observational learning and rule-governed behavior by children. *Psychological Bulletin, 81,* 29–42.

CHAPTER 12

Bernard Weiner's
Attribution Theory

A central assumption of attribution theory . . . is that the need for understanding is a basic "spring of action" (Weiner, 1979, p. 3).

People typically express sympathy for others with physical disabilities, but sometimes react negatively to hyperactive children. In the achievement domain, students who are perceived to fail because of lack of ability receive sympathy. However, students who are able but who are perceived to fail because they did not try are punished. These different events, in addition to individual reactions to one's own achievement successes and failures, share some common psychological characteristics (Weiner, 1993, 1995). The basis for the commonalities in these events is their attributions or perceived causes. The theory that addresses the consequences of the perceived causes of these and similar events is Bernard Weiner's attribution theory.

Attribution research focuses on the ways that individuals arrive at causal explanations and the implications of those beliefs. For example, suppose that one's foot is stepped on during a subway ride. Attribution theorists first would ask, What are the perceived causes? (e.g., standing too near the door, an aggressive act, etc.). Second, they would ask, What information influenced this selection? (a clenched fist, the belief that one is clumsy, etc.). Third, What are the consequences of the attribution? (hitting the aggressor, moving away from the door, etc.) (Weiner, 1985b, p. 280). In other words, attribution theorists focus on the ways that people answer the question *Why?*

Understanding the perceived cause or causes of an event is important for several reasons. One is that effective management may be possible. Guidelines for future action may be suggested (Weiner, 1985a, p. 548). Moreover, when negative situations occur, such as academic failure or socially stigmatizing events, attribution theory can provide explanations of the effects.

Also important is that the search for causes is not restricted to a particular period in human history or a particular geographical region. Both the Japanese warrior in the Middle Ages and today's union representative seek such information. The warrior wanted to know the underlying causes of his wins in battle in order to survive the next one. Similarly, the union representative seeks to understand the successes and failures in the industry in order to urge appropriate actions in the future (Weiner, 1985a, p. 549).

Attribution theory began with the work of Fritz Heider. Born in 1896 in Vienna, Austria, Heider studied with several of the Gestalt psychologists in Germany and arrived in the United States in 1930. Heider's 1958 text, *The Psychology of Interpersonal Relations,* describes the basic purpose of his work as an "investigation of common-sense psychology" (1958, p. 79). He was concerned about the causes of events developed by the "man in the street."

The attributional theory developed by Bernard Weiner began with the variables identified in John W. Atkinson's (1958, 1964) theory of achievement motivation. According to Atkinson, motivation is a function of task variables and the individual's disposition to strive for success or to avoid failure. However, Weiner and Kukla (1970) found that the effects of task variables are not uniform. That is, success on a difficult task generates more pride than success on an easy task. In addition, individuals high in achievement motivation perceive themselves as more able than those low in achievement motivation, and they also expend more effort on achievement tasks.

Focusing on achievement outcomes, the early development of Weiner's theory consisted of the identification of the major causes typically selected by individuals for success and failure and the conceptual links to subsequent behavior (see Weiner, 1972, 1979). Then the properties or dimensions of the major causes of success and failure outcomes were identified. These dimensions have been found to influence emotional reactions to events, such as pride and shame. They also influence expectations about future outcomes (Weiner, 1980d, 1982).

In the 1990s, Weiner (1994a, 1994b, 1994c) extended the theory to the social domain. That is, the attributions that others make about individuals' stigmatizing events, social rejection, and academic failure share a common psychological foundation with the personal attributions individuals make about themselves.

Early research on the components of the theory was conducted in the experimental laboratory. In recent years, however, research in the classroom setting has increased. Among the issues related to attribution theory are the effects of different classroom goal structures on students' perceptions of competence (Ames & Archer, 1988; Anderman & Midgley, 1997; Covington, 1999; Dweck, 1989; Eliot, 1999; Elliott & Dweck, 1988). Recent developments include guidelines for establishing classrooms that can foster positive goal structures and motivational patterns (Ames, 1992a, 1992b), and developing appreciation for subject-matter learning (Brophy, 1999; Covington, 1999).

PRINCIPLES OF MOTIVATION

The prior chapters in this text discuss theories of learning that describe the factors necessary for the achievement of particular skills and capabilities. Attribution theory, in contrast, views human beings from the perspective of their search to understand the world and to achieve personal fulfillment and self-actualization. The primary focus of this chapter, therefore, is on the relationships among achievement-related outcomes, causal beliefs, and subsequent emotions and activities.

Basic Assumptions

The basic assumptions of the theory are found in two areas. They are the nature of causal inferences (attributions) and the relationship of attributions to behavior.

The Nature of Causal Inferences

An important characteristic of causal inferences is that they occur in a broad range of human activities. Attributions are developed for achievement outcomes, such as why one failed a test or received a poor grade on a term paper. In addition, attributions are developed in the affiliative and power domains. Examples are "Why was I rejected for a date?" and "Why did I lose the election?" (Weiner, 1982, p. 186).

A major assumption of Weiner's attributional research is that causal inferences are complex sources of information about outcomes. That is, they are not unidimensional.

One-Dimensional Perspectives.   The initial analysis of causal structure, developed by Fritz Heider (1958), was influenced by Lewin's statement that behavior is a function of the person and the environment, $B = f(P,E)$. The two sets of conditions responsible for the outcomes of human action, according to Heider (1958, p. 82), are factors within the person and factors within the environment.

A subsequent development, referred to as locus of control (Rotter, 1966), specified that the perceived causes of behavior lie on a continuum between the two extremes of internal and external locus of control. Individuals who believe that reinforcements (positive consequences) are the result of hard work and planning also believe that they control their own destiny. They are, therefore, inner-directed and take responsibility for events in their lives. Arriving late to class is likely to be acknowledged as the result of leaving home too late to find a parking place, rather than some vague external condition.

In contrast, individuals who are outer-directed perceive no relationship between their behavior and reinforcements. Instead, luck, fate, or powerful others are in control. Therefore, the student may believe that a D on a test is the result of lack of ability (internal locus) or the result of teacher bias (external locus).

A variation of this conceptual framework is described in the origin/pawn analysis by deCharms (1968). Origins initiate behavior intended to produce a change in the environment. Pawns, in contrast, perceive that they are pushed around by the environment.

Problems with a One-Dimensional Analysis.   According to Weiner (1972), the internal–external analysis of attributions does not adequately account for subsequent effects. For example, both lack of ability and lack of effort are internal attributions for failure. However, they lead to different expectations for future outcomes. A poor grade attributed to lack of ability will be expected to occur again. However, a poor grade attributed to lack of effort may not be expected in the future since the student's expenditure of effort is subject to change (see Eswara, 1972; McMahan, 1973; Rosenbaum, 1972; Weiner, Neirenberg, & Goldstein, 1976).

In addition, lack of effort is punished more than lack of ability. Both males and females have dispensed the greatest punishment to hypothetical able pupils for failure attributed to lack of effort. The least punishment for failure went to motivated students of little ability (Rest, Neirenberg, Weiner, & Heckhausen, 1973; Weiner & Kukla, 1970). This reward pattern also was observed in reward dispensers who were as young as 16 (Weiner & Peter, 1973). The differential consequences resulting from attributions in the same locus of causality (internal attributions) led to further analysis and the development of Weiner's theory of attributions.

The Relationship of Causal Inferences to Behavior

A primary assumption of attribution theories is that the search for understanding is a major source of human motivation (Weiner, 1979). Another major assumption is that future behavior is influenced by people's belief systems and their cognitive analyses of the causes of positive and negative outcomes. For example, the student who attributes failure to low ability is likely to expect future failures and to believe that he or she has no behavioral response that can alter subsequent events (Weiner, 1979). Therefore, little or no effort will be expended on achievement-related tasks. In contrast, a student who attributes success to ability expects continued success. An occasional failure for such a student is likely to be attributed to a temporary cause, and future effort is not jeopardized.

In the social domain, individuals make judgments about events in the lives of others and their behavior. For example, negative events that are beyond the control of the individual typically elicit sympathy and help. An example is a student who missed class because of an eye infection and needs the class notes. A typical response is to loan one's notes to the student. However, a student who missed class because he went to the beach is responsible for the problem of not having the notes. Student reactions are typically anger and a refusal of help. Thus, future behavior is determined, in part, by perceived causes of prior outcomes.

Related to the assumption that people search for causal understanding is the belief that research can identify individuals' causal inferences. In early investigations, research participants read scenarios about hypothetical individuals and then identified attributions for the situational outcomes. Some psychologists, however, suggested that participants would not have made attributions unless prodded by the investigators (Weiner, 1985c).

Three methods have evolved in recent years to assess spontaneous thinking. One approach analyzed newspaper articles on sports events and elections for inferences about wins and losses (Lau & Russell, 1980; Foesterling & Groenvald, 1983). A second approach is to examine causal statements made during or immediately following task performance (Weiner, 1985c). Verbal protocols taken at parole hearings as board members reviewed files are an example (Carroll & Payne, 1977). Parole board members typically attributed criminals' past offenses to an inadequate upbringing (external cause) or to the nature of the individual (internal cause).

The third method, the critical incident approach, asks participants to recall personally meaningful successes or failures and then identify causal attributions for the outcomes. According to Vispoel and Austin (1995), the requirement to identify a personally meaningful event increases the likelihood that the events addressed are familiar, valued, and gender appropriate.

Summary

Attribution research focuses on the ways that individuals arrive at causal explanations and the implications of those beliefs. Understanding individuals' attributions is important because the knowledge may suggest guidelines for future action.

Three basic assumptions support attribution theory. The first assumption is that the search for understanding is a primary motivator of action. The second assumption concerns the nature of causal inferences. The limitation of internal–external analyses, such as the locus of control construct and the origin–pawn perspective, is that they do not adequately account for subsequent effects. In other words, attributions are complex sources of information about behavior.

The third assumption is that future behavior is determined, in part, by the perceived causes of prior outcomes. For example, a student who attributes success to ability expects continued success and approaches achievement-related tasks with positive feelings. In the social domain, individuals make judgments about the causes of others' behavior and, as a result, may extend or withhold assistance.

Related to the assumption that people make causal inferences is the belief that research studies can discover these inferences. Early research relied on identifications of attributes for events in hypothetical scenarios by research participants. Three current research methods that have been used are the analysis of newspaper articles on sports and elections, verbal protocols, and the critical incident approach.

The Components of the Attributional Process

The attributional model of motivation includes several components. The basic building blocks of the model are (1) outcome attributions and their characteristics or dimensions and (2) the functions of attributional dimensions in the personal domain. These and other factors interact in somewhat different ways to form attributional models for achievement and social motivation.

Attributions and Their Defining Dimensions

A virtually infinite number of causal inferences may be made for human events. In the achievement domain, multiple determinants of outcomes may be identified (Weiner, 1995). For example, failure may be the result of lack of effort, the absence of ability, poor strategy, bad luck, the bias of teachers, hindrance from peers, and so on. In the social domain, social rejection may be perceived as resulting from poor interpersonal skills, parental obstacles, sloppy personal habits, and so on (p. 562).

Typical Attributions.   In the achievement domain, the typical attributions for success and failure outcomes are ability, effort, task difficulty, and luck (Weiner, 1972). Others that are cited include mood, illness, fatigue, and help from others. However, the most dominant causes for success and failure, according to Weiner (1985a), are ability and effort. That is, success is attributed to high ability and/or hard work, and failure is attributed to lack of ability and/or lack of effort. Several research studies with various school populations support the dominance of ability and effort as causal inferences (see Anderson, 1983; Burger, Cooper, & Good, 1982; Frieze,

1976; Frieze & Snyder, 1980; and Wilson & Palmer, 1983). One study of junior high school students, however, found that interest was the second most highly rated success attribution after effort (Vispoel & Austin, 1995, p. 400). Also, lack of interest was the most highly rated failure attribution. Nevertheless, ability attributions for success and failure were the best predictors of students' grades.

Attributional Dimensions.   Attributional content varies across individuals, and many perceived causes for achievement successes and failures as well as social acceptance and rejection may be identified. Therefore, attribution theory focuses on causal meaning rather than the particular causes (Graham & Hudley, 1992). Causal meaning of attributions is determined, in large measure, by the underlying properties or dimensions of perceived attributions.

The three bipolar dimensions of attributions in both the personal and social domains are locus of causality, stability, and controllability. That is, an attribution may be internal or external, stable or subject to change, and under the individual's control or controlled by other individuals or events (see Table 12.1). For example, ability is internal, stable, and is not controlled by the individual. In contrast, luck, although uncontrollable, is external and unstable.

The identification of the properties of causal attributions indicates a similarity across contexts (Weiner, 1982, 1985a). Examples of attributions that are external, stable, and uncontrollable include religious restrictions on dating (social rejection) and the non-support of conservative districts for liberal candidates (failure in the power domain).

The dimensions of each of the often-cited achievement attributions are illustrated in Table 12.2. As indicated, no two of the attributions are exactly alike in their properties. More important, the unique combination of dimensions for each attribution plays an important role in the dynamics of behavior.

TABLE 12.1
The three dimensions of attributions

| | | Examples | |
| | | Personal Domain | Social Domain |
Dimension	Description		
Locus of causality	Origin of the perceived attribution, the environment or the individual (internal/external)	Ability is internal; luck is external	Personal sloppiness is internal; one's desired date being busy is external
Stability	The constancy or durability of the perceived attribution	Ability is stable; effort is unstable	Physical unattractiveness is stable; one's desired date being busy is unstable
Controllability	Perceived attribution can or cannot be controlled by the individual	Effort is controllable; ability is not	Hyperactivity typically is perceived as controllable; shyness is not

TABLE 12.2
Dimensions of major attributions for achievement-related behavior

| | Dimension | | | | | |
| | Stability | | Locus of Causality | | Controllability* | |
Attribution	Stable	Unstable	Internal	External	Controllable	Uncontrollable
Ability	x		x			x
Effort		x	x		x	
Task difficulty	x			x		x
Luck		x		x		x
Mood, illness		x	x			x
Help from others		x		x		x

*From the perspective of the individual who experienced the positive or negative outcome

Functions of Attributional Dimensions

The dimensions of causal inferences or attributions may influence motivation in one of two ways. One is the *expectancy* for future goal attainments. The other is that particular attributional dimensions generate a specific set of emotional reactions. Included are pride and self-esteem, confidence, anger, pity, guilt, shame, gratitude, and hopelessness.

Expectancy for Future Goal Attainment.   Currently, stability appears to be the only dimension that influences future goal expectancy. For example, success in mathematics that is attributed to ability (a stable cause) will be expected again. Similarly, test failure ascribed to lack of ability, social rejection attributed to physical unattractiveness, and criminal acts attributed to a psychopathic personality are all expected to recur. Each of the attributions is a stable cause that is not expected to change.

Similarly, the intent to engage in particular activities such as reentering school after dropping out or resubmitting a rejected manuscript are greater when these outcomes are attributed to unstable causes, such as needing a break from school or poor manuscript reviewers (Crittended & Wiley, 1980).

Emotional Reactions to Positive Outcomes.   Following a positive outcome, the individual may experience feelings of pride and self-worth, confidence, or gratitude. The individual's identification of a personal characteristic, which is internal, is the cause of feelings of pride and self-worth (see Table 12.3). Kant described the locus of causality-pride linkage when he noted that everyone at a meal may enjoy the good food but only the cook could experience pride (Weiner, 1985a, p. 561).

In contrast, success ascribed to external causes, such as luck or help from others, does not influence self-esteem or future task engagement (Weiner, 1982). An example is receiving an *A* from a teacher who awards only good grades (external

TABLE 12.3
Emotions generated by the dimensions of causal inferences for achievement

Outcome/Dimensions Linkage	Emotional Reactions
Positive outcomes	
Internal cause	Feelings of pride and self-esteem
Controllable cause	Feelings of confidence
Stable cause	Maximizes feelings of pride, self-worth, and confidence (for internal causes)
Uncontrollable/external cause	Feelings of gratitude
Negative outcomes	
Internal cause	Feelings of embarrassment, guilt, and shame
Controllable cause	Feelings of guilt
Stable cause	Maximizes emotions of shame, apathy, and resignation associated with internal, controllable causes
Uncontrollable/external cause	Feelings of anger

cause); pride is not experienced for the success. Instead, success attributed to external causes typically generates feelings of gratitude.

Emotional Reactions to Negative Outcomes.   Success attributed to internal causes influences one's self-image. Similarly, failure attributed to internal causes contributes to negative self-image. Some studies (Brown & Weiner, 1984; Covington & Omelich, 1984; Jagacinski & Nicholls, 1984) have reported that shame-related affects (disgrace, embarrassment, humiliation, and/or shame) are associated with low ability, and guilt-related reactions are associated with lack of effort. The occurrence of shame, a more negative emotion than guilt, may be related to the stability and uncontrollability of ability (aptitude). In contrast, effort, which is controllable, may tend to generate guilt but not the stronger emotion, shame. Graham and Weiner (1996) note that "guilt tends to promote goal-directed activity, whereas shame gives rise to task withdrawal and is a motivational inhibitor" (p. 72).

Also of importance is that shame-related emotions often are followed by withdrawal and motivational inhibition. In contrast, guilt-related emotions often lead to reproach behavior and retribution (Hoffman, 1982; Weiner, 1985a). Thus, failure attributed to stable and uncontrollable factors generates strong negative emotions and exerts a debilitating influence on future achievement-related behavior as well.

Similar to success outcomes, the stability dimension maximizes the emotions generated by internal causes of failure, such as lack of ability. Feelings of apathy, resignation, and hopelessness for the future typically occur. However, emotions resulting from unstable causes, such as lack of effort, are unlikely to be extended to future events.

Note also the emotions generated for failure attributed to uncontrollable causes. An example is one's neighbor playing the stereo so loud that one fails a test the next day. However, this uncontrollable cause is also external. Thus, emotions of anger are likely to arise for uncontrollable and external causes but not for uncontrollable internal causes.

In summary, the basic building blocks of the attributional model are (1) the individual's attributions for success and failure outcomes and (2) the characteristics or dimensions of these attributions. In the achievement domain, the typical attributions for success and failure outcomes are ability, effort, task difficulty, and luck. Others are mood, illness, fatigue, and help from others. For junior high school students, interest or lack of interest appear to be salient attributions for success and failure.

Causal meaning of attributions is determined largely by their underlying dimensions. The bipolar dimensions for attributions in both the personal and social domains are locus of causality, stability, and controllability. The dimension that influences future goal expectancy is the stability dimension.

In addition, each of the attributional properties also generates particular effects (Table 12.4). The locus of causality is linked primarily to the individual's self-esteem.

TABLE 12.4
Summary of the properties of major achievement-related attributions

Attribution	Dimension	Consequence
Ability	Internal	Generates feelings of competence or incompetence and feelings of pride or shame
	Stable	Same outcome expected again; emotions of pride and shame magnified; for failure, resignation and apathy magnified
	Uncontrollable	For failure, magnifies feelings of resignation and apathy
Effort	Internal	Generates feelings of pride for success
	Unstable	Does not decrease success expectancy
	Controllable	Magnifies feelings of pride or guilt
Luck	External	Self-image not altered
	Unstable	No decrease in success expectancy
	Uncontrollable	Generates surprise for both success and failure
Others	External	Self-image not altered
	Unstable	No decrease in success expectancy
	Uncontrollable (by outcome recipient)	Generates gratitude for help and anger for hindrance
Task difficulty	External	No enhancement of self-esteem for success outcome
	Stable	Same outcome expected again
	Uncontrollable	Depression and frustration for failure outcomes

Causes attributed to the self either enhance feelings of self-worth or contribute to a negative self-image. In contrast, the primary association for stable attributions is the magnitude of expectancy change for success and failure. The secondary association is one of affect in which emotions generated by other dimensions are maximized.

The Attributional Model for Achievement Outcomes

The study of achievement motivation is the analysis of factors that account for goal-oriented effort in achievement situations. In the attributional model, the emotions that influence goal-oriented behavior are generated by (1) the success or failure outcome, (2) the attribution identified as the cause, and (3) the dimensions of the attribution.

In the attributional process, individuals first appraise performance and assign it a subjective rating on a continuum from success to failure. Next, either a cause is identified or the individual reflectively begins to look for the probable cause. A search is most often undertaken for unexpected outcomes, such as failure when success was expected, and for unfulfilled desire, such as interpersonal rejection (Weiner & Graham, 1985, p. 167). Documented examples of unexpected events that generate causal searches include a win by an underdog, a loss by a favored team, more or less profits than expected, and inconsistent behavior (Weiner, 1985c).

Information that assists the individual in the causal search includes specific informational cues, such as social norms and performance patterns, and individual characteristics, such as self-concept and need for achievement. Also, both the general emotions associated with the outcome and the specific emotions generated by the attribution influence subsequent behavior (see Figure 12.1). In athletic competition, for example, one tends to experience happiness for a victory whether the win resulted from additional training, a poor competitor, or luck (Weiner, 1985a).

When the specific cause is identified, the particular attribution and its constellation of dimensions generate the sets of emotions already described. For example, consider a Little League baseball player who performs poorly during a game. The boy has played poorly in the past, and the other children are playing well. The boy also has tried to improve by practicing many hours. On the basis of past history, social comparison, and expenditure of effort, the boy is likely to conclude that he has failed because he is not good at baseball (lack of ability) (Weiner, 1985b, p. 566).

The Little Leaguer attributes his poor performance to lack of ability, which generates feelings of incompetence. Also, lack of ability is internal, stable, and uncontrollable. The results are lowered self-esteem (the internality dimension), accompanied by feelings of hopelessness, an expectancy for continued failure (the stability dimension), and humiliation (uncontrollability of the attribution). These conditions promote withdrawal and other behaviors that do not contribute to attainment of the desired goal (Weiner, 1985a, p. 566). A likely subsequent action for the Little Leaguer is that he stays home from the next game.

Antecedents of Causal Inferences.   As indicated in Figure 12.1, the individual makes use of several sources of information in the search for a causal attribution. They are specific information cues, the individual's general beliefs about success and failure, and individual predispositions.

FIGURE 12.1
Major events in the attributional model of motivation

Specific information cues include past success history, social norms, and performance patterns (Weiner, 1977, p. 181). The individual's past success history is the primary determinant for the selection of ability or lack of it as an attribution (Weiner, 1974a). A consistent record of prior achievements leads to attributions of ability for success, whereas a moderate success record is likely to generate effort as a cause for success. On the other hand, success for an individual with a consistently poor achievement record is likely to be attributed to luck, and failure will be attributed to lack of ability.

Social norms and the performance records of others also provide information about ability. If one succeeds at a task at which others fail, then the individual will likely decide that he or she is able (Weiner, 1974a, p. 53). Similarly, failure on a task at which others succeed is viewed as the result of lack of ability. The percentage of others who succeed or fail at a particular task, however, contributes to the use of task ease or difficulty as a causal belief. The higher the percentage of others who succeed at a task, the greater is the likelihood of ease of task as a causal inference for success.

The higher the percentage of task failures, the more likely that the inference for failure will be task difficulty (Weiner, 1974a, p. 53).

Another source of information is the individual's general beliefs about events and associated causes (Weiner, 1977). One is the belief that success is produced by either ability or effort (referred to as a sufficient causal schema) (Weiner, 1974a, p. 53). Another common belief is that success depends on both ability *and* effort (referred to as a necessary causal schema) (Weiner, 1977). This combination is often the explanation selected for success on a difficult task. High-ability students tend to attribute their successes to both ability and hard work (Dai, Moon, & Feldhusen, 1998). Further, some studies suggest that the learner's personal theory of intelligence is important. Dweck (1986; Dweck & Legget, 1988) proposed that some learners view intelligence as a capacity or fixed entity that is affected somewhat by effort. Others view intelligence as a set of knowledge and skills that increase incrementally with practice and effort.

Individual characteristics also influence causal attributions. For example, individuals who are high in achievement needs tend to attribute their success outcomes to themselves, that is, to their skill or effort. Individuals low in achievement needs, however, tend to identify external factors as responsible for success (Weiner & Kukla, 1970). In addition, persons with high achievement needs tend to attribute initial failure to lack of effort (rather than lack of ability). Their persistence therefore increases, since they believe that increased effort will lead to success. In contrast, persons low in achievement needs often do not attribute the initial failure to lack of effort, and therefore they tend to cease trying (Weiner & Kukla, 1970).

Self-concept is also a characteristic that is related to the causal attributions made by children. Research indicates that elementary school students who are high in self-concept credit skill and ability for success. They also engage in more self-reward following success than do low self-concept children (Ames, 1978; Ames, Ames, & Felker, 1977).

The Role of Affective Reactions.   As indicated in Figure 12.1, a success or failure outcome leads to a general positive or negative emotion. Then the specific attributions and their dimensions generate particular sets of feelings. Emotions are important in the attributional model because they serve as motivators of subsequent behavior. "Attributions tell us what to feel, and feelings tell us what to do" (Weiner, 1983b, p. 69). An individual who has experienced apathy, resignation, and feelings of incompetence will cease trying in achievement-related situations. On the other hand, one who feels gratitude and relief is motivated to express thankfulness. The individual who experiences feelings of competence, however, will approach achievement-related situations with confidence.

In addition to one's own emotions, the emotional reactions of others often serve as cues for self-perceptions. For example, both children and adults, when given failure situations and "teacher" reactions of anger, inferred lack of effort as the cause. For "teacher" reactions of pity, they inferred the cause of failure to be lack of ability (Graham & Weiner, 1983; Weiner, Graham, Stern, & Lawson, 1982).

The relationship between the affective reactions of the teacher and the student's inferences is illustrated in Figure 12.2. The model illustrates the unintentional attributional cues that are conveyed by the teacher's affective reactions to his or her perceived causes for student failure. Although the sympathy reaction typically is motivated by the goal to protect the student's self-esteem, the results are quite different (Weiner et al., 1983). Instead, sympathy telegraphs a message of "hopelessness" (i.e., low ability), a trait that is both stable and uncontrollable.

The teacher's affective reaction may also influence his or her subsequent actions, which in themselves convey messages about ability (Rohrkemper & Brophy, 1983). Rohrkemper and Brophy asked teaches to evaluate vignettes about student behavior problems in the classroom. Teacher attributions as to locus of causality, controllability, stability, and intentionality of perceived causes were important determinants of teacher affect and the selection of solution strategies.

The Attributional Model for Social Motivation

The social motivation domain, as Weiner (1993, 1994b, 1994c) conceptualizes it, consists of (1) the attributions of others for a person's failure or other stigmatizing event, and (2) the affective reactions and subsequent behaviors generated by the attributions. The attribution–emotion–reaction linkage identified in the intrapersonal model also is found in the social model, with one additional inference. Specifically, inferences of perceived responsibility for the particular event (such as poverty or social rejection) follow the identification of the perceived cause (attribution), and the responsibility inference generates the subsequent emotion. Weiner (1993) notes that "the powerful and prevailing practice of judging others as responsible or not provides a foundation for the construction of a general theory of motivation" (p. 957).

Currently, three areas of social interaction have been identified in which the model functions. They are judgments about the academic failure of others, decisions about help-giving, and reactions to aggression.

Achievement Evaluation.   One role of classroom teachers is that of evaluating the achievement-related actions of the students in their classes. An early series of studies by Weiner and Kukla (1970) investigated the relationships between attribu-

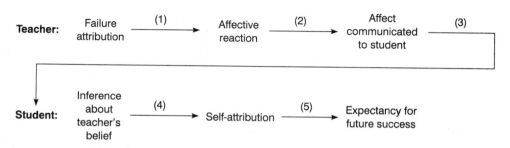

FIGURE 12.2
Attributional model of teacher affective cues for failure

Note: Summarized from "Social Cognition in the Classroom" by B. Weiner, S. Graham, S. Taylor, and W. Meyer, 1983, *Educational Psychologist, 18.*

tions for students' successes and failures and the assignment of rewards and punishments. In hypothetical situations, research participants rewarded high effort more than ability in the success conditions, and punished lack of effort more than lack of ability for failure.

The attributional explanation for the failure reactions is illustrated in Figure 12.3 (Weiner, 1993, p. 959). The controllability dimension is the key to the inference of responsibility or no responsibility. These inferences generate either sympathy or anger and the subsequent punishment or no punishment.

Other studies also document that responsibility following a negative event triggers anger (e.g., Reisenzein & Hoffman, 1990). For example, college students reported feeling anger when roommates failed to clean their rooms, lied, or should have taken a responsible action (Weiner, Graham, & Chandler, 1982; Weiner, 1993).

Help Giving.   Perceptions of responsibility also play a major role in giving or withholding help. Pity and helping behaviors usually are precipitated by infirmities or conditions that are not under an individual's control. That is, like low ability, the individual is perceived as not responsible for the condition. Included are serious illnesses and accidents (Weiner, 1982, 1993). On the other hand, negative outcomes that result from conditions perceived to be under the volitional control of the individual typically yield negative reactions and refusals of assistance (Weiner, 1980a, 1980c, 1982).

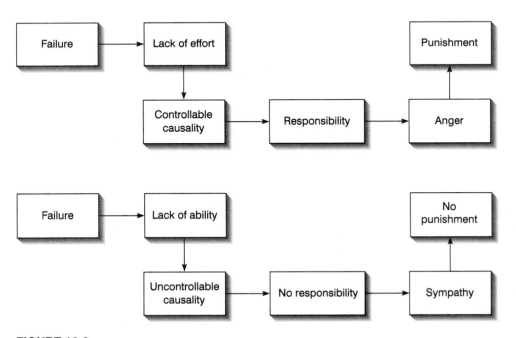

FIGURE 12.3
The relationship of controllability to affective reactions and administration of punishment

In one study, 40% of the research subjects reacted negatively to lending their notes to a hypothetical student who missed class to go to the beach. However, only 4% refused the classmate who missed class with a temporary eye disability.

Similarly, a person's fall in the subway from drunkenness (perceived to be controllable) elicited negative reactions, disgust, and neglect (Weiner, 1982). In contrast, a fall caused by an infirmity (uncontrollable condition) led to the positive reactions of sympathy and judgments of help. This characteristic of causal inference also may explain in part the difficulty experienced in the solicitation of funds for alcoholism as opposed to fund solicitation for catastrophic illnesses and child abuse (Weiner, 1979).

However, poverty, unlike the conditions just described, elicited diverse reactions. College students and adults classified as liberals and conservatives rated the importance of 13 dominant causes of poverty (Zucker & Weiner, 1993). The respondents also indicated the controllability of poverty, the extent to which the poor are personally responsible for their plight, their own emotional reactions (anger or pity), and decisions about giving help (Weiner, 1993).

Reactions to Deviant Social Characteristics and Behaviors. Two lines of research have been pursued in relation to deviant social characteristics and behaviors. One is teachers and children's reactions to nonnormative characteristics or behaviors of children. Data indicated that children rated hyperactivity, bragging, and rule breaking as the responsibility of the individual, and these categories elicited anger and dislike. In contrast, peers were viewed as not responsible for shyness and physical anomalies, such as epilepsy, and these conditions elicited sympathy and little anger (Juvonen, 1991, 1992).

The other area of research investigated the reactions of aggressive and nonaggressive children to negative events precipitated by other children. Studies reviewed by Dodge and Crick (1990) indicate that aggressive children typically infer hostile intent following a peer-initiated negative event, even if the intent is ambiguous or not clear. For example, a child is told to imagine that a peer spilled milk on him or her in the lunchroom, and no other information is provided. The respondent identified as "aggressive" is more likely to label the act as intentional than is a nonaggressive child (Graham & Hudley, 1992, p. 78). Further, the biased intentionality judgments are believed to precipitate retaliation. Graham, Hudley, and Williams (1992) found that aggressive minority youth made more attributions of biased intent in neutral situations by a hypothetical student, reported more anger, and were more likely to identify an aggressive behavior reaction than a comparable group of nonaggressive students. Attributional change efforts, therefore, should address mitigating the perceived responsibility of the negative act and the anger reaction in addition to tendencies toward retaliation.

In summary, in decisions about the achievement of others, help giving, or the aggression of others, perceived responsibility (extent of controllability) is a key element of the judgment. Failure outcomes, stigmatizing events, and aggressive acts perceived as the responsibility of the individual elicit negative emotional reactions and, sometimes, punishing behavior. Similarly, stigmatizing conditions and aggressive acts perceived as under the individual's control elicit negative reactions and a withholding of help giving behavior or a retaliatory action.

Summary

In the achievement domain, typical attributions for success and failure are ability, effort, task difficulty, and luck. Others are mood, illness, fatigue, help from others, and, for junior-high students, interest (or lack of it). A key component of attributions that influence both emotional reactions and subsequent behavior are three bipolar dimensions that characterize each attribution. They are stability, locus of causality, and controllability. Stability influences expectancy for future attainment, but locus of causality and controllability influence the emotions associated with success and failure.

Following an attribution of success or failure, the individual identifies a likely cause. Information that assists in this task includes specific informational cues, personal beliefs, individual predispositions, and the emotional reactions of others, particularly pity or anger following failure.

In the social domain, the attribution–affect–behavior linkage is proposed to explain others' reactions to one's academic failure or stigmatizing event. Teachers, for example, tend to punish lack of effort following a failure outcome more than lack of ability.

The Cumulative Effects of Attributions for Success or Failure

Over a period of time, the individual's success or failure history and the accompanying attributions exert a continuing influence on the individual's causal attributions in achievement situations and self-esteem.

Individuals with a consistent record of success in social and achievement situations have expectations for continued success and typically are high scorers on measures of self-esteem and self-concept. Conversely, individuals who have experienced a fairly consistent record of failures are low in self-esteem. They also tend to ascribe success to unstable factors and failure to internal, stable causes. They also have a low expectancy of success in the future. This pattern has been observed in several settings with different age groups. In one study, the researcher (Ames, 1978) found that the fifth graders who were low in self-concept did not respond favorably to their own successful outcomes.

The Concept of "Learned Helplessness".   Individuals low in self-concept who have experienced few successes are likely (1) to attribute failure to lack of ability and (2) to see no relationship between their success and their own actions. The belief that outcomes are independent of one's actions was researched originally as the construct known as "learned helplessness" (Seligman, 1975). In the initial experimental studies, dogs subjected to inescapable electric shock learned that no response, such as tail wagging, barking, or jumping, influenced the shocks. Then when placed in a situation in which knocking down a barrier terminated the shock, the animals first ran around frantically for a few seconds and then lay down, passively submitting to the shock. In other words, after the experience of uncontrollable trauma, the animals lost the motivation to respond, and depression and anxiety resulted. Further, even if a response was successful, the animal had difficulty in learning that the response was effective (Seligman, 1975, p. 22).

A major characteristic of helplessness in humans is whether individuals believe that outcomes are more or less likely to happen only to themselves or to relevant others as well. For example, a student may spend long hours studying, enroll in remedial courses, and still fail. The person eventually arrives at the conclusion that he is incompetent. In this case, important outcomes are available to others (they pass), but the student does not possess the behaviors to acquire them. The cause of the event is internal; this phenomenon is referred to as personal helplessness (Abramson et al., 1980, p. 11). The problem with personal helplessness, as in attributions for a single failure outcome, is that the internal nature of the attribution generates low self-esteem.

Comparisons with "Mastery-Oriented" Children.   Research indicates that children of equal ability often react to failure in very different ways (Diener & Dweck, 1978; Dweck, 1975). Learned-helpless children attribute failure to stable factors, such as lack of ability. They also react to failure with solution-irrelevant statements, stereotypic responses, and derogatory comments. Examples include "I am stupid" and "I never did have a good memory" (Diener & Dweck, 1978). In addition, a marked and rapid decline typically occurs in the sophistication and appropriateness of the children's problem-solving strategies. In one study, by the fourth problem in a discrimination-testing situation, over two thirds of the children made ineffectual responses.

In contrast, mastery-oriented children tend to acknowledge their errors but do not regard them as failures (Dweck & Licht, 1980, p. 199). They attribute the mistakes to unstable factors, such as bad luck, lack of effort, and unfairness of the experimenter. They also engage in self-instructional statements. For example, "I should slow down and try to figure this out" and "The harder it gets, the harder I need to try" (Diener & Dweck, 1978, p. 459). Mastery-oriented children also maintain mature strategies in the face of failure, and the strategies of some of the children increase in sophistication. The unflagging optimism of these children, however, is perhaps the most striking difference between them and the learned-helpless group (Dweck & Licht, 1980, p. 201).

The two groups also differ in their reactions to success. In one study, learned-helpless children were less likely to attribute success to ability, and they underestimated their number of successes. They also tended to state that other children outperformed them, and they predicted poor future performance for themselves (Diener & Dweck, 1980). Mastery-oriented children, however, attributed performance to ability, correctly estimated their number of successes, thought they were doing better than other children, and expected continued success.

The underlying problem for "helpless" children is that they do not view themselves as instrumental in the determination of outcomes. They are therefore likely to consider adverse circumstances as insurmountable. Thus, the important factor is not the occurrence of aversive events but, rather, the perceived relationship between the individual's behavior and the event (Dweck, 1975, p. 75).

Classroom conditions can place children at risk for developing learned helplessness. When normative performance evaluations prevail in the classroom, low-confidence children react with ineffective strategies and attributions of lack of ability. However, when tasks are presented in terms of learning, such as to sharpen one's mind, maladaptive responses tend to decrease (Elliott & Dweck, 1988). (See the section on Personal and Classroom Goal Structures.)

PRINCIPLES OF INSTRUCTION

In the formal educational setting, the young child soon learns that doing well in school is an implicit goal, yet an important one. Throughout the school years, in both formal and informal situations, students are faced with a continuing succession of success/failure assessments of their behavior. The nature of schooling, however, restricts those assessments to a narrow range of human knowledge that to a great extent is dependent on the learner's verbal proficiency.

The child's judgments about his or her successes and failures are relatively unsophisticated at first, but gradually become refined, and become an important factor in the further development of self-esteem. At the end of 12 years of schooling, students have developed beliefs about their skills, abilities, and potential for life success. These beliefs are developed in part from the causal attributions and emotional consequences generated by their achievement-related outcomes in the classroom.

The attributional theory developed by Bernard Weiner is relevant to the educational setting because it (1) addresses the range of effects of success and failure outcomes and (2) provides a framework for the analysis of teacher–student interactions in the classroom. Although specific principles for teaching are yet to be derived, guidelines for classroom practice can be identified.

Basic Assumptions

The assumptions on which attribution theory is based also apply to the classroom setting. They are that (1) the search for understanding is a source of motivation and (2) individual behavior is, in part, determined by one's beliefs about the causes of past outcomes. In the classroom setting, an additional assumption is also needed. It is that the beliefs and reactions of others are important contributions to the development of students' causal attributions for success and failure.

The Essentials of Attributional Formation in the Classroom

The classroom setting is one in which hundreds of interactions occur between teachers and students. These interactions are sources of information for both teacher and student beliefs about student abilities and effort on classroom tasks. These beliefs (i.e., attributions) generate affective reactions and serve as motivators for subsequent behavior. The essentials of attribution formation in the classroom are (1) the classroom model, (2) teacher and student characteristics, and (3) personal and classroom goal structures.

The Classroom Model

In the interactive classroom setting, the attributional model in Figure 12.1 and the interactive attribution sequence for failure in Figure 12.2 may be combined to illustrate the teacher influence on student attributions for success and failure. This sequence is illustrated in Figure 12.4, and it applies both to formal test situations and to more informal teacher–student exchanges. That is, student performance, whether completion of a test, submission of homework for grading, reading aloud in the reading group, or responding to teacher questions in a class discussion, provides the opportunity for evaluation of the student.

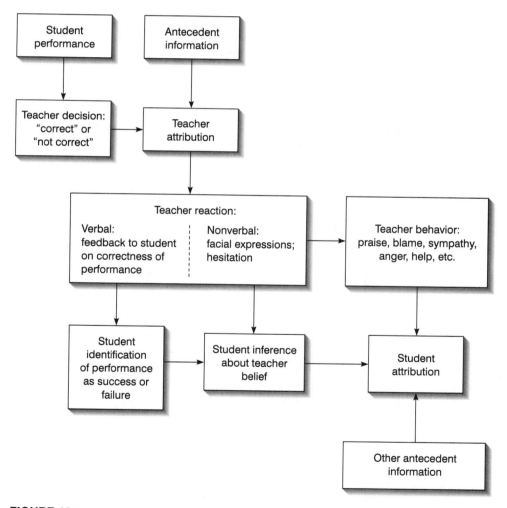

FIGURE 12.4
Teacher–student interactions in the formulation of attributions for success and failure

The teacher evaluates the student's behavior and contributes to the student's inferences about his or her ability through specific feedback to the student, nonverbal affective reactions, and subsequent behavior toward the student. The student combines this information, particularly the teacher's affective reaction (Graham & Weiner, 1983; Weiner, 1979, 1980d), with other information and makes inferences about his or her ability.

An important implication for educational practice is the need to analyze classroom events for the attributional messages that may be conveyed. Because ability typically is viewed as internal, stable, and uncontrollable, it takes on the characteristics (and importance) of the construct of aptitude (Weiner et al., 1983, p. 117). Classroom events are the source of both direct and implicit information to the student about academic performance and, therefore, ability.

Teacher and Student Characteristics

As indicated earlier in this chapter, student characteristics and the reactions of teachers are major factors in the formation of attributions.

Teacher Characteristics.   Already discussed in the first part of this chapter are the affective reactions of sympathy and anger. Sympathy extended to certain students following failure is one of the cues for low-ability inferences (Graham, 1984, 1988, 1990; Graham & Weiner, 1983; Weiner, 1982; Weiner, Chandler, & Graham, 1982). More important, the sympathy may (1) prevent the teacher from providing challenging tasks to the student and/or (2) lead to too much teacher help to the student, thereby removing student responsibility for learning (Weiner, 1980d, p. 10). Unsolicited aid may lead the student to conclude that the teacher perceives his or her ability to be low.

For the most part, teacher behavior has been researched from the perspective of teacher expectancy. That is, teachers who expect certain students to perform poorly will treat those students differently, thereby reducing their opportunity to learn and contributing to poor achievement. Good (1980) lists 11 ways that students designated as low achievers are treated differently in some classrooms. Referred to as reactive behaviors, they include seating low achievers farther from the teacher and/or in a group, demanding less work and effort from them, and paying less attention to them. Less attention includes less eye contact, fewer opportunities to respond to teacher questions, less time to answer questions, less detailed feedback on errors, and so on (Good, 1980, p. 88). From an attributional perspective, such teachers are identifying the cause of student behaviors in the classroom to be lack of ability.

A different perspective, referred to by Good (1980) as proactive, involves building classroom structures in which the needs of low achievers can be met without ignoring the needs of other students. From an attributional perspective, such teachers are likely to identify lack of effort as the cause for failure.

For both types of teachers, beliefs are translated into behaviors that can influence both student perceptions and the nature of the activities used in the classroom. The differential treatment sends different attributional messages to the students as well as providing different opportunities for learning. In one study, fifth-grade students asked to evaluate teacher expectations for a hypothetical smart student (G) and a low-ability student (E), indicated that the teacher would not expect the low-ability student to remain task involved (Thorkildsen & Nicholls, 1998).

Teacher feedback is an important factor in student perceptions of their abilities. Pintrich and Blumenfeld (1985) found that teacher feedback about work was a better predictor for children's ability and effort perceptions of themselves than other interactions with teachers or peers. Children who were praised more for their work thought they were smarter and also worked harder than the children who received less praise for their work.

Student Characteristics.   In addition to the individual predispositions discussed earlier, developmental level also influences attribution selection. Most children in kindergarten and first grade hold high perceptions of their ability and high expectancies of success. Their optimism holds even if they fail repeatedly at a task, and they also are more likely to attribute success and failure to luck than are older children (Wigfield & Harold, 1992, p. 102).

The subtle cues that indicate ability inferences often are not differentiated clearly by young children. Research indicates that young children interpret the success/teacher praise linkage as indicative of high ability (Barker & Graham, 1987), and only some children perceive the failure/sympathy linkage as inferring lack of ability (Weiner, Graham et al., 1982). Children in kindergarten and first grade also tend to rate their own ability independently of teacher and peer ratings (Stipek, 1981).

By the second or third grade, children begin to make normative evaluations of their ability. By that age, children are able to use concepts such as effort, ability, task difficulty, and luck in an adultlike way, even if they cannot explain their reasons (Thorkildsen & Nicholls, 1998). Their ratings are more consistent with their report cards, their confidence is likely to decline under failure, and success expectancies decrease (Dweck, 1989; Nicholls, 1978; Ruble & Rhales, 1981). In one 3-year study, children's ability perceptions and their valuing of academic activities in seven areas declined by the third grade (Wigfield & Harold, 1992).

Factors proposed to account for children's perceptions include differences in processing various sources of information and changing views of the ability/effort relationship. That is, young children tend to believe that success is related to working harder. Other factors related to young children's ability perceptions are the concrete nature of their classroom tasks (as opposed to abstract) (Dweck, 1989) and the nature of classroom feedback. In the early school years, more than half of the feedback addresses adherence to classroom procedures and conduct (Pintrich & Blumenfeld, 1985), and children's attributions reflect the combined emphasis on social and academic performance.

Personal and Classroom Goal Structures

An achievement goal describes the purposes of achievement behavior. It also defines an integrated pattern of beliefs, attributions, and affects that are represented by different ways of approaching, engaging in, and responding to achievement activities (Ames, 1992b, p. 261). Different types of achievement goals that represent different conceptions of success, different reasons for engaging in achievement activity, and different ways of viewing oneself, tasks, and task outcomes have been identified and researched in recent years (Ames, 1992b; Anderman, Greisinger, & Westerfield, 1998; Eliot, McGregor, & Gable, 1999; Midgley, Kaplan, Middleton, & Macke, 1998; Thork-ildsen & Nicholls, 1998). Classroom goals and task demands are an influential factor in the development of students' personal goal structures.

Types of Goal Structures. The original conceptualizations of students' goal struc-tures identified two contrasting types. They are performance (or ego involved) and mastery or learning goals. Performance goals (Ames & Archer, 1988; Ames, 1992b; Dweck, 1986; Elliott & Dweck, 1988), or ego-involvement (Jagacinski & Nicholls, 1987; Jagacinski, 1992; Maehr & Nicholls, 1980) involves demonstrating superior per-formance. This objective is accomplished by either outperforming others or by doing well with little effort. This type of goal reflects a focus on one's ability, and self-worth is based on perceptions of one's ability to perform. Social comparison information (how well others are doing or how much effort they are expending) is the standard for self-judgments about ability. In this goal structure, learning functions as a means to achieve a particular performance goal; learning is not an objective (Nicholls, 1989).

In contrast, the orientation referred to as learning goals (Dweck, 1986; Elliott & Dweck, 1988), task-involvement (Jagacinski & Nicholls, 1987; Jagacinski, 1992; Maehr & Nicholls, 1980), or mastery goals (Ames & Archer, 1987, 1988; Ames, 1992b) involves demonstrating ability through mastering new skills. One's prior learning and perfor-mance are the standards for judging ability, which is viewed in terms of improvement and progress. A core belief associated with mastery goals is that effort and outcome co-vary, and this belief maintains achievement-oriented behavior over time.

The original conceptualizations of goal structures, according to Elliott (1999), are insufficient to explain the data on achievement-related behaviors and achieve-ment outcomes. Specifically, neither a performance nor a mastery orientation can account for negative processes such as disorganized studying, low absorption during task engagement, procrastination, and unwillingness to seek help. He proposes a third goal structure labeled performance-avoidance. Examples include avoidance of asking the teacher a "dumb" question, fearing being thought stupid, and often wor-rying about doing badly in school (p. 180).

Two similar goal orientations measured by researchers are work avoidance and failure avoidance. Work avoidance seems to represent the absence of an achieve-ment goal and the endorsement of just "getting through" requirements (Archer, 1994; Eliot, 1999, p. 184). Briefly, examples are feeling successful when all the work is easy and not having any tough tests (Thorkildsen & Nicholls, 1998). Failure avoid-ance involves avoiding looking stupid in one's classes through self-protecting strate-gies, such as not responding to teacher questions (Middleton & Midgley, 1997). Bro-phy (1999) suggests that students who attribute failure to uncontrollable causes then seek to defend against perceptions of incompetence or to hide their incompetence from others (p. 76).

The type of goal structure influences students' future attributions, learning strategies, task selection, and perceptions of competence (Ames, 1992a; Ames &

Archer, 1988; Dweck, 1989; Elliott & Dweck, 1988; Jagacinski & Nicholls, 1987) (see Table 12.5). One study of 176 secondary school students found that the mastery-oriented students reported that they used more learning strategies, preferred challenging tasks, and held a more positive attitude toward class than their performance-oriented counterparts (Ames & Archer, 1988). Research also indicates that a performance-goal orientation sets up a win–lose situation in which performance deteriorates rapidly following failure, and negative feelings are generated (Dweck, 1989; Jagacinski & Nicholls, 1987; Elliott & Dweck, 1988). In addition, Stipek and Daniels (1988) found that children in several performance-oriented kindergartens rated their competence lower than children in learning-oriented kindergartens.

Related Classroom Structures.   The personal goal structure of each student is influenced by the goal structure of the classroom. One of the changes that typically

TABLE 12.5

Comparison of performance-goal and learning-goal orientations

	Performance-Goal (ego-involved) Orientation	Learning or Mastery-Goal (task-involved) Orientation
Definition of success	Judgments of high ability through high normative performance or the appearance of success with little effort	Learning new skills; mastery of new tasks; improvement, progress in learning new skills
Teacher orientation	How are students performing?	Are the students learning?
Major focus by the student	How can I best validate my competence?	How can I best acquire this skill or master this task?
Cognitive set	Intelligence is likely to be as a fixed trait or static entity (referred to as an "entity theory" orientation [Dweck, 1989]).	Intelligence is a dynamic, growing set of abilities (referred to as the "incremental theory" of intelligence [Dweck, 1989]).
Task choice(s)	Sacrifice learning and choose moderately difficult or moderately easy task to display competence or to avoid display of incompetence. Individuals with low expectancies of success: excessively easy task (ensure success) or excessively difficult (failure does not signal low ability).	Choose learning to increase competence at the risk of displaying mistakes. Challenging tasks chosen regardless of self-perception of ability as high or low
Reasons for effort	High grades; performing better than others	Learn something new
Views of errors	Anxiety eliciting	Part of learning
Reactions to failure	Low effort investment in the face of threatened failure; attributions to task difficulty or other external factors (preserves image of competence) Repeated failure: Attribution of lack of ability.	Signal to redirect effort and to change strategy

occurs from the elementary grades to the next level is the shift in grading practices. Elementary school classrooms focus on task mastery, improvement, and intellectual development. However, middle and junior high schools are perceived by teachers, students, and observers to be performance-focused with the emphasis on competition and social comparison (Anderman & Midgley, 1997; Covington, 1999; Wigfield, Eccles, & Pintrich, 1996). Specifically, grading practices tend to be stricter at the middle school and junior levels and grades often are determined relative to the performance of others. Covington (1999; Covington & Teel, 1996) refer to this structure as the "ability game." In such a competitive zero-sum situation, an inadequate supply of rewards (good grades) is available to only a few students. When one player "wins" (receives a high grade), then other students must lose (receive lower grades). Classrooms with this focus are oriented toward competitive performance among students.

Classrooms in which only a few high grades are available tend to foster the perception that self-worth is related to success (Covington, 1999). Two motivational patterns that are generated in such an environment are a performance-orientation (outperforming others or appearing to do well with little effort) and failure avoidance. In contrast, classrooms that establish achievable criteria and assign good grades to all students who meet the criteria can facilitate a more positive student focus, i.e., a mastery or learning goal orientation.

The types and forms of evaluation as well as learner perceptions of the purpose of evaluation also influence children's motivation (Mac Iver, 1987). Social comparisons, for example, tend to lower children's views of their competence when the comparisons are unfavorable. Examples include announcements of highest and lowest scores; posted charts of students' projects, scores, and progress; ability grouping; and public displays of selected projects and achievements (Ames, 1992b, p. 264). Frequent use of written assignments that are graded, the display of only *A* or mostly correct papers, and the use of both positive and negative feedback in a public context also should be avoided (Stipek & Daniels, 1988). Such practices provide many opportunities for students to question their ability and to judge themselves inadequate (Ames, 1984, 1992a).

When students are evaluated for mastery, the methods of evaluation typically are varied, and students have opportunities to improve their performance. Effort then becomes a credible attribution for achievement, and the "performance equals ability" equation is nullified. Also important is that evaluation is private, rather than public (Ames, 1992b, p. 266).

Two other classroom characteristics that influence goal orientation are the types of classroom tasks, and distribution of authority and responsibility in the classroom (Ames, 1992a, 1992b). Tasks that are varied and diverse facilitate the development of mastery goals because they provide few opportunities to engage in social comparison. Particularly important, however, is the teacher's focus for classroom tasks. They should be structured as learning experiences (Brophy & Merrick, 1987), and presentations should address personal relevance of the content (Ames, 1992b).

Characteristics of learning-oriented classrooms reported by Stipek & Daniels (1988) include flexible instructional groups, variations in assignments according to the students' skill levels, discouragement of normative comparisons, frequent group projects, encouragement of peer assistance, and substantive comments rather than grades on report cards.

Important in the learning-goal orientation is developing independent thinking and self-directed learning. Research reviewed by Ames (1992b) indicates a positive relationship between the autonomy orientation of the classroom and intrinsic (internal) motivation. That is, providing children choices such that the choices are guided by interest (and not to protect feelings of self-worth or to avoid failure) enhances children's engagement and investment in learning. However, simply assigning responsibility to the child for completing long-term tasks does not imply meaningful direction for the student. Instead, student input into the selection of tasks, materials, and, if possible, method of learning is a way of enhancing student responsibility for tasks.

Planning Classroom Environments

Planning for classroom instruction typically focuses on the identification and selection of activities important in learning. The implications of attributional theory, however, are that planning also should include activities to enhance students' achievement-related efforts. Figure 12.5 illustrates the instructional strategies consistent with a learning goal structure and the motivational patterns that are generated. Of major importance is that classroom structures are interdependent. For example, teachers may be effective in designing challenging and varied tasks for children. However, if the evaluation practices encourage social comparison, the learning goal emphasis is compromised (Ames, 1992b, p. 266). Implementing grading policies based on specific, clearly defined criteria was effective in discouraging negative achievement goals in at-risk middle school students (Teel, DeBruin-Parecki, & Covington, 1998).

Another mechanism that can contribute to a positive learning environment is the implementation of some form of cooperative learning. Examples include small-group teaching; the Jigsaw method; Teams, Games, and Tournaments (TGT); and Student Teams and Achievement Divisions (STAD). In small-group teaching, students typically select subtopics within a general area and then organize themselves in groups of two to six to prepare for presentation to the total class. In the Jigsaw method, groups of students who are working on the same portion of the material help each other learn and prepare the material for presentation to their original group (Aronson, Stephan, Sikes, Blaney, & Snapp, 1978). Teams, Games, and Tournaments and Student Teams and Achievement Divisions are group study approaches that each conclude with a formal method of evaluating student learning on a weekly basis.

The cooperative group structure can reduce some of the pressure to achieve and can provide opportunities in which students can develop positive self-images. However, providing success experiences and removing negative consequences of failure are not sufficient to enhance the self-esteem of low-self-concept children (Ames, 1978). An essential ingredient, according to the linkages established by Weiner (1980d; Graham & Weiner, 1983), is the set of attributional messages conveyed by the teacher.

Summary

The attributional theory developed by Bernard Weiner addresses classroom conditions that contribute to student attributions for success and failure outcomes. It also

FIGURE 12.5

Classroom structure and instructional strategies essential for mastery goal orientation

Note: From "Classrooms: Goals, Structures, and Student Motivation" by C. Ames, 1992, *Journal of Educational Psychology, 84(3)*, p. 267. Reprinted with permission of the American Psychological Association.

provides a framework for analyzing teacher–student interactions. The factors that explain attributional formation in the classroom are the classroom model, teacher and student characteristics, and personal and classroom goal structures.

The classroom model indicates that specific teacher feedback, the teacher's nonverbal reactions, and his or her subsequent behavior toward the student are key factors in the student's identification of attributions. Teacher characteristics that influence student attributions are the type of teacher—reactive or proactive—and teacher perceptions of low achievers. Student characteristics that influence personal attributions are individual predispositions and developmental level. Most kindergarten children have high expectations of their ability and high expectations for success. By the second or third grade, however, their perceptions change and expectancies decrease.

Finally, personal and classroom goal structures, which represent different views of success and different achievement-related actions, also influence attributions. A performance or ego-involved goal structure involves demonstrating superior performance. Maintaining positive judgments of one's ability and public recognition of one's performance are important. Two other nonproductive personal goal orientations are work avoidance and failure avoidance. The former seeks relief from academic pressure by endorsing "just getting through" requirements, whereas the latter involves strategies to prevent an impression of incompetence.

In contrast, a learning or mastery goal structure focuses on mastering new skills and is based on the belief that effort and outcome are related. Students typically use a variety of strategies and prefer challenging tasks because the purpose is not to publicly validate performance.

A pervasive influence on the development of student goal structure is the task and goal structure of the classroom. Competitive classrooms with a focus on achievement, social comparison practices, stable learning groups, and display of only the most outstanding work contribute to individuals' ego-involved or performance goals. However, flexible instructional groups, diverse assignments, discouragement of normative comparisons, and authority structures that emphasize student autonomy and decision making foster learning goals. Planning classroom environments to facilitate positive student attributions involves restructuring tasks to emphasize learning, providing diverse and challenging tasks, and recognizing student effort and individual progress.

Designing Programs for Attributional Change

Implications of attribution theory apply to two areas of program development. One is programs for failure-oriented students. These students are those who exhibit the learned-helplessness characteristics, bright students who are easily debilitated by failure, and those who have low expectancies for success on school tasks, such as students with learning disabilities.

Most attribution retraining programs are designed to change undesirable or maladaptive attributions for failure from lack of ability to lack of effort. However, according to the attributional model, both success and failure outcomes should be addressed (see Figure 12.6). In other words, instead of being viewed as a random event, success becomes predictable when related to ability *and* effort. Both are internal factors, and extent of effort is controlled by the individual. On the other hand, failure is changed from an expected (highly predictable) event to one that is under some individual control through the control of effort.

However, building the high, stable, and resilient expectancies that accompany challenge seeking and persistence requires attention to several variables. Among them are an environment that supports risk taking and tasks that include challenge, and even failure, within a learning-orientation setting (Dweck, 1989, p. 118).

Planning an attributional change program should include at least three steps. The first step is to develop an analysis of the attributional cues that currently signal fail-

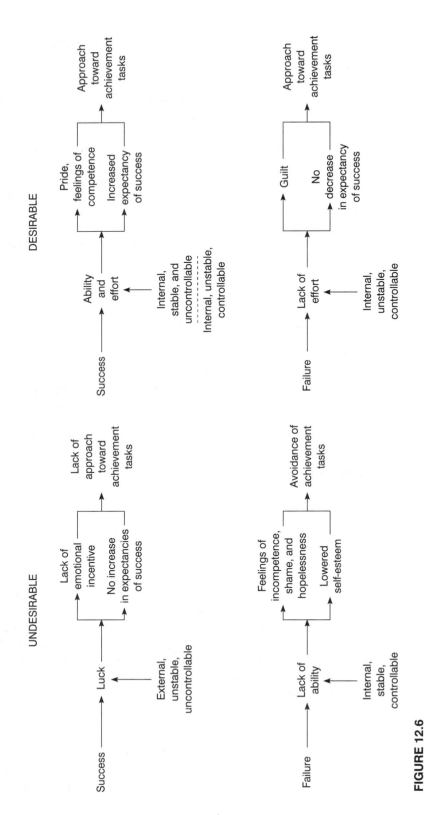

FIGURE 12.6
Desirable and undesirable causal inferences according to the attributional model

ure in the child's experience. The second step is to identify and implement alternative teacher behaviors that can serve as attributional cues to the student. Examples are legitimate, positive comments for both effort and partial activities completed correctly. The third is to identify group activities that foster beliefs in the importance of developing alternative strategies to reach a goal and that emphasize realistic goal setting.

The second area of program development is that of addressing childhood aggression. Hudley & Graham (1993) developed a set of 11 lessons to train aggressive boys not to infer hostile peer intent in negative social encounters with ambiguous causes. Lessons 2 through 6 used role play, discussions of personal experiences, and other activities to interpret and appropriately categorize the verbal and behavioral cues in social dilemmas (p. 127). Lessons 7 through 9 used negative encounters portrayed as ambiguous. Students then discussed likely causes, identified them as intentional or unintentional, and then selected the more likely causes given the ambiguous nature of intent. Lessons 10 and 11 involved practice in generating attributions to nonhostile intents and in generating decision rules about ways to respond given attributional uncertainty. Pre- and posttest measures of the students indicated a decrease in attributions of hostile intent, anger reactions, and selection of retaliatory behaviors in ambiguous situations.

EDUCATIONAL APPLICATIONS

A major contribution of attribution theory to education is related to the analysis of classroom interactions. In the classroom setting, researchers have applied the attributional framework to analyze both student and classroom goal orientations and to suggest remedies (Ames, 1992b; Ames & Archer, 1988; Covington, 1999; Dweck, 1989; Eliot, 1999; Elliott & Dweck, 1988; Jagacinski & Nicholls, 1987; Stipek & Daniels, 1988). On a broader scale, attribution theory has implications for the ways that our culture defines success. Frieze et al. (1983) describe several analyses of the American definition of success. It is viewed as attainable by the individual who outperforms others in competitive situations. Such a societal value, by its very nature, relegates some people to failure status. In contrast, other cultures define success in terms of group accomplishment and cooperation. At the very least, attribution theory suggests success definitions that emphasize accomplishment through effort and the exercise of learned skills (Frieze et al., 1983).

Classroom Issues

Since the theory is a theory of motivation, the issues of student characteristics, cognitive processes and instruction, and the social context for learning are viewed from that perspective.

Learner Characteristics
The characteristics of major concern to education include individual differences, readiness for learning, and motivation. They are viewed by attribution theory in terms of their relationship to students' causal beliefs about success and failure.

Individual Differences.   The theory developed by Bernard Weiner is one that seeks to identify the factors that influence the selection of personal attributions for success or failure, the judgments of others about failure and stigmatizing events, and the subsequent effects. The theory describes a general attributional model rather than individual differences in the selection of attributions. However, the developmental level and level of self-esteem of the student have been identified as characteristics that influence attribution selection for personal success or failure.

Readiness for Learning.   Although readiness is yet to be researched in the attributional framework, the implications for the classroom are clear. Students who consistently attribute failure to lack of ability experience rapid performance deterioration accompanied by ineffective problem solution strategies following errors. Readiness for new learning in terms of the capability to benefit from instruction for new skills is therefore influenced by the student's prior attributions for success or failure.

Motivation.   Theories of learning typically treat motivation as a concept that is an adjunct to the principles for generating learning in the student. For the most part, these theories focus on some environmental manipulation that may lead to student motivation, such as arousing the student's attention, examining the role of incentives, or making the material relevant, meaningful, or interesting (Weiner, 1974b).

In contrast, attribution theory views the student, and particularly the student's causal beliefs about success and failure, as primary sources of motivation. Therefore, in the classroom the important motivating events are not the "add-ons" to the instructional materials. Instead, the classroom events that contribute to motivation are teacher and peer reactions to student behavior in achievement-related activities.

Sources of information in the classroom that influence student motivation include (1) informational feedback about success or failure from the teacher, (2) the teacher's affective reaction to the outcome (pity, anger, and so on), and (3) the disposition made regarding the student following the outcome.

Cognitive Processes and Instruction

The three cognitive issues of importance to education are transfer of learning, teaching problem solving, and students' learning how-to-learn skills. Of these three constructs, transfer of learning plays a role in the theory.

The student's past record also influences the individual's "problem attack" skills. Research described earlier indicates that failure-oriented students execute stereotypic responses and inappropriate strategies when faced with failure, but mastery-oriented students undertake search and correction activities.

The Social Context for Learning

Attribution theory addresses the types of information used by individuals to construct perceptions of their abilities in a variety of situations and of their judgments about others. In the classroom setting, the theory has identified the teacher as an important source of information for the students' beliefs about their abilities. Specifically, in failure situations, the affective reaction of sympathy conveys the message of lack of ability, but anger signals lack of effort as a cause. In addition, research studies indicate that differential rewards and punishments and other subtle differences in treatments are dispensed to students on the basis of perceived causes for failure.

The full range of classroom factors that significantly influence student self-perceptions is beginning to be identified. Preliminary studies indicate some positive influence resulting from different types of goal structures and different classroom groupings that facilitate cooperative learning.

Relationships to Other Perspectives

Unlike the learning-process and cognitive-development theories, attribution theory is a theory of motivation. Although those theories refer to specific activities that may enhance learner interest or motivation, attribution theory identifies the learner as a major factor in developing motivation for school learning. Through the interpretation of information in the social setting and past experiences, the learner identifies causes of success or failure outcomes and is thereby motivated to or discouraged from attempting similar activities.

Some concepts in attribution theory and social–cognitive theory are complementary. Learners who attribute success to effort or ability and effort also hold positive self-efficacy beliefs and are self-regulated learners. Both theories also briefly discuss reprehensible conduct. Social–cognitive theory identifies mechanisms whereby the individual disengages from self-evaluative reactions. Attribution theory focuses on methods to redirect attributions of aggression for others' social actions in a positive direction. The purpose is to defuse incitements to aggressive behavior.

Developing a Classroom Strategy

The application of attribution theory in the classroom implies a need for proactive strategies rather than a reliance on reactive responses to students' achievement-related activities. It also implies a classroom climate that fosters an emphasis on the process of learning rather than on competitive achievement. Such a classroom climate minimizes the number of success-failure judgments with their accompanying self-worth assessments and expectancy consequences. Instead, classroom goals emphasize improved learning strategies, class time is structured to minimize interpersonal competition, and feedback to students minimizes ability or lack of ability as an attribution for classroom outcomes. In other words, the classroom is structured to reinforce the belief that learning is acquired through constructive effort. The following strategy is suggested for the development of a positive proactive environment.

Step 1: Restructure classroom objectives in terms of learning processes or strategies.

1.1 Which objectives can be rewritten to emphasize a learning strategy?

1.2 Which classroom tasks currently in use can be varied to provide novelty and diversity and enhance student interest?

Step 2: Identify appropriate evaluation methods.

2.1 Where can formative evaluations or tests be implemented that focus on identifying mistakes to improve learning?

2.2 Does the classroom contain wall charts or progress or grades that can be replaced with rotating displays of all students' work?

2.3 Are classroom rewards consistently distributed for effort, not ability?

2.4 Are students given a variety of opportunities to demonstrate what they have learned?

Step 3: Identify classroom activities that (1) deemphasize interpersonal competitiveness and (2) facilitate the development of effective task-approach strategies and effort.

3.1 Is the percentage of time devoted to class activities as compared with small-group and individual seatwork activities too high, for example, 80% as compared with 20%?

3.2 What changes can be made in tasks to increase student decision making?

3.3 Which small-group activities may be used to increase the cooperative nature of learning?

3.4 What individual or group games are available that can enhance student effort and/or improve learning strategies?

Step 4: Develop verbal feedback statements that convey appropriate attributional messages.

4.1 Is praise appropriately used (i.e., avoided for success at easy tasks, provided for persistence and appropriate strategies as well as success at difficult tasks)?

4.2 What constructive teacher strategies may be used instead of sympathy for unsuccessful performance? Are external factors, such as luck, avoided as explanations for success and failure?

4.3 What strategies may be used to encourage students to take responsibility for their own learning?

Classroom Examples

Two classroom strategies are discussed. The first is an academic learning game known as STRATAGEM (Bell, 1982), and the second is a group learning arrangement.

STRATAGEM

STRATAGEM was developed to ease the pressure of studying for examinations and to increase student effort in thinking through issues in the subject area. The game has been used successfully by the author with high school and college students. Other teachers have reported success with middle school students.

The game is a cooperative learning activity in which teams of two to four students take turns in answering questions typed on 3 × 5 cards placed face down in front of the players. Each game requires a banker and two teams of players. Thus, a classroom may have as many as five games operating simultaneously to accommodate the entire class.

Each team is given $1,000 in artificial money at the beginning of the game. The team decides, before seeing the question to be answered, the amount of money to be staked on the team's ability to answer the unseen question. Amounts from $10 to $50 may be selected. The information used by the team in this decision is the coding information provided about the question. This information is on the reverse side of the question card and, thus, is face up to the team. Questions are coded as one of three levels: 1 = recall; 2 = application; and 3 = inference. The topic of the question is also listed. An example is "Asking children to draw pictures about a story that they have just read is an example of _____," which is coded "Level 2—Application; Topic: Information-Processing Theory."

After the wager, one member turns the question card over and reads the question aloud. The team then has 3 to 4 minutes to discuss possible answers. Typically, the members of the other team in the game also are trying to determine the answer. If the team answers a level 1 question correctly, the bank matches the amount wagered. For a level 2 question, the bank pays double the wager, and it triples the amount for level 3 questions. Thus, the team, for a $10 wager, may receive an additional $10, $20, or $30. Similarly, for a $50 wager, the bank would pay $50, $100, or $150, depending on the level of the question.

To emphasize the learning process and to ensure that no team runs out of money, the teams lose only the amount of the wager for incorrect or incomplete answers. That is, the level of the question enters only into the reward for correct answers.

When the team announces the selected answer, it is either compared with a list of answers provided to the banker or evaluated by the teacher, who is circulating among the games. In practice, after learning the correct answer, both teams typically discuss the answer for a few minutes before the next team takes a turn on the next question. These brief discussions are permitted because (1) they do not lessen the enthusiasm for the game and (2) they contribute to the learning.

The teacher's role is to circulate among the games, clarifying questions or keeping the discussions from inhibiting the play. In a 45-minute class period, from 25 to 30 questions can be completed. Of the 50 questions developed for each use of the game, approximately two thirds are application and inference questions. The nature of the questions precipitates discussions that enhance learning.

The ideal time to implement the game is a week or two before a major examination, that is, before the students have begun their detailed study. This practice equalizes performance on the game questions and emphasizes learning.

Teaching Students to Identify the Main Idea

In this classroom strategy, the following instructional events are presented by the teacher (see chapter 6):

1. Gain attention.
2. Inform learner of the objective.
3. Stimulate recall.
4. Present distinctive stimulus features (topic + something special about the topic = main idea) plus two or three examples.

5. Provide learning guidance. This event is carried out with small groups. Each group is given the task of selecting four favorite movies or television programs, identifying the main idea of each and describing why the statement is the main idea. As each group progresses in the activity, the teacher provides feedback about needed changes in the choices. Differences between story details, sweeping statements, and the main idea are pointed out where needed. At the conclusion of the activity, each group presents its program choices and main idea identifications to the class.

6. Elicit performance.

7. Provide feedback.

Events 6 and 7 are completed in the form of a written diagnostic exercise. Children are given a set of eight story lines with four choices of the main idea for each. Feedback is given in the form of changes needed to realign the child's conception of *main idea* with the concept characteristics.

8. Assess performance.

9. Provide retention and transfer.

Events 8 and 9 make use of the academic game "Natural Topics," described in chapter 6.

Review of the Theory

Bernard Weiner's theory of achievement motivation applies the concepts of attributional theory to achievement-related tasks. Attribution theories seek to identify the ways in which individuals arrive at explanations for events. Weiner maintains that the search for understanding is a primary source of motivation for human behavior (Table 12.6).

The major components in the theory are (1) the likely explanations given to success and failure outcomes, (2) the characteristics of these causal inferences, and (3) the role of affective reactions in subsequent behavior. Typical explanations given for success and failure include ability, effort, task difficulty, luck, others, and mood or illness. These causal inferences vary on the dimensions of locus of causality, stability, and controllability. These dimensions generate different expectancies for the future and different emotional reactions.

Internal attributions contribute to the individual's self-image, whether positive or negative, and stable attributions lead to expectancies for recurrence of the experienced outcome. The controllability dimension, in contrast, influences emotional reactions, such as pity and anger, as well as the helping behavior of others.

In the classroom setting, continued attributions of lack of ability for failure lead to the phenomenon referred to as learned helplessness. Children in this category typically undertake random strategies for school tasks and they give up easily. Attribution theory suggests the implementation of change programs to alter failure beliefs from lack of ability to lack of effort.

TABLE 12.6
Summary of Weiner's attribution theory

Basic Elements	Definition
Assumptions	The search for understanding is a primary motivator of action. Attributions are complex sources of information about outcomes. Future behavior is determined, in part, by perceived causes of prior outcomes.
Motivation	Expectancies, self-esteem, and the tendency to engage in achievement-related behaviors are influenced by perceived causes of outcomes.
The attributional process	Outcomes are identified as success or failure and perceived causes are identified. Emotions and expectancies are generated by both the nature of the outcome, the particular attribution, and the dimensions of the selected attribution.
Components of motivation	Major attributions (ability, effort, task difficulty, mood or illness, luck, and others) and the dimensions (locus of causality, stability, and controllability).
Designing instruction for complex skills	In order to alleviate the phenomenon of learned helplessness, develop programs to change failure attributions from lack of ability to lack of effort.
Major issues in designing instruction	Effects of teacher attributions for success and failure; teacher cues that signal attributions; attributions that influence self-esteem and effort.
ANALYSIS OF THE THEORY	
Disadvantages	Specific classroom procedures for the implementation of attribution theory in the classroom are yet to be developed.
Contributions to classroom practice	Identifies classroom practices that contribute to failure and the psychological links to children's beliefs and actions. Identifies problems inherent in the competitive nature of much of classroom learning. Provides a framework for the research and analysis of many affective events operating in the classroom.

Disadvantages

Specific classroom procedures are yet to be developed for the implementation of attribution theory in the classroom. Although some promising directions have been identified by the research, further exploration is needed.

Contributions to Educational Practice

Weiner's attribution theory has identified a major problem in the American classroom. It is the competitive nature of learning and the effects that such an atmosphere can have on many children. Competitiveness, by its very nature, relegates someone to last place, often in a race that has limited long-term value. The theory provides a framework for the research and analysis of many affective events operating in the classroom.

CHAPTER QUESTIONS

1. What is the relationship between attributions for success and failure and Bandura's concept of efficacy?

2. How would Skinner view the teacher's expressions of sympathy following a student's academic failure if the failure-oriented behavior continued?

3. Suppose that a teacher is planning a program to redirect children's failure-oriented behav-iors. In implementing Weiner's attribution theory, what are some of the kinds of information that the teacher would ascertain about the children's characteristics and behaviors?

4. How might a learner's theory of intelligence interact with classroom events to influence attributions for achievement outcomes?

REFERENCES

Ames, C. (1978). Children's achievement attributions and self-reinforcement: Effects of self-concept and competitive reward structure. *Journal of Educational Psychology, 70*, 345–355.

Ames, C. (1984). Competitive, cooperative, and individualistic goal structures: A motivational analysis. In R. Ames & C. Ames (Eds.), *Research on motivation in education* (Vol. 1, pp. 177–207). New York: Academic Press.

Ames, C. (1992a). Achievement goals and the motivational climate. In D. Schunk & J. Meece (Eds.), *Student perceptions in the classroom* (pp. 327–348). Hillsdale, NJ: Erlbaum.

Ames, C. (1992b). Classrooms: Goals, structures, and student motivation. *Journal of Educational Psychology, 84*(3), 261–271.

Ames, C., & Ames, R. (1984). Systems of student and teacher motivation: Toward a qualitative definition. *Journal of Educational Psychology, 76*, 535–557.

Ames, C., & Archer, J. (1988). Achievement goals in the classroom: Students' learning strategies and motivational processes. *Journal of Educational Psychology, 80*(3), 260–267.

Ames, C., Ames, R., & Felker, D. W. (1977). Effects of a competitive reward structure and valence of outcome on children's achievement attributions. *Journal of Educational Psychology, 60*, 1–8.

Anderman, E. M., & Midgley, C. (1997). Changes in goal orientation, perceived academic competence, and grades across the middle-school levels. *Contemporary Educational Psychology, 22*, 260–298.

Anderman, E. M., Griesinger, T., & Westerfield, G. (1998). Motivation and cheating during early adolescence. *Journal of Educational Psychology, 90*(1), 84–93.

Anderson, C. A. (1983). Motivational and performance deficits in interpersonal settings: The effect of attributional style. *Journal of Personality and Social Psychology, 45*(3), 1136–1147.

Anderson, C., Horowitz, M., & French, R. (1983). Attributional style of lonely and depressed people. *Journal of Personality and Social Psychology, 45*, 137–144.

Archer, J. (1994). Achievement goals as a measure of motivation in university students. *Contemporary Educational Psychology, 19*, 430–446.

Aronson, E., Stephan, C., Sikes, J., Blaney, N., & Snapp, P. (1978). *The jigsaw classroom.* Beverly Hills, CA: Sage.

Atkinson, J. W. (1958). Towards experimental analysis of human motivation in terms of motives, expectancies, and incentives. In J. W. Atkinson (Ed.), *Motives in fantasy, action, and society* (pp. 288–305). Princeton, NJ: Van Nostrand.

Atkinson, J. W. (1964). *An introduction to motivation.* Princeton, NJ: D. Van Nostrand.

Barker, G., & Graham, S. (1987). Developmental study of praise and blame as attributional cues. *Journal of Educational Psychology, 79*, 62–66.

Bell, M. E. (1982). STRATAGEM: A problem-solving game for use in revision. *Simulation/Games for Learning, 12*(4), 157–164.

Brophy, J. (1999). Toward a model of the value aspects of motivation in education: Developing appreciation for particular learning domains and activities. *Educational Psychologist, 34*(2), 75–86.

Brophy, J., & Merrick, M. (1987). *Motivating students to learn: An experiment in junior high social studies classes.* East Lansing, MI: Institute for Research on Teaching.

Brown, J., & Weiner, B. (1984). Affective consequences of ability versus effort ascriptions: Controversies, resolutions, and quandaries. *Journal of Educational Psychology, 76,* 146–158.

Burger, J. M., Cooper, H. M., & Good, T. L. (1982). Teacher attributions of student performance: Effects of outcome. *Personality and Social Psychology Bulletin, 4,* 685–690.

Butler, R. (1987). Task involving and ego involving properties of evaluation: Effects of different feedback conditions on motivational perceptions, interest and performance. *Journal of Educational Psychology, 79,* 474–482.

Carroll, J. (1978). Causal attributions in expert parole decisions. *Journal of Personality and Social Psychology, 36,* 1501–1511.

Carroll, J., & Payne, J. (1977). Judgments about crime and the criminal: A model and a method for investigating parole decisions. In B. D. Sales (Ed.), *Perspectives in law and psychology: Vol. 1. The criminal justice system* (pp. 191–240). New York: Plenum.

Covington, M. V. (1999). Caring about learning: The nature and nurturing of subject-matter appreciation. *Educational Psychologist,* 127–136.

Covington, M. V., & Teel, K. M. (1996). *Overcoming student failure: Changing motives and incentives for learning.* Washington, DC: American Psychological Association.

Covington, M. V., & Omelich, C. L. (1984). Task-oriented versus competitive learning structures: Motivational and performance consequences. *Journal of Educational Psychology, 76,* 1038–1050.

Crittended, K. S., & Wiley, M. G. (1980). Causal attributions and behavioral response to failure. *Social Psychology Quarterly, 43,* 353–358

Dai, Y. D., Moon, S. M., & Feldhusen, J. F. (1998). Achievement motivation and gifted students: A social cognitive perspective. *Educational Psychologist, 33*(2/3), 45–64.

deCharms, R. (1968). *Personal causation.* New York: Academic.

DeVries, D., & Edwards, K. (1973). Learning games and student teams: Their effects on classroom process. *American Educational Research Journal, 10,* 307–318.

Diener, C. I., & Dweck, C. S. (1978). An analysis of learned helplessness: Continuous changes in performance, strategy and achievement cognitions following failure. *Journal of Personality and Social Psychology, 36,* 451–462.

Diener, C. I., & Dweck, C. S. (1980). Analysis of learned helplessness II: The processing of success. *Journal of Personality and Social Psychology, 39,* 940–952.

Dodge, K., & Crick, N. (1990). Social information-processing bases of aggressive behaviors in children. *Personality and Social Psychology Bulletin, 16,* 8–22.

Dweck, C. S. (1975). The role of expectations and attributions in the alleviation of learned helplessness. *Journal of Personality and Social Psychology, 31,* 674–685.

Dweck, C. S. (1986). Motivational processes affecting learning. *American Psychologist, 41,* 1040–1048.

Dweck, C. S. (1989). Motivation. In R. Glaser & A. Lesgold (Eds.), *The handbook of psychology and education. Vol. 1* (pp. 187–239). Hillsdale, NJ: Erlbaum.

Dweck, C. S., & Licht, B. G. (1980). Learned helplessness and academic achievement. In J. Garber & M. Seligman (Eds.), *Human helplessness: Theory and application* (pp. 197–221). New York: Academic.

Dweck, C., & Leggett, E. (1988). A social–cognitive approach to motivation and personality. *Psychological Review, 95,* 256–273.

Eliot, A. J. (1999). Approach and avoidance motivation and achievement goals. *Educational Psychologist, 35*(3), 169–189.

Eliot, A. J., McGregor, H. A., & Gable, S. (1999). Achievement goals, study strategies, and exam performance: A mediational analysis. *Journal of Educational Psychology, 91*(3), 549–563.

Elliott, E. E., & Dweck, C. S. (1988). Goals: An approach to motivation and achievement. *Journal of Personality and Social Psychology, 54*(1), 5–12.

Eswara, H. A. (1972). Administration of reward and punishment in relation to ability, effort, and performance. *Journal of Social Psychology, 87,* 139–140.

Foesterling, F., & Groenvald, A. (1983). Attributions for election results: A study of attributional hypotheses in a field study of Lower Saxony community elections. *Zeitschrift für Socialpsychologie, 14,* 262–269.

Frieze, I. H. (1976). Causal attributions and information seeking to explain success and failure. *Journal of Research in Personality, 10,* 293–305.

Frieze, I. H. (1980). Beliefs about success and failure in the classroom. In J. H. McMillan (Ed.), *The social psychology of school learning* (pp. 39–78). New York: Academic.

Frieze, I. H., & Snyder, H. N. (1980). Children's beliefs about the causes of success and failure in school settings. *Journal of Educational Psychology, 72,* 186–196.

Frieze, I., Francis, W., & Hanusa, B. (1983). Defining success in classroom learning. In J. Levine & M. Wang (Eds.), *Teacher and student perceptions* (pp. 3–28). Hillsdale, NJ: Erlbaum.

Good, T. (1980). Classroom expectations: Teacher–pupil interactions. In J. H. McMillan (Ed.), *The social psychology of school learning* (pp. 70–122). New York: Academic.

Graham, S. (1984). Communicating sympathy and anger to black and white children: The cognitive attributional consequences of affective cues. *Journal of Personality and Social Psychology, 47*(1), 40–540.

Graham, S. (1988). Can attribution theory tell us something about blacks? *Educational Psychologist, 23*(1), 3–21.

Graham, S. (1990). Communicating low ability in the classroom: Bad things good teachers sometimes do. In S. Graham & V. S. Folkes (Eds.), *Attribution theory: Applications to achievement, mental health, and interpersonal conflict* (pp. 17–36). Hillsdale, NJ: Erlbaum.

Graham, S., & Hudley, C. (1992). An attributional approach to aggression in African-American children. In D. Schunk & J. Meece (Eds.), *Student perceptions in the classroom* (pp. 75–93). Hillsdale, NJ: Erlbaum.

Graham, S., Hudley, C., & Williams, E. (1992). Attributional and emotional determinants of aggression among African-American and Latino young adolescents. *Developmental Psychology, 28,* 731–740.

Graham, S., & Weiner, B. (1983). Some educational implications of sympathy and anger from an attributional perspective. In R. Snow & M. Farr (Eds.), *Aptitude learning, and instruction: Vol. 3. Conative and affective policy analysis* (pp. 199–221). Hillsdale, NJ: Erlbaum.

Graham, S., & Weiner, B. (1996). Theories and principles of motivation. In D. C. Berliner & R. C. Calfee (Eds.), *Handbook of educational psychology* (pp. 63–84). New York: Macmillan.

Heider, F. (1958). *The psychology of interpersonal relations.* New York: Wiley.

Hoffman, M. L. (1982). Development of prosocial motivation: Empathy and guilt. In N. Eisenberg-Borg (Ed.), *Development of prosocial behavior* (pp. 281–313). New York: Academic.

Hudley, C., & Graham, S. (1993). An attributional intervention to reduce peer directed aggression among African-American boys. *Child Development, 64,* 124–138.

Jagacinski, C. M. (1992). The effects of task involvement and ego involvement on achievement-related cognitions and behaviors. In D. H. Schunk & J. Meece (Eds.), *Student perceptions in the classroom* (pp. 287–306). Hillsdale, NJ: Erlbaum.

Jagacinski, C. M., & Nicholls, J. G. (1984). Conceptions of ability and related affects in task involvement and ego involvement. *Journal of Educational Psychology, 76,* 909–919.

Jagacinski, C. M., & Nicholls, J. G. (1987). Competence and affect in task involvement and ego involvement: The impact of social comparison information. *Journal of Educational Psychology, 79,* 107–114.

Juvonen, J. (1991). Deviance, perceived responsibility, and negative peer reactions. *Developmental Psychology, 27,* 672–681.

Juvonen, J. (1992). Negative peer reactions from the perspective of the reactors. *Journal of Educational Psychology, 84,* 314–321.

Kelley, H., (1973). The processes of causal attribution. *American Psychologist, 28,* 107–128.

Kun, A., & Weiner, B. (1973). Necessary versus sufficient causal schema for success and failure. *Journal of Research in Personality, 7,* 197–203.

Lau, R. R., & Russell, D. (1980). Attributions in the sports pages: A field test of some current hypotheses in attribution research. *Journal of Personality and Social Psychology, 39,* 29–38.

Mac Iver, D. (1987). Classroom factors and student characteristics predicting students' use of achievement standards during self-assessment. *Child Development, 58,* 1258–1271.

Maehr, M. L., & Nicholls, J. G. (1980). Culture and achievement motivation: A second look. In. N. Warren (Ed.), *Studies in cross cultural psychology* (Vol. 3, pp. 221–267). New York: Academic Press.

McMahan, I. D. (1973). Relationships among causal attributions and expectancy of success. *Journal of Personality and Social Psychology, 28,* 108–114.

Middleton, M., & Midgley, C. (1997). Avoiding the demonstration of lack of ability: An underexplored aspect of goal theory. *Journal of Educational Psychology, 89,* 710–718.

Nicholls, J. G. (1978). The development of the concepts of effort and ability, perception of academic attainment, and the understanding that difficult tasks require more ability. *Child Development, 49,* 800–814.

Nicholls, J. G. (1989). *The competitive ethos and democratic education.* Cambridge, MA: Harvard University Press.

Pintrich, P. R., & Blumenfeld, P. C. (1985). Classroom experiences and children's self-perceptions of ability, effort, and conduct. *Journal of Educational Psychology, 77,* 646–657.

Reisenzein, R., & Hoffman, T. (1990). An investigation of the dimensions of cognitive appraisal in emotion using the repertory grid technique. *Motivation and Emotion, 14,* 1–26.

Rest, S., Neirenberg, R., Weiner, B., & Heckhausen, H. (1973). Further evidence concerning the effects of perceptions of effort and ability on achievement evaluation. *Journal of Personality and Social Psychology, 28,* 187–191.

Rohrkemper, M., & Brophy, J. (1983). Teachers' thinking about problem students. In J. Levine & M. Wang (Eds.), *Teacher and student perceptions* (pp. 75–103). Hillsdale, NJ: Erlbaum.

Rohrkemper, M., & Corno, L. (1988). Success and failure in classroom tasks: Adaptive learning and classroom teaching. *Elementary School Journal, 88*(3), 197–312.

Rosenbaum, R. M. (1972). *A dimensional analysis of the perceived causes of success and failure.* Unpublished doctoral dissertation, University of California, Los Angeles.

Rotter, J. B. (1966). Generalized expectancies for internal versus external control of reinforcement. *Psychological Monographs, 80* (1, Whole No. 609).

Ruble, D. N., & Rhales, W. S. (1981). The development of children's perceptions and attributions about their social world. In J. Harvey, W. Ickes, & R. Kidd (Eds.), *New directions in attribution research* (Vol. 3, pp. 3–26). Hillsdale, NJ: Erlbaum.

Seligman, M. E. P. (1975). *Helplessness.* San Francisco: Freeman.

Slavin, R. E. (1980). Cooperative learning. *Review of Educational Research, 50*(2), 315–342.

Stipek, D. J. (1981). Children's perceptions of their own and their classmate's ability. *Journal of Educational Psychology, 73,* 404–410.

Stipek, D. J., & Daniels, D. H. (1988). Declining perceptions of competence: A consequence of changes in the child or in the educational environment? *Journal of Educational Psychology, 80*(3), 352–356.

Teel, K. M., DeBruin-Parecki, A., & Covington, M. V. (1998). Teaching strategies that honor and motivate inner-city African American students: A school university collaboration. *Teaching and Teacher Education, 14,* 479–495.

Thorkildsen, T. A., & Nicholls, J. G. (1998). Fifth-graders' achievement orientation and beliefs: Individual and classroom differences. *Journal of Educational Psychology, 90*(2), 179–201.

Vispoel, W. P., & Austin, J. R. (1995). Success and failure in junior high school: A critical incident approach to understanding students' attributional beliefs. *American Educational Research Journal, 32*(2), 377–412.

Weiner, B. (1972). *Theories of motivation from mechanism to cognition.* Chicago: Markham.

Weiner, B. (1974a). An attributional interpretation of expectancy-value theory. In B. Weiner (Ed.), *Cognitive views of human motivation* (pp. 51–69). New York: Academic Press.

Weiner, B. (1974b). Motivational psychology and educational research. *Educational Psychologist, 11,* 96–101.

Weiner, B. (1977). An attributional approach for educational psychology. In L. Shulman (Ed.), *Review of research in education* (Vol. 4, pp. 179–209). Itasca, IL: Peacock.

Weiner, B. (1979). A theory of motivation for some classroom experiences. *Journal of Educational Psychology, 71,* 3–25.

Weiner, B. (1980a). A cognitive (attribution)-emotion-action model of motivated behavior: An analysis of judgments of help-giving. *Journal of Personality and Social Psychology, 39,* 186–200.

Weiner, B. (1980b). *Human motivation.* New York: Holt, Rinehart & Winston.

Weiner, B. (1980c). "May I borrow your class notes?" An attributional analysis of judgments of help-giving in an achievement-related context. *Journal of Educational Psychology, 72,* 676–681.

Weiner, B. (1980d). The role of affect in rational (attributional) approaches to human motivation. *Educational Research, 9,* 4–11.

Weiner, B. (1982). The emotional consequences of causal ascriptions. In M. S. Clark & S. T. Fiske (Eds.), *Affect and cognition: The 17th annual Carnegie symposium on cognition* (pp. 185–208). Hillsdale, NJ: Erlbaum.

Weiner, B. (1983a). Some thoughts about feelings. In S. G. Paris, G. M. Olson, & H. W. Stevenson (Eds.), *Learning and motivation in the classroom* (pp. 165–178). Hillsdale, NJ: Erlbaum.

Weiner, B. (1983b). Speculations regarding the role of affect in achievement-change programs guided by attributional principles. In J. Levine &

M. Wang (Eds.), *Teacher and student perceptions* (pp. 57–73). Hillsdale, NJ: Erlbaum.

Weiner, B. (1985a). An attributional theory of achievement motivation and emotion. *Psychological Review, 92*(4), 548–573.

Weiner, B. (1985b). *Human motivation.* New York: Springer-Verlag.

Weiner, B. (1985c). "Spontaneous" causal thinking. *Psychological Bulletin, 8,* 226–232.

Weiner, B. (1993). On sin versus sickness: A theory of perceived responsibility and social motivation. *American Psychologist, 48*(9), 957–965.

Weiner, B. (1994a). Ability versus effort revisited: The moral determinants of achievement evaluation and achievement as a moral system. *Educational Psychologist, 29*(3), 163–172.

Weiner, B. (1994b). Integrating social and personal theories of achievement striving. *Review of Educational Research, 64*(4), 557–574.

Weiner, B. (1995). *Judgments of responsibility: A foundation for a theory of social conduct.* New York: Guilford.

Weiner, B., & Graham, S. (1984). An attributional approach to emotional development. In C. Izard, J. Kagan, & R. Zacone (Eds.), *Emotions, cognition, and behavior* (pp. 167–191). Cambridge: Cambridge University Press.

Weiner, B., & Kukla, A. (1970). An attributional analysis of achievement motivation. *Journal of Personality and Social Psychology, 15,* 1–20.

Weiner, B., & Peter, N. (1973). A cognitive-developmental analysis of achievement and moral judgments. *Developmental Psychology, 9,* 290–309.

Weiner, B., Frieze, I., Kukla, A., Reed, L., Rest, S., & Rosenbaum, R. (1971). *Perceiving the causes of success and failure.* New York: General Learning.

Weiner, B., Graham S., & Chandler, S. (1982). Causal antecedents of pity, anger, and guilt. *Personality and Social Psychology Bulletin, 8,* 226–232.

Weiner, B., Graham, S., Stern, P., & Lawson, M. (1982). Using affective cues to infer causal thoughts. *Developmental Psychology, 18,* 278–286.

Weiner, B., Graham, S., Taylor, S., & Meyer, W. (1983). Social cognition in the classroom. *Educational Psychologist, 18,* 109–124.

Weiner, B., Neirenberg, R., & Goldstein, M. (1976). Social learning (locus of control) versus attributional (causal stability) interpretations of expectancy of success. *Journal of Personality, 44,* 52–68.

Wigfield, A., & Harold, R. D. (1992). Teacher beliefs and children's achievement self-perceptions: A developmental perspective. In D. Schunk & J. Meece (Eds.), *Student perceptions in the classroom* (pp. 95–121). Hillsdale, NJ: Erlbaum.

Wigfield, A., Eccles, J., & Pintrich, P. (1996). Development between the ages of 11 and 25. In R. C. Calfee & D. C. Berliner (Eds.), *Handbook of educational psychology* (pp. 148–187). New York: Macmillan.

Wilson, V. L., & Palmer, D. J. (1983). Latent partition analysis of attributions for actual achievement. *American Educational Research Journal, 20,* 581–589.

Zucker, G. S., & Weiner, B. (1993). Conservatism and perceptions of poverty: An attributional analysis. *Journal of Applied Social Psychology, 23,* 925–943.

Epilogue

Competing perspectives progress and degenerate, or coexist indefinitely, depending on their capability to generate new hypotheses that lead to empirical discoveries (Lakatos, 1970).

Early in human history philosophers and educators sought to understand the events that explain the process of learning. Philosophers approached the task by first defining the nature of knowledge consistent with a particular belief about the nature of reality. If knowledge is defined as the innate ideas present in the mind at birth, then learning must be the process by which those ideas acquire form and substance. In contrast, if knowledge is defined as sensory experience, then learning is the process whereby the information derived through the senses becomes organized in a systematic way.

In the early centuries of civilization, knowledge was a commodity reserved for an elite group—priests, kings, and philosophers. Society was not required to educate large numbers of citizens in a variety of complex skills in order to survive. Therefore, explanations of learning were not viewed as prescriptions for educational practice.

Since that time, however, societies and cultures have evolved and changed. Included in these changes were continued expansion of the available knowledge base of the culture and the ways that knowledge is to be transmitted to future generations.

Progress in the sciences in explaining physical phenomena in the 18th and 19th centuries led to interest in the derivation of learning principles from empirical data. Also, education, however rudimentary, had become a process whereby individuals received some instruction in at least the basic skills of reading, writing, and arithmetic (ciphering). Thus, the acquisition of organized knowledge, however simplified, was no longer the province of a few.

In the climate of expanded scientific investigations of physical phenomena, researchers interested in mental events pressed for experimental investigations of the human mind. The result was the emergence of psychology as the discipline that applied the experimental method to analyses of learning.

CONTRIBUTIONS OF LEARNING THEORY

The early theories of learning were charting new unexplored territory, and in many ways seem quite primitive from the perspective of the late 20th century. Nevertheless, they provided experimental paradigms for research and introduced basic constructs that could be studied systematically in the laboratory or in the school setting. Moreover, they were appropriate for the learning needs of society at the beginning of the 20th century. For the most part, individuals were expected to acquire rudimentary skills in ciphering (arithmetic) and reading. Only a few became scholars or thinkers. Pavlov's classical conditioning and Thorndike's instrumental conditioning addressed these basic learning situations, which involve the linking of a stimulus and a response. Classical conditioning demonstrated the association of a response to a stimulus through stimulus pairing, and instrumental conditioning demonstrated the linking of stimuli and responses through the use of consequences. Although Gestalt theory addressed the role of perception in problem solving, the problems were either of the puzzle type or relatively rote school problems. Functional fixedness and problem set, two Gestalt concepts, refer to difficulties that can arise in these situations.

Classical conditioning failed to fulfill Watson's bold promise that it would explain all behavior. Nevertheless, the paradigm addresses the attachment of emotional responses to otherwise neutral stimuli, such as calendar dates and particular locations.

Unable to explain the acquisition of complex skills, behaviorism was foundering in the late 1930s when B. F. Skinner introduced operant conditioning. Focusing on response consequences as the key to behavioral change, operant conditioning led to programs in behavior modification, the teaching machine, and programmed learning materials in reading and other areas. The widespread popularity of Skinner's principles led to many misapplications; nevertheless, reinforcement is a powerful principle that plays a key role in efforts to develop new behaviors.

The training needs of World War II and the later perceived threat from the USSR raised new questions about learning. Efforts to teach individuals to operate and repair complex equipment revealed that teaching the component skills of a complex task is essential. The role of component skills, a variable previously unaddressed, became the nucleus of Robert Gagné's conditions of learning.

The 1960s curriculum reform, precipitated by the launch of Sputnik, raised the issue that U.S. schools had failed to produce sufficient numbers of scholars and scientists. Gagné's domain of intellectual skills, which differentiated problem solving from less complex interactions with symbols, addressed this priority.

The communications research emerging after World War II and the advent of the computer raised another issue in human learning. If computers process information for a specific task, are humans engaged in a process no less complex? These developments validated the concerns of theorists and researchers interested in the long-neglected issue of mental processes. What followed is referred to as the cognitive revolution because the focus on the internal cognitive operations in information processing and problem solving was a major paradigm shift.

A different dimension of cognitive processing was introduced by the discovery of Piaget's theory and research in the 1960s. Piaget described the richness and complexity of the development of natural logic and the broad qualitative transformations from the preverbal logic of the infant to the cognitively complex thinking of the scientist. Piaget's research demonstrated that the thinking of children was not simply that of little adults, but, instead, was a very different set of processes.

Of interest is that the cognitive revolution of the 1960s and 1970s was a major discontinuity for psychology, and especially educational psychology (Pintrich, 1994). The interest in cognitive development generated by Piagetian theory and the attention to cognitive processes initiated by information-processing theory had a profound effect on both theory development and recommendations for educational practice. That is, the cognitive revolution changed the basic constructs addressed by psychology and educational psychology. Instead of observable events in the form of stimuli and responses, the basic constructs became the mental structures, activities, skills, and processes that represent the inward life of the mind (p. 138). Currently, perspectives on learning disagree on the best ways to represent the inner workings of the mind. Nevertheless, this focus addresses an issue raised by William James and other early psychologists.

The prevalence of electronic media in the decades following the 1960s has introduced another dimension into both society at large and educational institutions. Specifically, the images, ideas, settings, beliefs, and actions transmitted by television have changed the larger social reality with which individuals have contact. Albert Bandura's social–cognitive theory addressed this new reality in his analyses of the effects of models on observers. According to Bandura, much of learning is an indirect process in which the reinforcements and punishments accorded to others are influential in the observer's acquisition of particular behaviors.

Western society has become more complex in other ways as well. As computers become mainstays of business and industry, individuals in the work force are expected to become much more proficient at processing information and solving problems. Thus, cognitive psychology has a major role to play in addressing learning essential for such tasks.

In addition, the prevalence of the computer for both communication and work has extended both learning and work beyond the confines of a particular setting. Some businesses presently are exploring the use of computers by employees in their homes to generate communication with others and to carry out their basic activities.

The use of computers in the home setting to carry out one's work depends on individuals who are highly skilled, motivated, and self-directed. However, until the late 20th century, motivation was not a pivotal issue in theory development. Currently, both Bandura's social–cognitive theory and Bernard Weiner's theory of attribution address motivation as integral components of learning and achievement. Bandura describes the role of personal efficacy and the development of the individual's self-regulatory system as major components in acquiring both expertise and self-direction. Weiner, in contrast, analyzes the learner's causal inferences for success and failure outcomes and the effects of these attributions on subsequent achievement-related efforts.

As the 21st century unfolds, the number of individuals from diverse cultures who are becoming part of the mainstream are raising new questions for both education and the workplace. Vygotsky's cultural-historical theory describes the role of the signs and symbols of one's culture in determining the substance and form of one's learning. It places new emphasis on the ways that signs and symbols are learned and the ways that they are used to direct one's own learning. The implication is that individuals from different cultural backgrounds can come together to solve community problems, but developing mutually understandable forms of communication within educational and work settings is essential.

Each of the seven theories has addressed particular issues relevant both to learning and to education. Each has developed principles based on particular assumptions about the nature of learning or cognitive development. Further, each theory has provided insight into different issues in the classroom, and each has made a major contribution to an understanding of human learning (see Table 1).

CURRENT ISSUES

In recent years, theory and research have begun to address the many complexities inherent in the learning process. However, theory development and research face conceptual, theoretical and social issues in their efforts to contribute to our understanding of learning and instruction.

They are (1) the gap between theory development and understanding (conceptual), (2) the importance of affect and motivation (theoretical), (3) the role of technology in learning (theoretical), (4) the gap between the reality of many classroom settings and the theory (social), (5) the disparity among children entering school (social), and (6) the tension between universalistic and particularistic theories.

The Gap Between Theory Development and Understanding.   The rapid popularity of a theory often leads to misconceptions and misapplications. Valsiner (1998) notes that the depth of understanding of a theory is inversely related to its popularity. If the misconceptions are not corrected, the theory often is questioned or discredited. An early example in the 1960s was the rush to publish so-called programmed learning materials. On the surface, they resembled Skinner's mode of programming instruction. However, the developers simply left blanks in sentences from textbooks instead of carefully designing the instructional sequence. The problems generated by the poorly designed materials led to criticisms of operant conditioning as a basis for developing individualized instruction.

More recently, the attempted application of the Piagetian stages of cognitive development to the design of curriculum and the stated mandate that Vygotsky advocated group-directed school instruction are examples. The result is curriculum or instruction that fails to meet the potential suggested by the theory.

This issue is difficult to address in an era of prolific publications and rapid information dissemination through the Internet. Methods of addressing this issue include verifying the source of the theoretical interpretation, e.g., an established Vygotskian or Piagetian scholar, checking original sources (or translations by established scholars), and comparing suggested implementations with verified sources about the theory.

The Importance of Affect and Motivation.   Self-regulatory constructs are likely to become even more important as educators and others attempt to address the almost overwhelming problems in school and society today (Pintrich, 1994, p. 140) (see the following sections). Further, the rapid increase in knowledge and information as well as rapid transformations in the workplace place a premium on self-directed learners who value learning for its own sake and who can make use of new information. Brophy (1999) notes that a challenge for theory is to address ways to develop learners who value the subject matter and learning. His suggestion of the need for models who exemplify enthusiasm for the subject as well as the structuring of reinforcements for student development of insights about the subject area are useful. Nevertheless, theory and research also must explore other individual and social factors that influence the development of positive dispositions toward learning.

The Role of Technology in Learning.   Bandura's social–cognitive theory refers to models in the electronic media; however, most theories address the learning of the individual student in interacting with objects or events in the environment. Yet to be developed are learning principles that address teacher–student interactions, student-to-student communication, and student-to-subject-matter interactions for various uses of computer technology. The structuring of information, the nature of questioning, the nature of informative feedback, and the scheduling of reinforcements are among the many issues to be addressed in relation to technology. Complicating these issues is the potential of telecommunication exchange projects among classrooms in different cultures to promote simplistic and sanitized views of others (Fabos & Young, 1999). For example, in one project, computer exchanges among students in the United States and New Zealand revealed that the students watched the same television shows and listened to the same music. Such exchanges may indicate the dominance of U.S. media in the world, but they do not foster in-depth understandings of their backgrounds and cultural contexts.

The Gap Between the Reality of Many Classrooms and Theory.   Typically, learning-process theories identify specific components of learning in isolation and the processes required to learn complex skills and capabilities. They are, in one sense, the "ideal" components of learning.

In many classrooms, however, the pressure of standardized testing and suggestions to base teacher remuneration on student performance have introduced other variables into the learning process. Content coverage and test achievement are pervasive, if unstated priorities. Principles of instruction are often a secondary, not a primary, goal for theories of learning and cognitive development. Nevertheless, in addition to identifying differences between novices and experts, developments are needed that can address optimum ways for teachers (1) to identify key concepts and (2) integrate "learning-how-to-learn" strategies into subject matter learning.

The Disparity Among Children Entering School.   Programs that teach basic concepts about the nature of print and books and the nature of numbers to children were described in prior chapters. The need for these programs indicates the disparity

TABLE 1
Brief summary of seven contemporary theories

Theory	Summary of Assumptions	Basic Components	Major Issues In Designing Instruction	Major Contributions
B. F. Skinner's operant conditioning	Learning is behavior; behavioral change, represented by response frequency, is a function of environmental events and conditions.	(S^D)-(Response)-$(S^{reinf.})$	Transfer of stimulus control, timing of reinforcement, avoidance of punishment	Analysis of states, such as readiness; analysis of aversive classroom practices; individualized learning materials
Robert Gagné's conditions of learning	Human learning in all its variety is the focus of study. Learning is more than a single process, and these distinct processes cannot be reduced one to the other.	The five varieties of learning, each with its own set of internal and external conditions	Identification of capabilities to be learned; selection of appropriate instructional events; task analysis for cumulative learning	Identification of the psychological processes in cumulative learning; accounts for the diversity of human learning; linked instruction to phases in information processing
Information-processing theories	Human memory is a complex and active processor and organizer of information that transforms learning into new cognitive structures.	The processes of perception, encoding and storage in long-term memory, metacognitive knowledge and processes, and problem solving processes	Linking new learning to schema; providing processing aids in comprehension, developing metacognitive skills, and problem solving	Identification of the active processes in the learning of new information, developing learner-directed skills, and development of models of problem solving
Jean Piaget's cognitive-development theory	Intelligence constructs the cognitive structures that it needs to function. Knowledge is an interactive process between the learner and the environment.	Assimilation and accommodation, regulated by equilibration; physical experience and logico-mathematical experience	Provide rich opportunities for experimentation with physical objects with peer interaction and support from teacher questions	A rich description of the world through the child's eyes; identifies current curriculum problems; operationalizes discovery learning

Lev Vygotsky's cultural-historical theory of psychological development	The processes of human cognitive development are part of the process of historical development.	The processes of mastering the signs and symbols of the culture; also, learning to use symbols to direct and master one's own behavior	The role of subject matter concepts in developing higher cognitive skills; the creation of zones of proximal development during teaching	Recognition of the psychological contributions of created stimuli in cognitive development; the importance of social interaction and social collaboration in learning
Albert Bandura's social-cognitive theory	Learning is a three-way interaction among the environment, personal factors, and behavior.	Modeled behaviors, direct, vicarious, and self-reinforcement, and the learner's cognitive processes	Provide models, reinforcement, and rehearsal; develop efficacy and learner's self-regulation	Description of learning from models in the social setting and influence of mass media; development of the self-regulatory system
Bernard Weiner's attribution theory	The search for understanding is a primary motivator. Attributions are complex sources of information about outcomes, and future action is derived in part from perceived causes of prior outcomes.	Expectancies and self-esteem are influenced by six major attributions and their three dimensions.	Attributional messages conveyed by the teacher and the classroom; the role of helping behavior	Identification of the psychological linkages between beliefs and action and the linkages between classroom activities and children's beliefs about themselves

in basic pre-instructional concepts among children entering school. Prerequisite capabilities are discussed in Gagné's conditions of learning and readiness is referred to in other theories. Further, Vygotsky identified the differential use of signs and symbols in different cultural settings as setting broad parameters on cognitive development.

Nevertheless, specific constructs that address the nature of learner readiness in terms of world knowledge, observational strategies for noting and recording data about events and objects in the environment, and other related issues are needed.

The Tension Between Universalist and Particularistic Theories.   The learning-process theories, Piagetian theory, social–cognitive theory, and attribution theory are universalist perspectives. That is, the goal is to define principles of learning, cognitive development or motivation that universally apply across settings, contexts, and learners. Vygotsky's theory, in contrast, identifies setting, in the form of a cultural context, as a major variable in cognitive development. That is, the extent of sophistication of the symbol system of the culture and the ways of thinking used in the culture establish broad limitations on learning. Further, social interaction with capable adults is an essential component of learning. Thus, his theory breaks down the barrier between the individual learner and the context.

Vygotsky provided a new perspective in the form of the role of one's culture in learning. However, theorists and researchers must guard against further development that becomes so particularistic that generalizability is not possible. Bronfenbrenner (1993) notes that both universalist and particularistic theories are needed. Universal theories can provide information about the processes, activities, and skills that are to be found across learning settings. Particularistic theories then flesh out the details and fill in the gaps for various applications of the universal theories. In other words, each needs the other, and work should not proceed one without the other.

Finally, the world at the beginning of the 21st century is experiencing rapid and major shifts in political relationships and world economies. The centuries-old shift from an agricultural/industrial basis of production to an industrial/cybernetic basis is dominated by electronically mediated political economies (Gordon, 1991, p. 99). One result is that education is likely to become critical to society's survival and to be appreciated as an increasingly complex process. In addition to the prior issues, some of the new realities that theory development is facing are as follows:

1. A redefinition of culture to address the electronic dimensions of interpersonal interactions

2. The complexities involved in learning to harness a changing technology to master one's thinking and learning

3. The role of human support in rapidly changing work and learning environments

In other words, the increasingly complex needs of society in the area of learning will require theory development that addresses ever-more complex issues. This effort, however, has just begun, and, we hope, the best is yet to come.

REFERENCES

Bronfenbrenner, U. (1993). The ecology of cognitive development: Research models and fugitive findings. In R. H. Wozniak and K. W. Fischer (Eds.), *Development in cognition* (pp. 3–44). Mahwah, NJ: Erlbaum.

Brophy, J. (1999). Toward a model of the value aspects of motivation in education: Developing appreciation for particular learning domains and activities. *Educational Psychologist, 34*(2), 75–86.

Fabos, B., & Young, M. D. (1999). Telecommunication in the classroom: Rhetoric versus reality. *Review of Educational Research, 69*(3), 217–259.

Gordon, E. W. (1991). Human diversity and pluralism. *Educational Psychologist, 26*(2), 145–155.

Lakatos, I. (1970). Falsification and the methodology of scientific research programmes. In I. Lakatos & A. Musgrave (Eds.), *Criticism and the growth of knowledge* (pp. 59–89). Cambridge, U.K.: Cambridge University Press.

Pintrich, P. R. (1994). Continuities and discontinuities: Future directions for research in educational psychology. *Educational Psychologist, 29*(3), 137–148.

Valsiner, J. (1988). *Developmental psychology in the Soviet Union.* Brighton: Harvester Press.

Glossary

Abstraction, empirical. The process of constructing internally the physical characteristics of objects.

Abstraction, reflective. The process of reorganizing or coordinating one's actions on a higher level.

Accommodation. (1) The adjustment of internal cognitive structures to particular characteristics of specific situations; (2) the modification of internal cognitive structures that takes place when thinking is reorganized.

Adaptation, active. The adaptation to the environment undertaken by the human species in which nature is controlled and mastered. The two results of this process are (1) the creation of new natural conditions of existence and (2) altered internal psychological structures.

Adaptation, passive. The adaptation to the environment undertaken by animals in which tasks are mechanically executed according to inherited experience and materials available in the environment.

Advance organizer. An "umbrella" statement that provides a conceptual link between the learner's existing knowledge and the new learning.

Affect. The general and specific emotions that result from a particular outcome. General emotions include happiness and frustration. Specific emotions include gratitude, pride, incompetence, and guilt.

Antecedent information. The sources of information available to the individual prior to the causal attribution about success or failure. They include past success history, the individual's beliefs about events and associated causes, and individual predispositions, such as need for achievement.

Applied behavioral analysis. The application of Skinner's experimental analysis of behavior to real-world settings such as classrooms and hospitals (also referred to as *contingency management*).

Assimilation. The process by which information from the environment is integrated with the subject's internal structure; not a matter of passive registration of characteristics, however.

Attention. The processes of dealing with incoming stimuli; may be automatic, such as attending to usual household sounds, or deliberate, such as attending to unusual noises, a question, a problem, a television program, and so on.

Attitudes. The internal capabilities that govern the individual's disposition toward or away from events, objects, and individuals.

Attribution. An inference made by an individual about the causes of a particular outcome.

Autonomy. The capability of existing independently; a process or activity carried on without outside control.

Aversive stimuli. Those stimuli from which an individual seeks avoidance or escape.

Behaviorism. The term applied to the study of the relationships among environmental conditions and events and behavior.

Capabilities. The changes in states of memory that make possible the prediction of many instances of performances by the learner; the outcomes of learning.

Causality dimensions. The characteristics of attributions that lead to different consequences. The three causality dimensions are *locus* (source of the cause), *stability* (temporary or permanent cause), and *control* (internal to the individual or external). Attributions that are internal and stable, for example, strongly influence the individual's feelings of self-worth in contrast to external or unstable causes.

Class inclusion. The ability to deal simultaneously with a general class defined by a general property (e.g., flowers) and with subclasses of the general class that are defined by a restrictive property (e.g., roses). Included are combining classes (A + A' = B) and the reverse operation (B – A' = A).

Classical (reflex) conditioning. The procedure by which physiological reactions to particular stimuli (e.g., salivation, finger retraction) are trained to respond to new stimuli.

Cognitive behavior. An outward sign of the assimilatory and accommodative capacities of a living organism.

Cognitive strategy. An activity undertaken to facilitate understanding, such as comparing, describing, or summarizing.

Cognitive structures. Internal structures that govern the individual's interactions with the environment; internalized actions.

Concept learning. The skill of classifying objects or events into categories.

Concrete operations. The first forms of logical thought that begin at age 7 or 8 and continue until age 11 or 12.

Conditional procedure. A set of steps (procedure) that requires decisions about alternative steps at certain points in the sequence.

Conditioned response (CR). A reflex reaction that has been trained to respond to a new stimulus.

Conditioned stimulus (CS). After training, the new stimulus that elicits the reflex reaction.

Connectionism. A synonym for Thorndike's theory of learning, implying that connections are established between stimuli and voluntary behaviors. Also, a view of learning that approximates the neural networks in the brain. Memory is described as consisting of interacting connection nets composed of elements (units) and links referred to as connection weights. Processing occurs in the elements, and knowledge is stored in the connection weights.

Constructivism. Several related perspectives that view knowledge as a human construction. Radical constructivism, derived from Piaget's perspective of learning, views the learner's knowledge as adaptive. The teacher's role is to challenge the child's way of thinking. Social constructivist views, in contrast, view knowledge as a social product.

Contingency-governed behavior. The changing consequences of behavior that bring about behavioral change.

Culture.

> *In operant conditioning*—a set of social practices defined as the contingencies maintained by a group. Such contingencies shape the behavior of each member of the group and also transmit social practices and rituals to new or younger members.
>
> *In Vygotskian theory*—the society that (1) transmits the verbal and other codes essential for self-directed thinking and (2) serves, through the interactions inherent between individuals, as the agent of cognitive development.
>
> *In Vygotsky's cultural–historical theory*—the particular social setting in which the child grows up. It includes both past historical achievements and contemporary customs and rituals.

Developmental (genetic) epistemology. The study of the growth of logical thinking from infancy to mature thought.

Differential reinforcement. The reinforcement of particular responses to the exclusion of others.

Discriminative stimulus (S^D). The stimulus that gains control over a subject's behavior by its continued presence when responses are reinforced. Examples include red and green traffic lights and verbal stimuli such as "Please pass the salt."

Disequilibrium. A state of nonbalance in the individual's cognitive development that leads to equilibrium on a higher level; for example, the child's recognition that his or her judgments about a situation are in conflict.

Drive reduction. The satisfaction of a biological need that strengthens the link between the drive (hunger, thirst, etc.) and the response.

Dual-code model. The position that maintains that the information stored in long-term memory may be in either visual or verbal form.

Einstellung. See Problem set.

Elaboration. One of the mechanisms by which stimuli are transformed for storage in long-term memory and later retrieval. Included are stimulus substitution, association, and other stimulus modifications (also referred to as *secondary* or *constructive rehearsal*).

Elicited responses. Responses that are triggered by a particular stimulus. Included are reflexes and conditioned emotional reactions.

Emitted responses. Behaviors for which no known correlative stimulus can be identified; operants.

Encoding. The process of transforming stimuli so that the information may be stored in long-term memory and retrieved for later use.

Environment. The situation in which behavior occurs. It includes both *potential environment* and *actual environment*. The potential environment includes the range of possible consequences that can occur following an individual's response. Actual environment includes all the changes in the situation that occur as a result of the actions of the individual. The learner's behavior transforms the potential environment into the actual environment.

Equilibration. The set of processes that coordinate cognitive development in the individual's search for "true" equilibrium. Included are alpha, beta, and gamma reactions and reflective abstraction.

Equilibrium. A temporary level of understanding to be surpassed by later constructions; for example, concrete operational thought is the equilibrium toward which preoperational thinking is striving.

Events of instruction. The set of stimuli in the environment that supports the internal processes of learning; each learning event has a parallel stimulus situation. The set of instructional events comprises the external conditions of learning.

Expectancy. The anticipation that some performance will lead to a particular consequence.

Experimental analysis. The methodology used to identify the variables of which behavior is a function; accounts for behavior in terms of physical conditions that are both observable and manipulable.

Experimental–genetic (developmental) method. The experimental method that permits psychologists to study the causal-dynamic roots of a process.

Included are (1) placing subjects in tasks somewhat too difficult for them and introducing other factors into the process, such as auxiliary stimuli or possible disruptions, and (2) comparing the behavior of young children with that of older subjects.

External conditions of learning. The set of events deliberately planned to support the phases of learning; also referred to as *instructional events*.

Extinction. The weakening and eventual disappearance of emitted responses through nonreinforcement.

Formal operational period. Mature hypothetical reasoning.

Fossilized behavior. An action or behavior that has had a very long history in human development and therefore is executed in a mechanized or atomized fashion. The problem for research is that of discovering the internal features of such behaviors and the causal-dynamic roots.

Functional fixedness. The inability of the problem solver to perceive elements of a situation in a new relationship or a new way.

Functional method of double stimulation. The experimental method that provides both a typical stimulus and a neutral stimulus for the subject and then tabulates uses and applications of the neutral stimulus.

Functional value. The utility of a particular behavior. The utility of a behavior is established when the observed behavior leads to positive consequences.

General law of genetic development. Every function in the child's cultural development appears first on the social level between people (interpsychological) and then inside the child (intrapsychological).

Higher psychological (mental) functions. The psychological processes that are uniquely human. Included are logical memory, voluntary attention, and the activities of generating artificial or self-generated stimuli and mastering and regulating one's own behavior.

Implicit reinforcement. Behavior that is praised in one individual and disregarded in others may be regarded by the teacher as implicit reinforcement. However, it may be perceived by the students as punishment.

Inhibition. The reduction in a response caused by the introduction of new stimuli.

Insight. A particular reorganization of the perceptual field such that it is seen in a new way.

Instantaneous matching. Imitative learning in which the learner copies the behavior immediately after the presentation.

Instructional event. See External conditions of learning.

Instructional systems design. The development of instruction for specified goals and objectives in which (1) the organized sequential selection of components is made on the basis of information, data, and theoretical principles at every stage and (2) the product is tested in real-world situations both during development and at the end of the development process.

Instrumental conditioning. The term applied by Thorndike to his theory to indicate that it addressed the association of voluntary behaviors to new stimuli.

Intellectual skills. The organized set of human capabilities that involves the use of symbols in interacting with the environment. Included are discrimination, concepts (concrete and defined), rules, and higher-order rules (problem solving).

Intelligence. The individual's adaptation to the physical and social environment; a growing, developing, changing process that is represented moment by moment in the ways that the individual deals with the world.

Internal conditions of learning. The learner's internal states, such as motivation, and the processing steps that facilitate learning.

Intersubjectivity. The term used by James Wertsch to signify the sharing of situation definitions between knowledgeable adult (or peer) and the student in a learning task. Typically, this "temporarily shared social reality" may occur at several levels, and therefore, several levels of intersubjectivity may exist.

Keyword method. A mnemonic method for learning new vocabulary, particularly foreign languages. The word to be learned is encoded in a visual image that combines its meaning and its pronunciation (or some other distinguishing feature).

Knowledge. In Piagetian theory, the constructive interaction between the individual and the object. Knowledge is neither some predefined entity in the environment, nor is it a preformed innate cognitive structure.

Explicit knowledge. *In information-processing theory*—knowledge that is easily available to consciousness and is the object of thought.

Tacit knowledge. *In information-processing theory*—knowledge that typically operates below the level of conscious awareness.

Latency. The length of time between a stimulus and a response.

Latent learning. The acquisition of skills that may or may not be performed.

Law of contiguity. The principle that a combination of stimuli accompanied by a movement will tend to be followed by the same movement on its recurrence.

Law of equivalence. Any concept may be expressed in any of a variety of ways using other concepts at the same level of generality. For example, "1" may be expressed as "3 – 2," "4 – 3," "5 – 4," "2/2," "4/4," and so on.

Learning. The process(es) by which humans acquire the range and variety of skills, knowledge, and attitudes that set the species apart from others.

> *In operant conditioning*—a change in the likelihood or probability of a response.
>
> *In Gagné's conditions of learning*—the process by which humans acquire unique capabilities.
>
> *In information-processing theories*—the set of cognitive processes that transforms a state of the individual's memory from one state to another, resulting in one or more capabilities.

Learning hierarchy. An organized set of intellectual skills from simple to complex that indicates the set of prerequisites for each capability to be learned.

Learning task analysis. The process by which the true (i.e., essential) prerequisites of an intellectual skill are determined.

Measure of generality. Position of a concept within the total system of concepts in terms of its coordinate, superordinate, and subordinate relationships. It determines both the equivalence of concepts and the intellectual operations possible within a given concept.

Memory, episodic. Personal or autobiographical information characterized by the vividness of the memories.

Memory, long-term. Information in an inactive state that, unless forgotten, may be recalled for future use.

Memory, procedural. Information that enables the individual to respond adaptively to the environment.

Memory, semantic. General information that is part of the common store of knowledge (e.g., historical facts, technical information, addresses, phone numbers, and other bodies of knowledge).

Memory, short-term. Sometimes referred to as *working memory;* refers to information that is in the active state.

Metacognition. Knowledge about and awareness of one's own thinking and learning and the use of strategies to guide, monitor, and redirect one's thinking and learning.

Method of loci. An associative mechanism for aiding the encoding and storage of stimuli in memory. It involves the construction of bizarre visual images that link the stimuli with familiar, related locations, such as rooms in a house or landmarks on a familiar walk.

Microworld. A context or environment in which the learner can construct knowledge; usually refers to computer software.

Model. Any stimulus organized so that an observer can extract the principal information conveyed by environmental events without first performing overtly.

Modeling. A process in which a demonstrated behavior is the stimulus for learning. The primary function of the model is to transmit information.

Motor skills. The capabilities that govern the individual's execution and performance of particular physical acts.

Natural history (law) of the sign. The series of transformations that sign-using activity in directing one's own behavior undergoes. Included are the transitional stages between elementary mental functions and the development of higher mental functions.

Natural or primitive development. The domination in the early months of the child's life of biological principles of development. Included are the development of perception, simple or natural memory, and involuntary attention.

Natural selection. The process whereby certain behaviors are reinforced by survival of the species.

Negation. A form of reversibility; for example, in class inclusion, negation is expressed by $B - A' = A$. The action negates the combining of classes. Also, the characteristic of an object that must be constructed by the child; for example, the positive characteristic of lengthening a ball of clay is accompanied by increasing thinness (negation). The construction of operational structures depends on the child's development of both affirmations (positive characteristics) and negations.

Negative utility. A variable-ratio schedule of reinforcement in which the ultimate outcome is the long-term detriment of the subject. Compulsive gambling and drug addiction are examples.

Operant. Any response that acts or operates on the environment to produce some consequence or change.

Operant conditioning. The process of modifying a subject's behavior through the reinforcement of appropriate responses in the presence of the appropriate stimuli.

Operations. Cognitive structures described by Piaget that govern logical reasoning in the broad sense.

Perceived self-efficacy. The belief that one can perform successfully the behaviors that lead to positive outcomes.

Personal helplessness. Identified by Seligman, this state is the perception that outcomes inaccessible to the individual are nonetheless accessible to others.

Phases of learning. The nine internal phases of information processing that transform stimulation from the environment into a new capability. The set of events constitutes the internal conditions of learning and is executed in different ways for different capabilities.

Phi phenomenon. The projection of two brief illuminations of light such that they are perceived as light in motion.

Philosophy. An organized belief system that provides a consistent and unified view of the external world and the inner world of the individual. A philosophy is developed by defining the nature of reality first. Then questions such as "What is truth?" and "What is knowledge?" are answered consistent with the definition.

Prägnanz. The Gestalt law that states that a psychological organization can be only as "good" as prevailing conditions permit.

Precurrent responses. Activities often referred to by others as "thinking"; behaviors that make other behaviors more probable (e.g., reviewing a problem).

Premack principle. The rule that describes the relative power of certain reinforcers. Specifically, preferred activities may be used to reinforce less preferred activities.

Preoperational thinking. Prelogical thought processes that are governed by perceptions. This type of thinking takes place from about the age of 2 to 7 or 8. During these years, the child also develops representational thought and social relations with peers.

Primitive psychological (mental) functions. The basic psychological processes that are continuations of the basic process in animals. Included are perception, simple memory, involuntary attention, and practical tool-using intelligence, such as pulling a string to reach the object at the end of it.

Problem set. A view of a problem or situation that immediately predisposes one to a particular conscious act.

Problem solving. In general, problem solving involves dealing with new and unfamiliar tasks or situations that present some obstacle, and relevant solution methods are not known. In Gagné's conditions of learning, problem solving is the skill of recalling and applying a set of rules in the proper sequence to solve a problem. Also referred to as *higher-order rule learning.*

Procedures. The organization of discrete motor skills into complex activities; usually requires the learning of related concepts and rules. Examples include administering an injection and dissecting a frog.

Program. A series of changing contingencies that shapes behavior until the identified terminal behavior is generated.

Propositional network theories. The position that information is stored in long-term memory only in verbal form. This perspective describes networks of verbal information composed of nodes and the pathways that link the nodes.

Punishment. The withdrawal of a positive reinforcer or the addition of a negative reinforcer to a behavioral situation.

Reciprocal determinism. The mutual influence of the individual and the environment on each other.

Reciprocity. The reversibility of an ordered series; for example, if A >B >C, then C <B <A.

Rehearsal, elaborative. Also referred to as *constructive rehearsal* or *elaboration;* the process of modifying stimuli for storage and later retrieval.

Rehearsal, primary. Also referred to as *maintenance rehearsal;* the process of repetition in order to preserve information in memory.

Reinforcement. Any consequence of a response that increases the probability of the behavior's recurrence.

> Negative reinforcement—the withdrawal or termination of a stimulus that strengthens behavior; also known as *escape conditioning.*
>
> Positive reinforcement—the situation in which an organism's behavior "produces" a new stimulus that increases the frequency of the behavior.
>
> Vicarious reinforcement—according to Bandura, observation of positive consequences received by the model.
>
> Conditioned or secondary reinforcers—stimuli that acquire reinforcing power through repeated association with primary reinforcers. Examples include rocking and cuddling an infant while feeding it.
>
> Contrived reinforcers—artificial reinforcers that are not normally provided by the environment.
>
> Generalized reinforcers—reinforcers that function in a variety of situations.
>
> Natural reinforcers—nonaversive feedback provided by the environment.

Representational systems. The symbolic codes that are stored in the learner's memory. *Visual codes* are vivid images. *Verbal codes* include language symbols, numbers, and musical notation.

Resistance to extinction. The tendency of a response to persist after the supporting conditions are withdrawn.

Reversibility. An essential characteristic of operational structures; the capability of returning an operation to its starting point. For example, addition is reversed through subtraction.

Rule-governed behavior. Verbal stimuli, such as advice, maxims, rules, and laws, that can alter behavior. Unlike reinforcement contingencies, the probability of behavioral changes remains undetermined.

Rule learning. The skill of recalling and applying a rule to make a prediction, determine an effort, or deduce a consequence.

Scaffolding. A term introduced in recent years to describe the process of controlling task elements that are initially beyond the learner's capacity.

Schedules of reinforcement. The delivery of reinforcement according to different specifications.

    Interval schedule—delivery of reinforcers based on elapsed time; may be fixed (e.g., every 5th second) or variable (e.g., every 5th, 8th, and 12th second).

    Variable-ratio schedule—delivery of reinforcers based on emitted responses; may be fixed (e.g., every 5th response) or variable (e.g., every 5th, 10th, and 13th response).

Schema. A term with no fixed definition that is used to refer to knowledge structures; typically used as a synonym for prior knowledge.

Scientific concepts. The domain-specific concepts that are learned in subject areas in formal schooling, according to Vygotsky.

Scientific empiricism. The accumulation of facts through carefully designed experiments or "controlled experience."

Self-efficacy. The sense that one can execute successfully a behavior required to produce a particular outcome.

Self-perception. An individual's ability to respond differently to his or her own behavior.

Self-reinforcement. Anticipated and evaluative consequences that are generated by the individual for his or her behavior.

Sensorimotor thinking. The action schemes developed by infants to solve problems in their environment. An example is grasping the edge of a blanket and pulling it toward oneself to get the object lying on it (i.e., reaching-grasping-pulling).

Seriation (serial ordering). The operational structure by which individuals are able to place objects in a linear sequence from shortest to longest, smallest to largest, and so on. Included is the ordering of both a series A <B <C and its reciprocal C >B >A.

Shaping. The process of developing complex repertoires of behavior through (1) specifying the terminal skill to be learned and (2) reinforcing successive approximations to the terminal behavior.

Signalization. The system of connections that is a copy or the reflection of the natural ties among all kinds of natural events that indicate the appearance of immediately beneficial or destructive events.

Signification. The creation and use of signs, that is, artificial signals.

Signs. Artificial or self-generated stimuli that become the immediate causes of higher mental functions.

Social behavior. The tendency for an individual to match the behaviors, attitudes, or emotional reactions that are observed in actual or symbolic models.

Spontaneous concepts. The concepts—such as "dog," "cat," "hungry," and countless others—that are learned naturally in a child's daily interactions with family members and others.

Stimulus generalization.

    In classical conditioning—the tendency of similar stimuli to elicit the same reflex.

    In operant conditioning—the tendency of two or more stimuli that share a common feature to acquire control over an operant response (e.g., a child's verbal identification of "*p*" and "*P*").

Stimulus-response (S-R) theories. Behaviorist theories that define learning as an associative link between a particular stimulus and a particular response.

Strategy. A set of actions over and above the processes involved in a task.

Symbolic codes. The representations of information in long-term memory. Theorists disagree as to their forms (i.e., verbal only or visual and verbal [see Propositional network theories and Dual-code model]).

Symbolic model. A visual image of the live model, such as a film or televised presentation.

Teacher efficacy. The extent to which the teacher believes he or she has the capacity to affect student performance.

Terminal contingency. The complex set of behaviors expected as the outcome of a series of differential reinforcements for related subskills and/or approximations of the complex behavior. Such behaviors have an almost zero probability of occurring naturally in the environment. Instead, behavior must be shaped through a carefully planned sequence of behaviors and reinforcements. Examples include a pigeon bowling and a student writing a term paper.

Transfer of learning. The increased ease of a particular learning task that results from the prior learning of a similar task.

Transitivity. The property that represents the relationships among objects in a series; that is, if A > B > C, then A > C. Similarly, if A = B and B = C, then A = C.

Unconditioned response (UCR). The reflex reaction that naturally occurs following a particular stimulus.

Unconditioned stimulus (UCS). The stimulus that naturally is followed by a particular reflex reaction.

Varieties of learning. The five categories of human learning that (1) are differentiated by at least one unique requirement for learning, (2) result in different classes of performance, and (3) are generalizable across subject areas, grade levels, and learners. The five varieties of learning are verbal information, intellectual skills, cognitive strategies, motor skills, and attitudes.

Verbal information. The variety of skills that includes the acquisition of (1) labels and facts, (2) meaningfully connected selections of prose or poetry, and (3) organized bodies of knowledge.

Name Index

Subject Index